Horst H. Geerken

Hitler's Asian Adventure

Horst H. Geerken

Hitler's Asian Adventure

The Third Reich, the Dutch East Indies and British India,

the Creation of German Naval Bases

and the Beginning of the End of the Colonial Era.

A Documentation

Translated by Bill McCann

A BukitCinta Book

Jacket Design: Concept by Horst H. Geerken,
                  Execution by Sabine Berner
Photo Rear Cover: Annette Bräker
Maps: Sabine Berner based on sketches by Horst H. Geerken
Editing: Dilys McCann
Layout and Design: Barbara Bode
Typeset in Adobe Garamond Pro

Publisher: BoD · Books on Demand GmbH,
Überseering 33, 22297 Hamburg, bod@bod.de
Print: Libri Plureos GmbH, Friedensallee 273,
22763 Hamburg
ISBN: 978-3-8448-1963-2

In memory of my many Indonesian friends
who risked their lives as freedom fighters
for the independence of their motherland Indonesia
and
for Annette

Contents

Thanks

During my long stay in Indonesia and as I was researching for my book "A Gecko for Luck" I kept coming across connections that had existed in the Third Reich between Germany and Indonesia – in those days the Japanese occupied the Dutch East Indies. My interest aroused, I researched in German and Indonesian archives and national libraries and found new documents, previously undiscovered and unpublished, from the period 1942-1945, the period of Japanese occupation of the Dutch East Indies.

I owe especial gratitude to the National Library (Perpustakaan Nasional Republik Indonesia) and the National Archive (Arsip National Republik Indonesia) of the Republic of Indonesia in Jakarta and the Soekarno Archive (UPT Perpustakaan Proklamator Bung Karno) in Blitar (East Java).

My thanks for friendly and effective support must go to the Archive of the Foreign Ministry in Berlin. A great deal of the information that I acquired from the Institut für Zeitgeschichte in Munich is also included in this book.

I would also like to express my thanks to the journalist Iwan Ong Santosa and the historian Didi Kwartananda in Jakarta. My conversations with them led me along new paths.

Thanks to my friend Jürgen Graaff for his research into the transmitters that were sent from Germany to the Dutch East Indies and Shanghai. With the help of his private archive and his "historical transmitter list" it was possible to reconstruct the technical date and the routes by which the transmitters reached the Far East and Australia.

My thanks as well to Hardy Zöllner, who attended the former German School in Sarangan, for friendly conversations and information.

Friedrich Flakowski, an eyewitness who was interned with his mother and sister in the Dutch East Indies and was then moved to Japan, provided me with important information, pictures and original documents which have been included in this book, for which I am very grateful. Sadly, he has since died.

The diary of my friend Günther Fust, another eyewitness who died some time ago, was kindly placed at my disposal by Dr Walter Jäcker, for which much thanks. I have included some interesting historical material from Günther Fust's time in China in the book.

My especial thanks to my friend Horst Jordt, President of the Walter Spies Society in Germany and Baronin Victoria von Plessen for providing documents and photographs from the private archive concerning Victor[1] Baron von Plessen in Wahlstorf and for information about the "Queen of the Amstel".

I would like to give posthumous thanks to the Asia expert Professor Hans Bräker and the staff surgeon of the Indian Legion Dr R. Madan for a great deal of information about Subhas Chandra Bose, the Indian freedom fighter. Many thanks for information and photographs about the activities of the Borgward motor company in Indonesia go to Frau Monica Borgward and Peter Kurze, the author of several books about the Borgward company.

I must thank Frau Ayumi Schürmann for her help in translating Kiyokazu Tsuda's Japanese book about the project to reconstruct the Würzburg Radar Station. Telefunken engineer Heinrich Foders, a personal acquaintance of mine, was sent to Japan via Singapore by U-boat to bring it about.

My very special thanks and deep respect go to the many Indonesian freedom fighters who at the beginning of the 1960s provided me with information about the time of the Japanese occupation, the beginnings of Soekarno's volunteer army, the Defenders of the Fatherland, PETA (Pembela Tanah Air) and the subsequent almost five-year-long struggle for independence. I have discussed the subject many times with my dear Indonesian friends Wibowo, General Otty Soekotjo, Lt. Col. Daan Jahja, Umar Kayam and General M. Ng. Soenarjo. Much of this information is included in this book. Daan Jahja and Wibowo – with whom I worked in harmony for eighteen years – were particularly active in the creation of PETA, the country's first army, from 1942-43 and in the struggle for Indonesian independence to the end of 1949.

Posthumous thanks too to Admiral Martadinata, the Commander in Chief of the Indonesian Navy (ALRI) for interesting conversations about the German naval base in Surabaya and the German school in Sarangan. He was one of Indonesia's first officers and from 1945 received instruction as a young cadet in the branch of the first Indonesian military academy (SORA) at the German School in Sarangan in German and sport. He was also taught by German naval officers in the provisional military academy in Yogyakarta.

It is unfortunately impossible to list all the many Indonesian and German eyewitnesses from whom I received information in the 1960s and subsequently. But I owe them my special thanks for our many open and honest conversations.

---

1   In the literature, von Plessen's first name Victor is often spelt Viktor. In the frequent references to him in this book I have always used the correct version with 'c', as did von Plessen in letters and documents.

Finally, I would like to thank my beloved Annette. She always supported me with good advice and suggestions. Annette was the perfect travelling companion who coped with everything - even the most difficult situations - without complaint. As I was writing my books - including this one - she was always beside me with her help and professional knowledge. Sadly, my beloved Annette died a few months ago. She was a most extraordinary and brave woman. I owe her my deepest affection. I will never forget her.

Horst H. Geerken
September 2015

Ill. 1
Map of the "Southern Region" (Dutch East Indies and Malaya)
The Netherlands to the same scale

The Netherlands to the same scale

1. Foreword

When my book *A MAGIC GECKO, CIA's Role Behind the Fall of Soe-karno* was published in Indonesia in the Summer of 2011, I visited the big GRAMEDIA bookshop in Kuta on Bali with Annette. We were shocked to see that a display of about fifty copies of my book in both English and Bahasa Indonesia had been placed right next to a pile of copies of Hitler's *Mein Kampf* which had recently been translated into Bahasa Indonesia and was a current bestseller in Indonesia.

Quite close to my display there was another bestseller entitled *Hitler mati di Indonesia (Hitler died in Indonesia)*. How has it come about that Hitler – in spite of the war crimes and atrocities he was responsible for – still holds such great fascination for the Indonesians, that sometimes even goes as far as veneration?

I had often noticed this when I was working in Indonesia in the years 1963 to 1981, but my professional duties did not allow me the leisure to follow this up in detail.

Now, however, I decided to investigate the phenomenon of veneration for Hitler and I began my researches. New evidence and information that I uncovered in both Germany and Indonesia led me to commit the results of my research to a book. To my great surprise, the relationship between Hitler and the Third Reich and Indonesia – at that period the Dutch East Indies – was considerably more extensive and intensive than I had at first assumed. I was equally surprised to discover that the key to this relationship was one of Hitler's closest confidants, the importance of whom had previously been unrecognised by those working on the history of the Third Reich.

Even I have been surprised by some of the newly discovered information collated in this book. For example, how many of us are aware today that German naval personnel were stationed in the Dutch East Indies, Malaya and Singapore? Or that Indian troops fought on Hitler's side in Europe? Or that German U-boats and auxiliary cruisers penetrated into the Pacific, as far even as Australia and New Zealand?

The focus of this book is not on Hitler's well-known crimes and their moral significance, but rather on the political, technical and logistical aspects of the German theatre of war in the Far East.

This should in no way give rise to the impression that Hitler is being shown in a positive light. His crimes against humanity are a matter of historical record and in no way to be condoned. Much has been written about them, and they are not the theme of this book, which deals solely with the Far Eastern theatre of war, the hardship suffered by German personnel on their U-boat journeys (which lasted several months) and the technical challenges which had to be overcome. Respect for historical truth also demands that we do not ignore historically documented war-crimes committed by the Germans' opponents – the Allies.

For historical reasons one cannot, of course, avoid frequent mentions of Hitler, as head of state and supreme commander, and the members of his intimate circle in a book about the Third Reich. Some of the illustrations in this book also show the swastika, the Nazi salute and other Nazi symbols. This is not intended as any kind of glorification of the Nazi era. These historical images are often of very poor quality, but have been included because of their importance as documents.

The war in the Atlantic has already been described in hundreds of books. In the naval archives there are documents about almost every ship that took part in the Battle of the Atlantic, detailing their missions and their personnel, whereas the presence of the German Navy in South East Asia, Australia, off the coast of New Zealand and particularly in the Dutch East Indies during the Second World War is hardly ever mentioned; and yet the involvement of the Third Reich together with its Axis partner Japan had a major impact. The colonial powers were driven out and many countries achieved independence. The balance of power in this area underwent fundamental change.

During the Second World War the area comprising the Dutch East Indies and Malaya was described as the "Southern Region". Very little information about this theatre of war in far-off Asia can be found in the naval archives. The documentation concerning the activities of German U-boats in this area is also extremely fragmentary. All actions in this theatre were classified top secret by the German Navy, several of them being so secret that no documents were created. Even the Head of the German U-boat fleet, Admiral Karl Dönitz, seems to have forgotten the naval war in South-East Asia. In the more than 500 pages of his memoirs of the period from 1935 to 1945, *10 Years and 20 Days,* Dönitz only mentions German U-boat actions in South-East Asian in passing in a paltry 40 lines.

Perhaps the South-East Asian theatre was too far from Germany to be reported. Among the approximately six-hundred German war reporters I found only one who had travelled to the 'Southern Region'. This was Heinz Tischer, who travelled on the auxiliary cruiser *Thor*'s second voyage to Japan. The ship was destroyed in a fire in the port of Yokohama. His pictures and reports were all destroyed in the blaze. There may have been a second war reporter, Lieutenant Hermann Kiefer, who travelled to South East Asia on board of the U 861 in April 1944. The submarine did not reach Penang until the end of September 1944. The fact that this was only a few months before the German capitulation probably explains why I could not find any reports by him. Kiefer initially remained in Penang and became a British prisoner of war in Singapore after the capitulation of Japan.

Another reason why the distant 'Southern Region' was not as widely covered as the other fronts is surely the state of communications, which were not as good at that period as they are today.

Unfortunately the majority of contemporary witnesses who could have provided credible and reliable information are now dead. The German naval war in South-East Asia has become a forgotten war. Luckily I had already begun to investigate – if only marginally – this material at the beginning of the 1960s, when I was able to collect a lot of evidence from contemporary Indonesian and German witnesses.

The German military presence in the Dutch East Indies has a long history. As early as the 17th century many thousands of adventurous young German-speaking men set off for the East Indies to enter Dutch service as sailors or soldiers – or as artisans, merchants or civil servants. Often more than half of those in the service of the VOC (*Vereenigde Oost-Indische Compagnie* – the Dutch East India Company) were foreigners: Germans, Austrians, Poles, Swiss. The German soldiers were always in the majority.

At the end of the 18th century, Duke Carl Eugen of Württemberg sent a mercenary army of 2,000 of his officers and men to support the VOC in its colony for a sum of 300,000 gulden. They were mostly adventurers who were seeking their fortune in this unknown tropical country, but many were driven into the clutches of the recruiting officers by utter destitution. The soldiers were exploited and humiliated. Their rations, equipment and medical facilities were catastrophic, malaria, cholera, the vitamin-deficiency disease beriberi and other tropical illnesses decimated their ranks. There were no recreational facilities, though cheap arak, a spirit made from palm sugar juice and rice mash, flowed plentifully. Alcohol and gambling addiction were rife.

The mortality rate was extremely high as a result of the hot, damp tropical climate, unknown tropical diseases and poor hygiene. 10 to 20% of the passengers died on the sail voyage out, which took several months. More soldiers died of disease than in any military action. The Duke of Württemberg even sold his own sons to the Dutch, though they were at least officers. The family name of these sons – von Franquemont –, derived from a small county in eastern France which then belonged to Württemberg, could be found in Indonesia until the Second World War. Most of the von Franquemonts – like the other ranks – settled down in the tropics with a pretty Javanese woman and remained in the tropics for good.

The navy of the North German League, the Royal Prussian Navy and later the Imperial Navy were also present in South East Asia and the Pacific to foster German interests in the area. Up to that time the British, the French, the Dutch and the United States had made successful territorial claims in the region.

From 1859 the sailing frigate *SMS Thesis*, the schooner *SMS Frauenlob* and the transport vessel *SMS Elbe* operated in East Asia under the command of the flagship *SMS Arcona*. The German Empire constantly increased the power and the number of warships which led, via the 'East Asian Cruiser Division' to the 'German East Asian Squadron'. From 1896 ironclads and large cruisers like the *SMS Kaiser*, the *SMS Deutschland*, the *SMS Kaiserin Augusta*, the *SMS Fürst Bismarck*, the *SMS Scharnhorst* and the *SMS Gneisenau* served in these waters. There were up to 20 warships in the 'German East Asian Squadron'. They were compelled to use foreign ports for maintenance and repairs. This changed when Germany occupied Tsingtao in China in 1897 and built a naval base there.

After 1885 Germany acquired territory in New Guinea and in the Pacific, creating the following protectorates which from 1899 were administered directly as colonies by the German Empire and also contained German naval bases:

- Kaiser Wilhelm's Land (the north eastern section of New Guinea, the second largest island in the world)
- the Bismarck Archipelago of hundreds of islands, of which the best known were Neu-Pommern (now: New Britain), Neu-Mecklenburg (now: New Ireland) and Neu-Hannover (now: New Hanover).

Kaiser Wilhelm's Land and the Bismarck Archipelago together formed the colony of German New Guinea. Further German protectorates were:

- the Bougainville Islands, which are all now part of Papua New Guinea
- the Solomon Islands (now independent)
- the Northern Mariana Islands (now a commonwealth of the USA)
- the Marshall Islands, the Palau Islands, the Caroline Islands and Nauru (all now independent)
- German Samoa, now independent West Samoa (not to be confused with the eastern Samoa Islands, which are now American Samoa, a major US military base).

Ill. 2
German colonial territories in China, South East Asia and the Pacific before the First World War.

Before and during the First World War many German warships cruised the waters of the Dutch East Indies. In 1910 *SMS Scharnhorst, SMS Leipzig* and *SMS Luchs* visited Sumatra and Borneo (now: Kalimantan). In 1911 *SMS Scharnhorst* visited Batavia (now: Jakarta). In 1913 *SMS Scharnhorst* returned to Batavia together with *SMS Gneisenau*. Both ships then also visited the Lesser Sunda Islands. In 1914 the battleship *SMS Scharnhorst* was back in Sumatra and Borneo. During this period Germany still had its colonies in South East Asia and the Pacific: there was a strong German naval presence of up to 24 warships and 17,000 crew in the area.

After the First World War the new cruiser *SMS Emden III* visited Batavia in 1927 and 1931. In 1926, 1927 and 1931 the light cruiser *SMS Hamburg* visited several ports in the Dutch East Indies, as did *SMS Köln* in 1933 and *SMS Karlsruhe* in. In 1937 *SMS Emden III* was in Surabaya and in Belawan, East Sumatra. The frequent visits to the Dutch East Indies by German warships after the First World War fostered the community spirit of the Germans living and working there.

The *SMS Emden III* with its 665 man crew docked in the port of Belawan on the 11th of December 1937 during a round the world voyage. This visit was the cause of great celebration, the high-point of which for some German families was the christening of their children on German territory on board of the ship, which remained there for five days. All visits to the Dutch East Indies by German ships were greeted with great enthusiasm by the German population there.

Why was Hitler's interest in the Dutch East Indies – so far from Germany – so much greater than his interest in the former German colonies in the region? And who provided Hitler with such good information about the Dutch colony?

17

This question was what initially spurred me to write this book – and the answer soon revealed itself to be Walther Hewel. Even though no one else except Eva Braun shared Hitler's private life as intimately as this man, little research into the history of the Third Reich has considered him. We will meet Walther Hewel frequently in this book. It is astonishing that no historian has yet investigated the documents about Hewel, which are to be found in several separate archives. Hewel played a key role in Berlin in all actions that concerned the Dutch East Indies.

Unfortunately, in spite of several attempts, it has not been possible for me to make contact with Hewel's descendants and relations. They probably do not want light cast on the role played by him in the Third Reich, which is otherwise almost unknown. And yet, as we will see, Walther Hewel did in some respects play a quite positive mediatory role during this time.

Much of the information in this book is based on interviews with contemporary Indonesian witnesses who had themselves served in the German bases on Java and Sumatra and in the army founded by Soekarno during the Japanese occupation, the PETA (Pembela Tanah Air/Defenders of the Fatherland). In more recent times I have had further interviews with Indonesian experts, collectors and historians who are prepared to speak more openly with a foreigner like me who is, in their eyes, neutral, than they ever would to a former Dutch colonial master. I have therefore faithfully reproduced the attitudes and feelings of my Indonesian informants when speaking about the Dutch when reporting the events of those times.

The deeper I delved into Indonesian and German archives, the more interesting were the findings that emerged. Unfortunately many documents concerning the German military presence in South East Asia were lost in the confusion of the Second World War.

In contrast to the large number of books that have been written about the naval war in the Atlantic in the Second World War, I have found hardly any literature dealing with German naval operations in South East Asia. My many recent conversations with officers of the Indonesian navy (ALRI) who had only entered the service long after the end of the war remained fruitless. They had all experienced the Second World War either as children or not at all, and had had to devote all their energy to the rebuilding of their nation and its new armed forces after international pressure had forced the withdrawal of the Dutch colonial power in December 1949.

There is also the fact that under the presidency of Soeharto, the second Indonesian president, an attempt was made to wipe previous political events from the memory of the Indonesian people. Soeharto was always in the shadow of the first president, Soekarno, who had fought for the country's independence. Soeharto attempted to change this by suppressing all information about Soekarno: even Indonesian schoolbooks were altered to this effect. However, he did not succeed in minimising his predecessor's role: To the people of Indonesia, Soekarno was and still is the real hero who led their country to independence.

Several conversations at the beginning of the 60s with Admiral Martadinata, the Commander in Chief of the Indonesian navy, who was also a fellow-fighter and supporter of Soekarno, provided a lot of information about the German naval base in Surabaya and the German school in Sarangan. Unfortunately he lost his life in unexplained circumstances shortly after Soeharto seized power in a coup d'état supported by the CIA.

In the 1960s and 70s I visited all the former German naval bases: Surabaya, Batavia (now: Jakarta), Sabang, Singapore and Penang. I was not able to find any traces worth mentioning of the brief German naval presence in any of these places.

The Dutch colonial period, which lasted almost 350 years, together with the subsequent five-year independence struggle against the returning Dutch, is a time of pain and shame for all Indonesians, which they would much rather forget. In order to exclude this dark era, Indonesian historical consciousness only really begins in 1950. In the 1960s I therefore had to resort to acquiring information from contemporary eyewitnesses who had served in Soekarno's volunteer PETA army. Happily, I was able to make many friends among them. In the course of the years many of them had risen to responsible positions in the Indonesian administration and army. They were able to tell me a great deal about the South East Asian theatre of war.

I have failed to find any German eyewitnesses still alive today who served on a U-boat or a German blockade-breaker in Indonesian waters or on one of the German bases in the "Southern Region". When I arrived in Indonesia in 1963 it was still possible to interview a few former German submariners. However, at the time I did not have the leisure to deal with this topic more deeply because of my job as the representative of a German company. Moreover, themes harking back to the Second World War were at that time practically taboo.

I knew two people who worked at the German Embassy. One of them had remained on Java after serving in the crew of a U-boat, the other had served in the base at Sabang. A leading employee of Siemens-Indonesia had been a submariner and another U-boat commander worked for a German chemical company in Bandung in the 60s. All but one of them remained in their new home, Indonesia, until the end of their lives. A large number of them had fought beside the Indonesian freedom fighters, first against the British and then against the returning Dutch forces, until Indonesia finally achieved independence.

I knew two U-boat commanders who visited Indonesia frequently in the 1960s and 70s. Their boats had both been stationed at the base in Surabaya. During their time there they had made friends with Indonesian families, whom they were now visiting. I was able to talk to one of these commanders on several occasions.

On the Internet and also in historical works I have found much confusion and many errors concerning the numbers of the German U-boats and the names of their commanders. After a great deal of detailed research I have presented here the names, and data that are, in my opinion, correct, though 100% accuracy cannot be guaranteed. There is often a difference in the times and dates quoted, which may well derive from the time difference between Germany and Indonesia, depending on the place where the data was recorded.

The name 'Indonesia' for the former Dutch colony of the Dutch East Indies was first used officially after the declaration of independence on August 17th 1945. It was the German ship's doctor and scientist Adolf Bastian who first coined the term at the end of the 19th century: it then gained international currency. The term, which encompassed the whole archipelago, was taken up by the Indonesian independence movement. It was politically loaded and could not be used publicly during the Dutch colonial period: the Dutch regarded it as an attack on their claims to hegemony. Every attempt to unite the inhabitants of the archipelago with no concern for tribal affiliation, race, religion or language was blocked by the colonial government with all their might. "Divide and Rule" was the principle by which they hoped to maintain their power. But the name "Indonesia" reinforced the national consciousness and the unity of the nation.

I use the term officially in use for the Indonesian archipelago during the period of the Third Reich – Dutch East Indies –, and for the area comprising the Dutch East Indies and Malaya, where the German bases were situated, the term used by the German navy: 'Southern Region'.

In the interests of historical correctness I only use the word Indonesia for the period after the declaration of independence, even though the term was often used during the Second World War by Germans, Japanese and the people of Indonesia.

War and politics destroyed so many young lives on both sides, lives that were surely intended for something finer and better. Everyone, victors and defeated alike, suffered after that war. There were ruined souls and ruined landscapes on both sides – even in the far off theatre of war in South East Asia. The still, blue Java Sea became a watery grave for many a sailor.

2. Hitler Seizes Power.
The Beginning of the Second World War and
How my Interest in the Dutch East Indies was Awakened

I was born exactly 195 days after Hitler's seizure of power put an end to the Weimar Republic. After a period of serious unemployment, inflation and general poverty the majority of the German population celebrated Hitler as the "Saviour of the Fatherland". Defeat in the First World War, the humiliation that followed and the Weimar Republic's problems smoothed the way for Hitler's initially overwhelming success.

All over Germany autobahns were built, within only three years millions of unemployed found work again and you could order a *Volkswagen* for only 1,000 reichsmarks. Hitler created the most modern army in Europe. Everything was on the way up! As early as the mid-1930s Germany recorded the highest standard of living in its history. Everything seemed to be going right for Hitler. After the disgrace of the Versailles Treaty the Germans had regained their pride and praised him to the skies.

As a child I only heard positive and admiring things said about our "Führer Adolf Hitler": no unemployment, a change of world, a change of era. The chaos of the Weimar Republic was at an end and something new was coming. No wonder National Socialism attracted so many at first glance. They hoped for better times, and believed that only Hitler could bring about the miracle. He'd already made a beginning.

Hitler coined the slogan *"Neue Ordnung"* (New Order), which was then taken over by the other Axis powers. In Italy Mussolini spoke of the *Ordine Nuovo* and the Japanese Prime Minister Prince Konoe Fumimaro of *Shintesai*. Even the second Indonesian president Soeharto named his programme for restructuring the nation *Orde Baru*, New Order!

Hitler intended the 1936 Olympic Games to confirm his international acceptance, in spite of threats of a boycott by the USA, the United Kingdom, France, Sweden, Czechoslovakia and the Netherlands because of increasing alarm at the nature of his regime. Visitors reported on the exciting development of the capital, Berlin, the hordes of people from many different nations, the large number of cars, the impressively swirling sea of flags and the great successes of the German athletes. The new Olympic Stadium with its 100,000 seats, built in just two years, was particularly impressive – it was a masterly achievement by the architects, planners and builders.

Though the stadium was itself gigantic, Hitler and his architect Walter Speer had plans to create even larger buildings. In the vicinity of Nuremberg a stadium that was by far the biggest in the world was being built even after the war had begun. It was to be 90 metres high and have a capacity of 405,000. Lifts holding 100 people were to take the spectators to the upper rows. It was only towards the end of the war that work on this gigantic project ceased.

The plans and models for Berlin that Hitler revealed in 1936 were even more gigantic. Berlin was to be rebuilt as the "World Capital Germania". Monumental buildings were planned. The "Great Hall" was to become the biggest hall in the world with a surface area of 315 metres square, a dome 320 metres high and a capacity of 180,000. It was to be an architectonic masterpiece. A triumphal arch four times bigger than the one in Paris was also planned. Hitler's megalomania was beginning to show itself.

The ostentatious "New Reich Chancery" with a frontage of 420 metres was completed to Hitler's own plans in a record time of just about a year at the beginning of 1939. The interior fittings were all of marble and other valuable materials. This "World Capital Germania" was a demonstration of power. Nazi ideology was to be carved in stone.

The New Reich Chancery was only slightly damaged by Allied bombing and the battle for Berlin just before the end of the war, but on the orders of the Soviet Union it was gradually demolished and razed to the ground between 1949 and 1953. The Olympic stadium on the other hand survived the war almost undamaged. After refurbishment, modernisation and the addition of a partial roof the Berlin Olympic Stadium now holds 75,000 spectators. It is the only building from the planned "World Capital" that has remained standing till today and is still in use.

When I went on errands for my mother, I used to love going to the grocer's shop (*Kolonialwarenladen*) on our street. The very name "*Kolonialwarenladen*" conjured up associations with distant, exotic lands, and the name persisted even though the German colonies had ceased to exist after the First World War.

This was the eldorado of my young fantasy world. A world of brightly-coloured enamel signs showing tropical landscapes, of exotic aromas and strange foreign foods. The sago packet had "Bismarck Archipelago" as the country of origin and showed a picture of two dark-skinned natives hollowing out a tree trunk. As a child I was fascinated – you could even eat the tree trunks there.

Other enamel signs advertised "Hollandia Cacao", or soup cubes or coffee from the former German colony of Togo. Products from overseas like coffee, rice, brown sugar, coconut flakes, semolina and exotic beans stood around in open sacks on the floor. There was paraffin and sweet port wine from the barrel. Sometimes there were even bananas. All kinds of spices, tobacco and many other things were kept loose in big drawers behind the counter. Next to wooden coffee mills with a crank handle there were gaudy tin canisters on the shelves. This made my child's eyes shine, and the aroma of the strange spices awoke dreams and longing for the big, wide world in me even then. I was fascinated by the dusky-skinned people and the exotic tropical land-scapes with blue seas and simple huts under palm trees.

We were – and still are – a cosmopolitan family spread over several con-tinents. It was not unusual for my mother – even from a comparatively young age – to spend longer periods abroad in Europe. We also had rela-tives in Holland. My mother visited them frequently in Amsterdam and had even learned Dutch: my parents had very close contacts with Holland. This was probably how my mother awakened my interest in the Dutch East Indies very early on, an interest which has continually grown to this very day. Though far off, that fascinating country was closest to me from my young childhood onwards.

My parents encouraged my love of music and of literature. Their well-filled library was like a magnet to me. There were lots of illustrated books about the former German colonies in Africa and the Pacific and, probably because of my mother's family connections with Holland, numerous books in Dutch about the East Indies. I was constantly surrounded by books whose illustrations enchanted me. Even before I could read, I was fascinated by the photographs and drawings of rice terraces on Java or the tropical jungle of Sumatra: in this way I first came into contact with what is now Indonesia when I was three or four years old. This stimulus bore fruit, since I learned to read very early. Even as a little boy the pictures of the Netherlands Indies enabled me to visualise the tropics. Unfortunately very few of these books survived the war.

1939 was particularly eventful. I was now six years old and can remember many details quite clearly. Throughout that whole year the whole country was tense: we sensed that something was about to happen.

Signs proclaiming "No Entry for Jews" were displayed on many public buildings, and on our grocer's shop there was also a sign saying "Jews not wanted here".

And on the 1st September 1939 the day arrived. From first thing in the morning till late at night Hitler's announcement droned from the radio: *Since 5.45 A.M. we have been returning fire, and from now on bombs will be met by bombs.* For months beforehand we had been told that the Poles had been mistreating the Germans who lived in Silesia for no reason at all: they were expelling them and killing them, and had mobilised their troops there since March with the intent of making war on Germany. Now the Germans said that Hitler had warned the Poles often enough to stop their attacks on the Germans in Silesia. The Führer's patience was at an end, and if the Poles *would not hear, they would end up by being made to feel.* Hitler said: *I have, therefore, resolved to speak to Poland in the same language that Poland for months past has used toward us.*

The beginning of the Second World War also brought decisive change to the lives of the Germans in South East Asia. In the British territories of Malaya, Singapore and Burma all German citizens were interned. Some managed to escape to the Dutch East Indies, which were at the time still neutral. These men, women and children escaped internment by the British, but when the Germans invaded the Netherlands they ended up moving from the frying pan into the fire in the Dutch East Indies. Their fate in the Dutch internment camps was far worse.

Today of course it is clear to me that Hitler's policy of expansion to the east had been planned for a long time. The German people had been prepared for war by targeted propaganda. Hitler wanted to create a corridor to East Prussia, which was separated from the main part of the country. Only 17 days after the German army invaded from the west, the Red Army marched into Poland from the east: Hitler and Stalin had just signed their non-aggression pact.

As in every war both sides lied: successes were magnified and defeats concealed. But at the time I, as a child – and obviously many adults too – was unaware of this. It is only modern communications media that make it possible to acquire wider and more varied information.

I was six and a half when I started school in Stuttgart in the spring of 1940. The school day began with a loud, clear "Heil Hitler!" In the Third Reich this greeting was compulsory. School was a place where you did what you were told and its main aim was the promulgation of National Socialist ideology. All over the world young people are the easiest to influence, and the Nazi regime knew how to win over children: hiking, sport, romantic adventure, camp-fires, singing, comradeship.

Almost every day in school we were presented with a list of the territory lost after the First World War because of the Versailles treaty: the Sudetenland, Pomerania, Lorraine, the former German colonies. They were to be reconquered for the German Reich. The teachers talked of the "colonial lies" of the victorious Allies. We children didn't understand any of this, but we felt the tension. When Hitler reoccupied the Rhineland in 1936, Great Britain and France accepted this breach of the Versailles treaty without much protest. Hitler felt secure in his expansionist policies and hoped that these two powers would back down once again.

The Blitzkrieg against France was essentially a continuation of the First World War. It lasted from the 10th May to the 25th June 1940. The victory parade of the German troops in Paris actually took place on the 14th June. On the 22nd, the armistice with France was signed in the historic railway carriage in Compiègne in which Germany had signed its surrender in 1918. This time Hitler dictated the conditions. He screamed into the microphone: *I have thrown down the Treaty of Versailles at the feet of the French!* After defeat in the First World War and their humiliation by the Treaty of Versailles the German were proud again – and feared again. The German people rejoiced.

The armistice was the equivalent of a surrender by France, and divided France into the free Vichy regime in the south under Marshal Pétain and a German occupied zone in the north. Pétain shook hands with Hitler and offered to cooperate with the Nazis. He regarded the Jews and the Communists as responsible for the defeat of France. Without much resistance from the general populace the transport of French Jews to Germany began, and French citizens started to work for the German war industry. After the end of the war, Pétain was sentenced to life imprisonment for his collaboration with Germany.

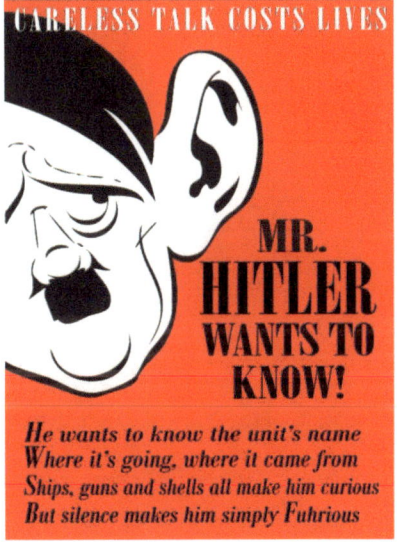

*Ill. 3 German poster Feind hört mit
1941*

*Ill. 4 British posters also warned
against espionage*

We had to be economical with our resources in Germany: they were needed to supply the military. The radio broadcast slogans like: *Save gas to bring victory! Don't heat with electricity! Combat extravagance!* Posters everywhere in towns and villages also encouraged energy saving. Posters like *The enemy is listening* warned against espionage, just as they did in the counties that were our opponents.

The Second World War was now at our door. At first it was only enemy reconnaissance planes, but then came the bombers with their fighter escorts. Then it was the roar of the bomber squadrons as they flew over in large formations. Churchill's announcement that the air war would now come to the cities of Germany was being fulfilled. He hoped to encourage resistance to Hitler by means of the air-raids, but they achieved the direct opposite. The raids made the links between the German people and the regime much stronger. Even people who had until now been sceptical about the Third Reich wished to hold out in the face of these attacks. The USA did not enter the war until the end of 1941, but it had supplied Great Britain with vital war materials even before that.

3. Dream Destination Dutch East Indies

As I have already said, I became familiar with the Dutch East Indies as a child because of my parents' books. In school, adventure novels set in Sumatra and Celebes went the rounds. But my very special interest in the islands on the Equator was encouraged by my geography teacher's stories about the gigantic archipelago. Many Germans were enchanted by the East Indies, especially by Bali. From the beginning of the last century Bali worked like a magnet on painters, musicians, film-makers, writers, actors and the upper ten thousand.

But the charm of the many islands of the archipelago derives not only from the volcanoes, the mountains, the long beaches, the beautiful tropical landscape, the exotic rituals or the unique Hindu culture that can be found only on Bali. The main reason is the gentle, friendly, attractive people. Bali, for example, is a land of born artists, even though every Balinese mainly works as a rice farmer or an artisan. Their whole life is imbued with magic and religion. Every job becomes a work of art for a Balinese, whether it is building rice terraces or a temple. Bali is a picturesque island which has managed to preserve its unique culture for centuries, even during the 350 years of Dutch colonial rule.

In 1931 there was a Colonial Exhibition in Paris, the *Exposition Coloniale Internationale*, which was open for six months. It was visited by 35 million people from all over the world – the colonial nations proudly showed off their colonies and their products at the *Exposition*. They wanted to show the rest of the world how "well" the native populations were doing under their rule. There was of course no mention of profit, exploitation or humiliation of the natives.

The Netherlands had a pavilion which presented the various styles of the colonial Dutch East Indies. There was a Javanese mosque, and also a Balinese Hindu temple. A dance group from Bali performed in a Balinese theatre. They were directed by Tjokorde Gede Raka Sukawati, the Prince of Ubud on Bali and a member of the *Volksraat* (People's Council) of the Dutch colonial government. In Paris he married a European woman as his second or third wife, which gave rise to a certain degree of sensation back home in Ubud when he returned.

Contrary to what has appeared in the literature and the Internet, Walter Spies – the German painter and musician who lived on Bali – was not himself at the exhibition in Paris, although it is certain that the dances presented by the Balinese group were influenced by Spies, who was a close friend of

Tjokorde Gede Raka Sukawati. They always worked closely together on artistic projects. I will return to Walter Spies later.

In connection with the exhibition, R. Goris, a Dutch official who loved Bali, produced the beautiful brochure *The Island of Bali: Its Religion and Ceremonies* (Batavia 1931), including photographs by Walter Spies. Its main purpose was to be an advertisement by the Dutch government to promote tourism on Bali.

From the 17th century onwards, the Indonesian archipelago had played an important part in literature written in German, and the Paris exhibition also inspired a boom in German literature about the East Indies which reached its high point during the Third Reich. This included adventure novels, children's books, non-fiction, travel writing, art books, language guides, novels, penny dreadfuls, Christian missionary books and many more.

Between 1930 and the end of the war well over 300 publications about the Indonesian archipelago appeared. Even during the war years from 1939-45 there were almost 90 publications, although the numbers did fall off sharply during this period. It is striking that many authors used the word "Indonesia", coined by the German doctor and scientist Adolf Bastian, for the archipelago, even though it was still under Dutch rule and the word was strictly forbidden in the colony.

Many authors also used the picturesque name invented by the German doctor, zoologist, biologist, philosopher and painter Ernst Haeckel: "Insulinde". Unfortunately this did not catch on internationally.

The works of Baron Victor von Plessen (published 1936 and 1944) and Hans Hasso von Veltheim-Ostrau (published 1943) gave rise to considerable interest in Germany, even though the war was already in its final phase.

Veltheim-Ostrau stayed with Walter Spies on Bali in 1938. His *Tagebücher aus Asien 1937-1939* (Asian Diaries 1937-1939) speaks enthusiastically about Bali as the "paradisiac, peaceful and unworldly island". When the book was published in 1943, German U-boats were already operating in Balinese waters and German sailors and a German air squadron were stationed only a few hundred kilometres west of Bali, in Surabaya. In the waters around the Dutch East Indies thousands of sailors, prisoners of war, internees and forced labourers had already died. No trace of "peaceful" and "paradise": the war had arrived in the East Indies.

The number of books for young people in which the region played a role was striking. We passed around from hand to hand books whose adventures were set on Java, in the jungles of Sumatra or on the island of Nias. Through reading these books we learned many words in Malay as children: *Tuan, Mau apa?* (Lord, what do you want?), *Selamat pagi* (Good morning) or *Toko Obat* (Pharmacy): they then became part of our youthful vocabulary as a "secret language".

The many new publications during the Third Reich included countless comic book series with adventure stories, scientific themes and historical events. There was a vast selection. All of these series – some of which had over 300 titles – provided a great deal of information about the Dutch East Indies.

Wilhelm Reinhardt's penny-dreadful series *Jörn Farrow's U-Boot-Abenteuer* (Jörn Farrow's U-boat Adventures) ran to over 350 numbers from 1932 to 1940. It narrates almost exclusively adventures in an U-boat around the islands of the Dutch East Indies. Although even those at the very top in Nazi Germany could not at the time have imagined that German U-boats would operate in these waters, these stories were about a U-boat which was continually being pursued by the Allies in the First World War. Since the Netherlands were neutral in that conflict, the submarine could always seek sanctuary in their East Indian Waters.

We boys knew all about the islands and cities of the region, because there were always maps of the relevant regions on the back of the comics. In terms of geography and other factual knowledge this series (and many others) were very educational. The inside of the cover always had factual knowledge about the language, the script or the culture of the country. Many magazines also reported on the Hindu culture of Bali. The Germans, young and old, were better informed about the Dutch East Indies during the Third Reich than they are today about the country called Indonesia. The tropical archipelago, whose islands wind round the Equator like a string of pearls, was very familiar to us in those days.

In Germany a real Bali myth was created by several films that reached German cinemas after 1931. First was the film *Der Kris* (The Kris) or *Das flammende Schwert* (The Flaming Sword, English title: Goona Goona) shot by André Roosevelt and Armand Denis on Bali in 1928/29. Walter Spies was an advisor on this film, which was premiered in the USA in 1930 and seen in German cinemas in 1931.

An even earlier film was mentioned by Robert Genin in his 1929 book *Die Ferne Insel: Aufzeichnungen von meiner Fahrt nach Bali* (The distant island: sketches of my trip to Bali). On his way to Bali he crossed Java as well. He says:

[...] The most glorious Buddhist monuments are nearby, and the Kraton, the seat of the Sultan, has recently become a great attraction for Europeans. A great film "At the Sultan's court" has already been shot – and it is reported in all the newspapers! We are as interested in the Sultan of Dyokya (now: Yogya, abbreviation for Yogyakarta), *as if he were actually our cousin. [...]*[1]

---

1   Genin, *Die Ferne Insel*, p. 125

Unfortunately I have been unable to find any details about this early – perhaps even the first – film about Bali.

Victor von Plessen knew a great deal about the Dutch East Indies. His first expedition to Bali took place in 1924/25, when he rediscovered the wonderful bird Bali Mina (Leucopsar). His second expedition took him to Celebes (now: Sulawesi) and the small islands of the Flores Sea. The premiere of von Plessen's film *Insel der Dämonen* (The Isle of Demons) took place in 1933, only a few days before Hitler seized power.

He had filmed it on Bali from 1930 to 1931 with his cameraman Dalsheim and in collaboration with Walter Spies.

In 1934 and 1935, during his fourth and last expedition, he filmed *Die Kopfjäger von Borneo* (The Headhunters of Borneo) which was premiered in German cinemas in 1936. Both his films were a success worldwide, and not just in Germany. In 1941 – in the middle of the war – there was a new cut of *Insel der Dämonen* with the title *Bali - Kleinod der*

Ill. 6
Film poster 1933

Südsee (Jewel of the South Seas) in German cinemas. It had been remastered with a new sound track and was shown until the end of the war. In the middle of a war, this film about a magical landscape with peaceful people in an idyllic world was a welcome contrast to horrific experiences at the front and in the ruined cities.

The Nazi party also attempted to use cultural films and radio programmes, like for example *Bali, das Paradies* (The Paradise of Bali, 1934) for their aims. Those responsible even went so far as to emphasise the 'Indo-Aryan blood-line" of the Hindu population of Bali![1]

In a letter of the 24th December 1940 Dr Hans Heinrich Hiller, "General Commissioner for Cinema and Theatre in the General Government of the Occupied Areas in Eastern Europe" wrote to "Privy Councillor and Envoy" Walther Hewel about an operetta with the title "Bali":

When I last saw you we spoke about Bali and my planned operetta. I have now completed it. And what better thing could I do than to dedicate it to the man who knows Bali and its beauty from personal experience. And so I present this first copy to you as a Christmas gift, coupled with sincere wishes for a happy Christmas, Heil Hitler, signed Hiller.

All attempts to discover the fate of this operetta in both German and Hungary were unfortunately unsuccessful. However, a film entitled *Mámoros Báli éj* (Enchanted Bali) was shown in Hungarian cinemas in 1939. It was impossible to discover, even from Hungarian sources, if this film was identical to the operetta.[2]

The films, books and reports about the tropical Dutch East Indies were clearly a kind of surrogate travel during the isolation of the war years. In the German media's presentation during the Third Reich Bali was an earthly paradise, a place to be longed for. The Germans sought a peaceful edenic alternative to the modern western way of living and the constant sense of threat and anxiety caused by the war that Hitler had brought upon them.

German films were received with great enthusiasm by the native population in the East Indies. During the Third Reich German films were shown with increasing frequency in cinemas there. The 1933 U-boat adventure film *Morgenrot* (Dawn, 1933) was particularly popular. Cinemas were full to the last seat when German films were shown. It was a form of propaganda intended to strengthen the population's sympathy for Germany. To draw the attention of the Dutch, the posters for German film premieres in Batavia were often bigger than the cinema itself.[3]

---

1   Gottowik, *Die Ethnographen ...*, pp. 202f
2   www.szineszkonyvtr.hu
3   Wilson, *Orang dan Partai Nazi ...*, p. 110

Ill. 7
Walter Spies with monkey and
cockatoo

The German painter and musician Walter Spies, whom we have mentioned several times above, came to Java in 1923 and then moved to Bali in 1927, where he was active until his death in 1942. Although he was an extraordinary artist, Walter Spies is known in Germany almost exclusively in connoisseur circles, whereas in the international art world, and particularly in Bali, he is very much admired. He was a bridge-builder between the two cultures.

The German architect Curt Grundler designed the ethnographic "Museum Bali" in Denpasar in 1910. As early as 1917 the museum was destroyed by the eruption of the volcano Gunung Batur and the subsequent earthquakes. It was through Spies' initiative that the museum was rebuilt in its present form, and he was its first curator on its reopening in 1932. In 1936, together with Tjokorde Gede Agung Sukawati, the Balinese painter I Gusti Nyoman Lempad and the Dutch painter Rudolf Bonnet he founded an artists' association, Pita Maha, which had nearly 150 Balinese artists in its membership.

Vicki Baum's 1937 novel *Life and Death in Bali* was written while she was staying with Spies using him as an advisor. It was an immediate bestseller and has become a classic which is still a fascinating read today.

Not only during the Third Reich but also after the end of the war there was continued enthusiasm for the new Republic of Indonesia. There were a large number of children's books and adventure novels from the war years about Java, Sumatra, Celebes, New Guinea and Bali were still on the market. New books and re-issues of old ones added to their number.

While a terrible colonial war was being waged against the freedom-loving Indonesians by the Dutch, we schoolboys would greet each other with the Malay phrase *Tabeh Tuan*. We were unaware of the atrocities committed by the Dutch in their attempt to reconquer their former colony – and so

Ill. 8
Walter Spies, The Village Street

were the adults in Germany at the time. The Dutch were very skilled at concealing their crimes against the Indonesians for many decades.

But this flood of books and films cannot be the only explanation for Hitler's especial interest in the Dutch East Indies. As well as the abundance of raw materials to be found in the archipelago there must have been something else that drew his attention to the area.

Walther Hewel, already mentioned above, became possibly Hitler's closest advisor and intimate, in fact their friendship developed into a lifelong relationship. Hewel remained one of Hitler's few personal friends until the latter's death. This man captured my imagination, and I began to research his life.

Was Walther Hewel the key to Hitler's interest in the archipelago with its rich natural resources? That seems to be the case! Hitler was never in the Dutch East Indies himself, but the land of the many thousand islands was – as we will see – introduced to him by Walther Hewel.

As well as my mother and my grammar school geography teacher, it was the large number of children's books and adventure comics of the period that aroused my interest in the region. And that was why as a schoolboy in a little town in South Germany I was already dreaming of the exotic Greater and Lesser Sunda Islands. My dream came true: I was to spend 18 years working in that beautiful country with its friendly and cultivated people.

Although literature about the Dutch East Indies played so great a role in the Third Reich, the German people were given little or no information about the activities of the German military in South East Asia. All attention was on the naval war in the Atlantic and on the Western and Eastern Fronts. Even today the majority of the German people have little idea of the theatre of war in the Indian Ocean and the Java Sea. This book is intended to fill that gap.

4. Walther Hewel and Adolf Hitler with Emil Helfferich, Freiherr von Trott and Ernst A. Bohle

Because of his family Walther Hewel had very close connections to the Dutch East Indies. His father, Anton Hewel, was partner in a cocoa factory in Java. After his death, Hewel's mother Elsa, née Freiin von Lindenfels, continued to run the firm. His mother's family had extensive family connections with England.

Walther[1] Hewel himself said that he was born on the 25th of March 1904 in Cologne. In the index of the Federal German Archive the date is wrongly given as the 25th of April 1904, and on the Internet the date of the 2nd of January 1904 is current. These differences in themselves demonstrate how little research was done into this man in the past. After successfully passing his Abitur and an internship in Cologne he studied Technology and Industrial Engineering at the Technical University in Munich.

Ill. 9
·Walther Hewel (October 1940)

Walther Hewel was an early adherent of National Socialism and became a member of the paramilitary Nazi organisation *Stoßtrupp (Shock Troop) Hitler*, a predecessor of the SS which was initially founded as Hitler's personal guard. As a student Hewel took part in Hitler's putsch in Munich in November 1923 as a standard bearer and was subsequently sentenced to a fine of 30 Gold marks and a suspended prison sentence of three months for being an accessory to high treason. When he took part in further Nazi activities the suspension was rescinded and he had to serve his sentence in prison at Landsberg.

1in some letters and documents also 'Walter''

In this fortress prison Hewel became much closer acquainted with his fellow prisoners Hitler and Rudolf Hess. During his time in jail, Walther Hewel, who was in the cell next to Hitler's, acted as Hitler's valet. Rudolf Hess, Hitler's secretary, became Hitler's deputy from 1933 onwards, and thus Hewel developed from early on a close and intimate connection to the two most powerful men in the Third Reich.

After all the frenzied activity and confusion preceeding the putsch in November 1923 Hitler made use of his enforced leisure and exclusion from political activity. During his term in prison he dictated his two-volume work *Mein Kampf* (My Struggle) to Hess. This was also the time that he thought up the concepts of the autobahn and a *'Volkswagen'* car that would be affordable by everyone.

Hitler and his roughly forty fellow participants in the putsch had comfortable conditions and a great deal of freedom in the prison – it was rather a pleasant stay. They were able to forge new plans and celebrate birthdays: Hitler turned 35 there, and the event was celebrated with flowers and presents. The prison administration met any special requests he made: he could receive visitors for up to six hours a day, and take his meals together with his fellow-prisoners at a long table beneath the swastika banner.[1]

Hewel was released early from prison on probation on the 30th of December 1924 at Hitler's instigation. Hitler himself was released ten days later.

During his time in jail Hitler not only wrote *Mein Kampf* but also converted the prison staff to National Socialism: as he left the prison, the Governor, Leybold, said, *"I think that I am today a National Socialist myself."*[2]

Since their time together in prison there was a lasting, close relationship between Hewel, Hitler and Hess. Rudolf Hess, born and growing up as the son of a German merchant family in Alexandria in Egypt, spoke fluent Arabic. He was open-minded and interested in distant countries, just like Hewel. The subsequent course of Hewel's life was definitely affected by his friendship with Hess as much as his family's connections with the Dutch East Indies. They were on common ground with their National Socialism, their admiration for Hitler and their mutual enthusiasm for exotic lands.

After their prison term, Hewel was very soon adopted into the inner circle of Hitler's advisors, and his close friendship with Hitler and Hess laid the foundation for his meteoric career in the Third Reich. But how did Hitler become interested in the then Dutch East Indies? How can it be that research on Hitler has until now more or less ignored the life of Hewel and his

---

1   Fest, *Hitler,* pp.287ff
2   Document imprisonment of Manfred Deiler,
     www.buergervereinigung-landsberg.de

close connection with Hitler? That is what inspired me to undertake my own research, and I was surprised what extraordinary material came to light in German and Indonesian archives. I am sure that in the future further material will be found about this man: my investigations can only be a beginning. But first, we must look at Hewel as a young man.

After graduating at university, Hewel went to Great Britain in 1926 to perfect his knowledge of English. There he made contact with Anglo-Dutch Plantations of Java Ltd, 5 & 7 East Cheap, London. On his own initiative he travelled to Java in order, as he said, to get to know the world. On the 9th of March 1927 Hewel set sail from Amsterdam on the *SS Rembrandt,* a ship of the Dutch line *Stoomvaart-Maatschappij Nederland*, his destination Batavia.

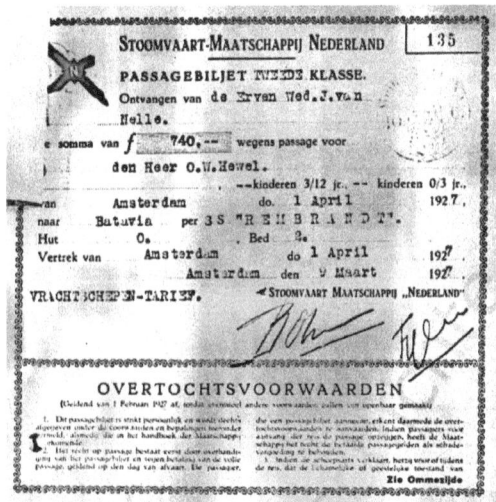

Ill. 10
Walther Hewel's ticket from Amsterdam to Batavia on the SS Rembrandt

Hewel worked for ten years precisely on the Neglasari Estate at Garoet (now: Garut) in West Java. In the hierarchy of Anglo-Dutch Plantations of Java Ltd he rose to become the Chief Assistant, an important position just below that of the manager.

A friendly letter sent by Hewel from Neglasari to Dr Karl Aloys Schenzinger on the 7th of October 1933 is extant, in which he hands over letters from his time in prison in Landsberg. Hewel and Schenzinger must have known each other since the 1920s. As well as being a doctor, Schenzinger was one of the Nazi movement's star authors. Between 1932 and 1945 his book for young people, *Der Hitlerjunge Quex* [Hitler Youth Quex] had a print run of more than half a million copies. Filmed in 1933, it was the first Nazi propaganda film aimed specifically at German youth. Schenzinger's sympathy for Hitler could be seen clearly in his books and the goals of National Socialism were always emphasized, even though he was never a card-carrying member of the party.

Hewel must have owned shares in the company he worked for (Anglo-Dutch Plantations of Java Ltd) because among his private correspondence I found letters from the company concerning dividends paid from Great Britain for the years 1936, 1937 and 1938, a period in which Hewel was already back with Hitler in Germany.[1]

Hewel also played an important role in the founding of local branches of the Nazi party in the Dutch West Indies. As early as 1931 organisations that supported Hitler began to be amalgamated. Eye witness reports tell us that in November 1933 around 1,000 Germans were queuing outside the party office in Batavia to sign up for membership.[2] As well as the Nazi party there was also at that time the right-wing *Vaterländische* [Patriotic] *Club* with almost 10,000 members.

After Hitler seized power in 1933 the various amalgamated Nazi and other extreme right-wing groups were tightly organised into local groups. Hitler was trying to gain a foothold in selected countries, particularly in North and South America, India and the Far East, by means of his National Socialist ideology. There were firmly established Nazi organisations in India, Japan, China, Australia and the Dutch East Indies. German schools, churches and newspapers in these countries received financial support from the German government.

At the end of the 1920s there were about 357,000 *Reichs* Germans and *Volks* Germans living in Asia and the Pacific islands. The Hitler regime divided the Germans into *Reichsdeutsche*, people with German citizenship, and *Volksdeutsche*, people of German descent, such as those Germans who had taken Netherlands citizenship. They tried, by means of the naval visits mentioned above and financial support of German-language newspapers and organisations, to strengthen the links between Germans living abroad and their homeland, Germany.

Because of the established trade links with the Dutch East Indies, Hitler was particularly interested in boosting his influence in the region. As well as food like coconut oil and sago, Germany imported rubber, tin, oil, tobacco and quinine from the area, not to mention bauxite, the aluminium ore that was so important for German industry.

The German consulate in Batavia was the operational centre for the spread of National Socialist ideology in the Dutch East Indies. It was subordinate to the German embassy in Tokyo, Japan. F. K. Trautmann was the Deputy National Group Leader of the *NSDAP Niederländisch-Indien*. He worked as administrator of the Kedondong Plantation at Lampong in southern Su-

---

1   AA, R 27480
2   Wilson, *Orang dan Partai...*, p. 109

matra. The head of the consulate was Konsul Tiemann. Parts of the former German consulate in Batavia survive to this day in the US embassy complex in Jakarta.

Long before the Third Reich there were Germans in the Dutch East Indies, Singapore and Malaya with nationalist attitudes and organisations that promoted their ideology. For example, in the Dutch East Indies there were from 1915 onwards the twice-monthly periodical *Deutsche Wacht* [German Guard], the *Deutscher Bund* [German League] also founded in 1915 with 3,000 members and the *Deutsches Haus* [German House] inaugurated on the 26th of November 1926 in a prime position on the Koningsplein in the Weltevreden area of Batavia. The founder and instigator of all three was the German merchant Emil Helfferich.

Ill. 11
Inauguration of the Deutsches Haus, 26 November 1926,
Emil Helfferich is in black in the centre of the front row

Helfferich was a striking example of the nationalist attitude of many Germans in the Dutch East Indies. He initially traded in pepper, and was later head of the Straits and Sunda Syndicate. He was an important personality among German merchants in the Dutch East Indies at the beginning of the 20th century.

Ill. 12
Emil Helfferich, Batavia 1927

Helfferich arrived in Penang in Malaya in 1899 and shortly afterwards moved to southern Sumatra, where he set up his first company. Later he was active in Batavia, which was also his most successful period. As well as his work for the *Deutscher Bund* and his regular contributions to the *Deutsche Wacht*, he worked tirelessly to promote German trade relations with the Dutch East Indies. In 1924 he founded the first German overseas Chamber of Trade in the Dutch East Indies. In 1928 he returned to Germany.

When the *Deutsche Wacht* was first published in January 1915, Helfferich said: *To counter the hostile war propaganda aimed at the Germans it was necessary to found an organ that would represent the German national standpoint.* Helfferich's speeches and contributions to the journal were full of glowing nationalism.

Deutsche Wacht

Schriftleitung und Geschäftsstelle:
Batavia-Centrum,
Keban Sirih 12.

Bezugspreis im voraus zahlbar für
Niederl-Indien jährlich fl 12.- für ...
Ausland fl 15.-

No. 5   Batavia, 14. März   1939

Kolonialpolitik und Rassenfrage
Die Kolonialgesetze der europäischen Nationen.

In der ausländischen Presse hat man verschiedentlich versucht, die Erörterungen in der Kolonialfrage damit abzutun, dass der deutsche Rassenstandpunkt die Übertragung eines Mandates von vornherein verbiete und unmöglich mache. Denn, so sagte man, aus allgemein menschlichen Gründen könne man den Eingeborenen eine deutsche Schutzhoheit nicht zumuten. Selbst die Engländer, die einen ausgesprochenen Rasseninstinkt besitzen und diesen in ihrer kolonialen Praxis nie verleugnet haben, wenn sie auch weniger davon gesprochen haben, haben diesen Vorwand aufgegriffen und glaubten damit, die Angelegenheit im Keime zu ersticken.

Diese bekannten Ablenkungsmanöver können auch nämlich getauft oder nicht getauft — unterschied, blieben dennoch dank dem meist vorherrschenden Instinkt und dank der persönlichen Disziplin der Mehrzahl der Weissen die Rassenunterschiede allgemein erhalten. Erst im 18. Jahrhundert reifte die grundsätzliche Änderung heran. Man besann sich nun, im Zeitalter des aufkommenden Liberalismus und der Aufklärung, der „allgemein menschlichen Verpflichtungen", die ein Herrenvolk gegenüber seinen Kolonien besitzt.

Auf Grund seiner rassisch bedingten Weltauffassung, dass nämlich er allein der Träger der wahren Kulturerkenntnis sei, erkannte z.B. der Franzose seine Aufgabe zur „Menschheitsbeglückung". Für

Ill. 13 ‚Deutsche Wacht', Batavia, 14th March 1939, Colonial policy and the race question

After his return to Germany Emil Helfferich became chairman of the board of the *Hamburg-Amerikanische Paketfahrt-Actien-Gesellschaft* (HAPAG) as well as chairman of the influential *Ostasiatischer Verein* (OAV: East Asian Society) in Hamburg. He retained these positions even after the end of the war.

Since Hewel arrived in Batavia a year before Emil Helfferich's departure it is almost certain that they met personally because during their time in the Dutch East Indies they were prominent figures in the German community. In any case, when Hewel arrived in 1927 he found that the ground had been well prepared by Helfferich and that there was a strongly nationalist German community.

Hewel and Helfferich must even have become good friends, because after Hewel returned home there was a lively and friendly correspondence between them. The Christmas and New Year's greetings that Hewel sent at the end of 1938 included among others one to Gretl Braun, the sister of Hitler's mistress Eva Braun and another to Emil Helfferich.

In Hewel's letter of the 24th of August 1940 to *Dear Staatsrat [State Councillor] Helfferich* he thanks the latter for two postcards he had sent him from Japan. Hewel writes:
[...] I was delighted and no less honoured that you should think of me in that far-off country in spite of the onerous tasks that you had in hand there. [...][1]

In a further letter of the 30th of September 1940 he asks Helfferich to send him a copy of a summary of statistical information about the Dutch East Indies because *[...] I would like to learn more about the Dutch East Indies in order to be able to inform the Führer, who often asks questions about the Indies.*[2] *[...]*[3] He did not have long to wait for Helfferich's response containing the desired information, which was sent on the 2nd of October 1940. In a further letter Hewel requests two notebooks containing travel sketches and the speeches that Helfferich had given in Japan, as he wished to show them to the "Führer".[4] All correspondence concerning the Dutch East Indies and the Far East crossed Hewel's desk.

In 1938 Helfferich travelled on the Trans-Siberian Railway for trade discussions in Manchukuo (now: Manchuria) and Japan. He tried in vain to invigorate trade between Germany and East Asia. His speeches in Japan were not only about economic matters, they also glowed with nationalist enthusiasm:

---

1   AA, Handakte Hewel 2, R 27469
2   The Dutch and the Germans living in the Dutch East Indies called the colony simply 'Indien' in contrast with British India.
3   AA, Handakte Hewel 2, R 27469
4   AA, Handakte Hewel 2, R 27469 and IfZ, Hewel's personal documents

[...] Hitler has succeeded in leading his people out of the depths, from the swamp of existence to the heights of humanity. [...] He has helped a poor, down-trodden, distressed and demoralised people which was in deep despair to stand upright again. [...][1]

In the Third Reich Helfferich was deeply involved in National Socialism. Even before he seized power, Hitler got Wilhelm Keppler, chairman of the board of *Braunkohle Benzin AG* [Lignite and Petroleum Company] and a member of the board of *Continentale Öl AG* [Continental Oil Company] to arrange a meeting of the most important Hanseatic business figures. This took place in Berlin in the presence of Hitler and Rudolf Hess on the 30th of April 1932. Helfferich participated in the meeting, together with the industrialist Friedrich Flick, the banker Hjalmar Schacht, the heads of IG-Farben and other business and banking experts. This was the birth of the Keppler Circle, later renamed the *Freundeskreis [Circle of Friends of] Himmler* or *Freundeskreis Reichsführer SS*, which provided substantial financial aid to Himmler. Helfferich remained a member of this circle until the end of the war. Wilhelm Keppler was a member of the *Reichstag* and a secretary of state in the Foreign Ministry from 1933 onwards and was one of the most important contacts with the Indian freedom fighter Subhas Chandra Bose, of whom more later. In spite of holding high office in the Third Reich Keppler continued as chairman of the board of *Braunkohle Benzin AG* and a member of the board of *Continentale Öl AG* after the end of the war.[2]

In 1933 Hewel became a member of the National Socialist Foreign Organisation as head of the Dutch East Indies overseas section, head of business activities in the Bandung local group and press officer of the Dutch East Indies national group. The National Socialist group in the Dutch East Indies was the second largest in the Asia-Pacific region after China.

Hewel does not appear to have been particularly active as press officer: in the many copies of the *Deutsche Wacht* preserved in the National Library Jakarta I could only find very few references to Hewel, although, given the large volume of material, it was not possible to conduct a truly searching examination. Here are two examples of references to Hewel:

Wickel, the head of the National Socialist national group in the Dutch East Indies, presented the group's greetings personally to Hitler and his deputy Rudolf Hess in 1934. As he departed, Hitler said to Wickel: *Greet Hewel from me.*[3]

---

1   Helfferich, *Vorträge in Japan, März – April 1940, vor der Japan Economic Federation,* Tokyo
2   Bucher Gruppe, *Freundeskreis Himmler,* Books Llc 2010
3   ANRI, *Deutsche Wacht,* No. 1, 1935

Further evidence is found in a copy of an extract from a newspaper, presumably *Deutsche Wacht*, with a letter from Houston Stewart Chamberlain to Hitler.[1] The introduction states:

The following transcript of the letter, made during the time spent together with Hitler in the fortress prison of Landsberg, was provided to us by Herr W. Hewel, Neglasari. This letter was written to Adolf Hitler by the then 68-year-old and seriously ill Houston Stewart Chamberlain, well-known author of "The Foundations of the Nineteenth Century".

The text of the letter follows. Since Chamberlain had written the letter to Hitler on the 7th of October 1923 and Hewel only arrived in Neglasari of Java three and a half years later in March 1927, I assume that Hewel only provided his transcript of the letter for publication in the paper in 1927.

The head of the NSDAP/AO (*Auslands Organisation* [Foreign Organisation]), who organised all overseas activities of the party from Hamburg (later Berlin), was Ernst Wilhelm Bohle. This section reported to Joachim von Ribbentrop, later Foreign Minister in the Third Reich. Bohle was a British citizen, born in Bradford, educated in South Africa, where his father was a professor of electrical engineering. Bohle studied politics and business in Cologne and Berlin. Married to a German, Bohle was so fascinated by Hitler and his ideology that, even though he was British, he joined the Nazi Party as early as 1932. He was convinced that with his knowledge of Great Britain, Africa and other countries, as well as being a native speaker of English, he could be of great use to the Nazi leadership. Bohle was convinced that only Hitler could save Europe from the "Red Plague", as he called Communism, and the Jewish Conspiracy. In 1933 he also joined the SS. From 1931 onwards he worked in the NSDAP/AO and from 1937 until the end of the war he was "Head of the Foreign Organisation in the Foreign Ministry" with the high rank of *Gauleiter*. Bohle was an unusual member of the Nazi hierarchy and it is astonishing that, as a British subject, he managed to achieve so high a position. At the end of 1937 he gave up his British passport and became a German citizen.

Bohle had an exceptionally good relationship with Hess, Goebbels and Himmler. His relationship with Ribbentrop, on the other hand, was problematic. As a leading member of the Nazi Party in the Dutch East Indies and press officer of the national group Hewel must have been in contact with Bohle from early on. Later, when Hewel was the Foreign Ministry's contact with Hitler, this would have been urgently necessary in view of their positions. However, I have found no evidence to support this in those documents of Hewel's that I have seen so far.[2]

---

1   ANRI, In Documents *Deutsche Wacht*, p. 18f, no date or place of publication.
2   Hausmann, *Ernst Wilhelm Bohle, Gauleiter*

The aim of the NSDAP/AO was to mobilise the roughly 30 million German expatriates round the world in support of the Nazi movement's goals. Hitler, Hess and Bohle even saw it as their mission to unite all Germans living abroad in a *Volksgemeinschaft* [People's Community].

There were local groups of the Nazi Party on Java in Batavia, in Bandung, Semarang and Surabaya; on Sumatra in Medan and Padang and on Celebes in Makassar. The swastika banners fluttered in the wind even in the Far East – over the local party group headquarters, and the German Clubs and German Associations that were to be found in all larger towns. Hitler's portrait hung in German living rooms, just as that of Queen Wilhelmina did in Dutch homes.

As I was told in the 1960s by Indonesian veterans who had fought in the War of Independence from 1945 to December 1949, a large number of Indonesians made efforts at the beginning of the Second World War to become members of one of the NSDAP local groups. They wished to position themselves on the side of the Germans, expecting that Hitler would support their struggle for independence. The Dutch naturally wished to maintain their position of power and severely punished any Indonesians who made contact with the Nazi Party.

There were also, of course, German nationals who did not agree with Hitler and his Nazi ideology and turned their back on the Third Reich, many of them taking Dutch citizenship. As we will see, this change of nationality did not help them very much. And there were also Germans in the Dutch East Indies who said to themselves: *What does a war in Europe have to do with us – it's so far away?* They too were making a mistake.

After the German army marched into the Netherlands the Dutch colonial rulers did not care whether someone was a *Reichs* German or a *Volks* German – for them all Germans, even those who had become Dutch citizens were *Duitsers* – worse, they were all *verdomde Moffen* [Damn Krauts].

A two-class society developed among the Germans in the Dutch East Indies. Those who were *Reichsdeutsche* joined the Nazi Party in large numbers during the war. The *Volksdeutsche*, the naturalised Dutch, were regarded by the former as half Dutch and therefore not to be trusted. After the invasion of Holland, it was not only the German citizens who were interned, but also the others, even if they did have a Dutch passport. The Dutch still regarded them as being half German. But more of that later.

Because of his broad experience abroad in Great Britain and the Dutch East Indies, as well as his education and his linguistic competence (German, English, French, Spanish, Dutch and Malay) Hewel was well placed to comprehend international matters. As well as having excellent professional knowledge he was a good conversationalist and sociable, and with his social graces was thus able to move confidently in the highest international circles. Hitler did not fail to notice these valuable qualities – this may have been the reason that Hitler maintained contact with Hewel after their time in Landsberg.

Hitler seems never to have forgotten Hewel's birthday, even when he was on the plantation in Neglasari: there are several letters from Java among his documents thanking Hitler for birthday gifts. Later, even during the war, Hewel thanks Hitler every year for birthday greetings and presents.[1]

At the end of 1935 Hewel received a personal invitation from Hitler to work for him in Germany. He offered an important position, and Hewel answered the call. In January 1936 Hewel began his sea voyage back to Germany, which, since he had secret messages for various Nazi organisations in the Far East, took him via Hong Kong to Shanghai, and via Nagasaki, Kobe and Tokyo to Yokohama.

The NSDAP/AO in Berlin informed the national groups in China and Japan about Hewel's impending visit in writing on the 21st of January 1936 through three channels: airmail, sea mail and land mail over the Trans-Siberian Railway. The airmail and sea mail messages contain the following addition:

The above-mentioned redacted version has been chosen because of the postal route via Siberia [Author's note: Fear of Russian censorship?]. I repeat that the summons to Pg. [Parteigenossen: Party Comrade] Hewel to join the higher ranks of the A.O. comes as the result of instructions from a higher instance [Hitler]. Pg. Hewel has until now been press agent for the National Group in the Dutch East Indies and has performed his duties extremely well. He accompanied the Führer on the 9th of November 1923 and was his loyal companion during his imprisonment in Landsberg.

I wish it to be known that he should be informed, without any reserve about the organisation of both national groups [Author's note: China and Japan] and any important matters of a local nature and that he should be introduced to all political leaders, insofar as this is attainable, and also the local representatives of the Reich. AO stamp.

The signature was indecipherable. The addressees were Siegfried Lahrmann in Shanghai and Rudolf Hillmann in Tokyo.[2] A similar letter of recommendation was given to Hewel by the NSDAP national group in Batavia.

---

1 IfZ, ED 100/79, Fa 74/39 and IfZ, ED 100/78, entry for 25th of March 1941
2 IfZ, ED 100-79-30 and ED 100-79-31

After the conclusion of his mission in China and Japan Hewel boarded another ship in Yokohama and sailed via Honolulu to San Francisco. He arrived in Cologne in April 1936 having travelled from New York via Hamburg. Then he was called to Berlin, where he registered with the police on the 5th of June 1936.

Hewel's rise in the Nazi Party in Berlin was meteoric. He began in charge of the head office of the Foreign Organisation of the party. At first he was Ribbentrop's main advisor on Great Britain. Hewel writes: *A job that brings me to England almost every week.*[1]

Even before Hewel returned to Berlin, Ribbentrop had been heavily involved with Britain. Hitler wished Ribbentrop to interest Great Britain in a pact with the German Reich and prepare a treaty with Great Britain. Great Britain refused, but he did succeed in bringing about the Anglo-German Naval Treaty in 1933. During this period, Ribbentrop founded the Anglo-German Society in London. Though he was initially a great friend of Britain, Ribbentrop became a bitter enemy in the course of time because of numerous disappointments.

Hewel also tried to encourage a strengthening of Anglo-German relations. He promoted the exchange of large groups of school pupils and students with Newcastle in England. This was commented on positively even in the British press, as a report in the *Newcastle Journal* on the 15th of June 1938 shows. Nevertheless, Hewel also had some doubts. He writes:

[...] Although I am very much in favour of promoting Anglo-German relations as we have done in recent years, it is of course justifiable to ask whether this work, which demands so much effort, really has any point politically today. We have all too often found that the British government is prepared, disregarding the natural feelings of its people, and young people as well, to pursue a policy which is directed against us, or rather against the strengthening of our fatherland. I myself, knowing England well, and having previously been of a different opinion, now also believe that English politics is governed exclusively by two or three hundred people or families, who go their own way and have the politically naive population so much under their control that to work against this step by step as we have done has no effect on the direction of their policies. [...] Only recently, the Führer spoke in his intimate circle about the problem of what England would have become if it had accepted his suggestions and entered into political agreement with Germany. In its whole world-wide empire, England would have no problems that it could not solve very easily with the strongest military power in the world at its side. Instead, the English with their incorrigible

---

1   IfZ, ED 100/78, Appendix

arrogance still believe that they could bring the flourishing of the German state to a halt whenever they wish. [...][1]

In the context of an attempted alliance with Great Britain, we should also mention Ferdinand Adam Freiherr von Trott zu Solz. From his earliest youth von Trott – influenced certainly by his English nanny – was very anglophile. In 1929 at the age of 20 he entered the University of Oxford to study political science. After graduation, he received a scholarship from the university for post-graduate study. He joined the Labour Club and made many friends in the House of Commons.

When Hitler came to power in 1933, Trott initially made efforts to promote closer collaboration between Great Britain and the German Reich. When this did not succeed, he decided to organise resistance against Hitler. He returned to Germany and took part in paramilitary sports camps for appearances' sake. He made several major journeys to the USA, Japan, Korea, Manchukuo and China. In 1938 he returned to Germany and was given a post in the Foreign Ministry in Berlin, where he made contact with other members of the resistance, including Claus Schenk Graf von Stauffenberg.

Hewel and von Trott met in 1939. His mother, Elsa Freiin zu Lindenfels, was a distant relation of the von Trott zu Solz family. Hewel welcomed and supported von Trott's suggestion that he make use of his good contacts to promote an alliance, or at least a non-aggression pact between Germany and Britain. Von Trott travelled to Britain on the 1st of June 1939. He actually met Lord Halifax, the British Foreign Minister at his country seat, Cliveden, as well as the Prime Minister, Neville Chamberlain, in Downing Street and one of Churchill's four daughters. On his return to Berlin he spoke – presumably to ward off suspicion – of his *bitter disappointment with English policies.*[2]

The Astors' country seat, Cliveden, gave its name to the Cliveden Set, a clique of important and influential British Politicians. Its members included, as well as Lord Halifax, Neville Chamberlain, Sir Samuel Hoare (Foreign Secretary in 1935 and Home Secretary from 1937 to 1939), Lady Nancy Astor (an American-born British politician who also had links with the Astor family USA through her husband) John Simon (Home Secretary in 1935 and Chancellor of the Exchequer from 1937 to 1940), Geoffrey Dawson (Editor in chief of the Times) and many other influential people. They were all closely connected with the Anglo-German Fellowship – whose aim was to promote friendship between the two countries – and their policy was to promote Britain's restraint with regard to Hitler's plans. One result of this

---

1   AA, R 27468, p. 368223-25
2   Dönhoff, *Um der Ehre willen*, p. 156

was Chamberlain's signing the Munich Agreement which left Hitler free to occupy the Sudetenland in Czechoslovakia. On the one hand the Cliveden Set wished to avoid conflict and on the other they saw Germany as a bulwark against Bolshevism. The best-known opponents of their policies were Winston Churchill, Anthony Eden (Foreign Secretary from 1940 to 1945) and the British politician and diplomat Alfred Duff Cooper.

In October 1939 von Trott was invited by Edward C. Carter to a conference in the USA. Carter had contacts to the Sorge Spy Ring through American and Chinese Communists. Hewel again intervened with Hitler to allow von Trott to travel to America even though the war had already started.[1] Von Trott was received in the US Foreign Ministry and was invited to tea in the White House by Eleanor Roosevelt.

In 1940 von Trott joined the Nazi Party as a cover for his double game. In the Foreign ministry he was made head of the India Bureau. Here he had regular meetings with Subhas Chandra Bose, the leader of the Indian resistance movement. Next to Keppler and Alexander Werth, von Trott was Bose's most important contact person.[2]

After Winston Churchill decreed on the 20th of June 1941 that there were to be no more negotiations between Britain and Germany von Trott's freedom to travel was at an end. Churchill's aim was the unconditional defeat of Germany.

When the attempted assassination of Hitler on the 20th of July 1944 failed, the leaders of the plot were court-martialed and shot. Adam von Trott zu Solz was tried at the People's Court in August 1944 and hanged. It is surprising that Hewel's relationship with Hitler did not suffer as a result in spite of Hewel's frequent interventions with Hitler on von Trott's behalf.

In 1937 Hewel became head of the East Asia division in Berlin, thus also becoming responsible for dealing with the local groups in the Dutch West Indies. In the same year he moved to the *Dienststelle Ribbentrop* [Ribbentrop Office], an extension of Hitler's staff that dealt with foreign affairs. He started as head of Anglo-German relations, and then from 1938 to the end of the war Hewel was Reich Foreign Minister Ribbentrop's Permanent Representative on Hitler's staff.

At that time Hilmar Bassler was also working in the Foreign Minster as legation secretary (Dept. P VIII). Bassler wars responsible for Nazi propaganda in East Asia. He was also close to the Security Service (SD) and the Secret State Police, the Gestapo, Amt IV. After the end of the war Bassler returned to a key position in the Foreign ministry in Bonn. He became head of the East Asia division and then German ambassador in Indonesia. He should

---

1   McDonogh: *A Good German: ...*, pp. 139ff
2   More details on Subhas Chandra Bose will appear later in this book

actually not have been allowed to take the post in Jakarta, because he was, according to the Foreign Ministry medical officer, only capable of taking a post in the tropics with some reservations because of serious diabetes. Both within and outside the embassy he played a somewhat inglorious part. He was not allowed to remain in charge of the running of the inner workings of the embassy, something almost unheard of in the Foreign Service.[1]

Bassler was not the only Nazi who moved directly from Ribbentrop's Reich Foreign Ministry to the Federal German Foreign Service in Bonn. Former Nazi diplomats played an important role in the Bonn Foreign Ministry. As well as Bassler (in Jakarta from April 1968 until August 1970), they included Dietrich von Mirbach (in Jakarta from March 1959 until May 1963) and Dr Luipold Werz (in Jakarta from November 1964 until April 1966).[2]

In the SS too Hewel rose with startling speed. On the 12th of September 1937 he joined the SS as a Sturmbandführer (the equivalent of an army major) with the number 283985.[3] From 1942 on he was already an SS-Brigadeführer (an army major-general). In the Foreign Ministry Hewel was a Legation Counsellor First Class in 1938, but from 1943 he was ambassador without portfolio with the rank of a Secretary of State.

Hewel was a typical Rhinelander, with a jovial nature and a love of comfort, always ready for a joke. He was a likable and intelligent, good-looking, tall, well-built man with broad shoulders and dark hair. He made a fresh, sporty impression and with his social graces he could move in society at all levels. Society ladies sought his company, and he seemed to be a stranger to misery. In Hitler's more intimate circle and among friends Hewel, because of his connection with Java, was nicknamed Surabaya Wally (a reference to Brecht's song *Surabaya Johnny.* Hewel met with Hitler almost every day to report on Ribbentrop's behalf on foreign affairs and to take down Hitler's decisions in writing to pass back to Ribbentrop.

Ribbentrop was a wealthy wine merchant and Hitler a convinced teetotaller – at least publicly, though in the private films that Eva Braun made of Hitler a wine glass can sometimes be seen near to him. Ribbentrop's success in the import and export business made him one of the most important in his field in Germany. He was a skilful diplomat, though many thought him arrogant. That may be why Hitler and Ribbentrop did not get on very well – and may be the reason that Hitler appointed his friend Hewel as Ribbentrop's "Permanent Representative".

---

1   Cf also: Geerken, *A Gecko for Luck,* pp. 279, 281ff and 358
2   *Braunbuch,* pp. 233-278 and
     http://www.ag-friedensforschung.de/regionen/Deutschland/ausw-amt3.html
3   IfZ, Fa 74-18

Ribbentrop was well-travelled. Before the Third Reich he lived in England, Canada and the Ottoman Empire. He spoke English, Turkish and French fluently. There is an amusing anecdote about his time in the wine trade:

When the German licence for Johnnie Walker whisky became vacant in 1920 he saw his chance. However, he heard that two of his rivals were already on their way to Scotland, which would have meant that his chances of success, if he arrived third, were minimal. His hobby – he was an amateur pilot – now turned out to be useful. On the spur of the moment he bought an old military plane from the First World War and flew to Scotland. He landed on the lawn right in front of Alexander Walker's castle. The whisky baron was so surprised that all he could say was, "You're my man!" Ribbentrop had won the race for the Johnnie Walker licence.

When Rudolf Hess, the Führer's deputy and likewise a keen amateur pilot flew solo to Lord Hamilton in Scotland to negotiate a separate peace with Britain he was not so successful. Hess wanted to use Lord Hamilton to get his plan to King George the 6th and Prime Minister Churchill. In so doing he must surely have been thinking of Ribbentrop's earlier exploit.

Even before the war Hess sought peace with Britain. He wanted to avoid a war on two fronts and combat Communism in Europe alongside the British. However, Hess's efforts for peace did not succeed with Hitler. Hitler felt that he was entitled to acquire *Lebensraum* [Living Space] in the east for Germany – the *Volk ohne Raum* [People without space] – even if this ran the risk of incurring the enmity of Great Britain.

Hewel and Hess frequently visited Schenzinger – the doctor and author mentioned above – in Berlin. It has also been suggested that Schenzinger and Hewel helped with the composition of the letter of recommendation in English to Lord Hamilton which Hess took with him on his flight. The letter refers to Hess's friendship with Schenzinger, Albrecht Haushofer (1903-1945), son of Karl Ernst Haushofer (see below), and Hewel. Lord Hamilton, Schenzinger and Haushofer, who was in the diplomatic service, were personal friends. Hewel had also corresponded with Lord Hamilton, though I was unable to discover if they knew each other personally.

Haushofer's father, Karl Ernst Haushofer (1869-1946) was the son of the Munich economist Professor Max Haushofer. He studied in Japan for several years and visited several Asian countries, including Korea, Japan, China, Tibet and India. In 1906 he married Martha Mayer-Doss, the daughter of a Jewish tobacco magnate. Karl Haushofer spoke English, French, Russian and Japanese fluently. In the Third Reich he became Professor of Geophysics at der Munich University and spiritual father of the idea of *Lebensraum*.

He was the founder of geopolitical studies. In his academic works *Geopolitik. Studien über die Wechselbeziehungen zwischen Geographie und Geschichte* [Geopolitics. Studies on the interrelationships between geography and history] (1938) and *Deutsche Kulturpolitik im indopazifischen Raum* [German cultural policies in the Indo-Pacific region] (1939) he mentions the Dutch East Indies. He regards Japan as playing the same power-political role as the German Reich in Europe. He prophesied that whoever possessed the world's energy resources would rule the world, a theory vindicated by the USA's wars in the 21st century.

Karl Haushofer also wrote an article in the *Deutsche Wacht* in Batavia (14th February 1939): *Die weltpolitische Bedeutung des Feldzuges der Japaner im Fernen Osten* [The world-political importance of the Japanese campaign in the Far East]. This reflects the German attitude to the second Japanese-Chinese war. From 1933 onwards Karl Ernst Haushofer's monthly report on world politics was broadcast to Germany and the world by the Reich radio station. From 1934 to 1937 he was President of the *Deutsch-Englische-Gesellschaft* [Anglo German Fellowship].

Rudolf Hess was a student of Karl Ernst Haushofer's in Munich from 1919 onwards. They became friends for life. When Hess was imprisoned in the Landsberg together with Hitler and Hewel after the 1923 putsch, he was visited by Haushofer several times. This was when Haushofer also got to know Hitler and Hewel. These conversations led to the inclusion of geopolitical themes in *Mein Kampf*.

Rudolf Hess may have spoken perfect Arabic, but his English was not so fluent. This is presumably why Hewel and Schenzinger helped with the letter to Lord Hamilton. That would, however, also mean that Schenzinger and Hewel were fully aware of Hess's plans, which would lead to the conclusion that Hitler also knew about them, given that Hewel, with his great loyalty to Hitler, would hardly have supported such an action without Hitler's agreement.

Further evidence that Hitler was aware of this is the fact that Hess discussed all the plans for his flight with his adjutant Karlheinz Pintsch, and that his bodyguard and chauffeur also knew. From the beginning of the war Hitler banned all his top officials from flying – except Hess. Hess very openly got Messerschmitt to fix auxiliary tanks to his Messerschmitt Me 110 and made regular test flights from Augsburg. His Me 110 was a secret model of the twin-engined fighter with more powerful engines and better manoeuvrability. Hess made two false starts in the direction of England but was forced back by bad weather after a few hours. It was only his third so-called "Peace flight" that succeeded. Is it likely that no one noticed all these events?

Hess failed to find a hearing in Britain. Churchill said that he would not negotiate with a war criminal. The news of the failed flight reached Hitler at Obersalzberg in the German Alps. He put on a fine display of feigned outrage. When no news came from Hess after several days, Hitler declared him to be 'mentally confused'. Hewel had no contact with Hess from this time on.

It was not only the consumption of alcohol that Ribbentrop and Hitler disagreed about: they simply could not get on with one another. Hitler would rebuff Ribbentrop at every opportunity. Hitler also discussed most matters concerning the Foreign ministry, not directly with Ribbentrop, but rather with Hewel.[1] Hewel was one of the very few people who worked with Hitler who was able to contradict him and whose opinion was often accepted by Hitler: Hitler frequently even took Hewel's advice. He was probably the most important person in Hitler's entourage – perhaps even a friend. It is probable that since their time in Landsberg they used the familiar 'du' with each other, as is shown by a silent film which was deciphered by lip-readers.[2] According to information contained in a top secret file on Hewel from the 11th of October 1945 – after the end of the war – the Dutch Lieutenant General Hendrik Alexander Seyffardt said: *Hewel was Hitler's best friend.*[3] We will return to Lieutenant General Seyffardt and his collaboration with Nazi Germany later.

No one in Hitler's immediate circle – apart from Eva Braun – was as close and intimate as Walther Hewel, as becomes clear in entry after entry in Hewel's diary. Thus it is all the more astonishing that the most famous historians and authors writing about Hitler were not aware of this most influential person, or did not recognise his importance. They may have grossly underestimated Hewel. For example, in Sebastian Haffner's biographies of Hitler I have never knowingly come across the name Hewel. And in his work *Anmerkungen zu Hitler* [Notes about Hitler], in which he writes about Hitler's friends, Hewel only appears once in an unimportant context. He is only mentioned in passing twice in the 1190 page biography *Hitler* by Joachim C. Fest.[4]

Although Hitler always listened to him, Hewel always felt that he was misguided where British policies were concerned. Because of his education, his experience and his cosmopolitan attitude Hewel was always pro-British. He continually – like Hess – tried in vain to achieve a peaceful conclusion to the conflict with Britain. Hewel wanted an alliance with Britain which

---

1   IfZ, ED 100/78, Appendix
2   TV Phönix, *Eva Hitler,* 18.12.12, 21.00 h
3   IfZ, ED 100/78
4   Fest, *Hitler,* pp. 288 and 836

would allow the undisturbed acquisition of the *Lebensraum* Hitler so desired in Eastern Europe. His attitude to the war with Russia was also very sceptical.[1]

As can be seen from documents preserved in the Political Archive of the Foreign Ministry in Berlin and the Institut für Zeitgeschichte in Munich, Hewel corresponded frequently with many influential people both at home and abroad from industry, the nobility, with ambassadors and government representatives, and also private persons from the worlds of politics, the arts and the theatre. He corresponded particularly frequently with his friends and acquaintances in Britain, Lord Hamilton and Mrs. Therbia Thornburg, the sister of the American writer Lowel Thomas, who lived in England. He wrote to a person named Grant and another Cornwell-Evans – both on the 6th of July 1938:

I would like to come over to see all my friends. [...] You know how keen I am in promoting a better understanding between our two countries [...].

Hewel also wrote frequently to a Lady Cory in England: it has not been possible to trace who she was. Among Hewel's documents there are many letters from home and abroad containing personal wishes: requests, pleas for clemency, and countless letters from women asking him to get them a signed photograph of Hitler, some of them even from Britain. It seems that Hewel answered all the letters, and helped where he could, though I suspect that he could not fulfil the vast number of requests for photographs.

Hewel was not just a good conversationalist, he was also a good listener. This, together with his other good qualities was no doubt the reason that Hitler always wished him to accompany him to social occasions and state receptions. He was even one of Hitler's party on the historic occasion when the armistice between France and Germany was signed in the fateful railway carriage in Compiègne on the 22nd of June 1940. Recently discovered film material shows that Hewel was always very close to Hitler on this occasion, showing how important he was to him. On many occasions when Hitler's chief interpreter Paul Otto Schmidt was unavailable, Hewel took over his duties. When Hitler had extremely confidential conversations with foreign partners he usually used Hewel rather than an official interpreter.

On official and private occasions, Hewel must surely have told stories of his time in the Dutch East Indies. He loved that tropical country and its lovable people, with whom he had worked for so long. As Hitler's permanent advisor on East and South East Asian matters, one can see from several surviving documents that Hewel chatted to Hitler in private about the gi-

---

1   www.zukunft-braucht-erinnerung.de

ant archipelago that is now Indonesia, providing him with information and making him more familiar with the islands.

How great Hitler's interest in the East Indies was is shown in a message from State Secretary Ahrens on the 30th of September 1940 asking for a copy of the Dutch East Indies report. He wrote that he wished to inform Hitler who often enquired about India (Author's note: Dutch East Indies).

The Stuttgarter Illustrierte contained in its March 1942 issue a photo-report by Antonescu about Java, Bali und Sumatra. Helmut Laux pointed this out to Hewel on the 3rd of March 1942. Hewel wrote in reply (5th of March 1942) that this magazine was already in Adolf Hitler's office in the Führer Headquarters and that Hitler had already read some of its contents.[1]

Hitler's interest in the Dutch East Indies was probably due less to the culture and the people than the inexhaustible and multifarious raw materials of that rich region. The German Reich had an ambitious four-year plan aiming to eliminate dependence on imported materials, but at the beginning of the war Germany was far from having fulfilled it.

The propaganda minister Joseph Goebbels must also have been interested in the Dutch East Indies – Emil Helfferich, who was a personal friend, probably also talked to him about his may years of East Indies experience. Helfferich's partner, the painter Dina Uhlenbeck-Ermeling, was often present at their meetings. Dina was an Indo: her father was Dutch and her mother Javanese. Like most female Indos, Dina was statuesque, beautiful, attractive and intelligent. With her expressive face, her slender lips, her dark complexion and her luxuriant black hair she must have appeared as an exotic bloom in Germany. As Helfferich mentions in his books, Goebbels was very taken with Dina and displayed an unconcealed interest – womaniser as he was – in her even though she was not an Aryan.[2]

I heard by chance at the beginning of 2012 that Goebbels was fond of talking about the Dutch East Indies on private occasions. Goebbels, also a Rheinlander, was a close friend of the owner of a well-known toyshop in Bonn. This businessman's grandson told me that his grandfather used to enthusiastically repeat to him the stories he had heard from Goebbels about the Dutch East Indies, and proudly tell him about the German U-boats and sailors in the Archipelago.

---

1   AA R27471, Ahrends and Laux
2   Helfferich, e.g. *Ein Leben,* Band 1

5. Hitler's Pianists

Hitler loved classical music and frequently held private concerts at home, The world-famous Beethoven interpreter Elly Ney, who adored and venerated Hitler, gave frequent piano recitals for Hitler and his guests at his holiday home in Obersalzberg.

Ernst Hanfstaengl (1887-1975), two years older than Hitler, was a gifted pianist who became Hitler's permanent entertainer, though more in the field of light music. They met in Munich in 1922 and he fell straight under Hitler's spell. After the failure of the Munich putsch in 1923 Hitler took refuge in Hanfstaengl's villa on the Staffelsee in Bavaria, where he was arrested.

Hitler was said to have had a relationship with Erna Hanfstaengl, Ernst's sister. In the spring of 1923 German media even spread a rumour that they were engaged. Hitler denied this: *I am only engaged to the whole German people!* He was, however, considered to be, as the left-wing *Münchner Post* reported, a Lothario and the erotic king of Munich.[1]

Hanfstaengl, whose father was a rich publisher, owning the Kunstverlag Franz Hanfstaengl in Munich and the Fine Arts Publishing House in New York, aided Hitler financially at the beginning, including help with the publication of Mein Kampf.

He studied at Harvard, where he made the acquaintance of the future President, Franklin D. Roosevelt – an acquaintance that later deepened due to the fact that they were both members of the New York Harvard Club. He graduated in 1909, and after a training period in Munich he took over the running of his father's US company. In the USA he married Helene Niemeyer, an American of German origins.

He returned to Germany in 1919, where he studied at Munich University, becoming a Doctor of Philosophy in 1930. In 1931, because of his knowledge of languages and his good contacts in the USA and Britain – he was a friend of Randolph Churchill, Winston Churchill's son – Hitler appointed him head of the Foreign Press Bureau. In 1932 – even before Hitler seized power, Hanfstaengl tried to organise a meeting between Churchill and Hitler, but Churchill's reluctance meant that nothing came of this.

The Hanfstaengls frequently visited Obersalzberg and Helene introduced Hitler to the Munich 'upper classes' and the intellectual and artistic elite of the city.

---

1   Haffner, *Anmerkungen zu Hitler,* p. 9
     DER SPIEGEL, 46/1977

In 1936, after the Hanfstaengls' divorce, his relationship with Hitler began to break up. There were wide differences of opinion between Propaganda Minister Goebbels and Hanfstaengl, and Goebbels lost no opportunity to defame Hanfstaengl to Hitler. The final straw in Hanfstaengl's relationship with Hitler came about because of Unity Mitford, an attractive young British woman, who denounced Hanfstaengl to Hitler. She was a close friend of both men, and it has been suggested that after his divorce Hanfstaengl made unambiguous advances to Unity which displeased Hitler.

Hanfstaengl fell into disgrace and, in fear of his life, fled to Switzerland. After he managed to get his son, Hitler's god-child, to join him he moved to Britain. When the Second World War broke out he was interned, but, after an interval in Canada, he was sent to the USA at the request of President Roosevelt in 1942. Here he changed sides and became Roosevelt's political advisor on matters pertaining to Hitler and Nazi Germany. Among other things he worked with US experts on a dossier of 400 major Nazis and psychological profiles of Hitler and his closest colleagues.

In 1946 he returned to Germany, dying in Munich in 1975. He was probably the only person who was a close friend of both Hitler and Roosevelt, entertaining them both with his piano-playing.

But who was Ernst Hanfstaengl's successor? There were no clues in Germany, but I came upon traces of him purely by chance – in Indonesia! At meetings in Jakarta with my Indonesian publisher I made the acquaintance of the well-known journalist Iwan Ong Santosa, who told me an extraordinary story that shows another connection between Hitler and the Dutch East Indies.

Hitler loved having private concerts at Obersalzberg. Precisely at the point when Hanfstaengl left the scene at Obersalzberg at the beginning of 1937, a new pianist enters, a musician from Java who stayed at Obersalzberg for a long time, entertaining Hitler and Eva with his skill. Iwan Ong Santosa and his mother remember:

At the beginning of the 1990s Iwan Ong Santosa's mother wanted to buy a house in Bogor in western Java. She was offered a property in the Jalan Tajur. Iwan Ong Santosa, then around 18, accompanied his mother on her first viewing. The house looked rather dilapidated, but might well have suited them after some renovation. They really liked the – somewhat neglected – garden. During negotiations about the purchase Iwan Ong Santosa became extremely interested in the house's owner and his stories.

The owner was Abu Bakar, who was then probably about 80 years old. His skin colouring was relatively light, probably because he was an *Indo,* of mixed race. He supported himself by giving private violin and piano lessons.

Young Iwan Ong Santosa was particularly interested in the living room. It was dominated by a large grand piano, and there were violins standing in the corners. The walls were plastered with photographs from Indonesian and German newspapers, showing Abu Bakar with Hitler and Abu Bakar playing the grand piano with Hitler and Eva Braun near him. Abu Bakar proudly told them that he had lived in Germany in 1937 and during the war, most of the time in an annex to Hitler's residence in Obersalzberg. He had regularly entertained Hitler and Eva Braun when they wanted to relax by listening to music in the evening. As a young man Iwan Ong Santosa was deeply impressed because – like many Indonesians – he was fascinated by Hitler.

In the end the sale of the house fell through. Abu Bakar was said to be very eccentric, and when the negotiations for the sale were quite advanced, decided that he did not want to leave his home. Iwan Ong Santosa's mother bought another house. This was all that she and her son could remember, but I wanted to find out more about Abu Bakar.

In September 2011 I set off with Iwan Ong Santosa to search for clues in Bogor. When I lived in Indonesia there was only a narrow road to Bogor via Tjimanggis (now: Cimanggis), where there were frequent traffic jams. Today there is a toll road of motorway standard which gets you to Bogor, about 45 kilometres away, in half an hour.

Abu Bakar's house in Jalan Tajur street had vanished. All we found was an overgrown garden full of tall bamboos, trees with gigantic papayas and a few cocoa palms. However, the older neighbours and a retired civil servant from the district knew a little about him: Abu Bakar had moved out of the house in 1994 and sold it to his neighbour, a car salesman. He had been very old at the time, and had probably died in a nursing home in Jakarta. Abu Bakar remained a bachelor his whole life and had been very lonely in his old age – no relatives had ever been seen to visit, and it was assumed that he had no family in Indonesia. His only relief from loneliness had been playing the piano and giving piano and violin lessons, which he had continued to do until he moved out.

In the 1930s his life had been much more active. He had often been engaged to give piano concerts for the isolated white planters and their families on various plantations around Bandung. Such concerts were quite popular with the plantation bosses.

Abu Bakar was – as Iwan Ong Santosa had correctly guessed – an *Indo*, with a Muslim father from West Java and a Dutch mother. People of mixed race often fell between two stools in Indonesian society: they were not accepted by the white Netherlanders and had to fight for recognition; among the indigenous population they were seen as arrogant and part of the white race. It was much more difficult for them to rise up the social ladder than it was for the *Blanken,* as the whites were called by the natives. Like Abu Bakar they often suffered from loneliness and isolation – and therefore his role as Hitler's pianist was something very special for him.

The neighbours told us that in his old age Abu Bakar had frequently boasted of his time at Hitler's place in Obersalzberg and shown photographs of himself with Hitler and Eva Braun. The neighbours thought he regarded this as the most important time of his life.

Unfortunately the photographs and newspaper cuttings had vanished by the time we visited Bogor. And we could not find any contacts or any information about where he had ended his days. Presumably these documents went to the grave with Abu Bakar or disappeared under the ruins when the house was pulled down.

But how did Abu Bakar get to Germany to work for Hitler? It will probably never be possible to give a definitive answer to this question, but in my mind the key has to be Walther Hewel. Until 1936 he lived on the Neglasari Estate plantation near Garoet (now: Garut) in West Java, not far from Bandung. Hewel was a great classical music lover, as can be seen from many entries in his diary. Is it not obvious that Hewel got to know Abu Bakar at concerts on the plantation he was managing and got him to come to Germany, because Abu Bakar left the Dutch East Indies for Germany only a short while after Hewel? If Hewel had heard of Ernst Hanfstaengl's flight before he left the East Indies, he could have arranged for Abu Bakar to move to Germany.

Like Abu Bakar, Hewel was frequently at Obersalzberg. The private films that Eva Braun took there often show Hewel with Hitler or with other guests. However, I have never been able to see an Indonesian in these films. Pure chance, or did they just not want to show Abu Bakar? A non-Aryan near to Hitler, and a man of mixed race to boot? That would be unheard-of. But compared with Hanfstaengl Abu Bakar had some great advantages: he was neutral. He could presumably speak Dutch, but could hardly understand what was said in the "Inner Circle". And it was only with Hewel that he could converse in his own language.

After 1950 Abu Bakar returned to Indonesia safe and sound. He did not get rich as a result of playing for the Nazi elite, but his time in Hitler's entourage made him a much respected person in Bogor and his stories about Hitler and Obersalzberg were always well received in his neighbourhood.

6. Hitler's Anti-Smoking Campaign

In 1863 the cultivation of tobacco was introduced to the Dutch East Indies by the Dutch tobacco planter Nienhuys. During the Third Reich the tobacco market was controlled by the "Big Four: the Deli Maatschappij, the Deli-Batavia Maatschappij, the Sempah Maatschappij and the Tabak Maatschappij Ahrensburg. In 1936 a total of 50,000 tonnes of tobacco were exported. The main market for Sumatra tobacco was Germany: although it was up to four times dearer than Java tobacco, Sumatra tobacco, especially the Sumatra wrapper, was preferred by German smokers.

At first glance it almost looks as if dictatorial regimes look after the health of their citizens better than democracies: Hitler started what was probably the first anti-smoking campaign in the modern world. As a non-smoker, teetotaller and fanatical vegetarian, Hitler wished to present a positive example of healthy eating and a healthy life. He loathed meat and dismissed soups containing meat stock contemptuously as 'corpse tea'. When he was ill his personal physician Dr Morell usually followed Hitler's wishes by providing naturopathic treatment.[1]

Indonesia' first president, Soekarno, advocated the vegetable *Daun Singkong*, which grows and flourishes on every street corner in Indonesia, as *the best, the healthiest and cheapest vegetable*. Soekarno was not a vegetarian, but he despised the meat of animals with four legs. I got to know *Daun Singkong* at the beginning of the 1960s at a dinner with President Soekarno in the palace at Tampaksiring on Bali, and it has remained one of my favourite Indonesian dishes.

Still, I suspect that these health campaigns – both Hitler's and Soekarno's were not motivated simply by a concern for the people's health, but also by economics. Hitler wished to cut down on tobacco imports from the Dutch East Indies and other regions: he needed the hard currency to pay for rearmament. In Germany, the amount spent annually on the import of tobacco from the East Indies would have bought two million *Volkswagen*.

Today's campaigns all over the world are very similar to Hitler's. Hitler wanted a smoke-free Nazi Germany. The Nazis forbade all advertising for tobacco products and tried, with a targeted anti-smoking initiative, which particularly emphasised the health risks, to wean smokers from their addiction. Great emphasis was laid on the dangers in pregnancy and the risk of

---

1   Bernhard Meyer, *Die letzten Tage des „Patienten A', On Hitler's state of health*, p. 5

cancer. From 1938, in some places only from 1939, onwards there was a strict ban on smoking in universities, post offices, hospitals, hotels, air-force premises and in Nazi Party buildings and offices. From 1941 on this ban was extended to public buses and trains. On the state radio – in Nazi Germany the only one permitted – they regularly broadcast advertisements against smoking. At the same time heavy taxes were put on tobacco products in the hope of reducing consumption. They even considered a ban on smoking in private cars. In the Third Reich they definitely did a lot for what Hitler called *die Volksgesundheit* [The People's Health] and the *duty to be healthy*, which applied to all Germans.

Ill. 14
No-smoking sign for offices

The Third Reich had the strongest anti-smoking movement in the world: their actions would be seen as exemplary by present day opponents of tobacco and health fanatics. American scientist Robert N. Procter writes in his book *The Nazi War on Cancer* that the health policies enforced by Hitler were decades ahead of those in other Western countries.[1]

It was not only tobacco that was targeted in the public health campaigns: measures were also taken against asbestos and radiation as well as pesticides and food colourings. There were health and safety regulations for the workplace. Healthy foods like wholemeal bread were constantly advocated and *Körperertüchtigung* [body toughening], as sport was called, was integrated into daily routines.

---

1   Procter, *The Nazi War on Cancer*, pp. 218ff,
    Loeber, *Das niederländische Kolonialreich*
    www.bundesarchiv.de
    www.deathby1000papercuts.com
    www.alifrafikkhan.blogspot.com/2012/02/gerakan-anti-merokok-zaman-nazi-jerman

In the Nazi press reporting was strictly controlled. In the daily press conferences journalists were given instructions on how certain themes were to be handled. Formally, this was only a request from the government, but what journalist would fail to recognise these requests as orders? For example, on the 21ˢᵗ of March 1941 the instruction was: *The promotion of wholemeal bread should be strengthened much more in future.*[1]

In 1941 a "Scientific Institute for Research into the Dangers of Tobacco" was founded in the University of Jena. Even in the midst of war, Hitler was prepared to devote money and time to the project. The head of the Institute was Fritz Lickint Professor of Food, Alcohol and Tobacco Science, who was heavily engaged in the anti tobacco campaign. His 1200-page book *Tabak und Organismus* [Tobacco and the Organism] (1939) is still relevant today. As early as 1929 Lickint recognised the link between tobacco and lung cancer, and he is still regarded as a pioneer in research into the health risks of smoking: it was he who invented the term "passive smoking" and warned against being near smokers. He was the doctor most hated by the German tobacco industry.

Franz H. Müller (1939) and E. Schairer (1943) also carried out studies on the connection between cancer and smoking, establishing that smoking causes a significant increase in the risk of cancer. Only a few days before the end of the war in spring 1945 the University of Jena published an anti-smoking leaflet entitled *Reine Luft* [pure air]. At that time Germany was already lying in ruins and there was no such thing as pure air. Smoke, ashes, dust and the smell of corpses hung over German cities.

Soldiers could only cope with the horrors of the front by means of their beloved cigarettes. Archive pictures show generals, officers and other ranks in the trenches puffing contentedly on their cigarettes. The soldiers at the front received a ration of six cigarettes a day. Non-smokers and female personnel received chocolate and fruit instead.

Hitler's anti-smoking campaign had some success: while in Germany in 1944 annual tobacco consumption was 743 grams per head, in the same year in the United States it was 3,039 grams per head – almost five times as much. However, none of these measures reduced the expenditure of hard currency for tobacco significantly, even though this may well have been one of Hitler's main aims.[2] Nevertheless it was a responsible and far-sighted health policy aimed at producing as strong and healthy German people.

---

1   Frei/Schmitz, *Journalismus im Dritten Reich,* pp. 30ff
2   Procter, *The Nazi War on Cancer,* pp. 218ff
     Loeber, *Das niederländische Kolonialreich*

For centuries Indonesian tobacco from Sumatra and Java was auctioned in the Dutch ports of Amsterdam and Rotterdam, contributing millions to the Dutch economy. After independence and in the train of national emancipation the young Indonesian republic no longer wished to do business with their former colonial masters. Dutch exports to Indonesia had already fallen to almost zero, and so at the request of Indonesia and much to Holland's annoyance the *Deutsch-Indonesische Tabakhandelsgesellschaft* (DITH – German-Indonesian Tobacco Trading Company) was founded in 1957 and the auction moved to Bremen. In 1959 the Netherlands stopped the tobacco ship *Ulysses* which was laden with Indonesian tobacco for Bremen. The Dutch lodged an interlocutory ordinance on the basis that there was Dutch tobacco on the ship and that this must be confiscated and unloaded at a Dutch port. Incredible arrogance on the part of the former colonial rulers. Even 14 years after independence the Dutch still regarded the country as theirs. Indonesia resisted and rightly won a decision in their favour from an international court. That did not by any means signify that Dutch gave up: they continued to try by multifarious means to cause difficulties for the young state. However, the Indonesian tobacco market in Bremen still functions perfectly.[1]

---

1   Geerken, *A Gecko for Luck,* pp. 119ff

7. Trade Relations Between the Third Reich and the Dutch East Indies

Since Germany has hardly any sources of raw materials, Kaiser Wilhelm II founded the *Königliche Institut für Seeverkehr und Weltwirtschaft* [Royal Institute for Maritime Transport and World Trade] in Kiel in 1914 to research the worldwide distribution of resources. Shortly after Hitler seized power the institute was renamed the *Institut für Weltwirtschaft an der Universität Kiel* [Kiel University Institute for World Trade] in 1934, a title it bears to this day. In the Third Reich the information that the institute acquired about international trade relations was an important part of the Nazi war machine. To ensure the security of supplies of raw materials, sources of raw materials in the conquered areas as well as other relevant areas worldwide were researched under the auspices of the Ministry of World Trade and Armaments. Several hundred secret reports were produced for the German armaments industry, and of course particular attention was paid to the vast resources of the Dutch East Indies and New Guinea. They also prepared reports on likely foreign export destinations for German products, such as, in 1939 a report on "The Dutch East Indies as an export market for German vehicles".[1]

In German technical literature written during the Third Reich concerning the Dutch East Indies, the Dutch colonial empire is always presented in a positive light, as for example Irmgard Loeber's 1939 book *Das niederländische Kolonialreich* [The Dutch Colonial Empire]. Particular attention was paid to the enormous resources of raw materials and the main export products. Interestingly enough there was no criticism at all of the way the native population was treated. Even the school education provided by the Dutch was praised, even though it was only available to the local population to a very limited extent.

In 1922 the Dutch constitution laid down that the Netherlands and the Dutch East Indies existed side by side as equal partners in the kingdom to produce – theoretically – a unified empire. In reality, however, the Dutch East Indies were ruled by the mother country and Dutch officials were in charge of the administration.

In the 1930s two thirds of the total surface area of the Dutch East Indies was covered in valuable forest. Many species of trees grew there, including

---

1   Archiv des ‚Instituts für Weltwirtschaft an der Universität Kiel', Verfasser: Zottmann, Dokument C 6461), Info durch Herrn Prof. Dr Frederico Foders

teak, ebony, mahogany, camphor and sandalwood, and also valuable palm species such as coconut palms, Palmyra palms, sago and rotang palms, there were also bamboo, fig and banana trees. Spices such as nutmeg, pepper, cinnamon and vanilla were in worldwide demand. The Dutch East Indies was one of the most important export countries for all tropical agricultural produce.

There had been a large volume of trade between Germany and the Dutch East Indies for many years. They ranged from heavy machinery to Solingen knives and sewing needles. At the beginning of the last century Germany exported steam locomotives, rails, and even Batavia's first tram system. AEG electrified the railway line from Batavia to Bogor. Telefunken built transmission and receiving systems, such as the major transmitter "Malabar" near Bandung, which enabled the first radio connection between Java and the Netherlands. Power stations and power distribution plans were built by German firms, as were the first telephone networks. Many German trading companies were also represented in the Dutch East Indies. They could provide everything an Indonesian man or woman's heart could desire.

The main exports to Germany in the 1930s before the outbreak of war were sugar, tobacco, coffee, tea, rubber, coconut products, palm oil, tapioca products, kapok, maize, spices, bauxite, oil, stannite and other raw materials.[1]

There were vast mineral resources in the Dutch East Indies. In Sumatra there was coal and tin; in central and eastern Java there was manganese ore. By far the greatest proportion of the 11,300 tonnes of manganese ore exported in 1936 went to produce alloys in German steelworks. The exploitation of nickel, iron and chrome ore was just beginning in that year.[2]

In the 1930s the Dutch Mijnbouw Maatschaapij had extensive mines in the Toli-Toli region in North Celebes, producing nickel, chrome, cobalt, magnesium and especially molybdenum. In 1939 they produced 23,000 tonnes of nickel ore, in 1940 as much as 55,000 tonnes. In 1942, after the Japanese occupied the Dutch East Indies, the Japanese firm Sumitomo Metal took over these mines. At first they only extracted 27,000 tonnes, but this was increased to 58,000 tonnes in 1945.[3] Germany's main interest in these mines was in molybdenum. From 1942 all the metal and ore from these mines was shipped to Tokyo and then to Germany. Today the molybdenum mines in the Toli-Toli region are run by the British, Australian, Spanish and American Rio Tinto company and the Australian Santos mining company.[4]

---

1   Loeber, *Das niederländische Kolonialreich*, pp. 66ff and 90
2   Loeber, *Das niederländische Kolonialreich*, pp. 76f
3   Museum Geologi Bandung, Daftar
4   The Malala Molybdenum Project, www.abnnewswire.net

The giant Rio Tinto mining company has its origin in the Minas de Riotinto copper mine in southern Spain, where copper was already being mined in the second century BC. When General Franco took control in Spain in 1937 he made a treaty with Hitler whereby copper from the Minas de Riotinto was used to pay for the supply of German aircraft. In order to gain direct access to other copper supplies from the mine Franco began to buy up shares in Rio Tinto on the London and Paris stock exchanges using dummy companies in Spanish Morocco.[1]

The oil industry in the Dutch East Indies, both production and refining, was already the fifth largest in the world. There were refineries for petrol, diesel, fuel oil and lubricant in production in Sumatra and Borneo, and others were planned.

The export of cinchona bark for the production of medication against malaria – epidemic at that time and still one of the major causes of death in developing countries – reached 10,000 tonnes in 1937, almost all of it going to the chemical giant IG-Farben in Germany.

Exports of gold and silver were also not inconsiderable in the 1930s: 2.3 tonnes of gold and 20.6 of silver exported in 1936, most of it to Germany.

In 1934 the Nederlandsch-Indische Bauxiet Exploitatie Mij began the extraction of bauxite in the Riouw Archipelago (now: Riau Archipelago) to the south of Singapore. They intended to export their entire production to a planned Japanese aluminium factory in Formosa. When the realisation of this project was continually delayed, Germany took over as main importer. In 1936 127,640 tonnes of bauxite were extracted and exported to Germany. An increase in production to between 300,000 and 400,000 tonnes per year was planned.

Japan had been trying since the beginning of the 1930s to acquire more influence in the Dutch East Indies. Japanese imports tripled in value between 1928 and 1934. Many of the commercial-political measures introduced in the Dutch East Indies were directed against Japanese commercial influence, because Japan was unbeatable in the production of cheap mass products because of its low wage level. This cheap competition was felt most of all by textile manufacturers in the Netherlands.[2]

Since Japanese ships with their low freight charges were also continually gaining more influence, foreign ships were only allowed to put in to a small number of 'open ports' to protect the Dutch merchant fleet.

The step-child of the Netherlands – as Dutch New Guinea was called – now became the focus of Dutch attention because of this Japanese influence.

---

1   www.lanzarote37.eu

2   Loeber, *Das niederländische Kolonialreich*, p. 89

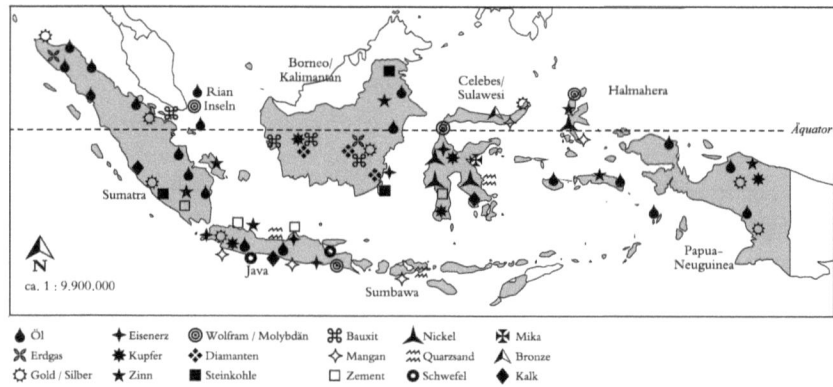

Ill. 15
Distribution of the main raw materials in Indonesia

Before this time only the coastal regions had been explored. Dutch New Guinea alone – the western half of the second largest island in the world – was twelve times bigger than the Netherlands. In the interior of the island the indigenous inhabitants still lived as if in the Stone Age in an area that no white person had set foot in by the beginning of the 1930s.

Thus far New Guinea had only been known as the land of the bird of paradise, a species unique to the island. At the turn of the last century rich Europeans were fascinated by the plumage of these birds – in the 1920s ladies who wished to make a fashion statement would adorn themselves with their feathers. Fortunately the bird of paradise became a protected species in 1931 which has ensured its survival until this day.

Exploration of Dutch New Guinea began in the mid-1930s. They expected to find large deposits of gold, copper and other ores, which turned out to be the case. Emil Helfferich, mentioned above, had presented the Dutch government with a German plan for developing and exploring the island in the 1920s, but it had been rejected. The Dutch could, in fact, have made use of the experience of the Germans in their former colony of German New Guinea – in the Bismarck Archipelago and Kaiser Wilhelm Land. There had been German trading stations there since 1874, and in 1884 the Imperial Navy had raised the German flag which continued to fly there until the First World War.

The Dutch began exploring in earnest in the mid-1930s. It was here in this isolated, forest-covered island, inhabited only by what they called "savage aboriginals", that the British and Australians wished to set up a homeland for the Jews of Europe and the whole world. At the end of the 1930s there were an estimated 330,000 native inhabitants and only 286 Europeans.[1]

The Japanese needed space and raw materials for their constantly expanding population, and these were present in abundance in the Dutch East Indies. This meant that the Netherlands regarded the expansion of Japanese policies towards the south and their arms build up with some concern. As a result of a memorandum from the Dutch defence minister van Dijk, the naval presence in the East Indies was expanded. The naval forces there were reinforced by 3 cruisers, 2 flotilla leaders, 12 destroyers and 18 submarines. The naval air force received 72 new aircraft, including 42 German Dornier flying boats. The USA supplied 4 million dollars' worth of armaments to the Dutch colony in 1938.[2] To protect against a possible Japanese attack the port defences on Sumatra, Borneo and Java were strengthened, and submarine bases and new airfields were built in New Guinea. As the tension in East Asia continued to grow, the Dutch government decided to increase their fleet-building programme yet further in 1939. The increase in expenditure was financed by an increase in taxes and the imposition of a 1% "defence export tax" on all goods exported from the Dutch East Indies. The Netherlands wished to support their interests in world politics out of their own resources. Unfortunately these measures did not in the end benefit them substantially.

---

1   Loeber, *Das niederländische Kolonialreich,* pp. 94f
2   Loeber, *Das niederländische Kolonialreich,* p. 138

8. German-British Relations

Internationally Adolf Hitler was mostly either laughed at or avoided before he seized power in 1933, but one of his greatest admirers in the early 1920s was the British writer Houston Stewart Chamberlain. In the First World War Chamberlain had accused England of war-mongering: he thought that Britain's entry into the war was a *betrayal of our common race*. Hitler said something similar in the Second World War: *Strange that we are, with the help of Japan, destroying the position of the white race in East Asia.*[1]

In a letter to Hitler on the 7th of October 1923 Chamberlain honoured him *as the precursor of a greater one, the saviour of the German counter-revolution.*[2] A copy of this letter was made available to the periodical Deutsche Wacht by Hewel during his time on the plantation at Neglasari on Java. Unfortunately there is no date or acknowledgement of source on the copy in the National Library in Jakarta.[3]

After taking power in 1933 Hitler suddenly became a star on the world stage. Politicians, statesmen and royalty now took notice of him and visited him. As the documents in the Foreign Ministry archive in Berlin and in the Institut für Zeitgeschichte in Munich show, Hewel was present at many meetings, receptions and official dinners.

There were frequent contacts between Hitler and representatives of Great Britain. Good relations with Britain were particularly important to Hitler: the Indian Ocean was surrounded by British possessions from South Africa to the Malay Archipelago and Singapore – it was essentially a British sea. Germany imported vital raw materials from the region, and so good relations were important to prevent the interruption of these supplies.

Hitler's guests from Britain included, among others, Sir John Simon (British Foreign Minister), Anthony Eden (Minister without Portfolio), the Duke and Duchess of Windsor, Lord Halifax (later British Foreign Minister), and Neville Chamberlain (Prime Minister until 1940). Hitler and Chamberlain met several times: in Munich, in Berlin, in Bad Godesberg, at Obersalzberg in the Bavarian Alps and in Hitler's "Eagle's Nest". Chamberlain could almost be said to have been a regular guest of Hitler's. Hitler held discussions with him in the Hotel Dreesen in Bad Godesberg in September 1938, in preparation for the Munich Agreement.

---

1   Entry in Hewel's diary for 16.12.1941
2   Fest, *Hitler,* p. 259
3   AA R 27480, Botschafter Hewel 13 (here without source or date)

Ill. 16
In the Hotel Dreesen in Bad
Godesberg, September 1938
Preparing the Munich Agreement
From left: Joachim von Ribben-
trop (German Foreign Minister),
Paul Schmidt (Interpreter),
Hitler, Neville Chamberlain
(British Prime Minister)

On the 29th and 30th of September talks took place between the heads of government of Britain, France, Italy and Germany. Neville Chamberlain (Britain), Edouard Daladiere (France), Benito Mussolini (Italy) signed the Munich Agreement which, based on the principle of a people's right to self-determination, assigned the Sudetenland, the German-speaking area of Czechoslovakia, to Germany. Hitler had achieved his goal.

Modern historical discussions of the effects of the conference do not seem to know about one item: during the talks, Great Britain urged the Netherlands to cede Sumatra in the Dutch East Indies to Germany.[1] It is not clear what the reasons for this pressure were, or on whose initiative it was applied, but the result would have been to allow Germany direct access to the territory of the East Indies.

Edward, Prince of Wales, later King Edward VIII – and after his abdication Duke of Windsor – was particularly well-inclined towards the Third Reich. The British royal family was German in origin: in the 18th century George I (Elector of Hannover) had become King when the last of the Stuarts, Queen Anne, died without a direct heir. And in the 19th century, the German house of Saxe-Coburg-Gotha cleverly managed to marry members into the royal houses of many European countries such as Britain, Greece, Russia, Romania, Sweden, Portugal, Bulgaria, Austria, Italy and Luxemburg – not to mention Mexico.

---

1   Wilson, *Orang dan Partai Nazi di Indonesia,* p. 71

Ill. 17
Special postcard commemorating the signing of the Munich Agreement
From left: Neville Chamberlain/Britain, Edouard Daladier/France, Benito Mussolini/
Italy and Hitler

Until the First World War the first language of all the English royal family was German, but during that war the all too German-sounding name Saxe-Coburg-Gotha was replaced with the invented "Windsor".

Edward, the future head of an empire on which the sun never set, was infamous for his amorous adventures until in 1934 he met Wallis Simpson, an American femme fatale who had already been divorced twice. Through her he got to know Sir Oswald Mosley, founder and leader of the British Union of Fascists, which had over 50,000 members. Through his first marriage with Lady Cynthia Curzon, daughter of the former Viceroy of India, Mosley had an entrée to the upper ranks of British society. His second marriage – to Diana Mitford, sister of Unity Mitford – took place in Germany in 1936 in the home of the Propaganda Minister Joseph Goebbels, in the presence of Hitler. I will return to the Mitford sisters' relationship with Hitler later.

On his father's death in 1936 Prince Edward ascended the throne as Edward VIII. He wished to influence British politics, then taboo for British royalty. He particularly favoured an alliance between Britain and Germany.

Edward's and Wallis Simpson's contacts with the Third Reich and Mosely made them suspect to Churchill and the British government. It was suspected that Wallis Simpson had handed secret British information to Ribbentrop. Winston Churchill also distrusted the King, and became his greatest opponent, particularly where an alliance with Germany against Communism was concerned. The King had fought against Germany in the First World War and wished to ensure that there was no recurrence of that hostility. His aim was the same as Hitler's: Britain should give Hitler a free hand in Europe, and in return Germany would leave Britain and its dominions and colonies in peace.

The British government's pressure on King Edward and his lover increased. Although many in Britain wished Edward to remain on the throne, he had to abdicate after only 10 months. The pretext was his romance and planned marriage with a divorced woman, but the true reason was his pro-German attitude and his closeness to National Socialism in Germany and to Mosley and his British Union of Fascists.

The Duke and Duchess of Windsor, as they became, were courted by all the top Nazis, and were even guests in Herrmann Göring's house. The leading elite of the Third Reich hoped that after a successful war they would put Edward VIII back on the throne and produce the desired alliance between the two countries. The Windsors visited Hitler in Obersalzberg, in October 1937. Edward said to journalists on this occasion: *It would be a tragic thing for the world if Hitler was overthrown.*

Even Philip Mountbatten, Duke of Edinburgh, the consort of the Queen of England, herself of German descent, comes from a German family, the Battenbergs, who had also changed their German name during the First World War.

As is generally known, Hitler had a large number of female admirers from among the upper ranks of society and business. Of these, one of the most glittering was the young British aristocrat Unity Valkyrie Mitford. She was the fifth of the seven children of Lord and Lady Redesdale. Her mother was a cousin of Churchill's wife Clementine. The family had long been pro-German, as Unity's second name Valkyrie, with its echoes of the Aryan heroine of Wagner's opera *Die Walküre,* shows.

The eccentric Mitford family hosted visits by the Queen and also consorted with both Churchill and Hitler.[1] Their daughters, the six "Mitford Girls" achieved an amazing degree of both fame and notoriety.

---

1   Die Welt, 04.12.2007, *Sechs Leben voller Glanz, Skandale und Elend*

Ill. 18
The leader and founder
of the British Union
of Fascist, Sir Oswald
Mosley, salutes members
of his party on Royal
Mint Street in London
in October 1936.

At Ernst Hanfstaengl's invitation Unity and Diana Mitford attended the Nazi Party conference in Nuremberg in 1933. This was their first meeting with Hitler and their previous admiration for the Führer now became adoration: from now on Unity wished to be as close to Hitler as possible.[1]

Unity Mitford began a German language course in Munich in 1934. For several days she sat in his favourite inn, the Osteria Bavaria, observing him from a distance. Hitler noticed her and, on the 2nd of February 1935, invited her over to his table and they quickly became close friends. Unity wrote to her father: *I am the happiest and luckiest girl in the world. For me he is the greatest man of all time.* Hitler also felt attracted to Unity, even though in comparison with Diana she was no great beauty. But she was tall, blonde, blue-eyed and typically English – Hitler described her as *a perfect specimen of Aryan womanhood.*[2]

Ill. 19
Diana Mosley, née Mitford,
with Ernst Hanfstaengl
at the Nazi party conference
in Nuremberg in August/Sep-
tember 1933

Hitlers British Girl, Part 2 and 4, Channel 4, Documentary 2007, www.youtube.com

2   *Hitlers British Girl*, Part 3, Channel 4, Documentary 2007, www.youtube.com

Ill. 20
Unity Mitford. Hitler had a special party badge, engraved with her name, made for her

Unity and Diana travelled to London several times with Ernst and Erna Hanfstaengl to meet their friend, Churchill's son Randolph. Randolph made several attempts to arrange a meeting with his father, but it is unlikely that any such meeting took place, given Churchill's attitude to Germany, which had always been one of aversion and envy. Nevertheless he had spent a holiday in Germany with his wife before the First World War. My father told me that this was when he produced the statement: *You want colonies? You wish to rule the ocean with your fleet? We'll have to put a stop to that!* A further visit to Germany followed in 1932, which must have been to some larger cities, since he recalled *the pompous and passionate parades of the National Socialists.* It was also said that he told brusquely former Chancellor of Germany, Heinrich Brüning, in 1934: *Germany must be defeated – and this time conclusively.*[1] There seemed to be no way of winning Churchill over to rapprochement between Germany and Britain.

In Germany Unity Mitford always remained in close proximity to Hitler: several hundred meetings between them are documented. Unity was actively engaged in promoting Hitler's ideas, and received a medal from him for that reason. In 1935, together with Julius Streicher, a member of the *Reichstag*, she gave a fiery anti-Semitic speech in Berlin. Streicher was also publisher of the hate sheet *Der Stürmer* [The Attacker]. In one of her letters Unity wished that England had a paper like *Der Stürmer*. In this Nazi organ she published several articles with headlines like:
The English have no notion of the Jewish danger!
England for the English! Out with the Jews! Heil Hitler![2]
In 1935 Unity was visited by her parents in Munich. At Hitler's invitation they spent a few days at Obersalzberg near Berchtesgaden and in Hitler's favourite home, the Kehlsteinhaus. There was a party there with the Mitford

---

1   www.entlarvendeZitate233513.com
2   *Sechs Leben voller Glanz, Skandale und Elend ...*, Die Welt, 04.12.2007

family, Adolf Hitler, Eva Braun, Magda Goebbels, Gerda Bormann (wife of Martin Bormann) and others.[1] Hitler's devoting so much time to Unity's parents seems to suggest that he had a special affection for her.

Hitler provided Unity with a private box at the 1936 Olympic Games in Berlin, and a trip in the state carriage to the Wagner Festival in Bayreuth. When Austria was annexed to Germany in 1939, Unity even appeared with Hitler on the balcony of Vienna Town Hall. Whether Unity was, like Eva Braun, Hitler's mistress is unproven, but seems likely. Entries in Eva Braun's diary show that Eva was more than jealous of Unity, and with good reason because she, unlike Unity, was not allowed to appear in public with Hitler. This jealousy led to a suicide attempt.

In 1938 Unity Mitford moved into a luxury apartment provided by Hitler in Agnesstraße 26 in Schwabing in Munich.[2] Unity's dearest wish was to bring about rapprochement between Germany and Britain. The stumbling block was on the British side: Winston Churchill. Unity was torn between her homeland England and Germany. She believed that Britain could only repel the Communist menace from the East in alliance with a racially pure Germany. Her conversations with Hitler show that he – as we will later confirm from Walther Hewel's diary – was not essentially anti-British.

Over 12,000 letters between the Mitford sisters have survived. Unity ended the majority of her letters to her parents and sisters with Best love & Heil Hitler. Charlotte Mosley, Diana and Oswald Mosley's daughter in law, published an 800-page selection of the sisters 'letters.[3] Unity to Diana, 8 February 1936:

He [Author's note: Hitler] talked a lot about England & Germany & said that in 2 years time the German army will be the strongest not only in Germany but in the WORLD. Isn't it wonderful. And he said that with the German army & the English navy we could rule the world. Oh if we could have that, and what wouldn't be worth doing to help the cause of friendship between the two countries even a little.

Unity to Diana 2 September 1939:
Chamberlain & co are criminals and should be hanged. [Author's note: Hitler said in a speech] I have proposed friendship to England again and again and, where necessary, the closest collaboration. But love cannot be all one-sided, it must be reciprocated.
A letter to Diana on the 29th of March 1939 shows how close Hitler and Unity had become. No wonder Eva Braun was jealous. Unity had access to Hitler to a greater extent than almost anyone else:

---

1   http://einestages.spiegel.de/static/entry/_heil_hitler_love_bobo/20087
2   *Sechs Leben voller Glanz, Skandale und Elend ...*, Die Welt, 04.12.2007
3   Mosley, *The Mitfords: Letters Between Six Sisters*

I had lunch with the Führer on Sunday & Monday. [...] Both days he was in his very best mood [...] he held my hand most of the time & looked sweet & said "Kind" [child] in his sympathetic way because he was so sorry about England and Germany being such enemies. However he said nothing but wonderful things about England and he completely gave me faith again that it will all come right in the end.

On one occasion when Hitler was very busy she wrote [July 1934]: *Poor sweet Führer, he's having such a dreadful time.*[1]

During the Bayreuth Festival in 1939 Hitler warned Unity and Diana about the impending war and suggested that they should both go back to Britain. Diana went back and was imprisoned for collaboration with Germany. Unity preferred to remain in Germany.

On the 1st of September 1939 the German invasion of Poland triggered the Second World War, and on the 3rd of September Britain's declaration of war on Germany followed. Unity could not bear the thought that Germany and Britain, the two countries she loved, were going to tear each other apart. On the day of the declaration of war, Unity went to the English garden in Munich, sat down on a bench and shot herself in the head. Though severely injured, she survived. The bullet remained in her head and she spent weeks in a Munich hospital. Although Germany was already at war she received regular visits from not only Hitler but also Ribbentrop, Goebbels and other top Nazis. Hitler frequently sent her flowers and paid all her bills.

Hitler suggested she be moved to Switzerland and then back to Britain. In January 1940 she was taken to Switzerland in a special railway carriage fitted out like a hospital ward. She was met by her sister Deborah and taken back to England.

Since 2007 there has been a rumour that Unity gave birth to Hitler's illegitimate child soon after her return to Britain. It was said to have been given up for adoption by a family in the North of England. All the British papers reported on these rumours. Unity Mitford died at the age of 33 in 1948 from the effects of her injury. It would be really strange if there were actually a direct descendant of Hitler were living in Britain today.[2]

---

1   Zitate aus den Briefen: Die Welt, 04.12.2007, *Sechs Leben voller Glanz ...*
2   Joachimsthaler, *Hitlers Liste. Ein Dokument persönlicher Beziehungen*
    Sigmund, *Die Frauen der Nazis*
    Lowell, *The Saga of the Mitford Family*
    Mosley, Charlotte, *The Mitfords: Letters Between Six Sisters*
    Die Welt, 04.12.2007, *Sechs Leben voller Glanz, Skandale und Elend*
    www.adel-genealogie.de/Mitford
    Hitler's British Girl, Channel 4 Documentary 2007, Part 1 – 4
    http://www.youtube.com/watch?v=Z9kBH47Ohlg

9. The Beginning of the Second World War, the Dutch Reaction and Japan's Entry into the War

During almost 350 years of colonial rule thousands of German scientists, doctors, researchers, sailors, craftsmen and planters served the Dutch colonial government in the East Indies loyally. They were hard-working and appreciated by the government. But after Hitler seized power in 1933 the majority of the Dutch in the colony made the Germans living there feel unwelcome. Even opponents of Hitler and Germans who had adopted Dutch citizenship – as we have said above, *Volksdeutsche* in Nazi terms were treated the same. On the other hand, there was a strong National Socialist movement in the Netherlands. Anton Adriaan Mussert and Cornelis van Geelkerken founded a Dutch Nazi Party, the *Nationaal Socialistische Beweging NSB*, in Utrecht in 1931.

Ill. 21
Anton Mussert's
NSB Membership Card.
Party Member No. 1

The NSB was at first a fascist, and then after 1933 a national socialist party that was very close to the German Nazi Party, the NS-DAP. Their uniforms were based on the German Nazi uniforms. Up to 1933 the NSB had only about 1,000 members, but by 1936 there were already 52,000: they received 8% of the vote in that year, and therefore had four seats in the Dutch parliament. By the time Hitler's troops marched into the Netherlands, the NSB had about 100,000 registered members and many more fellow-travellers.

In the Netherlands Anton A. Mussert was called the "Führer of the Dutch People". He was hoping to create a "Greater Netherlands", which after Hitler's victory would include Belgium and parts of northern France. Mussert had several meetings with Hitler: there is an interesting short report in the

Netherlands weekly newsreel about Mussert's visit to Hitler in the Chancery in Berlin in 1942: Walther Hewel, who of course spoke perfect Dutch, received Mussert and led him to Hitler.[1]

In 1935 Mussert travelled throughout the Dutch East Indies as the leader of the NSB. He was received as a statesman and welcomed everywhere with an enthusiastic *HOU ZEE! (Sieg Heil!)*. He filled the halls, gave inflammatory Hitler-style speeches: thousands of Dutch colonists cheered him to the rafters. It became fashionable for Dutch supporters of the NSB in the East Indies to greet each other with *Heil Hitler* or *Heil Führer*.[2]

Ill. 22
Mussert's Arrival in Batavia, 1935

Mussert was received several times by Governor General de Jonge.[3] De Jonge's successor, Tjarda van Starkenborgh-Stachouwer, even guaranteed state employees and officials in the Dutch East Indies the right to be members of the NSB. In the colony people flocked to become members of the *Nationaal Socialistische Beweging* – Dutch, native inhabitants, Indos and *Volksdeutsche* who lived and worked there.[4]

Hendrik Alexander Seyffardt was a former Chief of the General Staff of the Dutch army. He was an active member of the NSB and wrote regularly for their weekly paper *Volk en Vaderland*. From the early 1930s onwards he was an enthusiastic follower of Hitler. After the German

---

1   www.youtube.com/watch?v=iawadSo9Mal, Anton Mussert outmoet Adolf Hitler
2   Wilson, *Orang dan Partai Nazi* ..., pp. 177f
    http://www.oorloginblik.nl/lijst/AANKOMSTVANDE%20HRE0002FF57_2894
    Historical film (15 minutes) of Anton Musserts' 1935 visit to the Dutch East Indies. Content: Arrival by air in Batavia, welcome by Gouvernor in Batavia and the summer seat of government in Buitenzorg (now Bogor), tour of Batavia, visit to the Dutch Harmonie Club etc.
3   Mak, *Das Jahrhundert meines Vaters,* pp. 203ff
4   Wilson, *Orang dan Partai Nazi*..., pp. 70f and 117

army occupied the Netherlands, Seyffardt collaborated openly with Hitler and led a campaign to recruit Dutch volunteers for the German forces. Seyffardt worked to achieve a purely Dutch unit within the German army. Individual units like the SS-Freiwilligen-Standarte Nordwest [SS-Volunteer Unit Northwest] or the Nederlandse SS were integrated into the SS-Freiwilligen-Panzergrenadier-Division Nederland [SS Volunteer Mechanised Infantry Division Nederland]. After Seyffardt's murder in 1943 this Netherlands division was renamed General Seyffardt. The unit, whose soldiers wore German SS uniforms, was about 50,000 strong. It was under the command of the German commander of the Waffen-SS in the Netherlands and saw action mainly in the Netherlands. At the end of the war there were still between 5,000 and 10,000 members of this division. As Indonesians who were present at the time told me, there was within the division an Indonesien Zug [Indonesian Unit] which was made up of Indonesians who lived in the Netherlands. I was unable to discover how big this was, though my informants' information suggests somewhere between one and three thousand. Indonesian soldiers fighting on Hitler's side? Not as absurd as it might seem, when we consider the role of the Indian freedom fighter Subhas Chandra Bose and his Indian Legion.

Other national socialist organisations in the Netherlands were the *Nationale Jeugdstorm* (NJS), the Dutch equivalent of the Hitler Youth and the *Weerbaarheidsafdeling* (WA), an organisation based on the German paramilitary *Sturmabteilung* (SA).

There was of course also a Dutch resistance movement. Dutch historical sources estimate their numbers at around 25,000.[1] Although the NSB was very popular at first after the German invasion, solidarity with Germany crumbled when the German army passed the peak of its success. The underground resistance grew. Young resistance fighters founded the magazine *Vrij Nederland* [Free Netherlands] which still survives as a weekly magazine. Its fascist counterparts were *Het Hakenkruis* [The Swastika] and *Het Licht* [The Light).

Especially after the outbreak of the Second World War all Germans in the Dutch East Indies suddenly became suspect and subject to increased reprisals. Even the men, women and children who had fled Singapore before the beginning of the war with the permission of the British suffered as well. Postal contact with home became more difficult. Letters from Germany were no longer carried by the Dutch airline via Amsterdam. The long journey letters had to take can be seen by the illustration below of a German letter from Danzig to Bandoeng (now: Bandung)

1   Jong, *The German Fifth Column ...*

The airmail letter was posted in Danzig on the 16th of January 1940 passed via the Brenner Pass and Italy to Batavia. From there the letter went to Kilometre Stone 86 at Buitenzorg (now: Bogor) and was then sent on from there to Bandoeng. It finally reached its destination of the 11th of February 1940. All in- and out-going German post was censored by the Dutch. At that time it was usual to address post to people living outside the towns to the kilometre stone closest to where they lived, which is why the letter is addressed to "Km 86".

Ill. 23
Censored Airmail Letter from Danzig to Bandung

Dutch anti-German sentiment in the colony grew ever stronger. Even before the invasion of the Netherlands the German Consul in Batavia reported to the Foreign Organisation in Berlin that 19 German citizens had been arrested and imprisoned without trial. Official German protests were ignored.

When the Germans invaded the Netherlands on the 10th of May 1940, Queen Wilhelmina and the government fled to exile in England. Hitler naturally managed to find a justification for his invasion: the "Venlo Incident". The German secret service had discovered that the Dutch government had been cooperating with the British secret service. British spies working for the Dutch were captured in the Dutch-German border area, thus giving Hitler an excuse for invasion since this cooperation breached Dutch neutrality.

The NSB branches in the East Indies had only a few thousand Dutch members between 1934 and 1941. Nevertheless the local party organ *HOU ZEE* (Sieg Heil) abounded in words and slogans that were also in use by the Nazis.

Die *Nationaal-Socialistische Nederlandsche Arbeiderspartij* NSNAP was founded in 1931 by van Smit, van Waterland-De Joop and van Rappard. Van Rappard joined the Waffen-SS after the Dutch invasion of the Netherlands. The NSNAP called itself the *Hitlerbeweging* or *Groote Duitsche Beweging* [Hitler or Greater German Movement]. Their anti-semitic slogans were even worse than those of the NSB.

There were other nationalistic organisations in the Dutch East Indies, like the *Nederlandsch-Indische Fascisten Organisatie* NIFO. Frans Schomper, who founded the Nazi party NSDP in Batavia, lived in what is now the Menteng area of Jakarta. His home, Gedung Juan, today houses an army museum. The party had several thousand members with branches on all the major islands of the archipelago. After the German air raids on Rotterdam Dutch people attacked and ransacked the party headquarters in Bandung.

Among the Indonesian population the attitude to Hitler's policies was exceptionally favourable. They saw in Hitler a saviour who would finally free them from the colonial yoke. Nationalist groups received a noticeable boost in membership after the German army occupied the homeland of their colonial masters, which gave them hope that they could soon break the bonds of colonial rule. In 1927 Soekarno, who was later the first president of Indonesia, together with other freedom fighters, founded the *Partai Nasional Indonesia* PNI. Soekarno refused to cooperate with the Dutch colonial authorities and was therefore imprisoned in 1929 and later exiled.

One of the most important parties for the Indonesian population was the *Partai Indonesia Raya* PARINDRA founded by Sartono, Amir Sjarifuddin and M. Husni Thamrin in 1935. On the 6th of January 1941 Husni Thamrin was accused by the colonial authorities of having too close ties to

Nazi Germany and Japan. He was sentenced to house arrest, but only five days later, on the 11th of January, he died under circumstances that have remained unexplained to this day. The youth wing of PARINDRA was an exact copy of the German Hitler Youth, including its uniform and the "Hitler salute".

Ill. 25
Funeral of M. Husni Thamrin 15th January 1941, led by the head of the PARINDRA party, Woerjaningrat Soekardjo Wirjopranoto. The guard of honour was formed by Indonesian boys from the PARINDRA youth wing.

Other Nazi parties among the native population were the *Partai Fascist Indonesia* PFI and the *Sejarah Fascisme di Nusantara* SFN, both funded in 1933 by Dr Notonindito, who had studied in Germany from 1924 onwards, receiving a doctoral degree in economics from Berlin. PARINDRA was founded in 1935, in 1936 the *Gabungan Politik Indonesia* GAPI, and in 1937 *Gerakan Rakyat Indonesia* GERINDRA.

The extreme right wing *Indo-European Union* with around 12,000 members allowed Indonesians as well as Dutch and Germans to become members – they were even in a majority. All these nationalist and Hitler-friendly parties had the same aim: independence and a free Indonesia – *Indonesia Merdeka!* And they saw this goal approaching ever closer when Hitler's troops marched into the Netherlands. In their eyes the Germans were fighting side by side with them.

As we see, it was not only the Indonesians: there were quite a few Dutch who supported Hitler and the Nazi movement at home and in their colonies – hundreds of thousands of them enthusiastically raised their right arms in the Hitler salute. When the heir to the Dutch throne, Princess Juliana, married the German Prince Bernhard in 1937 the German swastika flag flew beside the Dutch flag in the Dutch East Indies.

Many Dutch people back in the Netherlands probably took the side of their German occupiers out of opportunism or the instinct for self-preservation. They simply accepted the situation as it was and tried to lead a normal life. Others saw in the occupation and the plans of the German Reich an attempt to establish a European economic system and were – with their centuries-old merchant tradition – enthusiastic about Hitler's plans. Such a system would have brought many advantages for the Netherlands.

It was different in the East Indies: even though there were hundreds of thousands of supporters of Hitler, particularly among the native population, the forces that were working against Hitler had the upper hand. The colonial government and the entire administration declared for Hitler's opponents right from the beginning of the war. They received their orders and financial support from the exiled Dutch government in London.

Even before Great Britain declared war on Germany, many British agents in plain clothes were active in the East Indies either with the agreement of or on behalf of the colonial administration. However, these agents were quickly unmasked by the native population because they spoke neither Dutch nor Malay. What actual missions they were on can no longer be ascertained. According to the contemporary witnesses the British agents' headquarters were in Sarangan, a health resort on the border between central and eastern Java that during that time was largely sealed off. Sarangan will play an important role later in this book for the Germans who remained in Java.

After the German invasion on the 10th of May 1940, the code word *Berlijn* was transmitted from the radio station at Kootwijk in Holland to all military and civil stations in the Dutch East Indies. Among other measures, this meant the internment of all Germans and the confiscation of German property and German ships in Dutch East Indian waters. The Dutch colonial government then set about all Germans and nationalist Indonesians in a very brutal manner. It became a real witch hunt.

The German nationalist paper *Deutsche Wacht* was banned – the last edition no. 8/1940 appearing on the 23rd of April 1940. German men and boys over sixteen were interned in various camps on Java, Sumatra and Borneo, the Dutch making hardly any distinction between *Reichs* Germans and *Volks* Germans – the latter were regarded by the Dutch as still being half-German and therefore suspect. No account was taken of the fact that they had become Dutch citizens and served loyally in the colonial administration and the colonial army KNIL *(Koninklijk Nederlandsch-Indisch Leger)* for many years. Officers and other ranks of the KNIL with German connections were taken out of the barracks and put in the internment camps still wearing their uniforms.

The Dutch feared that a "Fifth Column" might be formed by the German members of the NSDAP in the Dutch East Indies as well as by Dutch and Indonesian nationalists. As a result, not only were thousands of Dutch members of the NSB and Indonesian nationalists put behind barbed wire, but also women, children, and Jews who had just managed to escape from Nazi Germany. They all suddenly became *Landesverrader* [traitors]. Lies and denunciations were the order of the day. At first the *Volks* Germans thought there must be some mistake, after all they were Dutch citizens and had always done their best in the service of the Netherlands. But they were punished because they once had been Germans, ten, twenty or more years before: they were evil Duitsers and therefore *Landesverraders.*

The Dutch colonial minister fanned the fear of a fifth column in the East Indies by reporting that the German paratroops and soldiers had received massive support from Germans living in the Netherlands and from Dutch members of the NSB during the invasion. German merchants, inspectors or workers were taken directly from their workplaces, German doctors from their practices, by Dutch policemen with rifles and fixed bayonets without being given the chance to say goodbye to their families.[1]

Even prominent geologists and scientists like the world-famous German palaeontologist Dr Ralph von Koenigswald were interned. Von Koenigswald had come to Java in 1930 at the invitation of the Dutch government to take part in a geological expedition. He remained in the East Indies and made ground-breaking discoveries, such as that of Java man in Saringan, one of the oldest "human" fossils ever discovered at about 1.9 million years old. Because of his German roots Koenigswald was first taken to the internment camp at Ambarawa and later imprisoned in Fort Ngawi on Java.[2] When the Japanese occupied the Dutch East Indies von Koenigswald hoped in vain for release. The Japanese kept him interned because of his Dutch citizenship. It was a bad time for Germans who had become Dutch.

Dutchmen destroyed the German clubs, including their interiors, as in Bandung. There was no limit to the humiliation: dozens of Germans were driven naked through the streets of Batavia on the 10th of May 1940.[3] The rage of the Dutch colonial rulers did not even spare the German diplomatic representatives in Batavia. The German Foreign Ministry in Berlin sprang into action. Telegrams, telex messages and telephone calls arrived from all around the world. Walther Hewel seems to have played a key role in the affair, since all the information came together at his desk. A telegram from the

---

1   Interview with eyewitness Fred Flakowski, 18.03.2014
2   Keppner, *Wie weit bis Airmolang*, p. 116
3   Interview with eyewitness Fred Flakowski, 18.03.2014

German Embassy in Rome to Hewel on the 19th of May 1940, only a few days after the invasion, says:

[Italian] Foreign Ministry reports following message from Italian Consuls Batavia: Offices of German Consulate General and private homes of personnel searched by police. Safes broken open. Documents, private correspondence and private objects of value confiscated and removed. Response to protest: police seeking material about national socialist organisation. Consul General and Consulate personnel interned. Accommodation inhumane and insanitary. German Consul General requests immediate transfer of protection of interests to foreign, preferably Swiss Consul. Signed Mackensen.[1]

In Hewel's documents I found the transcript of a telex sent by Ribbentrop on the 28th May 1940 from his special train:

State Secretary Bohle (Author's note: Head of the Foreign Organisation of NS-DAP-AO):

I completely agree with your suggestion of severe reprisals on Dutch soil to bring about the release of German citizens interned in the Dutch East Indies. However, I think it is justified not to threaten these reprisals but to carry them out immediately [...] I would think it right to carry the reprisals out as follows: for every German man interned in the East Indies a Dutchman, for every German woman a Dutch woman, for every German child a Dutch child should be arrested immediately. The people to be interned should be taken from circles hostile to us, especially the court and the aristocracy as well as the sphere of finance and trade, since they have major holdings in the East Indies. [...] Signed Ribbentrop[2]

Many important people in the Netherlands were then arrested by the German army. The *Nederlandsche SS* led by Henk Feldmeijer, who also took part in the detection and imprisonment of a hundred thousand Jews and members of the Dutch resistance, were particularly active in this operation.

When the situation of the Germans in the internment camps failed to improve, the reprisals against the Dutch were increased: ten Dutch were now imprisoned for every German held in the colony. Germany suggested an exchange of prisoners, but the colonial administration in Batavia refused to accept.[3] Walther Hewel summarizes the details of the arrest and internment of the *Reichs* Germans in a detailed four-page report entitled *The treatment of the Germans on Java,* of which a copy has survived (without a date). Some extracts follow.

---

78   AA, Akte 84547
79   AA. Akte 84560 and 84561
3   McKale: *The Nazi Party in the Far East, 1931-45*, p. 304f
        Journal of Contemporary History, April 1977, Vol. 12

On the 10th of May 1940 from 1 p.m. onwards all German men were interned.
[...] The German men were taken from their homes by 2-3 Police officers with
loaded guns [...] They were not allowed to dress themselves fully.
Ships' crews who were on duty were, some of them only in bathing costumes,
taken away from their workplaces with hands above their heads. All the intern-
ees were brought to the Jaarmarktterrain [market place] where they had to sleep
overnight on the ground.
The next morning the internees were taken by train to Ngawi – a fort [Author's
note: in east Java]. [...] For the first 8 days they were locked in, in groups of 80
to 90 to a room. They were not allowed to use the WC, a bucket was placed in
the corner for that purpose.
Only after 2-3 weeks did the internees receive a small case with washing materi-
als which their wives had packed. Toothpaste, toothbrushes, razors, cigarettes and
books had been removed by the Dutch guards.
A man with severe asthma had his medicine taken away and died on the second
day. Inoculations were carried out in the room where the dead man was lying. At
night they had to sleep on mats on the floor with the lights on. After the difficul-
ties of the first eight days there was some small improvement.
Prof. Dr Leber [Author's note: A German doctor, pioneer in ophthalmic and
tropical medicine] from Malang near Soerabaia [now Surabaya] suffered greatly
from this treatment. He was not allowed to treat the sick, this was strictly forbid-
den. [...] The internees were totally cut off from the outside world. The smallest
things were severely punished.
Most of the men suffered severely because of the uncertainty about their wives
and children. At Banjoe Biroe near Ambarawa (East Java) 370 women were
interned with their babies and children. [...] A Frau Liebisch was taken away
and is in solitary confinement in the barracks at Oedjoeng, Soerabaia [...] She is
Swiss by birth and had been a doctor.
On the first day the German women had their radios and cars taken away, also
their driving licences – the Dutch said they would have no further need of them
– as well as jewels, silver and objects of value. On the third day all private cor-
respondence as well as passports and all documents were removed [...] The houses
and household goods of these women were auctioned, and the money given to the
Weeskamer [Estates office]. [...]
We have the descriptions of events in the Ngawi camp from Herr von Plessen, who was
recently German Consul in Soerabaia, but was also interned with the others since at the
time he had not received his accreditation from the Queen, even though he was every-
where recognised as consul. [...] Herr von Plessen was released on appeal after 6 weeks.
As he left [...] some people loudly shouted "Heil Hitler". All internees were imme-
diately called together, the whole camp was surrounded by heavily armed men.

[...] Herr von Plessen had to join the others. He was then ordered before the commandant. [...] Herr von Plessen pacified the commandant, pointing out that the shouts had not been a demonstration, just the way we Germans greet each other. [...]

The German men from Batavia are on the island of Onrust. [...] From Onrust a first transport was taken to Atjeh [now Aceh] – North Sumatra – where a large camp is planned. [...] These first 500 men are technicians and builders etc who are to build the camp. [...] The prisoners are now being given prison uniforms, including shorts![1]

On the 11th of May 1940 the above mentioned Professor Leber and his second wife, a nurse called Lotte, were interned by the Dutch in separate camps. He was later moved from the camp in Ngawi to the Dehra Dun camp in northern India. His wife Lotte was allowed to travel to Shanghai, at that time occupied by the Japanese, where she killed herself on the 7th of March 1943.

Professor Leber never returned to Germany. After his release from internment in India he first worked as the head of a hospital in Bhopal and then in 1952 became Dean and head of the Ophthalmology Department in Aligarh, northern India. After the war, Leber got to know Dr R. Madan, Staff Surgeon to the Indian Legion and personal doctor of the Indian freedom fighter Subhas Chandra Bose, in New Delhi.[2] He died in New Delhi in 1954. Before the First World War he had led two South Sea expeditions in 1910/11 and 1913/14, accompanied on the latter by the painter Emil Nolde.[3]

Consul von Plessen was Leopold Baron von Plessen, who should not be confused with Victor Baron von Plessen the ornithologist, traveller, film

---

1   AA, Handakte Hewel 2, R 27469
      Handbuch des deutschen Auswärtigen Dienstes 1871-1945, Bd. 3, Paderborn
      2008
2   Interviews by H. Bräker with R. Madan on several occasions in New Delhi
3   Prof. Dr Alfred Theodor Leber was leader of the first South Sea Expedition in
      1910/11, which took him to Sumatra, Samoa and Saipan. A second expedition under the auspices of the Imperial Colonial Ministry, in which the artist
      Emil Nolde and his wife Ada took part, took him in 1913/14 to the Far East
      on the Trans-Siberian Railway and then by sea to German New Guinea. From
      1916 he was head of the Soekoen Central Hospital for Ophthalmology and
      Tropical Medicine in Malang/East Java. In 1918 his friend, writer and artist
      Max Dauthendey (cf. Geerken, *A Gecko for Luck,* p.130) died in the hospital.
      In1922 Leber returned to Germany, but was once more in charge of the hospital in Malang in 1930. As letter no. 55 from Walter Spies to his mother shows,
      Leber and his first wife Dorothee were in contact with Walter Spies. Dorothee
      had even visited Spies for several days in Bali. In 1912 Emil Nolde created a
      signed woodcut portrait of Prof. Leber.

maker and author mentioned above. Leopold Baron von Plessen was honorary consul in Surabaya from 1939-1940. After his release from internment he was from 1940 to 1941 head of the German Embassy's Chungking (now: Chongqing) branch in China, where the headquarters of the German press agency DNB (*Deutsches Nachrichten Büro*) for Nationalist China was also located. From 1941 he was in the Embassy in Bangkok. After the war he was not retained by the Federal German Foreign Service. In 1949 he married an American woman in the USA and died in Bangkok in 1971.

On the 15th of July 1940 Hewel received a telegram from Manila with information from the Italian Consul General in Batavia, who was travelling through the Philippines at the time:

Condition of Germans including consular officials in Dutch East Indies not improved beginning of July. Internment camp central Java [Author's note: Fort Ngawi] to be moved to new camp to be built in north Sumatra.

In Dutch Borneo about 30 German citizens [Author's note: mostly missionaries] said to be interned and at least until recently imprisoned with native criminals. Confiscated German merchant ships not yet sailed.

Dutch administration very nervous. Defence works, trench digging, black out exercises in train. Signed Lautenschläger [1]

On the 26th of July 1940 Dr Albrecht[2] reported to Hewel that Ch. H. J. Wilhelm, an engineer and a Dutch citizen, had travelled to the Dutch East Indies to use his connections with the Governor General and other prominent members of the colonial administration to have the German internees freed. All he achieved was that conditions in the internment camps improved slightly.[3]

On the 3rd of August 1940 Eugen Ott, who was first from 1933 Military Attaché and then until 1942 German Ambassador in Japan sent Hewel a telegram containing information based on a report by the honorary German consul Schneewind.[4] The report had been smuggled form Padang to Tokyo on a Japanese ship:

Arrest and internment of Reichs Germans which took place on 10 May following a secret code word sent by radio and telegram was most carefully prepared. About 400 male Reichs Germans, including sick and old, from within a radius of 500 km from Padang, as well as naturalised Dutch, taken to long-prepared intern-

---

1   AA, Dokument 84583
2   Presumably Dr phil. agr. Herbert Albrecht, NSDAP politician and expert on finance and business matters.
3   AA, R2968 and 84587
4   Not to be confused with the U-boat commander Fritz Schneewind, son of the honorary consul, who was born in Padang (West Sumatra) and who will be mentioned later.

ment camp Fort de Kock, 90 km from Padang, where they were kept behind barbed wire and treated like criminals. [...] A number of German women who protested against these arbitrary measures were arrested and interned in a separate camp on Java, those known so far are [Author's note: here follows a list of names and descriptions, such as missionary's wife with 4 children, wife of the missionary doctor, missionary nurse etc] [...] Countless so called "defensive measures" have only one aim: the lasting destruction of German economic interests. [...] Un-bridled hostile press campaigns have totally poisoned Dutch minds. Signed Ott[1]

Honorary Consul Schneewind was a businessman. Shortly after he had filed his report his business in Sumatra was confiscated and he was imprisoned by the British in Singapore. When he was freed by the Japanese he became an industrial representative in Singapore supplying materials and spare parts for German naval bases in the Southern Region. He met his son, the U-boat Commander Fritz Schneewind, there at this time.

Since the Dutch East Indies administration refused to countenance any German suggestions about the release of the internees, Germany's retaliation became more brutal. On the 15th of October 1941 Dr Albrecht reported to Hewel on the basis of a telegram from the German Embassy in Tokyo that there were still 2,400 German men in the Alas Vallei camp and 118 German women and children in the Raja camp.

In retaliation, Dutch people who had acted against the Germans in the Netherlands were taken to concentration camps where conditions were much more severe:

241 men to Buchenwald (of whom 14 died)
710 for subversive actions also to Buchenwald
650 Jews with Dutch citizenship to Mauthausen (of whom 400 died)
Internment was in preparation for a further 400 Dutch citizens[2]

In a letter to Emil Helfferich on the 24th of August 1940, Hewel enquires about Dr Mengert (a medical doctor):
Dear State Counsellor! [...] There is no good news from the Dutch East Indies. We are doing everything we can here to help our good friends who have been interned by the Dutch. You will have heard of the reprisals that we have undertaken in Holland, but even they seem to have had no effect as the Dutch authorities in the East Indies appear to be completely under British control.
I received news via Japan yesterday that was totally shattering. [...] According to the report our good Dr Mengert was shot by the Dutch in an attempt to swim for

1   AA, Hewel, Akte 84591 and 84592
2   AA, 740/84657

supplies from the island of Onrust for the internees. [...] It would be an infinitely sad thought for me if his beneficent and self-sacrificing life should have ended in such a senseless fashion. [Author's note: Dr Mengert had actually been shot] With best wishes and Heil Hitler, Yours ever [Unsigned copy][1]

Many further reports describing the appalling state of the German internees reached Walther Hewel. For example, on the 16th of September 1940 there was a report from the German merchant house Arnold Otto Meyer (AOM) of Hamburg known throughout east and South East Asia. In the Foreign Ministry Archive there is a further report from H. E. Menche on the 19th of August 1940 containing a copy of a report from Dietmar Petersen in Kobe in Japan. Petersen's report (written on the 12th of July 1940) was directed to W. Kellinghusen the head of AOM's Dutch East Indies branch, who had remained in Germany since the beginning of the war. In Menche's covering letter to *Dear party comrade Hewel*[2] he writes of the worrying conditions in the Dutch internment camps and the pitiable state of the internees. Further:

I hope that the reprisal measures that have been introduced at last in terms of imprisoning the same number of prominent Dutch people in Düsseldorf will finally bring about some improvement of the situation of our compatriots in Java [...] A reunion with your lady sister was unfortunately not possible last week. Hopefully it will work out better next time. To you in the old way a hearty, comradely salute! Heil Hitler!

Yours ... signed Menche.

(This is the first hint that Walther Hewel had a sister, Thesi Hewel).

More extracts from Petersen's report from Kobe, which mention for the first time the arrest and internment of Dutch Citizens resident in the Dutch East Indies who were members of the NSB:

As a result of the exceedingly swift internment methods, the police and the military had so much to do when dealing with the large number of Germans and NSB-Dutch (about 1200 of the latter) that their accommodation on the island of Onrust [Author's note: in the Bay of von Batavia] was most unsatisfactory.

Summary of the rest of the report's content:

During the first three days no food at all, barracks not prepared, journalists not allowed to visit the camp, all written or spoken communications forbidden. Then follow references to the shooting of Dr Mengert. Another doctor and four other Germans said to have been shot.

Among those shot was the German Jew Rudolf Frühstück, a consular official from Singapore. He was shot by the Dutch guards for approaching the barbed wire

---

1   AA, Handakte Hewel 2, R 27469
2   They must have been personally acquainted from Hewel's time in the East Indies.

fence of the camp too closely. Eyewitnesses reported that he was refused all medical help, even though German doctors in the camp rushed to help him. They were held back with rifles until Frühstück had bled to death.

[It confirms] the German internees were now being taken to Atjeh (now Aceh). The Dutch nationalists are being held in normal prisons (used for natives and Chinese) spread around the country. [...]

Mr Kubo[1] confirmed that there was no doubt that there were English military personnel on Java. Shopkeepers everywhere report that officers in Dutch uniform speaking English but ignorant of Dutch and Malay, are all over the place and there were rumours that the mountain resort of Sarangan was the English head-quarters. In any case it was impossible for anyone to get near to the town.

According to Kubo these incredible situations were due to fear of a revolution by the Dutch NSB on the one hand, or riots among the native population on the other. He reports that no one Dutchman trusts another and that the Jews in particular have a serious influence on the measures taken by the authorities. [...]

More often than I would like my thoughts are drawn to my many friends down there in Java. Best wishes, your obedient servant

Signed ... Petersen[2]

None of the reprisals against the Dutch in their occupied homeland seem to have been very successful, because, according to Albin von Schenk, Director of the Deutsche Bank in Hamburg, they were not carried out rigorously enough, as his letter of the 3rd of December 1940 to Hewel in the Foreign Ministry in Berlin shows:

[...] Even if many prominent Dutch people have been interned here in Germany, the German authorities in Holland seem to have a strange view of the necessity for rigorous measures to be taken against the Dutch. As I hear, the major Dutch indus-trialist Herr Heinecken [Author's note: Heineken, Brewer], of Amsterdam, was quite correctly arrested with the others to be interned here in Germany. His arrest is said to have lasted just 24 hours until the German Reichskommissar, I think his name is Seiß-Inquart [Author's note: Seyß-Inquart], freed him again.[...]

If one now considers that in reality it was possible to imprison very few prominent Dutch industrialists because the majority of them, like the Philips family, escaped to England in time, then it is hardly possible to understand this behaviour of our German authorities in Holland which seems to be in total contradiction of the view of the authorities in Germany [...] In the interest of our interned German compatriots in the Dutch East Indies this really should not be happening. I hope that the Foreign Ministry will look more closely into this matter and as ministry

---

1   Director of Ch. Takeda & Co. Ltd., Osaka/Japan
2   AA, Handakte Hewel 3, R 27471

responsible for foreign affairs bring the gentlemen in Holland to their senses. Heil Hitler! Signed V. Schenk[1]

Walther Hewel also made an effort to answer all private letters from the Dutch East Indies. For example, in a letter of the 14th of May 1941 to a Frau Jaissle, who had enquired about the whereabouts of her husband (they knew each other from Hewel's time there):

[...] Your letter saddened me greatly because you can imagine how attached I am to all good friends from over there. [...] I have done everything I could with the relevant authorities to achieve better treatment for the Germans over there. [...] Nothing could be achieved by means of reprisals, because the Dutch East Indians do not care very much about what is happening in Holland. They are completely under English influence and live in an atmosphere of English and American propaganda! [...] Signed Hewel[2]

The "Dutch East Indians" mentioned in the letter (Dutchmen living in the East Indies colony) had cared very little during the centuries of colonial rule about the interests of their homeland, and still less about the needs of the native populations. For them the East Indies were a colony to be exploited and nothing more. The hierarchy in Dutch colonial society was much more marked than that in their homeland. In the colony everything revolved around rank, status, affairs and increasing one's private income. As an "upper class" they felt privileged and superior compared with the society in their homeland, and even higher when compared with the natives. Very few had any interest in the centuries-old culture and interests of the natives. And they intended to stay there a long time. Governor General de Jonge (1931-1936) said:

The Dutch must rule the country for centuries more until the native population is mature enough for independence.[3]

It wasn't even ten years until the collapse of the Dutch colonial empire and the Indonesian declaration of independence.

In another letter of the 27th of May (year illegible, probably 1940) Hewel thanks a Fräulein Maria Ludwig, who was trying to find out about her parents in the Dutch East Indies, for a letter:

[...] You can imagine that the fate of the Germans living out there is very close to my heart and that nothing which might help them is left untried. [...] The latest news was that their treatment, which initially was very bad and mean, is now

---

1   AA, Handakte Hewel 5, R 27473
2   AA, R27492 Hewel 15/H-Q
3   Geerken, *A Gecko for Luck*, pp. 144ff

acceptable. [...] At this moment in Holland a large number of prominent people are being arrested. I expect [...] that these measures will soon effect the desired response in the form of the release of all Germans in the Dutch East Indies. [...][1]

All the Germans living in the East Indies – Nazis and non-Nazis, Jews who had fled Germany, doctors, missionaries, nurses, engineers, businessmen, even mixed-race children with German fathers who didn't speak a word of German – were put into internment camps by the Dutch. The Swiss consul, who had taken over concern for German interests after the closing of the German Consulate in Batavia listed in a letter to the German Foreign Ministry in Berlin the following camps where Germans were interned:

On Sumatra: *Fort de Kock, Taroeroeng (for German women only), Pematang, Siantar, [Author's note: several hundred woman and children were interned here in a hospital alienated from its true purpose], Raja near Brastagi, Koeta Tjane in Atjeh, (Fort Kotatjane), Pagar Alam in South-Sumatra, Lahat, Medan, Takengon.*
On Java: *Onrust, Bandoeng (for German women and children only), Banjoe Biroe (for German women and children only), Batavia, Berg en Dal near Soekabumi, Blitar, Buitenzorg (only for German women and children), Magelang, Fort Ngawi, Salatiga (only for German women and children), Sindanglaja (only for German women and children), Soekabumi and Tjibuduk (only for German women).*
On Celebes: *Macassar, Sasaran, Menado, Singkang*
On Borneo: *Hendangan, Long Iram, Sintang, Teloek Najoer*[2]

All post from the internment camps was strictly censored. On the cards, which could be sent to relations every two weeks, only 75 words were allowed. Anything that exceeded this and any mention of conditions in the camps was blacked out.

Ill. 26   Censored Postcard from the Allas Vallei Internment Camp 4th August 1940

1   AA, Handakte Hewel (without document number)
2   AA, Pol. Archiv, R27492

According to a report from the Swiss Embassy in Jakarta to their government in Bern, German women in the camps on Java had their watches, jewellery, money and even their wedding rings taken from them.[1]

The camp where the conditions were worst was probably the internment camp on the small island of Onrust off Batavia. The commandant was Mijnheer de Vries, who was seldom seen without a pistol in his hand. There were not only about 1200 Germans from Batavia and the surrounding area squeezed together in a very small space, but also 1200 Dutchmen, members of the NSB.

There had been a Dutch shipyard on Onrust in the 19th century, where over 1,000 slaves and free workers were employed. Before the Second World War Onrust had first been a leper colony and then a quarantine station for pilgrims returning from Mecca. When the internees arrived there, there were no sanitary facilities, no mats and not even enough drinking water – instead there were plenty of rats, fleas and lice, mosquitos and diseases. The buildings were absolutely filthy and there weren't even any brooms available for cleaning. The internees had to sleep on the bare concrete floor without blankets, as a result of which many of them suffered from lung problems and asthma for the rest of their lives.[2] They were being treated like dangerous criminals.

When the men were dragged off to the internment camps there were only the German mothers and school age children left behind. They were treated somewhat better, even though their houses and possessions were confiscated. They too were interned – in so-called *beschermingkamps* [protection camps]. Since the family breadwinners had been interned and the colonial government no longer paid their salaries or offered any financial support, many of these women and children lived in pitiable circumstances: they only received the minimum absolutely necessary from the Dutch. Some *Reichs* German women and children found refuge with Indonesian friends – unlike the Dutch, the Germans had often fostered contacts with the native population.

In May 1941 when it was clear that war was approaching in the Pacific as well, this time with Japan, the Swiss Consul, working together with the Red Cross, managed to persuade the Dutch authorities to allow some of the German women and children to be moved from the Dutch East Indies to China and Japan. Before German troops invaded Russia it would still have been possible for them to return to Germany on the Trans-Siberian Railway. But

---

1   AA, Akte 4.879/Bern
2   like the father of Fred Flakowski. Interview with eyewitness Fred Flakowski, 18.03.2014

after the invasion on the 22nd of June 1941 this route was blocked. The German women and children could opt for China or Japan. On the 4th of July 1941 the Japanese passenger liner *Asama Maru* – a ship of 17,000 tonnes belonging to the N.Y.K. line (Nippon Yusen Kaisha Line) and known in East Asia as the "Queen of the Pacific" set sail from Batavia's Tanjung Priok port with 740 German women and children on board as well as some of the German consular staff.

Before the Germans were allowed to board their luggage – they were allowed a meagre 20 kilograms each – was searched again by the Dutch. Cameras, photograph albums, even shoes were confiscated. This was pure harassment, but it was the only way to freedom.

118 women and children had to be left behind because the *Asama Maru* was overfull. They were consoled with hopes of places on the next transport, but it never came. The *Asama Maru* was the only ship that transported Germans to China or Japan. Some women found another way to get to Japan with their children.[1] Many who wished to stay in the East Indies or who could not manage to escape to Japan continued to be interned in the camps.

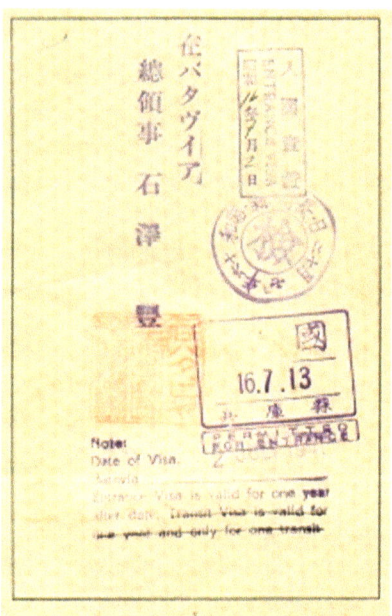

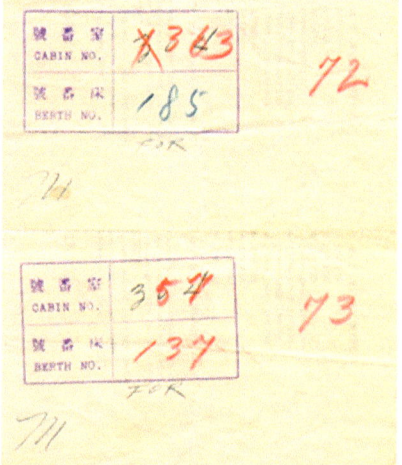

Ill. 27
Entry Visa for Japan, Date according to Japanese Showa Period reckoning

Ill. 28
Boarding Card for the Asama Maru

---

1   eyewitness Friedrich Flakowski

Two weeks before the departure of the *Asama Maru* there was a mass medical screening of German women and children in some camps, during which blood was taken from their ear-lobes. This caused the infection of a large number of these people with a mixture of malaria tropica and malaria tertiana. Since the incubation period for malaria is between 9 and 14 days, the first severe attacks of the disease coincided exactly with the departure of the *Asama Maru*. The Dutch were suspected of having deliberately infected these civilian prisoners. Did they wish to prevent them from leaving, or just to give them a 'souvenir'? One could believe anything of the Dutch at that time! Many who were severely ill had to remain behind because of their high fever – it was only when they reached Japan that this combined malaria infection could be diagnosed and treated.[1]

Japan was not really interested in accepting these German refugees. The captain of the *Asama Maru* tried in vain to hand them over to the Americans in Manila. Some of them were landed in Shanghai. Those mothers and their children travelled by train to the former German enclaves of Tsingtau (now Qingdao) or Tientsin (now Tianjing), where they remained for another three years until the end of the war.

Ill. 29
Arrival of the Asama Maru in Kobe with German Women and Children

---

1   Statement by F. Flakowski, who was infected and suffred from the after effects of the malaria for the rest of his life.

The *Asama Maru* arrived in Kobe in Japan on the 13th of July 1941. The German women and children were at first housed in hotels until apartments or houses could be assigned to them. Until the end of the war they were supported by the German state through the German Embassy in Tokyo, not only with money and food, but also with social activities. There were regular events and ceremonies in the Club Concordia in the *Deutsches Haus*. This was also where meetings of the Nazi Party, the Hitler Youth and the organisation for girls, the *Bund Deutscher Mädchen*, took place. The German Ambassador in Tokyo wrote (in his book *Japans Niederlage – Asiens Sieg* [Japan's Defeat, Asia's Victory]:

A pleasant enrichment of our simple social activities was provided by a film projector which we had acquired from the Lloyd-line steamer Scharnhorst. Individual blockade-breakers supplied us with a relatively broad selection of films so that we were able to provide the members of the German colony and our foreign guests with a pleasant diversion without dipping too deeply into the funds available for food.[1]

The Dutch forbade any schooling for the German children during their internment in the East Indies. It was different in Japan: here the children from the East Indies were enrolled in the German school in Kobe (*Zeiden Hojin Kobe Doitsu Gakuin*). At the same time they joined the *Deutsche Jugend Japans DJJ* [German Youth of Japan], which was similar to the *Hitlerjugend* and the *Bund Deutscher Mädchen*. Order now returned to their everyday lives. Over 700 German women who were separated from their husbands and fathers had to spend the years from 1941 to 1947 in Japan.[2]

Ill. 30
German School Kobe, 1943

---

1   Stahmer, *Japans Niederlage – Asiens Sieg,* pp. 190f
2   eyewitness F. Flakowski

Ill. 31
The Deutsche Jugend Japans in the Club Concordia Hall in Kobe, 1943

The German men had to follow another path. So that they could not be freed from the internment camps in the Dutch East Indies by Germany's allies the Japanese, who were approaching ever closer, they were deported by sea to British India, Ceylon and Dutch Guyana in South America.

Walter Spies was also interned even though he had utterly rejected the first stirrings of Nazism very early on. He was one of the most famous Germans in the Dutch East Indies to die during his internment in the Second World War. As he was being transported to British India with many others on the ship *Van Imhoff,* his life came to a tragic end. Several hundred Germans, including Spies and Hans F. Overbeck were drowned, as I shall describe in more detail later.

Only a few days after the *Van Imhoff,* the *Tjisadane,* pride of the former Dutch Java-China-Japan Line set sail from Surabaya. On the steerage deck 146 Germans – *Reichs* Germans, *Volks* Germans and German Jews were crammed together in a cage made of strong iron bars reaching from floor to ceiling. The conditions were appalling. The portholes and hatchways were closed, there was no fresh air and the open latrine smelt terrible. Bright electric light shone day and night. The Dutch guards said that this was a fair punishment for the bombing of Rotterdam. After the war the Dutch managed to forget very quickly that only a few years after the inexcusable bombing of Rotterdam they themselves had bombed towns and villages on Java and Sumatra in a brutal colonial war that was contrary to international law.

The *Tjisadane* was at sea for over five weeks; it was a hellish voyage. Its destination was Paramaribo in Dutch Guyana (now Surinam) in the north east of South America, where it arrived on the 1st of March 1942. The Germans were first held in prison in Nieuw Amsterdam and were then moved to Joden-Savanne (Jews' Savannah) a camp deep in the jungle where the conditions were utterly inhumane. It could only be reached by boat along the River Suriname. The camp commandant, Lieutenant van Baalen, was a brutal sadist. Forced labour in burning heat was the order of the day. The internees were harassed every day, sometimes even driven along with salvoes of machine-gun fire.[1] The hellish voyage in the *Tjisadane* was barbarously continued in the tropical hell of South America. The Red Cross was far away and the Dutch ignored the Geneva Convention anyway. Malaria, cholera and typhus raged in the camp. Medical treatment or transfer to the hospital in Paramaribo was either refused or only allowed when it was already too late. Many Germans remain buried forever in South American soil in the Joden-Savanne camp.[2]

After many years in Dutch prisons and five years' exile on the island of Flores, Soekarno was transferred to Bengkulu in south Sumatra in 1938. When German troops marched into the Netherlands in May 1940, the Dutch commandant called on Soekarno, the architect and engineer – in fact the only engineer and 'artist' in Bengkulu – to design a monument commemorating this terrible event. Soekarno responded:

You torment and torture me because I desire freedom for my people and now you expect me, your prisoner, to build a monument for you because another country has taken away your freedom?[3]

1941 was an extremely eventful year. Although the USA was still neutral, warships of the US Navy shepherded British and Canadian convoys across the Atlantic. These convoys carried millions of tonnes of food and important military material, to the value of 31 billion US dollars to Britain.[4] Without this immense and unlimited help Britain could not have held out for long in a war with Germany and so Churchill continually badgered Roosevelt to enter the war on the British side. Without the USA it looked as if Britain would lose the war.

The general sentiment of the US population – unlike President Franklin D. Roosevelt – was against entering a European war – only 8% were in favour. Roosevelt continued to provoke Hitler, in that warships of the neutral USA entered into combat with German submarines contrary to international law.

---

1   Keppner, *Wie weit bis Airmolang*, pp. 517ff
2   Keppner, *Wie weit bis Airmolang*, pp. 508ff
3   Adams, *Sukarno*, p. 145
4   Comparison: The post-war Marshall Aid Plan in the period from April 1948 to December 1952 involved a sum of 12.4 billion dollars for the whole of Europe.

Japan has no natural resources: no oil and no iron ore for the production of steel. Oil, iron ore and other important materials were mainly imported from the USA. Roosevelt put pressure on Japan by reducing exports to almost nil. Japan was suddenly deprived of many crucially important raw materials. Great Britain joined in the USA's embargo. Consequently, Japan tried to increase their supply of oil from the Dutch East Indies and sent their business minister Kobayashi to negotiate in Batavia. The German Ambassador in Tokyo, Ott, informed Hewel in Berlin of this in a telegram on the 27th of August 1940. An extract:

In view of American oil embargo main purpose of negotiations increase of oil imports from Dutch East Indies. Signed Ott[1]

The Japanese Prime Minister Prince Konoe Fumimaro, his Foreign Minister Yosuke Matsuoka and the very pro-German War Minister General Tojo were forced to look around elsewhere for raw materials. Their eyes naturally fell on the relatively close Dutch East Indies with their rich resources. At the end of 1941 President Roosevelt froze all Japanese assets in the USA in unequivocal breach of international law.[2]

When Japan tried once more to negotiate with the USA to secure further deliveries of oil, ore and steel and so achieve a peaceful solution to the conflict, Roosevelt brusquely refused any further talks. Even the Japanese government's suggestion that Prime Minister Prince Konoe should be sent to negotiate directly with Roosevelt was refused.[3]

Because of this provocative strangulation policy Japan was forced to expand to the south where raw materials were available. Japan felt compelled to take this step because it saw no further possibility of coming to a peaceful solution with the USA. Roosevelt goaded Japan into taking the decisive step in order to justify entry into the war. He wanted to lead America out of isolation and after the war in Europe and the Pacific by the back door.

Because of this rebuff from the USA and the consequent loss of face (so important in Asia) Japan wanted to teach the USA a lesson – which they did in the surprise attack on Pearl Harbour on the 7th of December 1941.

Sherwood, a close collaborator of Roosevelt's, wrote:

Roosevelt knew very well what it meant for the Japanese to 'preserve face', and so an action that gave them no chance to preserve face would practically make war inevitable.[4]

---

1   AA, Handakte Hewel 5, R 27473, Document 84595
2   Stahmer, *Japans Niederlage – Asiens Sieg*, p. 57
3   www.deutsches-marinearchiv.de (*Report on visits to Japan by Admiral P. W. Wenneker, Naval Attaché Tokyo*)
4   Stahmer, *Japans Niederlage – Asiens Sieg*, p. 60

Ill. 32
Japanese Special Issue Stamp on First Day Cover Celebrating the Attack on Pearl Harbour, Date according to Japanese Showa Period reckoning

Now Roosevelt had the first shot he needed and a good reason for entering the war. After Japan invaded South East Asia Roosevelt said:

If we had cut the oil off from [Author's note: Japan] earlier they would probably have gone to the Dutch East Indies a year earlier and we would have had war.[1]

President Roosevelt played a more than dubious role in this macabre drama. According to witness statements in the War Crimes Trial in 1948 the Americans were in possession of the Japanese radio code key and could thus decipher the secret orders for the attack on Pearl Harbour. The US Navy was also informed by the Royal Australian Navy that Japanese aircraft carriers were sailing in the direction of Hawaii.[2]

The spy Richard Sorge in Tokyo had also warned the Allies about the forthcoming attack. Roosevelt and his advisors were warned, but probably deliberately failed to do anything to warn the US naval command in Pearl Harbour. Roosevelt was looking for a reason to go to war. During the Teheran conference (28th November – 1st December 1943) Roosevelt opened up to his friend Stalin and explained his silence in spite of the alarming radio messages as follows:

It would have been impossible to send American troops to this war in Europe if the Japanese had not attacked Pearl Harbour.[3]

In the Axis pact Hitler had promised the Japanese Empire that if there was a war between Japan and the USA he would also declare war. After the Japanese attack on Pearl Harbour and the subsequent US declaration of war on Japan, Hitler kept his promise – at least that was the argument presented in the Third Reich. But is it true? In no way!

1   Stahmer, *Japans Niederlage – Asiens Sieg*, p. 69
2   Stahmer, *Japans Niederlage – Asiens Sieg*, pp. 68f
3   Stahmer, *Japans Niederlage – Asiens Sieg*, p. 67

The German-Japanese-Italian Tripartite Axis Pact was signed in September 1940. It was a purely defensive alliance. When it became clear to Japan that Hitler was shortly planning to attack the Soviet Union, Japan made a secret neutrality agreement with the Soviet Union in April 1941, i.e. a few months before Hitler invaded the Soviet Union, with the result that Japan could not join in Hitler's war against the USSR. Japan stabbed Germany in the back with this agreement, since Stalin could now withdraw his troops from the east to deploy them against the Germans in the west. Thus Hitler would have had good reason not to stick to his agreement with Japan.

The US now supported the Soviet Union with tanks, planes and other military equipment which they delivered to Vladivostok in eastern Siberia. From there it went to the western front on the Trans-Siberian Railway. US military aid to the USSR in the Second World War amounted to ten billion US Dollars. But their friendship soon came to an end, and in 1949, during the Cold War, the US had plans in place which could have led to 150 atom bombs being dropped on Soviet cities.[1]

Hitler's declaration of war on the USA was self-destructive megalomania. He was doing Roosevelt a big favour, since he would never have been able to declare war on Germany against the will of the American people. Roosevelt had achieved his goal, and Hitler was now fighting an unwinnable war on two fronts: in the West against the Allies, including the greatest power in the world, and in the east against the giant power of the Soviet Union.

Hitler declared war on the USA on the 11th of December 1941. Only a few days before there had been a massive offensive by Russian troops on the Eastern Front. The German troops were already suffering heavy losses and had to withdraw. It should have been clear to Hitler at this point that the war could no longer be won. Hitler's declaration of war on the USA sealed Germany's final downfall.

At the time of the Japanese bombing of Pearl Harbour, Japanese troops were already firmly entrenched in French Indo-China. Indo-China had taken the side of the Vichy regime in the French homeland and was thus an ally of Germany and Japan. No Dutchman at that time believed that the Japanese had the strength to force their way down to the Dutch East Indies. Japanese oil supplies were too limited, and they were also certain that as the Japanese advanced they would find the fortress of Singapore impregnable.

---

1   ZDFinfo, 10.02.2014, 22.30h, *Krieg der Spione*

10. The Beginning of the U-Boat War in the Atlantic

At this point we will briefly discuss the naval war in the Atlantic in order to make the general situation behind the submarine war easier to understand. At the beginning of the Second World War the German Navy was a dwarf in comparison with the Japanese war fleet – let alone those of Britain and the USA. Japan, for example, had much larger submarines than Germany. Submarine cruisers of type I-400 had three aircraft in a hangar on board that could take off when the submarine surfaced.

The reason for this small German navy was the Versailles Treaty after the loss of the First World War. There was a strict limit to ship building in Germany in terms of the number of ships, their size and tonnage, their armament, top speed etc. The treaty only allowed a German navy of a *quantité négligeable,* a negligible size. It was only when Germany left the League of Nations and, from 1934 onwards, disregarded these restrictions, that they began moderate rebuilding of the navy.

Hitler was never particularly interested in a strong German navy. For him, as for Goering, tanks and aircraft were more important. He thought that if a navy was necessary, then it should be made up of large battleships and not submarines. This was a fatal mistake. A decision in favour of submarines was not taken until it was too late and it could be foreseen that the war could no longer be won. The naval battle in the Second World War showed that it was no longer a matter of battleship against battleship. Far more effective was war on the enemy's merchant fleet to block supply lines. This was particularly true of Britain, which was dependent on regular supplies from America and Australia. And submarines were ideal for blocking trade routes. As early as the spring of 1939 Dönitz wanted to have 300 submarines mass produced. But Hitler and Admiral Raeder, who was commander in chief of the navy at the time, continued to prioritise surface fighting ships and overruled Dönitz, who was initially only responsible for the submarine fleet.

In 1936 the German Navy's modern ships comprised 3 heavy cruisers, six light cruisers and 35 submarines. There was planning provision for four battleships, four heavy cruisers, two aircraft carriers, 19 destroyers and only one submarine. These were to be produced by 1949 (!).[1] At the beginning of the war in 1939 the German Navy was far from being properly equipped and it was folly to begin a war in those circumstances.

---

1   Krug, Hirama, Sander-Nagashima, Niestlé, *Reluctant Allies,* pp. 91f

The activities of German U-boats in South East Asia and Japan were overshadowed by the initially spectacular successes and subsequent crushing defeat of the German submarine fleet in the Atlantic. For that reason there is hardly any literature about the war waged by the blockade-breakers, auxiliary cruisers and U-boats in the Indian Ocean and in Dutch East Indies waters – admittedly only starting a few years after the beginning of the war. The few German ships that were deployed in South East Asia were tasked with blocking British trade routes and keeping Allied naval forces occupied in the area. U-boats were also supposed to carry freight and passengers to South East Asia and Japan and pass on modern German submarine technology to the Japanese Navy.

Although the submarine campaign in the Atlantic began shortly after the outbreak of war, German U-boats were only deployed in South-East Asia after Germany's ally Japan had occupied the Dutch East Indies and Malaya so that the German Navy could set up naval bases in the area.

Dönitz wished to strike the USA with a surprise submarine campaign while they were still suffering from the shock of Pearl Harbour. He was convinced that submarine superiority in the Atlantic could decide the result of the war, but Hitler preferred to use the necessary steel for building tanks. Finally Hitler gave in to Dönitz's entreaties and authorized *Operation Paukenschlag* [Bombshell] with the few U-boats available.

Until the French capitulation in 1940, German ships and submarines had to take the long way round the north of Britain to reach the Atlantic. The narrow North Sea was controlled by Britain and France, and it was practically impossible for German ships to get through. The strategic situation of the German Navy changed decisively with the occupation of Denmark and Norway in 1940, as well as the French capitulation two months later. The Germans now had a coastline that stretched from the North Cape in Norway along the French west coast and the Bay of Biscay to the Spanish border.

They immediately began to build a number of bomb-proof U-boat pens of different sizes along the west coast of France. From then onwards German ships had free and direct access to the Atlantic and voyage times in the Atlantic and to the Indian Ocean and to South East Asia reduced considerably. As a result, smaller submarines of type IX C could operate alongside the larger long-range submarines of type IX D.

At first Dönitz could only send five long-range U-boats from Lorient in the Bay of Biscay in western France to the east coast of the USA. Lorient and other ports on the French Atlantic coast were later to play an important part in the story of the 'East Asia Boats'.

The U-boats Dönitz sent to America were very seaworthy 'Atlantic' submarines of type IX B. With bigger fuel tanks than any previous U-boats they had a considerably greater range. Without refuelling, they could sail to America, engage in action off the east coast and then return to their home bases on the west coast of France. They were 77 metres long and seven wide. On the foredeck in front of the conning tower there was a 10.5 cm cannon and astern there was a 2 cm anti-aircraft gun. The Atlantic boats were normally armed with only six torpedoes. For Operation Bombshell this was increased to up to 23, each with 300 kilograms of explosive. The lower cabins were removed to increase torpedo storage, considerably decreasing the already cramped space in the submarine – the crew had to share cabins.

The US Navy's lack of proper preparation enabled these five submarines to cause Allied losses that were far greater and more critical than those caused by the Japanese at Pearl Harbour.[1] The raid on Pearl Harbour did, however, have a greater effect as the US Navy was able to conceal the initial large scale of their losses in the Atlantic, in terms of freight and tanker ships, which were not reported in the US media. The US Navy and its commander in chief, Ernest King, had failed completely. People in America were asking 'Where is our Navy?'[2]

Because of ever-increasing public pressure the US Navy Ministry reported on the 1st of April 1942 that up to that point 28 German U-boats had been sunk off the US coast.[3] This was a downright lie, intended to reassure the American public. In fact, not one German submarine had been sunk off the US coast, in the Caribbean or the Gulf of Mexico until then. In war, both sides lie. It is a battle not just of weapons, but of words. Enemy losses are exaggerated and one's own losses played down.[4]

The German U-boats were taking the war right to America's doorstep. The German U-boat commanders were surprised to meet with no opposition. New York and the other cities along the east coast were blazing with light, lighthouses, buoys and beacons transmitted their signals as they had done in peace time. For example, U 123, commanded by Reinhard Hardegen, operated directly outside the entrance to New York harbour. The inhabitants of the city could see the burning wrecks of the torpedoed ships right in front of their own beaches. Even within sight of the US coast the U-boat commanders felt so secure that they almost always operated on the surface in waters which, with a depth of only eight to nine metres, were dangerous for submarines.

---

1   Gannon, *Operation Paukenschlag*, p. 169
2   Gannon, *Operation Paukenschlag*, pp. 274 and 276
3   Farago, *The Tenth Fleet*, pp. 69f
4   Gannon, *Operation Paukenschlag*, p. 390

There was a rumour among the US public that the crews of German U-boats were shopping for fresh supplies in supermarkets along the east coast and visiting cinemas in the evening. However, only two landings are known to have taken place in inhabited areas of the US coast – on Long Island (New York) and in Florida. On both occasions groups from the *Spezialeinheit [Special Unit] Brandenburg* were being landed to carry out sabotage in the US interior.

On the 22nd of October 1943 U 537, which later operated on several missions in the Java Sea, made another landing on the coast of North America in the vicinity of the uninhabited Martins Bay in Labrador/Canada to set up an automatic weather station. After this dangerous operation it returned safely to its base in Lorient on the 8th of December 1943. On the 25th of March 1944 U 537 set out to sea once more, this time round Africa and across the Indian Ocean to Batavia on Java, where it arrived safely after 131 days at sea – of which more later.

As the first five submarines of Operation Bombshell set course for home to refuel and load new torpedoes, a second wave of German U-boats sailed up to the east coast of North America. These were smaller boats of class IX which could not operate alone as they needed supply submarines, which provided the smaller U-boats with fuel, provisions and new torpedoes. One of these supply submarines could provide 14 U-boats in action with 700 tonnes of oil. In this way the time the smaller submarines could remain in action off the USA, in the Caribbean and the Gulf of Mexico was increased by four to eight weeks. Without the supply submarines they could not have managed the journey from the old world to the new and back.

Submarines now sailed up the St Lawrence River in Canada, where the convoys carrying vital supplies to Britain assembled. 100 kilometres deep in enemy territory, the German submarines sank many British and Canadian freighters. After this the St Lawrence was blocked to shipping. Canadian support for the British war effort was almost brought to an end. This disaster led the British to nickname the Royal Canadian Navy (RCN) the 'Royal Collision Navy'.

In the first six months of Operation Bombshell the German U-boats operating off the US coast and in the Caribbean, though few in number, sank 397 Allied cargo ships without loss. In June 1942 alone there were 127. The US naval historian Michael Gannon wrote in 1990:

The numbers [Author's note: of ships sunk by the Germans] are evidence of one of the greatest maritime catastrophes in history and the worst defeat that the United States have suffered at sea. For Germany it was the most successful U-boat operation of the entire war. [...] For America's main ally, Britain, the losses proved to be so serious that the contribution of this island nation, so dependent on imports, to the further course of the war was temporarily in question.[1]

By the end of 1942 more than 1,000 enemy ships lay on the bottom of the Atlantic, the worst defeat the Allies had suffered. Dönitz's surprise attack had succeeded without any real opposition from the US Navy. The supply of goods and materials to Britain was as good as cut off by the success of the U-boats. Some 2,000 supply ships were heading for Britain from all over the world, and at least 20 ships had to reach UK harbours every day if the country was to survive. It looked as if the Allies were about to lose the Battle of the Atlantic.

Admiral Dönitz wanted to exploit German naval superiority in the Atlantic, which had resulted from the initial incompetence of the US Navy. He wished to send a further 50 submarines to the American coast and force Britain out of the war. But in spite of Operation Bombshell's success Hitler thwarted Dönitz's plans, even though he was himself surprised by the German U-boats' success.

In spite of their great success off the US coast, Hitler weakened the U-boats' position in the Atlantic by a further seriously bad decision. Against Dönitz's objections Hitler moved U-boats from the Atlantic to the North Sea and refused to build the 300 new submarines Dönitz was requesting. The British naval historian Roskill shared Dönitz's view:
The weight of the offensive off the American coast declined just at the time when it had proved highly profitable. [...] but the small total [Author's note: of U-boats] [...] now seems to have been a decisive factor in the Atlantic battle.[2]

Hitler weakened the German Navy. When he later – still hesitantly – gave the green light for the construction of more U-boats and U-boat production was in full swing, it was already too late. The trump card of surprise had been played. The British had taken vital steps forward in U-boat detection with new radar and sonar devices. From late summer 1942 the destruction of the German U-boat force in the Atlantic began. The British had developed a new 9 cm Magnetron H2S radar device. These short waves could not be detected by the German Metox warning devices. Research into radio waves shorter than 50 cm had been abandoned in Germany shortly after the beginning of the war, since these high-frequency waves were felt to be of no use. This was a serious error, because Germany – until now the leading

---

1   Gannon, *Operation Paukenschlag*, p. 403
2   Roskill, *War at Sea*, Vol 2, pp. 101-104
     Gannon, *Operation Paukenschlag*, p. 318

nation in radar engineering – was being beaten by Britain. German high frequency specialists worked feverishly to solve the problem. A series of devices with resonant names like Borkum, Naxos, Wanze [Bug], Fliege [Fly], Mücke [Mosquito], Gema or Hagenuk were produced but none of them solved the problem because they could only work in an area of longer wavelength.[1]

Even in the dark the Allies could now surprise and destroy any German U-boat. From the middle of April to the end of May 1943 912 Allied freighters, tankers and troop-transporters crossed the Atlantic. The U-boats sunk 24 of them for a loss of 27 submarines. From June to August 1943 74 U-boats were sunk in the Atlantic, while the number of Allied ships sunk decreased significantly.[2] The British also made great progress in deciphering the radio traffic between the German submarines.

In Bletchley Park, 50 miles north west of London, there was Government Code and Cipher School, a centre run by the British secret service. There were large numbers of personnel to intercept the Morse code radio communication of the U-boats and the supply ships. They were all trained radio operators. Using the 'handwriting' of all the Morse transmitter operators – which hardly differs from one to another – they were able to assign almost all the messages to their particular U-boat. Initially the messages themselves were of little use since in spite of all their efforts they had not been able to break the German codes.

Only when the British managed to capture an ENIGMA code machine from U-boat U 110 in the Atlantic did they begin to have some success. They now gradually began to succeed in breaking into the ENIGMA keys and acquiring some idea of the content of the radio messages. With time they began to decipher the plans of action, the co-ordinates and the movements of the U-boats. In effect, the capture of the code machine and the deciphering of German radio traffic had a serious influence on the course of the war from then until its end. Now the Allies could inflict more German naval losses.

German code breakers also had great success with the deciphering of Allied radio traffic. For example, Germany was able as early as 1940/41 to unscramble scrambled conversations between President Roosevelt and Prime Minister Churchill and to listen in.[3]

From the end of 1942 there was also a change in the situation of the convoys, which sometimes contained thirty or more freighters. They were now

1   Terraine, *The U-Boat Wars*, p. 459
2   Brennecke, *Jäger - Gejagte*, pp. 237ff
3   Bartolomew Lee, *KV6LEE – WP2DLT, Radio Spies: Episodes in the Ether Wars*, p. 58
     www.scribd.com/doc/92110767/Intelligence-Analysis

protected by warships and aircraft. Dönitz deployed his 'Wolf Packs', groups of ten or more submarines who would attack a convoy simultaneously. But now the Allies were able to use SONAR and Radar to locate and pursue the German U-boats. A devastating war on the U-boats began. After the USA began to mass produce Liberty Ships, far more were made than the U-boats could sink. The number of Allied ships sunk declined from week to week while the number of U-boats sunk climbed rapidly. The Battle of the Atlantic was lost.

This was a short summary of the terrible naval war in the Atlantic to which 3,000 Allied ships with 36,000 officers and men fell victim. During the same period Germany lost 32,000 members of the U-boat crews.

After losing the naval war in the Atlantic the German leadership was forced to try and block British supply routes in the Indian Ocean and at the same time to secure supplies of raw materials for their own industry. From a military viewpoint the operations of the German U-boats in the Indian Ocean and Dutch East Indies waters were far less spectacular. However, given the long distances involved and the concomitant logistic problems, as well as the dangers involved in operating in unknown terrain with monsoons and a tropical climate without reliable weather data, meant that these operations were far more adventurous and impressive.

Although there was very wide coverage of the Eastern and Western Fronts as well as the naval war in the Atlantic or Rommel in Africa, there was hardly any coverage of South East Asia.

11. Merchant Ships and Captured Ships as Blockade Breakers

When war broke out on the 1st of September 1939, 858 German merchant ships were under way on the world's oceans. About 19 of them were in the Dutch East Indies and 14 in Japan and other East Asian countries, such as Japanese-occupied Manchuria. Suddenly, although their captains had no military experience, they were all faced with a completely new situation.

Until the outbreak of war there had been frequent and regular passenger and freight traffic between South East Asia and Europe carried by the Hamburg-America Line HAPAG and the North German Lloyd Far East Express NDLFEE. Notices in the *Deutsche Wacht* in Batavia regularly announced forthcoming departures. They were modern ships built for the tropics with bars, tea rooms, cinemas, sports decks and open-air swimming pools. Wm. H. Müller & Co. in Batavia held the General Agency for the Dutch East Indies.

Sailings from Batavia were normally every 14 days on the *Heidelberg, Karnak, Freiburg, Kurmark, Menes* and *Uckermark*. The *Duisburg, Sauerland, Leverkusen, Burgenland* and *Oldenburg* sailed from Singapore at rather more frequent intervals. The NDLFEE Line fast liners *Potsdam, Gneisenau* and *Scharnhorst*[1] reached Genoa from Singapore in just 15 days. They took a good week longer to reach Southampton and Bremerhaven.

These first class fast liners were also popular with the British because of their speed and the excellent service on board. It enabled them to reach their colonies in Asia swiftly, and for this reason the ships called at Southampton on both the outward and inward voyages.

In the 1930s Günther Fust was the representative of IG-Farben in China. In the 1960s I met him in Indonesia, where he was the first representative of the Hoechst company. He enjoyed telling tales of his adventurous time in China over a cool cocktail or beer on a warm tropical night.

In 1937 Herr Fust sailed from Shanghai to Bremerhaven on the *Gneisenau* for his home leave. In his diary he describes his return journey to Hong Kong on the *Scharnhorst* in detail.[2] On the 7th of February 1938 the *Scharnhorst* set sail from Bremerhaven. The ship, 199 metres long, with its modern turbo-electric engines, its black hull, white superstructure and yellow fun-

1   This is the passenger ship Scharnhorst. The battleship Scharnhorst entered service in January 1939 and was sunk in the North Atlantic in December 1943.
2   Fust, Günther: short summary from the diary

nel was an impressive sight. Fust was delighted with the cabins, sparkling clean and outfitted in the most modern style including a telephone, with the white-tiled bathroom and the main hall with its panoramic windows. It was all clean and bright. Of course there was a sun-deck with a swimming pool, a sports deck, a cinema, several bars, concerts and dancing.

A first small breakfast was served from 6:30. The main breakfast at 8 o'clock boasted a long menu with everything the heart might desire: fruit, rolls, eggs, ham. Coffee from Guatemala, Costa Rica, Java or Sumatra. An embarrassment of choices. There was a third small breakfast at 11, then lunch at two o'clock. Afternoon tea was served under the awning at 5 o'clock and the Lucullan dinner, where the ladies wore elegant evening dresses and the men dinner jackets, at 8 o'clock. Attentive stewards served in tail-coats and white gloves: at the end of the 1930s life on board the German liners of the NDLFEE was elegant and the service unequalled anywhere on the world's oceans. After Southampton and Genoa they sailed through the Suez Canal. Suez was the point where one's wardrobe changed: up to here men wore black suits, but in the tropics after Suez they had to be white. The colour of evening dress also changed: black dinner jacket before Suez, white afterwards. The rules on those liners were very strict.

Before and after meals it was the custom to enjoy a glass of Champagne or a cocktail in one of the bars. After Suez the favourite cocktail was the Gimlet, known from Batavia to Shanghai. A Champagne glass is filled with half gin, half lime juice, served with a lot of ice, sugar and a slice of lemon.

After Colombo, Singapore and Manila the *Scharnhorst* docked in Hong Kong on the 10th of March 1938. Outside the port lay the wreck of the Japanese *Asama Maru,* which had been dashed on the rocks by a typhoon in September 1937. The ship was later repaired and in July 1941 – as I have already described above – brought hundreds of German women and children from the Dutch East Indies to China and Japan.

The *Scharnhorst* continued its voyage via Shanghai to Yokohama or Kobe, before taking the same route in reverse back to Bremerhaven. For Herr Fust the journey ended in Hong Kong. After the luxury and excess of life on board everyday life in China came as a shock. Peace ruled on the *Scharnhorst,* but there was already a war on in China and even in Germany there was a hint of war in the air.

Three or four days before the outbreak of war the captains of all the ships received a radio message informing them that they were no longer to be controlled by their respective shipping lines but by the German Ministry of Transport. All further orders would now be issued by them. These turned out to be
:

1. sail for home waters immediately and as quickly as possible.
2. if point 1 not possible, immediately make for a neutral port so that the ship and its cargo could not fall into enemy hands.
3. if point 1 and 2 not possible, destroy the ship by opening the flooding valves or using explosives. The ship must on no account fall into the enemy's hands as a prize.

Many of these ships returned unharmed to Germany in the months that followed. Others made for neutral ports and in the course of the war were used as supply ships – for U-boats, for example – or blockade breakers. Some of the ships were sunk by their own crews to avoid capture. After the end of the war there were serious debates about the fact that Britain in particular, but also the USA, had attacked and also captured German merchant ships in neutral waters in contravention of maritime law and the laws of war.

One example of this is the North German Lloyd freighter *Franken*, which on the 6th of September 1939 – just a few days after the war had begun – was sailing within 1.5 nautical miles of the west coast of Sumatra. Since at that time the Dutch East Indies had not joined the Allies, the *Franken* was sailing in neutral waters.

A British aircraft dropped depth charges to force the *Franken* out into the open sea. The captain of the *Franken* sailed at full speed to within 500 metres of the coast. There was less than a metre of water beneath the keel. Now a British destroyer also pursued the *Franken* inside neutral waters, but because of its greater draught could not follow her. Although the destroyer's gun-barrels were aimed threateningly at the *Franken*, the captain sailed on undeterred. Only when the safety of the port of Padang came into view did the British abandon their pursuit.

For months there was no opportunity for the *Franken* to attempt to break out and escape to Japan. When the German invasion of the Netherlands began on the 10th of May 1940, a boarding party from the Dutch cruiser *Java* took over the ship. The German crew was interned, and the ship, renamed *Wangiwangi*, taken into Dutch service. A year later it was sunk in the Atlantic by a German U-boat.

At the outbreak of war the following German ships were in Japan and China:

Yokohama: *MS Regensburg, MS Elbe, MS Odenwald* and *MS Spreewald*
Nagasaki: *MS Anneliese Essberger* and *MS Else Essberger*
Kobe: *MS Burgenland, MS Kulmerland, MS Münsterland,* the fast liner *Scharnhorst, SS R. C. Rickmers* and *SS Ursula Rickmers*

Dairen/ Manchukuo: *SS Havenstein*
Shanghai: *MS Ramses*, which was later moved to Kobe.[1]

The German merchant ships which were in the ports of the Dutch East Indies at the outbreak of war – when the Netherlands and the East Indies were still neutral – were renamed and then, mostly with Malay names, sailed back to Germany as blockade breakers. Thus the *MS Wuppertal* as *Noesaniwa*, the *MS Kassel* as *Mendanan*, the *MS Bitterfeld* as *Mariso*, the *MS Essen* as *Ferkulei* and the *Monie Rickmers* as *Salando* sailed back towards Germany with their cargoes. The *MS Wasgenwald,* renamed *Sumbilaanga* sailed from the port of Sabang at the northern end of Sumatra towards Europe. The *MS Sophie Rickmers* was sunk very close to the port of Sabang.[2]

The German ships that found themselves in Dutch East Indies harbours after war broke out had to cope with reprisals, harassment and delays in documentation by the colonial authorities, but it was only after the invasion of their homeland by the German army and the sending of the code word *Berlijn* that German ships were seized. The freighters were confiscated and, if unable to escape, sailed on under Dutch colours.

Dairen (now: Dalian) was at that time, during Japanese rule over Manchukuo (now: Manchuria) from 1905 to 1945, an important port. Manchuria has important ore deposits and in Dairen itself, with its extensive port area, there was a major industrial complex for the chemical industry and for machine construction.

German merchant ships mainly brought machines and machine parts to Dairen, such as several gigantic 85-tonne transformers to equip an aluminium factory that was being built there. The auxiliary cruiser *Kormoran* brought a complete power station produced by AEG to Dairen for this factory: its generator alone weighed 90 tonnes.

Dairen, where at the outbreak of war the only German ship was the *SS Havenstein*, was a popular port for German ships and an entrepot for German goods during Japanese rule over Manchuria. It had a large port on the Pacific near the Korean border and was only about 1,000 nautical miles from the ports of Japan.[3]

During the first years of the war German ships were still being laden in Dairen with chemical products and various ores, such as manganese and chrome ore, to be transported back to Germany. In Japan itself freight for

---

1   Brennecke, *Schwarze Schiffe – Weite See,* pp. 126 and 176
2   AA, R 29.680/740, 84695f, secret telegram from the Dutch East Indies on 17. 11.42
3   Brennecke, *Schwarze Schiffe – Weite See,* p. 12

Germany consisted of whale oil, rubber, tin and copper. Japanese war materials were also exported to Germany via Dairen, such as Japanese aerial torpedoes, which could be launched against enemy ships from the air. Food such as coffee, tea, powdered egg, nutmeg, coconut oil and peanuts were exported from there to Germany. Until the attack on Pearl Harbour Japan frequently bought tropical products for Germany in the Dutch East Indies since German ships could no longer land there after the German invasion of Holland.

The ships' cargoes were organised by Admiral Wenneker, the German naval attaché who had been in Tokyo since 1940, using German firms who had branches all over the Far East. In the course of time his duties in respect of the blockade breakers became too much for Wenneker, and so Captain Vermehren was sent to Tokyo on the *MS Dresden* as head of the *Marine-Sonderdienst* [Naval Special Service] MSD to deal with all the tasks connected with the blockade breakers, such as the purchase of raw materials by the German Trade Delegation and the distribution of the cargoes among the ships.

There had always been a lively trade between Japan and Germany, although sea connections had always been of secondary importance. The main channel for trade had been – until the German army invaded the Soviet Union – the Trans-Siberian Railway, which was considerably faster.

Losses among the German freighters which were bringing ever more urgently necessary raw materials from Japan and South East Asia to Germany during the war continued to increase. For example, on the return voyage to Germany the *MS Elbe* was sunk, the *MS Odenwald* captured and the *MS Ramses* was damaged and had to be brought back to Kobe. The blockade breaker *MS Spreewald* was disguised as a British *Blue Funnel* liner. The German U-boat U 333 took it for a British ship and sank it by mistake.

Recognising their own ships was often difficult for the U-boats, since the German blockade breakers had strict radio silence and during a voyage often changed their identity and their livery several times. To minimise the possibility of meeting an enemy ship, the German blockade breakers travelled alone and away from the main seaways. They sailed mostly under foreign flags, the Union Flag or the Stars and Stripes. Only the fastest ships with a speed of at least 15 knots were employed to bring valuable cargoes from the Far East to Germany.

These merchant ships had no armament on board. To avoid possible encounters with enemy ships there were several observation posts which were continuously manned. If you saw them first, you could act first. For this purpose relatively uncomfortable crow's nests were attached to the mastheads.

Though there were many losses, they were initially outweighed by success-es. Before Japan entered the war the ships sailed, almost without exception, across the South Pacific and round Cape Horn to reach Germany. Their voy-ages were not easy, as they traversed many climate zones. They left Japan in the winter, only to encounter bad weather in the North Atlantic which was swarming with enemy ships. They came through the tropics in the Pacific, crossing the Equator, before reaching the cold currents and storms of Cape Horn. Then they crossed the Equator again in the Atlantic before hitting the stormy and icy North Atlantic with its hurricane force winds and fog on the final stage of their voyage home.

Enemy merchant ships captured by the German Navy were particularly useful. They mostly simply altered the ship's name, allowing the ship to con-tinue operating unrecognised. Good examples of this are the auxiliary cruiser *Pinguin* and the minelayer *Passat*, whose operations will be described in the chapter on operations off Australia and New Zealand.

One ship that long went undetected was the captured British ship the *Speybank*, since it resembled its three sister ships in every detail. The *Spey-bank* continued to sail under the British flag with a German crew, continu-ally changing its name to that of its sister ships, the *Levernbank*, *Doggerbank* and *Inverbank*, acting as a minelayer and supply ship. The captain's mission was to mine the waters off the Cape of Good Hope and to supply German U-boats in the Indian Ocean with fuel and provisions. Even British aircraft and the British destroyer *HMS Cheshire* failed to see through the deception. After carrying out its missions off South Africa and in the Indian Ocean the ship returned under British colours round the Cape of Good Hope, in spite of obsessive British observation.

The mining of the waters off South Africa by this captured ship caused the British great concern because of the WS-Convoys (Winston's Special Con-voys), all made up of British luxury liners such as the *Queen Mary*, the *Queen Elizabeth* and the *Aquitania*, which sailed round the Cape as troop transports. The mines off the South African coast caused the loss of one ship and severe damage to three others.

12. The Occupation of South East Asia by Japan

Japan had long regarded with disapproval the way that the Europeans and Americans had settled in East and South East Asia and continually expanded their sphere of influence. The Americans were firmly settled in the Philippines and to the east of that on the island of Guam in the Pacific, where they were building ever larger naval and air bases. The British were in Burma, Malaya, West Borneo and Singapore, the French were in Indochina and the Dutch in the East Indies.

Japan's goal was to end white colonial rule in Asia. The peoples of Asia needed to take their fate into their own hands. "Asia for the Asians" was Japan's slogan. Japan planned and promulgated a "Greater Asian Co-Prosperity Sphere" (*Daitoua Kyoueiken*), on the basis of equal rights and self determination for all nations. It goes without saying that Japan's aims were not merely altruistic: they were aiming at a Greater Asian Empire under their own hegemony. The countries thus annexed were to be Japan's "little brothers", just as Hitler aimed for a new Europe under German rule.

Because of Japan's centuries of isolation as an island nation the Japanese regarded themselves as a "pure race" and believed that they were a privileged nation or – as Hitler said of the Germans – a "master race". They saw it as their mission to lead the nations of East and South East Asia.

In February 1940 Takeja Fushimi in Tokyo published his "Plan for Educational Mobilisation" aimed at the nations of Asia:

We want to free you from your European and American chains and give you your own history with the imperial nation of Nippon as its centre and the myth of a new world based on Shinto, the way of the Gods.[1]

But Asia for the Asians hadn't looked very peaceful up to that point. It was not just the western powers who were fighting for their share of the raw materials those countries were so rich in – Japan was there too. Everyone was trying to get as big a slice of the cake as possible, even if it meant using force.

For years Japan had been waging war on its direct neighbours. Karl Hausdorfer writes in the *Deutsche Wacht* on the 14th of February 1939: *Finally there is only one open door in East Asia through which we can all flee – if we're lucky, still with bag and baggage. If we don't have anything left, then with our bare lives or without that last commodity.* How right this prophecy was to prove!

---

1   Eckert-Rotholz, *Wo Tränen verboten sind*, p. 227

Ill. 33
The Chinese cake is divided among kings and emperors. French cartoon 1898: En Chine – Le Gâteau des Rois et des Empereurs.

From left: Queen Victoria of the United Kingdom, the German Kaiser Wilhelm II, Tsar Nicholas II of Russia, the French "Marianne", Japan's Meijing emperor.

Manchuria with its considerable resources of raw materials returned to China in 1904 in the Russo-Japanese War. In 1931 Japan invaded Manchuria again and the land was practically integrated with Japan as the "Japanese Empire of Manchukuo" (*Manshu teikoku*) During the Japanese period Manchukuo's economic growth was enormous.

A large part of China, Nationalist China with its capital at Nanking (now: Nanjing), was already under Japanese occupation after the Sino-Japanese war of 1937. Tientsin (now: Tianjin in North China) was in Japanese hands from 1938. Since 1860 Tientsin had been an open and important treaty port. Eight foreign nations, including Britain, France, Russia, Japan and Germany, had concessions in the city which were practically protectorates of these foreign powers. Since Germany had a concession in Tientsin and many Germans already lived there, many of the German women and children who were expelled from the Dutch East Indies and were landed in Shanghai in 1941 by the Japanese ship *Asama Maru* made their way there. On Kaiser Wilhelm Straße the building of the German Concordia Club is still standing.

After the bloody conflict between Japan and China in 1937 and 1938 the situation was once more calm. Germany had close and friendly connections with Nationalist China under the government of Wang Jingwei and had an Embassy in Nanjing. Until the end of 1942 the ambassadors were Heinrich Georg Stahmer and then Dr Ernst Woermann.

Ill. 34
Head of the Chinese government that collaborated with Japan Wang Jingwei and German Ambassador Stahmer toast each other in 1941. To the left of the German flag the flag of the Republic of China, since Wang claimed to represent the whole of China.

A private letter of the 7th of August 1941 from the German Embassy's office in Chungking to *Geheimrat Walther Hewel* in the Foreign ministry in Berlin shows that friendly relations between Nationalist China and Germany should be expanded in spite of occupation by Germany's ally Japan:

Dear Party Comrade Hewel!

This letter should be delivered to you by Mr Chi Tsun. Mr Chi is a close confidant of Marshal Chiang Kai-shek and is being sent by him on a special mission to Germany.

Chiang Kai-shek urgently desires to return to a closer relationship with Germany and Mr Chi has been sent to Germany to investigate the possibility of bringing this about, to explain the Chinese Marshal's views to leading figures in the Reich and above all to arouse the Führer's interest in China and if possible to bring about a personal link between the Führer and Marshal Chiang Kai-shek.

Mr Chi wishes above all to make clear in Berlin what a decisive role the Reich can play in East Asia after a victorious conclusion to the war in Europe, the settlement of the Far East conflict and the restoration of ordered conditions in East Asia.

I recommend Mr Chi to you because he has fought for years to bring about a closer relationship between China and Germany and is also the main representative of the tendency here, mainly found among the officer corps, to try to bring about

an end to dependency on America. [...] Please listen to Mr Chi and, if it seems right to you, present him to the Foreign Minister.
With best wishes and Heil Hitler! Yours [signature illegible] [1]

Since at the time the letter was written Leopold Baron von Plessen[2] was head of the office in Chungking it can only come from him or his deputy. The tone of the letter leads us to suspect that the writer was a friend of Hewel's.

In the 1930s Germany wavered between an alliance with China or Japan. Since Germany urgently needed raw materials from China for her industry, Hitler supported Marshal Chiang Kai-shek, the opponent of the Communist Mao Zedong, with military materials and advisors: for example, Germany sent several military trainers and advisors to Chiang Kai-shek, such as Hans von Seeckt (Colonel-General and previously Chief of Staff of the army) and Alexander Freiherr von Falkenhausen (Infantry General). Even the uniforms and steel helmets of the Kuomintang soldiers imitated those of the German army. German combat aircraft were also supplied. Since there were hardly any trained Chinese pilots, the Russians offered pilots and aircraft mechanics. The Russians already had their own airfield in Hankow and they more or less took control of the Chinese air force.

At the same time, Chiang Kai-shek's second wife, Song Meiling, who had grown up in the USA and was very politically active, was soliciting the USA's aid in the battle against the Communists. She had excellent contacts, reaching up to the Roosevelts.

By the time of the letter quoted above, Germany's support for Chiang Kai-shek was at an end. Since Japan was extremely critical, help for China from the German Military Mission ended in 1938. Moreover, Germany's Foreign Minister Ribbentrop ideologically tended more towards Japan.

Although expansion by the Japanese in the East and Germany in the West had already come to a halt by then, Nationalist China under Wang Jingwei declared war on the Allies on the 9th of January 1942.

From the beginning of 1940 a short wave and a medium wave transmitter were constructed in Shanghai. Although it primarily broadcast National Socialist propaganda, it also contributed to the strengthening of German-Chinese friendship. There was even a plan to expand the short-wave station into a high-power transmitter which could reach the whole Greater Asian Co-Prosperity-Sphere. At the end of 1940 Dr Erich Wickert was appointed "Radio Attaché" by the German Foreign Ministry and sent to Shanghai as head of the radio station.

1   AA, Handakte Hewel 5, R 27473, Document 373238
2   previously German Consul in Surabaya

The many years of Japanese occupation in China still affect relations between the two nations. Anti-Japanese resentment constantly flares up in China, leading to mass demonstrations by the people – which are tolerated by the government. The atrocities and humiliation inflicted by the Japanese during their invasion of Manchuria and the massacres in Shanghai and Nanking, with the death of millions are still remembered in China. Japan is still regarded as the arch-enemy in China. The Chinese do not forget any humiliation – or any demonstration of friendship.

When British and Dutch forces were caught up in the war in Europe from 1939 onwards, Japan saw this as a good opportunity to strengthen its position on the Asian continent even further and to plan the seizure of territory in South East Asia, particularly the Dutch East Indian archipelago with its rich natural resources.

In this context, there is a telegram from the German Ambassador in Tokyo, Eugen Ott, sent on the 27th of August 1940:

Dispatch of Minister for Economic Affairs Kobayashi to Dutch East Indies is widely discussed in press. Papers emphasize that unusual dispatch of active minister shows how strong Japan's interest in acquiring Dutch raw materials. Beyond that Kobayashi's mission is to prepare the ground for Japan's much-desired Greater Asian Co-Prosperity-Sphere in Dutch East Indies as well. Negotiations must begin immediately to prevent England and America getting in before Japan. Territorial claims far from Japan's thoughts: as Jomiuri reports their only aim is to free East Asian nations from previous exploitation by European powers.

As I hear, government has decided after weeks of negotiation to cancel the originally intended despatch of the former Colonial Minister, General Koiso, who is known as the proponent of an alarming Japanese expansion in the South Seas and by sending the Economy minister to emphasize the purely economic purpose of the mission. In view of American oil-embargo negotiations will primarily aim at acquisition of oil in Dutch East Indies. Signed Ott [1]

I venture to doubt if the Japanese minister's mission was successful. The Dutch Colonial Administration in Batavia was against any extension of trade relations with Japan and – as we will see – attempted to undermine Japan's influence in the East Indies as much as possible.

Initially Japan's plans for a Greater Asian Co-Prosperity-Sphere were received positively by the native population in south East Asia. Their watchword was to take up the struggle against colonial paternalism in concert with Japan. The concept of the Co-Prosperity Sphere was meant to embrace a community of Asian and Pacific nations including Japan, Siam (now: Thai-

---

1   AA, Handakte Hewel 5, R 27473, Document 84595

land), Burma (now: Myanmar), Malaya, Singapore, the Philippines, the Dutch East Indies and various small Pacific states.

Ill. 35
Japanese 10 Sen stamp showing
the extent of Greater Asian
Co-Prosperity-Sphere

After Germany's initial successes in Europe and North Africa, the Asiatic world began to look to Germany and Tokyo. They were proud that Japan – an Asiatic country – was succeeding in standing up to the white race.

The realisation of the Greater Asian Co-Prosperity-Sphere was brought within reach by the capture of the British freighter *Automedon* by the German auxiliary cruiser *Atlantis* in the Indian Ocean on the 11ᵗʰ of November 1940. Important secret British Cabinet documents fell into the hands of the Germans, describing the strength of British troops in South East Asia and their defence strategy. These documents were handed over to the Japanese government. For this, the captain of the *Atlantis*, Bernhard Rogge, was awarded the highest Japanese medal, the "Samurai Sword".

This secret information increased Japan's readiness to enter a war against Britain and its South East Asian colonies. At the end of February 1941 the German Foreign Minister Ribbentrop also ordered Ambassador Ott in Tokyo to work on the Japanese government to attack and take the British fortress of Singapore as soon as possible, doubtless with a view to the acquisition of ever more necessary supplies of raw materials from the area.[1]

The Japanese promised the oppressed peoples of Asia that they could have a better life without their white colonial masters and that what was important about a person was their abilities, not their descent or skin colour. Japan's slogan "Asia for the Asians" was on everyone's lips. Japan laid the foundations for the independence of these South East Asian peoples.

---

1 AA, Akten zur Deutschen Auswärtigen Politik 1918-1945, Akte D XII, Doc. No. 100; Telegram from Ribbentrop, Berlin to Ott, Tokyo

Japan is – as I have already said – extremely poor in raw materials. With a population density of about 220 inhabitants per square kilometre it could not survive on its own resources and felt practically forced to bring colonial imperialism to an end in order to acquire the raw materials that the white colonialists claimed for themselves alone. The Japanese were forced – especially after the USA placed them under embargo – to extend their hegemony. On its own the country could not ensure that could support itself.

Whether the dream of a peaceful Greater Asian Co-Prosperity Sphere would have come true with a Japanese victory is extremely doubtful. Japan surely initially believed that it was inspired by an honourable mission, but as in every war, there were negative side effects. On their way south the Japanese fighting troops left a trail of atrocities which reached a climax in the Dutch East Indies.

The Japanese army advanced at lightning speed. Between the 8th and 10th of December 1941 the island of Guam fell. It had been under American administration since its conquest by the USA in January 1898. The Americans had built massive naval and air bases there. The rapid capture of the island by the Japanese was therefore more than surprising for the USA. On the 11th of January 1942 Hong Kong and Menado on Celebes (now: Sulawesi) fell into the hands of the Japanese, as did the oil fields on the island of Tarakan off Borneo.

Siam, which was renamed Thailand, "Land of the Free" by the Japanese was on the side of the Axis powers and declared war on the Allies. From 1893 onwards France and Britain had wished to divide Siam with its rich resources between them and integrate it into their colonial empires. This was prevented not least by the fact that German railway engineers under King Rama IV had built a railway network in 1891, enabling the country to remain strong and independent. It was therefore quite understandable that there was a degree of reserve towards France and Britain and a preference for Japan.

Japan had already negotiated skillfully with the Siamese monarchy and entered into a pact with Siam as early as 1941. Several smaller states in the south of the country, which Britain had incorporated into Malaya in 1909, were returned to Siam. This is still a bone of contention in the border regions. Chinese influence in the country was also reduced by the expulsion of Chinese citizens, something welcomed by the Siamese population.

The British colony of Burma also co-operated with the Japanese. The British had occupied and colonised Burma in three wars between 1824 and 1886. Burma was regarded as British India's fourth province and was ruled from there. On the outbreak of war in Europe the independence movement in Burma had spread rapidly. Aung San, father of the world-famous pro-democracy activist in Burma and Nobel peace laureate Aung San Sun Kyi, was general secretary of the Freedom Block which fought for Burmese independence. Burma saw this as a chance to throw off the British colonial yoke. When the Burmese refused to accede to British demands to enter the war on their side against Germany and Japan, all leading politicians who had advocated independence were arrested and imprisoned. However, Aung San succeeded in escaping to Japan where, together with other freedom-loving Burmese, he received military training.

After Japan declared war on the British and partially occupied Burma, Aung San returned to Burma and with Japanese help set up the Burma Independence Army (BIA), becoming its commander. Japan promised the Burmese immediate independence after the final expulsion of the British.

With the help of the BIA Japan advanced swiftly. In spring 1942 the British fled the country together with several hundred thousand Indian soldiers. An endless stream of refugees tramped through uninhabited jungle towards the Indian border. Ten thousand exhausted Indians and Britons died on this march. It was no better for the Indians who remained in Burma. About a million Indians controlled financial and commercial life in Burma. In the period between the British leaving Burma and the arrival of the Japanese most of the Indians – who were hated as usurers and exploiters – fell victim to Burmese vengeance. Shops and warehouses were plundered and the villas of the British and Indians destroyed and set on fire. Only when the Japanese arrived was order restored.

In July 1942 the BIA was renamed the BDA (Burma Defence Army) and reorganised. The BDA now had the strength of a division with about 15,000 men under the command of Major General Aung San. However, their fighting power was not very great as the troops were poorly armed and supplied.

The rights of the small principalities in Burma were respected by the Japanese and wherever possible Burmese were included in the administration, which already existed. In the administration and the military the Japanese merely played the role of advisors. Unlike the British, these advisors did not seclude themselves in their clubs but lived among the native population and adapted themselves to their customs. The Japanese had a free and open relationship with the native Burmese.

Ba Maw, a Burmese, was made head of state in Japanese occupied Burma. Aung San was his Secretary General. Under British rule Ba Maw had already been Burmese Prime Minister from 1937 to 1939. Their own army was now officered exclusively by Burmese and was no longer under the oppressive leadership of British officers. The Karen ethnic minority in North Burma felt disadvantaged and organised a revolt which was put down by Japanese troops. However, the Japanese also made severe psychological mistakes. For example, the Burmese had to address the Japanese as "Master", an English word that smacked of imperialism.

On the 1st of August 1943 Japan kept its promise, even though it was in the middle of the war, and granted Burma independence. The new Burmese government finally freed itself from the British Empire and immediately joined the Greater Asian Co-Prosperity Sphere. On the same day the now independent Burma declared war on the Allies.

There were many names for French Indo-China, the colony which continued in existence until the fall of Dien-Bien-Phu in 1954: Cochin China, Tonkin (also Tongkin), Vietnam, Khmer, Cambodia and Laos. Even today this causes many misunderstandings. For information purposes I will take a step back into the history of the region.

The name Tonkin was used in the 17th century by the Dutch East India VOC (*Vereenigde Oost-Indische Companie*) for the north of today's Vietnam. It was still often used in the 20th century for the whole area that is now called Vietnam.

French military expeditions in South East Asia began as early as 1856. After the Franco-Chinese war of 1884/1885 this whole area came under French control and was divided into three protectorates. That in the north continued to be called Tonkin, in the south was Cochin China and in the centre Annam. A very short time later the three protectorates were united and came under French colonial rule. The name *Union Indochinoise* came into official use. In the years between 1891 and 1893 the areas to the west of this, Khmer, now Cambodia, and Laos were integrated into the *Union Indochinoise*. This gigantic area was now known internationally as French Indochina.

Only three months after the fall of Dien-Bien-Phu and the armistice, French Indochina was abolished at the Geneva Indochina Conference in July 1954. New boundaries were drawn: the long coastal state of modern Vietnam was divided along the 17th parallel into Communist North Vietnam with its capital at Hanoi and the Western-supported South Vietnam with its capital at Saigon, thus dividing the province of Annam. Khmer, modern Cambodia and Laos became independent states. Subsequently both countries were involved in long-drawn-out bloody battles between royalist and Communist groups. In 1975 the Communists seized power in Laos. North and South Vietnam were reunited in 1976. For simplicity's sake I use the name Vietnam for Tonkin, Annam and Cochin China, Cambodia for Khmer and Laos for the Kingdom of Laos.

But now back to the Second World War and the Japanese conquest of South East Asia. The colonial authorities in French Indochina had joined with the Vichy Regime under Marshal Pétain, which was collaborating with Hitler, and therefore Indochina was recognised by Japan as part of collaborating France. The country was immediately linked with Japan and put its military bases and territorial rights at the disposal of the Japanese fleet, army and air force. From here followed the conquest of the British colonies on the Malay peninsula by the Japanese army. The city of Saigon, which remained peaceful and flourishing in the midst of war, was the centre from which the first Japanese operations in South East Asia set forth.

The governor general of French Indochina travelled through the Dutch East Indies in March/April 1940. Marc Chadourne[1] sent a long report on this journey, dated 10th of May 1940, to the colonial ministry in Paris. Walther Hewel received a copy. Here are some extracts:

[...] The southern expansion of Japan is justified simply by the fact that the Japanese originate from this area. Holland is blocking Japanese imports to the Dutch East Indies; England is securing its interests by expanding its base in Singapore. Japan is stronger today than in the last war.

The fact that the Western powers are engaged in Europe and cannot be everywhere at once must be exploited. The Nanyo [Author's note: Japanese for the "Southern Region"] is rich in natural resources and a suitable reception area for excess population. [...] It is impossible to watch these related peoples suffering under the yoke of European powers. [...] Japan can wait calmly for the right opportunity [Author's note: for an invasion].

Before occupying South East Asia Japan tried to win over the loyalty of Muslim organisations and the mainly Muslim population of this area. The report continues:

[...] Then the French report describes the activities of the Japanese-Mohammedan Society which was founded in September 1939. [...] It publishes a broad range of literature. An Islamic Congress recently took place in Tokyo. The aims of the society are: humanity, world peace, studies and research about Islam, close relationships with the Mohammedan peoples. They build temples, libraries, archives, support travel and pilgrimages to Mecca, trade delegations, exhibitions, schools. The exhibitions in Tokyo and Osaka in November 1939 and the Islamic Con-

---

1   It is questionable if this is the writer and translator of Joseph Conrad, Marc Chadourne (1895-1975). His novels are indeed set in Vietnam and the Pacific, and he was considered knowledgeable about the region. He was also a senior member of the French Colonial Ministry. However, there is also evidence that he fled to the USA on the outbreak of war.

gress in Tokyo in January 1940 were attended by Mohammedans from Manchu-
kuo, China, Afghanistan, India and the Dutch East Indies. [...]
In the opinion of knowledgeable people the army of the Dutch East Indies is not
in a fit state to defend against a Japanese landing for very long.
Japanese "infiltration" by agents etc. has been halted, partly by limits on immi-
gration and partly by limits on the distribution of concessions.[1]

This report by the governor general of French Indochina agrees with the assessment of the situation by Japan and the Third Reich.

When that letter was written there were already 6,700 Japanese in the
Dutch East Indies. Their propaganda activities were guided by the Japanese Consulate. Japanese agents had been active in the Dutch East Indies
since 1930. The Japanese Nanyo Warehousing Company in Batavia seems
to have been the centre of this activity. An employee of the company, Naoju
Aratame, was an officer in the Japanese Navy and under the command of the
Japanese Consulate General in Batavia. He directed the operations of Japanese spies. After 1939 almost all Japanese companies and merchant houses
and their Japanese employees were involved in espionage. They collected
military information, organised acts of sabotage and bribed civilians to acquire confidential information. Information exchange took place mainly in
hotels and brothels.[2]

After French Indochina allied itself with the Axis powers, there was a
Communist underground movement, strongly supported by Moscow, and
led by Ho Chi Minh, which continually hindered Japanese attempts to keep
order. Ho Chi Minh had returned from exile in Moscow in 1941. Since
he and his underground movement were operating against the Japanese
the USA provided them with generous supplies of arms and ammunition –
which he later used against their American donors. He was fighting for a free
Vietnam, without French, Japanese or American hegemony.

The mountain villages in Laos, which were inaccessible in the rainy season,
were a favourite refuge for political exiles and opponents of the Japanese. The
administration – on the French model with indigenous officials – functioned
extremely well, as it did everywhere in French Indochina. Many Vietnamese
officials had studied at the École Coloniale du Havre in France and returned
on graduation to take up important administrative posts. It was no wonder
that they showed little inclination to accept Nippon and resisted – even if

---

1   AA, Handakte Hewel 6, R 27474, Document 376143-6
2   Anwar, *Penetrasi Ekonomi ...*, pp. 61f
     Wilson, *Orang dan Partai Nazi ...*, pp. 133f

mostly passively – re-education. The hostility of this section of the population towards the French and Japanese increased with every year.

The Philippine Islands had been under American administration since the Spanish-American war (1896 -1898), and from 1901 they were ruled by an American occupation government. Any attempt on the part of the people to achieve independence was severely dealt with by the USA. Since the USA had built major naval and air bases, their neighbour Japan felt increasingly threatened. Missions could be flown from here to attack Japan or the Japanese occupied areas in China. The American-Philippine army under General MacArthur consisted of about 23,000 men, half of them Filipinos and half Americans. After Japan began its hostile actions on the 8th of December 1941, the army was reinforced by a further 18,000 Americans.

Japanese bombers first destroyed Clark Airfield in Manila. The Americans were totally unprepared. All their aircraft were on the ground and were destroyed. In subsequent waves of attacks other air-bases and ports were bombed. The naval port of Cavite near Manila and the American air-bases were in flames. Those aircraft that were undamaged fled to Mindanao, the most southerly Philippine island, but they were discovered by the Japanese and destroyed from the air. Ships fled to British North Borneo or to the Dutch East Indies where the Dutch colonial government was still in charge.

By the 2nd of January 1942 the capital Manila was in Japanese hands. Fighting between the Americans and Japanese lasted until the 9th of April 1942, when the American-Philippine troops were forced to yield to the Japanese. The Philippines voluntarily joined the Greater Asian Co-Prosperity Sphere and the Japanese in return granted them their independence from the USA. As a result of this Japanese action the USA was forced to grant sovereignty to the Philippine people after the end of the war.

Everywhere in South East Asia, in French Indochina, in the Philippines and in The Dutch East Indies, the USA supported Communist independence movements in their fight against the Japanese. After the war, when the Japanese had to leave those countries, their *de facto* independence could not be reversed. Now the Americans fought bitterly against the Communists. For example when the Communist Viet Minh proclaimed the independence of the Democratic Republic of Vietnam in the summer of 1945, this ultimately led to the terrible, long-drawn out, and – for the US – disastrous Vietnam War: the Communists they had previously supported against the Japanese were now their enemies.

Russia had expanded its territory throughout Siberia and eastwards to the Pacific in the 19th century and thus was regarded by the Japanese as a dangerous neighbour. At the end of the century Japan, feeling threatened, pre-empted a Russian occupation of Korea, which was at that time part of China. In the Japanese-Chinese war of 1894, Japan defeated the Chinese so soundly that they were forced to cede not only the Korean peninsula but also the island of Formosa to Japan in the "Peace of Shimonoseki".

The Japanese view was that they had annexed a Korea that was neglected and sinking into chaos and civilised it. The inhabitants, on the other hand, constantly organised violent resistance to the occupiers. Under Japanese rule railways and roads were built. Land reform was linked to the obligation to plant and care for trees, producing extensive re-afforestation whose positive effects on the climate can still be felt. Modern industries raised the Korean standard of living, but the Koreans seemed not to appreciate these "gifts" from Japan. The forced recruitment of Korean women as "comfort women" for the Japanese soldiers is still the subject of charges against Japan, and there is deep and lasting resentment until this day.

Formosa and Korea were thus under Japanese rule from 1895 onwards. The Japanese achieved major economic and health-service successes during this time, particularly on Formosa. Since the climate and landscape of Formosa differ considerably from those in Japan and Korea, Japan took a particular interest in Formosa and invested much more in education and infrastructure than they did in Korea. Formosa is a tropical island off the southern coast of China, with cocos, rice-terraces, sugar cane plantations and many tropical fruits. Its Portuguese discoverers called it Formosa "The Beautiful" and the Chinese and Japanese name is Taiwan, "the land of terraces". Its capital Taipeh was known during the Japanese occupation as Taihoku. Taiwan became Japan's granary. Schools were built in every village and in a very short time illiteracy decreased considerably. Japanese was introduced as the first foreign language. The Japanese also improved transport on the island, building a railway network of 4,000 kilometres and many roads. Dams were built to harness water power for electricity. In the Second World War this made it possible to create a major armaments and fuel industry.

A large number of Taiwanese are still grateful to Japan for this extraordinarily extensive development, particularly in the field of education, even though they had to sacrifice a great deal during the war. The older generation in Taiwan still speaks and sings in Japanese. Unlike in Korea, the Japanese are – as many Taiwanese both young and old affirmed to me – welcome in Taiwan. So, unlike the Koreans, the Taiwanese were on the side of Japan from the beginning of the war. The relationship between Korea and Japan today, however, could best be described as a state of cold war.

The ground was cleared for further advances by the Japanese Imperial Army in the direction of the Dutch East Indies – by far the largest state in the region next to China. But the relatively positive factors in Japan's advance so far were eroded with time.

On the 10th of December 1941 the British battleships *HMS Prince of Wales* and *HMS Repulse* were sunk by the Japanese air force as they attempted to ward off the Japanese invasion of the east coast of Malaya. British reports stated that 327 men lost their lives in this incident.

On the 11th of December 1941 the strategically important island of Penang off the Malayan coast was bombed by the Japanese for the first time. Many inhabitants of Penang fled into the countryside. On the 16th of December 1941 all Britons in Penang were evacuated to the apparent safety of Singapore. This privilege was not extended to the native population which led to outrage on the part of the Malay and Chinese inhabitants, who were being left in the lurch by the British. Even when the Magistrate of Penang, Lim Khoon Teck, tried to board a ship for Singapore he was told that it was reserved for "whites" only. At this time there were already a million refugees from Britain and other nations in the densely populated city. On the 17th of December 1941 Japanese troops landed in Penang and raised the banner of the Rising Sun over the British colony of Malaya.

Singapore was – as the British said – an impregnable sea fortress which was meant to symbolise the power of the white colonial rulers in South East Asia. It was the base of the British Far Eastern Fleet, from which they could control all shipping movement between the Indian Ocean and the Pacific. It was also close to the oil fields in Sumatra and Borneo. Singapore was thus a key British position in this region. Under General Yamashita Japan quickly succeeded in taking it. The western colonial rulers now finally began to lose what was so important in Asian eyes: Face.

On the seaward side Singapore was secured by heavy artillery batteries, but the Japanese army made what seemed impossible possible. They fought their way through the almost impenetrable jungle, which at that time had no noticeable gaps, towards Singapore from the north and stormed the fortress at its weakest point. The battle for Singapore lasted from the 31st of January to the 15th of February 1942, when Lieutenant General Percival surrendered to General Yamashita (Commander of the 25th Japanese Imperial Army) in the Ford factory in Singapore, even though the British outnumbered the Japanese by three to one. They had simply run out of ammunition. Important military facilities, naval arsenals, docks and repair workshops fell almost unscathed into Japanese hands. More than 100,000 British and Australian troops became Japanese prisoners of war in Malaya and Singapore. It was one of the greatest defeats in British military history.[1]

---

1   ZDFinfo, *Der Zweite Weltkrieg in Fernost*, 27.10.2013, 21.00

Members of an anti-Japanese movement were executed. English was forbidden in public and Japanese introduced as the main language in schools. Malay, the language of the indigenous population, was encouraged. The Japanese renamed Singapore *Shonanto*, "Light of the South". The German navy it was rechristened *Shonan*.

Western civilisation was still clung to their age-old prejudice about their technical and civilisatory superiority over Asia. At a secret sitting of the British House of Commons on the 23rd of April 1942 Churchill said: *I frankly admit that the violence, fury, skill and might of Japan has far exceeded anything that we had been led to expect.*[1]

From Singapore Japan, with the support of the Indian freedom fighter Subhas Chandra Bose, began to prepare for the invasion of India. The volunteer Indian National Army (INA) was recruited largely from among Indian prisoners of war who had been captured in Malaya and Singapore. The INA was under the command of the Japanese army. Even before the Japanese forces began their great offensive in the Pacific region and the fall of Singapore, a large proportion of the Allies moved to the safety of Australia. Now the way was free for the Japanese army to move against Java and other Dutch East Indian islands.

As the Imperial Japanese Army under the command of General Hitoshi Imamura advanced towards the borders of the Dutch East Indies, the Dutch colonial officials became very worried and their reactions became increasingly frantic. They feared for the survival of their colony, as well as their own existence and their colonial life style. Many Indonesians who now saw a chance of independence for their country within reach made this visible and were arrested by the Dutch and mostly executed without proper legal process.

Without much opposition the Japanese invasion of the Dutch East Indies began in the final days of 1941. For the defence of the colony the Royal Netherlands East Indies Legion KNIL (*Koninklijk Nederlandsch-Indisch Leger*) had 85,000 soldiers stationed, among them 1,170 Dutch officers and even more Dutch non-commissioned officers. Mercenaries were recruited to bring the total force up to 121,000.

In Sabang on the island of Weh and in North Sumatra the Dutch army attempted to defend themselves against the Japanese, but their resistance soon had to be abandoned because in the Aceh region in North Sumatra a revolt of the indigenous population against the Dutch had begun at the same time as the Japanese invasion. The Dutch army was not able to hold out on these two fronts for very long.

---

1   Stahmer, *Japans Niederlage – Asiens Sieg*, pp. 284f

The Royal Dutch Navy was well equipped in the colony, with three cruisers, eight destroyers, 14 submarines, eight minesweepers and five minelayers. The naval air force in 1939 had over 72 seaplanes and 18 small catapult aircraft.[1] There were also Allied units from the British, Australian and US armies. It is therefore all the more astonishing that the Dutch East Indies fell to the Japanese with so little resistance.

From December 1941 until March 1942 Borneo and Sumatra with their important oilfields and refineries were captured by means of Japanese paratroop attacks. The Dutch tried to destroy the oil wells and refineries. Those responsible were punished by the Japanese with torture and death. In spite of this sabotage, many facilities were soon able to function again. Now the Japanese had secured their supplies of oil and petrol. Bali also fell to the Japanese without any real resistance and the military airfield at Kuta was captured undamaged.

Shortly before the Japanese invasion, Soekarno had been brought from his exile in Bengkulu to Padang in West Sumatra to be deported to Australia. The Dutch regarded him as a collaborator with Japan who should not be allowed to fall into his "friends" hands. However, Soekarno managed in the chaos that reigned to escape and find shelter in the house of his friend Waworunto,[2] where he was when the Japanese troops marched in. The Japanese divisional commander Captain Sakaguchi, went straight to Soekarno and declared:

We consider it an honour to meet you here, Mr Soekarno, since you are famous throughout Asia. We know that you are a very influential person and the leader of your country.

Soekarno was surprised to be so quickly found in his hiding place. Sakaguchi responded:

We have the most efficient espionage organisation. We know everything about everyone, including where they live. When we took Bengkulu we already knew of your whereabouts and our first action was to come and find you here.[3]

About 500 kilometres south of Bali lies the Indonesian island of Sumba. A small airfield on a high plain at Waingapu, the main town in the east of Sumba, served in the Second World as a base for Japanese attacks on Darwin in northern Australia, which was about 1,000 kilometres away. The Japanese

---

1   AA, Document Dornier, Pol. Archiv VIII 1977/41, 740/84671,
     Die Stärke der niederländischen-indischen Wehrmacht
2   I was a friend of Waworunto's son, who confirmed the truth of the following story
3   Adams, *Sukarno,* p. 158 and personal conversations with Waworunto's son in
     Jakarta

air force raided Darwin several times from here, the first attack on the 19th of February 1942 producing the most Allied losses.

Darwin was a base for the British Royal Navy, the Royal Australian Navy, the Australian army, the US Navy and Air Force, the British Royal Air Force and the Dutch East Indies Air Force. 45 Allied warships had mustered here, including an aircraft carrier, as had a large number of merchant and supply ships. On Darwin's two airfields 30 Allied aircraft stood ready to launch an attack on the Japanese invaders of the Dutch East Indies. The Japanese wished to knock out this military base to prevent an Allied invasion of the Dutch East Indies, particularly the relatively close island of Timor. The Japanese Secret Service had discovered that a major invasion force was to start out from Darwin for the islands of Timor, Bali and Java on the 20th of February 1942. This was what the Japanese wished to stop.

At dawn on the 19th of February, just a day before the planned invasion of the East Indies, the inhabitants of Sumba were awakened by ear-splitting engine noise. One Japanese bomber after another took off and flew south towards Darwin. The evening before four Japanese aircraft carriers had set sail. The attack on Darwin began in the early morning. There were 242 aircraft in total, including D3A Val bombers, B5N Kate bombers and A6M Zero fighters. Before the bombing raid two Japanese submarines mined the harbour entrance to prevent the allied warships from escaping.

The attack caught the Allies totally unprepared and there was hardly any resistance. The attack was aimed mainly at the port, the two airfields and the oil bunkers. Allied losses were massive. The port was a sea of flame and both airfields, including runways and all their aircraft were destroyed.

After the last Japanese aircraft of the first wave left the air over Darwin, the second wave that had taken off from Sumba arrived. There were 54 bombers of types G3M and G4M. They also dropped their bombs on the port and the airfields. In the afternoon aircraft from the Japanese aircraft carriers made a third attack on Allied naval and merchant ships which had, during the attack on Darwin, anchored outside the port off Melville Island and Bathurst Island and were now making for the open sea. Several ships, mostly Australian, were sunk.

Japan had achieved its objective: an Allied invasion had been prevented and was never attempted again during the war. Since the bombing raids on Darwin were aimed at military targets there were 250-300 military casualties. Civilian casualties were minimal. The Australians still resent this attack even today, calling this Japanese trick "Australia's Pearl Harbour".

During the Second World War there was only one Japanese air-raid on a civilian target in Australia: on the 3rd of May 1942 they bombed the little town of Broome in Western Australia, causing 88 civilian casualties according to Australian reports.[1]

The invasion of Bali by the Japanese was a hard blow for the Allies since the Dutch naval base at Surabaya was now within range of the Japanese aircraft. All available Dutch, American, British and Australian ships were now ordered to Bali. The decisive naval battle took place on the 20th of February 1942 in the Strait of Badung off Bali, the Japanese defeating a clearly larger Allied naval force. Now the eastern and western flanks of Java were secure against Allied attacks. In a further battle in the Java Sea the Japanese navy sank two Allied battleships and three destroyers. The decisive combat took place the following day, on the 28th of February, in the Sunda Strait near the volcanic island of Krakatau. The Australian light cruiser *HMAS Perth* was involved in this action, as was the flagship of the Allied "Asian Fleet", the heavy cruiser *USS Houston*, the largest ship in the region. Because of its speed and fire power the *USS Houston* was known by its crew as "The Galloping Ghost of the Java Coast". These two ships were sunk in the battle: of the 1,061-man crew of the *USS Houston* only 368 were saved.

The loss of the *USS Houston* and the great loss of life were concealed until the end of the war by the US government. Only when the few survivors were released from Japanese captivity and were able to tell their story did the truth and the extent of the tragedy come to light.

Between the 1st and the 9th of March 1942 a major Japanese naval and air operation took place off the south coast of Java near Tjilatjap (now: Cilacap). At least eight American, British and Dutch cruisers, destroyers and gunboats and a Dutch passenger ship were sunk, as were two American tankers. At least 15 Dutch freighters were sunk or taken as prizes. An entire convoy of Australian mine seekers, tankers and transport ships was destroyed. In Surabaya 29 Dutch merchant ships were taken as prizes, and a further 11 in Batavia. Allied losses were frighteningly high.[2]

The invasion of Java, the most important and most densely populated island in the archipelago began on the 1st of March 1942. Only a few days later, Batavia was occupied. On the 10th of March 1942 at six o'clock in the evening Japanese troops marched into Bandung, a town whose altitude meant that it was inhabited by many Dutch people because of its moderate climate. In the next few days 1,500 Dutch civilians were captured and delivered to the Struiswijk prison in Batavia. Very soon there were 3,500 prisoners there. Others were taken to the Tjikoedapateuh internment camp which, with 10,000 civilian internees including 800 young people between 12 and

---

1   Axis naval activity in Australian waters
2   http://www.wlb-stuttgart.de/seekrieg/42-03.htm

14 years old, was one of the biggest Japanese camps during the occupation of the Dutch East Indies.[1] Two years later, on the 1st of April 1944 all Dutch civilian internees were reclassified as prisoners of war by the Japanese and treated accordingly.

On the 28th of March 1942, Java, the last bastion of the Dutch, was completely in Japanese hands. The military airfield at Kalijati near Subang in West Java is the place where the Dutch troops surrendered to the Japanese on the 8th of March 1942, a site that can still be seen today. The KNIL, the Royal Dutch East Indies Legion was beaten.

Ill. 36
Japanese special stamp celebrating the signing of the capitulation of the KNIL in Kalijati on the 8th of March 1942.

The Dutch who had colonised and exploited Indonesia for 350 years were beaten by the Japanese in less than three weeks even though the Japanese army had not used tanks or artillery. As in Singapore, the Japanese conquest of the islands of the archipelago was mainly done by bicycle. Japan lost only about 900 soldiers during the invasion.

One reason for the swift occupation of the Dutch East Indies was the fear among influential Japanese circles that the Germans, after invading the Netherlands, might lay claim to 'their territory' in South East Asia and set up a German protectorate. Nor could occupation by the USA be excluded at that time.[2]

The red and white Indonesian flag of the freedom fighters which had been outlawed by the colonial power as rebellious, now waved happily. The Japanese soldiers were greeted happily with loud shouts of *Banzai* and with

1   Journal of Olympic History, Summer 1998: Anthony T. H. Bijkerk, *How a Photograph saved Hermann van Karnebeek's Live,* pp. 27-30
2   Krug, Hirama, Sander-Nagashima, Niestlé, *Reluctant Allies,* p. 163

flowers as liberators. With the fall of Java the Dutch lost their colonial possessions in South East Asia.

Now Soekarno, the freedom fighter who was to become the first president of a free Indonesia after the declaration of independence in 1945, spoke of their Japanese brothers who had finally freed his country after 350 years of colonial oppression. He also spoke of "our friend Hitler" who had invaded the Netherlands and thus seriously weakened the Dutch position in the East Indies.

When the Japanese invaded, the Dutch radio stations of NIROM (*Nederlands Indische Radio Omroep Maatschappij*) came into Japanese hands. Their transmitters, which were distributed around the whole archipelago, were used intensively by the Japanese for propaganda purposes. Several stations had already been taken over by the freedom fighters, like the radio station in Jakarta, which transmitted the proclamation of independence on the 17th of August 1945. Soekarno had a mobile transmitter in Jakarta, *Radio Indonesia Merdeka* (Radio Free Indonesia), to promulgate his ideas and slogans to the people. Soekarno's aim was to unite the different population groups in the archipelago. These first beginnings afterwards became the state radio station *Radio Republik Indonesia*, which was later equipped with transmission and studio technology to a large extent by the German firm Telefunken.

In Malaya and Singapore the Japanese dealt rigorously with the British colonists and the Chinese section of the population, but in the East Indian archipelago the situation became even worse. Here the indigenous population suffered as well. After their initial enthusiasm at being freed from colonial oppression, the native population were as exploited and enslaved as they had been by the Dutch. Forced labour, hunger, and forced prostitution were the order of the day. Japan, with its lack of resources, urgently needed every grain of rice, every drop of oil, every scrap of material. The markets in the Dutch East Indies were suddenly empty. In order not to die of hunger, the Indonesians sold everything they had – furniture, jewellery, silver – on the black market at knock-down prices just to get something to eat. Japan was felt to be a burden and a threat, but Hitler was still a great hero to the Indonesians. He was not blamed for the situation. There was no interest in the atrocities committed all over Europe under Hitler. Europe was too far away. Their only goal was independence, and so it was necessary that the Dutch should be held in check by the German occupation of their homeland.

Unlike Korea and the Philippines, very little has so far been written in Indonesia about forced prostitution, although there too many young women and girls were used as *Jugun Ianfu* (comfort women). Recent historical research has suggested that the figures cited by the countries concerned have been exaggerated for propaganda purposes.[1] However, in Magelang in central Java and on the island of Flores there are said to have been mass rapes in the Dutch East Indies as well.[2]

Generally, according to contemporary witnesses, the Japanese were very disciplined. Misdemeanours by Japanese were severely punished by their superiors. But the fact that the Japanese ruled the Dutch East Indies with an iron rod can be explained by the completely different situation they found there from that in the countries they had occupied further to the north, which had been under British and French colonial rule.

In Burma, Malaya and Singapore the British colonial rulers valued thorough education of the population very highly. The final examinations that the natives sat in upper schools were evaluated in Britain, and gave the students a certificate which allowed them to study at a university – even one in Britain. There was a broad educated stratum who owed the expansion of their intellectual world to the colonial power. At all levels up to the highest, the British colonial administration was manned by educated members of the indigenous population. This meant that after the Japanese invaded the administration, after a short transitional phase, functioned smoothly as before. There was a similar situation in French Indochina: in colonial school and at the University of Marseille native officials were trained and then placed in leading positions.

Not so in the Dutch East Indies! Here racial differences played a decisive role in administration and the legal system. The Dutch colonial rulers had worked out an ingenious system to keep the natives under control – which means uneducated and undeveloped. They only allowed a small chosen few – preferably from among the nobility, who were well inclined towards them anyway – to have a school or university education. For centuries the native population were continuously fed the idea that they were an inferior race. Natives were only allowed at the very lowest level of the colonial administration. All important middle and higher positions were staffed by the Dutch. When the Japanese occupied the East Indies they had – at over 95% – one of the highest illiteracy rates in the world. In a country of about 70 million inhabitants, only 90 natives had received a university education according to Indonesian figures.

---

1   Jakarta Post, 25.02.2014, p. 10
2   Yoshimi Yoshiaki: *Comfort Women,* New York 2000
     Hartono & Juliantoro: *Derita Paksa Perempuan Kisah Jugun lanfu Pada Masa Pendudukan Jepang,* 1942 – 1945,
     Japan Times, 12 Mai, 2007: *Female forced into sexual servitude in wartime Indonesia*

During the colonial period the Dutch government saw improved education for the native population as nothing other than a threat to their power and so deliberately blocked the development of education at all levels for centuries. They had realised that education promotes self-confidence and so hindered any process that might encourage literacy. The natives were forcibly moulded to suit the interests of the Dutch and were told again and again that they were not capable of ruling themselves. The only aim of the Dutch was the exploitation of the country's rich resources. Clear evidence of the poverty of European colonial policies! Anton Adriaan Mussert, the Dutch Nazi leader said on visiting the East Indies before the Second World War: *The form of government prevailing here is one which corresponds to Fascist ideas.*[1]

When the Japanese marched in and the Dutch had either fled, gone underground or been interned, they found a collapsed administration and total chaos. These were not good circumstances in which to hand administration and power over to the Indonesians. The Japanese had to be much stricter here to bring back a certain degree of order than they had in the other lands they had occupied. To replace the white colonists Tokyo sent tens of thousands of engineers, teachers, policemen, administrators and other specialists to the East Indies. Of all the occupied territories in South East Asia, it was only here that the greater part of the administration could not be handed over because of a lack of qualified people. This gave the Japanese presence a much higher profile than elsewhere. It was a breeding ground for excesses, since many of the Japanese who had been sent at short notice were not qualified for the task and were not familiar with the Indonesian mentality. Many of them acted outside the control of the military authorities which often led them – like the Dutch before them – to feel like members of a master race and to act accordingly.

Since there was no functioning police force after the Dutch withdrawal, the Japanese secret police, the *Kempetai* had to recruit loyal natives from their other occupied territories to carry out simple duties. These auxiliary policemen were mainly trained military personnel from Korea and Formosa. They too felt themselves to be the lords of the land, and brutal treatment of the Indonesian native population was the order of the day. The Indonesians loathed them and refused to submit to them, especially since they had always had – and still have today – a great aversion to Chinese or Chinese-looking people.

One country after another in South East Asia had now fallen to the Japanese, a success that neither the USA nor Britain could have suspected of being within the abilities of the Japanese forces. Japan was a country that

---

1   Mak, *Das Jahrhundert meines Vaters*, p. 159

in US eyes had been living in the middle ages only a couple of generations before and was still backward, although Japan – unlike the USA – had a highly developed culture thousands of years old. Even before the war a higher percentage of the Japanese population could read and write than that of the USA.[1]

The Allies simply could not understand the Japanese successes. The Japanese soldiers in their shabby, baggy yellow uniforms that sagged around their bodies, poorly shod, with bicycles for transport and old-fashioned long-barrelled rifles made a very poor initial impression on the indigenous population. With their big round spectacles in black frames, making them look miserable all the time, and their inability to smile made a sharp contrast with the cheerful Indonesian attitude to life. This was supposed to be the successful and victorious Japanese army that had defeated the Dutch and the Allies? In their tattered uniforms they looked like the losers and yet they were the victors. How could this be?

In less than six months the Japanese had driven out all the white colonial powers that had ruled in East and South-East Asia for decades and centuries. Japan now ruled all the countries in the region – a population at the time of over 500 million. The dream of a Greater Asian Co-Prosperity Sphere was now for a short time a reality.

95% of the world's rubber and 90% of its quinine were now under Japanese control and it was also able to use the region's rich natural resources for its military purposes. For this incredible success Japan paid with 15,000 lives; the Allied forces lost several times more. The period of this great military success was called the "Imperial Chrysanthemum Miracle" by the Japanese propaganda machine.

After the occupation of the Netherlands by the Germans and the occupation of the East Indies by the Japanese the oppressed native population sensed a breath of fresh air. The Dutch had submitted to the Japanese without much resistance. The tall, blonde Dutch, whom the natives had always held to be invincible, had fled or gone underground, leaving the native population to its fate. The latter now saw their chance to throw off the chains of colonialism and continued to place their hope in Hitler. After the annexation of Austria and his occupation of the Sudetenland, as well as his swift successes on the western and eastern fronts he was much admired by the indigenous populations of South East Asia and India. The mood in the Dutch East Indies was: *If Hitler marches into Java, everyone will rejoice and bestrew him with flowers.*[2]

---

1   Stahmer, *Japans Niederlage – Asiens Sieg,* p. 147
2   Keppner, *Wie weit bis Airmolang,* p. 99

Ill. 37
Greater Asian Co-Prosperity Sphere

Every Indonesian wanted to see the end of centuries of Dutch servitude, even with Hitler's help, without thinking of the consequences that might possibly ensue.

Japan's swift successes had an almost immeasurable effect on the Asian peoples. Asians had defeated and driven out the white colonial rulers. No one believed in the superiority of the white race any more. Oppressed peoples no longer wished to fight against others for their white masters. This explains the throng of recruits for Subhas Chandra Bose's Free Indian Army (*Legion Azad Hind*) from the ranks of Indian prisoners of war in Germany and Asia. Indian soldiers no longer wished to risk their lives for British colonial interests. Britain and the Netherlands failed to see this development until it was too late. The Japanese seized on the opportunity it presented.

The Dutch East Indies had declared war on Japan on the 8th of December 1941 on orders from London, the seat of the exiled Dutch Government with Queen Wilhelmina. At that time the Japanese already held French Indochina and were beginning on the occupation of the Philippines. After the declaration of war the Japanese headed for the Dutch East Indies more quickly than planned because of their urgent need for the oil from Sumatra and Borneo.

The Dutch in the colony were hit not just by the fury of the occupiers, but also by that of the oppressed native population, *Inlanders.* Many Dutch colonial officials who had not been able to escape before the Japanese invasion had no desire to fall into Japanese hands and so disguised themselves in native costume and coloured their skin brown or tried to go underground. They wished to disappear, *onderduiken,* as the Dutch said. In vain. The native population did not offer them a refuge – quite the contrary, they were discovered, hunted and lynched. The hatred that had built up over centuries of colonial oppression boiled over in bloody massacres. Throughout the towns and villages one cry resounded: *Bunuh dia!* Kill them! Dutch men, women and children suffered this fate. The Dutch, previously the hunters, were now the hunted. The Japanese put a price on the head of every captured or betrayed Dutch person, and who would miss out on extra income in a time of great hardship?

The Germans, mostly mothers with children, were now freed from the Dutch internment camps by the Japanese. At the same time Dutch men women and children were thrown into the pre-existing camps, or others that were hastily constructed, as prisoners of war or internees. On their way to the camps the Dutch were mocked and spat on by the natives. Tens of thousands of Dutchmen were forced to work on the construction of the Burma or Sumatra railways by the Japanese.

Internment camps for Dutch and Allied prisoners of war were constructed all over the archipelago. There were camps in *Gloegoer* and *Aek Pamienke* in North Sumatra. The *Aek Pamienke* camp at Rantau Prapat, about 300 kilometres south of Medan, was built on an abandoned rubber plantation. Here alone about 7,000 Dutch, Australians and Americans were interned, including many Dutch women and children. In Siantar in North Sumatra the hospital, which had been used by the Dutch as an internment camp for women and children, was turned into a concentration camp by the Japanese. 800 Dutch women spent the rest of the war there in very cramped conditions.

Another internment camp on Sumatra was *Si Ringo Ringo* where 2.000 Dutch men and boys over 16 were held. There were five camps in Palembang in South Sumatra, and others in Aceh, in the north of the island. In the internment camp of *Pulau Brayan* on Sumatra over 2,000 Dutch women and children were held behind barbed wire. The internment camps on Java, which had previously held German prisoners, were now filled with the

Dutch – on Java alone 29,000 men, 25,000 women and 29,000 children.[1] In all these camps the sanitary facilities, the water supplies and medical treatment – as they had been previously under the Dutch – were far from satisfactory. Diseases like malaria and cholera raged, and every day there were deaths from sickness, malnourishment and exhaustion. The closer the approach of Japan's defeat came, the more brutal and inhumane was the treatment of the prisoners.

The mortality rate was very high. The lowest was in *Kampili* in south east Celebes: 1.5 %. In the internment camps on Java the average mortality rate was 16 % and on Sumatra 37 %. In comparison the death rate among Indonesian coolies working for the Dutch in North Sumatra over a period of three years was 20 %. And that was in peacetime. These figures reveal that Dutch treatment of their native coolies was not much better, if at all, than the treatment handed out to internees.[2]

The Japanese built a big prisoner-of-war camp in Tandjung Priok (now: Tanjung Priok), the port of Batavia. The prisoners here were Dutch, British, American and Australian. Among the Americans there were quite a few Japanese, some of whose families had emigrated to the USA several generations before. The Japanese wished to use these "Japanese US citizens" for their own purposes, but most of them were loyal to their new home and refused to cooperate. In the USA in contrast all citizens with a Japanese background were treated as spies and placed under strict surveillance or even interned.

The Allied PoWs in Tandjung Priok camp were largely guarded by local natives. As several veterans later told me with a smile the Indonesian guards thought it a great joke to humiliate their former Dutch rulers by making them clean their shoes.

The Japanese occupation of the East Indies improved the situation of the *Reichs* Germans considerably. They were now free. Not so the *Volks* Germans: they had previously been, in Dutch eyes, half-German and so suspect, but now in Japanese eyes they were half-Dutch and even less trustworthy. The *Reichs* Germans were also less forthcoming with the *Volks* German as they were not sure of their loyalty to the Third Reich.

The Japanese forbade the use of the Dutch language in public. Only a few of the Japanese officers spoke English or German, which made communication difficult. The natives had to show their respect for Japanese officers on the street by a deep kowtow. The *Reichs* Germans greeted them with a raised hand and a snappy "Heil Hitler". At the same time they also shouted *Doitzu,* German, to avoid unpleasantness. The Dutch and Allied prisoners

1   Doel, *Het Rijk van Insulinde*, pp. 272ff
2   Mak, *Das Jahrhundert meines Vaters,* p. 370

in the camps felt humiliated by the deep kowtow, although this is a normal greeting among the Japanese.

To try and catch any Dutch who might still be free, the Japanese instituted controls and raids. Since the Japanese had hardly any knowledge of foreign languages, some Dutch people initially tried to present themselves as German with a raised hand and a "Heil Hitler". Only when the Germans were given new papers by the Japanese and badges with a black swastika on a red background could they show unambiguously that they were German and receive friendly treatment as an ally.

Swiss, Scandinavians, Italians, Vichy-French and White Russians were called "free guests" and could move around Japanese occupied areas with some restrictions. The Germans were the only people who, as "Axis Brothers", were completely free. Nevertheless they still had to be careful not fall into their customary Dutch at control points, which would have aroused the suspicion of the Japanese.

German and Japanese newsreels were now shown in the cinemas. When an enemy ship was sunk on the screen, the Germans no longer shouted "Hurrah" or "Sieg Heil": together with the Indonesians they now shouted *Banzai!* They were quick to learn the first words of their allies' language.

As I have already said, the Japanese were initially greeted joyfully by the Indonesian population as liberators from the colonial yoke. The red and white Indonesian flag was happily waved and Soekarno accepted the Japanese offer to set up an Indonesian government under the Japanese military, of which he would be the head. However, the Indonesians only enjoyed the feeling of liberty and independence for a short while. Hundreds of thousands of young men were separated from their families and, like the Dutch men and Allied PoWs, put to forced labour. Many Indonesians also volunteered to work on building the railways in Sumatra, Siam and Burma out of economic necessity. Women were enslaved as prostitutes and often held in the Japanese barracks for months.

Since Japan was dependent on a high level of imports even in peacetime, the situation in the homeland got considerably worse during the war. Sea routes had become unsafe and the blockade imposed on Japan by the USA even before the war made the situation even worse. Now basic foods like rice, sweet potatoes and other products were taken from the occupied countries with as much enthusiasm as had been previously shown by the western colonial powers. The fertile East Indies suffered particularly badly: they were ruthlessly exploited. Agricultural products, food, textiles and much more were seized and taken back to Japan. The Japanese took whatever they needed: houses, cars, rice and women. They did not understand the considerate mentality and social customs of the normally very patient and undemanding South East Asians. In the eyes of the natives, they behaved like elephants in a China shop. They had clearly initially had the lofty intention, as "the older and more experienced brother", to help the oppressed and impoverished colonised peoples of Asia back on their feet, but they very soon squandered the positive feelings with which they had been greeted at first. The "Sons of the Rising Sun", the purposeful and hard-working Japanese, who had announced themselves as fatherly friends, treated the native population simply *kasar*, which one could translate as harshly, coarsely or ruthlessly, which was totally alien to the Indonesian mentality and customs. As a result the Indonesians suffered greatly even after colonial rule had ended.

Because of this and the psychological errors and arrogance of the military authorities and their auxiliary troops, the Indonesians' initial feelings of welcome for the Greater Asian Co-Prosperity Sphere under the banner of the Rising Sun swiftly vanished. "Asia for the Asians" became a farce. It is always a disadvantage in the Far East if you forget to be polite – even for just a second. In the excitement of the war and victory the Japanese had forgotten this.

Of course this was not uniquely Japanese. In every war the threshold of inhibition falls to a level one would not believe possible – in all countries. Lack of discipline among fighting troops runs like a thread throughout history, from the indescribable crimes of the Germans in the Third Reich and of the Russians down to the USA's behaviour in the Iraq War.

As time went by even Indonesian nationalists regarded the Japanese occupation with mixed feelings. Dutch oppression and exploitation had been replaced by the same thing under Japan, and this is still resented. But as Japan lost the good will of the native population the freedom movement under Soekarno gained in strength and numbers.

During the Japanese occupation people had no need to worry about thieves or plundering. The Japanese authorities punished the smallest offences with torture or even death. The Indonesians nevertheless still kept heir heads down in their huts. Peace on the streets was only interrupted by the marching feet and marching songs of passing Japanese troops. You didn't dare provoke a Japanese person if you met one on the street. The deeper you bowed to them, the greater the chance of avoiding problems.

All private cars vanished from the streets. They were hidden or confiscated by the authorities – all that could be seen were Japanese military vehicles. Even though there were ration cards for rice and sugar, these basic commodities could no longer be found on the official markets. Provisional Japanese bank notes were issued –people disparagingly called them *duit pisang* (banana money). Rice had become increasingly scarce and hardly available even at scandalous black market prices. Every patch of earth round people's houses became a vegetable plot. The main food crop was the quick-growing *ubi singkong* and its leaves. In order not to starve, the native population ate everything: tortoises, snakes and even snails. The majority of the archipelago's harvest was shipped to Japan.

Tjokorda Ibu Adun, the daughter of Tjokorde Gede Agung Sukawati, the Prince of Ubud on Bali told me the following story: during the Japanese occupation the soldiers particularly liked staying on Bali. The Japanese were and are a culture-loving people, and were fascinated by Balinese culture. Almost every Balinese person is an artist: they paint, make music, dance, or carve beautiful works of art from any piece of wood. There were not hundreds, but thousands of Hindu temples on Bali, where festivals take place almost every day. On Bali the Japanese could almost forget the war because of the many-facetted culture and art on the island. And the Japanese love painting.

At this time the Indonesian painter Affandi (born in 1907 in Cirebon) lived in Yogyakarta on Java. He had begun as a self-taught painter in 1934. He was a gifted, fanatical and at the time completely unknown painter. There was starvation on Java and he could not feed his family. He heard that because of the Japanese presence on Bali there was a better market for art. He went there and made friends with Tjokorde Gede Agung Sukawati in Ubud. The latter was a great art lover and a close friend of the German painter Walter Spies. Affandi was a member of POETRA, a society of artists whose aim was to promote indigenous art. Among many others, Soekarno and Mohammad Hatta, the freedom fighters and founders of the Indonesian Republic, were also members.

Affandi was allowed to display his paintings and drawings along the wall of Tjokorde Gede Agung Sukawati's palace in Ubud, opposite the big market. Japanese art lovers were attracted by his modern style and he sold his works for ever higher prices. He became so well-known in the Japanese art scene that he was allowed to hold his first solo exhibition in the *Gedung Poetera* in Batavia in 1943.

Many of his works were bought by the Japanese occupying troops and taken back to Japan. The Japanese occupation was a threshold for Affandi's fame and the beginning of a great career. More than 2,000 of his art works survive and are to be found in museums all over the world, including the Fukuoka Asian Art Museum in Japan. In 1973 the Affandi Museum in Yogyakarta was founded and still displays a comprehensive collection of his works.

After the end of the war, Indonesia declared its independence. But the Dutch came back to regain control of their former colony. Affandi was a devoted and fanatical freedom fighter at Soekarno's side. He painted the slogan *Merdeka atau Mati* (Freedom or Death) on railway waggons and designed posters for the independence movement. His best-known motif from that period is a man tearing off the chains that fetter him. I am sure that many of his paintings are still slumbering in Japanese back rooms or attics without the owners being aware what a valuable treasure their father or grandfather acquired back then as a soldier in Bali, because these early works of Affandi's, mostly signed simply with an 'A', are sold on the international art markets today for many tens of thousands of Euros.

Although the Japanese treated the Indonesians with a severity that they had previously only been used to from the Dutch but had not expected from an Asian 'brother nation', Japan continued to support the Indonesian independence movement.

The view of most Indonesians, that Hitler contributed decisively to the speed with which Indonesia became independent, has hardly changed even today. Soekarno, the first President of free Indonesia, had prophesied this long before the beginning of the war. He argued that a war in Europe started by Hitler would so weaken the Dutch colonial power that the freedom movement would gain enough strength to lead Indonesia to independence. In 1938, while still in exile on the island of Flores, he even prophesied that independence would be achieved in 1945 – he wrote a play entitled "Indonesia 45" at the time.[1]

This assessment by Soekarno is one of the reasons why Hitler is still so popular in Indonesia. There is also the fact that Indonesian historical consciousness only really begins in 1950 when the last Dutch withdrew. They have heard little or nothing about the atrocities committed by the Nazi regime – or they just do not want to know. A further reason is the testimony of contemporary witnesses who took part in the independence struggle from 1945 until December 1949. According to them Hitler massively supported the independence movement and the arming of PETA (*Pembela Tanah Air*), the army founded by Soekarno during the Japanese occupation, with military supplies, and after the German capitulation with military trainers as well. I shall deal with these matters later.

The gates of the infamous Dutch concentration camps *Tanah Merah* and *Tanah Tinggi* in New Guinea, where Indonesian nationalists were imprisoned, were also now opened by the Japanese. The camps had been called

---

1   Adams, *Sukarno*, p. 145
     Anwar, *Sejarah Kecil*, p. 123

Boven-Digoel by the Dutch. Among many thousands of others, Mohammad Hatta, the first Indonesian Vice President and Sutan Sjahrir, the first Indonesian Prime minister, were freed. The camps were a good 450 kilometres upstream of the mouth of the river Digoel (now: Digul) in the south east of Dutch New Guinea, surrounded by impenetrable jungle. At the beginning of the 1930s there were already over 2,100 Indonesians imprisoned there under terrible conditions with a murderous hot damp climate for their resistance to the colonial power. Diseases like malaria, measles and pneumonia were rife and the death rate extremely high.[1]

Now that the Dutch East Indies were Japanese territory, the German auxiliary cruiser *Thor* visited Batavia on its second voyage. Heinz Tischer, the war reporter, published a work in 1983 which gives details of the voyage:

The Hamburg freighter *Santa Cruz* was transformed in 100 days into the auxiliary cruiser *Thor*, also known by the German Navy as *Schiff 10* and by the British as "Raider E". On both sides of the ship there were two guns concealed behind shutters, and there was one camouflaged gun in both the bow and the stern. In the stern there was also a twin anti-aircraft canon. On both sides there were twin torpedo tubes behind armoured protection. 30 metres above the ship there was an extendible mast with a rotating seat for a lookout. In the bow there was a hydraulic lift for an Arado 196A reconnaissance seaplane whose wings could be folded when on board the ship. They also had a mechanism for ripping out the aerials that were suspended between the masts of merchant ships. This prevented the enemy from sending a message describing the position of the attack. The aircraft had machine guns and could carry two 50-kilogram bombs. When fully fuelled it had a range of 1,000 kilometres.

Since auxiliary cruisers often had to spend much more than a year at sea, the *Thor* was equipped with a first rate hospital with an operating theatre and a ward with several beds. Captured sailors could also be treated here. The surgeon was Dr Buchinger, the general practitioner Dr Lehmann, the dentist Kurt Grobe and the rating in charge of nursing was called Hollmann.[2] To entertain the crew there was a cinema on board and a canvas swimming pool. Live pigs were kept in the stern of the ship to ensure a supply of fresh meat. The *Thor* looked at first sight like a harmless merchant ship but could be transformed into a heavily armed auxiliary cruiser in a matter of seconds.

The *Thor* set sail in November 1941 under Captain Günther Gumprich. Their route took them from Kiel via Le Havre to Bordeaux. She set out twice from Bordeaux, but had to return damaged to Bordeaux after encountering

---

1   Loeber, *Das niederländische Kolonialreich,* p. 50
2   Tischer, *Die Abenteuer des letzten Kapers,* pp. 33ff

hurricane weather in the Atlantic. A third foray into the Antarctic Ocean was more successful. For four weeks the *Thor* searched in vain for whaling ships and then set course for the Cape of Good Hope. In the South Atlantic she was refuelled by the *Regensburg*. With her tanks full the *Thor* was now capable of sailing round the world without refuelling, as the work of adapting her to her new status as auxiliary cruiser had included building in supplementary fuel tanks.

In the Indian Ocean the *Thor* captured the British passenger ship *Nankin*, which was sailing from Fremantle in Western Australia to Colombo. As well as her crew, she was carrying Australian military personnel and 365 passengers, mostly women and children. With the ship the Germans captured 56 sacks of courier-mail which provided valuable information and 184 chests of Chinese currency (*Yüans*).[1] A recreation and play area was set up on the deck for the women and children. There was even a child born on the *Thor*: its mother called it Fritz in gratitude for the good treatment she received from Dr Fritz Lehmann. The *Nankin* was sailed by a German crew as a captured prize under the name *Leuthen* to Yokohama, where it was used as living accommodation for German naval personnel.

There were now over 800 prisoners on board *Thor*, including the crews of ships previously captured: they now by far outnumbered her own crew. Admiral Wenneker in Tokyo organised a rendezvous with the blockade breaker *Regensburg*, which was on its way to Yokohama, for a handover of the prisoners. The Australian women and children handed Captain Gumprich a letter of thanks for the hospitality and politeness they had received on board.[2] The ship arrived safely in Japan with its prisoners.

When the *Thor* reached "Japanese territory" in the eastern Indian Ocean she rendezvoused with the blockade breaker *Tannenfels* to take on fresh potatoes and a final year student from the German School in Tokyo. He spoke perfect Japanese and German and could act as an interpreter. In the Sunda Strait, just before they reached Batavia, the Imperial Japanese Naval Attaché to the commander in Chief in Batavia, Captain Count Maeda came on board to welcome the *Thor* to Japanese territory. He was mad about dogs. Eyewitnesses tell me that his favourite dog was allowed to eat from his plate – even at official dinners for naval officers. In 1940 Count *Maeda* was Military Attaché in the Hague, and during this time was received by Hitler in Berlin. This was the first time the *Thor* had touched land for almost 300 days. She had sunk or captured 10 enemy ships. Among the ships sunk were the British ships *Wellpark*, *Willesden*, *Aust* and *Kirkpool*, which were carrying military supplies to Britain. They sank with almost 100 aircraft, many tanks and

---

1   Tischer: *Die Abenteuer des letzten Kapers,* p. 53
2   Tischer, *Die Abenteuer des letzten Kapers,* p. 61

military vehicles, over 500 machine guns, 16,000 boxes of ammunition and 200 boxes of British uniforms, among other items.[1]

On the 10th of October 1942 the *Thor* arrived in Yokohama for maintenance – the men were allowed to take leave in a lakeside hotel in the spa resort of Hakone. The doctor on board the *Thor* was very busy, because in Yokohama and Tokyo a dozen men had caught sexually transmitted diseases.

The auxiliary cruiser's end came on the 30th of November 1942 as it was lying beside the *Uckermark* before starting on a new mission. The *Uckermark* had been carrying aviation fuel from Singapore to Yokohama, and its tanks had already been emptied when a moment of carelessness caused the fuel fumes to explode. This was followed by the explosion of the torpedo warheads on board. The *Uckermark* and the *Thor*, the Japanese ammunition ship *Unkai Maru III* and the *Leuthen*, which had recently been captured by *Thor* were totally destroyed. 57 German sailors were killed on the *Uckermark* and the *Thor*. The survivors from both ships were taken back from Japan to Bordeaux on the blockade breaker *Pietro Orseolo*.

---

1   Tischer, *Die Abenteuer des letzten Kapers*, p. 30

13. Radio XGRS (German Radio Station), "Shanghai Calling"

National Socialist propaganda spread as far as Asia: in China there was a whole range of German printed media in German and English. Examples of German newspapers and magazines were *Deutsch-Chinesische Nachrichten* [German-Chinese News], the *Deutsche Zeitung in Nordchina* [German Newspaper in North China], the *Deutsche Shanghai Zeitung* [German Shanghai Newspaper], the *Ostasiatische Beobachter* [East Asian Observer], the *Bühnenspiegel im Fernen Osten* [Stage Report for the Far East], *Die Brücke* [The Bridge] or *Die Dschunke* [The Junk]. In the Dutch East Indies it was the *Deutsche Wacht*. However, the English language monthly journal *The XXth Century* was the most successful instrument of German foreign propaganda in Asia. Germans and the international community with an interest in Germany had a wide choice.

Information and propaganda also reached the Far East via the ether. The German Transocean news agency had already been broadcasting news from Germany in English and Chinese four times a day for many years using the Chinese station XHHB in Shanghai. From Königs-Wusterhausen near Berlin powerful short wave transmitters with the call-signs DJA to DJE had been broadcasting programmes in German to Asia since 1933. It was possible to get good reception for this throughout East and South East Asia.

Günther Fust, already referred to above, worked in China as a representative of the Bayer pharmaceutical division of IG-Farben. On the 20th of November 1936 he travelled on the *SS Tungwo* through the gorges of the Yangtzekiang, the longest river in China, which is navigable by steamship for 3,000 kilometres into the Chinese interior. In a letter to Germany he writes: *The Berlin transmitter can be heard extremely well everywhere here on board ships, on the coast and in the Chinese interior.*

On another occasion he writes from his house in Chungking after purchasing a new radio set for 750 dollars at the end of 1938:
An excellent 10-valve Philips radio set supplies us with music and news from all over the world. Reception here is excellent. We hear music and news from German transmitters here as well as we would if we were in Germany.

His Neighbour, the American Ambassador, had bought the same radio but had paid 900 dollars for it. He writes of him:

Our house is on the side of a hill. On the other side of the hill lives our neighbour, the American Ambassador who is constantly annoyed by our swastika flag which flies provocatively under his nose.

In a report written from his home in Chungking at the end of 1938, Herr Fust describes his daily routine, including his listening habits::

At 4.30 you drive home, then drink tea and listen to the midday music from the German Station from 5.30 to 8. At 8 o'clock there is news from Berlin, at 8.30 from London and then you can listen to music from London, Berlin, Paris, Moscow, Prague, Rome, Hanoi, Tokyo and other cities.

The German news broadcast from Moscow daily at noon CET is always amusing. The programme opens with the Russian national anthem and the words "Workers of the world unite!" The content makes you laugh. They talk such nonsense that you wonder if these people can be taken at all seriously.[1]

Research has shown that Germany had a long history of providing Shanghai with transmitters. Between 1907 and 1914 three "quenched spark transmitters" were sent to the German Concession in Shanghai by the German firm Telefunken in Berlin. They were presumably used for communication with the East Asia Squadron of the German Imperial Navy. In 1930 several 2 kilowatt medium wave valve transmitters with a wavelength of between 16 and 60 metres were sent to Shanghai by the same firm. The clients were the German Concession and other foreign concessions in Shanghai.[2]

At the beginning of 1940 Germany had begun to use a small medium wave transmitter of only 300 watts for local radio in the German Kaiser-Wilhelm-Schule on Great Western Road in the German Concession in Shanghai. The British had their radio station XMHA, calling itself the Voice of the Orient. The Japanese radio station was XQHA, the Russian XRVN and the Italian XIRS. Altogether about 40, mostly rather weak private radio stations competed for the ether in Shanghai. All the broadcasts by these stations could only be heard within the city area.

During the war years Germany strengthened its radio presence in East Asia to a considerable degree. In 1940 a new German transmitter began broadcasting in Shanghai which now transmitted its programmes in the 49,

---

1   From Herr Fust's diary, kindly placed at my disposal by Dr Walter Jäcker. All italicised text is directly quoted from the original

2   Jürgen Graaff, previously head of the Radio Transmitter Department of Telefunken, private and unpublished Historical List of Transmitters

31 and 25 metre bands. It was a short wave transmitter which could be heard all over East and South-East Asia and beyond. With a strength of 10 kilowatts this German transmitter was now the most powerful in the Far East.

The call sign of the German radio stations was XGRS. "X" for China and "GRS" for **G**erman **R**adio **S**tation. Radio XGRS identified itself at the beginning and end of each programme section with *Deutscher Rundfunksender Shanghai – The Call of the Far East.*

The radio station and its activities were financed by the Reich Foreign and Propaganda Ministry in Berlin. It operated within the German Concession, but even so required the permission of the Japanese occupying force.

Radio XGRS was initially a German cultural broadcaster primarily serving to entertain the German community. This was soon to change. The Foreign Service and the Propaganda Ministry in Berlin recognised Radio XGRS' importance for the spread of Nazi ideology and fostering the feeling of solidarity among the many Germans in the region. Both ministries agreed that the schedules should be altered accordingly. Radio XGRS should become a propaganda weapon and broadcast mainly in English. Although the broadcasts could be heard perfectly well from Tokyo to Batavia, they announced at the beginning of 1940 that the capacity of the 10 kilowatt transmitter would be increased to 100 kilowatts.

At the end of 1940 Dr Erwin Wickert was sent to Shanghai as Radio Attaché by the Foreign Ministry to take over the running of Radio XGRS and to attempt, together with Martin Fischer, the German Consul General, to speed up the project of increasing the transmitter's capacity by agreement with Japan. Wickert was the first diplomat to fill the position of Radio Attaché in the Third Reich. His employment in Shanghai was obviously due to his knowledge of the region as well as his technical qualifications.

Erwin Wickert was a diplomat, philosopher and writer. He had studied politics and economics in the USA. After graduating there he travelled through many countries, including Japan, Korea, Manchukuo and China. He then took a doctorate in philosophy in Germany. In 1939, at the age of 24, Wickert joined the Foreign Ministry in Berlin, being appointed to the post in Shanghai just a year later.

XGRS played a prominent role in the East and South East Asian region, not just by providing war news and commentaries, but also as a Nazi propaganda station broadcasting from 7 a.m. to midnight every day in German, English, Chinese, Japanese and later in Hindustani and Russian as well. It also broadcast short coded messages to Germany's many agents in the region. Later, after the Japanese occupation of the East Indies the German naval bases on Java, Sumatra and the Malay peninsula also received coded messages via Radio XGRS.

Shanghai was swarming with agents from all nations. This is where in 1934 Richard Sorge the Soviet spy met "Sonja" who was later to become "Stalin's best spy".[1] The city was a hive of rumours, but there was also useful information to be had – this was then passed on by Radio XGRS in coded form to the Germans agents working underground. For example, the message *10,000 tonnes of cotton are ready in Bombay* might mean *10,000 British Soldiers have mustered in Singapore.*

By December 1940 Wickert was able to inform Berlin:

To all intents and purposes the transformation of a German cultural station aimed mainly at entertaining the German community into a political propaganda station is [...] complete.[2]

Radio XGRS attracted notice and gained an even greater international audience through its satirical political programme "A Briton's Point of View", presented by Peter Waldbauer, an Austrian whose commentaries were produced in totally exaggerated Oxford English. All commentaries on Radio XGRS were generally anti-British and anti-American, presumably with the intent of encouraging hostility to the British among the native populations of the mainly British colonies in the region – from Hong Kong to Singapore.

Herbert May, an American of Chinese descent, was Radio XGRS' "Slogan Maker". His biting commentaries were often printed in "Shanghai Calling!", Radio XGRS's programme listing magazine. In one programme, for example, May said:

The war began because Great Britain refused to recognise the German nation's right to existence [...] The war in the Pacific began because Mr Roosevelt insisted on meddling in matters that had nothing at all to do with him or the United States.[3]

In the course of time his tone became more aggressive and he now began to emphasise the racist world-view of the Third Reich. For example:

Roosevelt's war is not for the benefit of the American people, but serves the restoration of the Jewish position in the world. Roosevelt is the advocate of world

---

1   cf. chapter "The German Embassy in Tokyo"
2   Rundfunk und Geschichte, Mitteilungen aus dem Deutschen Rundfunkarchiv, 29. Jahrgang Nr. 1/2 – Januar/April 2003, Article by Astrid Freytag: *XGRS – Shanghai Calling*, p. 40 footnote 18, Wickert to the AA, 17.12.1940
3   Rundfunk und Geschichte, Mitteilungen aus dem Deutschen Rundfunkarchiv, 29. Jahrgang Nr. 1/2 – Januar/April 2003, article by Astrid Freytag: *XGRS – Shanghai Calling*, p. 42, Footnote 39, Programme listing for 6.1.1942, p. 3f

*Jewry and is surrounded by Jewish advisors. [...] But the crafty Jew does not fight
– he simply profits from the war.*[1]

Other Radio XGRS commentators were Frederick Wiehl, a German, the
American Robert Fockler and the Australian John Holland, all outstanding
propagandists for the "German cause". After the war, Holland was sentenced
in Australia to several years in prison because of this active support of Germany.

The British radio station XMHA and the German XGRS waged a war of
words. Erwin Wickert was also partly successful in his attempts to influence
other, non-German stations in favour of the Third Reich. Chinese stations
in particular rebroadcast a large proportion of Radio XGRS' programmes.

In February 1942 Wickert set up a monitoring station in Shanghai as
a subsidiary of *Sonderdienst Seehaus* [Special Service Seahouse] in Berlin,
which was a news-gathering operation run by the Foreign Ministry and the
Ministry of Propaganda. Around the clock 700 staff monitored news and
commentaries that might be of use to the military or political leadership in
37 languages. This material was summarised in a daily bulletin.

Besides *Sonderdienst Seehaus* in Berlin there were in Germany about a
dozen other monitoring stations, run for example by the army and the air
force. Probably the largest was the "Military Monitoring Service" which had
about 3,000 staff in Berlin and Nuremberg. Allied military radio traffic in
speech and Morse code was monitored and deciphered. However – and after
the war this was shown to be the security service's biggest failure – there was
little or no co-ordination between these different services.[2]

Wickert handed the management of the monitoring service in Shanghai
to Walter Leo Meyer, a Swiss, and reported to Berlin:

*I have given Herr Meyer the task of regularly monitoring and observing all
broadcasters in the Pacific region. I have instructed him to pay particular attention to broadcasts from San Francisco, Honolulu, Tokyo, Chungking, Hong
Kong, Sidney, Manila, Singapore, Saigon, Bangkok and Batavia.*[3]

---

1   Rundfunk und Geschichte, Mitteilungen aus dem Deutschen Rundfunkarchiv,
     29. Jahrgang Nr. 1/2 – Januar/April 2003, Aufsatz von Astrid Freytag: *XGRS
     – Shanghai Calling*, p. 44, Footnote 50, Office of Strategic Services, China,
     Report on German Radio Station XGRS, 7.10.1945
2   Bartolomew Lee, *Radio Spies: Episodes in the Ether Wars*, pp. 58 and 117
     Flicke, *War Secrets in the Ether*
     www.trft.org/TRFTPix/spies9eR2006.pdf
3   Rundfunk und Geschichte, Mitteilungen aus dem Deutschen Rundfunkarchiv,
     29. Jahrgang Nr. 1/2 – Januar/April 2003, Article by Astrid Freytag: *XGRS –
     Shanghai Calling*, p. 44, Footnote 53, Wickert to AA, 12.2.1941

TUNING IN

PROGRAM OF STATION XGRS IN SHANGHAI

570 kc   *25 m. band*

(Unless otherwise stated, the program will be transmitted by both long and short wave)

ON WEEKDAYS:

7.00	Choral—Folksongs—Marches	4.00	Chinese Program (Kuo Yu)
7.15	Physical Fitness Program	4.45	German Lessons for Chinese
7.30	Light Music	5.00	Afternoon Concert
7.45	News in English	6.00	Light Music
8.00	Light Music	6.15	Commentary by David Lester
8.15	Women's Half-hour with Anne Collins	6.25	Light Music
8.45	Light Music	6.30	Asia's Views on the News
9.00	Children's Hour with Pamela Anne	6.45	La demi-heure francaise
9.30	Light Music	7.15	Commentary in English
10.15	News in English	7.30	Shanghai Walla-Walla
10.30	Hindustani Program	7.45	News in English
11.00	Chinese Program (Cantonese)	8.00	American Program
11.30	News in French	8.30	Commentary by Herbert Moy
11.45	Italian Program	8.45	News in Russian
12.15	German Program	9.00	Ukrainian Program
12.40	Light Music	9.15	Classical Concert
12.45	News in English	10.15	News in English
1.00	Russian Program (Long Wave)	10.30	Light Music
1.00	Half-hour of American Dance Music (Short Wave)	10.35	Commentary by Herbert Moy
1.30	Light Music	10.50	Light Music
1.55	Program Preview	11.15	Late News in English
2.00	Broadcast for Overseas Listeners (Short Wave)	11.30	Dance Music
		11.45	Asia's Views on the News
		12.00-1.00	Broadcast for Overseas Listeners (Short Wave)

ON SUNDAYS:

8.00	Choral—Folksongs—Organ Selections	6.30	Light Music (Short Wave)
8.45	News in English	6.35	Asia's Views on the News (Short Wave)
9.00	Sunday Morning Concert	6.45	Request Program
10.15	News in English	7.00	German Program
10.30	Hindustani Program	7.15	Weekly Review in German
11.00	Chinese Program (Cantonese)	7.30	German Waltzes
11.30	News in French	7.45	News in English
11.45	Italian Program	8.00	Popular French Music
12.15	German Program	8.10	Durand et Dupont
12.40	Light Music	8.30	Reginald Hollingsworth
12.45	News in English	8.45	Commentary in Russian
1.00	Noon Concert (Short Wave)	9.00	Light Music
1.00	Russian Program (Long Wave)	9.30	Bill & Mack
1.30	Noon Concert	9.45	Light Music
1.55	Program Preview	10.15	News in English
2.00	Broadcast for Overseas Listeners (Short Wave)	10.30	Dance Music
4.00	Opera Concert	11.15	Late News in English
6.00	Request Program (Long Wave)	11.30	Dance Music
6.00	Light Music (Short Wave)	11.35	Bill & Mack
6.15	Flight Lieut. David Lester (Short Wave)	11.50	Concert Program
		12.00-1.00	Broadcast for Overseas Listeners (Short Wave)

Ill. 38
Programme Listing in the Magazine The XXth Century, Shanghai

His duties were, however, not confined to listening to radio stations. American military traffic in the Pacific was also monitored. If you consider that, as well as monitoring duties round the clock, up to 2,000 messages a day had to be decoded, it becomes obvious that the duties of this Shanghai subsidiary of *Sonderdienst Seehaus* were extremely labour-intensive.

The Germans were not the only ones to maintain monitoring services. The Americans had set up monitoring stations in the Pacific on the Aleutian Islands, the Philippines, Samoa and Hawaii which intercepted Morse as well as radio transmissions.

Australia had two monitoring stations on its territory, the British one in Singapore and the Dutch one in Batavia. As the Japanese army advanced ever further south in 1942, the Singapore and Batavia stations were also moved to Australia: there were therefore four stations in Australia in Darwin, Perth, Melbourne and New Guinea.

After completing his mission in Shanghai Dr Wickert moved to become the Radio Attaché at the German Embassy in Tokyo in 1942. His successor in Shanghai was Rudolf Grau. Wickert also set up a subsidiary of *Sonderdienst Seehaus* in Tokyo. His son, the well-known television presenter, author and journalist Ulrich Wickert was born there in December 1942.

In 1955 Erwin Wickert entered the Federal German diplomatic service. Among other postings, he was Deputy Ambassador in London and Ambassador in Bucharest and Beijing.

During Radio XGRS' propaganda period there was another prominent German in Shanghai: Klaus Mehnert, well known in Germany after the war as a broadcaster, political commentator and author. After graduating from university Mehnert travelled while still comparatively young in China, Japan and America. He visited China and Japan again during his time as a correspondent in Moscow from 1934 to 1936. After a guest professorship in Berkeley in the USA and a full professorship in Honolulu, he founded *The XXth Century*, the English-language magazine mentioned above in Shanghai under the auspices of the German Foreign Ministry. It was financially supported by Goebbels' Propaganda Ministry, and this was reflected in its character. *The XXth Century* was a great success in East Asia and was very successful in promulgating German propaganda on an international scale, publishing anti-British reports and commentaries as well as the programme listings for Radio XGRS.

Klaus Mehnert and Erwin Wickert worked closely together. After the war Mehnert was, like all Germans in China, interned. Back in Germany in 1950 he became foreign commentator for South German Radio. He was an advisor on Eastern and Asian policy to all German Chancellors from Konrad Adenauer to Helmut Schmidt.

Radio XGRS was very important, especially during the Japanese occupation of East and South East Asia, as its broadcasts could be heard as far away as Australia and the west coast of Canada and the USA in spite of its relatively low 10-kilowatt capacity.

The East Asia Committee of the Foreign Ministry was shown a copy of the American magazine *Amerasia*, in which the German station in Shanghai was highly praised because it could be received in California. Hilmar Bassler, later German Ambassador in Jakarta, sat on the committee representing the Press Department and commented *that the importance of the station was greatly overestimated in the article, but that the view expressed there certainly did Germany no harm.*[1]

The increase in XGRS' capacity to 100 kilowatts was not realised before the end of the war. After the German capitulation Radio XGRS was taken over by Japan and, under its new call sign XGOO, broadcast anti-American material. When Japan also capitulated some months later the station fell into Chinese hands. With its call sign XORA, this was the only radio station that broadcast from Shanghai after the war. An episode of German radio history in East Asia had come to an end.[2]

---

1   Rundfunk und Geschichte, Mitteilungen aus dem Deutschen Rundfunkarchiv, 29. Jahrgang Nr. 1/2 – Januar/April 2003, Article by Astrid Freytag: *XGRS – Shanghai Calling*, p. 44, Footnote 52, minutes of the meeting of the information service for East Asia and the South Seas, Berlin 22.8.1944

2   Astrid Freyeisen, XGRS, *Shanghai Calling: Deutsche Rundfunkpropaganda in Ostasien*, pp. 38-46
    http://rundfunkundgeschichte.de/assets/RuG_2003_1-2.pdf
    www.pateplumaradio.com, Radio Scene in Shanghai

14. The Nanking Massacre

Japan intensified its efforts at colonising China in the 1930s. In the First Japanese-Chinese War of 1932 Japanese troops attacked Shanghai. In the Second Japanese-Chinese War of 1937 there were considerable losses on both sides. With hostile smiles and a false sense of superiority, the Chinese initially made fun of the "Japanese island dwarfs" and their exaggerated urge for conquest. But Japan, the most modern industrial nation in the Far East, soon claimed the respect that was their due and took uncompromising action. The great battle of Shanghai lasted from the 13th of August to the 9th of November 1937 and ended in a Japanese victory. Japan was aided in its conquest of China by the fact that China was at the time – a year after the death of Sun Yat Sen, the father of the Chinese revolution – riven with unrest and revolts.

This Second Japanese-Chinese War was started by the bombs which fell on Shanghai, some of them on the international concessions.

Günther Fust gives a lively description of the outbreak of war in his diary:
I thought I was going to spend a quiet summer in Shanghai. [...] But the tension increased visibly. A Japanese officer was shot near the Chinese airfield and that was the signal to strike. [...]
At 19:00 the first shots rang out. At 19:30 we all met in the Garden Club. We old warriors of 1932 knew the ropes, we could distinguish clearly between artillery fire, mortars, rifle fire and the rattle of machine-guns. We wet the war's head heartily in the club. [...]
The next morning was the first time that we heard anti-aircraft fire and bombs in Shanghai. [...] We heard alarming news of panic on the streets. But why should that bother us? We were sitting safe in the Concession. And then the terrible disaster in the afternoon. Bombs on the Cathay Hotel, the Palace Hotel, the focal point of the International Settlement of Shanghai. (Author's note: Hotels which were mainly patronized by diplomats, foreign visitors, newspaper correspondents and wealthy Chinese.) And bombs on the Avenue Edward VII near the New World. Over 1,200 dead in the Concession on the first day. Wagons with human remains and wounded. Panic! Dreadful days followed, with indescribable tension in the whole city. [...][1]
The Cathay Hotel mentioned by Fust, only four years old, with its colonnades, roof garden and excellent restaurants and bars must surely be the

---

1   Diary of Günther Fust, p. 52

one that appears in Vicki Baum's 1939 novel *Hotel Shanghai*, in which she describes the horrors and human tragedies of the war.

The bombing continued every day, but from now on the International Concessions were spared. People felt safe there. After one bombing raid Fust writes: *Swimming in the afternoon, and tennis, and then the usual drink on the terrace.* It was a firm rule that the concessions in the middle of the city could not be subjected to military action. The Chinese and Japanese accused each other of the bombings. Protests followed which ultimately led to fatal military consequences. The conflict in Shanghai cost many tens of thousands of lives, mostly Chinese civilians.

Shanghai was overcrowded with refugees. About 15,000 German Jews had fled there when Hitler came to power, but they were not free for long, because after Shanghai was occupied by Japanese troops in November 1937 all Jews were arrested and interned in camps – so-called "residences for state-less aliens". It was only eight years later, when US troops freed them at the end of 1945, that they were able to leave the camps. Many of them died or suffered from diseases which affected them for the rest of their lives. It was not until some months after their liberation that the survivors were taken by ship from Shanghai to Vladivostok and from there on to Moscow by the Trans-Siberian Railway. From there they were distributed to various Eastern European cities.

After the Japanese conquest of Shanghai the way to the Nationalist Chinese capital Nanking, the capital of Marshal Chiang Kai-shek, was open. Chiang Kai-shek, a protégé of Sun Yat Sen, was basically pro-Western and anti-Communist and at first received direct support from Germany. However, he vehemently resisted Japanese occupation.

Chinese soldiers who were captured by the Japanese were immediately executed by imperial command. The Japanese left a trail of devastation, murder and rape behind them on their advance to Nanking. The "Sons of Tenno" were commanded by a power-mad, brutal military machine that soon consigned the Japanese reputation for natural politeness to oblivion. The Japanese secret service, the *Kempetai*, ruled with a rod of iron. Out of Nanking's population of 1.2 million 800,000 fled into the surrounding areas. The river boat *Kutwo* chanced to be at Nanking. The German Embassy chartered it to carry the German residents of Nanking to safety. Nearly all other foreigners had already left the city.[1]

In December 1937 the bloody battle for Nanking began. The city was bombed and shelled without let-up. After six days, on the 12th of December 1937, the Japanese had taken the city and the Massacre of Nanking began.

---

1   Diary of Günther Fust, part II: China

The Japanese military commanders ordered that no prisoners should be taken. Tens of thousands of Chinese soldiers, innocent men and youths were indiscriminately shot or killed with bayonets. There were mass rapes of women and children. In the Japanese war crimes trials after the Second World War figures of 300,000 Chinese victims and 80,000 rapes were given.

There was one ray of light among all these atrocities. John Rabe, the German commercial head of the Siemens-China Corporation in Nanking, set up a safety zone for civilians in the grounds of the factory. Because of the German government's bilateral agreement with Japan he could claim that the factory grounds were a neutral zone. He protected the area from Japanese bombing with a massive swastika flag. Up to 250,000 people found protection in the safety zone, and Rabe's home, with a plot of only 500 square metres, housed more than 650. Rabe saved these people's lives and because of his great humanitarian achievement he is honoured to this day in China as the "good German of Nanking" or the "living German Buddha".

The heads of the Siemens company were – possibly under pressure from the Nazi government – opposed to Rabe's involvement in these brutal Japanese actions and Rabe was replaced as manager by a convinced Nazi. When on his return to Germany Rabe tried to report on the atrocities committed by the Japanese, he was interrogated by the Gestapo (the secret police) and forbidden to say anything about the matter. In Nazi Germany nothing that might alter attitudes to their Asian ally and "Brother Japan" was allowed.

Rabe had a hard time after the end of the war. He had been a member of the Nazi Party and, after a long-drawn-out process of denazification, was only allowed to work in a subordinate position in Siemens. He died in poverty in Berlin in 1950. His gravestone is today honoured in the city museum in Nanking.

Erwin Wickert, the Third Reich's first Radio Attaché in Shanghai, was German Ambassador in China until 1980 and set up a memorial to Rabe in Nanking, where in 2003 a further monument was inaugurated and a John Rabe and International Safety Zone Memorial Hall opened in his old home. The city of Nanking also honoured John Rabe by erecting a bronze bust of him in Berlin. He is still held in great honour in China. The massacre is commemorated by seventeen memorials in Nanking.

John Rabe's diary was discovered and a translation was published in the US under the title *John Rabe, The Good Man of Nanking*. The New York Times also published an article about him, entitled *The good Nazi*, on the 13th of December 1998.

In his homeland Germany John Rabe was, in spite of several tributes, almost forgotten until Erwin Wickert published his book *John Rabe: Der gute Deutsche von Nanking* [The good German of Nanking] in 1997, and Florian Gallenberger brought out his successful film "John Rabe" in German cinemas in 2009. This was followed by a detailed documentary on German television in 2011. These things finally brought John Rabe the recognition he deserved in Germany.

15. The Sinking of the *Van Imhoff*

The extraordinary painter and musician Walter Spies was one of the best known of the Germans who, in the 1920s and 30s found a new home in the Dutch East Indies. During his internment in the Second World War his life came to a tragic end on board the *Van Imhoff*. There is no space in the present work to deal with his career adequately, so I will only describe the sinking of the *Van Imhoff*. Unfortunately Spies is almost unknown in Germany except in expert art circles, while his name is mentioned with reverence in the Indonesian art world even 70 years after his death.[1]

So that the German men could not be freed from the internment camps by the Japanese, who were approaching ever closer, they were taken to British India in several transports. The first group of 975 left Sumatra at the end of December 1941 and the second with 938 at the beginning of January 1942.[2]

On the 18th of January 1942 the Dutch ship *Van Imhoff* of the KPM (*Koninglijke Paketvaart Maatschappij*) line set sail.

Ill. 39

The Van Imhoff of the KPM

---

1   cf. Geerken, *A Gecko for Luck*, pp. 130ff
2   Keppner, *Wie weit bis Airmolang*, pp. 162ff

The prisoners were German merchants, missionaries, artists and scientists anti-fascists and German Jews who had already been living in the Dutch East Indies for a long time or who had fled there after the beginning of the war. One of the prisoners was Walter Spies. The *Van Imhoff* was the last Dutch ship that managed to leave the East Indies before the Japanese invasion. Apart from the German internees there were a crew of 84 Dutch sailors and 62 soldiers as guards on board. The prisoners were to be taken to the camp of Dehra Dun in British India.

The ship was not – as international and maritime law required – marked as a prisoner transport ship and was therefore bombed by a Japanese naval aircraft in the Indian Ocean only one day later, on the 19th of January 1942. The Japanese pilot must have thought the ship was a Dutch troop transport. The 477 German prisoners were locked below decks in barbed-wire cages.[1] The Dutch crew made for safety in a steam launch: the captain was the first to board. Before he and the crew left the ship, they destroyed the radio, which had already been damaged by the Japanese attack. They also demolished the pumps and smashed the water containers. The lifeboats and oars, which they did not need, were made unseaworthy, except for one boat which was stuck on the derricks and had to be left in their haste.

As the *Van Imhoff* slowly sank, the prisoners managed to free themselves. 66 men got into the overloaded lifeboat and rowed without water or food in the direction of Sumatra. Since the Dutch had destroyed the oars, they rowed with simple planks and their bare hands.

The next day the Dutch motor vessel *Boelongan* approached the lifeboat on the high seas. The *Boelongan* was also a KPM ship, the *Van Imhoff*'s sister ship. When the captain discovered that there were only Germans in the lifeboat he wished them all to hell and turned away without even leaving them any water.

One man swam towards the Dutch ship. His despairing cries that he was a Jew and begging for help were ignored. It was the jeweller Arno Schönmann from Java. He swam desperately after the *Boelongan*, but when he tried to grab a line dangling from the ship he was ruthlessly turned away. Exhausted, he drowned.

On the 25th of January 1942 the survivors – almost dead of thirst, burned by the tropical sun and near to madness – reached the island of Nias off Western Sumatra. Two of the exhausted Germans died in the surf close to the shore. Walter Spies was one of the 411 German victims on the *Van Imhoff*.

---

1   The survivors gave somewhat differing figures. The passenger lists of the Dutch authorities were also incomplete.

Ill. 40
The Island of Nias showing the point where the Van Imhoff sank

Another extraordinary man went down with the ship: the Bremen merchant, orientalist, Malay expert, and researcher in languages and insects Hans Friedrich Overbeck. He had been living in the Indonesian-Malay archipelago since 1903, and as well as collecting insects had devoted himself to the study of the region's literature. He published several books and wrote over 60 articles in scientific journals such as the *Journal of the Malayan Branch of the Royal Asiatic Society*. Shortly before his death he published a book in which he had collected and translated 1,500 Javanese children's songs and rhymes. He was also an important entomologist and several species of ants and other insects were discovered by him, which now bear the name *overbecki*. Overbeck was South East Asian Director General of the Hamburg merchant house Behn, Meyer & Co, but he was actually more of a researcher than a businessman.

Overbeck seemed always to be in the wrong place at the wrong time. At the beginning of the First World War he was in Singapore. He was arrested and imprisoned by the British. In 1915 he was transferred to Australia, where he was interned in several concentration camps until he was able to return to Germany in 1919.

Ill. 41
A photograph of Hans F. Overbeck, taken during his internment in Australia during the First World War.

At the beginning of the Second World War Overbeck was in the Dutch East Indies and was this time interned by the Dutch. After the internment camp at Ngawi on Java he was transferred to the Alas Vallei camp on Sumatra. Here met Walter Spies. The two of them made optimistic plans for the future and worked on a joint publication. Both of them were on the *Van Imhoff*, which became the grave for them and the sketches and other material they had taken with them.

On the 25th of January 1942, the same day the survivors reached Nias, the Foreign Ministry in Berlin received the first news about the sinking of the *Van Imhoff*. Graf Rosen of the Swedish Embassy handed them a report which he had received from the Swedish Foreign Ministry in Stockholm. They had been informed of the sinking by the Dutch Embassy in Stockholm. A copy of the report was given to Walther Hewel. Some extracts:

Subject: Sinking of a ship carrying German internees from the Dutch East Indies by Japanese forces.

The final group of internees from the Dutch East Indies, who were being taken to British India, 473 internees in total, had set sail from Sibolga on the 18th of January on board a Dutch liner [...]. On board were an escort of about 92 persons and a security force of 75. The ship had telegraphed on the 19th of January at

12.30 that [...] it was sinking. A group of Dutch East Indies aircraft and a ship were immediately sent to the location to bring help to those shipwrecked. This ship too was bombed as it was on its way. The aircraft had seen lifeboats with people on board but could not land on the water because of the bad weather. [...] 75 internees remained in the Dutch East Indies. [...]
Legation Secretary Graf Rosen informed us that the Swedish Embassy would send a verbal note to the Foreign Ministry tomorrow to give the German Government written notice of the above information.
Berlin, 25 January 1942, signed: Ruhe[1]

As the testimony of the few survivors shows, the Dutch Embassy's report was simply false. The Dutch motor ship *Boelongan* sent to rescue the survivors refused to help the Germans in the lifeboat, and was not bombed. The weather was also not bad, the sea was extremely calm. The Dutch were sure that the men in the boat would not survive to report their disgraceful behaviour. They wished to cover up this war crime.

Then began a hectic series of telex, telephone and telegram communications between the Foreign Ministry in Berlin and Tokyo and the Swiss Embassy in Batavia, which was protecting German interests. The Japanese Embassy was informed by telephone and the agreement of the Japanese Government that rescue measures could be undertaken was requested. On the 26th of January there was a provisional answer communicated by the Japanese diplomat Kase and recorded by the Foreign Ministry as follows:

The Japanese army and navy had been informed immediately. The army reported that on the 19th of January no Japanese military aircraft had been in the vicinity of the island of Nias. The navy reported that a reconnaissance aircraft had on the day in question seen a Dutch ship about 100 nautical miles south of Nias and dropped bombs. It had not been possible to establish the result of the bombing. However, since a reconnaissance aircraft only carries light bombs and bombs of this kind are not capable of sinking a liner it cannot be assumed that this reconnaissance aircraft destroyed the ship on which the German internees were travelling. According to the Japanese naval command one should not exclude the possibility that Netherlands sources have interpreted the incident for propaganda purposes to conceal an act of violence of their own. [...]
Berlin, 28 January 1942, signed: Eisenlohr [2]

Now, however it is clear that the Japanese aircraft did sink the *Van Imhoff* with its light bombs. Ernst Heinrich Freiherr von Weiszäcker, First Secretary

1   AA, Akte Hewel, Document 84673 and 84674
2   AA, Akte Hewel, Document 84675 and 84676

of State to Foreign Minister Ribbentrop – the father of the later German President Richard von Weiszäcker – entered into the affair. On the first of February 1942 he reported by telex from the Westfalen Special Train to Ribbentrop with a copy to Walther Hewel:

News that a ship with German internees was sunk by an air attack on the way to British India was reported here towards noon on the 25ᵗʰ of January by the Swedish Embassy.

Thereupon following action undertaken without delay:

1. *Oral report to Japanese Embassy here concerning rescue measures by Japanese forces if possible.*
2. *Similar telegram to German Embassy Tokyo.*
3. *Request to Swiss Government to discover through their representative in Batavia the names of those lost and those rescued and to inform us by wire*
4. *Similar request to International Committee of the Red Cross in Geneva. So far we only have the two wire reports from the Embassy in Tokyo which naturally give no news of the numbers or names of those lost. Swiss Government and International Committee requested once more by wire to hasten their enquiries and to report on the condition and possible needs of the victims.*

The matter is being further pursued here.

Weiszäcker, by telephone on 1.2. on Special Train.[1]

The sinking of the *Van Imhoff* in the Indian Ocean was dealt with at the highest level in the Third Reich. Foreign Minister Ribbentrop was informed, Walther Hewel received copies of all documents and therefore Hitler was also in the picture.

The archives mentioned above contain further telephone notes, memoranda and other documents on the sinking of the *Van Imhoff* survive. The Foreign Office immediately made a detailed list of the names of 329 missing with their professions and dates of birth. The list was later increased to 412.[2] Walter Spies and Hans Friedrich Overbeck were already on the first list.

Telegram communication between the Foreign Ministry, and Tokyo, Bern and Batavia continued for some time until it could finally be established who had been saved and who was still missing. Telegrams and letters from relatives of the internees arrived daily at the Foreign ministry and the Central Information Office in Berlin, asking for information about their husbands and fathers. On behalf of the Reich Foreign Minister letters of condolence were sent to the bereaved. All the information came to Walther Hewel. It seems that – as with the internment of Germans in the Dutch East Indies –

---

1   AA, Akte Hewel, Document 84677
2   AA, Akte Van Imhoff Kult. E/Nf. (Zv.) 4986, 007

he also took over the co-ordination of efforts to deal with this catastrophe, playing a central role.[1]

As was only recently discovered, the Foreign Organisation [*Auslandsorganisation/AO*] of the Nazi Party under Ernst A. Bohle extorted a reparation sum of four million gulden from the KPM shipping line because of the serious charges against them and the two captains. Arthur Seyß-Inquart, *Reichskommissar* for the occupied Netherlands was brought into the affair. KPM did actually transfer the four million gulden to the account of the *NSDAP Auslandsorganisation* at the Berlin *Stadtbank* on the 29th of January 1944. The money was supposed to be distributed among the heirs of the victims of the *Van Imhoff* tragedy. Contemporary witnesses, however, reported that none of these heirs received any money – it simply disappeared into the Nazi Party's coffers.

Even while the war was still continuing KPM demanded the payment of half of this sum (2 million gulden) from the Dutch government in exile in London since as KPM ships were under the command of the Dutch Navy at the time of the incident, they were actually on state service. The fight between the two parties went on into the 1950s. Bert Röling, an internationally recognised Professor of Criminal Law and International Law at Groningen University, gave an expert opinion that the shipping line had a claim for compensation but that the actions of the two captains should be considered war crimes. Before the case came to trial, the Dutch government backed down and the Dutch Finance Ministry allowed KPM a tax abatement of 2 million gulden in September 1954. This settlement was to remain confidential. The Dutch government wanted to prevent the criminal actions of the two captains – and the admission of guilt that might be deduced from the payment being made – becoming public.[2]

Both Dutch captains, H. J. Hoeksema and M. L. Berveling should have been prosecuted for breach of the Geneva Convention and the international Search & Rescue Convention, but neither of them was brought to justice in the Netherlands. The crime was simply airbrushed out of history.

The *Van Imhoff* case entered the arena of current politics once more in the 1950s, causing tension between the Netherlands and the Federal Republic of Germany. At Christmas 1952 seven former Dutch Nazi collaborators and members of the SS succeeded in escaping from the Dutch prison in Breda.

---

1   Reports by survivors Albert Vehring, Gottlob Weiler and Bruder Aloysius;
     IfZ, Bestand Karl Helbig Signatur ED 353
     AA, Bestand Walther Hewel)
     Geerken, *A Gecko for Luck,* pp. 138 ff
2   Gräbner, *Die van Imhoff: Das Totenschiff,* pp. 83ff

They managed to cross the "green border" with Germany and went into hiding. The Dutch government requested their extradition from Germany. This was declined, based on a 1943 *Führererlass* [Decree of the Führer], still valid at the time, which automatically granted foreign citizens who had been members of the Waffen-SS German citizenship. Handing over German war criminals was against the German basic law and so the Federal Government refused to hand the Breda escapees over.

In return the state prosecutor in Düsseldorf presented a request from the *Interessenverbandes der vertriebenen Hollanddeutschen* [Association of exiled Dutch Germans] for the handing over of the captain of the *Van Imhoff*. On the 19th of August 1959 the Dutch Embassy reacted with a verbal note to the German Foreign Ministry and refused, twisting the evidential facts, to accept any responsibility. German witness statements were not accepted in the judgment and survivors of the *Van Imhoff* disaster were not questioned. The truth was not allowed to come to light. Until today, Dutch justice insists that there is no reason to investigate any wrongdoing on the part of the two captains, and the war criminals who escaped from the Netherlands lived, or still live, undisturbed in Germany.

The dreadful actions of the two captains must also be seen against the background of the preceding bombing of Rotterdam by the German air force. All Dutch captains at sea in Dutch East Indies waters were ordered by their commander, Admiral Helfrichs, not to rescue Germans. But according to Professor Röling's expert opinion, in international law orders that would lead to the commission of war crimes should not be obeyed.[1]

What happened to the German survivors from the *Van Imhoff*? After they reached the Island of Nias they were once more captured and imprisoned by the Dutch. But they were not behind bars for long. The Indonesian policemen who were supposed to be guarding the German survivors allied themselves with them and freed them on Palm Sunday, the 29th of March 1942. Now this alliance between the Indonesians and the Germans locked up the Dutch. Only a few days after their liberation the Germans, together with prominent members of the Indonesian population of Nias declared the Island of Nias to be the Free Republic of Nias (*Nias Merdeka*) with E. L. Fischer, who had represented the Bosch company in the East Indies, as Prime Minister.

The island of Nias was the first part of the archipelago that, with German help, achieved independence – more than three years before the official declaration of Indonesian Independence after 350 years of colonial oppression.

---

1   Gräbner, *Die van Imhoff: Das Totenschiff,* pp. 100 and 105ff
     In this book there is detailed documentary evidence

The Free Republic of Nias survived until the Japanese occupied Nias a few weeks later and took the Dutch prisoners to work on building the railways in Sumatra and Burma. This Free Republic with its German involvement was a unique event in Indonesian history. I will return to Prime Minister Fischer and his exciting experiences later.

Today a memorial in Hamburg commemorates those who died on the *Van Imhoff* in January 1942. The *Van Imhoff* was the last ship to leave the Dutch East Indies carrying German internees. Tragically, they were all classed as non-political and non-dangerous civilians, missionaries and artists – like Walter Spies. And they were the ones who suffered

A few days before the departure of the *Van Imhoff* the KPM ships *Plantius* and *Ophir* sailed to British India from western Sumatra, carrying German internees. They reached their destinations safely. On Ceylon and in British India there were several internment camps. The Germans from the East Indies were first placed in a transit camp near Calcutta and then finally sent to the Dehra Dun group of camps at the foot of the Himalayas near the Nepalese border. These compulsory residences for civilian prisoners, with their double fence of barbed wire, were known as the *City of Despair*. Every fifty metres along the fence there were grim-looking watchtowers holding British soldiers and Ghurkhas with loaded guns.

Among the 1,500 prisoners cramped into the camps – Germans, Italians, Bulgarian, Hungarians, Rumanians and Finns – the Germans were in the vast majority. One barbed-wire-fenced section of the camp housed the prisoners from the Balkan states and other huts were reserved for German Jews, but in general the British made no distinction between the different nationalities. To them, they were all just "bloody internees". Only men were interned in Dehra Dun; women and children were in separate camps in other parts of India.

Eyewitnesses report that the internees in the dark, straw-roofed huts of Dehra Dun – in spite of poor food, tropical heat in the summer and icy cold in the winter – were treated much more humanely by the British than they had previously been by the Dutch on Sumatra and Java.

The massive camp at Dehra Dun held, as well as many professionals, officials, craftsmen, professors, teachers, doctors and lawyers. There were also famous personalities like Heinrich Harrer and Peter Aufschnaiter, who had been arrested during a Himalayan expedition at the beginning of the war: they later succeeded in escaping to Tibet.[1] There were also the well known ophthalmologist Alfred Leber and the Indologist and writer Walther Eidlitz.

---

1   Heinrich Harrer, *Seven Years in Tibet*, London 1952

F. Flakowski, who was interned in the Dutch East Indies and spent the last years of the war in Japan, supplied me with a great deal of information and documentary evidence from that time. His father, who had had a homeopathic medical practice and pharmacy in Singapore and later in Bandung on Java, was in Dehra Dun until the end of 1946.

After receiving a tip-off, presumably from the local Nazi Party office, the father managed to flee from Singapore to the Dutch East Indies, which at the time were neutral, just a few days before the outbreak of war. After the war started, the British allowed his wife and their two children to follow him. The family was now reunited, but were separated when they were interned after the German invasion of the Netherlands. The father was sent to Dehra Dun in India; the mother was interned with her two children in the Sindanglaja (now: Sindanglaya) camp on Java. The mother was later sent to Japan with the children, where they spent the war years in freedom in the big German communities in Tokyo and Kobe. The family was only reunited in Germany in 1947 after seven long years apart.

Rolf Magener worked for I.G.-Farben in China and India before the war. He managed to stage a dramatic escape from Dehra Dun with his friend Have. Disguised as British officers, they both reached Japanese occupied Burma, where they were at first imprisoned by the Japanese military and subjected to days of interrogation by the *Kempetai*. The Japanese suspected that they were British spies as they could not believe that an overland escape through the impenetrable jungle on the way from India to Burma was possible. They were finally released.

In Rangoon Rolf Magener was invited to a meal by the Indian freedom fighter Subhas Chandra Bose.[1] The meal lasted until the early hours of the morning because of their intense and interesting discussions. From Burma, Magener travelled by bus, train and air via Bangkok, Saigon and Taiwan to the German Embassy in Tokyo. He was only able to return to Germany in 1947.

After the war Rolf Magener became chief financial officer of BASF. When his book went on the market in Britain the proverbial British humour and fairness came to light. His description of his escape from a British camp in a British officer's uniform was read and reviewed with smiles and the recognition of a successful prank.[2]

In the Dehra Dun camp there were many professionals, doctors, engineers and professors. They founded a German high school where it was possible

---

1   Details on Subhas Chandra Bose later in this book
2   Rolf Magener, *Die Chance war Null; Our Chances were Zero*
     Rolf Magener, *Prisoner's Bluff*
     Heinrich Harrer, *Seven Years in Tibet,* Chapter 4

to take *Abitur* exams which had been failed or missed earlier in life. There was also a pre-medical course. These qualifications were later recognised in Germany when the internees returned home after the end of the war.

16. The Burma and Trans-Sumatra Railways

As a result of the swiftness of its advance to the South, the Japanese army had severe logistical problems. In Siam there was already a railway network, built by German engineers between 1891 and the beginning of the First World War. The network between north and south and east and west could be used immediately, but there was no link from Siam to the rich natural resources of Burma and the port of Rangoon.

To get to Rangoon Japanese freighters had to sail round Singapore and through the Strait of Malacca, which was becoming increasingly dangerous because of the increasing number of allied submarines. This meant that supplying Japanese troops and exporting raw materials from Burma were both risky and time-consuming. A particularly large number of Japanese ships were sunk by the Allies on the last stretch between the Strait of Malacca and Rangoon.

For this reason Japan wished to build a direct rail link from Bangkok in Siam (now: Thailand) to Rangoon in Burma (now: Yangon in Myanmar) as quickly as possible. On the Burmese side there was already a roughly 300 kilometre line from Rangoon to Thanbyuzayat. There was also a multi-track line in the normal Siamese one-metre gauge from Bangkok to the junction at Nong Pla Duk, in the district of Ban Pong. They urgently needed to close the gap between the two.

Work began on this single track line with multiple passing loops in October 1942. There were two work troops. The first, starting from Rangoon, consisted of 3,000 Australian PoWs. In the second, on the Siamese side, there were 3,000 British. Massive labour resources were needed for this gigantic project since the planned line ran through almost impenetrable jungle. All aspects of the work, such as 300 bridges, cuttings, removal of rocks or digging tunnels, had to be done by hand. To save time, bridges were originally built of wood although some of them were later replaced by steel constructions.

It was soon necessary to provide replacements for the work troops. Many of the PoWs had dropped out because of disease, exhaustion or death. All Dutch internees from the East Indies who were capable of work, as well as Allied PoWs – British, Australian and Americans – were now pressed into forced labour. They amounted to more than 60,000 men. There were also about 200,000 native workers from Java, Sumatra and other islands in the archipelago. For the most part the latter were volunteer labourers, because they had been promised good wages and good living conditions.

It turned out that the food, the accommodation in camps in the middle of the humid jungle, the hygiene and medical treatment were totally inadequate and did not correspond to what the volunteers had been promised. Their work was hard forced labour, just like that of the PoWs. Amoebic dysentery, cholera and malaria ravaged the workforce, both European and Indonesian. The survivors had to work even harder to keep to the timetable. They were continually compelled to work harder and quicker. The Japanese absolutely refused to allow the Indonesian volunteers to give notice and return to Java. Japanese soldiers who had 'lost their honour' were also punished by forced labour. Most attempts at escape failed: either the escapees were recaptured and executed, or they died in the jungle with its snakes, leeches and scorpions. There were frequent suicides: desperate men – both Indonesians and Allied PoWs – threw themselves off bridges. In the euphoria of victory, human life had little value in the eyes of the 10,000 Japanese guards.

Of the more than 60,000 European and American forced labourers about 15,000 lost their lives on the line, but of the 200,000 Indonesian labourers only 50,000 returned home. Over 150,000 Indonesians died here, a terrible death toll.[1] Small wonder that the Burma-Siam railway became known as the Death Railway.

If one disregards the great human loss, this project was nevertheless a masterwork of Japanese engineering. After exactly 12 months the 415 kilometres of the Burma-Siam Railway were complete; jungles, swamps, passes, and gorges had been conquered. Now the raw materials so important for the war effort, such as rubber, some of which was also intend-

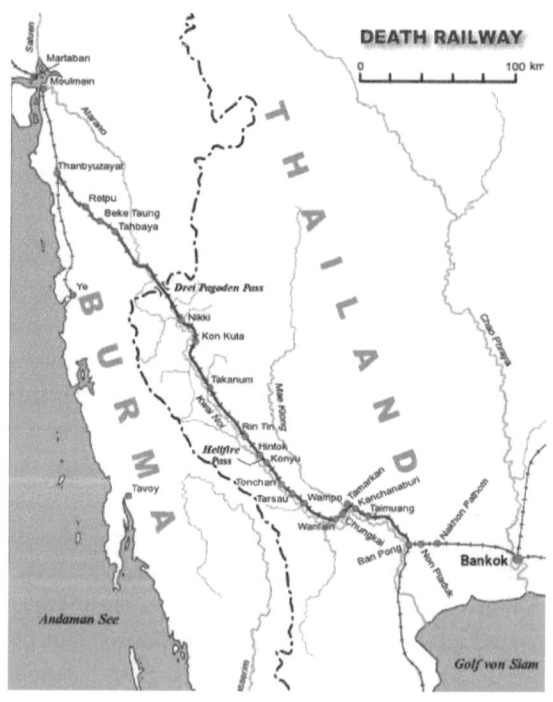

Ill. 42
Route of the Siam-Burma Railway

---

1   Mak, *Das Jahrhundert meines Vaters*, p. 340

ed for Germany, could be transported rapidly to the port of Bangkok. This railway line shortened the sea voyage by more than 3,000 kilometres.

In 1957 the film The Bridge over the River Kwai was made about the Death Railway. The line crosses the River Khwae Yai near the Thai town of Kanchanaburi, 111 kilometres from Bangkok. Both bridges, a wooden and a steel one, were destroyed by the Allies at the end of the war, and large sections of the track dismantled. The steel bridge was rebuilt by a Japanese firm in 1946 but never used. At the end of 1971 it was finally repaired and made operational. Today the bridge is a tourist attraction, and there are plans to rebuild the line to provide access to the international rail network by means of a Trans-Asian Railway.

Japanese forces had driven the British out of Burma with the help of Subhas Chandra Bose's Indian National Army. In the eyes of the Burmese, the British lost face because of this defeat, and they had to try to re-establish a presence in the lost territory. In Assam in the east of British India the British Major General Orde Wingate prepared the Chindit campaign. Specially trained special units of British, Indians and Ghurkhas were to carry out raids on railways behind the Japanese lines and cause confusion. They would be supplied with food and ammunition by air. Around 2,800 men were deployed in these operations.

Operation Longcloth began in February 1943. General Wingate commanded the northern group of 1,600 men and 850 mules. The group was divided into smaller units of about 400 men, each of which could operate independently of the others. The main aim was to sabotage the line from Mandalay to Myitkyina which was extremely important for Japanese supply lines. They succeeded in many places, cutting off Japanese supplies for four weeks.

Strong Japanese pressure on these British units meant that they had to beat a retreat through almost impenetrable jungle. Because of the strong Japanese presence it was no longer possible to supply them from the air. They now had two enemies to fight: the Japanese and the jungle. Hunger and malaria exhausted the British. Sick and wounded had to be left behind in the jungle – many of them were put out of their misery by their own side with a shot to the head. After four months Wingate finally reached British Indian territory with only 30 percent of his original force. The remainder were lost, had to be left in the jungle or were captured by the Japanese. For Churchill this failed mission was a great disaster. Nevertheless the temporary interruption of the Japanese railway line was the first positive news concerning British operations in the Far East and was highly praised by him. General Orde Wingate died in an air crash in the mountains of Assam in 1944.[1]

---

1   ZDFinfo, *Der Zweite Weltkrieg in Fernost,* 02.07.2013, 21.00h and 27.10.2013, 21.00h

A similarly spectacular railway project, though only half the length, was the Trans-Sumatra line. It is not as famous as the Burma-Siam project, but was just as demanding – and deadly.

The Japanese military headquarters in Sumatra was in Bukittinggi, about 70 kilometres north of Padang, a port in West Sumatra that could only be reached by sea. Because of the increased presence of Allied warships and submarines in the Indian Ocean the headquarters were becoming more and more isolated. And it was no longer safe to transport the coal which was mined in great quantities in the area using freighters sailing from Padang, so the Japanese engineers looked for a solution that would not only shorten the long diversion round the north or south tip of Sumatra for the freighters, but also secure the safe transport of the coal and other raw materials from the West Sumatra region that were so important to Japan.

Japan's coal-supply situation was already bad at the beginning of the war. The German Vice Consul in Osaka and Kobe, Dr von Braun, reported on the position to Hewel on the 19th of December 1939:

Supplies in the fuel sector are poor. There is no coal for newly built synthetic material factories. Electricity is being cut. The rice harvest was bad and transport is hard to come by.[1]

A swift improvement in the supply situation was urgently necessary. The answer was the Trans-Sumatra Railway. The Dutch colonial administration had begun on the construction of a railway network in West Sumatra in 1891. When the Japanese occupied Sumatra they found a line from Padang via the coal town of Sawahlunto 155 kilometres away, and ending in Muara after 177 kilometres in total. From there the line would have to be extended further north through jungle and swamp to Pekanbaru, in the middle of Sumatra. The River Siak flows through Pekanbaru and is navigable by larger ships from here to its mouth south of Dumai on the straits of Malacca. Pekanbaru was where the railway was to end. In the middle of the new section a short branch line to the coal mines of Sapa and Karu was planned as it had not been possible to exploit these major deposits previously. The Trans-Sumatra Railway was an important strategic project for Japan.

When the Japanese marched in they found not only the usable stretch of railway at Padang but also a large number of working German steam and diesel locomotives built by firms like Borsig, Hanomag and the Esslingen machine factory. The Japanese removed some of these locomotives for use in Cambodia and Burma.

---

1   AA, Akte Hewel, Document R 27.468

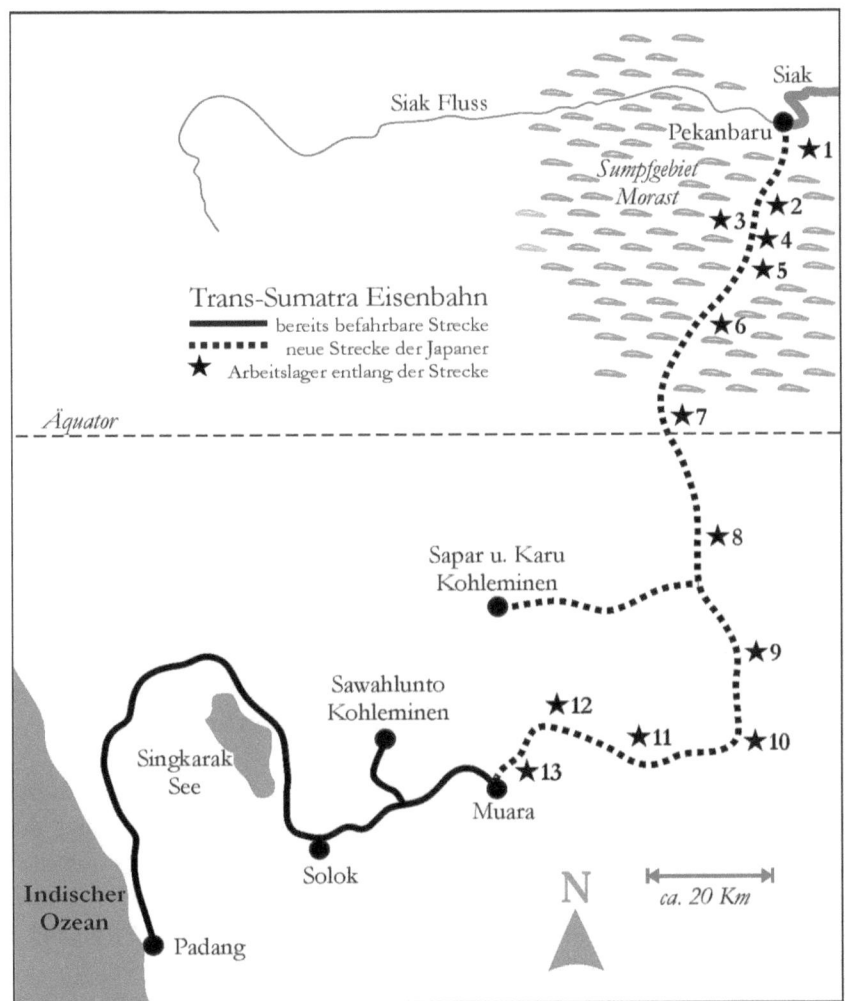

Ill. 43
The Trans-Sumatra Railway

Work on the extension of the track from Muara to Pekanbaru was begun in March 1944. Tens of thousands of Indonesian volunteer workers – mostly from Java – were recruited. They were promised good pay and working conditions, and were often tempted from their villages with band music and small gifts. When the working conditions turned out to be totally different and many of them wished to return to their home villages, they were forced to continue to work under catastrophic conditions. The Japanese called these forced labourers *Romushas* (Workers).

There was no proper provision for accommodation in the work camps along the line, food was in short supply and poor in quality, and there was hardly any medical attention in spite of the many tropical diseases. Working hours were from 7:30 a.m. to 6:30 p.m., with only a short meal break. The conditions were the same as those on the Burma-Siam Railway. It is estimated that between 100,000 and 150,000 Indonesians were deployed to build this railway, and the death rate was 75% here as well.

As well as the Indonesian forced labourers, thousands of Dutch, British, Australian and American PoWs and Dutch internees had to work under the same pitiless conditions. The basic daily food for all meals was rice, no bread, no potatoes, no pasta. This was normal for the Indonesians and Japanese but for the Allied prisoners it was extremely demanding. The mortality rate among this group was 35%. The loss of workers was continually made up by new batches of Indonesian forced labourers and Allied prisoners.

On the night of the 14th/15th of September 1944 the *SS Junyo Maru*, with the number 652 on the funnel, left the harbour of Tanjung Priok in Batavia. The *SS Junyo Maru* was already an old ship which had been launched in Liverpool in 1908. It was crammed with 6,800 "passengers", a 200 man Japanese crew and some guards. The passengers were 4,500 Indonesian workers from Java and 2,300 Allied PoWs and Dutch internees from camps on Java. The Dutch made up most of the second group.

The destination was Padang in West Sumatra, to take fresh workers to the Trans-Sumatra Railway's work camps. The *SS Junyo Maru* sailed through the Sunda Strait, past the volcano Krakatau and then northwards at a distance of 15 to 20 nautical miles along the western coast of Sumatra. To defend them against a submarine attack the ship was accompanied by two Japanese combat aircraft, a corvette and a gunboat.

On the 18th of September 1944 disaster struck. The ship was already just south of Padang level with Mukomuko, when it was torpedoed by the British submarine *HMS Tradewind*. After being hit twice the *SS Junyo Maru* sank within minutes. There were not enough lifeboats and life rafts on board. There was utter chaos. In the shark-infested waters very few survived.

Of the 4,500 Indonesian forced labourers, only 200 survived because they were locked in cramped conditions on the lowest deck and could not get off the ship in time. There was also the fact that many Javanese don't really like the sea and cannot swim. Of the 2,300 Allied prisoners just 680 were saved. The figures shift upwards and downwards depending on which source one is following or the accounts of the survivors. There was, of course, no passenger list. If you also add the dead Japanese crew and guards, the torpedo attack by *HMS Tradewind* under the command of Lt. Cmdr. Stephen Lynch Conway Maydon sent over 6,000 people to a watery grave off the west coast of Sumatra. Although this is hardly known in the western world, it was the biggest maritime disaster of the Second World War.[1]

The few survivors of the *Junyo Maru* who made it to the coast of Sumatra were set to work only a few days after the disaster for another eleven months eleven hours a day, seven days a week in the hostile Sumatran jungle. Many of them did not live to see the Japanese capitulation.

Work continued on the Trans-Sumatra Railway under extreme pressure. It is estimated that up to 100,000 lost their lives building this line. On the day of Japan's unconditional capitulation, the 15th of August 1945, the last rail on this line was laid. Now the first goods train could travel from Padang on the Indian Ocean to Pekanbaru on the River Siak. But no longer for Japan. The Trans-Sumatra Railway was built in a record time of 16 months, but at what human cost. Not a single train carried raw materials from West to East Sumatra for the Japanese. The war was over.

The Japanese were the first to suspect that there might be oil in the rain forest and the swamps around Rumbai, 10 kilometres north of Pekanbaru, and they drilled successfully during the occupation. Today there are major oilfields there. Since today's ocean-going oil-tankers are too big to sail up the River Siak to Pekanbaru, a pipeline was built linking Pekanbaru with the refineries in Dumai.

We should also note that the rails for the Burma-Siam Railway and the Trans-Sumatra Railway came from Java. The Dutch must have had massive reserves stored there. The German steel company Friedrich Krupp AG was the main supplier of rails and locomotives to the Dutch East Indies. To build the railway network on Java, 49,000 tonnes of rails were delivered from Essen in Germany to Java in the period to 1890. After that date the only lists are of exports to the Netherlands, without any indication of how much was intended for the East Indies. In the "Historical Archive" of the Friedrich Krupp AG (now: Thyssen Krupp) there are no more statistics about deliveries in later periods, for example the 1930s or the 1940s to the end of the war, because they were destroyed in the war.

You can still travel on some stretches from the time of Dutch colonialism and the Japanese Trans-Sumatra railway in West Sumatra. The PTKA Sumatra Barat, the West Sumatra Railway Company, has plans to revive the stretch built by the Japanese to Pekanbaru. There is also a new master railway

---

1   http://en.wikipedia.org/wiki/Hell_ship

plan to build a 2,168-kilometre line to cross Sumatra from north to south. Work is set to begin in 2014/15.[1]

1   William Wanrooy: *The Defining Years of the Dutch East Indies 1942-1949: Survivors' Accounts of Japanese Invasion and Enslavement of Europeans and the Revolution that Created Free Indonesia,* 1996
      Historisches Archiv Friedrich Krupp und Thyssen Krupp, Villa Hügel 1, Essen
      www.thyssenkrupp.com/en/asien/indonesien
      www.members.iinet.net.au/vanderkp
      ww.international steam.co.uk/trains/Sumatra

17. Second-World-War Maritime Disasters in South East Asia

A great deal has been written about naval disasters in the Atlantic. For example, on the 24th of October 1941 the German battleship *Bismarck* – Hitler's symbol of an imagined German naval superiority – sank the pride of the Royal Navy, the battle cruiser *HMS Hood*. Of the 1,419 man crew only three survived.

Britain was shocked. Churchill gave the order to *hunt the Bismarck* and sent the whole British fleet on the trail of the *Bismarck*. Only three days later the *Bismarck* was sunk in a sea battle about 1,000 kilometres west of Brest. 2,106 German officers and ratings were killed.

These are just two examples of the cruel naval war in the Atlantic, but who is aware that there were many comparable and even worse disasters in the waters around the Dutch East Indies?

I have already described the sinking of the *Van Imhoff* with 411 German victims and that of the *SS Junyo Maru* with 4,300 Indonesian and 1,620 Allied casualties. Bad as they were, they were not the only tragedies. Here is a list of the worst naval disasters in South East Asia during the Second World War:

- 1 July 1942: On its way from New Guinea to the island of Hainan in southern China with 1,053 Australian PoWs, the Japanese ship *Montevideo Maru* was torpedoed by the *USS Sturgeon* at the latitude of the southern Philippines. There were no survivors. This is Australia's worst maritime disaster to date.
- 28 November 1942: The British troop transporter *SS Nova Scotia* with around 1,200 men on board was on the way from Aden to Durban in South Africa. It was also carrying over 700 Italian PoWs who had been captured in North Africa. South west of Lourenço Marques (now: Maputo), capital of what was then the Portuguese colony of Mozambique in East Africa she was torpedoed by U 177, commanded by Commander Robert Gysae. The ship was not marked as being a prisoner transport. Only 117 Italians and 64 British were rescued from the waves of the Indian Ocean.
- 28 November 1943: The Japanese transporter *Suez Maru* was carrying 546 Allied PoWs from Ambon to Java when it was torpedoed in the Java Sea by *USS Bonefish*. There were no survivors.
- 21 January 1944: The Japanese ship *Ikoma Maru* was taking 611 Allied PoWs from the Palau Islands to New Guinea. It was torpedoed by the American submarine *USS Seahorse*. 418 men were killed.

- 25 February 1944: The Japanese transporter *Tango Maru* was sailing from Java to the island of Ambon with 3,500 Allied PoWs. It was torpedoed in the Java Sea by the *USS Rasher* with the loss of over 3,000 lives.
- 8 August 1944: The Japanese ship *Koshu Maru* was sailing from Batavia to Makassar, carrying 1,513 Allied PoWs: British, Australian, American and Dutch. It was torpedoed by the American submarine *USS Ray*. There were 1,239 casualties.
- 12 September 1944: As the Allies began recapturing more areas belonging to the Greater Asian Co-Prosperity-Sphere, all Allied PoWs and internees who were still in camps in the occupied areas were transferred to Japan. The Japanese ship *Kachidoki Maru* was on the way from Singapore to Japan with 900 British PoWs and a greater number of Japanese soldiers when it was torpedoed in the China Sea south of Formosa by the American submarine *USS Pampanito*. 250 British PoWs were killed. There is no record of the Japanese losses, which were at least as high.
- 12 September 1944: The *Rakuyo Maru* was also on the way from Singapore to Japan with 1,318 Allied PoWs, mostly British. It was torpedoed by the *USS Sealion II* with the loss of 1,159 lives.
- 24 October 1944: The *Arisan Maru* was sailing from Manila to Japan with 1,800 American PoWs on board. It was torpedoed by the American submarine *USS Shark*. Only eight Americans survived the disaster. With the loss of 1,792 American citizens this remains the USA's greatest maritime disaster.
- 17 November 1944: The *HIJMS Shinyo,* formerly the German liner *SS Scharnhorst*, but refitted by the Japanese as an aircraft carrier, was guarding a convoy of tankers and troop transporters from Japan to Singapore when it was surprised by the US Navy's submarine *USS Spadefish* and sunk by six torpedoes. Different sources suggest losses of between 950 and 1,130.
- 15 December 1944: *Oryoku Maru* was in the Bay of Luzon in the Philippines ready to sail to Japan. There were 1,620, mostly American, PoWs on board when it was bombed by aircraft from the aircraft carrier *USS Hornet*. 300 of the American PoWs were killed.

As you can see, the British, the Americans, the Australians and the Dutch caused the deaths of thousands of their own people since the Japanese – like the Allies and the Dutch – had not marked their ships as PoW transports in accordance with the Geneva Convention. The waters of South East Asia became a huge naval cemetery in the Second World War, for friend and foe alike. In the warm blue tropical sea thousands of soldiers, sailors and civilians went to the grave – a mass grave where no flowers grow.

18. Jewish Life in the Dutch East Indies and the Exodus of Jews from the Third Reich

There was a long tradition of Jewish life in the Dutch East Indies. There are reports by travellers as early as the 19th century of small Jewish communities in Batavia, Surabaya and Semarang. In 1850 Jacob Saphir from Jerusalem visited Batavia. He was informed of 20 Jewish families, originally from Germany and the Netherlands.[1]

In spite of some restrictions many Jewish families lived peacefully with the colonial rulers and the indigenous population. Most of them were merchants from the Netherlands. A second group were the "Baghdadi Jews" who were found in British India and the Dutch East Indies: their ancestors came mainly from the area which is now encompassed by the state of Iraq though at the time it was part of the Ottoman Empire. The number of Jews resident in the East Indies between the two world wars was somewhere between 1,500 and 2,000: they could be found in the larger cities such as Batavia, Bandung, Padang and Surabaya.

Although the Jews who had lived in the East Indies for generations co-operated peacefully with the colonial authorities, they were discriminated against in many ways. In Germany, racial laws were introduced under the Third Reich. In the Dutch East Indies they had been in force for decades. The Tripartite Racial Law (*Regeerings Reglement*) goes back 1854. It divides the population of the East Indies into three groups which were treated differently under the law. These *Bevolkingsgroepen* were:
1. European Subjects, i.e. racially pure Dutch and Europeans.
2. Foreign Orientals (*Vreemde Oosterlingen*), including Chinese, Japanese, all Muslims and unbelievers, but also most Jews.
3. Natives (*Inlanders*), i.e. the indigenous population.

From 1890 onwards all Chinese originating from Formosa – and that was the majority – were classed as Europeans. This led to a grotesque situation where Formosa Chinese who committed a crime were tried before the European court (*Raad van Justitie*) according to European law, while Japanese and Jews had to be satisfied with a local court (*Landraad*).Only in 1920 did the Japanese achieve European status – but not the Jews. The number of people of non-Malay racial origin we are concerned with here is shown

---

1   Encyclopaedia Judaica 1971, Vol. 8, p. 1363

by statistics from 1930. According to them, there were in the Dutch East Indies 240,417 Europeans, 1,233,214 Chinese and 71,355 Arabs.[1] There was apparently no census of the indigenous population. The statistics also fail to make clear which group the Formosa Chinese and the Japanese were assigned to.

No Chinese in Batavia, whether from Formosa or the Chinese mainland, could live outside the area designated for the Chinese. Compared with the Europeans, the Chinese paid double the amount of tax, could not own land – and only the Chinese had to be able to speak fluent Dutch to become Dutch citizens. There was a lot of harassment to make life difficult for the Chinese, the Jews and the indigenous population.

As Indonesian veterans who served in the Dutch colonial army KNIL (*Koninklijk Nederlandsch-Indisch Leger*) in the Second World War told me very bitterly, there is race discrimination in the Dutch government to this very day. It's *de Indisch Kwestie!* White skinned Netherlanders who were captured have the time they were in captivity included in the calculation of their pensions, and received compensation from the Dutch government. Indonesians and Netherlanders of Indonesian origin (the *Indos*), who served in the KNIL at the same time came away empty-handed. Even today, more than 65 years after the end of the war, they are still demanding equal rights.[2] The Dutch government's argument is that the Indonesian government should be made responsible. An absurd argument: the free Indonesian government defended their country against the returning Netherlanders. The Dutch Indonesians feel themselves to be discriminated against to this very day, and have recently handed another petition to the Dutch government.

In Britain, too, what could be seen as a racially motivated movement started in the 19th century. Where Hitler spoke of "Racial Hygiene" this much earlier movement used the term "Eugenics". The aim was the same. The British anthropologist Francis Galton suggested that people with a poor genetic make-up, like murderers or the feeble-minded, should be prevented from passing on those genes by sterilisation. This would lead to an improvement of what was regarded as positive genetic stock in Britain.

Winston Churchill was a major proponent of eugenics, although he sharply criticised Hitler's racial hygiene. He advocated the sterilisation of

---

1   Creutzberg and van Laanen, *Sejarah Statistik Ekonomi Indonesia,* p. 32,
       Wilson, *Orang dan Partai Nazi ...,* p. 100
       Furnivall, *Netherlands India,* 1944
2   Statements by people affected (like L. R. from the Netherlands. Name known
       to the Author)

100,000 "degenerate Britons" so that their genes could not be passed on to the next generation.[1]

In the USA such programmes were actually put into action. In 1909 in California alone 60,000 "mentally deficient" and epileptic people underwent forced sterilisation. Theodor Roosevelt was one of the supporters of this racial madness. American eugenicists like Lothrop Stoddart, were in personal contact with Hitler in the 1930s.[2] It is amazing how much Hitler adopted from the eugenics movement in Britain and the USA in his racial laws. As the danger of war became ever clearer and Hitler's rhetoric and the repressive measures taken against the Jews became ever sharper, an exodus of the Jews began. But where were they to find a new home?

To leave Germany and emigrate to Palestine was still possible at the beginning of the Third Reich, but also very complicated. As the travel documents of Eli Mayer show, the journey from Berlin to Italy via Austria and then on

Ill. 44
Travel Documents for Palestine for Eli Mayer, 29 May 1933
Stamps:
Exemptions for travel blocked. Berlin 1. 6. 1933, Foreign Exchange Control Office in the State Finance Office Berlin
1. 6. 1933: Exit Deutschland
21. 6. 1933: Exit Austria
21. 6. 1933: Entry Italy
11. 9. 1933: Visa for Palestine from the British Consulate in Trieste
13. 9. 1933: Exit Trieste/Italy
18. 9. 1933: Entry Palestine

---

1   3SAT, 20.01.2014, 22.25, *Der taumelnde Kontinent*
      Gilbert, Martin, *Churchill and Eugenics,* 2009
2   Spiegelonline, 05.01.2012

by ship from Trieste to Haifa lasted from the 1st of June to the 18th of September 1933. The Foreign Exchange Control Office in Berlin, at that time headed by Helmuth C. Wohlthat (mentioned above) allowed no exemptions, which meant that even at that time only limited financial assets could be taken out of the country.

Jewish emigration to another, presumably safer country was far more difficult than expected. Countries like the USA, Britain and the Netherlands baulked at the idea of taking in Jewish families from Germany. Britain even refused to allow most Jews entry to their mandate in Palestine and the Netherlands were the same about the East Indies. Roosevelt categorically refused to allow an increase in the immigration quota for Jews of all nations. Visa applications by Jews were deliberately delayed in the USA and Jewish families were subjected to insurmountable bureaucratic difficulties.

Decades before the Third Reich the British had been trying to find somewhere in the world where a Jewish state could be set up. They too wanted the Jews as far away from their own territory as possible. In 1917 Britain supported the idea of making Palestine the Jewish homeland. This was – as it turned out – merely lip-service.

At the beginning of the 20th century the British Uganda Proposal was the subject of great debate in the British Parliament. A Jewish homeland was to be founded in Uganda in East Africa. This proposal failed because it was unacceptable to the Zionist movement. Plans to settle Jews in Australia and New Zealand came to nothing because of the resistance of the local population.

Hitler revived the Madagascar Plan which had been developed at the end of the 19th century by the German orientalist Paul de Lagarde and energetically pursued by Henry Hamilton Beamish and Arnold Leese in Britain in the 1920s. Now it was Hitler who wanted to deport all European Jews to the island of Madagascar off the east African coast. This would – as Himmler wrote in his memorandum *Die Behandlung der Fremdvölkischen im Osten* [Dealing with the aliens in the East][1] – provide a final answer to the Jewish question in Europe. On the 25th of May 1940 Himmler handed this document to Hitler, who approved of the proposals it contained. In the negotiations for a peace treaty with the French Vichy Regime, the Madagascar Plan was one of the major points of discussion.

France was to make its colony in Madagascar available for the Jews of Europe. Over a period of four years 1 million Jews annually should be deported there. Madagascar was to become a Jewish state – or a super-ghetto? Italy's Mussolini, Marshal Petain of Vichy-France and Spain's General Franco sup-

---

1   DIE ZEIT Online No. 14, 4.5.1957, p. 3. In the English literature this transcript is entitled *Treatment of Alien Races in the East*

ported the plan. The confiscated valuables and bank accounts of the Jews were to pay for the cost of deportation.

In their daily press conference German journalists were given 'instructions' to keep them in line, and also told when they should correct what they had written. In an 'instruction' of the 28th of February 1939 we hear that a newspaper had published "Give Madagascar to the Jews". The instruction to the journalists was: *The German view is that the Jews should leave Germany. Where they go is a matter of relative indifference to Germany.*[1] After Free French soldiers, who were on the side of the Allies, regained control of Madagascar the Madagascar plan was abandoned by Hitler, setting off the long march to the gas chambers.[2]

As has already been said, during the Munich Conference in Munich in September 1938 Britain urged the Netherlands to cede the island of Sumatra to Germany. Did Britain wish to establish a home there for the Jews in concert with Germany? Possibly. But unfortunately no proof has been found as yet.

After Hitler took over in 1933 a wave of European Jews who were willing to move headed east. In Shanghai 15,000 German Jews arrived. In a very short time the Jewish community in Australia doubled in size. The British government which then also ruled Australia feared that the further "Import of Foreign Subjects" would also import a racial problem. Only 17% of Australians were in favour of allowing more Jews into the country. Australia only achieved independence in 1942 when the Australian parliament adopted the Statute of Westminster.

After "Crystal Night" in November 1938 the Australian quota for Jewish immigrants was raised – "on humanitarian grounds" but against the will of the population – to 4,000 per year, though limited to a period of three years. In actual fact only 7,000 Jews were able to settle in Australia between 1933 and 1939 as a result of bureaucratic obstructiveness.[3]

The Schacht-Rublee Plan, which I came upon by chance during my research in Jakarta into the activities of Hjalmar Schacht, the one-time President of the *Reichsbank*, is virtually unknown. Schacht was invited by President Soekarno to the young Indonesian Republic after the end of the Second World War to set up a new state bank and a stable finance system, of which more later.[4]

---

1   Frei/Schmitz, *Journalismus im Dritten Reich*, p. 30
2   Magnus Brechtken, *Madagaskar für die Juden*, 1895-1945, München 1997
      Heinrich Himmler, *Treatment of Alien Races in the East*, 1940
      www.forum.axishistory.com
3   Files Investigation Branch 1919-1946, Central Office, Canberra, File CA 747
4   Hjalmar Schacht's time in Indonesia is described later in this book

In July 1938 the Intergovernmental Committee on Refugees (ICR) came into being in Evian in France: it consisted of representatives from 32 states. Germany was represented on it, as were a British delegation led by Edward Turnour, 6th Earl Winterton, the politician Henri Bérenger representing France and Myro C. Taylor for the USA. The directors were the Americans George Rublee and Robert Pell. The aim of the committee was to ensure higher quotas in their respective countries for Jewish families from Germany and Austria.

It was not a success. No one could agree on quotas of any reasonable size. This failure led Ernst von Weizsäcker, First Secretary of State to Foreign Minister Ribbentrop, to refuse to take part in a second conference in August 1938 in spite of an official request from the British Ambassador, Nevile Henderson. Further internal negotiations between the ICR von Weizsäcker kept stalling because:

- Weizsäcker refused to agree to Jewish refugees being allowed to take valuables and cash with them,
- the states concerned – mainly Britain and the USA together with immigration countries like Canada and Australia refused to extend their quotas for Jewish refugees and
- Jewish organisations rejected the plans almost unanimously.

The Jewish side imposed a world-wide boycott of German goods and currency. This measure was used by the Nazi regime as an excuse to intensify the policy that had already been in force since 1933 of confiscating Jewish assets and excluding Jews from economic life in Germany. The tensions between the ICR and Germany as well as the other countries involved in the negotiations continued to grow. The result was that the borders of the countries bordering on the German Reich as well as those of Britain and the USA became much more impermeable for Jews who were driven out of Germany.

Shortly after the outrages committed against German Jews on the night of the 8th/9th of November 1938 – trivialised in popular parlance as "Crystal Night" – Hitler sent the President of the *Reichsbank*, Hjalmar Schacht, to London to try and achieve a breakthrough in negotiations. In London he negotiated with Rublee, the director of the ICR. He had good contacts with his friend Montagu Norman, the Governor of the Bank of England, who gave him his full support in the negotiations. Norman, like Schacht, was a member of the Anglo-German Fellowship, whose aim was to foster friendship between the two countries.

The result of the negotiations was the Schacht-Rublee Plan which now allowed for some financial concessions to the Jewish refugees. Although the plan was positively received by the US Department of State it was rejected by the Jewish organisations. In January 1939 Rublee came to Berlin to negotiate with Schacht once more. The result was a second Schacht-Rublee Plan whose provisions were somewhat more favourable for German Jews. Within five years all Jews were to be settled outside Germany. A trust fund was to make sure that all Jews should have help to start a new life in their new countries. As soon as the emigration began the Jews were to be freed from the camps. The Jewish view of this new plan was naturally divided, since it was still basically about expulsion and confiscation.

It is likely that Hitler found the concessions made by Schacht too generous, because on the 21st of January 1939, only a few days after the conclusion of the negotiations, Hitler personally removed Schacht from his post as President of the *Reichsbank*.

On the very next day Rublee met Hermann Göring, head of the Luftwaffe and Hitler's designated successor, in Berlin. Rublee wanted to see the second Schacht-Rublee Plan put into action as soon as possible. Göring promised to facilitate Jewish emigration, and in February 1939, only a few days later gave, Reinhard Heydrich, head of the Reich Security Service, the task of setting up a Reich Central Office for Jewish Emigration.

Helmut C. H. Wohlthat, who was responsible for foreign trade and currency procurement in the Third Reich, was directly answerable to Göring. Göring now ordered him to continue negotiations with Rublee. The effort to ensure greater entry quotas for Jews from Germany and Austria was renamed the Rublee-Wohlthat Plan.[1] We will meet Wohlthat again on numerous occasions.

When Rublee could not make even the slightest progress with the new German negotiator he resigned as Director of the ICR on the 13th of February 1939. The Schacht-Rublee Plan and the Rublee-Wohlthat Plan vanished for ever into the bureaucratic filing cabinet.

In 1941 Heydrich was entrusted by Göring with the organisation of a "Final Solution of the Jewish Question". The Holocaust and the murder of six million Jews in the concentration camps took their course. Hjalmar Schacht himself was imprisoned from 1944 until the end of the war in the concentration camps at Ravensbrück and Flossenbürg because of his suspected involvement in the attempt to assassinate Hitler on the 20th of July

---

1   *Das neue Universum*, Vol. 63, 1942, Union Deutsche Verlagsgesellschaft Stuttgart

1944 and his expressed criticism of the regime.[1] Schacht was opposed to the misappropriation of *Reichsbank* credits for armaments.

To solve the "Jewish problem", as it was seen by British and Australian eyes, Britain considered Jewish colonies in remote areas of Canada and Argentina, or even in the desert heart of Australia. In Australia, areas such as the torrid Kimberleys, on Melville Island, in the Northern Territory and in South Australia were suggested for the European Jews. The plan for a Jewish colony in South Australia initially had the best chances of success, but it was scotched by the veto of the then Australian Prime Minister R. L. Butler. Almost simultaneous with this rejection was the suggestion by the Australian businessman J. H. Catts that the plateau of Papua/New Guinea – 2,000 metres above sea level – could be used to settle Jews from all over the world. One argument was that this area was larger than Palestine and that it would make better use of the agricultural land available. No account was taken of the indigenous inhabitants of the plateau.

The South-Sea expert and businessman Heinrich Rudolph Wahlen used to send regular reports from this area to Walther Hewel. Wahlen frequently travelled for months on end in the Dutch East Indies, Australia, New Guinea, China, Japan and the South Seas. Hewel always found his reports very interesting. On the 28th of January 1939 he wrote to Hewel (extract):
Concerning settlement area for Jews: the British Government has asked their governors in the South Seas to investigate possible settlement areas in the South Seas. They are thinking of New Guinea's plateaus too.[2]

After 1944 no projects for Jewish settlement in Australia were pursued because the majority of the public were against them.

Today history seems to be repeating itself, but this time the plan has already become reality. Australia has once more used torrid Papua/New Guinea as a dumping ground – this time not for Jews from Europe but for refugees from Asia and other parts of the world. In the middle of 2013 the Social-Democratic Labour government decided to dump all refugees who were already in Australia and all future refugees in camps in Papua.

There are already Australian government refugee camps on the island of Nauru, to the east of Papua New Guinea. Until the end of the First World War

---

1   Yehuda Bauer: *Der Hüter meines Bruders. Eine Geschichte des Amerikanischen Jüdischen Vereinigten Verteilungskomitees,* Chapter 6: Der Beginn vom Ende
     Ralf Weingarten: *Die Hilfeleistung der westlichen Welt bei der Endlösung der deutschen Judenfrage. Das Intergovernmental Committee on Political Refugees,* Bern 1983
     www. geschichteinchronologie.ch/judentum
2   AA, Hewel, Akte 27.474

it was a German colony. It also played a role in the Second World War, as we will show later. Today the Republic of Nauru, with just 10,000 inhabitants on an area of 21 square kilometres, is the smallest Republic in the world. Australian phosphate extraction has done permanent damage to the environment: in 1989 Nauru took Australia to the International Court to claim restitution for the damage done. They tried to achieve an out-of-court settlement.

In 2005 Australia made an agreement with Nauru to take Asian refugees in return for financial support. In 2006, 2007 and 2012 refugees were sent to camps on Nauru. Today there are as many refugees as indigenous Polynesian inhabitants on the little island. Since the native unemployment rate is around 90%, this is a great burden and can only lead to social unrest. Nauru is 40 kilometres south of the Equator and has a murderous climate: the average daily temperature of over 30° C must be torture for refugees from, for example, the mountainous war areas of Iraq and Afghanistan.

At the end of 2014 Australia reached a secret agreement with Cambodia. For a payment of 40 million dollars Australia can now send its refugees there.

The Australian government now wants to force the refugees in Papua New Guinea and Nauru to settle there permanently. The Social Democrats and Conservatives in Australia's government are vying with one another to see who can produce the most inhumane measures for dealing with refugees. The former Labour Prime Minister Kevin Rudd said: *Asylum seekers who come here by boat without a visa will never be settled in Australia. This is our unshakable position!* Wealthy Australia is fobbing its problems off on poorer countries – as if they didn't have enough problems already!

The USA and Great Britain started an illegal war against Iraq. Australia was immediately ready to send troops as well. Tens of thousands of innocent civilians have since lost their lives. The country is in chaos and democracy is nowhere near. More is being destroyed than rebuilt. Hundreds of thousands of people from the region are trying to escape. The USA, Britain and Australia are responsible for this, so why is it precisely these countries that refuse to take in innocent refugees? The Iraq War started the firestorm in the Middle East. They wanted a war, but left chaos behind: the victims are simply collateral damage!

After the end of the Second World War the final turbulent years before the end of the British Mandate in Palestine led to further restrictions on Jewish immigration. The bloody anti-British demonstrations by Jewish nationalists in Palestine and the destruction of the King David Hotel in Tel Aviv clearly contributed to this.[1]

---

1   Isaac Nachman Steinberg, *Australia: The Unpromised Land*
     www.naa.gov.au

How is it possible to explain the fact that Britain wished to send the Jews to almost anywhere in the world except Palestine? After all, in November 1917 Britain had said in the Balfour declaration that it was prepared to accept a Jewish homeland in Palestine?

There was already tension there during the British Mandate because of Jewish immigration, and a new wave of Jewish settlers would have disturbed the balance between Palestinians and Jews, and it was feared that this might lead to a Palestinian Arab revolt. This would have led to an early loss of British power in the region. *Divide et impera* – divide and rule – was here, as with all colonial powers the principle by which they maintained control. Britain wished to postpone the formation of a Jewish state – Israel – as long as possible.

Here are some examples of the great difficulties faced by Jews even if they were among the lucky few who were able to leave Nazi Germany:

Until 1930 Jews were allowed to enter British-dominated South Africa, but as early as 1933 strict immigration conditions for Jews were introduced. In 1936 the *MS Stuttgart*, a *Kraft-durch-Freude* [Strength through Joy] cruise ship of the HAPAG line put in to Cape Town. On board were over 500 Jewish refugees from Germany who were met with loud anti-Semitic protest demonstrations by the South African right. This was the biggest single consignment of Jews to be allowed to immigrate to South Africa.

After the successful entry of this group the 1910 Alien Act was extended by the British-dominated South African government, making the conditions for Jewish immigration considerably stricter. The extended act came into force in 1937. Although between 1933 and 1936 around 3,600 Jewish refugees were allowed into South Africa, because of the Alien Act the number was reduced to practically nil after 1937.[1]

Within South Africa there were different opinions about the role the country should play with regard to the Third Reich. Ever since the territory had been colonised by the Dutch, the Boers, they had felt closer to continental Europe than to Britain. But British settlers obviously felt greater ties to Britain. There were major debates in the South African parliament during the Third Reich about which side the country should take. While some were unconditionally on the British side, the Nationalist Boers of the *Afrikaans Nasionale Party*, with their sympathy for Hitler, even went so far as to demand annexation of South Africa by the German Reich. In the Second Boer War of 1899 to 1902 the Boers' Orange Free State had wished to ally itself with the German colony of South West Africa (now Namibia). This was a major reason for the British to fight the Boers. After the British victory in that war South Africa was annexed to the British Empire.

---

1   Jüdische Zeitung, August 2006, Article by Brigitte Kirste and Susanne Zeller
     Brian Bunting, *The Rise of the South African Reich*

Four months before the beginning of the war the German ship *MS St. Louis* of the HAPAG line left Hamburg bound for the Caribbean with 906 Jewish refugees on board: men, women and children. The shipping line had got the Cuban government's agreement to take in refugees. You can just imagine how relaxed and happy the Jewish passengers were, how their eyes shone, how liberated they felt as the ship was finally on the high seas sailing westwards towards an assumed freedom. Their fear of humiliation, persecution and the concentration camps gradually dissipated.

But when the ship was already just outside the port of Havana the Cuban government changed its mind and forbade the *St. Louis* to put into a Cuban port. The ship was refused permission to land in any of the many Caribbean islands, and so the Captain, Gustav Schröder, decided to try his luck in Canada. There too the government refused to help. Now the *St. Louis* returned to the Caribbean and waited between Cuba and Florida in the hope that the USA would take pity on its Jewish passengers. President Roosevelt – whose commitment to human rights was as we know mere lip-service – was personally asked to intervene. The answer could not have been more dismissive: the *MS St. Louis* was forbidden permission to land in any US port and no help would be given to the passengers. No country in North and Central America would take in these Jewish refugees.

Fuel and provisions on the *MS St. Louis* were running out. The captain had no other choice: on the instructions of his company he would have to sail back to Germany with his Jewish passengers on board. You can imagine how great the passengers' disappointment and desperation must have been as the ship set course for the east, towards Germany. Some of the refugees unsuccessfully tried to take control of the ship. But where could they have gone?

On the way back to Europe Captain Schröder managed to get permission for the refugees to land in a neutral western European country. Schröder initially saved all 906 refugees, but when the German army occupied Belgium, the Netherlands and France in 1940 many of them fell once more into the Nazis' clutches and ended up in concentration camps – yet they had been so close to freedom.

President Roosevelt had many anti-Semitic advisors around him who had great influence on him. One of the most fanatical was Breckinridge Long, a diplomat in the State Department. He was mainly responsible for the rejection of the Jewish refugees on the *MS St. Louis*, and also for the delays and refusals of visas for Jews from Europe. Statistics were falsified to make the number of Jews who had already immigrated seem higher. During the 12 years of Third Reich he wanted to allow only one thousand Jews from Europe into the 'Promised Land'. These were to be kept in a closed camp and leave the USA after the war. They should not even be allowed to visit their relatives in the USA. But in spite of Breckinridge Long's negative attitude tens of thousands of Jews managed to make it to the USA.

In the USA the tragic fate of the Jewish refugees on the *MS St. Louis* was made into a film called *Voyage of the Damned* in 1976, based on the book of the same name by Gorden and Thomas. However, in this American film the dubious activities of the USA and Canada play a very minor role.[1]

Even in 1940 the Nazis were still allowing some Jews to leave Germany and Austria. On the 3rd of September 1940 four ships of the *Deutsche-Donau-Schifffahrts-Gesellschaft* [German Danube Shipping Company] left Vienna and Preßburg (now Bratislava in Slovakia), which is only 60 kilometres further downstream. They were the *Helios, Melk, Uranus* and *Schönbrunn*. There were about 4, 000 Jewish refugees on board, their destination was Palestine. When they reached the Black Sea, the refugees transferred to the *Atlantic, Pacific* and *Milos*, the Greek freighter *Atlantic* taking on 1,829 passengers. The three ships were to take the refugees through the Sea of Marmara and the Mediterranean to Palestine.

Though the *Pacific* and *Milos* arrived punctually in Palestine, the *Atlantic* was caught by a storm and had to be repaired. They were forced by the British to make an intermediate stop on Cyprus, then controlled by the British, and British troops came on board. The *Atlantic* finally reached the port of Haifa in Palestine on the 23rd of November 1940.

The disappointment was great when the British authorities refused the Jewish passengers on the *Atlantic* permission to land. The same fate had befallen the passengers on the other two ships which had arrived before. Immediately on arrival in Haifa they had been transferred to the requisitioned French liner *MS Patria* and were just waiting for the arrival of the *Atlantic*: then all 4,000 refugees were to be deported to Mauritius in the southern Indian Ocean.

On the 25th of November 1940 they had just begun transferring the first passengers from the *Atlantic* to the *Patria* when an explosion ravaged the *Patria*. Within 15 minutes the ship sank. There were hundreds of casualties, mainly because many of the refugees had been locked in on the lower decks and drowned.

All the surviving refugees were now taken to an internment camp on Cyprus and, a little later, deported to Mauritius, where they spent five years in the Beau Bassin prison near the capital, Port Louis.[2]

---

1   Reinfelder, *MS St. Louis. Die Irrfahrt nach Kuba, Frühjahr 1939*
     Schröder: *Heimatlos auf hoher See*
2   Ofer, *Escaping the Holocaust: Illegal Immigration to the Land of Israel 1939-1944*, p. 44
     www.wikipedia.org/Patria_Disaster

There are many examples of the way Britain prevented Jewish refugees from entering Palestine. For example, the Bulgarian ship, the *Struma,* carried 800 Jewish refugees to Palestine. The British refused to let them land there, and the Turks also turned them away. The ship sailed from port to port, from country to country on the Mediterranean. It was finally torpedoed by a Russian submarine and sank with the loss of all but one of the Jewish refugees and three of the crew.

There were also cases where German captains ignored orders from the German Ministry of Transport so that they could take Jewish refugees to safety. The passengers on the German freighter *MS Poseidon* (138 metres long, 5,864 tonnes) under Captain Nielsen were very lucky, given the circumstances. The ship set sail on the 4th of August 1939 carrying not freight, but Jewish families who were still allowed to leave Germany and hoped to make a new home in South America. When the war began on the 1st of September, the ship was near the South American coast when Captain Nielsen – like all German merchant captains – received the order to return immediately to Germany or to sink his own ship to prevent it falling into enemy hands. He was now under the orders, not of his own shipping line, North-German Lloyd, but the German ministry of Transport. Disregarding the order, Captain Nielsen sailed on towards South America.

The *MS Poseidon* had just reached the coast when suddenly the British light cruiser *HMS Ajax* appeared on the horizon and sailed towards the *Poseidon*. The warship, with a top speed of 32.5 knots (60 km/hour), was three times as fast as the *Poseidon* and was approaching rapidly. Captain Nielsen, sailing full steam ahead, managed at the last minute and without the help of a pilot to run into an unimportant Argentinian port. The ship and its passengers were saved.

The German authorities gave the Captain new orders to sail to Buenos Aires with his passengers. This seemed far too risky to him as the *HMS Ajax* was patrolling off the port day and night in the hope of capturing the *Poseidon*. He did not wish to endanger his passengers and refused to set sail. With the aid of the very helpful Naval Attaché at the German Embassy in Buenos Aires – also a captain – he managed to get permission for all the Jewish passengers to travel overland to their original destinations. With the help of the Argentinian harbourmaster and the pilot he supplied, the *MS Poseidon* succeeded in breaking the blockade by the *HMS Ajax* one night without being spotted, and set off back to Germany under foreign colours.

Near Iceland two British auxiliary cruisers caught up with the *Poseidon*. Now Nielsen followed orders and opened the valves and the fuel tanks, sinking the ship. The British reacted angrily, since Britain urgently needed captured ships: German U-boats had sunk 200,000 tonnes of the British merchant fleet in the first weeks of the war.

Captain Nielsen and his crew were initially taken to Britain, where they and other German sailors, German businessmen, 800 Italian PoWs together with Jewish refugees and British soldiers were put on board the *SS Arandora Star* of the Blue Star Line. The Germans and Italians were being taken to internment camps in Canada. There were also 500 wounded on board who were going to be treated in Canadian hospitals. There are differing accounts of the total number on board, but there were somewhere between 2 and 3,000. The *SS Arandora Star* (170 metres long) had been a passenger ship between London and South America and later, until the beginning of the war, a cruise ship.

The *SS Arandora Star* left Liverpool on the 2nd of July 1940. Shortly afterwards a torpedo struck her amidships. Nothing worked any more, the engines were destroyed, the electricity failed. Chaos broke out. Some of the lifeboats were destroyed or could not be let down into the water. Within just 35 minutes the ship had sunk.

The German U-boat that had torpedoed the *SS Arandora Star* was U 47, commanded by Lieutenant Günther Prien, famous for his daring escapade in Scapa Flow. Prien had slipped into the narrow bay of Scapa Flow in southern Scotland with his submarine on the 14th of October 1939 and sunk the battleship *HMS Royal Oak* with its crew of over 800 men. U 47 escaped unharmed. Nazi propaganda obviously made a great deal of this success. Prien had torpedoed the *Arandora Star* because he thought she was a British troop transport. The ship had not been marked with a red cross, which it should have been according to the Geneva Convention as a transport for PoWs, internees, civilians and wounded.

Of the up to 3,000 on board, only 800 survived, including Captain Nielsen. One of the victims was Captain Buhrfein. He had saved his ship, the freighter *Adolph Woermann,* from capture by the British by scuttling it. Before he drowned in the icy waves of the North Sea he had rescued many of the passengers. For his heroism he was posthumously decorated by the British government.[1]

The liner *TS Bremen* was a dream ship, the pride and joy of North German Lloyd and the whole German merchant fleet. With its four turbines, four propellers and 135,000 horse-power it won the Blue Riband for the fastest Atlantic crossing in 1929. On the 22nd of August 1939 the ship left

---

1   Brenneke, *Schwarze Schiffe,* pp. 97-101
      London Express News
      www.wikipedia.org/SS_Arandora_Star

Ill. 45
Article from the London Daily Express 1960

Bremerhaven for New York. On board, apart from the 1,000 crew members, were 1,800 passengers, almost exclusively Jewish families who wished to take this last chance of escaping from Germany.

Shortly before reaching New York and just before the outbreak of war, Captain Adolf Ahrens received orders from the shipping line to turn round and make for a German port with all speed. He ignored the order, and continued to New York where he landed all his passengers safely and punctually. He received a repeated order to return to Germany immediately and without passengers. The ship was being refuelled by Standard Oil, an American company that worked closely with Germany.

The departure of the *Bremen* was delayed by the interference and invented complaints of the British for almost two days. They wished to gain time to get their warships into position to capture or sink the *Bremen*. Finally, on 30th August 1939 – just one day before the outbreak of war – the *Bremen* weighed anchor for her homeward voyage. By this time the British Admiral Forbes had collected several warships together in the Atlantic. His orders were that the *Bremen* should not be allowed to get away. Immediately after leaving New York Captain Ahrens had the gigantic ship – 290 metres long – painted in camouflage grey. At the same time he made preparations to scuttle her – she was not to be captured, which would have been a great propaganda coup for the British.

At full steam ahead – 29 knots, almost 54 km/hour – the *Bremen* headed northeast towards the Polar Sea. Untroubled by the British fleet, the *Bremen* reached the Russian port of Murmansk in the Bay of Kola near the Norwegian border. She had succeeded in breaking the blockade.

At that time the Soviet Union was still neutral. When war broke out between Finland and the Soviet Union three months later the *Bremen* made another daring attempt to escape the blockade on a foggy, snowy, dark polar night. Captain Ahrens was lucky once again. He brought the ship safely back to a German port. These examples show how some German captains disobeyed orders to save Jewish families.[1]

The Dutch treatment of Jewish refugees who wished to escape to the Netherlands during the Third Reich was no better than that Britain and the USA. After Crystal Night in particular thousands of German Jews wanted to escape to the Netherlands. They were hoping to be safe from the Nazis there or in the Dutch East Indies. In 1930 F. A. Schöppel had produced a booklet entitled *Einreise, Aufenthalt und Ansiedlung in Niederländisch-Indien* [Entry, residence and settlement in the Dutch East Indies]. Presumably this was not meant simply as a guide for Jews who were willing to emigrate.

Masses of German Jews thronged to the German-Dutch border in 1939, but the Dutch government refused them entry. They had set a quota of 7,000 German Jews per year which could not be exceeded. That meant that only 20 people per day could enter. Dutch Prime Minister Colijn explained that the Netherlands would otherwise "become too full". They planned to have a camp near Ermelo for the Jewish refugees that they did accept, but this was vetoed by Queen Wilhelmina, who did not want a Jewish refugee camp near her summer residence.[2]

Of the roughly 140,000 Jews living in the Netherlands only 40,000 survived the Second World War. Next to Poland, the Netherlands had the highest death rate among Jewish citizens at 75%. The lowest death rate with 'only' 2% was in Denmark.[3] This does not, however, mean that the Dutch were more anti-Semitic than their neighbours. Quite the contrary: when the leader of the *Nationaal-Socialistische Beweging* NSB, Anton Adriaan Mussert,

---

1   Ahrens, *Die Siegesfahrt der Bremen*

     AA, Akte Botschafter Moskau, Graf von der Schulenburg

2   Mak, *Das Jahrhundert meines Vaters,* p. 211

3   Mak, *Das Jahrhundert meines Vaters,* p. 305

took over the party programme of Hitler's NSDAP, he omitted the anti-Semitic passages. In my view the behaviour of the Dutch was due to their submission to the authority of their German occupiers. They didn't wish to break any laws, and so in a disciplined and pedantic way registered their Jewish neighbours. The Dutch bureaucratic apparatus – admittedly now in the service of the Nazis – continued to function perfectly smoothly. The Dutch arrested Jews, collected them, and then the trains of the Dutch railway, *Nederlandse Spoorwegen,* transported them to certain death in the east. Acts of sabotage were rare and very few Dutch people gave Jews refuge. In the Netherlands – as in Germany – there was a lack of civil courage.

Very few Jews from Europe succeeded in emigrating to the Dutch East Indies after 1933, and even there they were subjected to persecution and terror. German Jews in the East Indies were in a paradoxical situation: they had fled Germany to escape Hitler's concentration camps, but the Dutch there made no distinction between Jews and Germans. When the Germans occupied the Netherlands in 1940, German Jews in the East Indies were arrested by the colonial authorities and interned in camps even though the Dutch East Indies were on the side of the Allies. It was a particularly ironic tragedy that Jews who had escaped from Europe to a country where they assumed they would be safe were now, like all Germans, treated by the Dutch as criminals and put behind barbed wire.

Many Jews were put in the internment camp at Tangerang, west of Batavia. Women and children were kept in separate accommodation. In the *Adek* internment camp in Batavia the "Baghdadi Jews" were separated from the new immigrants. Others were sent to the *Werfstraat* prison in Surabaya. In the infamous *Ngawi* camp in eastern Java Jewish and German men were crammed in together.

After the Japanese occupied the Dutch East Indies in 1942, the Germans were freed, but not the German Jews. Now the Dutch were put behind bars with the Jews. As many Jews later reported, in all the camps non-Jews were fed sooner and better than the Jews – first by the Dutch and then the Japanese. There was discrimination everywhere. The Jewish men were put to forced labour together with the Dutch by the Japanese occupying force on the railways in Sumatra and Burma. Many women and children never saw their husbands and fathers again.

After Indonesia's Declaration of Independence on the 17th of August 1945 there was total chaos on the streets. It was the time of *Bersiap* – Be prepared! Various Indonesian militia groups who had seized Japanese weapons plundered and killed every Dutchman or Jew they found on the streets. The Jews now felt safest in the detested internment camps.

There were cases where, as in Bogor in West Java, even after the Japanese capitulation, Dutch and Jews in the internment camps were protected from the Indonesian mobs by German sailors. The enraged Indonesians were trying to lynch their detested colonial rulers. German sailors and personnel from the German bases were armed by the British, who were the first to arrive on Java after the capitulation. Curious: the losers of the Second World War had to be armed to protect the winners from the indigenous population, the reason being that the British on Java did not have enough forces of their own to control the chaos that reigned after the end of the war.

It was a whole year after the end of the war before the Jews could leave the internment camps in what was now called Indonesia. At the first opportunity, many Jews returned to the Netherlands. When they met with rejection there as well, they tried to get to Israel. The voyage of the *Exodus* shows that this too was difficult.

One of the most spectacular post-war cases, which led to serious debate and was also filmed, was the journey of the *Exodus* to what was still the British Mandate in Palestine. The *Exodus* set sail from Marseille on the 10th of July 1947 carrying 4,515 Jewish passengers – families with children who had been fortunate enough to survive the Holocaust. Before sailing the *Exodus* had succeeded in attracting the attention of the whole world. When the captain refused to obey the British command to stop the ship off the coast of Palestine in the 18th of July 1947, British soldiers boarded the ship. There was a four-hour battle for possession of the ship with dead and wounded on both sides. The ship's radio officer reported live on the progress of the struggle. The *Exodus* arrived in Haifa on the 20th of July escorted by British warships. The Jewish refugees were transferred to three ships and sent back to Marseille, where they arrived on the 29th of July.

When the passengers refused to leave the ship for over three weeks, they were sent to Hamburg under pressure from the British. There the families were taken of the ships by force by British forces personnel under the eyes of the world's press, and taken to internment camps. Resistance was punished by withholding food. The reaction of the international press was devastating and contributed to the creation of the state of Israel earlier than the British wished. I have already explained the background to these unusually brutal British actions: they were aimed solely at preserving British power in their Palestine Mandate.[1]

To sum up, one could say that the USA and Britain with Canada and Australia reacted too indecisively to the systematic expulsion and mass murder

---

1   Siebecke, Horst, *Die Schicksalsfahrt der Exodus 1947*
     Halamish, *The Exodus Affair: Holocaust Survivors and …*

of the Jews by Nazi Germany. Although some Jewish refugees were allowed into these countries it was usually too little too late – which is not meant to relativise the unforgivable Nazi atrocities against the Jews.

The coup d'état of 1965, which led to the fall of the first President of the Indonesian Republic, was followed by a wave of Jewish emigration. Many headed for Israel, though a small proportion remained on Java.

The Indonesian government still does not recognise Israel and there are no diplomatic relations between the two countries. Indonesia says that Israel must give way on the Palestine question and give up the illegally occupied areas and settlements in Palestine. By 1957 the number of Jews in Indonesia had shrunk to 450, and by 1963 there were only 50. There is little or no Jewish immigration any more.[1]

The Asian Games in Jakarta, a sporting competition initiated by Indonesia's first President Soekarno in 1962, was planned to be a counter-Olympics for the developing nations. Soekarno felt that the Olympics were no longer about sport but about commercialism and wished to provide an alternative. The delegation from Israel was refused entry – a restriction that lasts to this day.

There is hardly any Jewish life in Indonesia now. Only in Surabaya and on Bali are there two small Jewish communities of about ten members each. In Surabaya a building dating back to the colonial period was acquired in 1950 and now houses a small synagogue and a small Jewish cemetery. Most of the members of these communities – if they have not become naturalised Indonesians – have dual nationality. The older Jews mostly have Dutch and Israeli passports, the younger ones German and Israeli. That surprised me, given the extreme suffering Germany has caused the Jews. The answer was simple: Germany is the only western nation that issues Jews with a German passport as a second passport without great bureaucratic complications. So they travel to and from Israel with the Israeli passport, and use the German passport in Indonesia and other Asian countries. This helps the Israelis, and the Germans try to assuage their conscience by the action. The Indonesian constitution, the five pillars of the *Pancasila*, actually guarantees religious freedom with the belief in one God, but "Jew" or "Jewish" is not allowed on Indonesian documents. They simply indicate Muslim or Hindu.

---

1   Encyclopaedia Judaica 1971, Vol. 8, p. 1363

19. Walther Hewel's Diary

Walther Hewel has appeared frequently in this book, and now we will look at him more closely. He kept a very detailed diary which tells us a great deal about Hewel as a private person, as well as Hitler as a private person. Unfortunately only a small part of the diary, from the 1st of January to the 31st of December 1941, has survived the war. It is now in the Irving Collection in the archives of the Institut für Zeitgeschichte in Munich.

Interestingly, Hewel did not write his diary simply in German, there are also entries in faultless, legible Malay and others in jargon that is a mixture of Malay, a West-Javanese dialect and Balinese. It is difficult, if not impossible, to make any sense of these last entries. I assume they are in a code that only Hewel could understand. With the help of the journalist Iwan Ong Santosa some of the text was deciphered. At first glance they look like trivialities that Hewel may have written down in this mish-mash merely for fun, though it is also possible that there is some as yet undeciphered message concealed in the text. Some examples:

9 May 1941: *Awewe uben pagoh sanur andjing.* (makes no sense)

1 July 1941: *Führer schimpft wieder über AA. Sau-AA* [Führer rants about AA (Auswärtiges Amt, Foreign Ministry) again. Bloody AA] *[...] Down katjida libak.* (makes no sense)

7 August 1941: *Führer sakit. Sudah envems dina Lage. Katjidoh ansah [oder susah]. Ntembh peogoch dina bunker. Ocrang lebak.*
Roughly translated this could mean "Führer is ill. For several days already. He seems unhappy. Tense atmosphere in the bunker (The last two words *Ocrang lebak* make no sense.)

7 October 1941: *Führer erra katjida. Nten datang kaun makanan. Ori parenta bullit Panzer nten bisa ai pake anoe katjida Anjar sama balik. Nten ai bira kana Soldado koe oj. K.*
Rough translation: "Führer is confused. He was put in an unpleasant situation. Something was wrong with the meal. Did not come to meal, neither lunch nor dinner, even though he whose birthday it was had invited him to lunch. The few that look brand new could not be used. They are only as good as the old ones.[1]

It was Himmler's 41st birthday. Hitler's daily diary shows that he issued the order not to accept the capitulation of Moscow under any circumstances and that the Reich Women's Leader Gertrud Scholz-Klink opened an interna-

---

1   IfZ: Archiv ED 100/78 and Microfilm DJ-75

tional women's conference in Berlin.[1] Perhaps a reader of this book can make some sense of this Babel-like confusion?

In the 1941 diary there is nothing out of the ordinary about the Dutch East Indies, but there is no doubt that Hewel regularly raised the subject with Hitler and other leading figures at headquarters. For example:

22 February 1941, Saturday: *Boss in good mood. Long conversation about Netherlands Indies.*

3 June 1941: *Oshima [Author's note: Japanese Ambassador in Berlin] talks about Japanese spies in Malaya.*

The whole of South East Asia was at the time infiltrated by agents of the Japanese *Kempetai,* in order to be able to find and liquidate "Nippon's enemies" immediately after the occupation.

Walther Hewel showed continued interest in his beloved Dutch East Indies and remained in contact with the film-maker and author Victor Baron von Plessen (see Chapter 3 above) after they both returned to Germany: from 1937 Hewel had been a member of the SS, becoming an *SS-Oberführer* in 1941. Von Plessen, on the other hand, was no friend of the Nazis. The members of the *Deutscher Auslands-Club* [German Overseas Club] – whose members apart from German notables were mainly foreign journalists and diplomats – were invited by Baron von Plessen and his wife Marie-Isabel to their estate in Wahlstorf during the Kiel Regatta in 1939. It is notable that none of the guests appeared in uniform.[2] As the "Egmont Reports" show, Hewel also did not always uncritically share Hitler's opinions.[3]

A diary entry shows how close Hewel was to Victor von Plessen:

3 May 1941: *Lunch with Thesi and Victor von Plessen. Prepared Führer's speech.* Thesi was Hewel's sister. She was also, as we see from Plessen's guest book, invited to stay at the Wahlstorf estate in 1942: *11. – 23. August were glorious days for me. A thousand thanks! Thesi Hewel*[4]

Hewel and Plessen and his wife Marie-Isabel seem to have been quite personally close. For example, they had a *pleasant evening* together in the middle of the war. In Hewel's documents I found the carbon copy of a letter from Hewel to Plessen thanking him for the evening and for a signed copy of Plessen's book *Bei den Kopfjägern von Borneo* [With the Headhunters of Borneo]. In his letter Plessen had obviously asked if Hitler had seen *Island of the Demons.* Hewel's letter of the 4th of April 1941 from Berlin:

1   www.chroniknet.de
2   A photo album in the Plessen Archive in Wahlstorf documents this
3   IfZ, Archiv ED 100/78
4   Entry in guest book, Plessen Archive, Wahlstorf

Dear Baron Plessen!
I received your book with its kind dedication today and was delighted. [Author's note: Plessens Bei den Kopfjägern von Borneo only appeared in paperback in 1944. So this must have been the 1936 hardback edition] I will dip into it on my next journey. It was really nice of you to think of it.
My circle of acquaintances tell me that the film "Bali" has been well received and regarded by many as beautiful – that of course is only from people who do not know your "Island of the Demons". In answer to your question I can tell you that Führer has definitely not seen the film "Bali" because since the beginning of the war the Führer no longer watches any films except newsreels and purely military films. The film was shown in the Reich Chancery for the Führer's entourage. I saw it on that occasion, but the Führer himself has not seen it.
I still think back fondly to that pleasant evening that I spent with you and your truly dear wife and hope that we can soon repeat it – I hope you will call to arrange it.
With very best wishes to you and your dear wife, yours [signed Hewel][1]

It is striking that Hewel does not end the letter with his usual "Heil Hitler".

The diary entries for 1941 show that Hewel met Hitler almost every day that year. He was present at all official occasions, conferences and dinners for foreign heads of state or diplomats, often as note-taker. Here Hewel benefited from his long years of overseas experience in England and the East Indies as well as his command of a wide range of languages.

Hewel was always near to Hitler even when he was flying or travelling on his special train. After dinner, Hitler usually requested Hewel's company, and they often sat up late into the night discussing and philosophising. Hitler was very interested in Hewel's reports on Asia – as Hewel was the only person competent to discuss the region, since all the information crossed his desk.

Hitler and Hewel often watched a film before ending their evening. Hitler, who rarely went to bed before three o'clock in the morning, was a film fan, like most of the Nazi grandees. German film production was in full swing in all their studios until the end of the war. Heinz Rühmann, the darling of the German film public, appeared in five films a year, mostly in the starring role.

Hitler did not just watch newsreels and military films as Hewel had told Plessen. He was an enthusiastic watcher of Hollywood productions and approved the release of many of them for public showing in Germany. Germany was one of the most important film markets in the world, and so all the bosses in Hollywood deferred to Hitler's wishes and readily cut anti-German

1   AA, Handakte Hewel 4, R27472

scenes from their films for screenings all over the world. The leading Hollywood producers from MGM to Fox lionised Hitler, ending their letters to the Third Reich with "Heil Hitler"! As Nazi stooges all the major studios produced propaganda for Nazi Germany, including newsreels. From 1933 to 1940 about 225 Hollywood films were shown in German cinemas: in Hollywood only money counted, and for that the Hollywood bosses were even prepared to collaborate with Hitler.[1]

When Charlie Chaplin produced his Hitler-parody *The Great Dictator*, the Hollywood bosses tried to prevent it reaching the cinemas. The American press baron William Randolph Hearst even accused Chaplin of warmongering. But Roosevelt insisted that the film be shown.[2] The premiere took place at the end of 1940 and was one of Chaplin's greatest successes. Documents from the German film archive show that Hitler twice requested the film.[3]

Hitler's conversations as shown in Hewel's diary show new and unknown sides of Hitler's personality:

2 June 1941: *The* Führer sa*id: As a private individual I would never break my word. As a politician, for Germany – a thousand times.*

On the 30th of April 1943, when Foreign Minister Ribbentrop requested a list of all the treaties he had signed on the occasion of an anniversary, Hewel reports that Hitler burst out laughing because *very few of those treaties had not been broken by Germany!*

2 July 1941: *In the evening with the Führer for a long time. Philosophising about the origins of mankind.*

11 July 1941, Friday: *Conversation with the* Führer *about [Author's note: the German philosophers] Kant, Schopenhauer and Nietzsche. Hitler's view:*
1) Kant: Utilitarian, practical reason. First step towards freedom from thought dominated by religion. But philosophy for the use of national governments etc.
2) Schopenhauer: the greatest clear mind that every German should have read. Masterful in argumentation. Writes the best German style. Political reasoning, but since it is also purely rational tends towards defeatism. Also goes too far.
3) Nietzsche: More intuitive than purely analytical. Affirms natural law and conflict. Positive directions for action. Therefore the actual philosopher of National Socialism. Mussolini also very great admirer of Nietzsche.

3 October 1941: *Lunch with the Führer [...] Then with the Führer to the Sportpalast. Great speech – off the cuff. Incredibly devout.*

---

1   3SAT, 16.10.2013, Kulturzeit, 19.20
2   Dokumentation ZDF Info, 29.01.2014, 20.15
3   ZDFinfo, 28.10.2012, 21.45, *Der Tramp und der Diktator*

10 October 1941: *Führer at table: Christianity is a revolt against creation. It is a perversion of all natural laws, which even in the smallest process of fertilisation are based on conflict and selection of the best.*

It is always surprising how positively Hitler spoke about England/Britain, even though it was generally assumed that he had nothing but hate for the country. His private view was different:

8 September 1941: *evening at table with the Führer. Führer: [...] We Germans only feel empathy with Finland, we could have it with Sweden and, of course, England. A German-English alliance would be an alliance of people with people. The English only need to keep their hands off the continent. They can keep their Empire and the world.*

At another point Hitler says of Britain: *We don't need their colonies.* In 1937 Britain had rejected Hitler's proposal of an Anglo-German alliance. Communism was Hitler's arch-enemy. He was convinced that he could be the saviour of the world if he could – in alliance with Britain – defeat Communism.

16 December 1941: *Führer about Japan: Strange that we, with the help of Japan, are destroying the position of the white race in East Asia and that England is fighting with the Bolshevist swine against Europe.*

The white race meant the Dutch in the East Indies, the British in Burma, Malaya and Singapore, the USA in the Philippines and the French in Indochina.

The British historian David Irving wrote: *Hitler wanted an alliance with England. He also tried to avoid war with the USA.*[1]

Hitler's remark about Japan on the 16th of December came a week after Japan began the occupation of South East Asia. It is surely connected with the statement broadcast at the time on Japanese radio and reported in the Japanese press that they were going to *wage a holy war on the white race with one thousand million Asian people.*

In 1938 the "Destruction of the White Race" had already been announced in the book *Nippon Kakushin nosho* [On the Renewal of Japan]. Even such unambiguous warnings from the Land of the Rising Sun were ignored by the "white colonial gods" from Hong Kong through Singapore to Batavia. The colonial rulers in their overweening self-confidence continued to drink their cocktails and play bridge in their clubs until the Imperial Japanese Army was standing at their front door and shook them out of their lethargy and complacency.

1   IfZ, Appendix ED 100/78

Hewel's last diary entry for 1941 was on New Year's Eve:
31 December 1941: *Bad news from the Front. [...] With the* Führer *in the evening. Subdued atmosphere.* Führer said: *I'm glad that I can solve the greatest difficulties. May 1942 bring as much happiness as 1941. The cares can stay behind. It has always been the case so far that very hard times were a preparation for great events. [...] Listened to Bruckner's Seventh Symphony.*

In the first days of December 1941 the Russians in Moscow began their counter-offensive. Hitler's luck and success had turned. By New Year's Eve Hitler must have known that it would now not be possible to win the war.

Towards the end of the war in spring 1945 Hitler fell into total lethargy. He said to Hewel at Führer Headquarters: *Politics? I'm not going to engage in politics any more. It disgusts me so much.*[1]

Shortly before he died in the Berlin Bunker Hitler warned Hewel: *If you fall into the hands of the Russians you will be squeezed until your eyes pop out of their sockets and then they'll drag you through the streets of Moscow and put you on show in an iron cage in a circus or in the zoo.*[2]

There was surely no-one influential working in close proximity to Hitler who was more often with Hitler than Hewel. He had the gift of mediating between the various interest groups that surrounded the Führer. Hewel was the only one whose company in private Hitler sought, even though he contradicted him often enough. In the course of the war Hitler was surrounded by more and more yes-men. Hewel was the only one that Hitler trusted completely until the bitter end. Hitler could be cheerful with him and relax.

You might imagine that Martin Bormann, who as Head of the Chancery and Hitler's private secretary also saw him almost daily, had as close a relationship with Hitler as Hewel had. This is not the case: Bormann rose, especially after Hess flew to England, to a position of very great administrative power. He decided who had access to Hitler and who did not, and for that reason was very unpopular with party members and the military – and also with Eva Braun. But Bormann never became personally close to Hitler as Hewel did.

A comparison of the positions of Werner Koeppen and Hewel in the Führer Headquarters also demonstrates this closeness. Koeppen had a role parallel to that of Hewel: he was permanent contact man for Alfred Rosenberg, the Reich Minister for the Occupied Countries of Eastern Europe and chief Nazi ideologist in the Wolf's Lair.

---

1   Haffner, *Anmerkungen zu Hitler,* Frankfurt 1981, p. 166
2   Statement by Hitler's aide de camp Otto Günsche, Der Spiegel 15/1955

Ill. 46
Hitler with his staff in the Wolf's Lair, June 1940. Directly above Hitler's cap you can see Walther Hewel's head.

After 1941 Hitler seldom visited the capital of the Reich, Berlin. From now on his headquarters was the Wolf's Lair at Rastenburg in East Prussia. Hewel and Koeppen had similar positions there, but there were still major differences. Martin Vogt says in *Herbst 1941 im Führerhauptquartier* [Autumn 1941 in the Führer's Headquarters]:

Koeppen was, however, not in a position to take on a parallel role to Hewel's: the latter was not merely the representative of the Foreign Ministry, between him and Hitler the link that existed between Hitler and the "Old Comrades" from the old days was particularly strong. Koeppen could not hope for such personal closeness and personal influence. Unlike Hewel he was at best of secondary importance in the Wolf's Lair.[1]

Every day at meals in the Führer Headquarters, even when the number of gusts was large or state visits were taking place, Walther Hewel always sat at Hitler's table, unlike Werner Koeppen who was one of those who were normally assigned a seat in another room.[2]

1   Vogt: *Herbst 1941 im Führerhauptquartier,* p. XIX.
2   Vogt, *Herbst 1941 im Führerhauptquartier,* p. XIX and
      Documentation *Berichte Werner Koeppens an seinen Minister Alfred Rosenberg*

Hitler really disliked his Foreign Minister Ribbentrop. He often tried not to see him for weeks and discussed all matters concerning foreign affairs exclusively with Hewel. Hitler said things to the latter that show that there was great tension between him and Ribbentrop. Hewel's diary again:

1 July 1941: *Führer rants about AA again.[Author's note: Auswärtiges Amt (Foreign Ministry)] Bloody-AA etc.*

14 October 1941: *The Russian front is cracking at all the seams. Führer very optimistic. In the evening Schulze and I tell funny stories about "kepala orang". Führer laughed a lot and very pensive.*

'kepala orang', which could be translated as "superior" is surely a reference to Hewel's superior, Ribbentrop, whom they must have been making fun of. The Schulze mentioned here was Richard Schulze (after the war Richard Schulze-Kossens). He was an SS officer and from 1941-1944 Hitler's 'orderly officer and personal aide de camp'. He had been present in 1939 when Hitler signed the non-aggression pact with Stalin in Moscow.

7 November 1941: *Führer: I couldn't work under your boss [Author's note: Ribbentrop] for three weeks!*[1]

Surviving documents show that Hitler continually wished to marry Hewel off, presenting to him one lady from "good National-Socialist society" after another. Without success.

23 March 1941: *Morning arrival in Vienna. On the platform Führer wishes me a happy birthday. Very cordially. Evening dinner with Schirach. [...] Führer talks continually about my getting married.*

Baldur von Schirach, the Reich Youth Leader, had been married since 1932 to Henriette, the sister of Hitler's personal photographer, Heinrich Hoffmann. Hitler had also had a hand in bringing this couple together. Their daughter Angelika Benedikta von Schirach, born in 1933, was obviously not yet a possible candidate for marriage to Hewel. Baldur von Schirach collaborated with Heinrich Hoffmann on a series of very successful illustrated books about Hitler.

Hitler also frequently brought the daughter of Fritz Todt, General Inspector of Roads, responsible for building the autobahns and the U-boat pens on the west coast of France, into the conversation as a good match for Hewel. When the latter continued obstinately to reject the idea, Hitler became annoyed. This was probably the only time that there was ill-humour between Hitler and Hewel.

---

1   All diary entries: IfZ, Archiv ED 100/78

Hewel never lacked female company. He was certainly not a misogynist – rather the opposite. In his diary there are several entries about visits to restaurants and bars everywhere in Europe: in Rome, Paris and Lisbon. There are constant mentions of dancing and beautiful women: *Very pretty Englishwoman, pretty girl in bathing suit, Sigi even prettier, fantastic women, etc.* He mentions in his diary the first names – unfortunately only the first names – of lots of women he met. There was a massive selection.

Perhaps Hitler thought that Hewel would "calm down" if he were married and for that reason wanted to pair him off. An anecdote shows a personal aspect of Hitler's character in this respect. When Hewel, at an official dinner in Vienna, was surrounded by a group of attractive women, Hitler pushed a menu across the table to him. On it he had written: *You ladykiller! Just you watch out!* Hitler seems to have been particularly jovial when he was with Hewel, because Hewel's documents include a number of menus on which Hitler has written a personal or joking message to him.[1]

Hitler's mistress, later his wife, Eva Braun and her sister Gretl had trained in photography with Heinrich Hoffmann in Munich. Hoffman joined the Nazi Party in 1920 and began to photograph the party leaders, which is how he came to meet Hitler, becoming his personal cameraman and photographer. They became firm friends for life.

Eva Braun was 17 and Hitler 40 when they met in Hoffmann's studio. She became his mistress. Eva and Gretl were keen photographers and film-makers and were responsible for an extensive collection of photographic and filmed material much of which has survived.

They were regular guests at Obersalzberg and the Eagle's Nest high above Berchtesgaden. They always had a camera in hand, and in the films they took, which are sometimes shown on TV, Walther Hewel can constantly be seen in close proximity to Hitler.[2]

At Obersalzberg Hewel also met Gretl Braun, and they had a short affair. Evidence of this is a telegram sent by Gretl on the 17th of June 1942 to Hewel, who was at the time staying in the Grand Hotel Splendito in Portofino on the Amalfi coast in Italy. *Arriving 20 June by sleeping car. Connection via Milan-Genoa.* Although on this day the rearguard action in Russia was raging and Rommel just beginning his attack on Tobruk in Libya, they seem to have managed a weekend or more off in a love nest in southern Italy.[3]

---

1   IfZ, Akz.4770/72, David Irving: Notes on a first interview
2   N24, 29.08.11, *Eva Braun*
3   Source: AA R2749,1 Handakte 14. This file also contains letters between Walther Hewel and Gretl Braun, unfortunately in old German shorthand/stenography, which I could not decipher.

Hermann Fegelein, Himmler's liaison officer with Hitler, frequently brought his girlfriend Blanda-Elisabeth Ludwig, who acquired the nickname Blondie (not to be confused with Hitler's German Shepherd bitch Blondi), with him to Obersalzberg. After a very short time there was an exchange of partners. In June 1944 Hermann Fegelein and Gretl Braun were married in the presence of Hitler. This wartime wedding party lasted three days!

Statements by Hitler's two secretaries Wolf and Schröder suggest that Fegelein had an affair with Eva Braun. If Hitler got to know this that would explain Hitler's unrelenting severity towards Fegelein in the incident described below.

Eva Braun was actually in love with Fegelein, whose marriage to her sister she encouraged. After the wedding Eva said that she was now "at least" his sister-in-law. Shortly before the end of the war she told her friend Marion Schönmann: *If I'd met Fegelein ten years earlier, I'd have asked the boss [Author's note: Hitler] to let me free.*

Hewel was the only survivor of an air crash in Austria in April 1944. He was treated in hospitals in Salzburg and Berchtesgaden. During his stay in hospital, he wrote a curriculum vitae which he must have needed in preparation

for his marriage to Blanda. Because of his injuries the document could only be typed or dictated.

After leaving hospital Hewel married Blanda Ludwig on the 12th of July 1944 in Schloss Klessheim near Salzburg. Adolf Hitler was guest of honour.

Ill. 47
Wedding photograph of Walther Hewel and his wife Blanda, 12 July 1944

Unfortunately Hewel's diary only survives for the year 1941. The following years leading to the end of the war would surely have brought a lot of fascinating information to light, especially about the war in South East Asia, which only began in 1942 with the building of bases and the deployment of U-boats. I'm sure that Hewel played an important role in these operations, especially in the support given to the Indonesian independence movement.

Documents in the archive of the Foreign Ministry in Berlin show that Hewel's devotion to Hitler was not unlimited. From July 1944 Hewel was firmly convinced that the war could not be won. A small group around Schellenberg and Wirsing wished to compel the Führer via Himmler to a partial abdication of powers and a partial capitulation in the west. Hewel was very close to this group, but also knew that Hitler could not be persuaded given his dualistic way of thinking. For him there was only light and dark, victory or defeat, and no compromises. None of those close to Hitler could persuade him. What he now wanted was "Total War". Walter Schellenberg repeatedly urged Himmler *to end things with Hitler and bring an end to the war.* Himmler also urged Hitler to negotiate with the Western Allies. Without success. From then on Himmler acted in secret without Hitler's consent.

At the beginning of 1945 Himmler held secret talks with the Swedish Count Folke Bernadotte, the Vice-President of the Swedish and International Red Cross about the release of Scandinavian internees. This led to the release and transfer of 8,000 prisoners of Scandinavian origin to Sweden and a further 12,000 of other nationalities from German concentration camps. among them were 5,000 Jews. When Hitler heard of this, he saw it as Himmler's first breach of faith.

On the 23rd of April 1945 there were further talks between Himmler and Count Bernadotte. On his own authority, Himmler made an offer of capitulation to the western powers which was transmitted to Dwight D. Eisenhower by Count Bernadotte. Himmler wanted only to capitulate to the western powers while continuing the fight against Bolshevism in the east. When Eisenhower demanded that they capitulate to all the Allies – including the Soviet Union – Himmler is said to have agreed to this as well. When news of this reached Hitler, he was outraged and dismissed Himmler from all his party and state offices.[1]

Himmler fled with forged papers, but was captured by British troops. While under interrogation by the British he committed suicide by means of a cyanide capsule.

Hitler suspected Herman Fegelein, Eva Braun's brother-in-law, of having been involved in the offer of capitulation. Fegelein fled the Führer Bunker

---

1   Büttner and Voss-Louis: *Neuanfang auf Trümmern,* p. 99

in Berlin shortly before the end of the war. He was arrested a few hours later, carrying a case containing money and papers that were proof of Himmler's secret negotiations. On the 24th of April 1945 Fegelein – in spite of pleas for clemency by his wife Gretl and Eva Braun – was executed after a short court martial.

Hewel held an important position among the upper ranks of the Third Reich. Although he was clearly the most important person in Hitler's entourage even he could not persuade Hitler to capitulate. Germany steered straight on towards disaster.

20. Reasons for Building German Bases
in South East Asia

German-Japanese relations were traditionally characterised even before the Second World War by mutual friendship and respect, and their cooperation in military matters also went back a long way. For example, there is in the *Yasakuni* military museum in Tokyo a mortar which the German gunner Hans Wolfgang Braun constructed in Japan in 1639.

After a roughly 250-year period of isolationism under the Tokugawa Shogunate, the Meiji government that followed realised that Japan should actively import western science and technology to ensure itself a place among advanced nations. By the 1868 constitutional Oath of Five Articles, scientists were to be sought all over the world to support imperial rule. The Japanese then took numerous foreign experts into its service, calling them *o-yatoi gaikokujin*. This included military men like Sergeant Carl Koeppen in 1870 or in 1885 the Prussian Brigadier General Jacob Meckel, who is honoured in Japan to this day. Meckel was a student of Field Marshal von Moltke. He was a pivotal figure in setting up the Japanese Military Academy which he created on the Prussian model.[1]

In my family, too, there are early connections with Japan. My great-great-great uncle Carl Schenk (born 1838) took advantage of the opening of Japan to the world. After studying in Stuttgart and San Francisco he quickly made a name for himself in the field of mineralogy. He was invited to take up a chair in the Imperial University in Yedo (now: Tokyo). He was one of the western experts who made a fundamental contribution to the development of western science in Japan. The Emperor made him his advisor and "Minister of Technology". He is still honoured in Japan as the "Father of Japanese Mineralogy."[2]

Both Japan and Germany were strongly anti-Communist and felt threatened by Russia. Hitler regarded the Communists as his deadly enemies, and the Japanese had acted continuously to oppose the expansion of Russian power in the Far East after the Japanese-Russian War of 1905.

On the 25th of November 1936 the Anti-Comintern Pact was signed between Nazi Germany and imperial Japan, with the aim of combatting Bol-

---

1   Kerst, *Jacob Meckel*
2   Takeshi Ozawa, *Carl Schenk, the First Professor of Mineralogy in Japan,* Proc. INHIGEO, Japan, pp. 157-159, 2012 and KAGAKUSHI, Vol. 39, 2012, pp. 199-202

shevist activity in both countries. This was Hitler's response to the alliances that the Soviet Union had made the year before with France, Czechoslovakia and the Communist part of China. Other countries, such as Italy, Hungary, Spain, Bulgaria, Denmark, Finland, Romania, Slovakia, Manchukuo and Nationalist China joined the Anti-Comintern Pact a few months later. This was the first step in the direction of the Tripartite Power Pact.

Initially, however, the relationship between Japan and Germany was characterised by distrust. There was a fatal collision of cultures. Germans and Japanese lived in completely different cultures and worlds. Misunderstanding was rife. One reason for this initial distrust was China. The main aim of the Japanese moves towards occupation was to create a united Greater China under Japanese administration, while Germany had powerful economic interests in Nationalist China under Chiang Kai-shek. Germany was dependent of supplies of raw materials from Nationalist China and had running contracts worth a good 300 million Reich marks.

Japan's greatest reservation about Germany was the military aid and the provision of military advisors to Nationalist China. After the last military advisors, Colonel-General Hans von Seeckt and General of Infantry Alexander Freiherr von Falkenhausen, were withdrawn from Nationalist China in the middle of 1930s the relationship between Japan and Germany improved.

Günther Fust describes the events of the time as follows:

For the Germans recent days and weeks have been made particularly exciting by the impending recall of the German advisors. The German government had requested the release of the advisors from Chinese service, but there were always new difficulties. It almost looked as if it would give rise to a serious conflict between Germany and China.

One day in the middle of June [1938], as the situation became ever more tense, we were sitting in the Terminus Hotel: Colonel L., Colonel N., Major B., and we believed that conflict was inevitable. A telegram had arrived at the Embassy from the German government that left no room for doubt. That afternoon Marshal Chiang Kai-shek had given the general advisor Freiherr von F. [Falkenhausen] an equally clear answer. Freiherr von F. was also in the Terminus Hotel in a side room. And fresh news kept arriving: the German Ambassador will be recalled, a break in diplomatic relations.[1]

But it did not go that far. Chiang Kai-shek amicably released all the military advisors at a banquet. On the 5th of July 1938 the German advisors, accompanied by friendly words in the Chinese press, travelled to Hong Kong with their wives in a special train. Germany had decided for Japan.

---

1   Günther Fust, Diary part III, *War.*

Trust was built up by reciprocal naval visits, such as that of the German light cruisers *Karlsruhe* and *Emden* in Japan and the Japanese cruiser *Ashigara* in Kiel, but a fundamental improvement in relations with Japan only occurred when the pro-German and anti-Soviet General Tojo became Minister of War in Japan.[1]

Co-operation between Japan, Germany and Italy then led to the signing of the Tripartite Pact advocated by Hitler at the end of 1940. By 1941 Hungary, Bulgaria, Romania, Croatia and Slovakia had joined the pact.

Ill. 48
Japanese special stamp celebrating the signing of the Tripartite Pact.
Date according to Japanese calendar

Heinrich Georg Stahmer, who later became German Ambassador at the court of Tenno Hirohito, was in charge of the negotiations in Tokyo. In 1940 and 1942 he was also involved in the mediation of the Japanese-Chinese conflict.

After the signing of the Tripartite Pact it was Hitler who was annoyed with Japan. When he attacked the Soviet Union in June 1941 he had expected his ally Japan to support him and attack Russia from the East. There had previously been several major border conflicts between Japan and Russia. But then he discovered that Japan – without informing Germany – had concluded a non-aggression pact with the Soviet Union only a few weeks before the German attack, a pact that lasted till the end of the war.

From then on Japan and Germany seldom pulled together. Their relationship was plagued by mutual distrust. Another factor was that Japan was very concerned that after Germany's swift occupation of France and the Netherlands it would lay claim to their colonies in South East Asia.

Both nations acted more or less independently since they had different strategic interests. The German Navy's main aim was to destroy the British merchant and supply fleet, while Japan's main enemy was the USA and their target was the US Navy. Given the totally different command structure and organisation of the two nations, effective collaboration was very rarely possible. There were basically two wars being waged independently of one

---

1   Stahmer, *Asiens Sieg ...*, p. 56

another, one in the Far East and one in the West. The vast distance between the two allies played a crucial role in the exchange of war materials and technical specialists, passenger transport and the problems involved. The limited telecommunications facilities of the time also hindered the exchange of information.

Language was another barrier. Very few Japanese spoke German or English, and very few Germans spoke Japanese. Governmental talks always required interpreters. Nevertheless the Japanese Ambassador in Berlin, Oshima Hiroshi, spoke German and the Naval Attaché at the German Embassy in Tokyo, Admiral Paul Wenneker, spoke Japanese. The Japanese had a particular Asian mentality and a way of expressing themselves that was not always understood by their German partners, and the Japanese must have felt the same about the Germans.

However, co-operation between the German Naval command and the Japanese Naval Ministry Kaigunshō functioned better. They needed each other. Germany urgently needed raw materials that during the war were only available within the Japanese sphere of influence and Japan needed German technology for its war industry. Collaboration was particularly good in the "Southern Region", where German and Japanese personnel had to work closely together in the naval bases. This was particularly important, since the only way to exchange war materials, raw materials, personnel or military technology led through the Indian Ocean and the waters around the Dutch East Indies.

The main reason for the smooth running of the collaboration between the two allies in the "Southern Region" was the excellent relationships that the German Naval Attaché in Tokyo, Admiral Paul Wenneker, had built with his Japanese counterparts at the highest level and the fact that he had built up trust during his many years in Japan. The commanders of the German bases in the Dutch East Indies, Malaya and Singapore also fostered close personal contact with their Japanese colleagues.

Initially there were problems here too. The Japanese base commanders were higher in the military pecking order than the Germans. The Japanese were normally admirals, while the Germans were mainly recruited from the officer cadres of the blockade breakers and the submarine fleet. The Japanese, who were very concerned with preserving face, never met their German partners on an equal footing. This led at first to resentment among the Germans, but this was smoothed over by the intervention of Admiral Wenneker. With tolerance and loyalty on both sides naval co-operation generally functioned well. How great Wenneker's influence with the Japanese Navy was, and how well he was regarded by them is shown by the following incident:

At the annual dinner given by the Japanese navy minister Yonai for foreign diplomats and naval attachés, the Russian attaché had to give up the place next to the minister that was his by right as the longest serving attaché in Japan in favour of Admiral Wenneker. The Russian attaché left the dinner in protest.[1]

Collaboration between the German and Japanese navies began very early. Before the First World War the Imperial Japanese Navy ordered the armoured cruiser *Yakumo* from Germany. Several high ranking delegations of Japanese officers travelled to Germany to study the latest technology for use by the Japanese navy. Japan planned to have an eight-eight Fleet consisting of eight battleships and eight battle cruisers. By the terms of the Versailles Treaty, Germany was forbidden to build ships of that size, but they were able to give the Japanese a great deal of support in their planning. For this project the Krupp company delivered large amounts of armoured steel to Japanese ports. At this time several Japanese took up permanent residence in Germany. After 1933 the number of Japanese students at German universities grew considerably. There were also training programmes for Japanese naval personnel in Germany. More German delegations also visited Japan.

Efforts to expand the German navy were intensified towards the beginning of the war because the only ships that were ready for action were the "small battleships" *Deutschland*, *Admiral Graf Spee* and *Admiral Scheer,* which had diesel engines. The new heavy cruiser *Admiral Hipper* and the battleships *Scharnhorst* and *Gneisenau* had turbine engines and were not suitable for travelling long distances or for long periods of action, as would be the case in the "Southern Region". The German navy was very badly prepared for war.

The battleships *Scharnhorst* and *Gneisenau* should not be confused with the North German Lloyd liners of the same name: they were passenger ships. For example, the liner *Scharnhorst* made its maiden voyage at the beginning of 1935, while the battleship only entered service in 1938. The liner *Scharnhorst* was often called the *Scharnhorst II* to avoid confusion.

As a temporary solution the German navy created the "auxiliary" cruisers, which were intended to lurk "behind enemy lines" in disguise and destroy enemy shipping. They were normal fast freighters which had only temporary armour: they had been requisitioned by the navy at the beginning of the war and refitted. With minimal armament hidden behind camouflage, eleven German auxiliary cruisers were sent to distant waters as mine-layers and to capture enemy ships in 1941. To allow them to operate with the least chance of being discovered they operated almost entirely under radio silence. The experienced captains were given a free hand to operate as they thought best.

1   Krug, Hirama, Sander-Nagashima, Niestlé, *Reluctant Allies,* p. 137

At the beginning of the war the German Navy was far behind the Allies in terms of fighting strength. Hitler had completely underestimated this in his strategic planning. In spite of this, the Germans had a considerable number of initial naval successes.

Germany was well-disposed to Japanese expansion plans and the creation of a Greater Asian Co-Prosperity Sphere, and so it is no surprise that immediately after the beginning of the war, before Japan joined in, there was intensive military co-operation between Germany and Japan.

The luxury liner *SS Scharnhorst*, which entered service with North German Lloyd in 1935, was in the port of Kobe in Japan at the outbreak of the Second World War. The *SS Scharnhorst* and her sister ships the *SS Gneisenau* and the *SS Potsdam* were the pride of the German nation and symbolised the revival of German passenger and merchant shipping on the seas of the world. 190 metres long, a displacement of 18,184 tonnes – quite considerable for the time – and a speed of 21 knots (39 km/hour) they were among the giants of the sea.

Units of the German Navy travelled to Kobe to take the ship back to Germany, but since the risks of a voyage to Germany were too great the ship was first used as a depot ship for German blockade breakers. After the signing of the Tripartite Pact the *SS Scharnhorst* was handed over to the Japanese Navy. Japan intended to supply Germany with two valuable freighters in return when the war was over.

It was originally intended that the *SS Scharnhorst* should be used as a troop transporter in the Japanese Navy, but when Japan lost four big aircraft carriers in the Battle of Midway she was converted into an aircraft carrier with 32 fighters and bombers. From November 1943 the aircraft carrier, now renamed the *HIJMS Shinyo*, was in action as a supply ship escort. These supply ships collected raw materials vital for the war effort in South East Asia, some of which were then further transported to Germany by German blockade breakers.

HIJMS Shinyo was escorting a convoy of tankers and troop transporters from Japan to Singapore when she was surprised and sunk by the US submarine *Spadefish SS-411*, with the loss of almost the entire 1,200 man crew, as already described above in Chapter 17. The proud passenger liner *Scharnhorst* was now history.

The destruction of several large German ships in the port of Kobe, as previously described, and increasing losses among the blockade breakers required new ideas about how goods could be traded and personnel transported between Germany and Japan. When Germany declared war on the Soviet Union the mode of transport for raw materials that had been most important until then – the Trans-Siberian Railway – was removed from the equation. Sea transport by blockade breaker led to too many losses. The German naval command was forced to move to submarine transport, but this was extremely unproductive because of their limited load-carrying capacity.

When the Malay Archipelago and the Dutch East Indies fell into the hands of their Japanese allies, the Germans wished to build naval bases in the area in order to be closer to the raw materials that were so necessary, and which were mostly produced in South East Asian countries. Initially the Japanese government was very hesitant about agreeing to this request because they did not want to go against their own maxim for the Greater Asian Co-Prosperity Sphere – Asia for the Asians – by importing a new white race, namely the Germans. After Japan realised that the deployment of German submarines in the Indian Ocean and the waters around the Dutch East Indies was also in their interests, the building of bases for the German Navy began without delay.

The German naval command was well prepared for the deployment of its forces around the Dutch East Indies. In 1933 the navy had produced a *Handbook for the East Asian Archipelago*, dealing with the south western and eastern coasts of Sumatra, the Sunda Strait, the western Java Sea, the Banka, Riouw (now: Riau), Gaspar and Karumata Straits and the west coast of Borneo. With 715 pages, 304 illustrations and marine charts and 12 tables it was very precise and comprehensive. Supplements to the handbook were issued in 1934 and 1940, so that German ships were well-prepared for sailing in the waters of the Dutch East Indies.[1]

Several Malay phrase books were issued between 1933 and 1945: it was the *lingua franca* in South East Asia. In Germany at that time there were many families of which at least one member worked or had worked for the Dutch in their colony, and so an attempt was made to ensure that there was at least one crew member who could speak Malay on every blockade breaker – and later every U-boat. In some cases this was even the U-boat commander, like for example Fritz Schneewind, commander of U 511 and U 183, who had been born in Padang on Sumatra.

The officers and men of the U-boats sailing out to the "Southern Region" were extensively informed about and prepared for what they could expect in the area. A *Penang Booklet* and a *Shonan Booklet* are still extant.[2] The former was produced by the first commander of the Penang base, Captain Wolfgang Erhardt. Tolerance and loyalty towards their Japanese allies in spite of pos-

---

1   Werner Müller, *‚Bibliographie deutschsprachiger Literatur über Indonesien‘*, 1983, p. 63

2   www.die-feldpost-2-weltkrieg.de

sible misunderstandings are emphasised several times. The Shonan booklet was printed in Singapore by the Japanese "Navy Printing Department, 104-110 Anson Road". I was unable to discover whether similar booklets had been produced for the bases in Batavia and Surabaya.

The first page of both surviving booklets contains warnings about espionage: *Keep your mouth shut! – Be careful everywhere! – Trust no one! – Look out, there are spies about! – Strictest confidentiality!* This is followed by information about *geography, town plans, maps, climatic conditions, information about the town, and history* and in the Penang Booklet also about *the "glorious naval history of the cruiser Emden" in these waters,* about *facilities for recreation and excursions as well as convalescent leave,* about *local transport,* including for example the order: *It is strictly forbidden to stop passing cars.*

The chapter on *medical facilities* warns against unwashed food, impure water and ices and sexually transmitted diseases: *Be careful when eating and drinking. The slightest carelessness has the greatest consequences. Eating food from street stands is forbidden.* Consumption of locally produced alcoholic drinks – except beer – was strictly forbidden. *Every girl is a health risk! Without a condom disease is a certainty!* Ten per cent of the men in the first units to go to Penang and Singapore were infected with venereal disease.

The chapter on *Food* and *Behaviour in Public* includes the instruction: *Dress in Penang (Author's note: as in all the other base towns) must always be civilian. Suits must always be clean and the demeanour of personnel must be exemplary.*

All members of U-boat crews had to shave off the beards they had grown during the months of the voyage over before they were allowed to go ashore at the bases. This order had less to do with a neat appearance than with security: sailors should not be immediately recognisable by their beards. There were spies everywhere in the "Southern Region". In the section on *Shopping* there is a warning against using the black market, and so on. Officers and men were well-prepared for their posting. The same rules still make sense today.

After Japan gave its assent to setting up German bases in the region in the wake of the 1940 Tripartite Pact, preparations for bases in Penang and Singapore on the Malay peninsula began immediately. Batavia was already well-equipped because blockade breakers had previously been maintained and prepared and loaded for their journey back to Europe there. The construction of the base in Surabaya came a little later. Sabang on the island of Weh off the north point of Sumatra was primarily a Japanese base which was only shared by the German Navy.

Until the outbreak of the war the Indian Ocean was firmly in the hands of the British Eastern Fleet. The Ocean, completely surrounded by British possessions from South Africa via Aden and India to Singapore, was practically a British sea.

During British rule Singapore was the base of the Eastern Fleet and the seat of the Far East Command. In the period of Japanese occupation Singapore became capital of the Japanese "Southern Region". It was now renamed *Shonan*, meaning "Light of the South".

When Italy entered the war in June 1940, the British saw their transport routes for oil and other materials vital for the war effort threatened by the Italian-controlled ports in East Africa and the Red Sea. There was also the danger that after the occupation of the Malay peninsula the Imperial Japanese Navy would drive the British out of other areas like British India. The British Eastern Fleet was therefore reinforced by units of the Royal Australian Navy, the Royal New Zealand Navy, the Royal Dutch East Indies Navy and the United States Navy. German U-boats sailed the Indian Ocean, the Java Sea and the Strait of Malacca on the hunt for foreign naval and merchant shipping, initially with great success. As in the Atlantic this was not a war of conquest, but a war aimed at cutting Allied supply lines.

Documents seen so far do not show whether German ships also put in to Madagascar while it was still controlled by the French Vichy government or to the neutral Portuguese colonies in East Africa and Goa in India, but it seems unlikely. Mogadishu in Italian Somaliland (now: Somalia) was no longer available as a port for the U-boats because it was taken by British troops in 1941.

The Malacca Strait is today the busiest sea lane in the world with up to 2,000 ships passing through every day. About 25% of the entire world's seaborne trade uses this passage. It separates the land masses of Sumatra in the west and the Malay peninsula in the east. It is about 800 kilometres long, at its widest 300 and its narrowest a mere 3 kilometres wide. The most important towns on the Malay peninsula are Malacca and Georgetown on the island of Penang, with the island city state of Singapore at its southern tip. On the Sumatra side there is Medan with its port at Belawan and in the very north the island of Weh with Sabang. Even today this Strait between the Indian Ocean and the Java and South China Seas is made unsafe by pirates, but it is still the most important connection between the Atlantic, the Indian Ocean, China and Japan for trade and oil products.

It was therefore particularly important for Germany to control the Strait and the surrounding waters and secure access to the region's raw materials. Germany urgently needed tungsten, molybdenum, titanium, chrome, nickel and tin, as well as rubber for the production of tyres. The blockade breakers were suffering great losses and could no longer meet the demand for the war industry.

Tungsten and molybdenum were particularly important in the alloying of steel, the production of armour plating and shell-cases as well as aircraft and rocket parts. Although tungsten, the metal with the highest melting point, was extracted in small quantities in Austria, the supply was far too small to meet German demand. Tungsten came from mines in the Japanese occupied areas in China and Korea. Molybdenum ore was also shipped to Japan from Chile and Peru and then transported to Germany. There were deposits in the Dutch East Indies at Pulau Sinkap in the Riau Islands, in Halmahera, one of the Molucca Islands, in the north of Celebes and in East Java.

In March 1944 three Japanese submarines sailed for Europe to bring supplies of molybdenum to Germany. I-34 and I-52 were lost, only I-29 reaching Lorient on the western French coast. It was carrying between 30 and 50 tonnes of molybdenum and 150 tonnes of raw materials, which met the demand for molybdenum for a few months. There were also two tonnes of gold on board to finance Japan's expenditure in Europe. For the return voyage to Japan, she was loaded with remote controlled bombs, aircraft canons, ammunition and other war material produced in Germany. This was a successful example of how co-operation could work effectively and unbureaucratically, but this was not always the case. The loss of submarines I-34 and I-52 made Japan reluctant to send more ships to Europe.

In 1933 Rheinmetall acquired the Berlin locomotive producer Borsig AG and from 1935 onwards produced large quantities of tanks and artillery for the German army. During the war the company was merged almost in its entirety with the *Waffenschmiede Hermann Göring* [HG Armoury] (official name *Reichswerke Hermann Göring*)

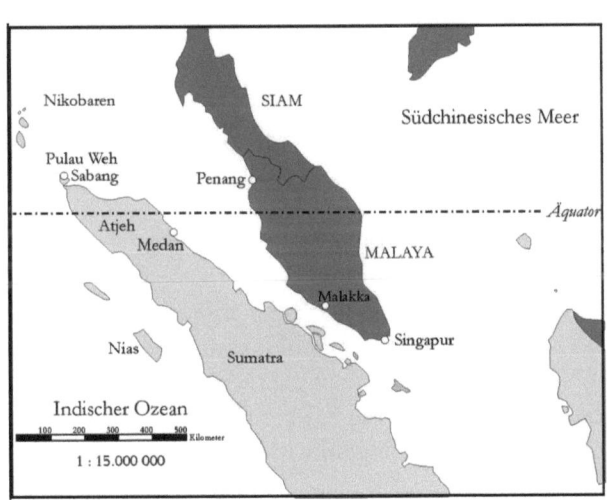

Ill. 49
Map of the Strait of Malacca

which fostered war production in the sphere of heavy industry. This was where molybdenum was most needed.

A further reason for sending the submarines was to meet the Japanese desire to study German submarine technology and use it for Japanese submarine production. There is only space here to mention in detail a few German U-boats that carried out spectacular actions. Over 50 U-boats reached the "Southern Region" and were deployed in Dutch East Indian waters. More of them operated in the Indian Ocean and on the east coast of Africa. Many were destroyed on the voyage out or the return journey. Since the exchange of newly developed war material and construction plans were mostly top secret operations there is hardly any documentation. Many transports to the "Southern Region" were so secret that no documentation was produced.

As the war grew more intense, the exchange of personnel and material between Germany and the "Southern Region" and Japan became much more difficult. Until 1942 German blockade breakers and merchant ships could still reach Japan, but after that this could only be done by submarine, which was much more demanding in terms of time and effort. The submarines often took many months to travel from Germany to the Far East, and a major disadvantage was the load capacity which was much lower than that of surface ships.

In the middle of 1943 The German air force planned a direct flight via the Bering Strait in Norway to Japan to speed up these exchanges. A four-engined Junkers Ju 290 long-distance reconnaissance aircraft fitted with supplementary tanks was originally meant to carry a crew of 4 and 2 passengers on the 7,700 kilometre flight. This plan was abandoned in favour of the further development of a larger version, the Ju 390. This had considerably bigger wings and six 14-cylinder BMW engines, each capable of 1,500 horse power. It was twice as big as the biggest US aircraft of the time, the B-29 Superfortress.

The Ju 390 made its maiden flight in October 1943. With a payload of 10 tonnes and at a speed of 500 km/hour the aircraft had a maximum range of 10,000 kilometres. From this point on it would definitely have been possible to reach China or Japan directly from Germany.

In American sources the technical specification of this aircraft and its operational capability seem extremely impressive. Their information is based on interviews with Anna Kreisling, a very successful Luftwaffe test pilot, who became known in the USA as the White Wolf of the Luftwaffe. She is said to have carried out the first test flights of the Horten Ho IX flying wing bomber and to have made several flights into Stalingrad with a Ju-52.

On the 27th August 1943 a Ju-390 with auxiliary tanks which would have allowed it to fly 25,000 kilometres without refuelling is said to have taken off from Norway with Anna Kreisling as co-pilot for a test and reconnaissance flight over the North American continent.

After a nine-hour flight at an altitude of 22,000 feet the aircraft is said to have been over Canada and then flown south. The mission was to photograph heavy industrial areas in Michigan. At about noon on the 28th of August the plane was sighted over New York by the US Air Force. They were totally surprised to see an unknown aircraft over the city which explains why it took far too long to send up fighter cover. The evening of the same day the aircraft was back in a German air base near Paris. If this information is correct, this would have been the longest reconnaissance flight of the Second World War.

American sources suggest that at the end of the war there were not two, but eleven Ju-390s in service. There was also at least one successful flight from Odessa in German-occupied Ukraine to Nationalist China and Japan. This flight to Japan or South-East Asia was confirmed by Albert Speer to the War Crimes Tribunal in Nuremberg. However, there is no information in German sources.

After the war Anna Kreisling is said to have worked for the USAF. She gave several interviews about her flight to America in the US press, for example in the November/December 1965 issue of the magazine *Air Progress*. In Germany I could find no clear evidence of her and her flight to America. Sensation, fiction or truth?[1]

One flight that is confirmed is that of an Italian aircraft to Japan. On the 30th of June 1942 a Savoia-Marchetti SM 75 trimotor with auxiliary tanks took off from Rome. After an intermediate landing in German-occupied Ukraine, the aircraft reached Japanese-occupied Nationalist China on the 2nd of July, and Tokyo a day later. On the 20th of July 1942 it returned safely to its home airfield in Rome. A planned second flight to take the Indian freedom fighter Subhas Chandra Bose from Rome to Tokyo did not take place.

The representative of the DNB [*Deutsche Nachrichten Büro*, the main German press agency] in Chungking (now: Chongqing), Wolf Schenke, presented a feasibility study for a flight-connection between Nationalist China and Germany via Russian Central Asia to Walther Hewel on the 7th of August 1940. Since Germany was already developing the relevant aircraft, he requested that it be swiftly implemented. I could not find a reply from Hewel.

---

1   http://www.myheimat.de/gersthofen/gedanken/luftwaffe-over-new-york-a-ww2-secret-d2522402.html

A Japanese air force aircraft carrying high-ranking General Staff officers took off from Singapore in 1944 heading for Germany. Some sources suggest that this first and only flight to Europe by the Japanese air force took place on the 1ˢᵗ of August 1943. Were there perhaps two flights? I trust the evidence of the German Ambassador, Stahmer, who said that it was in 1944. They were supposed to be attempting a non-stop flight on the southern route via India and Arabia to Europe. The aircraft never reached its destination and was declared missing.[1]

It is difficult to understand today why there were no regular German flights to the Far East, as Lufthansa and its pilots already had experience of the route. In 1926 Lufthansa carried out a Far-East expedition using a Junkers G 24. In 1934 Captain Gerstenkorn flew from Berlin to Shanghai in a Junkers W 34 in only four days, and in the same year a Junkers Ju 53 flew from Berlin to Shanghai.

In 1937, on the orders of *Reichsmarschall* Göring, Lufthansa carried out an amazing research flight that was intended to reconnoitre the air route to the Far East for regular air traffic. For the first time, a new route over neutral territory that diverged from the shortest route via Russia was to be tested. It crossed the Hindu Kush and the Pamir mountains. On the 14ᵗʰ of August 1937 the fully laden Ju 52 D-ANOY flew from Berlin via Damascus and Teheran to Kabul, a city at an altitude of 1,800 metres. In order to cope with the altitude over the Hindu Kush and the Pamir range the machine was equipped with stronger BMW engines and adjustable propellers. Five auxiliary fuel tanks were also built in to obviate the need for too many intermediate landings. The flight over the mountains to Jarkand and Sian (now: Xian) west of Nanking was successful. It was the first time an aircraft had crossed the Pamir mountains.

The return flight was somewhat more difficult. After a forced landing in Turkestan in western China because of engine failure, the crew was held for a few weeks by the Chinese military authorities because of passport problems. D-ANOY finally landed safely in Berlin 50 days after its departure. The aircraft survived the war and can still be visited at Munich Airport.[2]

---

1   Stahmer, *Japans Niederlage ...*, pp. 198f
2   Gablenz, *D-Anoy bezwingt den Pamir*

21. The Last Blockade Breakers and the Shortage of Rubber

Previously, German blockade breakers had preferred to use ports in Japan and Manchukuo. After the Japanese occupation of Malaya and the Dutch East Indies their strategy changed. Now German naval bases were built in the "Southern Region", where there was plenty of rubber, ores and important goods at reasonable prices. A further advantage was that the voyage to the region was 6,000 nautical miles shorter than that to Japan.

After 1942 the crisis years began for the German blockade breakers. After August 1942 ships from Japan and the East Indies could only sail through the Indian Ocean to the western French ports. The route around Cape Horn and across the Atlantic had become too risky. The route across the Indian Ocean had the further advantage that ships travelling from Japan could be revictualled, refuelled and have their cargoes replenished in Batavia.

However, the Allies had not only improved their radar systems to such an extent that they could turn night into day, they had also reinforced their naval forces on the new route through the Indian Ocean and round South Africa – particularly off South Africa and in the Bay of Biscay – that it was barely possible for the blockade breakers to get through. Admiral of the Fleet Dönitz, who now commanded the navy, discussed the problem with Hitler in February 1943 because blockade-breaker losses were becoming unsustainable. Dönitz's demands to Hitler were:

1. massive back-up by the navy to get the blockade breakers through the danger zones.

2. immediate construction of freight-submarines for the transport of raw materials and

3. the immediate deployment of Italian submarines to transport raw materials from South East Asia.[1]

When the Allied presence in the Indian Ocean was reinforced yet more, all ships coming from Japan had to put in to Batavia to wait for a favourable moment to break through the Sunda Strait. Because of this position on the Sunda Strait Batavia became the main port for ships travelling to and fro between Europe and the "Southern Region". This was where the blockade breakers – also called "rubber ships" by the sailors because of their cargoes of rubber – were refuelled and laden with rubber. The engines were also tested

---

1   Brennecke, *Schwarze Schiffe ...*, p. 219

here before the long return journey. The port of Menado in the north of the island of Celebes was also occasionally visited to load rice and other agricultural produce.

More and more American submarines were lurking in the Sunda Strait, lying in wait for German freighters, which often had to wait in Batavia for days for the opportunity to break through to the Indian Ocean. One passenger, Lieutenant Colonel Niemöller, who sailed on the 7,840-tonne freighter *Tannenfels* from Bordeaux to Yokohama in May 1942, wrote in his diary about the Sunda Strait:

[...] in the Sunda Strait with the – by chance inactive [Author's note: volcano] Krakatau. The China Sea [actually: Java Sea] is still and as smooth as oil, and also wonderfully clear. Non-stop submarine warnings. Submarine sighted here, submarine sighted there[...][1]

Blockade breaker losses in winter 1942 on the way from south East Asia were exceptionally high, as the following list of the most important ships shows:

Regensburg (North German Lloyd) sailed from Kobe on the 14.09.1942. Torpedoed by a US submarine in the Sunda Strait while attempting to break through to the Indian Ocean. But several tonnes of thick fat were stored just at the spot where the torpedo hit, and this sealed the leak. The ship managed to get back to Batavia and was then repaired in Singapore. She sailed from Batavia again on the 6.2.1943. Shortly before reaching her destination she was sunk by a British cruiser.

Rhakotis (HAPAG) sailed from Yokohama on the 27.9.1942.She was sunk by her own crew on the approach of a British cruiser on the 1.1. 1943.

Ramses (HAPAG) sailed from Kobe on the 23.10.1942. On her second attempt to break through into the Indian Ocean she was attacked by two British cruisers and scuttled by her own crew in the Sunda Strait on the 10. 12. 1942.

Hohenfriedberg (Captured Herborg) sailed from Yokohama on the 11.11.1942. Scuttled by the crew shortly before its destination in Western France on the approach of the British cruiser *HMS Sussex*

Rossbach (Captured Madrono) sailed from Kobe on the 12.11.1942. The ship was called back to Batavia from the South Atlantic and sunk by a US submarine in the middle of May 1943.

Irene (Captured Kota Nopan) sailed on the 10.10 1942 from western France to Batavia. On the 2.2.1943 it sailed again from Singapore for Eu-

---

1   Brennecke, *Schwarze Schiffe* ..., p. 197

rope. Close to her destination the crew scuttled her on the approach of a British cruiser.

Pietro Orseolo safely reached Bordeaux from Kobe on her first voyage on the 24.2.1942. On her second voyage she reached Kobe again on the 2.12.1942, sailing again on the 25.1.1943. Despite being hit by a torpedo, causing a large hole, the ship reached Bordeaux.

Rio Grande (HSDG: Hamburg Südamerikanische Dampfschifffahrt Gesellschaft, abbreviated Hamburg-Süd) made a successful voyage from Bordeaux to Osaka and back between the 21.9.1941 and the 16.4.1942. On her second blockade-breaking voyage she sailed from Kobe on the 4.10.1943. Further cargo was taken on in Singapore and Batavia. When she was attacked by the *USS Omaha* off the coast of South Africa, the crew scuttled her.

The loss of this ship was particularly painful for the naval command. It had taken on tyres in Yokohama and rubber in Singapore. In Batavia a large amount of agar-agar was also loaded. Agar-agar is a gelling agent produced from seaweed but during the war it was important for the production of aircraft paint. There was a great shortage of this material in Germany during the war.

Karin (Captured Silvaplana) arrived in Singapore from Bordeaux in January 1943. She set sail again on the 4.2.1943. She was scuttled off South Africa on the approach of a US cruiser and destroyer.

Burgenland (HAPAG) sailed from Kobe on its second Asian voyage on the 7.2.1943, but was ordered back to Japan because of increased Allied naval activity near the base at Batavia. On the 29.10.1943 the ship sailed once more from Yokohama for Batavia, where extra cargo of rubber, tungsten, quinine and iodine was loaded. The latter two materials were as important for the wartime economy as rubber or tungsten because there was nothing in Germany that could replace them. After the stop in Batavia the *Burgenland* started on its voyage home to Germany through the Sunda Strait.

On the 5th of January 1943 she was attacked off the South African coast be the US destroyers *Omaha* and *Jouett*. She was scuttled by her crew. The journalist Hoffmeier, a suspected spy who was being taken back to Germany from Japan for trial went down with the ship. More will be said about him in connection with Soviet spy Richard Sorge.

Weserland, ex Ermland (HAPAG) arrived in Yokohama on the 1.12.1942 from Bordeaux and sailed again on the 26.10.1943. She came under fire from a US destroyer and was scuttled by the crew.

Osorno was a HAPAG combination carrier. At the outbreak of war the ship was in Chile. She successfully escaped from Chile but then suffered an engine failure in mid-Atlantic that made her unmanoeuvrable. Her distress calls were received by the North German Lloyd blockade breaker *Bogota*, which hurried to her aid and towed her the 1,800 nautical miles to Yokohama. The *Bogota* then made a successful voyage from Japan to Bordeaux and back to Batavia. On her second voyage from Asia the *Osorno* sailed from Kobe on the 2.10.1943 and set off for home from Batavia fully laden. On the 26.12.1943 the ship struck a wreck in the mouth of the Gironde and was holed. The captain managed to beach the ship so that her valuable cargo of rubber could be saved. The *Osorno* was the last blockade breaker that managed to save at least some of her cargo.

Alsterufer sailed on the 4.11.1943 from Kobe via Batavia to Europe. She was the last blockade breaker to sail from East Asia. As well as urgently needed rubber the ship had 344 tonnes of tungsten on board, which would have filled the German war industry's demand for a year. The *Alsterufer* safely reached the North Atlantic. To ensure that the ship and its valuable cargo reached its home port of Brest[1], the navy sent a large force of eleven destroyers and two torpedo boats to escort her. Only a few hundred nautical miles from Brest the Allies attacked the *Alsterufer* with bombs on the 27.12.1943. It had been a very costly business and was the end of blockade running. The *Alsterufer* was lost, as were two torpedo boats. What a waste of men and material – for nothing. Four of the *Alsterufer*'s lifeboats carrying 74 men were rescued two days later by a Canadian corvette.

Other blockade breakers, like the *Cortellazzo*, the *Anneliese Essberger*, the *Benno* (ex *Ole Jacob*), the *Kota Pinang* and the *Elbe* were also scuttled by their own crews.[2]

A major naval operation to protect the blockade breakers in the particularly threatened area of the North Atlantic was undertaken for the last homeward bound ships, that is the *Irene* and the *Regensburg* as well as the

---

1   there are also sources which Bordeaux as home port

2   J. P. Mallmann-Showell: *Das Buch der deutschen Kriegsmarine 1939 – 1945,* 1982

     Hans Jürgen Witthöft: *Lexikon zur deutschen Marinegeschichte,* 1978,

     Bericht über Aufenthalte in Japan von Admiral P. W. Wenneker, Marineattaché, Tokyo

     www.deutsches-marinearchiv.de

Burgenland. However, they were all unsuccessful. With the aid of the new British ASV-radar equipment, which were first used in June 1942, the Allies had achieved air superiority in the western Atlantic. The Bay of Biscay in particular was under constant surveillance to prevent German ships reaching their home ports.

Most of the blockade breakers were scuttled by their own crews to prevent them falling into enemy hands. Some of them were called back to Batavia or Japan when it seemed obvious that it would not be possible to break through Allied lines. Of the eleven blockade breakers that had sailed to the "Southern Region" and Japan only one, the *Pietro Orseolo* – carrying the crew of the *Thor* which had been destroyed by fire in Yokahama harbour – reached the port of Bordeaux. After this series of failures the naval command abandoned the use of blockade breakers.

Next to the tungsten and molybdenum that were so vital for steel production, the blockade breakers' main freight was rubber. Without rubber, no wheels, without wheels no advances and no supply lines. But why was rubber suddenly as valuable as gold – it was even called "black gold"?

The chemist Fritz Hoffmann of IG-Farben had invented synthetic rubber and marketed it under the name Buna. Hitler said triumphantly *that the production of Buna has made us independent of foreign raw materials* and *we could survive the war for another ten years.* However, Hitler was by no means right.

The outside world observed the development of Buna production in Germany with eagle eyes. Among Walther Hewel's documents I found several letters from Heinrich Rudolph Wahlen, who sent him regular reports on economic affairs on South East Asia and the Pacific. On the 31st of July 1939, for example, he reports, using the trade magazine *Pacific Islands Monthly* from Sydney about the copra and timber markets, about gold mines and prospecting for oil in New Guinea. Of Buna he writes: *Buna as a product is feared by the pioneers of rubber plantation [...]* but says consolingly at the end: *But there will be always a market for natural rubber, vegetable oil, silk, wool and so on. Substitutes may live, but there are indications of an expanding market and ever-widening consumption.*[1]

Heinrich Rudolph[2] Wahlen was an expert on New Guinea. At the beginning of the 20th century he – an extremely successful merchant from Hamburg – was know as the "King of the South Seas". At the time he was Consul in German New Guinea and owned the Maron Islands, a group of 17 islands

---

1   AA, Hewel, Handakte 6, R 27474
2   also Rudolf

in the northern Bismarck Archipelago, where he had his grand estate. He made his great fortune from massive banana plantations and the export of South Sea shells to Germany for the manufacture of mother of pearl buttons. He died in Hamburg in 1970 at the age of 97. He was a first class source of information on the region for Hewel and was entrusted with colonial affairs under the Third Reich.[1]

The almost inexhaustible raw materials found in New Guinea still attract the covetousness of the industrial nations. From the end of the nineteenth century the Dutch, British and Germans fought for predominance in this area. Germany had lost all its colonies at the end of the First World War under the pretext that it was not capable of ruling a colony properly, which from a present-day perspective was a blessing in disguise for Germany.

With slogans like: *Heim ins Reich* [Home to the Empire] and *Volk ohne Raum* [A People without Living Space] Hitler now openly demanded the return of Germany's colonies. *Germany needs colonies too and will get them!* And there were still 30,000 German citizens living in those former colonies. Their economic interests and the preservation of German culture should be protected. In East Asia and the Pacific German schools, churches, newspapers and associations were given financial support, particularly in the Dutch East Indies.[2]

By the middle of 1939 there were already concrete plans for what was to be done with the former German colonies in the Pacific. Wahlen wrote to Hewel in his report on the 27th of April 1939:

I am referring to Java with a population of about 40 million. Java can no longer feed such masses of people. [...] It will surely be possible for Greater Germany to come to an agreement with Holland about settling and bringing a work force to New Guinea (Bismarck Archipelago, Salomon Islands). [...] An airport should be built on Samoa [...] Since New Zealand has not exactly earned any laurels by its methods of administration in Samoa, they are considering a plan to give up the mandate and hand it to Great Britain. No one is asking us. [...] We will accept the loss of Samoa in return for the annexation of Papua.[3]

Wahlen's prophesies were correct, as today Indonesia has, in New Guinea, the biggest gold mine in the world as well as the copper mine with the lowest production costs. The income from these mines comes to several billion dollars per year.

---

1   Hamburger Abendblatt, 7. Dezember 2008, Bericht ‚*Südsee-Ausstellung*‘ von Matthias Gretzschel
2   McKale, *The Swastika Outside Germany,* p.6
3   AA, Akte R27474

The former German colony of the Bismarck Archipelago is also to be the site of a new era in raw material extraction from 2015 onwards. In the Bismarck Sea, where in a Second-World-War battle between Japan and the USA in March 1943 6,100 Japanese and thousands of Americans and Australians went to a watery grave, gold, silver, copper and rare earths are to be mined from the seabed. The first licence for such a mine went to a Canadian company. The main customer will be China, with its hunger for raw materials.[1] In the 1930s Wahlen, the King of the South Seas, had – as his reports to Hewel show – a nose for where the hidden treasures lie.

The USA and Britain were in an extremely difficult position after Japan took control over the whole of South East Asia. Malaya and the Dutch East Indies produced about 80% of the world's rubber, and the USA and Britain acquired their entire supply from these areas. After the Japanese occupation, they were cut off from these sources of supply. Japan hoped that this would seriously affect its opponent's armament potential, but this turned out to be wrong. At the beginning of the war the German IG-Farben company had sold its patent for Buna, which was now ready to enter production, to the US company Standard Oil with Hitler's agreement. Was Hitler so sure that the USA would not enter the war, or was it the greed for hard currency that led him to take this incomprehensible action?

In the USA synthetic rubber had a meteoric rise after the IG-Farben patent was acquired. In 1941 only 8,200 tonnes were produced – by 1945 this rose to 833,500 tonnes. The quality of the US product was considerably better than the German. Using the amount produced, the USA and Britain could meet their entire demand and were not forced to rely on natural rubber from South East Asia.

But how did German synthetic rubber production fare at this time? Why did they have to import such huge quantities of natural rubber from the Dutch East Indies, and even ready-made tyres from Japan? As the inventor of synthetic rubber Germany should have had a great advantage!

In 1942 Germany produced about 110,000 tonnes of Buna. As a result of the effects of the war and Allied air-raids on IG-Farben's factories in Ludwigshafen and Leverkusen, capacity could only be increased to 170,000 tonnes by the end of the war. Of the total of 94,000 tonnes of natural rubber shipped to Germany by blockade breakers, only 44,500 reached their destination.[2]

The main reason why Germany was still so dependent on natural rubber was probably sabotage. While US synthetic rubber could be used for tyres

---

1   Süddeutsche Zeitung No. 198, 28.08.12
2   Brennecke, *Schwarze Schiffe ...*, pp. 224f and 259

without any problem and was already as good as natural rubber, there were major problems with German Buna. Although German Buna tyres passed quality controls in the factories without any difficulty, many tyres burst after only 100 kilometres' driving at the front. This particularly affected Rommel's North African desert campaign and the winter campaign in Russia. The Buna tyres were not adequate for these extreme conditions. To improve quality, natural rubber had to be combined with the synthetic product.

After the war there were whispered rumours in IG-Farben's successor company that a chemist responsible for the manufacture of the Buna tyres had committed sabotage. By adding a very small quantity of a chemical substance to the synthetic rubber recipe he had ensured that the tyres aged extremely quickly and could not stand up to the extreme demands of driving at the front.[1]

With the sinking of the last blockade breaker the naval war for rubber was at an end. The master spy Richard Sorge had done good work in Tokyo by informing the Soviet Union and the western Allies of every blockade breaker that left Japan or Batavia, together with its route.[2]

Even their own German U-boats made life difficult for the blockade breakers. They mostly travelled under foreign colours and for concealment purposes frequently changed the ship's name and its paintwork, so that it was not easy for the U-boat commanders to identify them as German ships. Several blockade breakers were sunk by them. An example:

In peacetime the *Goldenfels* transported break bulk cargo between Europe, India and Burma for the Bremen shipping line Hansa. In the war she was deployed as the auxiliary cruiser *Atlantis*. In 1941 the *Atlantis* captured the British ship *Speybank* in the Indian Ocean and it was put into service as a prize. The *Speybank* constantly changed its name to those of its similarly built sister ships *Doggerbank*, *Levernbank* and *Inverbank*. That was not just confusing for the Allies, but also for the German U-boats which were hunting British merchant ships. Further confusion was caused when the ship added false superstructures of wood and canvas.

On several occasions the *Speybank* laid mines of the South African coast. In the South Atlantic she supplied two German auxiliary cruisers and took 177 British and American PoWs on board, then passed the Cape of Good Hope and landed the prisoners in Batavia. Then she put in to Yokohama on the 19th of August 1942 to take on provisions and fuel.

---

1   Informatione from Günther Fust and other former employees of IG-Farben AG

2   Sorge espionage ring in Chapter *"The German Embassy in Tokyo"* later in this book

Disguised as the *Doggerbank* she put to sea once more on the 17th of December 1942 with a cargo of rubber and fats. While the ship was being maintained and loaded, the crew were allowed to take leave in shifts in the holiday resort of Hakone, where the German Navy had rented a row of bungalows for the use of the crews of ships moored in Japanese ports.

In Kobe, Saigon, Singapore and Batavia the *Doggerbank* took on more cargo. Heavily laden, she left Batavia on the 10th of January 1943; her destination was Bordeaux, 10,000 nautical miles away. There were 365 on board: the crew of 109 and some of the survivors of the crews of the *Uckermark* and the *Thor*, which had been destroyed in an explosion in Yokohama.

The war reporter Lieutenant Heinz Tischer had travelled on the auxiliary cruiser *Thor*'s second voyage from Bordeaux to Yokohama via Batavia and Balikpapan on Borneo.

Heinz Tischer's voyage to Yokohama has already been mentioned. After his arrival the Japanese authorities put him up in the New Grand Hotel. In the explosion of the *Uckermark* in the port of Yokohama all Tischer's photographic and sound material was destroyed on the *Thor*. Tischer left Yokohama on the 25th of January 1943 on the blockade breakers *Pietro Orseolo*, without any material for a war report. Before setting out into the Indian Ocean the ship docked at Singapore and Batavia to take on cargo. Here the sailors from the *Uckermark* and the *Thor* spent their last cash on souvenirs, because occupation currency was worthless outside the occupied areas. On the 1st of April 1943 the *Pietro Orseolo* returned safely to its home port of Bordeaux.[1]

The remaining survivors of the Yokahama disaster had less luck. On the 3rd of March 1943, sailing under the false name *Doggerbank*, the *Speybank* was sunk in error by the German U-boat U 43 using 3 torpedoes.

It was not until 26 days later that the bosun of the *Doggerbank*, Fritz Kuert, was found by a Spanish ship in the south west Atlantic after an Odyssey of 1,600 nautical miles in a small dinghy. The crew of the *Doggerbank* had bought the dinghy for fun in Japan and kept it on board. After the torpedo attack 13 men had been able to save themselves in the dinghy. They died one after another, of exhaustion, drinking sea water or suicide. 364 sailors were killed; only one survived, bosun Fritz Kuert. Kuert must have had a guardian angel, because he had previously survived the sinking of four ships in one year.

Kuert became a prisoner of war in America and was released back to Germany in 1944 under a prisoner exchange organised by the International

---

1   Date according to eyewitness Tischer, who sailed to Bordeaux on the ship. Other documents give April 2.

Red Cross. He was supposed to tell the German naval authorities about the disaster, but the interview became more of an interrogation because the BBC had exploited the sinking of the blockade breaker by a German submarine for propaganda purposes. Kuert was suspected of having blabbed during questioning in the USA, but it was only in Germany that he heard for the first time that it was the U43 that had sunk the *Doggerbank*.[1]

The total cargo brought from the "Southern Region" by the blockade breakers was a mere 220,000 tonnes, far too little for the German war effort. In transporting vital raw materials to Germany over 20 German freighters and tankers as well as a number of the warships escorting them were sunk in the years after 1943.[2]

The rate of losses among German auxiliary cruisers was also high. Seven of the nine put into service were lost, although they did cause major Allied losses: they sank 102 freighters and two cruisers and captured 27 prizes. The Allies lost almost a million tonnes of shipping because of them.[3]

1   Herlin, *Der letzte Mann der Doggerbank*
2   Brennecke, *Schwarze Schiffe* ..., p. 259
3   Tischert, *Die Abenteuer des letzten Kapers,* p. 104

22. The *Yanagi* Mission

Under the Tripartite Pact there was to be an exchange of strategic war materials, newly developed weapons and personnel between Germany and Japan. In Japan and in the German Navy this exchange was designated the *Yanagi*-Mission. As well as newly developed weapons, research results and construction diagrams were to be exchanged.

Since the use of surface blockade breakers had become too risky, Berlin planned to transport raw materials by submarine. On the 31st of March 1943 the Japanese Ambassador in Berlin, Oshima Hiroshi, reported that Field Marshal Erich von Manstein was suggesting the deployment of large submarines as transports for the *Yanagi*-Mission between the Far East and Europe. The shortage of raw materials was already seriously affecting the German war machine. Ambassador Hiroshi recommended the Japanese government to implement the plan as soon as possible. Initially Germany had no special transport submarines even though Admiral Dönitz had advocated the construction of such ships for some time. Hitler did not at first support the idea – or did so only reluctantly – as he needed front line ships for the trade war in the Atlantic more urgently than ever.

Dönitz therefore suggested to Hitler that the submarines of their Italian allies, which were stationed at Bordeaux and were little suited to front-line service, should be deployed as submarine transport vessels between South East Asia and western France. Hitler found this idea acceptable. The Italian Naval High command in Rome, the *Supermarina,* also consented to the use of all of their submarines except the *Ammiraglio Cagni* for freight transport purposes.

This was a great advantage for the German Navy. The Italian submarines, which were more cumbersome and slower than the German U-boats, were much more suitable as transport ships after refitting. At that time German shipbuilders were launching a new U-boat practically every day, but the navy could not train crews to man them quickly enough. The Italian submarines were handed over complete with crews, and were under German command, so that they could be used immediately.

Hitler's change of mind regarding sending German U-boats to South East Asia anyway was surely influenced by the successful voyage of the large Japanese submarine cruiser I-30. This was the first ship of the Imperial Japanese Navy, *Dai-Nippon Taikoku Kaigun,* to sail successfully from South East Asia to Lorient in western France.

I-30 sailed from Penang on the 22nd of April 1942 under Commander Shinobu Endo on a reconnaissance mission. Her on-board aircraft carried out reconnaissance over Aden, Djibouti, Zanzibar and Durban. On the 24th of June 1942 she was refuelled on the high seas south of Madagascar by the Japanese auxiliary cruisers *Kokoku Maru* and *Aikoku Maru* and loaded with raw material for Germany. She continued her voyage under the codename *Kirschblüte* [cherry blossom].

She arrived in the port of Lorient on the 5th of August 1942, having been escorted the last few miles by German naval ships and eight Junkers Ju-88 aircraft. The boat moored in one of the sixteen bomb-proof U-boat pens. Admirals in Chief Raeder and Dönitz, as well as the Japanese Naval Attaché from Berlin, Yokoi Tadao, welcomed the I-30 with martial music and flowers. Commander Endo was decorated with a medal. That evening there was an official banquet in honour of the Japanese officers and crew attended by German officers and diplomats.

In the days that followed the Japanese crew were allowed to visit and photograph German U-boats; however, the Japanese allowed only a select few to view the I-30. Her entire crew were invited to Berlin, where Hitler gave Endo another decoration. After a tour of Paris they returned to Lorient.

To the chagrin of the German Navy the cargo of raw materials was extremely small. I-30's voyage had been intended more as a reconnaissance of the maritime route to Europe. However, the I-30 did bring construction plans for the Japanese aerial torpedo type 91, although the Japanese did not reveal that their navy was already using the newer and more efficient type 95. Japan was much more reluctant to share secret information than Germany. Before returning to Japan the I-30 was equipped with a radar system and German experts fitted a modern Mauser four-barrel anti-aircraft canon.

On the 26th of August 1942[1] the I-30, with a new coat of paint and a cargo of important war supplies, set sail again for Japan. Commander Endo left behind a Japanese seaplane as a sign of gratitude for German hospitality. As well as her 110-man crew she was carrying General Suzuki, who was in charge of the project to replicate the "Würzburg Radar System", and a Japanese civilian radar engineer. They had both had training in the construction and running of the system at Telefunken in Germany. Japan was very keen to deploy this world-leading early warning system in their own region.

The German Navy provided the following material for the I-30 to take back to Japan: a complete Würzburg radar system with all the necessary construction drawings, five new German G7 aerial torpedoes, three electric-propelled G 7e torpedoes, rockets, glider bombs, anti-tank weapons, Zeiss

---

1   There are also sources which give the 22 August 1942

lenses for anti-aircraft systems, 50 Enigma code-machines, 1 million yen's worth of industrial diamonds and many other things.

The top secret Enigma machines were provided to Japan for encrypted communication with the German bases in the "Southern Region". For this region they had agreed on using the "Sumatra Code".[1]

Test flights over the Atlantic by the seaplanes carried by the I-30 were filmed for the German newsreel. This was seen by the Allies and caused great consternation. They suspected that Japanese submarines and the Japanese Naval Flying Corps would now be operating from the bases on the western French coast. The I-30's three aircraft were painted in a series of constantly changing colours and markings to give the false impression that there were far more than just three of them. This deception was supported by the German press agencies to disconcert the Allies.

On the 9th of October 1942 the I-30 returned safely to Penang, where some of her cargo was unloaded. The construction plans were sent directly to Japan by air. After refuelling, she sailed for Singapore, arriving two days later. Here ten of the Enigma machines were unloaded. On leaving Singapore for Japan the I-30 hit a British mine only three nautical miles from port on the 13th of October 1942 and sank. Commander Endo and 96 of the crew were saved, but 13 lives were lost. Some of the cargo could be saved because she sank in shallow water.

It was not until 1943 that a second Japanese submarine cruiser reached France. The I-8 left the naval port of Kure in Japan on the 1st of June 1943 under the command of Captain S. Uschino. On board, as well as the normal crew, were a complete 48-man replacement crew and three German engineers who had completed their mission in Japan. The replacement crew were to be trained in Germany on the German U-boat U 1224, one of class IX C. The intention was that they should sail the submarine back to Japan under Japanese colours when the training was complete. With around 160 men on board it must have been very cramped on board, with very little room for additional cargo, although it was loaded with several tonnes of molybdenum and other raw materials in Penang. She set sail for Europe on the 27th of June 1943, and after refuelling twice in the Indian Ocean the I-8 reached the Atlantic in the middle of July.

On the 24th of July the I-8 received a coded radio telegram from the German Navy, warning of an increase in Allied air-reconnaissance activity. South of the Azores she met the U 161, and Lieutenant Jahn and two radio officers were transferred from the U 161 to pilot the I-8 safely to the port of Brest. In the Bay of Biscay she received an escort of several destroyers and aircraft, and

---

1   Forum für deutsche Militärgeschichte, www.balsi.de www.combinedfleet.com

was welcomed in Brest with music and flowers on the 31st of August 1943. This example of German-Japanese co-operation was extensively celebrated in the German newsreels.[1]

A banquet was held for the officers and men. The German passengers must have been very happy to be on European soil after their many weeks at sea, since they complained bitterly about the monotonous food on board and the mentality of the Japanese crew.[2]

On the 5th of October 1943 I-8 set sail again with a cargo of torpedo motors, aircraft canons, chronometers, a "Rotterdam Sonar Apparatus" and 20-cylinder Daimler-Benz diesel speed-boat motors. Her passengers were the former Naval Attaché in Berlin, Rear-Admiral Yokoi Tadao and the former Naval Attaché in France, Captain Hosoya Sukeyoshi. There were also German passengers: three naval officers with Lieutenant Koch as a Japanese interpreter, four radar and sonar specialists, an army major and four or five civilian passengers, including a Dr Jakob and a Dr Müller. These last two were presumably German-Japanese interpreters who were going to work in the German bases in the "Southern Region".[3] After the war, in the 1960s, Dr Jakob was Cultural Attaché to the German Embassy in Jakarta.[4]

At the end of October the I-8 was pursued and attacked off the coast of West Africa by American aircraft. She survived the attack with only light damage by crash diving to a depth of 60 metre. Without any further incident she arrived in Penang on the 2nd of December 1943, reaching Singapore three days later. After an overhaul the I-8 returned safely to the port at Kure in the 21st of December. She was the only Japanese submarine to survive the 30,000 kilometre voyage from Japan to France and back undamaged.

In September 1944 the I-8 was back in Penang after an operation in the Indian Ocean. On the 9th of September 1944 Commander Heinrich Timm arrived there with his submarine U 862. The officers and men of the I-8 greeted the German submariners heartily. There were meals and visits to both boats in the interests German-Japanese friendship. In April 1945 the I-8 was sunk at Okinawa.[5]

---

1   Newsreel I-8, www.facebook.com/pages/japanese -submarine-I-8

2   Krug, Hirama, Sander-Nagashima, Niestlé, *Reluctant Allies,* p. 204f

3   Dr Jakob was Lector for Japanese in the Centre for Japanese Language and Culture. It seems almost certain that this is the same Dr Jakob described in my book A Gecko for Luck who was Cultural Attaché at the German Embassy in Jakarta in the 1960s. I knew him personally: he never wished to speak about the war. He spoke fluent Japanese and Vietnamese and Japan was, as he said, his second home.

4   Geerken, *A Gecko for Luck,* pp. 358-360

5   www.combinedfleet.com/I-8.htm

At Hitler's special request to increase deliveries of raw materials from Japan the Japanese Navy sent three large submarines – the I-29, I-34 and I-52 – to Europe between September and October 1943. Only the I-29 reached Lorient on this *Yanagi*-mission. She had previously picked up the Indian freedom fighter Subhas Chandra Bose from the U 180 in the Indian Ocean and brought him safely to Sabang in the Dutch East Indies. The details of this voyage will be given later in this book.

The I-34 left Japan on the 15th of September 1943 with a crew of 94, reaching Singapore on the 22nd of October 1943 to take on freight and passengers for Germany. Because of delays in loading the cargo – some tonnes of molybdenum, tin and quinine – the passengers travelled overland to Penang where they intended to board the I-34. In the Strait of Malacca the I-34 was torpedoed and sunk by the British submarine *HMS Taurus* on the 13th of November 1942 with only 14 survivors.

The voyage of the I-52 – the last of the three submarines to leave Japan– ended in disaster. I-52 was a special freight submarine of Japanese Navy type C-3. They had planned to build 20 of this type, but up to the end of the war only three had entered service. It was the most modern submarine of the Second World War and the biggest ever built. It was 108.7 metres long, 9.3 metres high and 5.1 metres wide. Her surface speed was 17.7 knots (33 km/hour), and submerged 6.5 knots (12km/hour). At a speed of 16 knots (30km/hour) she could cover a distance of 21,000 nautical miles (30,000 km) without refuelling. Type C-3 was armed with six torpedo tubes, while on deck there were a further four or five *Kamikaze*-torpedoes which would be steered towards enemy targets by sailors prepared to die in the attempt.

The considerably greater cargo capacity of type C-3 submarines would have secured Germany's raw material requirements, but unfortunately new developments in Allied radio direction finders, sonar, detection and radar equipment meant that transport by submarine was now as dangerous as by surface craft.

The I-52 was codenamed *Momi*, [evergreen] and her captain was Uno Kameo. 10 tonnes of molybdenum and over two tonnes of gold for Nazi Germany were loaded in Japan. The voyage was top secret, not just because of the gold, but also because there were numerous boxes of secret documents. The gold was intended to pay Germany for optical devices and other military material which had previously been delivered by blockade breakers or via the Trans-Siberian Railway. Before the voyage, which was the I-52's maiden voyage, tin, 60 tonnes of rubber, 55 tonnes of coffee, opium and quinine were loaded in Singapore. There were 95 crew and 14 Japanese engineers who were travelling to Germany to familiarise themselves with German submarine technology.

In the Atlantic, about 1,400 kilometres west of the Cape Verde Islands I-52 rendezvoused with the German U-530 under the command of Lieutenant Kurt Lange on the 22nd of June 1944. A German navigator and a pilot for the Bay of Biscay were transferred to I-52 as well as German radio officers Schulze and Behrend to install the German Naxos radio apparatus on the Japanese submarine to help it and its valuable cargo to reach Lorient safely.

Equipped with the new radar, Commander Uno Kameo felt so safe that he continued towards Lorient on the surface. The Allies were aware of the two submarines because of the radio traffic between them and sank the I-52 shortly afterwards with an aerial torpedo. The U 530 managed to escape and continued her voyage unharmed. More will be said about the U 530 and its operations later. The valuable cargo of two tonnes of gold is still lying on the bed of the Atlantic at a depth of 5,000 metres. Several unsuccessful attempts have been made to find it.

Unlike the I-34 and I-52, the I-29's voyage was more fortunate. She sailed from Penang on the 8th of August 1942 for her second Indian Ocean operation. Her field of action was Diego Suarez, the Seychelles, Zanzibar, Mombasa and the Gulf of Aden, sinking four British and one American freighter within four days. From the 5th of October 1942 she was overhauled at the base in Singapore.

On the 11th of November 1942 the ship left Penang and headed for the Gulf of Aden under Captain Terraoka Masao, where she sank the British passenger ship *Tilawa*. *HMS Birmingham* saved 678 victims, but 252 passengers and 28 crew lost their lives.

On the 14th of November 1943, after an overhaul at the Japanese military docks in Kure, the I-29 docked at Singapore again where she was loaded for a *Yanagi*-mission with 80 tonnes of rubber, about 50 tonnes of molybdenum, tin, quinine and other raw materials for Germany. She left Singapore on the 16th of December 1943 commanded by Commander Kinashi under the Japanese code name *Matsu* [pine tree](the German codename was U-Kiefer [pine]) and headed for Europe. There were 16 passengers on board, including Admiral Kojima Hideo, the new Japanese Naval Attaché for Germany and his deputy, Captain Ogi Kazuto. To support the Japanese officer there was a German navigation officer on board for the whole voyage from Singapore to guide the submarine safely through waters unfamiliar to the Japanese from the Indian Ocean and the Atlantic to the Bay of Biscay.

On the morning of the 23rd of December 1943 the I-29 took on fuel and provisions from the German supply ship *Bogota* in the western Indian Ocean. On the 16th of January 1944 she rounded the Cape of Good Hope and headed northwards along the west coast of Africa.

On the 12th of February 1944 the I-29 rendezvoused with the U 518 under Commander Offermann south of the Azores. Three German technicians came on board and installed the latest German radar system, FuMB7 Naxos, on the bridge. On the next day the I-29 took on about 1,700 tonnes of fuel from the German supply submarine U 488.

On the 10th of March 1944 she reached the Bay of Biscay and was escorted to Lorient by five Junkers aircraft, the destroyers Z-23 and ZH-1 and torpedo boats T-27 and T-29. She survived two attacks by the Allies unscathed just before she arrived, although one Junkers aircraft was shot down. The I-29 moored in one of the massive U-boat pens. The Germans were particularly pleased by the arrival of the molybdenum, which met their requirements for the next two or three months.

The Japanese crew was made welcome and given a grand banquet in the Château de Trévarez above the village of Château Neuf de Faou. They were also invited to take the train for a sight-seeing tour of Paris. Commander Kinashi travelled to Berlin, where Hitler gave him the Iron Cross, Second Class.

After his arrival in Lorient the German navigation officer, who had been on the Japanese submarine for nearly three months, complained about the monotony of the food on board. Rice with sausage and vegetables four times a day were not exactly to his taste.[1] By contrast, great emphasis was placed on a varied and healthy diet on the German submarines.

This was the fourth successful voyage by a Japanese submarine bringing raw materials and passengers to occupied France. If one thinks of the demands made on the Japanese submarine fleet by their conflict with the US Navy in the Pacific, then these transports were an unambiguous sign to Germany of positive collaboration between the two countries. In return for this help Hitler gave Japan several U-boats, although he was hoping to gain an advantage by doing so. By arming his allies with modern German technology, more Allied units would be kept busy in the Pacific.

On the 16th of April 1944 the I-29 left Lorient laden with the following modern German arms: parts for a V1 rocket, an engine for each of the two Messerschmitt jet fighters Me 163 and Me 262, a 37mm Krupp artillery piece, a Mauser four-barrel anti-aircraft canon, acoustic naval mines, bauxite and mercury. Many construction plans were also carried, as were 18 passengers, among them four German engineers. The voyage passed without any problems.

At the latitude of Sabang the I-29 rendezvoused with two Mitsubishi bombers which escorted her through the Strait of Malacca to Singapore,

1   Krug, Hirama, Sander-Nagashima, Niestlé, *Reluctant Allies*, p. 206

where she docked on the 14th of July 1944. From there the Japanese and German experts flew on to Japan. Some of the cargo was unloaded in Singapore. On the 22nd of July 1944 the I-29 left the port of Singapore, headed for Japan. On the 26th of July she was torpedoed and sunk by the American *Sawfish*. One single survivor managed to reach a small island in the Philippines.

23. German Naval Bases in South East Asia and the Arrival of the First Submarines

The home port of most of the U-boats that travelled to the German bases in South East Asia and Japan was Lorient, the biggest German naval base on the French Atlantic coast. Others sailed to the "Southern Region" from Bordeaux, Brest, La Pallice (La Rochelle's industrial port) and St. Nazaire.

In the spring of 1942 the Allies tried to wipe out the German U-boat bases, but even the biggest bombs available to them in the Second World War did no damage. The several metre thick concrete pens survived all attacks and can still be seen along the French Atlantic coast.

From summer 1941 the operational area for U-boats was extended to the entire West African coast as far as Cape Town. At the beginning of 1942 the naval command in Berlin decided in favour of extending operations to the Indian Ocean and Dutch East Indian waters, with the submarines being stationed for overhaul, refuelling and provisioning purposes in Malaya and the Dutch East Indies, the Japanese-occupied "Southern Region". One of the first missions of the boats was to intensify the exchange of materials, information and passengers between Germany and Japan. They were also to interfere with British supply routes from Australia through the Indian Ocean, which had so far been undisturbed. As many Allied warships as possible were to be caught up in this area to relieve pressure on the naval war in the Atlantic.

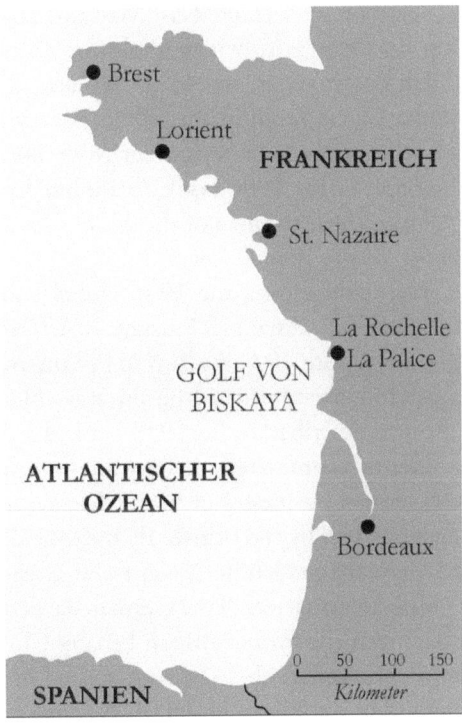

Ill. 50
German U-boat bases on the French Atlantic Coast

243

Preparations soon began for the construction of bases in Penang, Singapore, Batavia and Surabaya. The British naval base in Penang had fallen almost intact into Japanese hands when the British retreated towards India before the Japanese troops marched in. Only the floating dock had been towed away, so that Japan could use the port and its facilities immediately. Before the arrival of the first German personnel, Japanese submarines from Penang had already been in operation in the Indian Ocean, which is why Penang was the first base that was ready to take German U-boats.

Penang is an island in the Strait of Malacca with a large port. It is connected to mainland Malaya by a bridge. Its main city, Georgetown, is not only a tourist attraction with temples, mosques, churches and synagogues, but also a major trade centre for the region. There had been German merchants, engineers, architects and missionaries living in Penang since the middle of the 19th century. The merchant houses had successfully run import-export businesses to Europe and neighbouring North Sumatra. To the annoyance of the British, German shipping lines were well represented and successful: the Hamburg shipping line F. L. Laeisz had a fleet of ships known as P-liners, one of which, a three-master barque, they named *Penang*. A German Club was founded in Penang in 1898.

German writers like Karl May and Hermann Hesse visited Penang. During his Asian trip, which took him from Egypt to Colombo, Penang and Atjeh (now: Aceh) in North Sumatra Karl May stayed with his Egyptian butler Omar Sejjid in the still legendary Eastern & Oriental Hotel (P & O Hotel) in Penang in November 1899. He described the hotel and its grounds in detail in his 1904 book *Friede auf Erden* [Peace on Earth], in which he pillories the arrogance of the white race and the Chinese towards the indigenous Malay population.

Hermann Hesse, the 1946 Nobel Laureate for Literature, also travelled in South East Asia. His journey, which took him to India, Sumatra, Borneo and Singapore, brought him to Penang on two occasions. In September and again in November 1911 he also stayed in the Eastern & Oriental Hotel. The trip was described in his 1913 book *Aus Indien* [From India].

German commercial activity was interrupted during both World Wars since all German businesses in British Malaya and Singapore were confiscated and auctioned off by the British. By the time the German U-boats came to Penang all Germans resident in Malaya were already interned in camps in Australia.

The headquarters of the German base command in Penang was in Northam Road near the former British Penang Club. Other buildings and some villas to accommodate the staff were rented in Bell Road. The naval airmen were housed in the Elysee Hotel, in Penang's commercial quarter. Houses for the officers were in Rose Road. The swimming pools in the Springtide Hotel and the Penang Swimming Club were rented for exclusive use by the Germans.

In Penang port there was room for a maximum of five submarines, and since the Japanese also used Penang, German boats constantly had to move to Singapore and Batavia. Singapore became the centre for the maintenance and repair of the U-boats.

In Batavia there were already infrastructure and repair facilities, since the German blockade breakers used this port for preference. German officers were mainly accommodated in houses in Gambir-Selatan street, mostly houses belonging to Germans that been confiscated by the Dutch but returned to the Germans by the Japanese. The crews were mainly housed in Pulu Beton, a suburb of Batavia. The commander of the Batavia base, Captain Hermann Kandeler, who was also Germany's representative in the Dutch East Indies, initially took over co-ordination between all the German bases in the "Southern Region".

The naval base at Surabaya was the last that became available to German submarines, which is difficult to understand, since Surabaya was the central and biggest port of the Dutch East Indies Navy. The Dutch had probably destroyed the port facilities before leaving. When the base at Surabaya was once more available for use, the first U-boat from Europe arrived in October 1944: it was the U 537 commanded by Lieutenant Schrewe.

At the beginning of 1943 the blockade breaker *MS Quito* brought in material for the construction of the Penang and Singapore bases. Shortly afterwards she, together with the *MS Alstertor,* also took materials and provisions to Batavia.

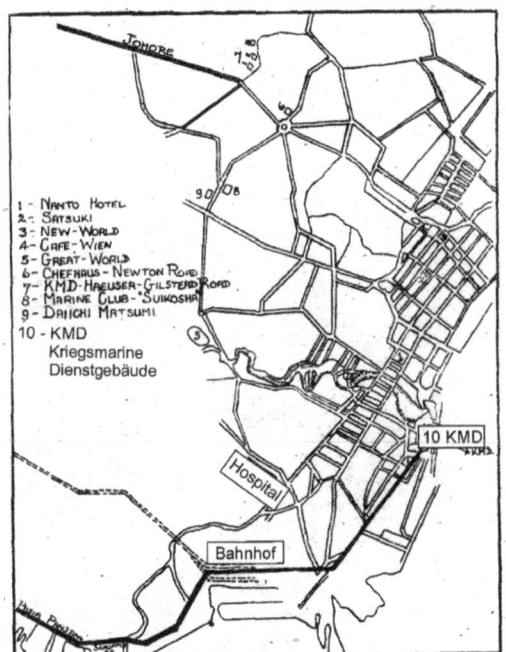

Ill. 51
Plan of Singapore from the Shonan Booklet, 1944 edition

On all the bases buildings and houses were made available to the German naval personnel by the Imperial Japanese Navy. The offices of the German Navy in Singapore were in the Union Building on Collyer Quay Number 12. It was in a central position near Raffles Place, outside the inner basin opposite the *Yamato Sambashi* landing stage.

The offices of the Japanese Naval Attaché were also in this building. Erected in 1924, it was, with its eight floors, the biggest and highest building in Singapore at the time. The German Navy's offices were on the 4th and 5th floor. It was demolished in 1981 to make room for a new building.

German personnel lived in three houses Gilstead Road: numbers 25, 31 and 39 (Houses numbers 1, 2 and 3, see Ill. 51). House number 3 also contained the receivers and transmitters for the radio station. The codename for the Singapore base in encrypted German radio traffic was "Point Siegfried". House number 4 was in 23 Newton Road 23 (see Ill. 51, 6) and contained the offices of the base commander Wolfgang Erhardt and the commander of the duty stations in Malaya.

About 12 kilometres west of these buildings was the *Pasir Panjang* camp on Singapore's Western Roads. There was Camp 1 (called Sack-Lager after the camp commandant Sack) and Camp 2 (called Maerz-Lager after commandant Maerz). The dock command was in House 3, House 4 was the camp commanders' central office and House 5 was the Officers' House. There was a barracks in House 6 and in House 7 was the "Tiger House", which was the night club for German officers which was run by Mrs Kadowaki, a Japanese ballet dancer. It was rumoured that she worked for the *Kempetai*. Espionage happened even among allies. Quite close to the Tiger House there was the

Skizze Pasir Panjang-Lager

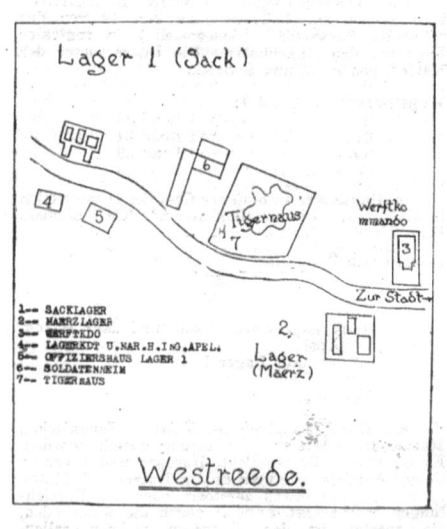

Ill. 52
Sketch of the Pasir Panjang Camp in West Singapore from the Shonan Booklet, 1944 edition, page 4

246

Jungle Club for the base personnel and the crews of the U-boats.[1] This latter was a large house in an extensive tropical garden in the most upmarket suburb of Singapore. Among the Germans the club was known as the "Jungle Pavilion". Since dancing is a favourite recreational activity among sailors, German-speaking Eurasian women and a band from Java were engaged. The women had firm contracts and were just there as dance partners. After curfew at 10.30 at night they were taken home by bus.

The naval base at Sabang on the Pulau Weh (Island of Weh), only a few nautical miles north of Sumatra in the Andaman Sea had a special position among the German bases. It was a Japanese base at the northern entrance to the Strait of Malacca and was often the first port of call for German submarines after months at sea. With its big natural harbour it was strategically important because it was an excellent place for monitoring the northern part of the Strait of Malacca.

The German boats arriving from Europe only spent a day or two in Sabang to await the arrival of an escort from Penang. They were then escorted back to Penang by ships and aircraft, because Allied submarines made the Strait of Malacca very unsafe.

In Sabang German submariners first set foot on terra firma after many weeks in cramped conditions. They were welcomed by the Japanese at the base and invited to a hot Japanese bath before a celebratory meal. After the long deprivation of their sea voyage the German submariners were hoping for a warm bath and a relaxing massage from delicate Japanese courtesans, but to their great disappointment they were scrubbed roughly by muscular Japanese men. The U-boats often brought valuable and eagerly awaited military material with them which was unloaded here and sent on by air to Japan.

There were very few German naval personnel stationed in Sabang, because there were no maintenance facilities and it was not possible to provision the ships there. Nevertheless – as we will see – Sabang played an outstanding role in both the First and Second World Wars.

The German Naval Special Service in Tokyo for the *Marine-Sonderdienst/MSD*, which up till then had been responsible for freight, fuel and provisions for the blockade breakers in Japan and Manchukuo, was now transferred to the "Southern Region" and based at Penang in Malaya. The MSD was directly subordinate to the Naval High Command. The Naval Attaché in Tokyo, Admiral Paul Wenneker and his Chief of Staff Captain Werner Vermehren were responsible for day to day operations. Because of the German bases in the "Southern Region" raw materials could be loaded in the places where they were produced and thus save the 6,000 nautical mile voyage to Japan and back.

---

1   Shonan-Büchlein, 1944 edition, p. 3

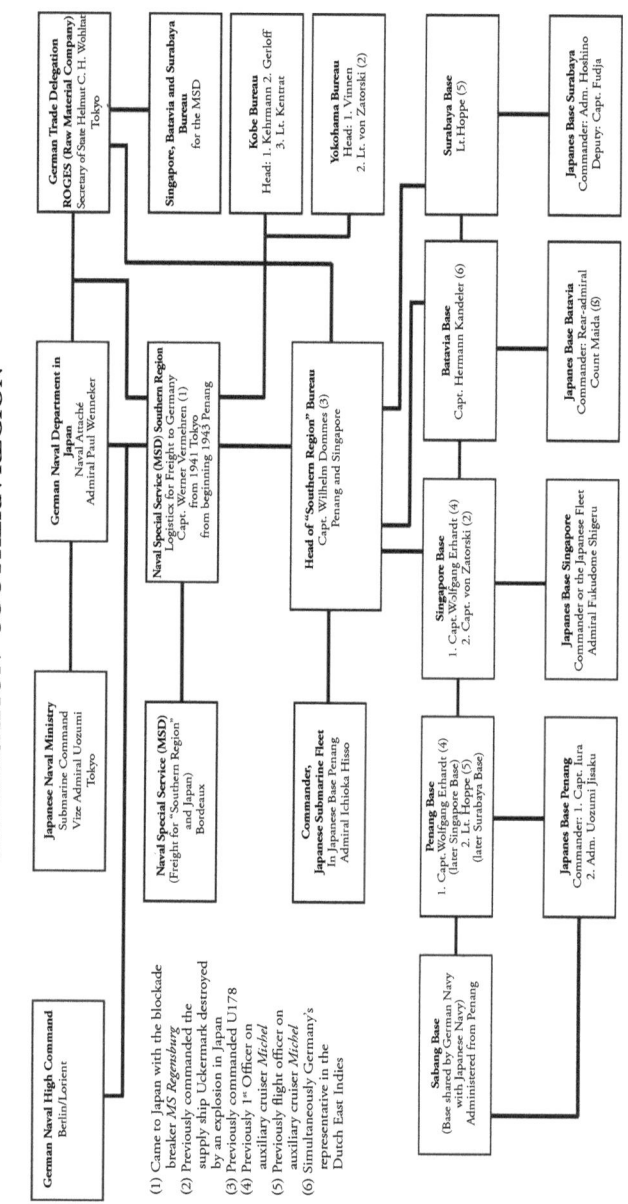

ORGANISATION "SOUTHERN REGION"

German Naval High Command
Berlin/Lorient

Japanese Naval Ministry
Submarine Command
Vice Admiral Uozumi
Tokyo

German Naval Department in Japan
Naval Attaché
Admiral Paul Wenneker

German Trade Delegation
ROGES (Raw Material Company)
Secretary of State Helmut C. H. Wohltat
Tokyo

Naval Special Service (MSD)
(Freight for "Southern Region" and Japan)
Bordeaux

Naval Special Service (MSD) Southern Region
Logistics for Freight to Germany
Capt. Werner Vermehren (1)
from 1941 Tokyo
from beginning 1943 Penang

Singapore, Batavia and Surabaya Bureau
for the MSD

Kobe Bureau
Head: 1. Kehrmann 2. Gerloff
3. Lt. Kentrat

Yokohama Bureau
Head: 1. Vinnen
2. Lt. von Zatorski (2)

Commander, Japanese Submarine Fleet
In Japanese Base Penang
Admiral Ichioka Hisso

Head of "Southern Region" Bureau
Capt. Wilhelm Dommes (3)
Penang and Singapore

Batavia Base
Capt. Hermann Kandeler (6)

Surabaya Base
Lt. Hoppe (5)

Penang Base
1. Capt. Wolfgang Erhardt (4)
(later Singapore Base)
2. Lt. Hoppe (5)
(later Surabaya Base)

Singapore Base
1. Capt. Wolfgang Erhardt (4)
2. Capt. von Zatorski (2)

Japanes Base Singapore
Commander or the Japanese Fleet
Admiral Fukudome Shigeru

Japanes Base Batavia
Commander: Rear-admiral
Count Maida (6)

Japanes Base Surabaya
Commander: Adm. Hoshino
Deputy: Capt. Fudja

Sabang Base
(Base shared by German Navy with Japanese Navy)
Administered from Penang

Japanes Base Penang
Commander: 1. Capt. Iura
2. Adm. Uozumi Jisaku

(1) Came to Japan with the blockade breaker *MS Regensburg*
(2) Previously commanded the supply ship Uckermark destroyed by an explosion in Japan
(3) Previously commanded U178
(4) Previously 1st Officer on auxiliary cruiser *Michel*
(5) Previously flight officer on auxiliary cruiser *Michel*
(6) Simultaneously Germany's representative in the Dutch East Indies

Ill. 53
Organisation of the German Navy in the "Southern Region"

After the disaster of the surface blockade breakers they had to move as quickly as possible to submarine transport for the urgently needed raw materials. However, the Germany Navy did not yet have any ships suited for the task and the construction of the new German freight U-boats of type XX continued to be delayed by Hitler's objections. They were supposed to be long-distance submarines numbered U 1601 to 1800 for voyages to South East Asia. They had no torpedoes and could carry about 800 tonnes of freight. The construction of these special freight U-boats was however shelved in favour of the newer and more modern electric-powered U-boats of type XXI and XXIII in 1944.

At the beginning of the Second World War Italy, with 120 submarines, was second in the world only to the Soviet Union's 160.[1] In comparison, at the beginning of the war Germany only had 51, mostly small, serviceable U-boats, with a further 78 under construction. Italy was proud of its navy, with which it intended to secure its hegemony in the Mediterranean. However, the Allies did not take the Italian submarine fleet seriously, since they were not technically up to date and the commanders and crews were not seriously enough motivated to fulfil their objectives.[2] Italy did in fact have a large fleet, but as Hitler is reported to have scornfully said to his admirals after viewing the Italian fleet in the Mediterranean, their *outward appearance was greater than their fighting ability.*

There were ten large Italian submarines in Bordeaux, which were too slow for the naval war in the Atlantic and had so far had little success. Hitler therefore thought that deploying them for the transport of freight between Europe and South East Asia would be more useful than an involvement in battle which was not at all sure of success. He exchanged them for nine German combat U-boats of type VII C. After a six-week refit the Italian submarines would be capable of transport operations. Their load capacity was 200 tons per boat.

At about the same time as the first Japanese submarines set off from Penang for Europe the first five Italian submarines set off from Bordeaux for South East Asia in May 1943 as Mission Aquila (Eagle), carrying freight and passengers. The freight was mainly material for the construction and fitting out of the naval bases.

The first submarine to reach Sabang was the *Commandante Cappellini* on the 9ᵗʰ of July 1943. She was presumably carrying Telefunken "Würzburg" radar equipment for Sabang. The *Reginaldo Guiliani* arrived in Singapore on the 26ᵗʰ of July 1943, and the *Luigi Torelli* in Sabang on the 26ᵗʰ of August

---

1   Brennecke, *Jäger - Gejagte,* p. 117
2   Brennecke, *Jäger - Gejagte,* p. 117

1943. The *Luigi Torelli* definitely had two "Würzburg"[1] radar systems for the "Southern Region" and Japan on board, as well as Telefunken radar engineer Heinrich Foders and another technician.[2] The *Barbarigo* was sunk near the Azores on the 19th of June 1943 with several "Würzburg" radar systems on board, and the *Enrico Tazzoli* was reported missing in the Atlantic.

Only a few days after the departure of the first Italian submarines they were followed by two German combat U-boats, the U 511 and U 178, as the vanguard of Operation Monsun [Monsoon]. The U 511 was the first of the two to reach Penang. She had already been engaged in several combat missions in the Caribbean, the Atlantic and of the West African coast, sinking several Allied freighters and a US tanker. She left Lorient for South East Asia under the command of Captain Fritz Schneewind on the 10th of May 1943: they had named her the *Marco Polo*. There had initially been a rocket-launcher fitted on her deck which could be fired either from the surface or underwater from a depth of up to 12 metres. The rockets had a range of four kilometres and had been tested on the U 511 by Dr Wernher von Braun in the Baltic near Peenemünde. The rocket launcher was dismounted for the long trip to South East Asia because it reduced underwater speed considerably.

The U 511 was carrying freight for the new German naval bases in Penang and several passengers. As well as several German officers, scientists and engineers, these included the Japanese Naval Attaché, Admiral Yokoi Tadao, who had been stationed in Berlin since 1940 as the Japanese representative of the Tripartite Pact, and the new German Ambassador to Tokyo, Heinrich Georg Stahmer. Stahmer had been appointed in spite of having a "non-aryan" wife, and was replacing Eugen Ott who had come to grief because of the Richard Sorge espionage affair, as will be related later in this book.

In the Indian Ocean the U 511 sank two US Liberty Freighters, before arriving at the Japanese base at Sabang, continuing to Penang by the 7th of August 1943. It was the first U-boat to be handed over to the Japanese Navy as a gift from Hitler for the purpose of replication, to show his gratitude for Japanese help in the acquisition of raw materials. The U 511 was welcomed enthusiastically by the Japanese in Penang with one celebration dinner after another, and then officially handed over to the Imperial Japanese Navy.

Fritz Schneewind was commanded to report to Admiral Wenneker in Tokyo for debriefing, arriving by Japanese aircraft. He was presented with an important decoration by the Japanese Emperor Hirohito in person for safely delivering Hitler's gift.

---

1   According to statement by radar engineer Heinrich Foders
2   Tsuda, Kiyokazu, *The Würzburg Project* (Translation of the Japanese title) CQ Verlags GmbH, Tokyo 15.12.1981. The book was kindly given to me by F. Flakowski

Ill. 54
Japanese-German banquet celebrating the arrival of U 511 in Penang

The German NCOs and other ranks were accommodated in hotels by the Japanese, and a number of villas were requisitioned for the use of the officers in Park Road. In these villas they were served by the same Chinese or Malay staff who had previously worked there. The German Navy Office paid for this board and lodging in Chinese dollars, which were also used to pay the German personnel's wages in South East Asia. For security reasons all the crew members had to wear civilian clothing, though to show the Japanese they were German they had to wear a black, red and gold cord on their jackets – of course this also made them instantly recognisable to any of the many Allied agents in Penang.[1]

In Penang and Singapore the Japanese submarine crew was familiarised with the U 511's technology, and some of her German crew were stationed in Penang as staff in the base. At the beginning of September 1943, now designated RO-500 and flying the Japanese Rising Sun banner, she sailed on to Japan with the new German Ambassador, the Japanese Naval Attaché and several members of the German crew. On this final stretch of the voyage the Japanese submariners received their final training from their German counterparts. 90 days after leaving Lorient the U 511/RO-500 arrived at the Japanese naval dockyard in Kure. In September 1943 RO-500 officially entered Japanese service under Captain Okuda. She operated in the Pacific until the end of the war, when she surrendered to the USA.

The German submariners sailed back from Kure to Singapore in the blockade breaker *MS Osorno*. In October 1943 they were distributed among the Italian submarines that had been taken over by the German Navy. This was because the Japanese Navy had confiscated them and handed them to

---

1   Brennecke, *Haie im Paradies,* p. 41

the Germans after Italy declared an armistice on the 3rd of September 1943 and then entered the war on the side of the Allies.

The *Commandante Cappellini*, the first Italian submarine to reach the "Southern Region", was taken over by the German Navy in Singapore in September 1943 and deployed as UIT 24 (*Unterwasser Italien Transport* [Underwater Italian Transport]) under the command of Lieutenant Heinrich Pahls. This was the first real transport submarine to sail under German colours, and was handed over in a solemn ceremony in Singapore attended by Admiral Wenneker and several high-ranking Japanese officers. She carried out transport operations between the bases in the "Southern Region" until the end of the war.

The *Emilio Tortelli* was taken over in Singapore at the same time, to serve under Captain Werner Striegler as UIT 25, as was the *Reginaldo Guiliani* under Captain Heinrich Schäfer as UIT 23. These two were mainly used for transport between Japan and the "Southern Region", a voyage normally lasting nine days.

The UIT submarines now had mixed German and Italian crews. Many of the Italian officers and men had not wanted to fall into Japanese captivity and volunteered to serve in the German Navy. UIT 23, UIT 24 and UIT 25 were the only Italian submarines to reach the "Southern Region". *Alpino Bagnoli* was taken over by the German Navy in Bordeaux and set sail for the "Southern Region" as the UIT 22. In March 1944 she was sunk by an Allied aircraft off the Cape of Good Hope with the loss of all 43 crew.

The remaining serviceable Italian submarines were sent to the "Southern Region" as the Mercator Group. The *Archimede* was sunk off the coast of Brazil and the *Leonardo da Vinci* in the Bay of Biscay. After Mussolini was deposed, the *Ammiraglio Cagni* surrendered to the British in Durban in South Africa with her Italian crew. *Guiseppe Finzi* was taken over by the German Navy in Bordeaux but could not be deployed before the war ended because of engine problems and was scuttled off Bordeaux by the German Navy shortly before the end of the war.

At the end of July 1943 the small Italian cruiser *Eritrea* arrived in Singapore to act as supply ship for the Italian freight submarines in the "Southern Region". After Mussolini was deposed, the Japanese regarded the Italians with great suspicion. They were not sure of the Italians' loyalty, and deliberately delayed the ship's departure several times. Italy's declaration of war on Germany on the 3rd of September 1943 led to an immediate break between Germany and Italy. Unnoticed by the German and Japanese port authorities in Singapore the *Eritrea* escaped from the port and sailed to Ceylon in British India, where the Italian captain surrendered himself and his crew to the

British, handing over to the Allies a great deal of top secret information, such as German and Japanese naval strength in the "Southern Region", positions of supply ships, encryption codes for radio communication and so on. This was a severe blow which made the German Navy's conduct of operations in the Indian Ocean and the "Southern Region" considerably more difficult.

A further German U-boat, U 1224, was to be handed over to Japan as a gift from Hitler, though this time with a completely Japanese crew, which was to be trained in Germany and Norway beforehand. With a double crew, her own and the crew designated for the U 1224, the Japanese submarine cruiser I-8 left Penang of the 27th of June 1943 and sailed to Brest. It loaded with cargo and several passengers and returned safely to Singapore.

When the training of the Japanese crew of the U 1224 in Norway was complete it sailed, now under Japanese colours as the RO 501, for Japan in April 1944. On the 13th of May 1944 it was sunk off the Cape Verde islands. There were no survivors.

Shortly after taking up office, Ambassador Stahmer, visited the countries of the Greater Asian Co-Prosperity Sphere with a high-ranking Japanese delegation. There is a memo from Walther Hewel to the Foreign minister about this visit:

On the 28th of January 1944 Stahmer began a fourteen-day visit to the Japanese southern regions at the invitation of the Japanese Foreign Ministry and the Japanese General Staff.[1]

Stahmer was already familiar with the base at Penang after his journey in the U 511, his brief stay having shown him the base in its construction phase. Now he briefly described the situation there and the morale of the U-boat crews as he found them at the beginning of 1944. There were now several German submarines moored at the quay in Penang, and Stahmer met a large number of contented German sailors.

In spite of oppressive heat I found the officers and men at the Penang station in good spirits and well-looked after when I visited. [...] A mountain railway that goes to a mountain plateau about eight hundred metres high, above the humid heat of the day is one possible form of recreation. [...] The submarines had a quite long waiting period in Penang until they could be overhauled and made ready for the return journey with the base's relatively primitive facilities. In 1944 these voyages were already very dangerous and the number of submarines that made it through the long journey in spite of the [Author's note: Allies] was becoming ever smaller.[2]

In a telegram to Hewel on the 24th of February 1944, Stahmer reported that he would return to Tokyo on the 25th of February. According to Stahmer's

---

1   AA: Hewel, Akte 147720/1420
2   Stahmer, *Japans Niederlage...*, pp. 197f

report, repairs could already be carried out in Batavia and the Italian UIT freight submarines should preferably be based there.[1]

To ensure that cooperation with the Japanese ran as smoothly as possible, German-Japanese interpreters were stationed in all the German bases. In Surabaya, for example, there wasa Dr Schreiber and in Batavia Dr Hupfer, who had been a lecturer in the University of Tokyo for many years before the war.

There may have been workshops in all the German bases, but there was a shortage of qualified staff. Since the big British naval floating dock had been towed away before the arrival of the Japanese, Singapore was the only base with dry docks for general maintenance of the ships, which meant that all German ships stationed in the "Southern Region" needing exterior maintenance work had to travel to the dry docks of the former British naval dockyard at Selatar in Singapore. The German Head of Station in Singapore had to negotiate timetables with the Japanese Naval Attaché responsible, Rear Admiral Watanabe. Since the Japanese boats could also only be overhauled here there were continuous bottlenecks. The docks were always occupied and work went on night and day. Even so, long waiting times for the German ships had to be accepted.

To clean the submarines that had just arrived from Europe took on average three days, general maintenance took 20 days, cleaning the outer surfaces and repainting at least 14 days, and for refuelling and loading ammunition, provisions and freight at least another fourteen days more. If a submarine was coming from another base, then at least another three days had to be added for the voyage to Singapore. Then there were test trips and at least one test dive. Until a German submarine was ready to sail back to her home port on the French Atlantic coast would take at least three months.

---

1   Stahmer, *Japans Niederlage ...*, p. 197

24. Operation Monsoon

It was not just freight submarines that sailed to the Dutch East Indies: many conventional combat U-boats also operated in the waters of the Indian Ocean and the Malay Archipelago. These were initially Class IX D2 long-distance submarines, also known as "East Asia Boats". The mission of the first submarines sent out, all members of the Monsoon group, was to take freight and passengers for the construction of the bases in South East Asia. They were also to sink Allied supply ships that were under way in the Indian Ocean, the Arabian Sea and Dutch East Indian waters. The seaways in this region were not yet adequately protected by the Allies, and Dönitz wanted to make a surprise strike here like *Operation Paukenschlag* [Thunderbolt] in the Atlantic.

The U 511, shortly followed by the type IX D2 U 178 under the command of Captain Wilhelm Dommes, arrived in the port of Penang in August 1943 after five months at sea. The Italian submarine *Luigi Torelli*, which was carrying freight and passengers, for example Telefunken "Würzburg" radar equipment and my personal acquaintance, Telefunken engineer Heinrich Foders, to Sabang and Singapore, had been refuelled east of South Africa by U 511. This mission will be described in more detail later.

The commander of the U 178, Captain Dommes, had already survived several operations, but now he was relatively exhausted. He had previously been a merchant captain, at the beginning of the war he became 1st Officer of the Watch on the battleship *Scharnhorst* and from April 1940 he commanded the U 431 in the Mediterranean. The long voyage to South East Asia took the U-boat commanders and crews to their physical and mental limit. Dommes was troubled by increasingly frequent stomach cramps so that his 1st Officer of the Watch, Wilhelm Spahr, gradually had to take over command of the U 178. After arriving in Penang, Dommes was allowed to stay ashore and, after his recovery, became Fleet Commander in the "Southern Region" in March 1944.

Operation Monsoon began in June 1943. Eleven U-boats of type IX-C and IX-D2 and a submarine tanker were despatched to the Indian Ocean. Initially, two type IX-D2 submarines were to operate in the Arabian Gulf to disrupt British oil transport before continuing to Sabang and Penang. Extremely sophisticated logistics were required to deal with the enormous distances between Europe and South East Asia. Depending on which port voyages started from and ended at, the distance round South Africa to the

"Southern Region" was between 11,500 and 13,000 nautical miles (21,000 to 24,000 kilometres). The length of the voyage lasted, depending on what operations were undertaken in the Atlantic and Indian Oceans, between 90 days for U 511 and 171 days for U 188.

Travelling economically on the surface at 10 knots (19 km/hour) the German long-distance U-boats of the Monsoon Group had a range of up to 46,000 kilometres; at their highest speed of 18.2 knots (34 km/hour) and when travelling below the surface this was naturally much less. So that they could operate in the Indian Ocean unhindered on their voyage round Africa past Ceylon to their target area, they were provided with fuel and fresh provisions by supply ships while under way and in their target area. This required detailed planning. The sea around Ceylon was a particularly important operational area for German U-boats. The Royal Navy's most important anchorage in the western Indian Ocean was at Trincomalee on the east coast of Ceylon and it was important to disrupt merchant shipping here as much as possible. The Japanese air force had already sunk several British cruisers and 23 merchant ships here.[1]

There were frequent incidents and delays because the slower and clumsier supply submarines often had to return to their bases on the French Atlantic coast to prepare for new supply voyages. They offered an easy target for enemy attacks. Later, supplies could be topped up at the bases in the "Southern Region".

The yearly strong monsoon winds also caused the "Asia Boats" problems. Unlike the Atlantic, there were no reliable weather data for the Indian Ocean and the waters further east. The submarine commanders were forced to rely on the forecasts of their own on-board meteorologists. Every voyage was a journey into the unknown.

First the strong south-west monsoon blew from July to August, then came the north-east monsoon. With strong winds and high waves U-boats often made very slow progress. The Indian Ocean is famous – if not infamous – for its high swells. One wave after another passed over the low-lying boat and crashed over the conning tower: it was tossed about on the water like a cork. Even old and experienced sailors were not safe from seasickness in seas like that. A contributory factor was no doubt also the perspiration of about 55 crewmen and the smell of diesel oil in the confined space of the U-boat.

The watch on the conning tower – fastened in with belts so that they were not washed overboard – were often standing up to their waists in water: many a man had been lost because of a sudden high swell. The watch were swathed in oilskin, which was surely not very pleasant in the tropical tem-

---

1   Tischer, *Die Abenteuer des letzten Kapers*, p. 55

peratures of the Indian Ocean, though the water temperature of about 27°C must have been more pleasant than the ice-cold Atlantic. The boats had often come from the Arctic ice and run through all possible climate zones, and for safety reasons they sometimes had to travel very far to the South as they rounded Africa, as far as the edge of the Antarctic ice floes.

In tropical waters the temperatures in the U-boats were murderously hot and humid. When travelling on the surface the temperature in the main body was up to 40°C, in the engine room even 60 to 65°C. There was no air-conditioning in submarines in those days.

By day the U-boats had to switch to the much slower underwater mode when danger threatened and sail under electric power. At night they could come to the surface and use the diesel motors. Now the ship could be aired and the batteries charged for the next dive. Apart from one of the last boats to be sent out, the "Asia Boats" had no snorkels, so that they could not rely on unlimited underwater travel.

In calms seas there was another problem: marine luminescence, which is particularly strong in the Indian Ocean. On a dark night the ship would often leave a light trail hundreds of metres long behind it through the phosphorescent plankton. In such cases they often had to travel under water even when there was no immediate danger.

The morning, when the red sun rose over the silky blue Indian Ocean colouring the feathery mists pink, was the loveliest moment of the day, but for the submariners also the most dangerous. The men on watch could not spare a single glance at the beauty of this natural wonder. Every one of the four-man watch had to scan his 90° segment with eagle eyes, ready to give the signal for a crash dive at any moment. It was precisely at this time, especially when they were travelling close to land or in a convoy with air protection, that enemy aircraft would suddenly appear out of the radiantly bright background of the rising sun. They were sometimes spotted very late, and then every second was a matter of life and death. Fortunately this precarious time did not last very because here, close to the Equator, the sun rises and sets with dramatic speed.

When the alarm klaxon began to sound and the water thundered into the ballast tanks the crew on deck and the bridge had exactly fifteen seconds to get into the boat and batten down the hatches. After 35 seconds she would already have dived ten metres. Of course, this only worked when a trained crew worked together perfectly. This meant in particular the men at the helm, the sailor at the periscope, the navigating officer, the chief engineer, the sonar man, the radio officer and above all the commander. They were all a team who concentrated on working closely together, a heterogeneous group – young and old, workers and educated men, bound together in life and death. In this cramped space they were all dependent on each other.

After a crash dive there was a deathly hush in the submarine. All that could be heard was the soft humming of the electric motors and transformers and the gentle vibration of the submarine itself. Because of the sensitivity of the enemy's listening devices all commands had to be given in a whisper. The silence was only broken by the clicking of switches, machines and relays. In the control room, the heart of the U-boat, the crew kept their eyes fixed on the dimly lit dials of the instruments. They checked the depth finder, the air pressure, the consumption of the electric motors; they adjusted the pumps for the balance tanks and regulated various equipment with buttons and hand wheels. A ghostly, tense silence reigned as they hoped not to be found and to return to the surface undamaged.

The cook had a very responsible role: he had to ration the provisions. In a tiny galley on a rocking boat he had to conjure up varied and tasty meals for between 50 and 60 men. Even in heavy seas, meals had to be ready on time. Bread was baked on board. On Sundays and holidays and on special occasions there would be a festive meal with several courses and a cake in the afternoon. If a crew was not satisfied with the food, positive morale could soon turn into its opposite. If U-boat crews had to spend months in a cramped submarine, Dönitz demanded that they should at least get the best food possible. Fresh food usually ran out after one or two weeks. Lemons were refrigerated and so kept longer. Fishing was allowed in calm seas on routes away from the main sea-lanes: many a large tuna or a four-foot bonito mackerel helped to make the on-board menu more varied.

As German passengers who travelled on Japanese submarines reported, food there was much more monotonous and often the same for weeks on end: rice with vegetables and sausage, three times a day. The Japanese crews did not mind.

During the months of the voyage to South east Asia the lack of fresh fruit and vegetables was compensated for by a daily dose of multivitamins. When the box of vitamin pills was accidentally forgotten on the U 66 under Commander Lüdde, after a few weeks the whole crew showed symptoms of scurvy: yellow skin, joint pains, lethargy and loose teeth.

On their voyages to Asia the submarines were packed to the decks with spare parts, food, ammunition and so on. There would be 15 to 16 tonnes of provisions for the long journey. Gigantic batteries for the electric motors when underwater, compressed air and oxygen cylinders, valves, pumps and hand-wheels left little space for the crew. When off watch the exhausted submariners would sleep in any possible position wherever there was space.

There were no chairs. They sat on food-cartons, even in the officers' mess. They slept with their clothes on. Life in the floating tin can was laborious and monotonous. The spare torpedoes were stored in the space in the bow and stern, in the spaces between the electric motors and the exhaust pipe in the stern. Every torpedo that was fired cheered the crew, because it meant there would be more space on board.

The dangerous life spent crammed together for months in the discomfort of the U-boats produced among the crew a spirit of solidarity and comradeship that was not found in other branches of the service. They all depended 100% on each other: they all survived together or they died together – and life and death were very close to each other.

To keep the crews fit and in good spirits all kinds of activities were organised: sporting competitions, games, craft competitions, singing together or listening to records. There was always someone on board who could get a song going with his harmonica. Pictures were painted and superb model ships were made. In the Indian Ocean some commanders even sailed to a remote atoll and allowed their crews to play around in the warm sea. However, when part of a crew was lost while swimming in the Atlantic because the submarine came under attack and had to execute a crash dive, swimming in the sea was forbidden by the naval high command.

Most U-boats had a weekly ship's newspaper with world news, general information, crossword puzzles and poems. Any crew member could contribute. On the U 861, commanded by Jürgen Oesten, they produced *Der Monsun Bote* [The Monsoon Messenger], edited by war reporter Lieutenant Hermann Kiefer on their voyage to Penang. I could not find any of his reports on the successful voyage, presumably because he arrived in Penang only a few months before the end of the war. Kiefer remained in the "Southern Region", becoming a British PoW when the war ended.

In the control room and the other sitting and sleeping areas, the steel hull was covered in white-painted cork to prevent condensation in the humid, oily-smelling atmosphere. The control room was the brain of the U-boat where all the threads came together. In the dimmed light you could see instruments, dials, valves and all kinds of hand-wheels. The rudder and the periscope were operated from here, and the bridge watch and the look out made their way to the conning tower through here as well. The commander's cabin, divided off only by a curtain, was accessible from here.

The bow end of the ship was separated from the control room by watertight hatches. It was here that you would find the officers' mess, though like everywhere else on board there was no luxury here, just a similar airless cramped space. There were two toilets for the 50 men, but on the long-distance voyages to South East Asia one of them could not be used because it was full of boxes of tinned food. The only shower on board and all washing facilities used only salt water direct from the sea. The limited supplies of fresh water could only be used for cooking and drinking.

The long-distance submarines often carried passengers in addition to the 55-man crew, and at first they usually had a ship's doctor and a medical orderly to treat injuries and other medical problems, including some quite serious cases. Several appendices were removed under far from sterile conditions on a table set up in the officer's mess.

Some very complex operations were carried out on the high seas. When Lieutenant Lask, Second Officer of the Watch on the U 861, delayed reporting a middle-ear abscess to the Ship's doctor, Dr von Gehlen, until it was far too late, the doctor decided to remove it by an operation on the skull, even though his medical equipment did not contain the necessary instruments. With the help of the Chief Engineer they manufactured from the contents of the engine room a small chisel with a rounded cutting surface and a kind of spoon. So that the ship would be perfectly still for the operation, they dived to 80 metres. There, in the middle of the Indian Ocean, the operation was successfully carried out. When the U 861 was waiting off Sabang for its escort to Penang ten days later, Lieutenant Lask was already fit to resume his duties.

Another complicated operation is recorded as having taken place on the U 859 under the command of Lieutenant Johann Jensen. The boat set sail from Kiel for the "Southern Region" on the 4th of April 1944. In the South Atlantic she sank a freighter and in the operational area between Madagascar, the island of Réunion and Zanzibar she sank some more freighters and a tanker. In a duel between the U-boat and a British Catalina aircraft one sailor was killed and the Second Officer of the Watch seriously injured: he had several pieces of shrapnel in his skull. The officers' mess was transformed into an operating theatre and the ship's doctor removed the splinters from his cerebellum. Another successful operation in a submerged U-boat.

Dr Erwin Kühn, the ship's doctor on the U 843, had to operate on the lung of radio operator Martin on the return voyage from Batavia. This operation was also successful. In Bergen he was taken to hospital, where he quickly recovered. This hospital stay was very lucky for him, because on the way from Bergen to Kiel the U 843 was sunk only 100 nautical miles from its destination. Of the 58 men on board only 12 survived.

The ship's doctor always had other duties beside his medical ones, but towards the end of the war a shortage of doctors meant that only medical orderlies were available for their long voyages.

On the U-boats there was a playful ceremony for the "new boys" on crossing the Equator for the first time, with a certificate to prove it. For the young sailors it was a crude test of manhood using shoe polish, herring brine or shaving soap. The Equator was crossed several times on the voyage to South East Asia, the first time on the way south along the West African coast, and then on the Indian Ocean of the way to Sabang or Penang and again between Singapore and Batavia.

If nothing unusual had happened during the course of the day, the men were allowed out onto the tower in small groups to enjoy some daylight, some fresh air or a cigarette. In the boat itself smoking was strictly forbidden.

The risk of being spotted and attacked when on the surface was very great. To widen the field of view of the U-boats, which were only a few metres above water level, some were fitted with tow-gyrocopters. Nicknamed "wagtails", these could be carried by the motion of the boat through the air or the sea breeze to a height of over 100 metres by autorotation. Built by the Focke company, they had a folding rotor with a diameter of four metres, and were fitted with a bosun's chair for a lookout. It must have been quite uncomfortable up there in the wind. Since an air attack meant a crash dive there often wasn't enough time to haul the lookout safely back on board. Men who were urgently needed on the boat were lost.

The visual range of the boat on the surface could be extended to up to 50 Kilometres using the "wagtail". This gave early warning of enemy attacks so

---

1 The "Crossing the Line" ceremony took place about 3,000 kilometres off the coast of West Aftrica at the latitude of Gabon. The sea voyage from Bordeaux to Batavia took 130 days. The certificate was signed by Lieutenant Fritz Steinfeld and the Chief Engineer, Lieutenant (Eng.) Weber. The name of the sailor who received the document was Dienst.

that they could take avoiding action, crash dive or plan a counter-attack in good time.

The Japanese navy was very interested in the "wagtail". Captain Wilhelm Dommes, head of the "Southern Region" office made a very advantageous exchange: in return for a wagtail he was given a Japanese seaplane of the *Reichiki* type for the German air base in Penang.

Using supply and tanker submarines the range and duration of the "East Asia Boats" could be greatly extended. For example, the U 862 (Type IX D2) sailed far into the Pacific and sank a merchant ship off the east coast of Australia.

Even the initial deployment of the first Monsoon Group was plagued with losses. Four U-boats were sunk, one U-boat and the U-tanker were damaged. Another boat had to offload its fuel to those U-boats that were still serviceable and return to the home port. Of the twelve U-boats that originally started out on Operation Monsoon only five reached the Arabian Gulf. Here the U 533 was also sunk. Only five of the original twelve, U 168, U 183, U 188 and U 532, reached port in the "Southern Region" between October and November 1943.

U 200, which set sail from Kiel for South East Asia on the 12ᵗʰ of June 1943 was sunk in the Atlantic with the loss of 68 men. On board there were also men of the Brandenburg Special Unit whose main mission was carrying out acts of sabotage behind enemy lines. Until that time the Special Unit had only been deployed in the Near East, in Afghanistan and South Africa. Two attempts to use them in the USA failed – they were captured shortly after landing. Whether the Special Unit was to be carried to the Dutch East Indies on the U 200 or landed before then in Africa or India is not shown in the surviving documents.

Many *Volks* Germans had volunteered for the Brandenburg Special Unit because they were highly valued for their perfect knowledge of local languages which qualified them for work behind the lines.

The U 533, which travelled from Kiel to Lorient in the Bay of Biscay, was most unfortunate. It sailed from Lorient for Penang on the 5ᵗʰ of July 1943. It was supposed to operate first in the Arabian Sea and the Gulf of Oman disrupting Allied shipping. In October 1943 the U 533 was surprised off the coast of Oman by a royal Air Force bomber and sunk. Only one of the 53 on board, Able Seaman Günther Schmidt, survived. He swam towards the coast for 28 hours before being rescued from the shark-infested sea by the British patrol boat *HMS Hiravati*.

What was a German U-boat doing in the Gulf of Oman? That was a question asked by the German magazine *Der Spiegel*. On the 8ᵗʰ of December

2009 it printed an article on the demise of the U 533 under the headline "*Untergang vorm Morgenland*" [Sunk in the Orient]. Little was known of what happened to the survivor, Schmidt. After he was captured and fed in the British sergeants' mess in Sharjah all trace of him was lost, reported *Der Spiegel*.

Other sources claim that Schmidt swam for 28 hours and reached land at Khor-Fakkam near Muscat in Oman, where he was looked after by an Arab tribe until being captured by the British. He had been taken from Basra to Cairo where all trace of him was lost.

The wreck of the U 533 still lies in the Gulf of Oman, only 25 nautical miles from the Emirate of Fujairah. The diving team of the Desert Sports Diving Club in Dubai identified and filmed the wreck at a depth of 108 metres. U 534, the twin sister ship of U 533 entered service on the 23rd of December 1942 and was sunk by air attack on the 3rd of May 1945 between Denmark and Sweden. It was raised and restored, and is now a museum ship in Liverpool, England.

The position regarding Germany's supplies of raw materials from South East Asia was becoming much more precarious. The chances of a conventional surface ship reaching her home port were practically nil, and therefore the last two years of the war saw a considerable increase in the deployment of submarines for raw material transport. This met with little success because new Allied developments in the field of radar and sonar had made the seas too dangerous.

Freight was transported by gigantic U-boats of type X, which had originally been intended as minelayers. From 1939 onwards eight of these were built. After a refit lasting only six weeks they could be deployed as freight U-boats. 90 metres long, over 9 metres wide and over 10 metres high, they were the German Navy's biggest submarines in the Second World War. Their range at economy speed was 30,000 kilometres, their surface speed was 17 knots, (31.5 km/hour) and submerged 7 knots (13 km/hour). The freight U-boats could reach their destination in South East Asia relatively quickly, given that they could travel on the surface in the South Atlantic and the Indian Ocean as long as they avoided the normal shipping lanes. Travelling on the surface was very economical in terms of fuel. They were crewed by 5 officers and 47 men. It could dive to an astonishing 220 metres. When they were fully laden, the Chief Engineer had to keep a sharp eye on the balance tanks because it as possible for a laden boat to plunge uncontrollably bow or stern first into the depths.

As minelayers they could carry 66 mines and 15 torpedoes. After refitting as transports they only had two torpedoes on board and a 2 cm four-barrel anti-aircraft canon on deck. The cargo was stowed in pressurised containers in the mine stores, the bow and stern spaces and the bilges. Every little space was used for cargo. Even the unused torpedo tubes were filled with raw rubber or other material needed in Germany. All eight of these submarines travelled the route to Japan and South East Asia.

Combat U-boats of class IX D2 were now increasingly used as supplementary transports in South East Asia. They were 87.5 metres long, 7.5 metres wide and 10.2 metres high. In some of them the torpedo tubes were removed to create more space for freight and extra tanks. They could carry up to 260 tonnes of freight. Their range at economy speed was over 55,000 kilometres, meaning that they could travel from Europe to Japan and back without refuelling. These submarines also supplied other U-boats with fuel en route from their own stock.

Freight from the "Southern Region" for Europe consisted mainly of rubber, molybdenum, tungsten and tin, as well as iodine, opium and quinine for medical purposes. The tin was cast in bars and stored in the keel, the tungsten and molybdenum kept in tin containers. Smaller U-boats of type IX C had a cargo capacity of only about 150 tonnes. They could probably have taken more cargo, but their maximum capacity was never tested.

In the "Southern Region" the submarines were supplied with fuel and lubricants from the restored refineries on Sumatra and Borneo. Since the high temperatures in the tropics placed considerable and incalculable strain on the submarines' batteries, they often had to travel to Japan, since batteries of that size were not available in the "Southern Region". They discovered that the batteries replicated in Japan were considerably better than the German originals. They had a longer life and a greater capacity.

The torpedo store was in Penang, and this is where the boats were loaded for their home journey. Normally very few torpedoes were loaded, on the one hand to provide more space for cargo and on the other because torpedoes were in short supply in the "Southern Region" because the blockade breakers were no longer bringing replacements. The torpedoes loaded for the return journey were intended to be fired at Allied shipping in the Indian Ocean before the boats returned home.[1] Then there was a bit more space for the crew.

Far too late, Hitler gave his blessing to the plan to build even bigger U-boats of type XX. Designed as freighters, they would have carried a payload of up to 800 tonnes. Because of other priorities the construction of these boats was continually delayed so that they were never deployed before the end of the war.

---

1   Brennecke, *Schwarze Schiffe* ..., pp. 230ff

Even before the First World War Germany had developed submarine freighters, the U-boats *Deutschland* and *Bremen*. *U-Deutschland* was an 1,860 tonne submarine and carried freight and post from Germany to America twice under the command of Captain König.[1] Type XX was a further development of *U-Deutschland*.

As already mentioned, only five of the 12 submarines in the first Monsoon Group reached the Indian Ocean, and after the U 533 was sunk in the Gulf of Oman, only four reached their destination in the "Southern Region". Dönitz wished to compensate for these major losses and so sent five further U-boats to South East Asia between the end of September and the beginning of November 1943. This was an even greater disaster: the U 219 had to distribute its fuel to the other U-boats and was called back to France; the U 848, U 849 and U 850 were sunk by the Allies; only the U 510 under Lieutenant Alfred Eick reached Penang.

Since the U 510's operations are documented with almost no gaps in the record I will describe her actions in detail. Lieutenant Alfred Eick took her over on the 17th of April 1943. In his first operation between the 3rd of June and the 29th of August 1943 in the South Atlantic and off the coast of Brazil he sank four Allied ships, including a tanker.

In Lorient the U 510 was equipped for another voyage which would take her to the waters of the Dutch East Indies and Japan. This was one of the first U-boats to be equipped with the new acoustic torpedoes, codenamed "*Zaunkönig*" [Wren]. They had a built in acoustic guidance system that sensed the sound of the enemy ship's propellers and headed for the target independently. Since acoustic torpedoes could be fired from a much greater distance and the U-boat could veer away or dive deeper immediately after firing, this made detecting and pursuing it much more difficult. The use of acoustic torpedoes was kept top secret and only revealed after the end of the war. The Allies had, however, got wind of this very early on and after the initial German successes deployed "sound buoys". Now the *Zaunkönig* would steer towards the sound buoy and miss the ship.

Armed with this new weapon, the U 510 set sail for South East Asia in the second half of November 1943. In mid-Atlantic she was refuelled and provisioned by U-boot tanker U 219 to extend her operational range as much as possible. The U 219 had actually been supposed to lay mines off Cape Town and Colombo, but when the supply ship of the second Monsoon Group was sunk, the U 219 had to take over that role and supply the other submarines with fuel so that they could reach their home ports safely. Only the U 510 continued on course for South East Asia. Near Madagascar it was refuelled,

---

1   Gannon, *Operation Paukenschlag*, p. 143

together with the U 178 which was also heading for South East Asia, by the German tanker *Charlotte Schliemann*.

Lieutenant Eick then operated in the Indian Ocean and the Arabian Sea during February and March 1944. By the time he arrived in Penang on the 1ˢᵗ of April 1944 he had sunk three Allied tankers and six freighters in the Indian Ocean. The new acoustic torpedoes had survived their baptism of fire. For his exploits, Eick was awarded the Knight's Cross in a radio conversation with Hitler.

In June 1944 the U 510 had to go to the Kobe dockyard in Japan for an overhaul. She needed replacement batteries. At the beginning of October she was back in Batavia on Java to be prepared for the voyage back to Europe.

While the boat was being loaded with tin, molybdenum, tungsten, raw rubber and quinine, the crew were relaxing in shifts in the *U-Boot-Wiese* [U-boat meadow], the submariners' recreation facility on the tea plantation at Tjikopo (now: Cikopo). It must have been very lively there, since the 136 rescued survivors of the supply ship and tanker *Brake* were at the plantation at the same time.

When the U 168 had arrived at her secret rendezvous point with the *Brake* in the Indian Ocean, there were only life-boats full of survivors. The commander took them all on board and landed them in Batavia on the 24ᵗʰ of April 1944.

Secret documents showing the positions of the supply ships must have fallen into the hands of Richard Sorge, the spy, in Tokyo. These ships were being sunk very frequently. The sinking of the supply ships meant that the mobility and operational radius of the U-boats were considerably reduced. Since the overloading of the submarines as transports meant a massive increase in fuel use, it was absolutely necessary to have supply ships to refuel them on their voyage home. At the same time the Allies were introducing effective measures to counter the German U-boats in the Indian Ocean and in the waters around the Dutch East Indies.

The Allies were beginning to notice that it was usually the ships with the most valuable cargoes that were being sunk in the convoys. It seemed obvious that espionage was the reason here too. And that was actually the case. The Indian freedom fighter Subhas Chandra Bose used his radio station in Berlin, *Radio Azad Hind,* to call on all Indians to support Germany in the war against the Allies. Tens of thousands of Indian dockers were employed in the ports, mostly controlled by the British, from Australia around the Indian Ocean to South Africa: in Dhaka, Calcutta, Ceylon, Goa, Basra, Aden, Lourenco Marques (now: Maputo in Mozambique) to Cape Town. They were the ones who provided information about the British ships' cargoes, their routes and their departure times to the local German agents who then passed it on to Berlin for transmission to the relevant U-boats. These Indian informers were not, however, pro-Nazi-Germany but primarily anti-British.

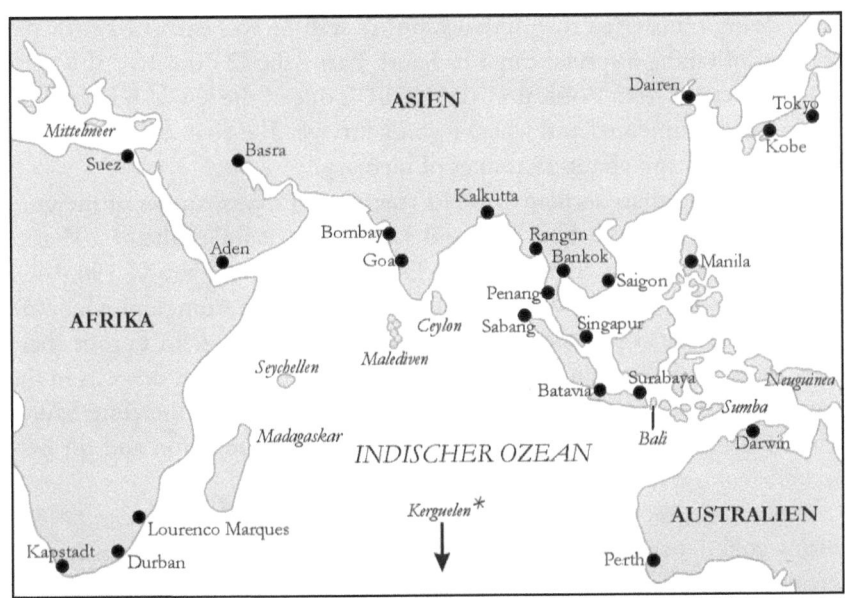

Ill. 56
Indian Ocean Map

At the end of December 1944 the U 510 set off from Batavia on her return voyage to Europe with only 2 torpedoes. Near Madagascar the U 510 was refuelled by U 861, which had just come from Surabaya. In the South Atlantic the U 510 sank a Canadian freighter before returning to the port of St. Nazaire. After the German capitulation she was taken over by the French Navy and renamed *U-Bouan*.

Shortly after the U 510, U 1062, which had been sent separately from the second group, also reached Penang. She was purely a supply ship, carrying among other things 39 torpedoes for the stores in Penang to equip submarines operating in the "Southern Region". After the disaster of the second Monsoon Group, Dönitz now dispatched the ships singly rather than in "wolfpacks". He sent sixteen of them off. More and more were being sunk on the voyage out or home in the area around the Bay of Biscay, which the Allies had under day and night observation with aircraft and the most modern radar technology. Six of the sixteen were lost, although some did actually reach the "Southern Region", including the U 181, U 183, U 196, U 532, U 861 and U 862.

The U 181 was commanded by the experienced Captain Kurt Freiwald. At the beginning of the war he had been on the staff of Admiral Raeder.

After being transferred to Admiral Dönitz's staff he was entrusted with the mission of taking a special cargo to South East Asia. On the 16th of March 1944 he set sail from Bordeaux. The U 181 is one of the few U-boats whose cargo was documented and where records survive. The boat was carrying 41 tonnes of lead and about 43 tonnes of mercury.

It is striking that German U-boats transported many tonnes of mercury from Europe to South East Asia and Japan. For example, the U 195 carried 250 tonnes of mercury, the U 234 65 tonnes, and the U 196 1404 steel bottles of mercury. Where did the mercury come from, and why were such large quantities needed in south East Asia and Japan? In Europe there were mercury deposits in Italy and Serbia, though the biggest deposits in the world were in Spain. Japan has no mercury of its own and therefore had to import it from Europe for detonator and weapon production and for batteries.

Some of the mercury also went to the Dutch East Indies. There are several major gold deposits there, but it is hardly likely that the large quantities of mercury that were delivered were used solely for the extraction of gold.

During the war some German U-boats sank off the coast of Japan. If they too carried a poisonous cargo of mercury, it would explain the prevalence of the *Minamata* disease – which causes massive nerve damage – along the Japanese coast. In the 1950s hundreds of people living along the coast of Japan died of this disease because of eating fish poisoned with mercury.

There was a further case in Japan in 1964. Excessive levels of mercury were discovered in the blood of the inhabitants of the fishing village of Taiji. Dolphins and whales are high on the food list of the fisher people of this village.

One German U-boat is still causing outrage in Norway. The new U 864 was supposed to carry a top-secret high-tech cargo to Japan via Java. On the 7th of February 1945, shortly before the end of the war, it set sail from Bergen in Norway. The cargo was a dismantled Messerschmitt Me 262 jet fighter, a large number of Junkers and BMW engine parts, construction diagrams and once more around 65 tonnes of mercury in steel bottles. There was a 73-man crew, and there were also some air force officers and three undesignated civilian passengers on board.

What Dönitz and the navy chiefs did not know was that British intelligence knew of their plans in advance and could make preparations. They were now able to decipher the –as the Germans believed – unbreakable Enigma code. The British sent the submarine *HMS Venturer* in pursuit of the U 864. Her mission was to sink the U 864 to prevent its valuable cargo reaching Japan. The U 864 initially managed to avoid the Allied blockade, but had to return to Bergen after two days at sea because of engine problems. She was sailing slowly at periscope depth in a zig-zag pattern because of the damaged engine. It had been followed by the British submarine, also submerged, for hours. On the 9th of February 1945, just off Bergen near the island of Fedje, *HMS Venturer* fired four torpedoes. The fourth torpedo hit its mark and the German submarine sank immediately with its dangerous, poisonous cargo to the sea bed 150 metres below. The ship was torn in two and there were no survivors.

The Norwegian Navy searched for the wreck of the U 864 for several years. At the end of 2003 it was found – divers recovered a cast iron bottle of mercury. They established that mercury had already leaked out of the wreck and that the sea bed and the sea around it were severely polluted. Fishing in the vicinity of the wreck was forbidden.

It is still not clear how an environmental disaster can be avoided. There have been several suggestions, ranging from covering it with a coffin of sand, stones and concrete to raising the wreck. This latter is, however, very risky because of the torpedoes on board. The cost of the various proposals are said to be around 110 million euros.

The long-distance type IX D2 U 196, carrying 1,404 steel bottles of mercury, over 9,000 aluminium bars, 105 boxes of optical glass and several tonnes of round-bar and square section steel, left the port of La Pallice in Western France for South East Asia on the 16th of March 1944 under the command of Lieutenant Eitel-Friedrich Kentrat. The U 196 had previously operated successfully in the Atlantic and especially off the coast of South Africa under Lieutenant Kentrat. 225 days at sea without touching land made this one of the longest submarine combat patrols of the war.

Now the U 196 was on a new voyage to the "Southern Region". In the Indian Ocean she sank an Allied freighter, then spent a day in the port of Sabang waiting for an escort on the last stretch of the voyage through the Strait of Malacca. The escort was made up of a Japanese ship and an Arado aircraft piloted by Lieutenant Ulrich Horn, commander of the naval air squadron in Penang. On the 13th of August 1944, after 152 days at sea, the U 196 reached Penang with its precious cargo. The U 18, which had arrived three days earlier, was also in the port.

In Penang Kentrat went ashore to carry out other duties in the "Southern Region" bases. Lieutenant Werner Striegler then took over command of the U 196, and sailed first to Singapore and then on to Batavia where the ship was prepared for a long operation right round Australia. On the 30th of November 1944 the U 196 left Batavia and sailed through the Sunda Strait to the open sea. Shortly afterwards radio contact with her was lost, and she was declared missing on the 12th of December 1944.

Rumours still abound about the fate of the U 196. After the German capitulation she is said to have been seen in Chilean territorial waters. The German submarine is said to have asked for and received charts of the South American coast from a Chilean cruiser. Her destination was apparently Peru, where she was travelling on a secret mission carrying a treasure of gold. A few years later someone met a member of the crew in Buenos Aires, and so on. There is no evidence for any of this information, which comes from several sources. Presumably it is little more than conspiracy theories.

If the U 196 left Batavia with full fuel tanks, then she would have been capable of travelling from Batavia to Peru either to the west or the east without any problem. The only certainty is that the U 196 remains missing to this day. She probably hit a mine in the Sunda Strait immediately after sailing.

The naval base in Batavia grew in importance in the course of the U-boat operations in the "Southern Region". Since the port of Penang was mined by the Allies and was subject to air raids that made it ever more unsafe, the headquarters of the bases and the telecommunications centre were moved to Batavia. U 195, U 219, U 537 and U 843, among others, were ordered to Batavia. In the course of 1944 only the combat U-boats U 168, U 837 and U 862 operated in Dutch East Indies waters. All the other submarines in these waters were to be loaded with raw materials and return to Europe without any intermediate stops.[1] In total about 55 U-boats reached the "Southern Region" and operated there. Several of them only managed one voyage, some even managed to travel both ways several times, but even more were destroyed on their way to the "Southern Region".

---

1   Brennecke, *Haie im Paradies,* p. 127

25. Sabang Base on the Island of Weh and the Italian Submarines

At the northern tip of Sumatra there is a city of about 300,000 inhabitants which during the Second World War was called Kota Radja. Today it is called Banda Aceh. The island lying directly opposite Kota Radja, Pulau Weh where the town of Sabang is situated, is the most north-westerly point of Indonesia, or one might also call it the northern outpost of Sumatra. The Indian Andaman and Nicobar Islands lie just to the north-west. The natives call the island Sabang after its main town. Pulau Weh is a beautiful, calm and peaceful volcanic island at the end of the world. With its palm-trees, white sandy beaches and coral reefs it is a picture-book South Sea paradise. There is a lot of rain and so the mountains at the centre of the island, over 600 metres high, are covered in impenetrable jungle. Here, on this little island up in the west, is where the Dutch colonial empire had its beginnings. The tourist island of Bali is about 36 times bigger. But who would guess that this little island, which had only a few thousand inhabitants during the Second World War, is of such historical significance?

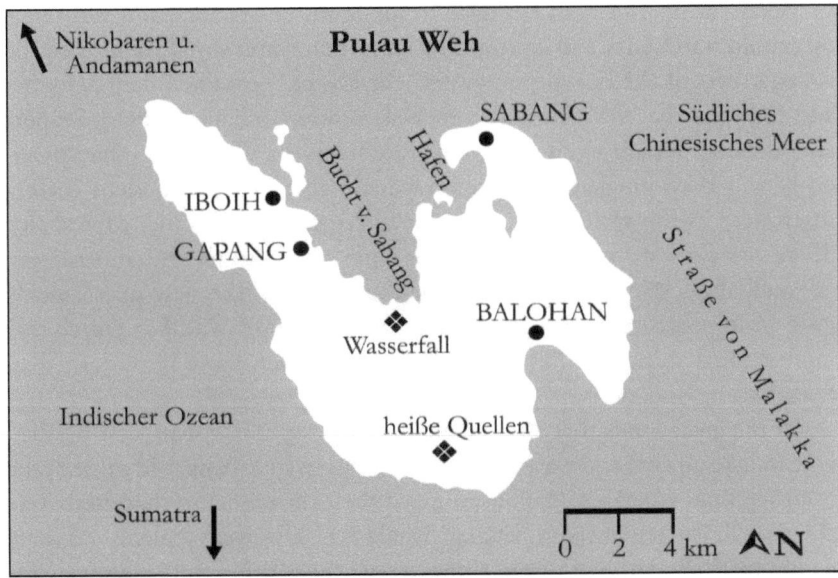

Ill. 57
Pulau Weh (Island of Weh) with Sabang

Today there are about 25,000 people living on the island, and its only larger town, Sabang, is a small, unimportant, forgotten place; but earlier, at the end of the 19th and the beginning of the 20th century Sabang, because of its strategic position, played a very important role and was even the site of violent battles, especially in the Second World War.

Sabang hit the German headlines just after the First World War. When Japan conquered the German Mandate of Tsingtao about 800 Germans were taken to Japan and interned there. After they were freed in 1920, these Germans were landed in Sabang, then belonging to the Dutch East Indies. Since the economic situation in Germany after the First World War was extremely bad, most of them stayed in the colony and found work with the Dutch colonial authorities.[1]

Indonesian sources suggest that Sabang has the biggest natural harbour in the world. As can be seen from the map, this harbour is protected from the monsoon winds by the spit of land that extends to the west of the island. Ships of the deepest draught could and can still berth here.

In 1895 the port was a bunker station for coal and water half way between the Suez Canal and the Far East. During the Russian-Japanese War at the beginning of the 20th century, which was the first time an Asian country had defeated a European power, the excellent strategic position of the island became clear. The port of Sabang was opposite the island of Penang in Malaya at the northern entrance to the Strait of Malacca, and from here one could watch over and control this important waterway. This aroused the covetousness of the European powers. The Dutch intensified their activities and founded the N.V. Zeehaven en Kolenstation Sabang [Sabang Seaport and Coaling Station Company], a private freeport. Where there had previously only been jungle there were now docks and the most modern coaling machinery in the world. Gigantic cranes thrust into the blue tropical sky. There was a dry dock, used not just for repairs but also for the construction of small ships. Housing was built for the workers. The new port quickly grew in importance, especially during the First World War. For Dutch and international shipping lines it was at that time even more important than Singapore.

All the great liners that sailed from west to east and east to west berthed here to take on coal and water. Older eyewitnesses in Sabang told me that the shipping lines wherever possible arranged their timetables so that there were always at least two liners in Sabang. While the ships were replenished there would be lively parties on both ships to pass the waiting time pleasantly for the passengers.

1   PNRI, *Deutsche Wacht*, 1922, No. 5

When Sabang experienced this boom, many German engineers, experts and technicians for the coaling machinery, officials and businessmen found work there. At the end of the 1920s there were still good restaurants, hotels, a German Club and a swimming pool in Sabang, but by the beginning of the Second World War its glory had begun to fade. There was still eternal summer and eternal green, but Singapore had taken over Sabang's place. Sabang was once more a small, peaceful, forgotten outpost. But that peace was soon shattered.

When the Second World War began the Dutch colonial authorities ordered the removal of the swastika flag from the German club. After the Germans invaded the Netherlands the German Club building was confiscated. All the Germans living on the island of Weh were interned in Sumatra and then sent to camps in British India. However, some Germans did escape into the jungle where they managed to hide for many months with the help of the native population, until the Germans' Japanese allies arrived.

Weh and its main town Sabang were the first bridgehead by which the Japanese arrived from Penang to invade the Dutch East Indies. Until recently, hardly anything was known about the naval base the Japanese built at Sabang, perhaps because it was the last Japanese base in the "Southern Region" to receive a German contingent. Even Jochen Brennecke, who had travelled in U-boats as a war reporter and written many books about the German U-boat war only mentions the base once in passing. And yet Sabang, as the first point of arrival for submarines after their long voyage from Europe, played, as we will see, a major role in the surveillance of the Strait of Malacca and as a hiding place for French Foreign Legionnaires of German origin, quite apart from its historical importance.

French troop transports which, until the Germans occupied France in 1940, sailed between their home port of Marseille and their possessions in French Indochina, had to pass through the Strait of Malacca between the island of Sumatra and the Malay Peninsula on every voyage. French Indochina was an enormous colony encompassing the modern states of Vietnam, Cambodia and Laos. There was constant military conflict, leading to severe losses against an enemy who fought guerrilla warfare and could not be pinned down. France had to compensate for these losses by regular reinforcement by the Foreign Legion. By far the majority of legionnaires were from Germany.

France said farewell to the legionnaires in Marseille with the words: *Vous êtes Légionnaires pour mourir! Vive la Légion!* (You have become legionnaires to die. Long live the Legion!). They were mercenaries – convicted criminals, failures, rootless, desperate – but none of them wanted to die, and so it was no wonder that many legionnaires took any opportunity to desert.

The Strait of Malacca is between 3 and 300 kilometres wide. For the legionnaires the stretch between Penang and Sabang was the best moment to jump overboard. On the northward shipping route the troop transports frequently came close to that coast of Sumatra. Although the French troops on the transport ships were particularly vigilant on that stretch of water, thousands succeeded in escaping. This freedom, however, was often of short duration, because the sea in that area is infested with sharks and poisonous sea snakes. Those who made it to the coast were still far from safe, because the flat, swampy coast of East Sumatra is largely covered with impenetrable mangrove jungle. Those who reached an inhabited area often joined the services of the Dutch East Indies, where the conditions were far better than those in the French Foreign Legion. But many lived in hiding in the jungle areas of North Sumatra and the island of Weh. The native population mostly accepted them and even sometimes sheltered them.

In Jakarta in 1963 I met a former German Foreign Legionnaire who had succeeded in escaping to Sabang on a voyage to French Indochina shortly before the outbreak of war. According to him, a posting to Indochina meant certain death in those days. He told me that there had sometimes been up to 100 deserters from the Legion hiding in the jungle on Weh, just waiting in the hope that a ship from their home country might berth in Sabang and take them home.

He didn't make it back to Germany – he was overtaken by the Second World War. He first hid from the Dutch among natives in Sabang, since he would obviously have been interned. After the Japanese occupied Sabang he initially worked on the Japanese naval base there. When the German Navy came to Sabang in 1943, he offered them his services. He was responsible for a diesel generator. After the Japanese capitulation he joined the freedom fighters under Soekarno and fought in Sumatra against the Dutch, who were trying to reconquer their former colony – by then the independent Republic of Indonesia. After 1950 he became an Indonesian citizen and, as a side-line, encouraged the development of boxing. He never saw his German homeland again, dying in Indonesia in the mid-1970s.

After the Imperial Japanese Army's rapid southward advance had subdued Malaya, they immediately occupied the strategically important island of Weh. The port of Sabang was the ideal place to set up a naval base from which to control shipping in the Strait of Malacca. Now the peace of this sleepy little island was at an end.

After the Japanese constructed the base, the Germans added a base for naval personnel. Sabang was mainly a Japanese base, but was also made available for German use. The German sailors stationed here must surely have led a quiet, contented life on this tropical island paradise. German vessels were not overhauled or provisioned here, it was simply the first landfall after the voyage from Europe. They then made their way under air and sea escort to Penang. Towards the end of the war this northern stretch of the Strait of Malacca was under increased threat from enemy submarines.

Before the First World War the Dutch had erected a military hospital in Sabang which also served as a medical base for the Imperial German East Asia Squadron. The hospital was staffed by Dutch doctors and Catholic nuns. During both World Wars it became a military hospital. It was regarded as one of the best hospitals in South East Asia, especially when it was thoroughly renovated and modernised by German medical staff during the Japanese occupation from 1942 to 1945.

German commercial shipping lines like North German Lloyd or the Hamburg-America Line always had their ailing staff or passengers treated at the Sabang hospital when they passed through these waters. Just before the Second World War, Siegfried Meyrich, a member of the crew of the Lloyd ship *Crefeld*, was being treated here. When war did break out, he was interned by the Dutch straight from his hospital bed. Later he was one of the few survivors of the sinking of the *Van Imhoff*.[1]

The Dutch hospital staff either fled before the Japanese or were liquidated by them. With the help of the doctors from the German U-boats, the hospital returned to service. It is likely that any serious medical problems among German sailors or the personnel of all the bases in the "Southern Region" were treated in Sabang.

It is not clear when the first Japanese submarine docked in Sabang, but the first submarine to reach the "Southern Region" from Europe was the Italian *Commandante Cappellini*, which had sailed from Bordeaux under German command and arrived in Sabang on the 10th of July 1943.

On the 20th of July 1943 the U 511 under Lieutenant Schneewind was the first German submarine to reach Penang, having sailed from Lorient. There is no documentary evidence to show whether she arrived in Penang directly or via Sabang. The U 178 under Captain Dommes and the Italian *Luigi Torelli* both reached Sabang on the 26th of August 1943. Shortly afterwards the U 178 sailed on to Penang.

The first German U-boat whose arrival in Sabang is recorded was the IX C type U 168 commanded by Lieutenant Helmuth Pich, which had sailed from Lorient on the 3rd of July 1943 with seven other submarines. Operating off the west coast of India, she was damaged by depth charges. It was not possible to carry out repairs with the means at their disposal on board,

1   See earlier in this book

and so the naval command in Germany ordered them to proceed to Penang. North of Sumatra the U 168 was met by a Japanese escort ship and brought initially to the port of Sabang. After 132 days at sea the crew of the U 168 finally stepped on to dry land.

Pich describes the arrival at Sabang as follows in his diary: *These mountainous islands that rise steeply from the crystal clear blue sea give you the feeling that you're just about to collide with them. But nothing of the sort – there are still another ten miles to go. The harbour was exactly the tropical island you imagine in your dreams. It was circular, a harbour in a crater; beyond the snow-white beach, huts under swaying palms. After 152 days in action, at last the order "Switch off engines!"*[1]

As we have noted before, the whole crew was invited to a reception by the Japanese admiral, which was to be preceded by a Japanese bath – where the attendants were, disappointingly, all muscular men. The crew then turned up, spruce and neat in clean khaki uniforms. Pich writes: *He [Author's note: the Japanese admiral] bows to us, and we bow back. We were so happy to have a day off at last and after the reception went to look at the native huts on the beach and the monkeys. For the rest, we had no idea what would come next. The admiral had smilingly asked us to be patient. Patience, a word that is written in capitals in Asia, but for us grinds like sand in the works.*[2]

But in fact they sailed on the next day. With an escort ship and an Arado 196 from Penang to spot enemy submarines, they reached Penang in safety, where they were welcomed by base-commander Lieutenant Konrad Hoppe with a Japanese marching band and a Japanese band from Tokyo which played alternate Japanese and German marches. After the first welcome ceremony, Pich writes: *We knew about the baths. Then, after I had made sure that my crew had everything they needed, I started with the visits. Twelve highest- and higher-ranking Japanese officers. Beginning with an Admiral and ending with a Captain. And every one of them offered us a small glass [...] I had to down 68 of them that morning. That meant that we arrived somewhat merry at the official visit. But they weren't annoyed, no, they were very pleased. [...] In the evening a big reception had been arranged in our honour in the Japanese Naval Club. First hearty words of thanks were exchanged and then finally, I could not believe my eyes, our gentlemen hosts, high and highest ranking officers, took off their jackets. And the banquet began. In shirtsleeves.*[3]

The Japanese submarine cruiser I-29 moored in Sabang on the 6th of March 1943 to land the Indian freedom fighter Subhas Chandra Bose, whom the

---

1   Brennecke, *Haie im Paradies*, pp. 49ff
2   Ibid.
3   Ibid.

I-29 had taken over from the German U 180 in the Indian Ocean. According to an eyewitness[1], the U 180 under Commander Musenberg arrived in Sabang at the same time. Both submarines had sailed together from a rendezvous in the Indian Ocean, of which more later.

The U-boat crews and the staff at the naval bases in Malaya and the Dutch East Indies had to work very hard in the hot, humid tropical climate, which they were not used to. For security reasons maintenance work on board the submarines had to be carried out by the crew. Nevertheless the general state of health was satisfactory. Initially a very high number of cases of malaria – up to 25% of the crews – were reported due to an error. The German medical staff, inexperienced in tropical medicine, had mistaken a harmless strong tropical fever for malaria. Only when Dr Schlenkermann, experienced in tropical medicine, took over responsibility for the whole "Southern Region" and senior registrar Dr Buchholz arrived in Singapore was the error noticed. Malaria was now diagnosed so seldom that it was possible to dispense with prophylaxis.

Nevertheless many thousand ampoules of the German anti-malarial drug Atebrin and many hundreds of thousands of Atebrin tablets were taken to South East Asia by U-boat. These were probably intended for use by the Japanese fighting in the jungles of Malaya and the forced labourers on the Sumatra and Siam-Burma Railways.[2]

Dysentery, skin lesions and ulcers needed regular treatment because susceptibility to disease was higher in the tropics than in Germany, although the availability of medication was far better in the "Southern Region" than at home in Germany or on the Eastern Front. The former military hospital in Sabang is today a general hospital, *Rumah Sakit Umum Sabang*, which has maintained its good reputation.

Italy was Germany's partner in the Tripartite Pact and transported material to and from South East Asia on behalf of the German Navy. The Italian submarine *Luigi Torelli* was – like other Italian submarines – refitted as a transport submarine. All eight torpedo tubes were converted into cargo space or fuel tanks, and some of the batteries for sailing submerged were removed to create yet more cargo space. After conversion the *Luigi Torelli* was also known as *Aquila IV*. On the 16th of June 1943 the *Luigi Torelli* commanded by Enrico Gropalli sailed from Brest for South East Asia on her 11th combat mission. She was heading first for Sabang and then Singapore.

The *Luigi Torelli* was carrying over 150 tonnes of cargo: special steel for ball bearings, mercury, a 2 cm-gun mount, several hundred Mauser MG

---

1   Dr Madan
2   Department of the Navy – Naval Historical Center, Washington DC, Report
     SRH-19, p.8

151/20 anti-aircraft canon, submarine optics, a newly developed 500 kilogram SC 500 blockbuster bomb and other munitions as models for the Japanese war industry. There were also some replacement torpedoes on board for Penang.

The most important cargo was two FuMG radar units, generally known as *Würzburg* radar apparatus, with which ships and aircraft could be detected at distances of up to 60 to 80 kilometres, and therefore could be used for surveillance in the Strait of Malacca. Allied attacks on Sumatra's natural gas and oil fields could be detected in good time and more easily dealt with.

After Italy capitulated and went over to the Allied side, the *Luigi Torelli* sailed on under German command as UIT 25 (Underwater Italian Transport boat). The majority of the Italian naval personnel continued in German service even after Italy had changed sides. Those who did not were interned by the Japanese in a prison in Singapore. As the German Legionnaire mentioned above told me, the Italians continued to work reliably for the Germans in the bases and on the submarines.

Either the *Würzburg* radar in Sabang had not yet been brought into operation or the men on the naval base in Sabang felt so safe on their isolated tropical island that they didn't bother to keep air or sea watch at night. The Japanese and Germans who had had such an easy time there were caught napping. Or at least no one was ready for an Allied attack.

The tropical paradise, 9 degrees north of the Equator, suddenly became a living Hell. On the early morning of the 19th of April 1944 the British aircraft carrier *HMS Illustrious* and the American aircraft carrier *USS Saratoga* neared the port of Sabang. They were supported by a further 20 warships, including the cruisers *HMS Ceylon* and *Gambia* and the destroyers *HMS Quillian, Quadrant* and *Dunlop*. The British battleship *HMS Queen Elisabeth* was the flagship of Admiral James Somerville, commander-in-chief of the Eastern Fleet, who was in command of the operation. It was a combined fleet with units from the US Navy, British Royal Navy, the Royal Australian Navy, the Dutch Koninklijke Marine and the Royal New Zealand Navy. Before the attack on Sabang the fleet refuelled and provisioned at Exmouth in Western Australia on the 6th of April 1944.

The French heavy battleship *Richelieu* (40,000 tonnes), which had been in West Africa when the French capitulated, was also with them as her captain had decided not to accept the Vichy regime but to operate within the British Eastern Fleet.

The USA ordered attacks on Japanese-German bases in South East Asia to relieve the pressure on their own operations east of New Guinea and other Pacific islands. The strategically important port of Sabang was chosen as their first and most important target, because it had newly extended port facilities with fuel tanks and docks as well as extensive telecommunications facilities, including the first *Würzburg* radar equipment.

There was also Sabang's airport Lho Nga (now: Maimun Saleh), which the Japanese used to supply their troops fighting the British 14th Army in Burma. The Allied attack was codenamed Operation Cockpit.

At 5:30 a.m. on the 19th of April 1944 46 bombers and 37 fighters attacked the port and the ships that were moored there. The airfield, the radar station, the telecommunications facilities, the big oil tanks and the power station were bombed. Sabang was in flames. The Japanese troops had been caught literally napping. By the time they managed to bring their anti-aircraft guns into action, everything had been destroyed. They only managed to shoot down one Allied aircraft.

After the attack the port was in ruins, and two Japanese destroyers, two freighters and an escort ship had been destroyed. The diesel generators, the telecommunications equipment and the radar station were flattened, the oil tanks were burning and 30 Japanese aircraft had been destroyed on the airfield at Lho Nga.

For the Allies Operation Cockpit was a complete success. Admiral Somerville said: *We caught the Japs with their kimonos up and their heads down and gave Sabang a good bang.*[1]

On the 27th of April 1944 the Allied fleet refuelled and loaded fresh ammunition again at Exmouth in Western Australia. There was another attack on Sabang, which from now on was allowed no peace, and nor were many other towns in Sumatra. Simultaneously with the US offensive on the Mariana and Palau Islands in the Pacific, there were renewed air attacks on Sabang on the 10th and 21st of June 1944.

Only four days later the Allies attacked Port Blair on the Andaman Islands north of Sabang. The Andaman and Nicobar Islands were the only British Indian territory that was occupied by the Japanese, who handed them pro forma to the exile government of Subhas Chandra Bose and the Indian National Army. Now the flag of *Azad Hind* waved over both island groups as the symbol of an India freed from British colonial power. The airfields in both were destroyed by Allied bombing since they served to support and supply the Japanese in Burma.

On the 25th of July 1944 a further air attack on Sabang was carried out by the British aircraft carriers *HMS Victorious* and *HMS Illustrious*. The Lho Nga airfield was once more the target. Then there were Allied air raids on the port of Padang in West Sumatra and the little town of Indaroeng a few

1   Water, *The Royal New Zealand Navy*, p. 359

kilometres inland of this to the west. Padang and other towns in Sumatra were bombed again from the 24th of August 1944. The aircraft carriers were protected by the British battleship *HMS Howe* and other warships of the Eastern Fleet. On the 17th of November 1944 the little port of Brandan on the Strait of Malacca, about 70 kilometres north of Medan was bombed. On the 20th of November there was another attack on Sabang. On the 17th of December 1944 Belawan, the port of Medan, was destroyed. The situation in the "Southern Region" was becoming increasingly precarious.

After these attacks the Sabang naval base was practically neutralised in operational terms. My information suggests that no German U-boats used this port after the middle of 1944. The Strait of Malacca had become too dangerous because of Allied mines. The safest way of approaching the "Southern Region" was now the Sunda Strait between Java and Sumatra with landfall at Batavia.

In March 1945 the *Richelieu* was tasked with destroying the harbour facilities and coastal defence batteries of the Japanese bases. Shortly after the Japanese capitulation she sailed through the Strait of Malacca for Singapore. On the 9th of September she hit a British mine and was holed, but managed just to make it to Singapore.

Between 1964 and 1975 I was regularly on the island of Weh in connection with the freeport project and – when my time allowed – looked for signs of the Second-World-War base. Apart from a few ruins in the port area I found nothing. The Allied attacks had done a good job!

There was, however, still an Indonesian Navy (ALRI) fast patrol boat in the port, which turned out to be a German wartime product, although it was not possible to discover what class the boat belonged to or how it reached Sabang: probably on a blockade breaker or a supply ship.

In 1969 my friend Jürgen Graaff, who was stationed in Sabang directing a project for the installation of new telecommunications facilities, managed to inspect the boat. He still remembers that she was in top-notch condition, looked after like a jewel. In the engine room the original engines – 24 years after the end of the war – were still in use: 3 Daimler-Benz petrol engines and 1 Maybach diesel engine. It was presumably one of the "light patrol boats" which were carried by German auxiliary cruisers like the *Kormoran*.

In the same year Jürgen Graaff was in an Indonesian customs store searching for a part that had been sent from Germany but not delivered to the site. He didn't find the part, but did find a well-preserved Telefunken 5-kilowatt quenched spark transmitter which must have come from the period of the First World War. It was a valuable historical set from the beginnings of wireless telegraphy. Jürgen Graaff's research in his list of historical transmitters revealed that it had been delivered to the Dutch Colonial Ministry in 1911. It had a wavelength of between 600 and 2,500 metres. Even the name of the Telefunken engineer, Herr Nicolas, who was in charge of setting up the equipment in Sabang, was recorded. Perhaps it was not so isolated and lonely on this remote island over a hundred years ago as it was in Jürgen Graaff's time in the 1960s. As we have already said, at that time almost all east-west passenger ships docked there to refuel and party.

As I was researching in Sabang I was made aware of a grave in the old graveyard at the edge of the town by an Indonesian teacher who had lived there through the Second World War. It was mostly Dutch colonial officials who were buried there. He felt that the grave he was talking about was that of a German sailor. It was a relatively neglected grave. There was no cross, but on the gravestone it was possible to decipher a few faded French words: ICI REPOSE...CARISSAN...MORT GLORIEUSEMENT...COMBAT... CROISEUR ALLEM...' and a date, 'LE 28 OCTOBRE...

So it wasn't a German sailor, but a Frenchman who had died in glorious battle with a German cruiser one 28th of October. How had a French sailor come to die in this way in these distant waters and to be buried in Sabang? My interest was aroused and the story that my subsequent researches turned up is quite exciting. But to follow it we have to leap back in time to the First World War.

The German Imperial Navy's cruiser *SMS Emden* sailed from Germany under the command of Captain Karl von Müller via South America into the Pacific to join the East Asian Squadron. The *Emden* was the smallest cruiser of the Imperial Navy in this region. Its initial mission was to sail to the naval base in the German Mandate in Tsingtao in China and then to cruise in the Pacific and in Dutch East Indian waters. In the Dutch East Indies the *Emden* was overtaken by the First World War. She was then supposed to capture British and French merchant shipping here and in the Indian Ocean.

Reserve Lieutenant Julius Lauterbach was also on the *Emden*. He was only supposed to have spent a few weeks as one of her officers. Lauterbach had spent many years as the captain of Hamburg-America Line passenger and merchant ships in East and South East Asia, where he was familiar with all the seaways and almost all the commercial ships that operated there.

On the 28th of October 1914 the *Emden* attacked the port of Penang in what was then the British Crown Colony of Malaya. Disguised as a British warship, she was even able to penetrate into the inner harbour in the darkness of the early morning. From very close range she fired two torpedoes at the Russian cruiser *Zhemchug*, which sank. There were also three French warships in the harbour, two destroyers and the torpedo boat *D'Iberville*, but they were all moored and unready for action.

The attack on Penang had serious consequences for the German commercial community. At the beginning of the war most Germans in Malaya and Singapore had been interned by the British, but this incident was the last straw, especially since the Singapore press claimed that August Diehn, the manager of the German company Behn, Meyer & Co., had been a spy and had guided the *Emden*. All German companies in British Malaya and Singapore were confiscated and their property auctioned, the proceeds going to the British Crown. Then the last remaining Germans were interned in Australian camps with their families, as well as British citizens of German descent.

Although the *Emden* had been pursued in the Indian Ocean for months by 20 enemy ships – British, French and Russian – her success and that of her excellent crew became legendary: in just two months she sank or captured over 30 enemy merchant ships and two warships. The British eyed these initial German naval successes suspiciously: they feared the loss of British naval hegemony, especially in the Pacific and the Indian Ocean. But Winston Churchill, at the time First Lord of the Admiralty, swore revenge and prepared to fight back.

When Captain von Müller left the port of Penang the French torpedo boat/destroyer, the *Mousquet*, suddenly appeared in the bay outside the harbour, returning from patrol in the Strait of Malacca. The *Mousquet* was hopelessly outgunned by the *Emden*, and after a short combat foundered and sank within a few minutes. 44 of the *Mousquet's* 80-man crew were killed, but the *Emden* managed to rescue 36, including 16 wounded. The commander of the *Mousquet*, Lieutenant Théroinne, survived, though severely wounded. Three of the wounded sailors died soon after being rescued and were buried at sea.

On the 30th of October 1914, as the *Emden* was steaming back south along the Strait of Malacca, she met the British freighter *Newburn*, which had a cargo of salt and corn. The captain of the *Newburn* was promised immunity if he would take the French prisoners to Sabang without delay. He agreed, and took them to Sabang, which with its excellent hospital was in the neutral Dutch East Indies.

The wounded were taken to the hospital and treated by the Dutch military doctor Blankenberg and two civilian doctors. Two of the wounded, Jacques Carissan and Joseph Hamon, died there of their wounds. They were buried next to each other in simple graves. Captain Visser, commandant of the Dutch garrison in Sabang and Baron Frederic Mari van Asbeck, head of the Constitutional and Political Department of the Dutch East Indies General Secretariat did the honours at the funeral.

After four weeks all but three of the wounded from the *Mousquet* were so much improved that it was possible to ship them out with the other survivors on the torpedo boat *D'Iberville*. Six days later they landed in Saigon.

What happened to the two graves in the meantime? On the 6th of June 1922, eight years after the burial, two French warships, the *Moqueuse* and the *Malicieuse* put into Sabang to raise a gravestone on the site of the burial. After that, especially during the Second World War and the Indonesian war of independence until the end of 1949, the graves were neglected, as might be expected in the circumstances. When the French frigate *Béarnais* visited Sabang in 1960, her commander could only find one grave, that of Jacques Carissan. The second sailor's grave had presumably been destroyed in the confusion of war.

In 1970 the wreck of the *Mousquet* was raised because it was a serious hindrance in the entrance to the port of Penang. The remains of those who had gone down with the ship were recovered and handed over to France by the Malaysian government. They were buried in Noumea in New Caledonia in August 1971 and a monument was set up. No one thought of the forgotten and neglected grave in Sabang on this occasion.

When the French Minister of Defence requested a list of all French military cemeteries abroad in April 1985, the grave in Sabang was remembered. On the 9th of March 1989 the restored grave was consecrated in its old position. This is the only – unfortunately now once more very weathered – official French military grave in the whole of Indonesia.[1]

I was unable to find any German sailors' graves in Sabang. As the Legionnaire mentioned above, who was there during the Japanese occupation, told me, German sailors had been killed during the massive Allied attacks, but because of the chaotic circumstances at the time they, like many Japanese, had been buried at sea for the sake of simplicity.

The *Mousquet* was the last ship sunk by the *Emden*. I would like to describe the end of *Emden* and the dramatic escape of some of her crew, even though it does not fit directly into the theme of this book. After transferring the wounded from the *Mousquet* to the *Newburn*, the *Emden* set course for the Australian Cocos Islands (also: Cocos-Keeling Islands) south west

---

1   Destins croisés entre l'Insulinde et la France, Archipel 54/1997, Jean Rocher: *Mort à Sabang*
Henri Moreau: *Le Port de Sabang*, Paris 1926
www.ww2db.com/battle_spec.php?battle_id=196
www.wikipedia.org/operation_cockpit

of Java. Captain von Müller's mission was to destroy a British marine cable junction and a big short-wave radio station on Direction Island.

On the 9th of November 1914 The *SMS Emden* sailed into the entrance of Port Refuge on Direction Island, disguised as a British warship with a false fourth funnel. Lieutenant Hellmuth von Mücke and 47 men were towed to the landing stage in two cutters by a steam launch. To their surprise, they were not resisted by the Australian and British forces there, but rather greeted politely by a welcome party.

The marine cable was cut by the German sailors and the marine cable relay station and the radio station were destroyed. What the Germans did not know was that the British radio operator had managed to send a message about the *Emden's* arrival. The Australian cruiser *HMAS Sydney* commanded by Captain John Glossop was operating in the vicinity, and when it received the message with the position of the *Emden* it made full steam ahead for Direction Island.

Only two hours after von Mücke landed, the *Emden* was surprised by the *HMAS Sydney* and a fight began. The *Emden* was outgunned from the start and, heavily damaged, had to ground herself on a coral reef on North Keeling Island. Captain von Müller and the survivors from his crew were captured and, after a long Odyssey, ended up in a PoW camp on Malta. On Direction Island the remains of the once so proud and successful German cruiser still stick up out of the blue sea.

How did the SOS from the Direction Island radio operator reach the *HMAS Sydney?* This is a curiosity in military history, and shows how receiver and transmission equipment supplied to Western Australia from Germany helped to sink a German ship: the government of Australia wanted to link Western Australia, then a distant and relatively new state, with the more developed east, and decided to install the necessary radio equipment in Perth and Sydney. In 1910 the German company Telefunken won an international competition for the contract. It took only twelve months to manufacture the equipment and ship it to Australia: brilliant work. Telefunken engineer Moens was in charge of setting the equipment up and bringing it into operation. That also proceeded very swiftly and by August and September 1912 the two stations, call signs POP (Post Office Perth) and POS (Post Office Sydney) were in action for the Australian Post Office.

Station POP was built on Wireless Hill south of Perth. The transmitter was a quenched spark transmitter with an antenna power of 25 kilowatts and a wavelength of between 600 and 3,500 metres for Morse telegraphy. An umbrella antenna was mounted on a 120 metre lattice mast. The station was state of the art for the time.

Radio communication between the west and east Australian coasts functioned smoothly. When international call signs were issued by the International Wireless Convention, Perth received the call sign VIP. Telefunken received further contracts for Melbourne and Macquarie Island, south of Tasmania. This isolated island in the Antarctic Ocean was used as a communications centre for the British and Australian Antarctic expeditions that were just beginning at that time. Telefunken equipment was also supplied for Wellington, Auckland, Bluff Harbour and Doubtless Bay in New Zealand.

The Telefunken equipment surpassed all expectations. Since several ships were equipped with it at the same time as the land stations at Perth and Sydney, it was now possible to communicate wirelessly with ships at sea. The Sydney Daily Telegraph reported on the 8th of April 1913 that the liner *Australia* heading for Europe was still in contact with the Sydney station even though it was already 1,970 nautical miles west of Fremantle in Western Australia. This was a distance of about 6,000 kilometres. They also reported that the New Zealand stations could receive signals loud and clear from ships sailing between Yokohama and Honolulu. This was a distance of 8,000 kilometres, a record for wireless range at the time.[1]

When the First World War broke out in 1914, the station in Perth was taken over by the Royal Australian Navy. From now on they monitored all frequencies to find German ships off Australia and in the Indian Ocean. It was this Perth station that received the distress call from Direction Island – using equipment supplied by a German company. They passed the message on, with the position of the *SMS Emden*, to *HMAS Sydney*. So German technology tolled the knell of a German ship, and fate took its course.

On Wireless Hill where the POP/VIP radio station once was there is now the Wireless Hill Telecommunications Museum. It is in a beautiful park setting on Telefunken Drive with a view over Perth and the Swan River. There is only the street name to remind us of the pioneering German engineering work of over 100 years ago.

The First-World-War *HMAS Sydney* was scrapped in 1928 and should not be confused with its namesake, a cruiser which entered service in 1935. The radio station on Wireless Hill played an important role in the sinking of the German auxiliary cruiser *Kormoran* and the new cruiser *HMAS Sydney* off the coast of Western Australia on the 19th of November 1941, of which more later.

---

1   TELEFUNKEN-Zeitung, 2. Jahrgang, No. 12 and
     private archive of Jürgen Graaff

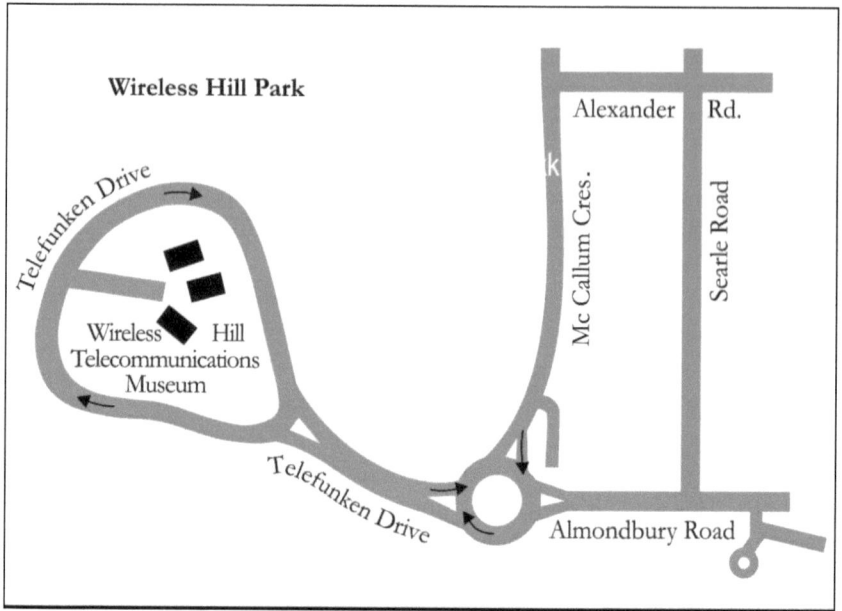

Ill. 58
The Wireless Telecommunications Museum on Telefunken Drive in Perth, Western Australia

A day after sinking the *Emden* the *Sydney* returned to Direction Island to capture Lieutenant von Mücke and his men. In the meanwhile, however, von Mücke had commandeered the only ship in the harbour, the schooner *Ayesha,* which was ready for the scrapyard and far from seaworthy. They shared what supplies there were with the cooperative British and Australians on the island. The schooner was only meant for a seven-man crew, but all 49 German sailors boarded her. Captain Partridge, the British commander on Direction Island, warned von Mücke that trying to escape in this rotting ship was tantamount to suicide, but the Germans could not be persuaded to abandon their plan.

Their escape voyage was adventurous: across the sea to the west coast of Sumatra and then on with a German freighter as far as what is now Yemen. From Hodeidah on the Red Sea they continued by camel across the desert to the terminus of the German-built Baghdad Railway. This journey is still known among the Arabs as the "Caravan of Sailors". In Constantinople von Mücke his men were given a grandiose reception. After a journey of more than seven months von Mücke finally brought his men safely home to Germany in June 1915. Six of them were lost to disease and conflict with rebellious Arabs. The German Kaiser granted the survivors the right to add the heritable suffix "Emden" to their names.[1]

In 1944 history almost repeated itself. Captain Oskar Herwartz, commander of the U 943, set his course for the return to Germany in such a way that he would pass close to the Cocos-Keeling Islands. He wanted – as had happened in the First World War – to destroy the radio station and the underwater cable. For this attack he requested Count Maeda to supply him with machine guns, automatic rifles, hand guns hand grenades and explosives. This sort of weaponry, which would be needed for the assault, was not part of a U-boat's normal equipment. Count Maeda refused the request, saying that Japan had no interest in the island – and if she did, Japan could take the island at any time.

The weapons were probably available at the German base in Batavia, but could not be given to Herwartz because they were part of the base's inventory. Herwartz and his officers and men were disappointed, because they would really have liked to repeat Lieutenant Mücke of the *Bremen*'s exploit. So the U 843, fully laden with raw materials, had to set sail on the return voyage to Germany without an excursion to the Cocos-Keeling Islands. She reached Bergen safely on the 2nd of April 1945, but on the 9th, 100 nautical miles from Kiel and only a few days before the war ended, she was attacked by Allied aircraft and sunk. Only twelve men, including Captain Herwartz, survived of the 58-man crew.

But now back to the Second World War to bring the story of the Italian submarine *Commandante Cappellini* to a conclusion. It only sailed under an Italian captain for one more week. Just as it reached Singapore on the 3rd of September 1943, Italy announced its capitulation, which led to an immediate break between Germany and Italy. On the 13th of October 1943 Italy declared war on Germany and changed over to the Allied side.

The Italian submarines were initially confiscated by Japan, but in Sabang on the 13.10.1943 the *Commandante Cappellini* and the *Emilio Tortelli* were handed over to the German Navy in the presence of the German Naval Attaché, who flew in from Tokyo for the occasion, becoming the UIT 24 and UIT 25 respectively. UIT 25 was now commanded by Captain Werner Striegler who had sailed to Penang on the U 511 as First Officer of the Watch.

---

1   TV Phoenix 05.06.2012, 20.15h, *Unter kaiserlicher Flagge,*
     Hellmuth von Mücke: *Emden und Ayesha*, Berlin 1915
     Julius Lauterbach: *1000 Pfund Kopfpreis tot oder lebendig. Fluchtabenteuer des ehemaligen Prisenoffiziers S. M. S. „Emden",* Berlin 1917

UIT 24 also sailed under German command with a mixed crew of Italians and Germans, as did the UIT 23 (formerly *Reginaldo Giuliani*). When Italy capitulated the latter was still in Singapore and was confiscated by the Japanese Navy. On the 23.10.1943 it was transferred to the German Navy by the Japanese. The majority of the Italian officers and crews decided for Germany. The rest were interned as PoWs by Japan.

UIT 24 now undertook transport and combat missions for Germany in the Java Sea and also carried out two transport missions to Japan. On the 25th of May 1944 UIT 24 unloaded in Singapore 34 tonnes of tin and tungsten from Penang and then sailed on to arrive at the Mitsui Dock in Tama, Japan, on the 8th of June 1944. She then continued to Kobe to load supplies for the U-boats in the "Southern Region". She left for Singapore on the 5th of September 1944, arriving 14 days later. After various combat missions in the Java Sea and the Indian Ocean, UIT 24 made a further voyage from Singapore to Kobe, arriving on the 18th of February 1945. She stayed there until Germany capitulated and was then taken over by the Japanese Navy.

Even today control over the Strait of Malacca is important because pirates from Malaysia and Indonesia still contribute to insecurity there. During the presidency of Soekarno Indonesia was in control here, which aroused the displeasure of the USA, because Soekarno and Admiral Martadinata, at the time commander-in-chief of the Indonesian Navy (ALRI) would not allow US naval ships unhindered and unannounced passage between the Indian Ocean and the Pacific..

After President Soekarno was deposed in 1965 by US-friendly General Soeharto, who came to power with the help of the CIA, Admiral Martadinata and other leading officers of the ALRI fell into disfavour. In 1966 Martadinata died in a mysterious helicopter crash in the Punjak Pass in West Java.

After an agreement was reached with an international consortium in 2006, the port of Sabang is to be expanded to become one of the biggest container ports in Asia. Can the sleepy Island of Weh once more experience a peaceful boom? One would hope so, for the sake of the native population.

26. The Telefunken Würzburg Radar Stations in the Far East

At the beginning of the 1930s there was little interest in radio direction finding technology in Germany, and the first developments did not begin until 1934. Telefunken started on development work in 1936 and the first prototype of the series FuMG 65, generally known as *Würzburg* was demonstrated to the German military in the summer of 1939. It was a good year later before the equipment entered operational use. Telefunken's MTI (Moving Target Indicator) technology, developed by Professor Wilhelm T. Runge gave Germany decided superiority over allied devices, and is still in use in all modern radar devices.

Würzburg was a ground based fire-control radar which was used with great success by the German air force and army from 1940 onwards. It was the first device to be built on the modular principle: the individual electronic units were inserted into separate slots which meant that if one of them was defective it could be changed by non-professionals.

Ill. 59
Surviving Würzburg Radar Station in Douvres-la-Délirande, France

This equipment could locate ships at a distance of 60 to 80 kilometres, and aircraft even as far as 250 kilometres. In Germany it was mainly used to catch enemy aircraft in a guide beam and then use the data to direct anti-aircraft fire. Accuracy was considerably enhanced by the use of *Würzburg*. Up to the end of the war about 1,500 *Würzburg* devices were produced. It was the first impulse radar in the decimetre wave range and was the most modern and most powerful radar equipment of the time. They weighed 20 tonnes and the diameter of the parabolic mirror antenna was up to 7.5 metres, which shows what weights and what dimensions had to be carried in the freight submarines, even when the parabolic mirror was dismantled.

Japan was extremely interested in using this effective equipment in Japan and the "Southern Region" as well, since they had nothing comparable. One attempt to send *Würzburg* radar equipment to Japan at the end of 1942 on the I-30, the first Japanese submarine to reach Europe, failed.

The I-30 sailed for Japan from Lorient on the 22nd of August 1942 under Captain Endo. The boat had to be refitted by German technicians to be able to accommodate the large sections of the *Würzburg* equipment. At the same time the hull of the boat was strengthened and the extremely loud engine noise muffled. I-30, which was black on arrival in Lorient was now repainted and left there white.[1]

On board the I-30 were the Japanese head of the *Würzburg* replication project, General Suzuki and a Japanese radar technician who had both been trained by Telefunken to set up and operate the equipment.

The submarine with its cargo safely reached Singapore, and was supposed then to continue to Japan. As she left the port of Singapore on the13th of October 1942 the I-30 hit a British mine and sank, with the loss of 16 lives. There were 96 survivors though it was not possible to discover if the two radar specialists were among them. The radar equipment was destroyed.

After this loss the decision was reached to replicate the *Würzburg* equip-ment in Japan. Parts that were not available in Japan would be supplied from Germany. However, because this radar equipment was urgently needed in the "Southern Region" and Japan, two complete installations were shipped to the Far East. The first submarines – the Italian UITs – to sail from Ger-man U-boat pens to the "Southern Region" almost all carried *Würzburg* radar in their cargo.

I know that at least eight of these complete radar stations were shipped east on submarines. Four were lost, and of the four remaining stations, one was set up in Sabang. It was probably the *Commandante Cappellini*, the first

---

1   Tsuda, *The Würzburg Project*, Chapter 2: The negotiations about handing over the *Würzburg* equipment and its transport to Japan (translation from Japanese)

submarine to reach Sabang from Europe, that carried the equipment for Sabang, because this was where it was most urgently needed to monitor the Strait of Malacca. It is also possible that it was the *Luigi Torelli* that carried the equipment for Sabang, but there is unfortunately no reliable evidence either way. It is, however, certain that the *Luigi Torelli* was carrying two *Würzburg* stations and also made landfall in Sabang.[1] The *Luigi Torelli* was also carrying the Telefunken engineer Heinrich Foders, who played a major role in the replication of the *Würzburg* in Japan. One of the complete *Würzburg* stations was put up in the Japanese naval port of Kure in Japan, but there is no evidence for the siting of the two others.

According to Alexander Werth – who looked after Subhas Chandra Bose during his stay in Germany – another *Würzburg* station which was transferred from a U-boat to Japanese submarine I-8 south of the Azores is said to have reached Japan.[2] In my opinion it would hardly be possible to load the cumbersome equipment – weighing tonnes – from submarine to submarine on the high seas.

Other submarines carried construction diagrams and spare parts such as transformers, vacuum tubes, and complete units to the Far East. More types of radar equipment such as a Hohentwiel FuG 200 (air force radar for detecting ships), an FuMO-61 for installation on ships and submarines and an FuMO 29 *Seetakt* ship-borne radar were shipped to East Asia in submarines, but never reached their destinations: they were all sunk by the Allies.[3]

When the I-30 went down off Singapore with the *Würzburg* equipment on board, a further attempt was immediately made with two Italian submarines that were travelling at the same time. Since Heinrich Foders of Telefunken, a personal acquaintance of mine, was on board the *Luigi Torelli,* I can here present the detailed facts about this operation. On the Internet and even in the pages of official naval histories there is a great deal of varying information about this submarine. There are major disagreements about dates, ports of departure in western France and routes followed. Problems with dating may well arise from the fact that the Japanese calendar differs from the European. But there were other, worse errors. Sabang – where the submarine made its landfall – was often mislocated in British Malaya or Borneo, although we know that it is on the island of Weh off the northern tip of Sumatra.

1   E.g. Italian naval information:
      http://www.regiamarina.net/detail_text_with_list.asp?nid=84&lid=1&cid=44)
2   Werth, A. *Der Tiger Indiens,* p. 175
3   Department of the Navy – Naval Historical Center, Washington DC, Report SRH-019, p. 6
      http://www.ibiblio.org/hyperwar/NHC/blockade_running_subs.htm
      Forum für deutsche Militärgeschichte, http://forum.balsi.de/index.php?topic=6572.0)

The following dates and facts are the only correct ones, since they are based on the evidence and documents of Heinrich Foders, who was actually there, and entries in the book published in Japan in 1981 by Foders' Japanese friend and partner Tsuda Kiyokazu, a copy of which is in my possession. I was also able to make contact with Foders' nephew, although he had no new information to add.[1]

The *Luigi Torelli* was carrying two *Würzburg* stations for the Japanese Navy, and the *Barbarigo* three; they were both also carrying complete sets of construction diagrams for the replication of the equipment in Japan. The *Luigi Torelli* and the *Barbarigo* were both Italian submarines that had been converted to freight submarines because they were not suitable for combat in the Atlantic, as mentioned earlier.

The *Luigi Torelli* was handed over to the German Navy together with her crew including her captain, Enrico Gropalli, and was under German orders. As already described every last space on board the submarines was crammed with cargo, even including two of the three toilets. Even at this early stage the Italian crew of the *Luigi Torelli* were extremely disgruntled, since their freedom of movement was severely limited and they were not under the command of their own navy. Captain Gropalli therefore began his voyage to the Far East with very little enthusiasm, since he had no power to make any decisions.[2]

The *Luigi Torelli* was also carrying passengers: Japanese Captain Satake Kinjo, a Japanese radio officer who had been training on the *Würzburg* system with Telefunken in Germany, two German engineers from the German ship and machine construction company Deschimag, which had a U-boat yard in Bremen, and Heinrich Foders and another Telefunken radar technician. According to Foders and Tsuda there were also German naval personnel on board to assist the Italian captain.[3]

Foders had accompanied Captain Kinjo's training in Germany. The *Würzburg* was produced in Berlin, Backnang near Stuttgart and Ulm. Foders was instructed to take charge of the project to replicate the *Würzburg* system in the Far East, setting it up with the Nihon Musen company in Tokyo. Foders took a lot of persuasion before finally agreeing to accompany Kinjo to Japan and manage the project there.

1   Information directly from Herr Foders in the 1960s and 1970s
     Tsuda, *Würzburg Project* and Professor Federico Foders, nephew of Heinrich Foders

2   Italian documents name Capitano di Fregata Primo Longobardo, who was said to have commanded the Luigi Torelli from the 7th of October 1940 until the 8th of September 1943

3   Tsuda, *Würzburg Project,* Chapter 3: *The Second Würzburg transport*

Foders left Berlin for Brest on the 7th of June 1943. On the 16th the *Luigi Torelli* and the *Barbarigo* sailed from Brest. Closely protected by the German air force and navy both safely reached the North Atlantic. For some stretches they even sailed in sight of each other. Only 8 days after leaving Brest, on the 24th of June, they were both attacked off the Azores by the British navy: the *Barbarigo* was sunk, the *Luigi Torelli* escaped unharmed. Keeping a safe distance, she sailed south along the coast of West Africa. On the 10th of July 1943, near St. Helena there was a massive Allied air and sea attack. The *Luigi Torelli* escaped unharmed once more by crash-diving. She survived a total of 6 Allied attacks.

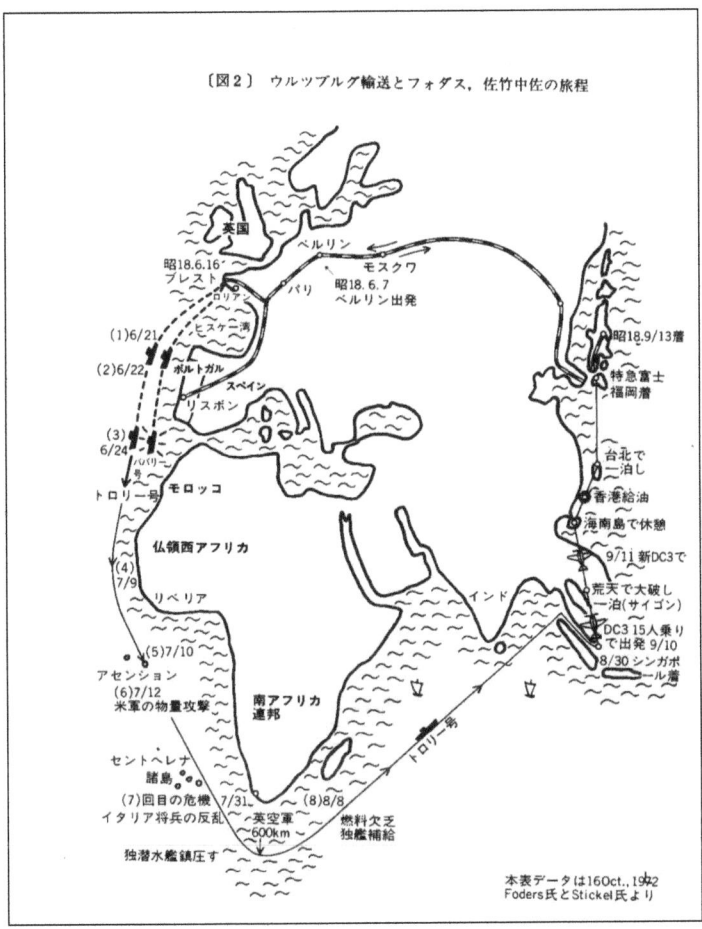

Ill. 60
Route of Luigi Torelli carrying Heinrich Foders from the Japanese Book Maboroshi no reda - Urutsuburugu [The Dream of Radar: Würzburg] by Tsuda Kiyokazu

In the night between the 24th and 25th of June 1943 Mussolini was deposed. Marshal Badoglio became Prime Minister and removed all Fascists from the government. It took some time for the news to trickle through to the *Luigi Torelli*, but then the Italian crew became increasingly unsettled, whispered to each other in groups and only reluctantly obeyed orders from the Germans. The relationship between the German and Japanese passengers and the captain and his Italian crew got worse day by day. On the 31st of July 1943, when the ship reached its closest point to the tip of South Africa, there was open mutiny. Captain Gropalli and his crew wanted to give up their dangerous mission for the Germans and hand themselves over to the British in South Africa. Attempts by the Germans to negotiate with the captain were unsuccessful, but the armed German sailors were able to prevent a change of course and desertion to South Africa.

Shortly after the mutiny a German U-boat came to the aid of the German crew of the Luigi *Torelli*.[1] Several German sailors and the German commander boarded the *Luigi Torelli* to negotiate with Captain Gropalli, who insisted that the German and Japanese passengers be transferred to the German U-boat so that he and his men could surrender to the British. Of course it was impossible to transfer the *Würzburg* equipment, and that could not under any circumstances fall into enemy hands. Only when the German commander threatened to sink the *Luigi Torelli* immediately after the transfer of her passengers did Gropalli reluctantly agree to continue his voyage to Sabang and Singapore.

The *Luigi Torelli* rounded the Cape of Good Hope at a distance of around 600 kilometres. In the Indian Ocean 700 kilometres east of the Cape she ran out of fuel, and on the 1st of August 1943 Captain Wilhelm Dommes of the U 178 received instructions from Berlin to provide the *Luigi Torelli* with fuel. He was operating in the Indian Ocean, and the two submarines met eight days later. Shortly before Dommes had sunk the British freighter *City of Canton* off the coast of Mozambique.

Although there were a number of problems, the *Luigi Torelli* was refuelled by the U 178 on the 8th of August 1943. The sea was relatively rough, and they had to maintain a safety distance of 80 metres. The U 178 had two water hoses for firefighting, but they were not compatible with the tank connection on the Italian submarine. Wiebke, the Chief Engineer of the U 178 was sent over to the *Luigi Torelli* with parts to make the connection work and finally enough fuel was pumped over for the voyage to continue. The weather then worsened to such a degree that the Chief Engineer was unable to return to the U 178.

---

1   Foders and Tsuda do not identify the U-boat. There were several operating in the vicinity at the time.

So that the Italian captain could not make another escape attempt, it had been decided that the two ships would travel on together. For several days they fought with extremely rough seas, but finally arrived in Sabang on the 26th of August 1943.

It is not absolutely clear if one of the two *Würzburg* installations that the *Luigi Torelli* had on board was unloaded at Sabang, or whether there was already one there from the *Commandante Cappellini*. Presumably the Telefunken radar technician left the *Torelli* at Sabang to manage the setting up procedures. Foders spent three days in Sabang and according to Tsuda Kiyokazu continued alone. On the 29th of August 1943 both submarines sailed on to Penang, but since there was only one berth available only the U 178 was able to dock. The *Luigi Torelli* sailed directly on to Singapore after a short pause to unload her cargo. Foders reached the Singapore base on the 30th of August 1943, just a few days before the Italian capitulation.

Foders had a ten-day break in Singapore to recover from his long, troubled and exciting voyage. The Japanese base command treated him exceedingly well. He was accommodated in the luxury Raffles Hotel, was given plenty of spending money and was even able to make a number of trips, including one to Johor Baru in Malaya. Foders writes that his time there was extremely pleasant.[1]

Presumably Foders missed the ceremonial handover, described in the previous chapter, of the *Luigi Torelli* to the German Navy on the 10th of September 1943, because that was the day he flew to Japan. The majority of the Italians remained in German service, possibly because they feared that if they became prisoners of war they might be court-martialled for their mutiny.

That day Foders flew to Saigon in a Japanese Air Force DC3. Since the aircraft was damaged by a tropical storm he had to spend a night in Saigon while the aircraft was changed. He next day he boarded a new DC3 and flew via Hainan in China to Hong Kong, where they refuelled. After another overnight stop in Formosa he arrived in Fukuoka in Japan. From there he went on by train to Tokyo, where he finally arrived after a nearly three-month journey, on the 13th of September 1943. He was accommodated in the luxurious Hotel Imperial.

In Tokyo he worked with the Japanese company Nihon Musen. Their head engineer for this project, Kiyokazu Tsuda, and Foders worked very closely and confidently together, and collaboration soon developed into friendship.

Collaboration with the other Japanese organisations that were responsible for the *Würzburg* replication project was by no means so unproblematic. He continually had to fight to get the financial resources and extra staff required.

1   Tsuda, *Würzburg,* Chapter 3, *Arrival in Singapore and the flight to Jap*an

Since the Japanese technical staff could not understand the drawings and circuit diagrams from Germany, they quickly had to be redrafted to Japanese standards. Kiyokazu Tsuda writes with great respect of the disciplined way that Foders followed his project plan, something unknown in Japan at the time. Foders regretted that the Japanese were very reluctant to reveal their developments in the field of radar. There were many failures, because he was not satisfied with the quality of the parts replicated in Japan, and also because the supply of parts from Germany was drying up since an increasing number of the submarines that were supposed to bring them were failing to arrive in the Far East. This meant that even German vacuum-electron tubes had to be replicated in Japan, an almost impossible task. Foders had to improvise more and more and replace German parts with Japanese ones. The plans and the whole concept of the equipment had to be changed and adapted to Japanese circumstances.

When the first prototype of the technically altered *Würzburg* system was ready, the Americans were already bombing Japan with their B 29 bombers, which obviously led to difficulties in the final preparation. A few days before Japan finally capitulated the first functioning *Würzburg* prototype was tested. It immediately brought down two American bombers. It was working perfectly, but by then the war was over. This prototype, all further developments and all technical documentation were destroyed. However, it is impossible to value Foders' commitment, his ability to improvise, his technical abilities and his adaptability adequately.

On the 15th of April 1945, shortly before the end of the war, the U 234, equipped with a Hohentwiel radar station, left the port of Kristiansand in Norway, heading for the Atlantic to take valuable freight to Japan.[1] Its cargo weighed 240 tonnes, and included jet aircraft engines, a dismantled functioning Me 262 jet fighter, parts for the rocket-propelled aircraft Me 163, parts for a V2 rocket, mercury and 560 kilograms of uranium oxide. The passengers included Naval Captain and naval construction consultant Heinz Schlicke, an expert in radar technology who had also been a consultant on the development of the *Würzburg* system, Lieutenant Fritz von Sandrart and Lieutenant Heinrich Hellendorn, both experts in radar assisted anti-aircraft systems. They were intended to support Herr Foders in speeding up the development of radar in Japan. The mission failed, because the U 234 had to surrender to the Americans in the Atlantic when the war ended.

The Nihon Musen electronics company, founded in 1915, still exists. It is better known under the name of the Japan Radio Corporation (JRC). Production sites were and still are Osaka, Tokyo and Mitaka. After the war Japan

1   See later in this book

was, of course, forbidden to research radar systems for military purposes. But with the knowledge gained from their work on *Würzburg* they were able to develop equipment like weather radar, ship-borne radar for fishery vessels and sonar devices for detecting schools of fish, which they still successfully produce.

After the Japanese capitulation in August 1945 Foders retreated to a simple wooden hut near Hakone, which was then a day's journey south of Tokyo. Here he could feel relatively safe. Hakone has a wonderful site in the middle of the mountains, surrounded by volcanoes and hot springs. The hut was very simple, the windows were draughty and as the first winter approached it became icy cold in the hut because there was no heating. He built himself a German-type stove out of scrap and odds and ends. There was enough fuel in the nearby wood, but he had to fell, saw and split the trees himself – but at least he was now comfortable on the warmth of the hut. Foders lived there in total isolation, but was still classed as a prisoner of war by the Americans. But for some reason he was allowed to continue living in his hut, though he was under close surveillance.

In the isolation of Hakone Foders naturally wanted to know what was going on in the outside world after the war, and so he built himself a short-wave radio with which he could receive international stations. He somehow managed to come into contact with a dubious Japanese black marketeer who asked him to build more radios – he would sell them and they would share the profit. Foders immediately agreed, as he needed a source of supplementary income. The black marketeer brought the parts and Foders kept on building. It was a lucrative business.

In his isolation in Hakone Foders had initially lost all contact with his partner and friend Kiyokazu Tsuda. Personal or mail contact were still not possible, and so he sent a message to Tsuda asking him to try and visit him in Hakone at Christmas 1945. Tsuda did manage to get there on the 24th of December 1945. Foders had prepared a traditional Christmas with a decorated pine tree and a German Christmas meal. For Tsuda it was his first German Christmas, an experience he never forgot.

Foders was occasionally visited by Germans who were interned in Hakone, including an engineer called Schüffner (a Sonar specialist from the Atlas company who had also been sent to Nihon Musen), a General Stöckelt (or was it a Herr Stickel, who drew the map of the submarine and air voyage to Japan with Foders?), Admiral Hans Koschella – whom Foders taught how to build a radio in February 1947– and a widow called Frau Lehnert.[1]

---

1   The names are not necessarily correct. They were taken down phonetically from the Japanese.

When in the spring of 1947 rumour began to spread in Japan that the Americans were soon going to send all German internees back to Germany, Foders made efforts to be allowed to stay in Japan. He was worried that he might be prosecuted in Germany because of his work for the Japanese forces. But the Americans would make no exceptions and in February 1947 Foders was taken from Hakone and, together with other Germans – former Nazi officials, women, children and the managers of German firms involved in the Far East – put on the American freighter *Marine Jumper*. She sailed from Yokosuka via Panama and Dover to Bremen, arriving in April 1947. In Germany Foders was put in a camp and interrogated ceaselessly for a year.

During the voyage on the freighter two Germans committed suicide: they saw no future for themselves in Germany after the war. Since communications were still poor, Foders' friend Kiyokazu Tsuda was not informed of his departure date. Four weeks after Fodors sailed Tsuda had a chance to visit him in Hakone. When he arrived, he found the widow Lehnert living in Foders' hut. He was told that Foders was one of the two suicides. Since no one could have known that this was not true, a Japanese funeral ceremony was held for Foders in Tokyo. Tsuda had an altar erected for Foders and in accordance with Japanese tradition Fodor was given the god-like name *Fodernomikoto*. There was great surprise and joy when Tsuda received a letter from the living Foders in 1951.

After a year in a German camp, Foders was finally freed on the 5th of April 1948. Since he could not at first discover if his wife and daughter in Berlin had survived the war, or whether they were now living somewhere else, he stayed with his uncle near Bremen. Foders had no money and it was still almost impossible to travel to Berlin, and so he worked in his uncle's electronic parts business. Although his house in Berlin had been destroyed, the search for his family was successful. He managed to fly to Berlin on an American military aircraft in June and was finally, after seven long years, reunited with his wife and daughter.

His former superior at Telefunken, the radar pioneer Professor Wilhelm T. Runge, had Foders reinstated in the company. In the 1960s I got to know and value Heinrich Foders personally. We met on several occasions because many radio link and radar projects for Sumatra and Java had led to contracts and he was the person responsible for these in Germany. At these meetings we often talked about his stay in Sabang and his voyage through the Strait of Malacca, since I by then also knew these areas very well.

In recognition of his services to Japan, Foders was invited to Japan in 1964. The president of Nihon Musen, Mr Naruyoshi, thanked him personally for what he had done. On a second visit to Japan in 1976, this time accompanied by his wife, Nihon Musen put him up in the fashionable Hotel Okura in Tokyo, and he was welcomed by the new president, Hasegawa.

Until his death, Foders maintained a close friendship with his Japanese friend Tsuda and his family, and they visited each other in Japan and Germany. When Heinrich Foders' funeral was held in Backnang in South Germany, Tsuda and some of his former Japanese colleagues and friends travelled to Germany to pay their last respects.

In 1942 an event occurred that was soon to reduce the *Würzburg* radar system's superiority. On the night of the 27th to the 28th of February a British special unit of 120 paratroopers and radar experts captured large parts of a *Würzburg* system near Le Havre on the French coast. The team of guards and operators were put out of action, only three German soldiers surviving. The British managed to take the most important parts of the system and a captured German radar technician to England, which meant that British engineers were now in a position to develop similarly powerful radar systems and from July 1943 to take measures against the *Würzburg* system by dropping strips of tinfoil or using jamming transmitters. By the end of 1944 Telefunken had developed new devices and regained its leading position in radar technology, but by that time the outcome of the war had already been decided and the end was in sight.

You can see a *Würzburg* radar device today in the Imperial War Museum in London. Could it be the one captured in Le Havre?[1] They are also on view in museums in Greding in Bavaria, and near Douvres-la-Délirande in Normandy.

US-Soldiers captured working *Würzburg* devices at the end of the war and they remained in American military use until 1957. By changing the wavelength to 11 centimetres the range for detecting aircraft was extended to almost 600 kilometres.

---

1   Information from my late British friend Michael Hudelist, who was himself involved in this action.

27. Subhas Chandra Bose and other Supporters of Hitler

The Bumi Sanguriang Club was on a hill above Bandung. It had previously been a Dutch club, but in the 1960s it was a regular meeting place for Indonesians and Germans. When I was in Bandung at the beginning of 1964, they were about to hold a German film evening for the first time in years. In those days a film from Germany was something special, and everybody who was anybody in Bandung and spoke German was there. For us Germans, however, the show was more than embarrassing, because the film was one from the time of the Third Reich and glorified Adolf Hitler. We wanted to stop the film evening, but the Indonesian audience protested and insisted that the film should be shown to the end: they were not offended by the film; quite the contrary, they were actually enthusiastic about it. How do we explain that?

From an Indonesian viewpoint, Hitler helped to speed up the process of Indonesian independence by his war against the Netherlands. The Indonesians argue that Hitler's European war weakened their colonial rulers so severely that the freedom fighters in Indonesia were able to gain the upper hand, and eventually achieve independence, for which they were grateful to Hitler. They also valued the Third Reich's support of PETA and the independence movement, which they ascribed to Hitler.

It is always embarrassing to hear, in former European colonies like Indonesia, Malaysia or India, how positively Hitler is regarded even today following this line of argument. Indians' positive attitude to Germany is based even today on the fact that Germany fought against the British in two world wars, in the second even under a flag bearing the 5,000-year-old Indian symbol of good fortune, the Swastika. Since the struggle for a free India is closely connected with Hitler, Japan, German U-boats and South East Asia, we will investigate Hitler's role in the Indian independence movement.

After the beginning of the First World War, Germany supported the independence movement in British India. The Indian revolutionaries found help and recognition in Berlin. Two students from Bengal founded the Indian Independence Committee and gathered Indian freedom fighters around them. Britain saw this committee, with the student Chatto at its head, as a serious threat. In 1918 the *Bund der Freunde Indiens* [Association of Friends of India], which also aimed for Indian independence, was founded in Berlin.

Germany was well thought of in India because after 1918 it had no more colonies and was, after Britain, India's second largest trade partner. German Indology was also – and still is – highly valued by Indian scholars. As a result of good technical and academic co-operation an increasing number of Indian students came to Berlin because they did not want to study in their colonial homeland. With a few exceptions, they all agitated against Britain's colonial hegemony.

In Berlin the Indian League against Imperialism published (in English) the journal *Indian Independence* and distributed it all over Europe. Leading pro-independence representatives of the Indian National Congress, like Jawaharlal Nehru and Subhas Chandra Bose, visited Germany even before the Third Reich to discover if there was any prospect of help from Germany.

Bose also wished to study the Sinn Fein movement in Ireland, seeing in it a successful model for India. During the First World War Germany supported the Irish struggle for independence, smuggling thousands of rifles, with ammunition, explosives and machine guns into the country. In India, too, the British were the enemy, and they hoped to be able to beat them using the same strategy. After a number of failed uprisings Ireland finally achieved independence from Britain in 1921, a model Bose wished to follow.

Bose was born in 1897 in Cuttack/Orissa, the ninth of fourteen children. His father was a lawyer. Bose studied in Cambridge and successfully passed the Indian Civil Service examination.

The British did not take the Indian independence movement seriously, but punished its leaders severely anyway, generally sentencing them to long stretches in prison. After his call for civil disobedience, Gandhi had a meeting with Lord Irwin, the British Viceroy, in February 1931. Winston Churchill regarded this meeting as "alarming and nauseating". A "half-naked fakir" should not meet the representative of the Crown on equal terms.[1]

When Gandhi accepted an invitation to talks with the new Viceroy Lord Wellington in December 1931, to bring about an easing of the tense situation and a peaceful solution to the independence question, he was arrested and imprisoned. The same fate befell Subhas Chandra Bose, Nehru and other Congress leaders.

Bose's health declined in prison, and when he became increasingly weak, a medical commission recommended a convalescent stay in Europe – but at his own expense. Bose was taken to the liner *Ganges* in February 1933 by a police escort, and was not allowed to say goodbye to his parents and siblings. According to an entry in his British passport his only permitted place of residence was Austria.[2]

---

1   Werth, Alexander, *Der Tiger Indiens*, p. 53
2   Ibid., pp. 57ff

However, after Czechoslovakia and Poland produced their own entry and exit documents for Bose and other countries such as Germany and Italy wished to follow suit, the British Consul in Prague felt forced to extend his residence permit to the whole of continental Europe. Now all borders were open to him. He wished particularly to learn from Hitler and Mussolini how they succeeded in electrifying the mass of the population.

Between 1933 and 1934 Bose wrote his book *The Indian Struggle 1920 – 1934* in Vienna, Karlsbad and Bad Gastein. In India its sale was strictly forbidden by the British authorities. Bose fell in love with his Austrian secretary Emilie Schenkl, whom he married in 1941. In 1942 they had a daughter, Anita Bose-Pfaff, later a professor of economics at the University of Augsburg.

Bose visited Berlin for the first time in July 1933. He wished to meet Hitler and persuade him to change his negative attitude to India, but nothing came of this. Hitler had written in *Mein Kampf: England will lose India only if it either falls victim to racial degeneration within its own administrative machinery (something which, at the moment, is entirely excluded in India), or if it is compelled to by the sword of a powerful enemy. Indian rebels will, however, never achieve this. We Germans have learned well enough how hard it is to force England. Entirely aside from the fact that, as a German, I would, despite everything, still far rather see India under English than some other rule.*[1]

Reichsmarschall Göring even described Gandhi as an "anti-British and Bolshevist agent".[2] Bose was not happy with this attitude on the part of leading German politicians. When Hitler emphasised the "supremacy of the white races" in a speech in 1936, Bose responded at a press conference in Geneva in May 1936: *During the last few weeks my mind has been greatly disturbed at the insulting remarks made by the German Führer. [...] It is quite clear that Germany today is determined to curry favour with England by insulting India. I can have no objection if the Germans desire to lick the boots of the Britishers, but if they think that [...] an insult hurled at India will be quietly pocketed by us, they are sadly mistaken.*[3]

At this time Bose was not given access to Hitler or any other high-ranking Germans. He only received the evasive answer that the German government would maintain a neutral stance with regard to the Indian independence movement. They did not wish to alarm the British government. It was ini-

---

1   Hitler, *Mein Kampf*, quoted from p. 956 of http://archive.org/stream/ meinkampf035176mbp/meinkampf035176mbp_djvu.txt
2   Werth, *Der Tiger Indiens*, p. 66
3   Netaji Collected Works, Vol. 8, p. 346, Press Conference in Geneva, March 1936

tially very difficult for Bose to win the Germans over to the idea of collaboration. They did not agree with him that India's problem was a world problem. Mussolini, on the other hand, had met Bose several times and offered his co-operation. In the Nazi Party offices, however, Bose met with a certain degree of support. They wanted to provide small arms and other technical equipment for his allies in Bengal.

When Bose returned to India from his European journey in April 1936, he was arrested on board ship in Bombay and imprisoned in the Arthur Road Prison in Bombay. He was later transferred to another prison near Poona: the British were aware of Bose's anti-British activities in Europe. Eleven months later, in March 1937, Bose had to be released again for health reasons. He underwent medical treatment in the mountains of the Punjab for several months.

Subhas Chandra Bose was elected President of the Indian National Congress in 1938 and 1939. Because of his extreme anti-British position he was imprisoned eleven times for up to three years – comparisons with Soekarno in the Dutch East Indies are obvious.

As in the First World War, Britain wished to bring India into the Second World War against Germany and Japan. Sir Stafford Cripps, a member of the War Cabinet, was sent to India by Churchill in March 1942 to demand India's unconditional solidarity. He negotiated separately with Mahatma Gandhi for the Hindus and Muhammad Ali Jinnah for the Muslims. The "Cripps Mission", as it was called, met with no success, since the Congress demanded immediate independence in return for their support. Britain would only offer to grant this after the war. India then refused to ally themselves with the colonial power and answered with open resistance, since India's politicians saw the chances of their struggle for independence being successful increasing after Hitler's successes in Europe and Japan's in South East Asian. In the satirical magazine *Kladderadatsch* the "Cripps Mission" was satirised in a cartoon:

Bose said contemptuously that the otherwise arrogant British Empire was begging all round the world for money, soldiers and arms – not just from free nations like the USA but also enslaved countries like India. The peoples who had been oppressed for centuries by the "iron hand" of the colonial powers could feel it losing its grip because of the war in Europe. The British quickly declared the Congress illegal and imprisoned the leading members of the independence movement – including Jawaharlal Nehru and Mahatma Gandhi – until the end of the war. Using the time-tested method of "divide and rule" the British now tried to stir up hostility and problems between Hindus and Muslims.

Ill. 61
Cartoon from Kladderadatsch 1942.
Text (translated):
Cripps: I'll probably give you your
freedom after the war. Is there
anything else you want?
Indian: Get out of my light!
(Author's note: The sun in the background
is the Japanese Rising Sun Banner)

Ill. 62
Japan's Rising Sun Banner

Subhas Chandra Bose was mayor of Calcutta and a leading light of the Congress Party. In spite of his admiration for Germany he was more than reserved with regard to Hitler and his ideas, especially his racial policies. However, he saw in Germany and Japan potential allies in the Indian battle for independence. Unlike Gandhi, who chose the peaceful path to independence, Bose wished to achieve it as quickly as possible, if necessary by military means.

Bose initiated a mass movement in India to prevent the deployment of Indian resources and soldiers by the British Empire in the war against Germany. He wanted to see no more Indian blood shed for British interests, as had happened for centuries. Britain claimed to be waging a war for freedom and democracy, but would not grant them to India. Bose managed to foster solidarity between all Indians, both Hindus and Muslims. In November 1940, when he began a hunger strike during his eleventh spell in prison and refused to accept forced feeding, the British authorities freed him, on condition that he did not provoke an uprising among the masses.

Bose avoided his twelfth prison sentence on the 16th of January 1941 by escaping from Calcutta to northern India in a 1937 Wanderer W24 car.[1] Disguised as a Pashtun insurance agent he received help and accommoda-

---

1   Wanderer was a daughter company of the German DKW/Auto-Union car and motor cycle manufacturing company.

tion from supporters. His disappearance was only noticed ten days later, since he used a number of carefully prepared diversionary tactics, including letters that were dated after his departure, and rumours that he had retired to a monastery. Bose had disappeared from the face of the earth, and the secret was only revealed a year later when he broadcast on the radio from Berlin.

Following lonely tracks over snowbound passes Bose reached Kabul in Afghanistan on the 31st of January 1941. He wasn't able to speak to the German Ambassador in Kabul, Herr Pilger, until the 6th of February 1941. Pilger immediately asked Berlin for instructions. For security reasons all further contact between Pilger and Bose was made via the Siemens representative in Kabul. The German Embassy there was already heavily involved in the activities of the Indian independence movement. There was an advance party of the Brandenburg Special Unit there to prepare an advance by German troops from Turkey towards India. Hitler was against the plan.

At the beginning of 1941 Iraqi troops started a major revolt against the British, which quickly became all-out war. The Iraqi Prime Minister Rashid Ali al-Gaylani and the former Afghan Foreign Minister Ghulam Siddiq Khan decamped to Germany. This war led Hitler to issue Führer decree no. 30, aimed at supporting anti-British Arab forces in Iraq and the Near East. An Axis victory would free the countries in the near and Middle East from the British yoke. All countries wishing for freedom should join the fight against England.[1] Hitler expressed himself much more clearly when referring to the freedom movements in the Arab countries than he did with respect to India. He regarded the Arab states as Germany's natural allies, but not India.

One important duty of the Special Unit Brandenburg in Kabul was to maintain connections with the anti-British underground in India. About 100 selected Indian underground fighters had been trained in Germany so that they could pass on their knowledge to others in India. The training included technical skills like radio and the construction and operation of espionage transmitters and the use of code machines, and also parachute jumping, riding and operating in mountain terrain. These German-Indian commando troops under the command of Captain Walter Harbich were to destabilise India by carrying out acts of sabotage. At the same time more fighters were to be recruited to the movement. The Northwest Frontier of British India, which was near to Kabul (it is now the border with Pakistan) and had always been unruly – the British called it the Tribal Territories – was particularly suitable for this kind of action. It was called Operation Tiger. In 1936 to 1937 the freedom fighter Mirza Ali Khan had started a campaign

---

1   Führererlass No. 30 of 23rd May 1941
     www.chroniknet.de

against the British army and was waiting for support from Nazi Germany. Ribbentrop authorised a million *Reichs* marks for Operation Tiger, half of the money being intended for the support of the rebels.[1]

Germany even planned to build a landing strip for the long-distance bomber Focke-Wulf Fw 200 Condor in the Tribal Territories, to speed up the dispatch of material, agents and troops to the area. The plan failed because of the unfavourable ground conditions in that extremely mountainous region, and so material and secret service agents were dropped by parachute.

On the 23rd of February 1941 Subhas Chandra Bose was informed via the Siemens representative in Kabul that he should contact the Italian ambassador, Alberto Quaroni. Previous to this there had been a lively exchange of diplomatic despatches between Germany, Italy and the Soviet Union. At that time, Germany and Russia were not yet at war. All three countries agreed to allow Bose to travel to Germany via the Soviet Union with an Italian diplomatic passport in the name of Orlando Mazzotta. Getting to Germany was his goal, since he saw -- in spite of Hitler's reservations – his best chance of gaining support there. It was felt that an Italian passport would be more sensible, given his "southern" skin colouring, which would not be likely in a German.

Bose left Kabul on the 18th of March 1941 in the company of three German soldiers, and travelled to Samarkand in a motor vehicle. From there he travelled to Moscow by train. A telegram from the German Embassy in Moscow on the 31st of March 1941 announced his impending arrival in Berlin with the intention of reporting directly to the Foreign Ministry. He arrived in Berlin by air on the 3rd of April 1941.[2]

When Bose arrived in Berlin, Germany was at the peak of its success. A vast area reaching from the Arctic to the Spanish border and from the west coast of France to the Black Sea was occupied by German forces. On the very day of his arrival in Berlin, Bose was received by Secretary of State Ernst Woermann in the Foreign Ministry. At this first meeting Bose asked for 100,000 German soldiers to attack India from the north – a request that obviously could not be fulfilled. Kabul became from then on the point of contact between the anti-British movement in India and Bose in Berlin.

Woermann was the son of the famous art historian Karl Woermann. At the time of Bose's arrival in Berlin he was head of the Political Department in the Foreign Ministry, and then from 1943 until the end of the war German Ambassador to the Nationalist Chinese government in Nanking (now: Nanjing).

---

1   Schnabel, Reimund, *Tiger und Schakal: Deutsche Innenpolitik 1941-43,* Wien 1968

2   Werth, *Der Tiger Indiens,* pp. 115ff

Because of the war, Bose found fruitful ground for his efforts to achieve independence. Even the government was now more approachable and was prepared to listen to his wishes. He had many German and Indian friends and supporters in Berlin, who called him *Netaji* [Führer] or King of Bengal. He was firmly convinced that his plans for a free India could only be achieved with Germany's political support.

Dr Adam von Trott zu Solz – later a legation counsellor, whom we have already met – and Dr Alexander Werth, son of an English father and a Russian mother, who had spent his school days in England, were responsible for the care of Bose in Berlin. Werth worked from 1934 to 1938 as a lawyer and consultant for German companies in Britain. During that time he also graduated in English law. In September 1938 he moved to Germany and, because of his good knowledge of Britain, was employed by the Foreign Ministry in Berlin in 1940. He became the deputy of von Trott, his friend from student days, in 1940 and was made responsible for liaison with Bose within the "Special India Section". After the war he wrote an impressive biography of Bose, *Der Tiger Indiens* [The Tiger of India].

Both von Trott and Werth were very knowledgeable about the situation in both India and Britain and treated Bose – unlike Hitler – with great sympathy and understanding for his plans. Because of his racial prejudices, Hitler continued to view the Indian problem from a British perspective.

Several departments in the Foreign Ministry now took an interest in Bose, leading to the creation of the "Special India Section" headed by von Trott and Werth and reporting to Secretary of State Wilhelm Keppler, who had direct access to Ribbentrop. Bose's first meeting with Ribbentrop on the 29th of November 1941 brought the breakthrough. Keppler now granted Bose total freedom in the realisation of his plans. Bose now received regular financial support for the preparation of the Provisional Government of Free India which came into being in Japan in 1943. This support was intended as a loan which would be repaid to Germany after the war by a free Indian government. One installment of half a million yen was in fact repaid in 1944 via the German Embassy in Tokyo. It was made up of donations from Indians which Bose had received during his time in South East Asia.

In Berlin Bose founded a radio propaganda station, Radio Azad Hind (Radio Free India), which broadcast successfully to India and to Indians living or fighting in the British sphere of influence. These daily broadcasts were in seven languages: English, Hindustani, Bengali, Pashtu, Telugu, Tamil and Gujarati. This required the employment of a large number of people in the Free India Centre in Berlin: journalists, editors, writers, translators, announcers and so on. German and foreign news material and news media also had to be analysed. News from India came via Kabul which was able to receive transmissions from several secret underground transmitters. All the employees of the Free India Centre were granted the same privileges as a diplomatic mission.

Radio Azad Hind's programmes were broadcast to India by the powerful transmitter in Huizen near Hilversum, with its rotatable curtain antenna. It came into service in around 1937 for the purpose of contact with the Dutch East Indies, 12,000 kilometres away, and had the identifier PHOHI (*Philips Omroep Holland Indie*). When the Germans invaded the Netherlands, the Dutch military tried to destroy the station, but the damage was so limited that German experts soon had it running again.

Only a few days after Singapore fell to the Japanese on the 15th of February 1942, Subhas Chandra Bose spoke to the Indian people on Radio Azad Hind from Berlin: *The fall of Singapore means the collapse of the British Empire, [...] and the dawn of a new era in Indian history. The Indian people who have [...] been ruined spiritually, culturally, politically and economically while under British domination, must now offer their humble thanks to the Almighty for the auspicious event. [...]One fifth of the human race has been ruthlessly suppressed and persecuted. For other nations, British imperialism may be the enemy of today, but for India, it is the eternal foe. [...] During this struggle, and the reconstruction that will follow, we heartily cooperate with all those who will help us in overthrowing the common enemy.*[1]

The United States increasingly took the British side in the Indian question. Roosevelt sent a Personal Representative, Colonel Louis John, to New Delhi. Around 100,000 American troops were already stationed in India in support of the British. Bose first made a sharp attack on the USA in a radio speech on the 13th of April 1942. He accused Roosevelt of playing the role of an "agent provocateur" in order to be able to seize power when the British were driven out.[2]

Unrest in India escalated, becoming the Quit India uprising. There were demonstrations and violence against British soldiers and civilians in the whole country. Policemen were drenched in petrol and set on fire; British officers were lynched on the streets. The Congress leaders, including Gandhi and Nehru were imprisoned. The British now tried to regain control by the use of force, imprisonment, public floggings and fines. There were many deaths on both sides.

Bose exploited the situation to fan the flames. At the end of 1942 more transmitters in various places in Germany were used for Bose to broadcast

---

1   Hayes, *Subhas Chandra Bose in Nazi Germany*, pp. 88f
2   Ibid., p. 102

not just Radio Azad Hind but also further agitatory programmes like National Congress Radio, intended to act for the Congress, which could no longer function in India, Azad Muslim Radio for the Indian Muslim minority and Waziristan Radio for the inhabitants of the tribal territories on the border between India and Afghanistan. These latter were encouraged to take up arms against the British in India. Bose even presented them with the prospect of German paratroops being dropped in the region to support them, though I doubt if he had Germany's agreement to this.[1]

Since very few Indians had their own radios at the time, dozens of them would crowd around a single set in the evening. Listening to the programmes of Radio Azad Hind became a daily ritual, although the British authorities tried in vain to forbid people to do so.

Another Indian freedom fighter, Mohammad Iqbal Shedai, ran the anti-British radio station Radio Himalaya in Rome from 1941 onwards. Shedai operated in Italy because he hoped for more support for the independence movement from the Italians than the Germans were prepared to give. Shedai was, however, less successful than Bose, and there was great rivalry between them. Radio Himalaya was run rather amateurishly and never attained the professionalism and popularity of Bose's Radio Azad Hind. Radio Himalaya did, on the other hand, manage to reach the Indian troops fighting for the British in North Africa with its propaganda.

Germany also had its own anti-British propaganda radio programme, *Germany Calling!* It was broadcast from Hamburg to Britain, Ireland and the USA. The announcers included Wolf Mittler, who worked for Bavarian Radio after the war, a former British army officer, Norman Baillie-Steward, and William Joyce, an American citizen of Irish origin who was a member of Mosley's British Union of Fascists and held a British passport as well as his American one.

Joyce was the most prominent announcer on the Lord Haw-Haw programme. Since it included messages from British PoWs in Germany, it was popular in Britain, reaching an audience of some 6 million. Even Churchill found the parodies it broadcast amusing. Hitler awarded Joyce the War Merit Cross.

To make *Germany Calling!* more attractive to English-speaking listeners it also broadcast high quality swing and jazz music – music that was forbidden in Germany. This was mainly played by Charlie and his Orchestra, a band specially formed for the purpose by the saxophonist Lutz Templin in Berlin in 1940.

---

1   Werth, *Der Tiger Indiens,* pp. 133f

William Joyce's last broadcast as Lord Haw-Haw on the 30th of April 1945, just a few days before the German capitulation, ended with a defiant "Heil Hitler". He was hanged for treason in Britain in 1946.

Through Adam von Trott, Bose met journalist and author Giselher Wirsing with whom he had a close and informative relationship. He also became friendly with the author Karl Haushofer, whom he met in Munich. Haushofer was a close friend of Walther Hewel and Wirsing was an acquaintance, but I can find no reference to a meeting between Hewel and Bose.

Bose's English periodical *Azad Hind* (Free India) mobilised all Indian groups throughout Europe. The Third Reich gave its full support to its printing and distribution. In Berlin Bose was also provided with studios and offices for the Free India Centre, whose main office was in Berlin's diplomatic quarter at Lichtensteiner Allee 2a. A villa in Sophienstraße in Berlin-Charlottenburg was provided for Bose and his wife. The British tried in vain to liquidate this, in their eyes, rebellious and awkward Indian.

On the 26th of January 1942 Bose organised an elaborate celebration of Indian Independence Day in the Kaiserhof Hotel in Berlin: the day had been proclaimed as early as 1930 by the Congress Party, much to the annoyance of the British.[1] Hundreds of prominent members of the Nazi Party, and the German Forces, politicians, leading businessmen, diplomats and journalists from many nations took part in the Indian celebrations. The ballroom was decked with bouquets of flowers and hung with hundreds of German and Free Indian flags.

Ill. 63
Celebration of Indian Independence day in the Kaiserhof Hotel in Berlin. Secretary of State Wilhelm Keppler on the rostrum

1   British rule finally ended on the 15th of August 1947

Following the motto "My enemy's enemy is my friend", Bose offered his services to the Third Reich. In May 1941 the first Indian troops captured in North Africa by Rommel arrived in Germany as prisoners of war. Bose recruited his first *Legion Azad Hind* /Free Indian Army from Indian students and about 3,500 of those Indian PoWs. Indians from all over Europe thronged to Germany to offer their fighting services to Subhas Chandra Bose and Indian independence. 14,000 more Indian PoWs from North Africa arrived in Germany in the course of 1942 to volunteer for the Free Indian Army.[1]

Ill. 64
The Indian Legion
with Subhas Chandra
Bose in Germany

The Indian PoWs, who had previously fought for the British, mainly in North Africa, came from PoW camps in North Africa and Italy and were now trained for their new struggle by Bose and several hundred German army officers and trainers. Infantry Regiment 950, colloquially known as the Indian Legion by the German army, consisted exclusively of Indian soldiers. Their training took place mainly in the Garrison at Königsbrück near Dresden. The regiment was provided with the most modern armaments, including anti-aircraft guns, anti-tank canons and light field artillery.

The Legion's soldiers wore German uniforms with an Azad Hind shoulder badge, so that they could not be regarded as deserters or partisans if they fell into British hands. The Indian Legion's banner also had the inscription Azad Hind, with the image of a leaping Indian tiger.

About two thirds of the soldiers were Muslims, and one third Hindus and Sikhs. The Sikhs were allowed to wear their turbans instead of the German steel helmet. They swore their oath of allegiance to both Subhas Chandra Bose and Adolf Hitler:

---

1   Hayes, *Subhas Chandra Bose in Nazi Germany,* p. XX

Ill. 65
Azad Hind banner and shoulder badge

I swear by God this holy oath, that I will obey the leader of the German state and people, Adolf Hitler, Commander of the German Armed Forces, in the fight for the freedom of India, in which fight the leader is Subhas Chandra Bose, and that as a brave soldier, I am willing to lay down my life for this oath.[1]

John Amery, a British citizen played a significant role in the formation and organisation of the Indian Legion, much to the annoyance of his father, Leopold Amery, who was Minister for Indian Affairs in the Churchill government. In broadcasts from Berlin John Amery called for the overthrow of the Churchill government: Britain should change sides and join Germany in the war against the Soviet Union. He also tried – with very little success – to persuade British PoWs to join a British Free Corps on the model of the Indian Legion

In December 1942 about 3,500 soldiers of the Indian Legion were divided into four battalions. The regiment's commander was Lieutenant Colonel Kurt Krappe, the company commander was Lieutenant General Hans Seifritz. Their first posting was the Dutch coast and the island of Texel. In 1944 the Indian Legion was incorporated into the Waffen-SS.

Members of the German army who had graduated in Indology were posted to the Legion to act as interpreters and mediators between the two cultures. For the German Indologists their service with the Legion was an

---

1   Mangat, *The Tiger Strikes,* pp. 124f

excellent opportunity to further their studies and to increase their command of the languages. Working with Indian experts, they developed a new language for army use, called Hindustani, which was meant to replace English as a command language. Hindustani was a combination of India's two main languages, Hindi and Urdu and was written in Latin script. It was the first step towards a common language for India, which unfortunately was not followed up after the war. Gandhi expressed his regret about this in one of his first speeches after independence: he said that he was ashamed to have to speak English, the language of the colonial power, to be understood by all his Indian listeners.

In contrast with the British practice of having separate units for Muslims, Sikhs and Hindus in the army, Bose made a special point of not dividing the Indian Legion in terms of religious, ethnic or tribal affiliation. Bose successfully insisted on a unified force to promote national unity.

On the 29th of May 1942 Bose was received by Hitler. For Bose, this conversation with Hitler was negative. Adam von Trott zu Solz was present as interpreter and reported that Hitler refused to comment on the prejudice against India expressed in *Mein Kampf*. He insisted – like Britain – that it would be 150 years before India was capable of ruling herself.[1]

Ill. 66
Subhas Chandra
Bose meets Hitler

Bose's plan was to send his Legion, together with German troops, to India via Persia to end British colonial rule by force of arms. The Special Unit Brandenburg had already prepared operations to that end in Kabul, but Hitler was under no circumstances prepared to send German troops to the Indian border. He had already conceded Britain the right to rule India in *Mein Kampf*, and suggested to Bose that he should ally himself with the Japanese, who had already occupied British, French and Dutch colonies in South East Asia and were therefore much nearer to India's borders than Ger-

1   Werth, *Der Tiger Indiens,* pp. 142f

many. He did however declare himself ready to give Bose all possible help to move to Japan.

Bose's efforts to bring about an invasion of India had failed. He did not want just to produce propaganda in Germany, he wanted to be active right on India's borders, and so he felt that he would have a better chance with Japan, especially since Japan was prepared – unlike Hitler – to countenance Indian independence after the war. He therefore accepted Hitler's proposal and began to make preparations for a move to Japan.

In July 1942 Bose met Himmler and Goebbels. He was surprised to find that Himmler was well-informed about Hinduism, ancient Hindu writings and the caste system – unlike Hitler, here was a man who would support his plans and who promised him all possible help.

Ill. 67
Subhas Chandra Bose
in conversation with
Heinrich Himmler,
1943

In September 1942, on the occasion of the foundation of the German Indian Society in Hamburg with Subhas Chandra Bose present, the Indian national anthem (still used today) was performed in public for the first time – by a German orchestra. It is a setting of Tagore's famous poem *Jana Gana Mana* (Ruler of the minds of all people).

When it was clear that Bose was just waiting for a favourable opportunity to travel to Japan but did not have a definite departure date, Ribbentrop threw a big farewell party in his honour in the Foreign Ministry in Berlin on the 14th of October 1942.

The annual Indian Independence Day celebration in the Kaiserhof Hotel in Berlin on the 26th of January 1943 (there were 600 guests) was Bose's last-but-one official appearance in Germany. His speech and the national anthem were broadcast on short wave radio to India and the world. Among the guests were the Grand Mufti of Jerusalem and the Prime Minister of Iraq, Rashid Ali al-Gaylani.

To conceal his intentions and whereabouts, Bose made several recordings which were broadcast at intervals on Radio Azad Hind. Several items were also filmed for German newsreels: all so that people would think he was still in Germany. His last official appearance took place two days after Independence Day, on the 28th of January 1943, before the soldiers of his Indian Legion. A. C. N. Nambir, who had been head of the Free India Centre since 1942 and was Bose's deputy, now took charge of all Indian matters in Germany.

After the war Nambir became the first Ambassador of the Republic of India in Germany in 1951. On the German side, the head of the Political Department of the Foreign Ministry, Legation Counsellor Wilhelm Melchers, who was closely connected with the Special India Section during the Third Reich, eventually became German Ambassador to India.

Even though Bose was no longer in Germany the Indian Legion continued to fight for Germany. It was mainly stationed in the Netherlands and on the French Atlantic coast.

A few weeks after the Allied invasion of Normandy the Indian Legion was withdrawn to the army camp at Heuberg in the Swabian Alps. While attempting to retreat to neutral Switzerland shortly before the end of the war, the Indian Legion, which had fought bravely for Germany to the very end, was captured by the Allies. The prisoners were taken by the British to New Delhi, where they were charged with high treason. This led to massive protests and demonstrations by the Indian populace and so the British courts did not convict them and released all members of the Indian Legion in 1946.

As the Indian Legion retreated, some of the soldiers were shot by French Moroccan troops in Bavaria. They were initially buried in the cemetery in Immenstadt in the Allgäu. The bodies were exhumed by the Americans in 1946, because they thought that the grave contained the bodies of the crew of an American bomber that had crashed in the vicinity. They were reburied in another part of the cemetery before finally being exhumed again and laid to rest in the British War Cemetery in Dürnbach (Bavaria).[1]

Not all the soldiers of the Indian Legion made the attempt to reach Switzerland. Some of them ended up in Berlin taking part in the final battle for the Reich Chancery. Soviet documents even mention a "Tibetan Company of the Waffen-SS". Many members of the Legion came from northern India, near the Tibetan border. The Indian region of Ladakh is even sometimes called Western Tibet or Little Tibet. Its population is ethnically Tibetan, with Tibetan features. The language is also closely related to Tibetan, although they are Indian by nationality. I have visited Ladakh several times and have been told of fathers and relations who fought in Germany during the war.

---

1   Information: Stadtarchiv Immenstadt, Herr G. Klein

Many readers will ask where I acquired much of this previously unpublished detailed information about Bose: it was in many conversations, often late into the night, with my late father-in-law the orientalist Hans Bräker, who sadly died far too early, that I received a great deal of this information about Bose and his personal physician Dr R. Madan.

The Bräker family in Cologne maintained a long, close friendship with Dr Madan in New Delhi, and they visited each other in India and Germany. My wife Annette met Dr Madan twice after 1984 – she well remembers conversations about the Indian Legion on those occasions.

Earlier generations of Dr Madan's family had worked for India's independence from Britain. From his youth he was convinced that it would not be long before the British Crown – like the British East India Company – would no longer have any power over India.

R. Madan was born in Kargil in the Punjab, in the present-day Indian state of Jammu and Kashmir. He studied medicine in Vienna, specialising in ophthalmology. Madan met Bose shortly after the latter's arrival in Germany in 1941. He was one of the first to join the Indian Legion and became Bose's personal physician and confidant. He shared the duties of medical officer to the Indian Legion with a German, Dr Ernst Koch-Grünberg.

In 1945 Madan was one of those taken back to India by the Allies and imprisoned as a PoW in the Red Fort in Delhi. Following popular mass protest, he too was freed in 1946. As well as acting as ophthalmologist to Mahatma Gandhi and Jawaharlal Nehru, he continued to work for a free India, which actually happened in 1947. Unfortunately Bose did not live to see it.

Nevertheless the Indians' great joy at receiving independence was short-lived. Britain's arbitrary division of India into the state of Pakistan – much desired by the leader of the Muslim League, Ali Jinnah – with its Muslim majority, and the Hindu-majority Indian Union led to one the greatest refugee and

Ill. 68
Dr R. Madan being invested with the Order of Merit by Dr Dirk Oncken, the German Ambassador, 18 June 1978

expulsion crises in history. Ten million Hindus and Sikhs were driven out of Pakistan and seven million Muslims from India. There was torture, murder, looting and rape: there were over a million victims of the disturbance.

The arbitrary border between Pakistan and India, drawn with a ruler by the British without any concern for those affected, is still the cause of diplomatic complications, border conflicts and military actions by both countries: a tragic legacy of colonial rule.

Madan's friendly relationship with Germany continued after the war: he became the medical officer of the German Embassy in India and was awarded the Federal Order of Merit in 1978. After the deaths of H. Bräker and R. Madan, there was still contact between my wife and myself and Dr Madan's son-in-law, Dr Vijay Arora.

Bose's desire to move to Japan now became reality – for his wife Emilie it was a final parting. Bose must have felt this, because before his departure he left his wife an emotional letter: *I do not know what the future has in store for me. May be, I shall spend my life in prison, may be, I shall be shot or hanged. But whatever happens, I shall think of you and convey my gratitude to you in silence for your love for me. May be I shall never see you again – may be I shall not be able to write you again when I am back – but believe me, you will always live in my heart, in my thoughts and in my dreams. [...]*[1]

How did he get from Germany to South East Asia and Japan in the middle of a war? It proved to be extremely difficult. It was intended at first to send Bose to Japan on an Italian flight, but the aircraft left without him. Bose was informed that it was only a test flight, and that others would follow.

The test flight was successful. A Savoia-Marchetti SM 75 trimotor military transport aircraft was fitted with supplementary tanks so that it could travel 8,000 kilometres without refuelling. The payload was reduced accordingly to just a few hundred kilograms. The machine took off from Rome on the 30th of June 1942 heading for the furthest possible airfield to the east in German-occupied Ukraine. In Odessa the aircraft was filled to its capacity of over ten tonnes of fuel and then flew over the Soviet Union to Japanese-occupied China. It reached Tokyo on the 3rd of July 1942.

On the 16th of July 1942 the aircraft began its return flight over Nationalist China and the Soviet Union. Since there were powerful headwinds on the westward journey, it took 29 hours to reach Odessa. On the 20th of July 1942 it was back in Rome. This is the only documented successful flight from Europe to the Far East during the Second World War. There is a memorandum about this flight in the Foreign Ministry Archive in Berlin written

---

1   The Telegraph, Calcutta, India, Sunday, June 5, 2011, Title: *To Emilie, with Love*

by Alexander Werth of the Special India Section on the 14th of July 1942. It concerns negotiations with "Orlando Mazzotta", Bose's cover name, and with the Italians and Japanese in Rome from the 7th to the 12th of July 1942. Point 1 states: *The Italian test flight to Tokyo was successful; it was in two stages, the first from Europe to China and the second from there to Tokyo. The first stage is said to have taken about 20 hours. In Tokyo the Italian airmen were received by Prime Minister Tojo. The same aircraft is about to start on the return flight in the near future along the same route. After its return the Italian government will consider setting up regular flights to East Asia and decide whether further test flights are necessary. In Rome Embassy Counsellor Kase and the Japanese military attaché, Colonel Shimutsu, spoke positively about the technical feasibility of a flight from Europe to East Asia, without there being any discussion about Mazzotta using this route.* [1]

Ill. 69
Arrival of the long-distance Italian Savoia-Marchetti in Japan

Bose was annoyed not to be able to avail himself of this first chance to get to Japan quickly. The Italian Air Force were unable to give him a date for the next flight. In the meanwhile the first Japanese submarine, the I-30, reached Lorient on the 5th of August 1942. Germany attempted to get Bose taken as a passenger on its return voyage, but Japanese naval command refused to do so because they were not allowed under any circumstances to carry civilians on their submarines.

1   Werth, *Der Tiger Indiens*, Dokument 10, p. 264

Bose tried his luck in Rome once more, but all efforts were unavailing because of technical and organisational problems on the Italian side. Finally, the Italian Air Force decided that a second flight would be too risky. Bose returned to Berlin disappointed, but Hitler assured him that Germany would see that he was taken to Japan by submarine. Secretary of State Weizsäcker sent a telegram on the subject to the German Ambassador in Rome on the 8th of February: *In order not to endanger the enterprise it is absolutely necessary that no other parties be informed. In particular, no wires even hinting about this are to be sent to the Italian mission in East Asia. [...]Since Subhas Chandra Bose's intended flight by Italian aircraft did not come about, Bose will make his way to East Asia in the next few days by other means. His arrival there to be expected only after a considerable time. Departure only to be known by very limited circle. Until further notice we are explaining that Bose is on an inspection trip. Records made by him will be played on the radio during his absence to make it seem he is still in Berlin.*

[...] signed Weizsäcker[1]

Germany arranged in strictest secrecy for Bose to be transferred from a German to a Japanese submarine in the Indian Ocean. On the 7th of February 1943 Bose travelled from Berlin to Kiel accompanied by Secretary of State Keppler, Bose's deputy Nambier and Alexander Werth. His secretary and confidant Abid Hassan had been taken to Kiel overnight by another route. Even Hassan had not been informed of the travel plans.

At the end of January 1943 the new type IX D1 U-boat U 180 under the command of Captain Werner Musenberg put in to Kiel after undergoing sea trials in the Baltic. She was refuelled and provisioned for a long distance voyage and kept ready to sail. Where she was to sail was highly confidential: the Führer had a special, top secret mission for the U 180.[2] This led me to some fascinating research.

At 8 a.m. on the 9th of February 1943, the U 180's screws began to turn. She cast off from Kiel with Captain Musenberg and a 55-man crew. The previous night, the luggage of two mysterious passengers had been brought to the officers' mess. There were also several boxes which were so heavy they could hardly be moved. We now know that they contained almost 500 kilograms of gold for the German Embassy in Tokyo, presumably for the purchase of rubber and other raw materials that would be acquired and loaded in the "Southern Region" to be shipped to Germany.

---

1   AA, Pol. VII, 140177

2   Only in Ambassador Stahmer's book, *Japans Niederlage – Asiens Sieg*, p. 96 is a brief mention of the fact that Subhas Chandra Bose arrived in South East Asia by U-boat.

Shortly after sailing the U 180's engines were stopped on the open sea. Two passengers in thick, dark woollen overcoats and dark horn-rimmed glasses were taken aboard and down to the officers' mess. For reasons of security, the captain introduced the passengers to the crew as specialists in the construction of U-boat pens. One of them was Subhas Chandra Bose: because he had been so frequently seen on German newsreels that he had acquired the nickname "the Indian Adolf", he was immediately recognised by the crew in spite of all attempts at secrecy.

The second passenger, Abid Hassan, was an officer in the Indian Legion and later held a leading position in the Indian National Army in Japan. He had studied engineering in Germany before the war, during which he became Bose's personal aide de camp, confidant and interpreter, since Bose spoke very little German.

In an interview with the *Augsburger Zeitung* on the 19th of August 2000, the U 180's chief engineer, Herman Wien, then 84 years old, described Bose as *a man who was polite and reticent. He did not want a lot of fuss and hardly spoke any German.* Captain Musenberg also mentions Bose very favourably in his diary: *He makes a very solid impression. If he speaks at all, then it is thoughtfully and shows that he is a man who is knowledgeable in many fields. He knows exactly what he wants.*[1]

After they had successfully made the dangerous transit of the narrowest part of the Channel the boat put in to Le Havre for an intermediate stop. They loaded fuel and provisions for a week's journey.

For Bose and Hassan life in the very restricted space of the U-boat was unfamiliar. In a storm with very high seas the U 180 passed through the strait between Iceland and the Faroes without hindrance in spite of heavy Allied surveillance. Because this surveillance was particularly heavy in the coastal areas of the Atlantic, they had to make wide detours. Bose spent the period of bad weather in his cabin with seasickness. His only comment was: *This is worse than prison.*[2]

As the sea grew calmer along the West African coast the two passengers were able to take an occasional breath of fresh air in the conning tower. Even Bose could not avoid the customary line-crossing ceremony at the Equator. To break the monotony of the long voyage, the two Indian passengers from time to time cooked Indian meals in the little galley of the U-boat, much to the crew's delight. They must have brought the spices required with them, since they were certainly not part of a U-boat's normal supplies.

---

1   Brennecke, *Haie*. p. 31
2   Ibid.

They rounded the Cape of Good Hope without enemy interference, and on the 18th of April 1943 U 180 sank the British tanker *Corbis* in the western Indian Ocean with two torpedoes. The tanker was carrying over 13,000 tonnes of diesel oil and 50 tonnes of aviation fuel from the Gulf States to Cape Town. Only ten of the 59-man crew survived. Here, off the coast near Madras (now: Chennai) the U 180 initially worked in concert with the U 195.

Finally U 180 sailed on alone to a secret rendezvous point agreed by the Japanese and German naval commands. When she surfaced at dawn on the 21st of April 1943 about 450 nautical miles south-east of Madagascar, the giant Japanese submarine cruiser I-29, commanded by Captain Yoichi Izu and carrying Captain Masao Teraoka, the commander of the fleet at Penang, was only three nautical miles away. She had arrived at the meeting point a day early.

On the 5th of April 1943 the I-29 had left the port of Penang with two tonnes of gold and 12 tonnes of freight for Germany. The gold was payment for war materials previously delivered to Japan. After the submarines exchanged the flag signals agreed by both foreign ministries, the U 180 steered towards the Japanese submarine cruiser.

Japanese submarine cruisers were far bigger and equipped with heavier artillery than German U-boats. They had a high top speed and a long operational range. In front of the conning tower there was a hangar for a Yokosuka E 14Y seaplane that was launched by catapult.

For security reasons the U 180 and the I-29 were not allowed to make radio contact. When they were lying close to one another the Japanese captain came over to the U 180 in an inflatable boat in spite of the high seas.[1] He was made welcome be the German captain and a toast was drunk in the mess. Because of the high seas it was not going to be possible to exchange the valuable cargo and transfer the Indian passengers from the German to the Japanese submarine. The Japanese captain suggested sailing to the Japanese naval base in Sabang to make the exchange. Musenberg rejected the suggestion because such a major diversion would mean that he did not have enough fuel for the return voyage. Both captains then decided to sail towards India in search of calmer waters.

After a day, on the 27th of April 1943, they reached calmer seas in the Strait of Mozambique. They began the transfer of the goods that the I-29 had brought for the U 180: boxes containing Japanese one-man torpedoes, a three centimetre self-loading canon, aerial torpedoes, other military equip-

---

1   Alexander Werth wrote that an officer and a boatswain swam from the German to the Japanese submarine. Werth, *Der Tiger Indiens*, p. 174

ment and the gold for the Japanese Embassy in Berlin. There was also a sack of mail for Berlin from the German Embassy in Tokyo.[1] To improve their rations the Japanese also gave the crew of the U 180 fresh potatoes and vegetables from Penang.

The freight from the Japanese boat was first piled on the deck and closely examined before it was carried below decks. They had to make sure that no cockroaches, fleas or other vermin were brought aboard – another German boat had had some bad experiences of that kind.

The Japanese submarine cruiser took on board the boxes of gold for the German Embassy in Tokyo, and boxes of aircraft engines, HHL 3 limpet mines and anti-sonar equipment from Germany. The U 180 also delivered many construction diagrams, especially for the new German IX C/40 U-boats, to the I-29. During these exchanges the men from the U 180 visited the Japanese submarine cruiser and the Japanese crew did likewise on the U 180.

After Bose and Hassan had said a grateful farewell to the crew that had brought them safely to the rendezvous, two new guests boarded the German boat: Captains Tetsuhiro Emi and Tomonaga. They were going to Germany to familiarise themselves with the latest developments in U-boat technology.

Before Bose left, he gave Captain Musenberg two radio messages to send to Germany. They were decoded and transcribed in the Foreign Ministry in Berlin on the 28th of April 1943. Extracts include:

1.) Transfer of Subhas Chandra Bose from German to Japanese boat has taken place.

2.) Bose sent following message to Foreign Minister before transfer:

To the Führer and Chancellor of the German People and Reich,

Before I leave the German boat, I would like to express my heartfelt thanks to your Excellency and the German government in my own name and in the name of the Indian freedom movement for the friendliness, support and hospitality shown to us. I would further like to use this occasion to emphasise our unwavering solidarity with Germany in the battle against our mutual enemy until the achievement of final victory. [...] Finally I send my wishes for a swift German victory and for your Excellency's personal well-being, signed Subhas Chandra Bose[2]

A similar telegram went to Foreign Minister Ribbentrop.

On the 29th of April 1943 there was a great celebration on the Japanese submarine in honour of the successful arrival of the two Indian passengers and the birthday of the Japanese Emperor.

---

1   It is not clear why this pointless exchange of gold took place. Perhaps it was a failure of communication.

2   Excerpt from Document 14 of the AA, Werth, *Der Tiger Indiens*, p. 269

Ill. 70
Subhas Chandra Bose (front row, 2ⁿᵈ from left) on the Japanese submarine cruiser.

In the sparse literature about Bose you always read that the two boats now parted, and that the U 180 sailed round the Cape of Good Hope back to the U-boat pens in Bordeaux without encountering the enemy, while the I-29 sailed east to Sabang. This is not true.

According to Dr Madan, who remained in contact with Bose until the latter's death and so had first-hand information, the U 180's fuel was so low that it would have been too risky to attempt a return to France. Madan was also certain that the U 180 sailed to the Sabang in convoy with the I-29. The base in Sabang was not prepared for this eventuality, and so fuel and provisions for the U 180 were sent specially from Penang.

In Sabang the entire crew of the U 180 was welcomed by the Japanese base commander. This was also confirmed by Alexander Werth, who had liaised with Bose in Germany and remained in contact with him.[1] From Sabang the U 180 sailed non-stop back to Bordeaux, arriving safely about two months later with its precious cargo.

On the 8th of May 1943 Bose and Hassan landed in Sabang, and were welcomed by Colonel Yamamoto, the head of the Hikari Kikan espionage section and the Japanese-Indian Liaison Group. Bose and Yamamoto knew each other from Berlin, where the latter had been the military attaché's deputy.

---

1   Werth, *Der Tiger Indiens,* p.151

After Bose and Hassan had had a couple of days in Sabang to recover from the long sea voyage in the cramped space of the submarines, they continued their journey. Since the Allies were making Penang and the Strait of Malacca unsafe, the commander of the I-29 did not wish to risk losing the Indian passengers, who were so important for Japan's future war plans, and so Bose, Hassan and Yamamoto flew via Penang, Manila, Saigon and Formosa to Tokyo, arriving on the 21ˢᵗ of May 1943. In Tokyo Bose was welcomed by Prime Minister Hideki Tojo and somewhat later even received by Emperor Hirohito.

In the few extant documents about Bose's travel to Japan the dates and places given vary considerably, especially on the Internet. The ones given above are correct, because they are based on original documents in the political archive of the Foreign Ministry in Berlin and statements by a contemporary witness, Dr Madan. Bose sent several telegrams from Tokyo to the Foreign Ministry in Berlin, in which he gives the dates I have quoted.

In a telegram on the 8ᵗʰ of June 1943 Ambassador Stahmer in Tokyo writes to Secretary of State Keppler in Berlin:

Top State Secret: Subhas Chandra Bose, with whom I had private discussions yesterday, requested me to send the following telegram together with his best wishes to Secretary of State Keppler in the Foreign Ministry. Bose Telegram begins:
Landed on 8th May (in Sabang) and met by Colonel Yamamoto. Flew to Tokyo. Arrived here 21ˢᵗ May. [...] Have already met leading figures including Foreign Minister, Navy Minister, Chief of the Army and Navy General Staff. [...]
Indian National Army here completely under Indian command with Indian officers. Daily paper Azad Hind already appearing in (Singapore) in Hindostani, Tamil and English. [...]Bose telegram ends.
Have the impression that Bose [...] lays great emphasis on maintaining the close relationship with Germany forged in Berlin. He expressed his determination to carry out his work in Asia according to what was discussed in Berlin and to stay in contact with German agencies. [...] signed Stahmer.[1]

On the19th of June 1943 Bose appeared in public in Japan for the first time. At a press conference with 60 Japanese and foreign journalists he said:
For many a year the British prisons in India and Burma were my home. But if, instead of rotting in the den of an Indian prison, I am standing in your midst today in the capital of Japan, it is only symbolic of the new momentum gained by the widespread movement for independence in my country. [...] Spiritual degradation, cultural degeneration, dire poverty and political slavery are the only things which India got from British imperialism. It is no wonder, therefore, that the Indian people have once and for all risen up boldly to smash the British chains and attain freedom.[2]

---

1   AA, Pol VII, 140323
2   Quoted from http://subhaschandrabose.org/speechcontent/id/843

Ill. 71
Subhas Chandra Bose in Japan

A few days later Bose received the following telegram from Ba Maw, Burmese head of state: *I sincerely congratulate you on your return to the East. Your first statement in Tokyo deeply impressed the Indian people here and gave them courage and hope. Both Indian and Burmese peoples have long awaited this opportunity. The time has come for us to rise. Burma hereby pledges herself to fight on your side in your fight for national honour and independence.*[1]

On the 1st of August 1943 Bose was a guest of honour in Rangoon at the celebration of Burma's independence.

The I-29 sailed on from Sabang without her two Indian passengers to Singapore, where the freight from Germany was unloaded. She then operated out of Penang off the coast of East Africa and the Gulf of Aden, where she sank the British freighter *Rahmani*. On the 8th of August 1943 she left Penang for Japan where she arrived on the 19th in the naval dockyard in Kure for maintenance.

Bose was fully supported by Prime Minister Tojo from the very beginning. Stahmer, the German Ambassador in Japan, met Bose regularly to exchange ideas: they even became close friends. However, Stahmer had to keep making it clear to Bose that Germany would not intervene militarily in India because it did not have the resources. Stahmer wrote about Bose: *the more I got to know this quiet, cultured man – medium in height with an interesting*

---

1   Werth, Alexander, ed. *A Beacon across Asia: A biography of Subhas Chandra Bose*, p. 142

face – the greater grew my liking for him. From our work towards common goals grew a friendship [...] He had firm ideas about the future of his country and saw his main task to be the reconciliation and collaboration of Hindus with Moslems. He gladly demonstrated that this was possible by the good relationship between his two secretaries, Swami and Hassan, one from each religion.[1]

When the Japanese army occupied Singapore in 1942, Japan began to prepare for the invasion of India from Singapore. By the middle of February there were 75,000 Indian PoWs who had previously fought for Britain in Burma, Malaya and Singapore, ready to volunteer for the Indian National Army (INA). They all aimed to achieve India's independence from Britain. In some cases, this was obviously the result of pressure, since if they did not volunteer for the INA they were threatened with working on the railway in Burma or Siam. Nevertheless, by far the majority of the INA was enthusiastic about Bose's idea of fighting against the British for Indian independence.

In Singapore he founded the Rani of Jhansi women's regiment, which was joined by thousands of Indian women. He then immediately set up a government Department of Women's Affairs to ensure that these female soldiers were properly treated. The Japanese government supported him with money and materials.

In Penang Bose gave a fiery speech to an audience of about 15,000 Indians in August 1943. He needed funds for his planned attack on India and was dependent on donations. Chinese and Jews, who played an important role in the Malayan economy, as they did in other regions in South East Asia, also answered the call for donations. Bose said: *England is today only surviving on outside help. She is fighting under American leadership and with American aid. The English hope to achieve short-term success in this way. But in the long run this war will not bring the English any luck. [...] Even if the enemy were to win the war Great Britain would not be one of the real winners. [...] It doesn't matter if the Axis powers win or lose, the English will be thrown out of India. [...] Before we achieve our goal we must deal with the following problems: we need soldiers, we need money and other material; at the moment we have too few weapons and have to borrow them from other countries.*[2]

The citizens of Penang donated money and gold. From here alone (in terms of modern spending power) about two million dollars flowed into Bose's war chest. Requests for donations in other cities like Bangkok or Shanghai were equally successful. The government of Siam also donated money to Bose and granted his troops the right of transit on their way to Bengal.

The Indians had harboured hopes of an end to colonial rule even in the First World War. Hundreds of German merchants from Malaya and Singa-

---

1   Stahmer, *Japans Niederlage - Asiens Sieg,* pp. 96f
2   Werth, *Der Tiger Indiens,* p. 195

pore were interned in the camp at Tanglin Barracks in Singapore, as were the captain of the freighter *Exford,* Julius Lauterbach, with his officers and men. The *Exford* was intended to supply the battleship *Emden* with coal, and Captain Lauterbach had only taken command of her for a few days to sail her to a neutral port.

The Germans in Tanglin Barracks were guarded by 20 British soldiers and 850 Indians. The Indians saw their chance, and fraternised with the Germans. Their hate for the British was fuelled by the fact that the latter took little notice of their religious and dietary requirements.

The Singapore Mutiny began on the 15th of February 1915. Telephone and telegraph lines were cut and the radio station destroyed. The British guards at Tanglin Barracks were shot by the Indians and the Germans released. With hatred in their faces, the Indians stormed into the city to slaughter the fleeing British. Only when the colonial authorities reinforced the garrison with new troops from India and Malaya did they regain control of Singapore.

The freedom-loving Indians held Singapore for four weeks. During this time many of the Germans escaped to neutral countries. For example, Captain Lauterbach made a daring escape via Sumatra, Java, the Philippines and the USA back to Germany, where he arrived a good six months later.

There were revolts against the British in all their colonies in South East Asia, like Burma in 1919 when British soldiers refused to remove their shoes before entering Buddhist temples – a gross disregard of Burmese culture which led to long-lasting discontent.

In the Second World War the Burmese independence movement entered an alliance with Japan. Burma, too, had a voluntary force, the Burmese Independence Army, BIA, which later became the Burma National Army BNA and fought beside Bose's INA against the British.

Bose had no trouble recruiting volunteers for his army: he now had a force of over 120,000.[1] His plan was to invade India as soon as possible in concert with the Japanese army. The Japanese military and influential politicians also had plans to include India in the Greater Asian Co-Prosperity Sphere. However, support for Bose was luke-warm, because if the enterprise succeeded the glory would go to the INA and not to Japan.

Japan had no definite plan – nor did it have the means – to open a new front in India. It was more that they hoped that India would throw off the colonial yoke on its own without outside help. Even before Stahmer was accredited as German Ambassador in Tokyo, the Japanese Foreign Minister, Togo Shigenobu, pressed Stahmer's predecessor Ott to give mutual recognition to India's independence after the war. Berlin's response was guarded.

---

1   Ibid., p. 204

In February 1942 Japan was considering unilateral recognition of the independence of India and Burma. On the 16th of February 1942 Prime Minister Tojo Hideki proclaimed: *[...] India now holds in her hands a golden opportunity to rise from her state of barbaric enslavement and march as comrades-in-arms towards Great East Asian co-prosperity. The Japanese Empire shall spare no effort to assist the people of India in their patriotic endeavours to regain their rightful independence.*[1]

A few days before the Japanese military had reached the following agreement with Bose: *Further strong measures should be taken towards India with the objective of disrupting her communications with Great Britain and the United States, thus urging her to abandon her cooperation with Great Britain and accelerating the anti-British movement.*[2]

But without German support Japan did not wish to attack India alone. They did, however, recognise the Provisional Government of Free India officially on the 21st of October 1943. The capital of Azad Hind was Port Blair on the Andaman Islands, since the Andaman and Nicobar Islands were the only British Indian territories occupied by Japan. The seats of government were Rangoon and Singapore. Subhas Chandra Bose was Head of State and Prime Minister of the provisional government. They even printed stamps for the new state which never, however, entered circulation. As well as Japan,

Ill. 72
Stamps of Free India/Azad Hind

1   Krug, Hirama, Sander-Nagashima, Niestlé, *Reluctant Allies*, p.74
2   Ibid., p.74

Germany, Italy, Croatia, Burma, Thailand, Manchukuo, the Philippines and Nationalist China gave diplomatic recognition to the Provisional Government of Free India. On the 23rd of October 1943, Free India declared war on Britain and America.

The chances of a successful invasion of India were at that time particularly high because Gandhi had made a speech demanding the withdrawal of British troops from India. When Britain refused, resistance to British colonial rule in India increased massively. But Japan no longer had the military or political strength to take advantage of this opportunity.

In spite of Japan's half-hearted support the INA invaded India from the east though Burma. In this Imphal Operation the Japanese troops were led by General Mutaguchi. After initial successes the operation failed because of fatal errors in planning and the long and difficult lines of communication through almost impassable jungle between Burma and Bengal: it was not possible to provide adequate supplies of food and ammunition to the troops, who could not subsist on local resources because of the Bengal Holocaust caused by Churchill. Admiral Ugaki Matome, the commander of the Japanese fleet, wrote in his diary: *Japan wishes to call itself the leader of East Asia. Is Japan prepared, and does it have the ability to help the Indians achieve their independence? If not, we are not worthy of being called neighbours, let alone leaders of Asia.*[1]

There was also a massive outbreak of malaria in the area of the front between Burma and Bengal, which led to exceptionally high numbers of Japanese troops being unfit for combat. Java in the Dutch East Indies had a monopoly on quinine: it was the German physician and tropical explorer Dr Franz Wilhelm Junghuhn, the "Humboldt of Java" who had laid the foundations for the cultivation of the cinchona tree in plantations there in 1850. It was the only place where this rare anti-malaria medication was available in large quantities. When the Japanese occupied Java, the quinine monopoly fell into their hands. In Germany the bark of the trees was processed into the anti-malaria drug atebrin by IG-Farben. Large quantities of atebrine tablets and ampoules were carried to the "Southern Region" by German U-boats. The troops could now be given a daily dose, and the malaria figures declined noticeably.

The Imphal Operation, lasting from the 15th of March to the 8th of July 1944 was condemned to failure because the Indian troops were poorly equipped and the relative strengths of the British forces involved were unequal. Requests to the Japanese for reinforcements and provisions went unanswered, and the Indian and Japanese forces had to withdraw after losing 65,000 men.[2]

---

1   Matome Ugaki: *Fading Victory,* p. 181 (Translated by H. Geerken)
2   Werth, *Der Tiger Indiens,* p. 207

Bengal, then the north-eastern part of India, whose eastern half is now the state of Bangladesh, was struck by famine in 1943. In spite of pleas from the Indians and even the Viceroy of India, General Wavell, Churchill firmly refused on strategic grounds to allow any British help to the Bengalis. Subhas Chandra Bose offered a large scale aid operation: the INA and Japan would deliver rice from Burma to the stricken regions. Both the colonial authorities and Churchill turned the offer down flat.

This was Churchill's strategic thinking: without food supplies on the spot a possible advance by the Japanese and the INA to New Delhi would be seriously hindered. According to recent research by Indian and Australian historians about 8 million Indians died in this famine, which has been called the Bengali Holocaust – an atrocity of which the British can by no means feel proud.

In 1944, when events in the war meant that Japan became more and more tied up in the Pacific and had to deal with defeat after defeat, they handed control of the INA, until then subordinate to the Japanese, entirely to the Indians. Three divisions, now entirely made up of Indians, immediately marched through Burma towards India: their way was now free to fight directly against their colonial rulers in India itself. Without opposition they crossed the Indian border and south of Imphal, capital of the present Indian state of Manipur, planted the flag of Free India on Indian soil for the first time. There is now a monument to Subhas Chandra Bose and the Indian National Army on that spot. Their advance on New Delhi nevertheless came to a halt in August 1945 when Japan surrendered unconditionally. The Andamans and the Nicobars were still under Bose's control, but with the collapse of Japan the INA also capitulated.

A few weeks before the Japanese capitulation the Soviet Union also joined the war against Japan. Since the result of the war was now clear, Bose dismissed all the employees of the provisional government and the INA stationed in Singapore – at this time there were still 23,000 of them. All the available state funds were distributed among the soldiers.

Now that Bose could expect no help from Germany or Japan, he tried to enter into an alliance with the Soviet Union. On the morning of the 15th of August 1945 Bose took off from Singapore with a number of companions and flew first to Bangkok and then on to Saigon and Taiwan, from where Bose was to be flown in a Japanese military aircraft – a Mitsubishi Ki-21, called Sally by the Allies – to the Soviet forces in Manchukuo. The pilot, Flight Sergeant Aoyagi, was very experienced. Any explanation of what happened to Bose next is based on speculation and conspiracy theories:

- The most likely version of how Bose died is the one that Alexander Werth favours. His research suggests that the aircraft had 13 on board and took off from Taipeh on 18th of August 1945. Immediately after take-off, the plane crashed and caught fire. Only a few of those on board survived. According to them, Bose was so severely injured that he died of his wounds a few hours later on the same day. His body is then said to have been cremated: ashes that are claimed to be Bose's are preserved in the Renkoji Temple in Tokyo.[1] Although this version sounds plausible, the evidence of the survivors was contradictory and the suspicion arises that Bose was not even on the aircraft. In May 2006 a Japanese commission re-examined the last days and the cause of death of Subhas Chandra Bose. They came to the conclusion that the air accident and the death in hospital in Taipeh are extremely dubious.
- In another version that appeared in the Japanese press it was claimed that the aircraft crashed on the Chinese coast with no survivors.[2]
- Yet other sources suggest that Bose reached Russian-occupied Manchukuo alive. His wife Emilie insisted until she died that her husband was still alive, but was being held by the Soviets in Russia.

After the war the Indian independence movement reached its zenith. The foreseeable conflict could only have been suppressed by military means if several extra divisions were sent from Britain, but Britain at the time was not in a financial position to be able to do so. Prime Minister Atlee finally agreed to hand over power to the Indians, but he only got the agreement of the opposition Conservative Party on condition that, on the principle of "divide and rule", the country be divided in two: the mainly Hindu India and the mainly Muslim Pakistan. Britain's goal was the national disintegration of India. As in so many similar cases, it was a fatal decision and resulted in hundreds of thousands of deaths. The conflict between Pakistan and India is still problematic today.

Two years after Subhas Chandra Bose's death, in August 1947 in New Delhi, Panditji Nehru proclaimed the end of colonial rule and the independence of India as first Prime Minister of India. Bose had made a major contribution to this with Germany's help. The British described him as a traitor and a collaborator with Hitler and Japan, but in India he is still regarded, along with Mahatma Gandhi and Jawaharlal Nehru, as a great patriot and national hero. I have travelled in India many times, and I have seen his por-

---

1   Ibid., pp. 223ff
2   Stahmer, *Japans Niederlage - Asiens Sieg*, p. 97

trait in all parts of the country. The credit he deserves for his contribution to India's independence is not forgotten.

On his 100th birthday in January 1997 Subhas Chandra Bose was posthumously honoured as a national hero. He was the third person after Mahatma Gandhi and Jawaharlal Nehru to receive this honour for his struggle for a free and independent India. He is still honoured on coins, stamps and monuments in India. As is also recognised by the Indians, Germany made a not inconsiderable contribution to the struggle.[1] The name Azad Hind, introduced by Bose, is also ubiquitous in India: several newspapers and radio stations bear the name. The express train between Kolkata and Pune is also called the Azad Hind Express.

It was not only Subhas Chandra Bose and his Indian Legion who fought against the British on Hitler's side. For German soldiers foreign volunteers and foreign units were nothing unusual.

For example, the Spanish *Division Azul* (Blue Division) fought against the Soviet Union from 1941 to 1943. If we add up all the officers and men who fought in the division over this time there were nearly 55,000 Spanish volunteers who fought "against Communism" with the division. They too wore a normal German uniform with a *Division Azul* arm badge.

Hendrik Alexander Scyffardt, former Chief of the Netherlands General Staff and President of the *Nationaal Socialistische Beweging* NSB and other Dutch parties favouring Hitler have already been described in this book.

There were also French volunteers: The 33rd "Charlemagne" Waffen Grenadier Division of the SS, had a strength of 10,000 to 15,000 men. They fought on the Eastern Front in the winter of 1940/41 and were later involved in the defence of Berlin, together with the Scandinavian 11th SS Volunteer Armoured Infantry Division, Nordland, until the capitulation.

The Nordland division was about 13,000 men strong, with the Danes at 7,000 forming the majority. There was a Hunyadi Waffen Grenadier Division of the SS from Hungary, a Lettish Waffen Grenadier Division of the SS and others.

One could continue with the list, but it is just meant to show that it was not just from India that Hitler received support, but that there were volunteers from many of his European neighbours.

---

1   Information for this chapter came, unless otherwise indicated from:
Dr R. Madan, New Delhi and Professor Dr Hans Bräker, Bonn
Günther and Rehmer, *Inder, Indien und Berlin*
Dr Lothar Günther, *Indien und Deutschland – Berichte und Analysen*, Nr. 4/2007
H. G. Stahmer, *Japans Niederlage - Asiens Sieg*, p. 96
www.lexikon-der-Wehrmacht.de

The Arabian Division played a major role in the war. Mohammed Amin el Husseini, Grand Mufti of Jerusalem and President of the Supreme Muslim Council, visited Hitler in Berlin in November 1941. He had already fomented several revolts between 1936 and 1939 to try and achieve Palestinian independence from British rule. He offered to aid Hitler in the fight against Britain by providing an Arab division. In return, Hitler was to guarantee Palestine's independence after the final victory. This saw the birth of the Muslim SS Division Khanjar (Scimitar). The division's banner and arm badge showed a scimitar. In 1943 the Division had nearly 22,000 men, deployed in southern France and the Balkans.

Ill. 73
Mohammed Amin el Husseini, Grand Mufti of Jerusalem inspects the volunteers of the Muslim SS Division Scimitar

The Germans called the Muslims the SS Division Scimitar or more colloquially the *Muselgermanen* [Musel is a derogatory term for a Muslim]. This term, as well as jokes about Islam or the Muslims, was forbidden by Himmler, the head of the SS, who was a great admirer of Islam. Himmler also ordered that the use of the word "anti-Semitism" should immediately cease, since the word Semite applied to Arabs as well as Jews. In a memorandum on the 17th of May 1943 he wrote: *The use of this word always insults the Arab world, which according to the Grand Mufti is overwhelmingly friendly towards Germany. Foreigners abroad use the fact that we work with the term Antisemitism to suggest that we put the Arabs in the same boat as the Jews.*[1]

Shortly before the end of the war, as the Soviet army marched into Berlin, Mohammed Amin el Hussein escaped to Switzerland in a German air force aircraft. He spent the last years of his life in France.

It is not very well known that Romania with more than 650,000 men had, after Italy, the third largest Axis force numerically. Hitler had signed a military pact with Romania before the war and in 1940 Romania joined the Tripartite Pact. The hard-hitting Romanian Army fought mainly in the east against the Soviet Union – about half their men fell on the Eastern Front.

Because of the many nations that supplied troops for the German Waffen-SS it was also called Himmler's European Army. In the course of the war the proportion of foreign volunteers from occupied or neutral countries grew considerably.

---

1   Himmler's memorandum to Dr Koeppen v. 17.5.1943, ns-archiv, Hans Hagemeyer

28. The Bengali Holocaust

For hundreds of years Bengal was not just a supplier of cotton: the cultivation of rice and wheat meant that Bengal was also the bread-basket of India. This changed dramatically in the mid-19th century when the British forced the introduction of indigo cultivation, which meant that Bengal became dependent of rice imports from British-occupied Burma. During the war the Japanese occupation of Burma meant that this source of supply was cut off. The quantities of rice produced in India would obviously have been sufficient to meet the increase in demand from Bengal, but the hoarding of rice by the Indian population and the state purchases of rice by the British for military and official purposes meant that the situation deteriorated. People were starving in Bengal, while at the same time the surplus of rice and wheat in Britain increased.

The famine in Bengal in 1943 was the result of human agency. On Churchill's instructions all help was refused for strategic reasons. For example, he refused to allow the provision of cargo space for shipping rice to Bengal. Subhas Chandra Bose's offer of help was, as I have already pointed out, turned down. Churchill hoped that the lack of food in Bengal would delay a Japanese invasion. The Japanese supply lines were constantly being blocked, and so the troops could not be supplied from Burma alone.

Churchill's instructions were given during the Casablanca Conference in1943, where he is said to have trivialised the problem by declaring that, famine or no famine the Indians would breed like rabbits. His actions deliberately caused the deaths of several million Bengalis and other Indians. Britain has successfully tried to keep this "Bengali Holocaust" a secret for many years, but that will not last much longer, because a number of historians, film-makers and authors are working to shed light on the subject.

During the war itself the Indian author N. G. Jog criticised the inglorious role played by the British in his book Churchill's Blind Spot. He was the first to call this atrocity a holocaust.

The renowned Indian director Satyajit Ray took up the theme in his 1973 film Ashani Sanket (Distant Thunder). In the film, which won the Golden Bear at the Berlin film Festival the same year, he talks of five million Bengalis who lost their lives in the famine

The Australian academic Gideon Maxwell Polya, in his book Jane Austen and the Black Hole of British History, even writes of the deaths of four million Bengalis and six to seven million Indians in neighbouring regions.[1]

The Bengali doctor and author Madhusree Mukerrjee analysed the latest evidence about Churchill's role in her 2010 book Churchill's Secret War. She describes Churchill as a mass murderer, a racist imperialist and a holocaust denier. In her view Churchill's six-volume 'history', The Second World War, is an air-brushed and mendacious story, since, among other things, it fails to mention that he caused the deaths of about 8 million Bengalis and other Indians.

The respected British historian and Churchill expert, Sir Martin Gilbert, has written several books about Churchill's role in the Second World War. In his most recent two-volume work about Churchill which appeared in 2004 he also completely fails to mention the British holocaust in Bengal. Just imagine a German historian publishing a new biography of Hitler without mentioning the European holocaust! The cries of outrage would echo throughout the German people and the international media!

Along with the German holocaust of the Jews, the British Bengali holocaust was a dreadful crime against humanity in the Second World War. It was committed far away from Europe, and in those days it was easier to prevent its being reported. But it will no longer be possible for Britain to blot out this crime and erase it from history.

In Indian books and films there has recently been increasingly serious criticism of the "Bengali Holocaust". More and more details of Churchill's disgraceful role in the matter are coming to light. The British are faced with a reappraisal of Churchill's part in this crime.[2] If an injustice has occurred, it must be permissible to talk about it!

---

1   Polya, Gideom M., *Jane Austen and the Black Hole of British History,* Chapter 14, p. 133

2   Short summary from the following sources:
Madhusree Mukerrjee, *Churchill's Secret War*
Gideon M. Polya, *Jane Austen and the Black Hole of British History*
N. G. Jog, *Churchills Blind Spot*
www.archiv.ub.uni-heidelberg.de/safiva.dok

29. The German Embassy in Tokyo and the Sorge Espionage Affair

German-Japanese relations were traditionally – except for the Japanese occupation of the German colony of Tsingtao in China during the First World War – characterised by friendship and mutual respect. When Japan's isolation from the outside world came to an end, many German academics came to Japan as teachers and advisors – *o-yatri haikokujin* – in the Meiji period (1868-1912). These included, as I have previously mentioned, my great-uncle Carl Schenk, who taught at the University in Yedo (now: Tokyo) from 1871 onwards and is still honoured as the Father of Japanese Mineralogy.[1]

In 1906 the Imperial German Legation in Japan was upgraded to an embassy, situated in the same building in Tokyo. This became the most important nerve centre of the Second World War in the Far East, where so many vital decisions about the naval war in the waters of the Dutch East Indies or the deployment and cargoes of blockade breakers were made. All the threads that made up the conduct of the war in South East and East Asia crossed here.

In the capital of an important ally such as Japan one would expect a huge imposing building. This was not so: it was a simple, somewhat run down building, and the embassy did not move in to a new, modern building until 2004.

In 1933 Major General Eugen Ott was sent to Tokyo, initially as an observer with the Japanese army. In February 1934 he was promoted to Military Attaché, and in March 1938 – as the man the Japanese most wanted in the post – was appointed German Ambassador to Japan by Foreign Minister Ribbentrop. In following the wishes of the Japanese in this way, Ribbentrop was hoping that in return the Japanese Military Attaché in Berlin, General Oshima Hiroshi – whom Germany found it extremely easy to work with – would also be promoted to Ambassador: this happened in 1940. Ribbentrop and Walther Hewel were close personal friends of General Hiroshi, and many documents in the political archive of the Foreign Ministry in Berlin show that they met regularly – privately as well as officially.

---

1   Kagakushi, The Journal of the Japanese Society for the History of Chemistry, Volume 37, Number 4, 2010, Note: Takeshi Ozawa, C. Schenk, the First Teacher of Chemistry and Mineralogy in the Predecessor of the University of Tokyo, p. 183

As a result of the Sorge espionage affair, Ambassador Ott was recalled to Berlin in November 1942, and Heinrich Georg Stahmer was named as his successor in Tokyo in 1943, in spite of having a "non-Aryan" wife: Helga Stahmer was Jewish on her mother's side.

Previously, from 1941 until the end of 1942, Stahmer had been German Ambassador in Japanese-supported Nationalist China. Ernst Woermann was his successor, appointed in July 1943. The seat of the Chinese Nationalist Government was then not Peking, but the more centrally situated Nanking (now: Nanjing). In Walther Hewel's papers there are copies of letters from Hitler to *His Excellency, the President of the Chinese National Government, Mr Wang Ching Wei* requesting permission to withdraw Ambassador Stahmer from Nanking, as well as a further letter from him to *His Majesty, the Emperor of Japan*, requesting him to accept Heinrich Georg Stahmer as German Ambassador to the Japanese Empire.[1]

Stahmer travelled to Japan in the U 511 commanded by Lieutenant Fritz Schneewind. She sailed from Lorient on the 10th of May 1943 and reached Penang on the 20th of July 1943. The U 511 was the first submarine presented by Hitler to the Japanese Navy as a gift. Japanese naval personnel were inducted into the U 511's technology. She sailed on as the RO-500 under Japanese colours – with nine top-notch German submarine engineers on board – to Japan, arriving at the naval port of Kure on the 7th of August 1943. Stahmer then took up his post as German Ambassador to Japan.

Lieutenant Fritz Schneewind was invited to Japan, where Emperor Hirohito awarded him a high honour for the safe navigation and delivery of the submarine. Back in Singapore he met his father, the former honorary German consul in Padang. The father's businesses had been confiscated by the Dutch at the beginning of the war, and he was later imprisoned by the British in Singapore. After being freed by the Japanese he became an industrial representative in Singapore, his main business being the supply of spare parts to the German Navy in the "Southern Region".

Stahmer had previously visited Japan many times and had been dealing with Far East problems in the Foreign Ministry in Berlin for some time. He had, for example, accompanied the Duke of Sachsen-Coburg and Gotha on a tour of Japan from autumn 1939 to spring 1940. He had also led the negotiations with Japanese Foreign Minister Matsuoka in Tokyo which led to the signing and promulgation of the Tripartite Pact. He was thus excellently qualified for his new post.

It was only discovered after the war that Stahmer, Ambassador Ott and Matsuoka had, without authorisation by Germany, added six secret addi-

---

1   AA, Pol. Archiv, private Unterlagen Hewel

tional protocols to the Pact in their negotiations in Tokyo from September to December 1940. This was how Stahmer and Ott succeeded in breaking down strong Japanese opposition to the Pact. The content of these protocols was as follows: after a Japanese victory in the Pacific, Japan would officially return the former German colonies in the region to Germany. Germany would then cede these possessions to Japan for compensation which was still to be negotiated. These secret protocols were only known to Stahmer, Ott and Matsuoka. It is likely, but not certain, that Foreign Minister Ribbentrop was also informed. Since renunciation of the former German colonies in the Pacific region was important to Japan, Stahmer and Ott did not want the Pact to collapse because of the issue, even though they doubted that Hitler would agree to the protocols.[1]

Since the Germans and the circles responsible in Japan knew that Hitler was really only interested in the former German colonies in Africa, the Japanese officer responsible for liaison between the Japanese and German navies, Captain Maeda Minoru, had already suggested in 1938 that if the Japanese conquered the former German colonies in the Pacific, they would return them to Germany, disregarding the Treaty of Versailles and the League of Nations. Japan would then buy these mandates back from Germany.[2]

It is impossible to write about the German Embassy in Tokyo during the Third Reich without mentioning the Sorge espionage case. Richard Sorge was a journalist with first-class contacts in the German Embassy, where he had also managed to worm his way into Ambassador Ott's confidence. He was a master spy for the Allies, particularly the Soviet Union. He worked as an advisor to Ott and had free access to the Embassy. It must have looked to outsiders as if he was a diplomat at the Embassy. No one was aware of his espionage activities, not even the Japanese military secret police, the Kempetai.

There were contacts between the Kempetai and the German Intelligence Service, the *Abwehr*, as early as the 1930s, and these became much closer after the signing of the Tripartite Pact. For example, Germany was informed of the strength of Soviet forces in the Far East before Operation Barbarossa – the German attack on the Soviet Union in 1941. Admiral Canaris, the *Abwehr* chief also did all he could to ensure that the neutral Portuguese colony of East Timor (in the south east of the Indonesian archipelago) was not initially occupied by the Japanese. Because of his espionage activity and his resistance to National Socialism Canaris was executed a few days before the end of the war.

Richard Sorge was a convinced Communist of Russian-German descent. As early as 1929 he was spying for the Soviet Union in China under the

1   Krug, Hirama, Sander-Nagashima, Niestlé, *Reluctant Allies,* pp. 250ff
2   Ibid., p. 157

cover of being a press agent. His espionage activity in Japan began in 1933. As a cover, he joined the Nazi Party and wrote for the *Frankfurter Zeitung*. For his own safety, he also provided material to the German secret service.

In China Sorge met the Japanese journalist Ozaki Hotsumi, who became his closest collaborator in Japan. Hotsumi provided him with contacts to the highest circles in Japan, including the Japanese Prime Minister Konoe Fumimaro. Sorge provided the Soviet Union with precise and extensive information: he warned in advance about the Japanese attack on Pearl Harbour, giving the exact date, and also informed Stalin about the impending German attack on the Soviet Union, including details of the date, the strength of the forces involved and the position of the attack. At the same time he informed the Soviet Union that Japan did not intend to attack their eastern flank, so that they could withdraw forces from Siberia and meet Hitler's advance in the west with greater strength.

Sorge reported all blockade-breaker sailings and their intended routes to the Allies, so that all they had to do was position their cruisers and destroyers in ambush. This explains the above average losses incurred by these supply ships: Sorge's information was of vital importance to the war effort of Germany's enemies.

In Shanghai in 1930 Sorge met the German Communist and Soviet agent codenamed Sonja, and from then on they worked closely together. Shanghai was crawling with spies, dubious characters and rumours – but also useful information. For Sonja, Shanghai was a fruitful field of action, because after 1933 15,000 Jews from Germany found refuge there, since their entry was not hindered, as it was in Britain, the USA and the Netherlands.
Sonja was Jewish, and worked under several cover names: Ursula Maria Kuczynski, Ruth Werner, Ursula Beurton, Ursula Hamburger and Ursula Schulz. Under Sorge's direction, she collected information from China and Manchukuo, and on his recommendation she went to Moscow in 1933 to perfect her espionage skills, after which she was deployed successfully in Europe and Asia.

In Germany in 1938 Sonja recruited several British citizens as spies, and in 1941 went to Oxford on Sorge's orders. Shortly after her departure 30 spies were arrested in Germany: German had developed mobile radio-location equipment to detect spy transmitters. Was only Sonja warned by Sorge, sacrificing the other agents in Germany?[1]

Even after the war Sonja sent vital information to the Soviet Union using her secret transmitter. After Klaus Fuchs, the "Atom Spy" was unmasked in

---

1   Bartolomew Lee, *Radio Spies: Episodes in the Ether Wars*, pp. 73 and 106
     www.trft.org/TRFTPix/spies9eR2006.pdf

England in 1949, she fled to the German Democratic Republic and worked in the Ministry of Information there. She received high honours from both the GDR and the Soviet Union, whose most successful spy she had been during the war. In 1980 a film was made of her life in the GDR, and she died in Berlin at the age of 93 in 2000. Which of her names was her true identity? She was born Ursula Maria Kuczynski and died as Ruth Werner.

Richard Sorge sent thousands of coded messages to the Soviet Union from his home and from a yacht out at sea. The Japanese civilian secret police, the Tokko, did not discover Sorge and his helper Hotsumi until quite late. It was more than embarrassing that the Police Attaché at the German Embassy had not noticed his espionage activities – he had even fraternised with him in a drunken night.[1] Sorge and Hotsumi were sentenced to death and supposedly hanged in Tokyo on the 7th of November 1944.

There are many mysteries and suggestions about Sorge's death. Since he was a German citizen, Germany demanded that he be handed over so that he could be tried for treason in Germany. The Japanese refused. The German Embassy received no written confirmation of Sorge's death, Ambassador Stahmer was not allowed to attend the execution or identify the body. The Ambassador was one of many people who felt it likely that Sorge had survived and been exchanged with the Soviet Union for Japanese spies who had been imprisoned there. It is quite possible that master spy Sorge lived on in the Soviet Union after the war, cheerfully indulging in the same excessive life style for which he was known in Tokyo, with copious quantities of alcohol and sexual adventures. The mystery persists: the machinations of the world's secret services are always devious!

Karl Hoffmeier, a German journalist working in Tokyo, was also accused of belonging to Sorge's spy ring. Since his guilt was more or less certain, it was decided to send him to Germany to face a court martial. He sailed on the *Burgenland,* the last blockade breaker to leave Japan.

The *Burgenland* was attacked off South Africa on the 5th of January 1943 by the Allied cruiser *Omaha* and the destroyer *Jouett.* Just before the ship was scuttled by the crew, Hoffmeier was shot by the SS- Hauptsturmführer who had been detailed to guard him. Admiral Paul Wenneker, the Naval Attaché in Tokyo, had ordered that Hoffmeier should be prevented at all costs from falling into the hands of the Allies. Wenneker was Admiral of East Asia and thus the highest ranking officer in the region. Because of this order and Hoffmeier's shooting, Wenneker was put on trial in 1966, but was discharged because of the statute of limitations.

---

1   Tischert, *Die Abenteuer des letzten Kapers*, p. 85

The German Embassy in Tokyo was extremely well-staffed during the war. Apart from the usual staff – the Ambassador and the sections dealing with politics, culture, trade and so on – there were also attachés for each of the forces – army, navy and air force, with their attendant officials. There was even a Police Attaché, Colonel Meisinger and a Party Attaché, initially Hillmann, and later Spahn. The Party Attaché's duties included protecting the interests of the Nazi Party and increasing the party's influence among the German community. Police Attaché Meisinger even put the crews of the blockade-breakers under surveillance in the bars of Yokohama and Kobe. He would have done better to keep a closer eye on Richard Sorge!

During his period of service in Tokyo Paul Werner Wenneker was promoted to Admiral and German Admiral of East Asia. He had already been Naval Attaché in Tokyo from 1934 to 1937, acting as liaison officer between the German navy and the Japanese navy, *Dai-Nippon Teikoku Kaigun* (Navy of the Empire of Greater Japan). With the USA and Britain, Japan was one of the greatest sea powers in the world, and the position of Naval Attaché in Japan was correspondingly important.

From 1937 to the end of 1939 Wenneker commanded the battleship *Deutschland*. He was reappointed Naval Attaché in Tokyo in 1940. He travelled to Vladivostok on the Trans-Siberian Railway and then by sea to Japan, arriving in Tokyo on the 27th of February 1940. Until Ambassador Ott was recalled, Wenneker worked well and closely with him, but his relationship with the new Ambassador, Stahmer, was plagued with tension from the very beginning. After the Sorge affair Stahmer was deeply suspicious of anyone who got on well with his predecessor. Another factor was that Stahmer and his Police Attaché Meisinger – a member of the SS and the GESTAPO – were convinced National Socialists, and directed their activities in the interests of the party.

Admiral Wenneker was also in charge of the experts sent from Germany to make Germany's technical advances in the sphere of armaments accessible to the Japanese research departments. There were one or two dozen submarine experts, diesel specialists and radio engineers, including Heinrich Foders, the head of the *Würzburg* replication project. Another German expert was supposed to develop radar equipment for Japanese aircraft. Germany constantly supplied Japan with the results of the latest research. Every German vessel that sailed to East Asia carried whole machines, individual parts, prototypes and construction diagrams for the Japanese military.

By contrast, the Japanese were much more reluctant to give out military information about new weapon developments. The Japanese probably – rightly – did not trust the German Enigma code, and feared that important information might reach the enemy if it was passed on to Berlin by radio. Requests for visits to technical facilities were also unwelcome. The Germans kept coming up against the inscrutable, indifferent and unapproachable smiles of their Far- Eastern brothers in arms. It took months before Wenneker was allowed to view the new battleship *Yamato*. Apart from a lot of deep, friendly but often ironic bows, not much happened.

Information about the movements of enemy ships in the "Southern Region" was only sketchily passed on to the Germans, leading to the loss of many German U-boats and auxiliary cruisers. The deployment of escort ships and air cover for German U-boats as they approached the bases in the "Southern Region" was utterly inadequate.

In the Second World War Germany and Japan were totally dependent on one another, but the Japanese do not seem to have realised this, even though they profited greatly from German operations in the area. You got the impression that the Japanese were only interested in their own empire

One of Admiral Wenneker's duties in Tokyo was to maintain contact with the German agents stationed in all the important ports in Japan and East and South East Asia. They were under Admiral Canaris and the *Abwehr* in Germany. There were agents in Shanghai and Harbin in China. The agent in Harbin, Lissner, is said to have heard from the Russians about the timing of the Allied landings in Normandy. A few days before the landings took place, the information was handed on to Canaris, but because he was working against the Nazis it never went any further.

Many of these agents were the heads of long established German companies and leading employees of merchant houses or heads of German shipping lines who were also trustworthy party members. Their job was to report the movements of foreign merchant vessels and the nature of their cargoes to Tokyo. They were also supposed to investigate possible sources of raw materials and food supplies. Each had a small transmitter and encryption machine. Messages to them were passed on by the local consulates or broadcast as coded messages on Radio XGRS in Shanghai. There were agents in Tokyo, Yokohama, Kobe, Dairen, Tientsin, Manila, Bangkok, Batavia, Surabaya and other important locations. Lissner also reported to Berlin from Harbin on the Sorge espionage case and the Japanese reaction to it. In the same report, of which Hewel kept a copy, he also recommended Wenneker as successor to the recalled Ambassador Ott.[1] As we have seen, this suggestion was not considered.

---

1   Information about Wenneker from the following sources:
    Berichte über die Aufenthalte in Japan von Admiral Paul Werner Wenneker, collected by G. F. Dose, nephew of Admiral Wenneker. Copyright Ilse Bosch, née Wenneker; www.deutsches-marinearchiv.de/organisatio/seegebiete/japan

Four weeks after the Japanese occupation of Java, Wenneker toured the newly conquered regions with the Italian Naval Attaché Admiral Balsamo at the invitation of the Japanese government. They visited China, Formosa, French Indochina, the Philippines, the Islands of Palau, Guam and Saipan as well as Malaya, Sumatra and Java.

Admiral Wenneker's most wide-ranging task was running the *Marine-Sonder-Dienst* [Naval Special Service] MSD. Branches with staff, radios, equipment and food stores had to be set up. The branches in Japan were in Yokohama and Kobe, in the "Southern Region" they were in Singapore, Penang, Batavia and Surabaya.

16 German merchant ships that were moored in Japanese, Chinese and Manchurian ports at the outbreak of war, and another lying in Bangkok, were taken over by the German Navy and brought together in Japan, as were ships lying in South America. Those that were suitable for use as blockade breakers were provided with armour for the bridge and anti-aircraft guns in Japan. Seven merchant ships that were unsuitable to act as blockade breakers were handed to the Japanese Navy as charter ships to be used as transport vessels in the "Southern Region".

As the tasks of the MSD became increasingly extensive, Captain Werner Vermehren was put in charge. He arrived in Tokyo on the blockade breaker *MS Dresden*. His office was initially in the German Embassy building, but was later moved, because of Allied air raids, to Kamakura, about 50 kilometres to the south west. The transmitters and receivers for the German Embassy's short-wave communications with Berlin and the bases in the "Southern Region" were also installed in Kamakura.

Werner Vermehren was supported by the German Trade Delegation and ROGES, the *Rohstoff-Gesellschaft* [Raw Materials Company].[1] ROGES was located in Tokyo from July 1942 and was headed by State Counsellor Helmut C. H. Wohlthat. Representatives of ROGES were stationed in Singapore, Batavia and Surabaya. The Trade Delegation was responsible for purchasing raw materials, general freight and provisions on the markets in Japan and the "Southern Region". These included especially rubber, tin, quinine and opium which were mainly sourced in the Dutch East Indies. The heavy metal tungsten and molybdenum ore were initially sourced mainly in Japan and Manchukuo, but also later on Java. Since the valuable freight was usually stored in the U-boats in the ballast tanks below the waterline, all sensitive items were sealed in watertight metal containers.

Fuel and oil for the submarines were acquired solely in the "Southern Region" and provided by the Japanese Navy. The quality of the lubricating

1   ROGES, see diagram on page 248

oil was however of poor quality, so that there was frequent damage to the U-boat engines. The small German tanker *Bogota* was deployed as a transport ship to carry fuel from Balikpapan – the oil extraction and refinery area in West Sumatra – to the bases. Sometimes it was necessary for the blockade breakers and U-boats to travel directly to the oil production areas in West Sumatra or East Borneo to refuel.

After the war the Sorge case occupied the German media and was generally known, but who is aware that there was a second, independent spy ring in Japan?

A German businessman in Kobe led a very active group of agents who passed on information, mainly about the Japanese Navy, to the Allies using a secret transmitter. After the German capitulation, the German staff at the base in Kobe and the crews of the U-boats that were caught by the end of the war were accommodated in the area of Kobe and Osaka. Japan continued to wage war for several months more.

Since Japanese naval targets were being very frequently attacked by the Allies, the German naval personnel were suspected of being the source of the information. The co-ordinates of these targets could only have been discovered by espionage. In fact the German U-boat crews were regularly invited to lavish dinners and drinking sessions by members of the group of agents so that they could be pumped for information. This group provided the information that led to a brand new 50,000 tonne Japanese aircraft carrier being attacked and sunk by the Americans the day before it entered service. It was their final act.

The German agents were unmasked and brought to trial. The German sailors who had conversed with them had to give evidence for many days. All the members of the spy-ring were sentenced to death, but since Japan capitulated immediately after the trial the sentences were not carried out.

Stahmer's successor as German Ambassador in Nanking from June 1943 was Ernst Woermann, who has already been mentioned several times. He travelled from France to Nanking via Penang in a German U-boat. Many sources suggest that Woermann travelled to Penang with Stahmer in the U 511. This does not agree with Stahmer's records.[1] Woermann travelled on another submarine, whose identification I could not discover. Other passengers included Japanese Admiral Nomura, until then the head of the Japanese Navy's office for liaison with Germany, and Spahn, who was to take over the post of Nazi Party Attaché in the Tokyo Embassy.

Helmut C. H. Wohlthat, whom we have already met in the context of the Rublee-Wohlthat Plan was also closely linked with the German Em-

---

1   Stahmer, *Japans Niederlage - Asiens Sieg,* pp. 198

bassy in Tokyo. From 1936 Wohlthat was involved in the implementation of the Four-Year Plan and was sent to Japan in 1941 as Head of the German Trade Delegation by *Reichsmarschall* Göring. The Trade Delegation's mission was to acquire raw materials in South East Asia. To meet German demand for these goods, rubber was purchased in the Dutch East Indies and Malaya, opium in Siam and Burma, quinine and agar-agar on Java. Opium and quinine were needed for medical purposes, and agar-agar for aircraft paint. Tungsten ore and molybdenum were initially acquired in Japan and then later in the Dutch East Indies.

Wohlthat remained in Japan until the end of the war. In spite of having been a high-ranking official under the Third Reich he had a prominent career in post-war Germany. He headed a trading company, was on the boards of many German business companies and was even suggested as Director of the World Bank in 1954.

30. Communication

In the high-frequency area of short-wave radio German developments occasionally lagged somewhat behind the British. By means of espionage and a large department for deciphering German radio traffic staffed by highly qualified experts, the British often acquired early information about German advances and were able to take counter-measures.

In the Second World War collaboration between the Axis powers, Japan and Germany, was often accompanied by shortcomings and hindrance on the Japanese side. From time to time Japan was less than forthcoming in the exchange of information. They were very concerned that the German code could be deciphered by the Allies – and that concern was justified. On the 9th of May 1941 the British had acquired an Enigma code machine from the U 110. From this time on the Allies gradually began to be able to decipher German radio traffic, which gave them an invaluable advantage right down to the end of the war. 28 survivors from the U 100 were rescued by the British destroyer *HMS Bulldog* and put under close guard so that the news of the machine's capture could not reach Germany. The German Naval High Command was convinced that the U 110 had sunk with all hands.

How did communication with the bases in South East Asia and the U-boats operating east of the Indian Ocean, practically at the end of the world off the east coast of Australia and off New Zealand, work at all? In 1936 the Naval High Command decided to set up a command centre for naval warfare. It was given the code name Koralle [Coral] and located in an intelligence bunker near Berlin. Transmitters remotely controlled by Koralle were set up in Nauen, Elmshorn, Königs-Wusterhausen and other sites in Germany. Several very powerful mobile transmitters were mounted on oversize lorries and there were several receivers, also remotely controlled by Koralle, at various sites on German territory.

Communication between the German Embassy in Tokyo and the German naval bases in South East Asia took place mainly by short wave. The radio stations in Japan were sited about 50 kilometres south-west of Tokyo at Kamakura on Sagami Bay. They were remotely controlled and keyed by the German Embassy's radio station in Tokyo.

The co-ordination of radio traffic between the individual German bases and the Embassy was mainly run from the radio station in Penang, commanded by Senior Midshipman Dechow. All the bases in the "Southern Region" had at least one set of radio equipment. They could communicate with each other and with Japan, and in case of necessity even reach Berlin directly. Radio communication between the base in Surabaya and Germany normally went via the base in Batavia, because the station there was more powerful. The German base in Batavia was also permitted to use the Dutch Post Office's radio station, which had been captured by the Japanese. Telephone and Morse signals were carried from Batavia to Bandung by an overhead telephone line.

The distances that had to be crossed were immense. For example, the outlying bases at Sabang and Surabaya were a good 3,000 kilometres apart as the crow flies. The distance from Batavia to Tokyo is 6,000 kilometres, and to Berlin 11,500 kilometres.

Because of the influence of the ionosphere on short waves and the connected changes in propagation conditions, short-wave frequencies had to be changed daily, sometimes also depending on the season. Messages for radio communication were enciphered using code machines by the military personnel in the security department at the German Embassy in Tokyo. There was an insecure telephone connection with Germany, but that was used only for unimportant communications.

Coded radio telegrams which were transmitted by short wave were frequently subject to interference from enemy agents' transmitters. Lieutenant Herwartz, commander of the U 483, reports that he was unable to send any radio telegrams to Penang und Tokyo announcing his safe arrival in Batavia. His radio operator informed him that there was interference from a nuisance transmitter on exactly the same crystal-controlled frequency as the one used by the Batavia base. When they informed their Japanese colleagues, their security service immediately deployed radio locators to find the source of the disturbance. The very next day they located the unassuming bungalow where the transmitter was hidden. Four Japanese soldiers stormed the house with drawn pistols and arrested a Dutch agent, Rooseman, at his transmitter. They found papers proving that Rooseman had been informing an Allied espionage centre in Shanghai about all movements of German and Japanese shipping. No wonder so many German ships and U-boats had been lost in Dutch East Indian waters. Now the Japanese took over the spy transmitter and successfully supplied the centre in Shanghai with false information for several weeks.

Near Wolfsburg there was a German Post Office transmitter station with several powerful short-wave transmitters. It had been intended for use in commercial communications with overseas, but after the beginning of the war was partially taken over by the naval high command. One of these transmitters was used exclusively for radio communication with the Embassy in

Tokyo. The German Navy's bases were equipped partly with German and partly with Japanese units.

The U-boats also carried short-wave equipment to communicate with each other and with Berlin and the South East Asian bases. In the Second World War radio communication grew in importance as a weapon: quite often, distress calls with false locations were deliberately sent to confuse the enemy.

The German companies Telefunken, Siemens and Lorenz were at the time the most innovative and important producers of telecommunications equipment. All U-boats that set out for South East Asia were equipped as follows:

- a Telefunken type T200FK 200 watt short-wave transmitter with a frequency range of 3- 23 MHz
- a 40-watt Lorenz Lo 40k emergency transmitter
- a type 2113S 150 Watt long wave transmitter with a frequency range of 300-600 KHz
- a type E52 "Köln" radio telegram receiver with a frequency range of 1.5-25 MHz
- a type E437S receiver with a frequency range of 0.3-15 MHz
- a receiver capable of receiving communications from the type T3PL Telefunken "Goliath" VLF transmitter with a frequency range of 5-33 KHz and
- a type E 1012 radio receiver with long wave, medium wave and two short wave frequencies to entertain and inform the crew
- a 10-watt VHF transmitter for communication with submarines in the vicinity

Since for physical reasons only traditional wire antennae could be used for short wave, U-boats were forced to surface to make radio contact. The exactitude of the frequency settings on the equipment made it possible to transmit "short signals" at high speed on previously fixed frequencies at fixed times for just a few seconds –"blindly", you might say. This made it considerably more difficult for the enemy to locate the submarines' positions by radio location.

These short Morse signals always contained a location and enciphered groups of letters and numbers containing information. All messages sent and received were coded or decoded using the ENIGMA machine. The U-boats were controlled by the headquarters in Berlin. Only when they entered the eastern Indian Ocean were information and commands communicated directly with the bases on the "Southern Region's" frequencies. Initially it was the most efficient communication system of the Second World War.

There was also supplementary communication with the submarines in the Indian Ocean and South East Asian waters using very low frequency. These electronic beams with extremely low frequency between 15 and 60 KHz, and therefore very long wave length, could penetrate salt water to some a certain degree. The transmitters for this purpose were in Nauen near Berlin. As a result of the very great distance (about 11,500 Km to Java), the connection was highly unreliable.

This changed after the occupation of the Netherlands and the French capitulation. Both countries had modern and well-equipped networks for communication with their overseas territories which fell into German hands ready for use and could now be connected with the "Koralle" control centre. In France 24 short-wave and 7 very low frequency transmitters were taken over by the Germans. The control centre now had a wide choice of stations and could transmit on several frequencies simultaneously.

In the Netherlands the Kootwijk transmitter, with several short-wave and one very low frequency transmitter, was now available to the German forces. Kootwijk's opposite number was the major Malabar transmission station on Java, in the mountains south of Bandung. Both Kootwijk and Malabar had been built by the German Telefunken company in 1922 with the most powerful equipment available at the time. These transmitters provided the first wireless communication between East Asia and Europe. An antenna suspended from peak to peak over a valley in Malabar was orientated towards Kootwijk in Holland. Malabar was the most important and most powerful radio station in the whole of South East Asia.[1] It is likely that the station was taken over in working order by the Japanese army when they occupied Java – all we know is that it was destroyed by the Japanese towards the end of the war.

A decided improvement in communication with the U-boats operating in the Indian Ocean and the Java Sea came about when the "Goliath" VLF transmitter came into service in spring 1943. It was developed jointly by C. Lorenz AG and Telefunken, and was the first and most powerful megawatt valve-transmitter in the world. The output stage contained several water-cooled Telefunken high power valves. Each valve was about two metres high and weighed 90 kilograms. It was several times more powerful than all previous transmitters. It was operated by the navy from 1943 until the end of the war. The head of the station was Naval Radio Officer Karl Wrackmeyer. Since "Goliath's" antenna required an area of three square kilometres, there was not enough space in Nauen, and so "Goliath" was constructed at Kalbe-Milde, between Hannover and Berlin. It was a massive construction. The antenna consisted of 15 steel lattice masts, each 170 metre high and three 203 metre high tubular masts with a diameter of 2 metres. Several motorised

---

1   Cf. Geerken, *Der Ruf des Geckos*, pp. 22 and 287ff

remote-controlled antenna tuning coils were controlled from the transmitter building. Each of these copper coils was five metres high, 3.5 metres in diameter and weighed 5 tonnes.

Using this VLF transmitter there was now reliable communication with all U-boats and warships anywhere in the world. Even commercial traffic with fixed stations, like that in Tokyo, now used "Goliath", since its power guaranteed absolutely reliable communication. The transmitter was mainly intended for Morse telegraphy at a frequency of 16 KHz. At a frequency of 30 KHz facsimiles could also be transmitted using the "Hellschreiber" – a precursor of the fax machine invented in the Third Reich. With frequencies from 45 KHz telephonic communication was possible, though with limited sound quality. It was in use for 20 hours per day.

To receive the VLF signals the U-boats were equipped with extendible loop antennae which could be used underwater at a speed of up to eight knots. Data from the Second World War suggests reception figures that still surprise radio technicians today: they suggest that U-boats in the Indian Ocean or the Strait of Malacca could receive "Goliath's" signals from Germany at a depth of up to 14.5 metres. A remarkable achievement for the time.

At the end of June 1945 the Soviet Army took over the site. They repaired the equipment which the operating team had partly destroyed on the arrival of the Allies and put it into service. The equipment was dismantled and taken to the Soviet Union in April 1947. "Goliath" was reassembled near Moscow and continued in service with the soviet Navy for many years.[1] However, it never reached its original transmission power of 1,000 kilowatts.

Because of its high fences the Americans used the site as a prisoner of war camp for 85,000 German soldiers. Today it has returned to agricultural use.

After the Japanese capitulation, when Singapore returned to British control, several dozen experts from among the staff of the base and the crews of the U-boats caught there at the end of the war were put to work by the British. In the naval dockyard at Selatar they repaired British warships or removed valuable parts from German submarines.

One German senior radio operator was set to repairing a British radio direction finder in the high frequency section. He discovered to his surprise that this device worked automatically and sent the co-ordinates discovered to a central point by radio. He suddenly realised why so many U-boats had been lost in the Indian Ocean in the last year of the war. All the territories along the coast of the Indian Ocean from Assam in the east to the Red Sea

---

1   Herold, Klaus, *Der Längstwellensender Goliath bei Kalbe an der Milbe von 1941-1945,* pp. 236-249

in the west and southwards to South Africa were under British control. Dozens of these automatic devices were installed along this coastline. Using the short signals sent by the U-boats their position could now be fixed precisely. Aircraft were then sent to destroy the U-boats with depth charges.

The German experts on the U-boats were used by the British in many different areas. Lieutenant (Eng.) Dietrich Hille of the U 181 and Machinist's Mate Walter Pfeiffer, who was very familiar with cooling systems, had to repair an ice factory. They were extremely successful: it was the first working ice factory in Singapore after the war, and within a few weeks was producing four tonnes of ice-blocks a day.

American firms played a willing role in Hitler's preparations for war, since this was very profitable for them. For many US industrialists, Hitler was the only bulwark against the spread of Communism. The Ford Motor Company and General Motors, with their German branch Adam Opel AG, provided hundreds of tracked vehicles and military trucks to the German armed forces. IBM (International Business Machines Corporation) provided equipment to Germany via Switzerland even during the war. Without their Hollerith punched card technology the racially-orientated censuses in Germany, Poland, Romania, Hungary and Czechoslovakia which enabled the removal of Jews, Sinti and Roma from the population, would hardly have been possible. The ITT (International Telephone and Telegraph Corporation) also took part. All the German Navy's warships and U-boats were provided with ITT communications equipment as well as that from German firms.

The head of ITT, US Army Colonel Sosthenes Behn, was one of the first American businessmen to visit Hitler on the 2nd of August 1933, shortly after he seized power. Behn was a pioneer in communications technology and founder of ITT. Right until the end of the war he was a great admirer of Hitler. He employed loyal Nazis in the leadership of ITT's two German daughter-companies, the *Standard Elektrizitäts-Gesellschaft* (SEG), which was already owned by ITT, and C. Lorenz AG, which ITT acquired in 1930. Both were active in the fields of telephone technology, telecommunications, radar and transmitter construction. After the war the companies merged under the name *Standard Elektrik Lorenz* (SEL).

ITT also acquired the Berlin company Huth GmbH, which produced radar and telecommunication parts for the German Army. In 1938 ITT used its daughter-company C. Lorenz AG to buy a 28% share in the Focke-Wulf aircraft manufacturers. The quicker the Germans rearmed, the more intensively ITT invested in Germany. After 1933 ITT invested all the profits from their German branches in new armament businesses. The outbreak of war in 1939 led to a world-wide decline in ITT's turnover, though in Germany it increased due to the production of telecommunications equipment for the German forces. Profit came before morality – then as now.

In 1938 the Berlin lawyer Dr Gerhard Alois Westrick[1], became chairman of the board of ITT's German holdings. The ITT companies in Austria, Switzerland and Romania were controlled by ITT Germany. During the war these companies produced exclusively for the German forces. Ships, submarines, aircraft and the army were equipped with telecommunications and encoding equipment by these ITT branches. Thus U-boats heading for the "Southern Region" were fitted with FuMu 61-65 (Hohentwiel) radar equipment specially developed for submarine use, Lo6L39 receivers and LO40K39 reserve short-wave transmitters. C. Lorenz AG was also the leading manufacturer of the "Goliath" VLF transmitter after 1941.

After the war, ITT in America was even compensated by the US government for armament factories destroyed in Germany by wartime air-raids. Colonel Sosthenes Behn was honoured for his "outstanding achievements for the USA" by being buried in the Arlington National Cemetery in Washington on his death in 1957.

---

1   Elder brother of Ludger Westrick, later State Secretary under Chancellor Ludwig Ehrhard. (I have mentioned Ludger Westrick's son, who behaved disgracefully in Indonesia in the 1960s and whom I knew personally, in my book *Der Ruf des Geckos* pp. 35f and 129). Gerhard Alois Westrick lived mainly in the USA, where he worked mainly in liaison with German firms for influential American companies. He was a close friend of Torkild Rieber, the Texaco boss. Westrick received massive financial support from Texaco. He was very influential and moved in the highest American circles. For example, he was a partner in the same Washington law firm as John Foster Dulles, later the US Secretary of State. Westrick was a member of the Rieber Rings, the aim of which was to support Nazi Germany and hinder America's entry into the war. Members of the Rieber Ring included Henry and Edsel Ford; GM Vice President James D. Mooney; Sosthenes Behn, founder and President of ITT; Ralph B. Strassburger, a financier and press baron from Herald and Times; Eberhard Faber, owner of the New York writing material company: representatives of Eastman Kodak and of the typewriter manufacturers Underwood-Elliott-Fisher and many others. The information the German secret service received from the Rieber Ring via Westrick was invaluable. In June 1940 Dr Westrick informed Berlin that the members of the Rieber Rings would intervene with President Roosevelt to bring about an improvement in relations with Germany and to bring the supply of aid to Britain to a halt. Westrick insisted to his American friends that interrupting aid to Britain would bring the war to an end within three months.

31. Provisions for the German U-Boats

Since food was either used up on the long voyages or spoilt in the damp tropical climate, fresh provisions for the U-boats' month-long operations or their journey home had to be acquired in Penang and the other German naval bases. It was not possible to get the right provisions at the local markets, since fresh food does not keep very long in a U-boat where space for frozen food was also limited.

Even on the black market it was not possible to acquire preserved foods suitable for western tastes in the quantities required, which led to problems. Initially canned food – especially canned meat – had been brought to Penang from Nanking or bought on the black market in Shanghai. Food captured from Allied shipping had also been used to feed the U-boat crews. After the sea route to China was cut off because of the blockade breakers' massive losses, there was no source of supply in the "Southern Region". As supplies ran out, new methods had to be found. In Penang the conditions for producing canned foods seemed favourable.

With the help of the Japanese a disused cannery was reopened and new personnel trained. Captain Dommes (responsible for the "Southern Region") and the station commander at Penang, Lieutenant Hoppe, were charged with organising the operation, even though neither of them had much experience of conserving food or dealing with native staff.

Fortunately they had Willy Vogel and a few merchant captains and prize-ship officers available, who knew how to deal with the natives' sensibilities. Vogel had lived in South East Asia for many years, and spoke Chinese, which he had learned in Nanking, and Malay. Some of the merchant captains also spoke Malay fluently. Vogel was the manager of a big Chinese bakery, which from now on worked exclusively for the Germans. The rye flour for German brown bread was bought in Shanghai.

Staff Sergeant Klossek came to Tokyo on the auxiliary cruiser *Thor*. He was an expert in food preservation and was posted to Penang for the new project. He began on the preservation of meat and bread. Even smoked meat and flour had to be canned so that it would not spoil on board. Production in large quantities meant that they needed tinplate to produce the cans. The Chinese, being pro-German and good businessmen, managed – in unimaginable ways – to get hold of everything the base needed, including tinplate.

They created a meat processing industry with smokeries for ham and sausages, and the bakery in Penang produced bread that was acceptable to German taste following recipes sent from Berlin by radio. All the provisions, from bread to vegetables to processed meat, had to be sealed in cans. For all this work they trained uneducated but skilful and hard-working native workers, who were very soon able to run and maintain all the German factories on their own.

Vegetables like celeriac, tomatoes, cabbage, carrots and potatoes were grown and harvested on Emil Helfferich's former tea plantation on Java, Tjikopo (now: Cikopo). The farm manager, Lieutenant Tangermann of the supply ship *Brake,* employed over 400 diligent and skilled Javanese gardeners and farmers to grow the vegetables.

On the local markets – even the black market – it was only possible to obtain the usual South East Asian sweet potatoes. Tjikopo was the first place on Java where the oldest German variety of potato, Sieglinde, was successfully planted. It is resistant to many diseases and became so popular with the native population that it is now found all over Indonesia. It has even found its way into Indonesian dishes like *gado-gado.* The potatoes and vegetables were transported by plane or U-boat from Batavia to Penang for processing and canning.

Fruit like pineapples and mangoes, as well as vitamin-rich coconut slices and bamboo shoots were bought on the spot in Penang for preservation. Now the U-boats could be well-supplied with freshly canned provisions; food was also frozen for the U-boats here. I have been to Penang many times, but could find no trace of this former German industry.

When fresh meat became practically unavailable in Malaya, they shifted to Java, where there were good supplies of chickens and ducks as well as cattle and water buffaloes. In their search for a suitable production site, the provision team found, to their amazement, a small, abandoned German meat and sausage factory in Bandung. But how had a German butcher got there?

Shortly after the end of the First World War, a young German-trained butcher and cook from the Black Forest left home and – like so many others – went to the Dutch East Indies to seek his fortune. In Bandung he found a job as chef in the famous Hotel Preanger, which used to be frequented by the planters – the managers of tea, palm oil and coconut plantations, like Walther Hewel. A few years later, the butcher began making his living with this small meat and sausage processing plant. His meat and sausage products were famous all over the East Indies. The business flourished, but all his plans came to nothing because of the Second World War.

When German troops invaded the Netherlands he was, like all the Germans, interned and taken to British India, ending up in the big internment camp of Dehra Dun, in northern India, at the foot of the Himalayas.

The Germans found the little meat processing plant in Bandung abandoned but still serviceable. Someone remembered a senior worker, a *Volks* German with Dutch citizenship: he had not been interned by the Dutch or the Japanese, since he had gone underground in a small village with his native wife. He and his assistant were brought back to work, filling the little factory with life again.

In Bandung the processed meat began to pile up: goulash, beef olives, chicken fricassee, duck breast à l'orange and all kinds of sausage were smoked, canned and numbered ready to supply the submarines. The navy was insistent that crews should be supplied with plentiful and varied provisions: Dönitz ensured that the submarine crews wanted for nothing to make their long and dangerous voyages as pleasant as possible.

When I arrived in Jakarta in the early 1960s the butcher from the Black Forest was back in his second home – which was now called Indonesia. He was a chef again, but now in the first and only luxury hotel in Jakarta, the Hotel Indonesia, a prestige project of the first President of Indonesia, Soekarno. I met him there for many talks, but can now unfortunately only remember his first name, Konrad.

At the time I arrived in Indonesia it was very hard to find foods that suited European tastes, because of a lack of the right ingredients. But Konrad could work magic! To order, he would make any dish the Germans in Jakarta wanted, even Swabian Maultaschen (a kind of ravioli). Spätzle were always on the hotel menu. Only when he reached 75 did he take his well-earned retirement after a life full of incident. Konrad told me many stories about the final years of Dutch colonial rule and his time in internment in Java and Dehra Dun.

With Willy Vogel's help a Chinese shoe factory in Penang specialised in producing U-boat shoes and army boots of all sizes. They were made by hand and supplied in any size and quantity required. German army boots were even supplied to the German Embassy in Tokyo from Penang. There is no proof of whether these boots were meant for the Imperial Japanese Army or not. Indonesian eyewitnesses report that German army boots were carried to Batavia and Surabaya by U-boat. They were intended both for the Japanese army, which had footwear that was totally unsuitable for the tropics, and for Soekarno's first army, the PETA, so that they would be well-equipped for the forthcoming war of independence against the Dutch. It was not possible to discover if these German army boots came from Germany or were produced in Penang.

The Hindu temple Pura Bukit Lan Pucak on Bali is regarded as a great oddity: instead of the usual pair of fearsome temple guardians at the entrance, there are two life-size, fully-equipped Japanese soldiers carved in stone, wearing German army boots. They were carved during the Japanese occupation, and demonstrate the Balinese sense of humour.

During their operations, which often lasted for months, fresh water was only used on U-boats for drinking and cooking. Sweaty bodies could only be showered in seawater, for which they needed a soap that would foam in salt water. Using a recipe from Germany and ingredients available in Siam this was produced under German auspices by Chinese manufacturers in Penang. By the end of the war, most German bases were more or less running themselves.

Best of all were the provisions in the base at Surabaya, where the black market provided almost everything the heart could desire. The German women in Sarangan, whom we will deal with later, also provided the base with fresh fruit and vegetables that they either bought from the peasants in the surrounding mountain villages or grew themselves.

When the British refrigerator ship, the SS *Nanking* – fully laden with preserved food, fruit and vegetables, beef and pork, flour, butter and other foodstuffs – was captured on its way from Australia, the Germans in the Penang base were very well supplied. The ship was brought into the port of Penang and was used there as a storage facility until the end of the war.[1]

---

1   Information received in conversation with Indonesian and Malayan eyewitnesses, see also Brennecke, *Haie...* pp. 135ff

32. Rest and Recreation for German Sailors

On their voyages to South East Asia the U-boats were often tossed about for days on end by the monsoon driven waves. The commander and crew had to be on duty day and night, seven days a week in a cramped space under great pressure for three to five months. There were only short breaks for sleep or rest, which were often interrupted by impending danger

The long, dangerous and suspense-packed voyage often took the crew to their physical and psychological limits. There were also the climatic conditions which were extremely enervating. It is hardly surprising that after months on duty the crew's spirits rose and their expressions brightened when the commander decided to head for Penang or Batavia to revictual and refuel and unload cargo from Germany. The crew's watchword was then: Off to South East Asia! Off to Paradise! Even the place names in this tropical world were evocative: Java, Surabaya, Malaya! When you hear these names, you immediately think of green rice-fields, tall coconut palms, exotic fruits and slim dusky South Sea beauties with sinuous bodies.

It must have been such a relief for the crews when, after such a long and arduous voyage, one of the westernmost bases, Sabang, Penang or Batavia – finally, finally – hove into view and they could look forward to a break on dry land with the fresh fruit and vegetables they had missed so much.

The period of at least three months that was spent in the ports of Penang, Batavia, Surabaya or Singapore to maintain, repair and re-equip the submarines was no less effortful. Since, quite understandably, there were hardly any local trained staff on any of the German bases in the region, the crew, although tired after their long voyage, had to do much of the maintenance work for themselves – often of course on the grounds of security. Most of the German welders, mechanics and electricians who had worked for the Dutch colonial government had been taken to internment camps in British India. There were no skilled Japanese personnel available because they not only avoided but rigorously refused physical labour in front of the indigenous population. As victors and new rulers they did not wish to lose the face that is so important in Asia.

Working in the submarines was hellish – the hot tropical sun beating on the steel colossi so near to the equator frequently produced inside temperatures of 50°C and more. But there was always some time for recuperation and there was a wide selection of activities provided by the base commandants. All the German bases had facilities for sports like golf, tennis, table tennis, swimming and football. German-Japanese sports competitions were arranged: the German sailors even tried traditional Japanese sumo wrestling, and many friendships grew up between Germans and Japanese. Hunting trips in the jungle were organised, and hiking in the cooler air of the mountains was surely also very welcome.

Ill. 74
German and Japanese sailors make friends

At regular intervals the crews were allowed to spend a few days in the cool hill resorts in Malaya or on Java. In Penang this was the lovely 830 metre Penang Hill, reached by a half-hour cable railway journey, where the officers and crews were accommodated in the luxurious bungalows which had previously been the weekend homes of the British. These spacious villas, surrounded by verandas, were set in spacious parks under gigantic shady trees with flocks of birds whose song the sailors had not heard for ages. Up there they had an enchanting view over the surrounding countryside and the Strait of Malacca. Every German sailor was allowed rest and recuperation in this paradise on the edge of the jungle. There were no rules and regulations here, just unlimited freedom. Chinese chefs and Malay servants looked after the Germans, treating them like kings. The Penang booklet[1] recommended long walks in the hills.

Mount Pleasant with its palm-shaded swimming pool was just down the road, and there were trips to the Cameron Highlands with their tea plantations and high-class hotels and restaurants. The Penang booklet also recommended visits to the many temples, and the botanic gardens which were very nicely laid out – but, says the booklet, more for those of a dreamy disposition. In Penang itself the following places were recommended: the Elysee Hotel, the Theatre Royal, the Queen's Cinema, the Majestic Cinema, the Fun and Frolic Park, Wembley Park and the Recreation Office. Typically German food was unlikely to be found in Penang – one should remember that initially things like potatoes were unavailable.[2]

1   see earlier in this book
2   www.die-feldpost-2-weltkrieg.org, Penang Booklet, pp. 4-6

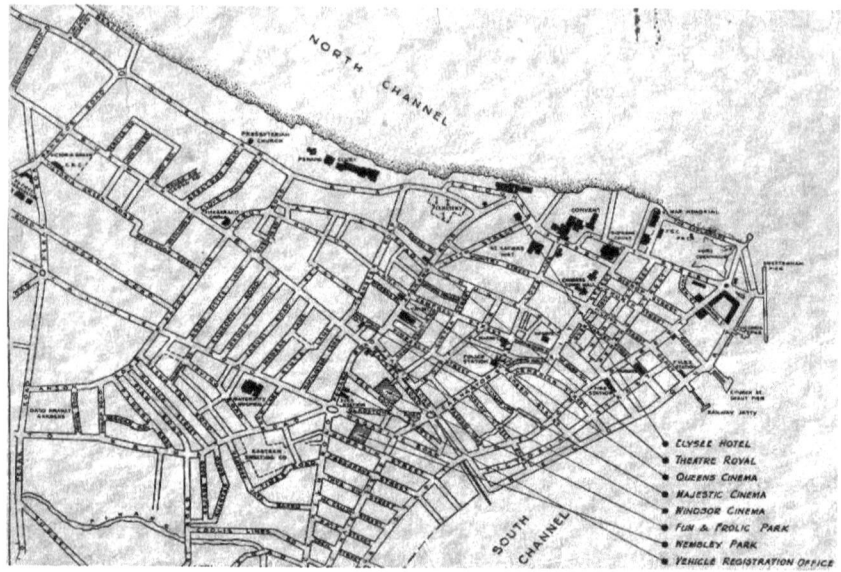

Ill. 75
Plan of Penang from the Penang booklet, 1944 edition

There were also many opportunities for leisure activities in Singapore. The Germans could visit any public establishment, but the Japanese Navy particularly recommended the places listed in the Shonan booklet:
For German and Japanese officers only:
Suikosha, the Japanese Officers' Club on Scotts Road
Daiichi Mutsumi, diagonally opposite *Suikosha*
Konan Club, previously the Cricket Club, opposite the Civic Hall
Nanto Hotel, previously the Adelphi Hotel[1]
Nanten Churo, on New Bridge Road
Minami-Sukiyaki-Restaurant, only by prior reservation
Goodwood Park Hotel[2]

---

1   After the Japanese capitulation the Nanto Hotel returned to its old name, the Adelphi Hotel. At the beginning of the 1960s the Adelphi Hotel was still working to its old standard. I frequently stayed there at the time. Some of the older waiters could still remember the parties the German officers had thrown there.

2   This was the former German Club Teutonia, which was confiscated by the British in 1914 when the war began, and turned into a hotel. Now the British had been thrown out and German officers could sip their cocktails there again.

For NCOs:
Nanmeiso, the former Dutch Club
Satsuki-Restaurant

For all ranks:
Daini Shukusha, previously the Union Jack Club
Daisan Shukusha, previously the Marine Hostel
Daini Mutsumi, on Battery Road
Aoitori-Restaurant, in the Union Building, which also held the offices of the German base
Swing-Restaurant, on Serangoon Road
Rising Sun-Restaurant, on Lavender Street

Dance Halls:
Great World (Japanese: *Daisekai*), an amusement park
Great Eastern Asia-Cabaret (Japanese: *Daitoa*)
Tien Yak Kei-Cabaret, on Maxwell Road

Civilian clothing was the rule for the dance halls. If one wished to make the closer acquaintance of a native lady, the Tiger Club was very popular. All the places restricted to Japanese military personnel had a sign with the letter M. German sailors were not to enter them unless accompanied.

The elegant Raffles Hotel, famous for the Singapore Sling cocktail and now renamed the *Shonan Hotel,* was also listed in the booklet. For coffee and cakes to remind them of home there was even a Cafe Wien in Singapore. There were film showings and concerts in the Shonan Civic Hall (Japanese: Shonan Kokaido). Trips to Johore Baru on the mainland to visit the Sultan's palace were another attraction. The sailors met for regular gymnastic exercises

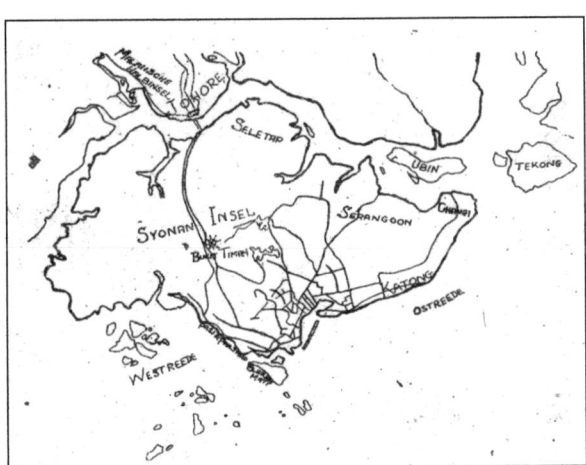

Ill. 76
Map of Singapore from the Shonan booklet, 1944 edition

on the lawns near the Pasir Panjang camp next to the docks on the western roads.[1]

As said before, the servicemen's club in Singapore was a large building that was known as the Jungle Pavilion. It was set in a big tropical garden. Since dancing was a favourite activity of the seamen friendly women were employed as dance partners there on fixed contracts. The ladies were only dance partners, and were picked up by bus and taken home at 10.30 on the dot.

In Surabaya the sailors mainly went to the cool village of Tretes with its delightful *Nimfenbad* [Nymph Baths], a Dutch luxury bath complex, full of fresh mountain water which cascaded into the swimming pool from a spring in the mountain above. Tretes, previously a mountain resort for the colonial rulers, was at an altitude of over 800 metres at the foot of the volcano *Arjuna*, was cool in temperature and only an hour by car from Surabaya on a road that wound through idyllic villages. The massive pool was impressive with its diving towers and slides, little streams and bridges all set in an evergreen landscape with flowering bushes, coconut palms and hundreds of orchids. All around the pool itself stood nymphs carved of pure white marble. Cool drinks and aperitifs were served with the spicy food in the garden. The sailors could really relax here. When I visited the baths at the beginning of the 1960s they had already lost some of their former glory. Near Tretes is the still active volcano *Bromo*, which must have been some people's favourite destination for a trip. The holiday resort of Sarangan with its German school was also not too far away.

While the submarines were being loaded in Batavia with tin, molybdenum, tungsten, rubber and quinine for the German war effort, or when they were forced to wait for spare parts from Germany, the German sailors relaxed in the many bars of Tanjung Priok, Batavia's port, or sauntered along the elegant Oranje-Boulevard, now Jalan Diponegoro. Here and in the Pasar Baru the upmarket shops were always filled with brightly coloured native and foreign goods.

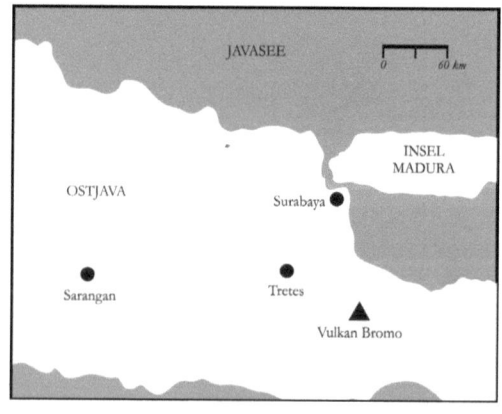

Ill. 77
Map of East Java (Extract)

If their stay was longer, the sailors took leave in shifts on the cool tea plantation of Tjikopo (now: Cikopo) at the foot of the volcano *Gunung Pangrango*. The plantation, which had previously belonged to Emil Helfferich, was nicknamed the *U-Boot-Wiese* [submarine meadow] by the sailors.

After the end of the First World War Emil Helfferich had bought this plantation near Bogor on Java. When he returned to Germany in 1928, he handed over the management to Albert Vehring. When the Germans invaded the Netherlands the Dutch colonial government confiscated the plantation and Vehring was interned. Vehring was one of the survivors of the *Van Imhoff*–disaster and became Foreign Minister of the "Free Republic of Nias".

When the Japanese occupied Java and the German Navy set up their base in Batavia, the base commander, Captain Hermann Kandeler, succeeded in persuading the Japanese military authorities to return the plantation to the Germans, and Albert Vehring was reinstated as manager of the plantation – now the sailors' U-boat meadow. They were able to rest and recuperate after their long and stressful voyages. Since replacement parts from Germany often took a long time to arrive, there were often several months of inaction. But in this tropical paradise with its pleasant mountain air, the delays were never too long for the crews.

In the grounds there were, as well as the bosses' houses, bungalows and a few rather neglected and abandoned little huts for the tea-pickers. With their walls overgrown with bright bougainvillea and hibiscus bushes in front of them, these huts – like all houses in the tropics – looked idyllic rather than squalid. The submariners, who were used to cramped conditions and bad air, were perfectly happy here.

With Vehring's assistance a farming business was set up on the plantation, producing fresh vegetables, potatoes and fruit straight from the tree. They kept chickens and bred pigs and cattle. This farm supplied the U-boats with provisions for their long voyage home. By day there were hikes, sports and games, and the silence of the night was broken only by the chirping of the cicadas. War? For the sailors the rest periods at the U-boat meadow were a carefree time in paradise.[1] But at home in Germany, the Allied air-raids had already begun, and Goebbels was shrieking: *Wollt Ihr den totalen Krieg?* [Do you want total war?]. And the people roared *ja* and cheered him to the echo.

It must always have been very lively here, as when for example the 136 crewmen rescued from the sinking of the supply ship/tanker *Brake* on the 24th of April 1944 arrived in Batavia on the U 168 and were allowed a long period at the U-boat meadow to recover.

---

1   www.bogor.indo.net.id

A walk through the local markets was always an experience for the sailors. Hardly any of them had seen Asia before. Whether it was the Malay Peninsula or Java, the unique atmosphere, the sounds, the smells and the wares on offer were the same all over South East Asia. When the sailors went out, they changed their uniforms for standard lightweight khaki civilian clothing. They were not allowed to be seen in uniform outside the port area so that they would not look like an occupation force to the locals. The Japanese even provided them with silk shirts – a luxury that had not been seen in Germany for some time. The only distinguishing feature was a cord fastened to the shirts, which identified them as Germans to the Japanese.

How exotic the brightly coloured and exuberant markets of South East Asia must have seemed to the young German sailors after the wartime austerity at home. Whether they were in Penang, Batavia, Surabaya, Sabang or Singapore, they were surrounded by an abundance of unfamiliar fresh tropical fruit and vegetables: juicy saffron-yellow mangoes, giant yellow papayas, brown scaly salak fruit, shiny purple aubergines, bright green limes and glowing red chilies, all carefully and artistically arranged in pyramidal piles.

Men and women in bright sarongs sat on the ground on raffia mats and sold peas and beans, rice, onions, sugar and flour from open sacks. Bright rolls of cloth fluttered in the wind on little stands. Amongst all this, pretty girls strolled around, protecting themselves from the sun with massive banana leaves.

On every corner there was the smell of Malay curry or coconut oil or the star anise so beloved all over South East Asia. The aroma that hovered over the market – cinnamon, ginger, cloves, vanilla, cardamom and many other spices – was intoxicating. Betel leaves, slaked lime, betel nuts, cardamom, cloves and a whole variety of spices were displayed on broad banana leaves: they were mixed to make a stimulant called *siri* – particularly popular with old women – which is chewed for hours and leaves the mouth a nasty blue colour.

On both sides of the street there were Chinese shops: bakeries, shoemakers, goldsmiths, tailors and countless little kiosks selling all kinds of trinkets and trumpery. In dark side streets there were piles of brightly coloured Indian and Siamese silk. All the businesses attracted the attention of passers-by with big signboards. Plucked ducks and chickens hung by the neck in rows outside butchers' shops and restaurants. A miasma of spices, bread, coconut – and also fish, smoke and garbage – hovered in the air. But there was always a heavy, sweet-spicy scent prevalent in the mixture – the smell of kretek cigarettes, a speciality very popular in Indonesia and mainly sold there. The tobacco is mixed with cloves, and since Indonesians are heavy smokers the sweet smell of cloves hovers over any gathering. During the war, however, the variety and quantity of produce on offer in the markets declined as Japan began to confiscate large amounts of food for their home population.

The markets were thronged with people, in Penang in particular, with a hectic mixture of peoples – Malays, Chinese, Indians, Arabs and descendants of the Portuguese, who were the first settlers – and a confused babble of all their different languages. How strange this exotic heaving throng of brightly dressed people must have seemed to the young German sailors in their drab khaki clothing.

Remarkably, there were a large number of products "Made in Germany" on offer in the markets at that time: toys, sewing machines, tools, kitchen utensils, screws and hinges were all imported from Germany. German knives from Solingen: the brand Tjap Mata (Eye Brand) stamped with an eye was produced specially for this region. These knives were very popular in South East Asia and were regarded for many decades as the best in Asia. Things look different now: everything is dominated by plastic and the trade mark "Made in China".

There was chatter and bartering all around. The lively conversation of the men and the smell of coffee drifted out from the coffee houses. On every corner people were frying, boiling and eating. Every nation offered their own speciality.

At night the life and activity of the markets was – and still is – even more impressive than by day, and the choice even more bewildering. Now there were hundreds of little mobile cookshops producing Malay, Chinese, Arab and Indian dishes by the flickering light of paraffin lamps. Each of them had its own speciality: noodles, fish or meat balls, dumplings, fried rice and soup. On the ground, instead of spices and food, there were displays of saucepans, crockery, clothes, books and all sorts of other goods

In those days the locals held their weddings out on the street in the open air. Then as now a *Pasar Malam,* a night market, was a scene of wild confusion. And later in the evening prostitutes of all ages, dressed to kill, would stroll around on the lookout for customers.

However, during the Japanese occupation the markets on Java were not as well-stocked as those in Malaya or Singapore. The Japanese siphoned off a far greater quantity for home consumption in Japan, so that the black market prices were far from affordable by the local population.

Every city had many cinemas, though what they showed was rarely to German tastes. However, the Malay theatres were different: young female dancers dancing to Gamelan music were a new and unusual experience.

At dawn and twilight the mullahs sang the praises of Allah, *Allahu-akbar, Allahu-akbar* in the call to prayer from the minarets of the mosques. For the Germans it was an exotic, unfamiliar and yet peaceful world – in the middle of the war.

Shortly after being appointed German Ambassador in Tokyo, Heinrich Georg Stahmer visited Malaya and the Dutch East Indies. He reported that the officers were in good spirits and well looked after. He wrote of the naval base in Penang: *The Japanese had made every effort to attend to their needs, including those of the heart.*[1] Stahmer is obviously circumspectly describing the provision of prostitutes, called comfort women by the Japanese, to satisfy the desires of the sex-starved sailors.

Sometimes there were three or four U-Boats in one of the ports at the same time. It was always an attraction, not just for the Japanese, but also for the local population, when a shark-like German submarine, with its sloping bow and the jagged net-cutter and the German flag fluttering behind the conning tower, was on view docked in one of the bases.

As well as the officers, there were between 150 and 300 German sailors stationed permanently in every base. They were submarine experts, engineers, radio operators, administrative staff, doctors, medical staff and craftsmen. There were also German civilian personnel, Germans and German-Indos, who had somehow managed to escape internment in British India or the Dutch East Indies. In Surabaya there were also young people who had not been interned because of their age and were living with their mothers in the nearby mountain village of Sarangan. The Japanese provided bungalows and other quarters for the permanent staff and the crews of the U-boats while in dock: these were mostly houses confiscated from Dutch internees. Local staff were also trained for auxiliary and service duties. Towards the end of the war there are reported to have been several thousand German personnel living and working in the "Southern Region".[2]

It was understandable that men who were tired out by work on the U-boats and the unbearable heat should long for relaxation – and the seductive arts of the graceful young Malay and Chinese women with their supple bodies were very powerful. The Japanese placed their 'houses' at the disposal of the Germans – like the Taifun Hotel in Penang with its Malay, Chinese and Indian prostitutes. Japanese soldiers were taken there by bus and then after a fixed time – usually an hour – picked up again.

There were several reasons why the Japanese set up military brothels employing *jugun ianfu* (comfort women): they wished to avoid mass rapes of

---

1   Stahmer, *Japans Niederlage – Asiens Sieg*, pp. 197f
2   Statements by Indonesian and German eyewitnesses.

local women and at the same time control the spread of venereal diseases. However, their visits to the brothels actually increased the number of infections. A visit to a brothel was intended to raise morale and be a reward. At the time, sexual laxity and infidelity on the part of husbands was not a serious failing in the eyes of Japanese men. This only changed after defeat in the Second World War when Japanese women made it clear that they were aware of what their rights were – and then Japanese cities were full of wives living alone after leaving their unfaithful husbands.

At first the Japanese authorities only employed professional prostitutes in their brothels: they advertised for them in the local papers. But when that source of supply ran out, they seized ordinary women and forced them into prostitution. In places close to the front, and because of the incompetence of local Japanese authorities, as well as the deployment of auxiliary policemen from Korea and Formosa, the system got more and more out of control. It is estimated that during the victorious Japanese advance through the "Southern Region" at least between 100,000 and 200,000 women and girls from China, Korea, Indonesia, Malaya, India and the Philippines were held as sex slaves in these brothels.

The Germans did not like the organised and time-limited nature of the "activity", but it was in particular the poor hygiene and danger of infection in the Japanese brothels that caused problems. The base doctor in Penang, Dr Schlenkermann, was becoming overloaded with cases of venereal infection, and so with the aid of station commander Hoppe and Captain Jürgen Oesten, of the U 861 they persuaded to Japanese to give the Germans their own "house" in Penang – the Hotel Shanghai.

The Hotel Shanghai, set in a park-like garden, was a massive villa, once the property of the millionaire Chinese captain Chung Thye Phin, "the richest man in Penang" who died in 1935. The building and its decoration were correspondingly lavish and luxurious. After his death it was sold, and now it was converted into the Hotel Shanghai.

The Hotel was on Kelawai Road (now Northam Road) in Penang. In 1964 it was demolished and replaced by the current large apartment building. The German sailors nicknamed the hotel the "House of a Thousand Delights".

Unlike the Japanese brothels, only women who voluntarily wished to work there were employed. There was a very positive response. Each of the ladies had an individual contract laying down what kind of activity she was there for, the period of service and the rate of pay. The contracts distinguished between those who were solely dance partners and those who were willing to sleep with the sailors. The dancing partners were given a green badge, and the sailors were requested to behave in a suitably disciplined and restrained way towards them. The ladies who were prepared to do more were given red badges.

The Malayan group, the Hawaiian Boys, who played for the dances in the Shanghai Hotel, were trained and managed by a Senior Radio Operator who was a musician himself. Only German hits and folk songs were played. Cash payments were not allowed: the German officers and other ranks had to buy a ticket for every drink, every dance with a dancing girl or other activity. A 20 cent green ticket bought you a dance, a one dollar yellow ticket a beer, and so on. Best of all was a delicate pink ticket for 8 dollars: *The choice is yours,* the ticket seller in the ticket window would say, *but please only a lady with a red badge – keep your hands off the others!* The women with the green badges were not examined by Dr Schlenkermann, but the ladies with the red badges were not allowed to leave the Hotel Shanghai during the run of their contract to ensure that they did not run the risk of infection. Each of them had her own room, with shared kitchen and sitting-room facilities.

The ladies in the extravagantly slit silk dresses were paid directly by the hotel management. Tips were not permitted, but the charming and single-minded ladies seemed always to be able to coax an extra gift or tip from their customers. They were mainly from China, Malaya and Indonesia.

There was no shortage of female company. Many a young German service-man – often only 20 years old – fell in love with one of the lovely ladies with the brown almond eyes, either in the club or elsewhere, and remained in South East Asia for ever.

German passengers and seamen who sailed from Japan or the "Southern Region" to the west coast of France on Japanese submarines complained after their return not only about the monotonous food on board, but also about the shameless and overt homosexual behaviour of some of the Japanese crew. In the cramped space of a submarine there was no privacy at all.

It was probably this life in close proximity to each other on the long months of the voyages to the "Southern Region" that awakened homosexual desires in the "Boys in Blue" as well. A well known gay Indo from Moluccan descent had been an adolescent in Batavia during the time the Germans were stationed there. After 1945 he left Indonesia and spent the rest of his life in Holland, where he achieved a certain notoriety as a legendary gay with the nickname Queen of the Amstel[1]. As my friend Horst Jordt – who knew the Queen of the Amstel personally – told me, he would always have a gleam in his eye when he talked about the young German seamen in Batavia. He would squeal excitedly and gasp with pleasure and delight as he remembered

1   His real name is known to Horst Jordt and the author

the randy, young, blond, sinewy German "Boys in Blue". They had been fantastic in bed. If Hitler had only known!

Nearby, in Penang's amusement park, the Tonga Park, you would find the Gamling Farm behind two native dance halls: this was where rich Chinese and poor Malayan coolies would meet at the same table to throw dice, to play mah-jongg or roulette. The German sailors also tried their luck there, although they had been warned against gambling by the base authorities.

When the U-boat maintenance and repair base in was ready for service, Lieutenant Hoppe, formerly the pilot of the aircraft on the auxiliary cruiser *Michel*, was transferred from Penang to Surabaya as base commander.

The headquarters of the German naval base in Surabaya were on Tunjungan Boulevard, which the sailors nicknamed Oranje-Boulevard[1] because of the grand colonial Oranje Hotel: today it is still there, a historical feature, though now renamed the Hotel Majapahit.

The extensive grounds of the German base, about five kilometres from the port, were surrounded by a bamboo hedge reinforced with barbed wire. Non-commissioned officers and other ranks lived in two groups of former villas. Bathrooms and toilets were outside the buildings, and several open garages served as a dining room. There was a separate building for the clinic and other rooms of the base doctor. The officers lived in a separate group of apartments. In the main headquarters building there were training rooms, and offices and conference rooms for the officers. In various neighbouring buildings there were store rooms, map rooms, the clothing store and workshops for diesel engineers, electricians, welders or battery overhauls.

The radio operators worked in a building surrounded with antennas in the southern part of the complex. Only a few people were allowed entry to this building, as it was the centre for radio communication with Berlin, the Embassy in Tokyo and the other German bases in the "Southern Region". It was also possible to make radio contact with the U-boats and auxiliary cruisers operating in East Asian or Australian waters via Surabaya. The rooms where messages were encoded and deciphered were particularly well-guarded.

There were also four concrete tennis courts which were used to drill newcomers in the glaring heat of the midday sun. Many a drop of sweat sizzled on the hot concrete floor here.

In the canteens on the base there were cigarettes, German chocolate, Eau de Cologne, Nivea soap and various alcoholic drinks, all brought from Germany by U-boat. The bases were supplied with beer by the former Dutch breweries in Batavia und Surabaya, which had been brought back into ser-

---

1   not to be confused with the street known as Oranje-Laan in the colonial era, now Jalan Papadayan.

vice by the Japanese.[1] After the war German brewers came out and brewed Bintang and Anker beer.

There was a brothel for Japanese soldiers in Surabaya too. Since base-commander Hoppe already had experience of setting up a German recreation centre in Penang, he also created the Taifun Hotel in Surabaya. It was reserved for German personnel. It had previously been the dream villa of a Dutch businessman who had been interned by the Japanese, but now it was equipped with a bar, a dance hall and a table tennis room.

There was dance music provided by Otto Kühn, a youth with bright ginger hair who had previously been at the German school in Sarangan, was a guitar virtuoso. At the request of the officers, he founded a band made up of German and Indonesian musicians. After a few practice sessions they were ready to play at dances in the Taifun Hotel. Berthold Brecht's song Surabaya Johnny, set to music by Kurt Weill and forbidden in Germany, was their biggest hit. Fittingly, given their current residence, the sailors would sing the chorus with great enthusiasm: *Surabaya Johnny, why are you so rough? Surabaya Johnny, I love you so much!* So that Kühn could recover from the long evening playing dance music, the base commander put him on light kitchen duties.[2]

Hoppe introduced the same rules in Surabaya that had proved successful in Penang. Tickets had to be bought for drinks, a dance or a visit to the upper floor – which was forbidden to young *Reichs* and *Volks* Germans under 21 who were on the base for training. In the Taifun Hotel in Surabaya as in the Shanghai Hotel in Penang great emphasis was laid on cultivated and formal behaviour. For example, a dance-companion had to be escorted back to her seat after a dance with a polite bow. The Javanese ladies liked good manners.

Indo girls, mostly born of Indonesian mothers by European fathers, were particularly popular with the submariners,. They were slim, tall, well-built and exceedingly pretty. With their light brown complexion and swaying gait they were particularly popular as dancing partners. Quite a few of them had German fathers who had been in Dutch colonial service and spoke German fluently. They were often driven to become dance partners by economic necessity, since the German head of the family had been interned by the Dutch. The others, who knew no German beforehand, soon learned.

In the mid-1960s I got to know two ladies[3] in Surabaya, who had worked as dancing partners in the Taifun Hotel during the war. They had remained

---

1 Synopsis of Keppner, *Wie weit bis Airmolang?*, pp. 337ff and 384
2 Ibid., p. 377
3 Name and address known to the author

friends ever since. Twenty years later they were still good to look at. They were married with children. They told me that they had not been forced to work there, and had always been treated correctly. They had had a lot of fun with the Germans, and said that it had been a carefree and happy time, the best time of their youth. They had particularly valued the Germans' good manners. They had not forgotten the German they learned there either.

Anyone who found the Taifun Hotel too stiff and formal went to the nearby Tabarin Bar and Dance Club in Palm Lane. This was mainly frequented by Japanese soldiers. The prices were lower here, but the women were just as pretty and attentive. Before the war the musician Bart Groenewoud had owned the Tabarin Bar and Dance Clubs. At the time he ran the dance and jazz band the Oriental Ramblers. I could not find out if this had continued during the Japanese occupation. The area around the Tabarin Bar was very popular in the evenings: the Chinese Shanghai Restaurant was opposite and the Maxim Cinema was also close.[1]

Ill. 78
Tabarin Bar and
Dance Club,
about 1939

The German officers, on the other hand, mostly went to the grand former Hotel Oranje, renamed Yamato Hotel during the Japanese occupation.[2] It had originally belonged to the Iranian Sarkies brothers, famous throughout South East Asia. It was built in the colonial style and opened in 1911. Between 1923 und 1926 two wings were added. Charlie Chaplin and his mistress, co-star[3] and later wife[4], Paulette Goddard and the writer Joseph Conrad were among the regular guests.

1   Information from eyewitnesses in Surabaya from 1963-1970
2   in English: 'great peace' or 'great harmony', but can also mean the Yamato race which is superior to all other Asian races and is the one from which the Japanese are said to be descended.
3   For example, in the films *Modern Times* or *The Great Dictator*
4   1936-1942

Ill. 79
Oranje Hotel, Surabaya, before the Second World War
.

Other world-famous colonial hotels owned by the Sarkies brothers in South East Asia include the Eastern & Oriental Hotel (known as the P & O Hotel) in Penang, Raffles Hotel in Singapore and the Strand Hotel in Rangoon. They are still among the best in the world.[1] For a short while the Hotel Oranje was used as an internment camp for Dutch women and children until the Japanese set up their headquarters there. Japanese and German officers were billeted there.

Ill. 80
Hotel Yamato
1942-1945

1   Information from the leaflet Brief History from the Hotel Majapahit

Ill. 81
Hotel Majapahit
2014

After Japan's capitulation the Dutch set up the provisional headquarters for their returning armed forces in room 33 of the hotel and flew the Dutch flag from the roof. They regarded the Indonesian declaration of independence as null and void. Indonesian freedom fighters led by Roeslan Abdul Gani[1] stormed their office on the 19th of September 1945 and asked for an explanation. After the Dutch made it clear that they were still the masters, the freedom fighters tore the blue stripe from the Dutch flag in a scuffle. The red and white stripes remained, the colours of the Indonesian freedom movement and the flag of the Republic of Indonesia to this day.

Ill. 82
Flag of the Indonesian Freedom Movement on the Yamato Hotel

1   Fought beside Soekarno and after independence first Ambassador to the United Nations and minister in the Soekarno era

For a short while the hotel was renamed Hotel Merdeka (Freedom Hotel), and then in 1946 the Sarkies brothers returned to Indonesia and changed its name to the L.M.S. Hotel, in honour of their founder, Lucas Martin Sarkies. In 1996 it was taken over by the Mandarin Oriental Group and was given the name Mandarin-Oriental Hotel Majapahit. Since 2006 it has had six stars and has received many international awards. In memory of the events of the 19th of September 1945 Roeslan Abdul Gani put up a flagpole and a memorial tablet in the hotel.

The commander of the Japanese base in Surabaya was Captain Fuja. To foster the best possible relationship between the Japanese and German base commands, Captain Fuja was the only Japanese permitted to enter the Tai-fun Hotel. He became a permanent guest! He ate and drank as much as he wanted at the German Navy's expense. He could also make use of the dancing and other girls to his heart's content. This German generosity was rewarded, as he always did everything in his power when the Germans needed help, spare parts or technical support.[1]

The native Malays and the Chinese in Malaya and the Dutch East Indies liked the fact that the disciplined Germans, unlike their Dutch colonial masters and the Japanese, always treated them with respect – and avoided excessive alcohol consumption. This positive view is still prevalent in Indonesia, because they still believe in good old German virtues like punctuality, thoroughness and discipline, virtues that are sadly less obvious in Germany today. The Germans' good behaviour in the "Southern Region" can surely be at least partly attributed to the good preparation provided by booklets like the *Penang Booklet* and the *Shonan [Singapore] Booklet* with their rules about correct behaviour and dress.

The exotic and peaceful way of life of the people of South East Asia must surely have left a lasting impression on the German sailors. It is no surprise, then, that when the war ended quite a few felt no urge to return to their ruined and flattened homeland. Many German sailors remained in their tropical paradise after their release from captivity. On Java many Germans – and also Japanese – joined the Indonesian freedom movement and fought against the returning Dutch until the end of 1949. Many Germans also found new happiness here until the end of their lives. But I am sure that many of them were constantly overcome with homesickness as they watched the sun sinking like a ball of fire in the west – the direction of their far-off home – colouring the sea blood red.

The others who returned to their ruined homeland must surely also have spoken longingly of the precious and enchanting years they spent in the "Southern Region". The blood-red tropical sunset was one of those moments the German sailors would remember for the rest of their lives.

---

1   Brennecke, *Haie...*, p. 162

33. German Naval Pilots in the "Southern Region"

In the 1930s many German amateur pilots, both male and female, made it their goal to fly to the Dutch East Indies. Elly Beinhorn, a pilot who became a legend, set out in 1932 at the age of 24 on her first solo round-the-world flight in her little open Klemm-Argus-L16 plane, registration D-2160. Its motor was only 80 horse power. She made intermediate stops in the Dutch East Indies in Batavia, Bandung, Surabaya and Kupang on the island of Timor. She was welcomed enthusiastically wherever she went as the first German to fly from Germany to the distant archipelago.

In Surabaya she was met by the director of the airport, the fattest man in the city, known because of his well-rounded figure as the *Reistafel* King. Before flying on to Australia she had her engine serviced at the Dutch naval air-station (*Marine Luchtvaart Dienst* MLD).[1] She used the time to take the overnight ferry to Bali, because Victor von Plessen had suggested a visit to Walter Spies in Ubud. Many of the pictures in her book *Ein Mädchen fliegt um die Welt* [A girl flies round the world] show that Spies did introduce her to the real Bali.

Lieutenant Colonel Horst Pulkowski and Lieutenant Rudolf Jenett made history with their flight to Australia. In their two-man Arado Ar 79 touring plane, at the time the fastest in its class, they set many records. They landed in Medan, Batavia and Surabaya. Between the 7th and the 15th of January 1938 these two Luftwaffe pilots also visited Bali – the visit is recorded in a photograph taken by the famous Swiss artist Theo Meier, probably on the airfield at Buleleng in the north of Bali. On their return flight to Germany they collided with a bird of prey over Madras in India and crashed, killing Pulkowski and an Indian passenger.

Ill. 83
The Arado
Ar 79 with
Balinese
children

---

1   Geerken, *Der Ruf des Geckos*, p. 149

For the duration of the war the Japanese air force was unable to guarantee total air surveillance of the Strait of Malacca between Sumatra and Malaya: they would have needed far more aircraft to deal with the long coastline of the large "Southern Region". The Allies were aware of these failings, and from the end of 1943 enemy submarines were constantly in action in the narrows to interfere with Japanese supply lines to Burma, where the Burma-Thailand Railway was still being built, and the arrival and departure of the German U-boats. This Allied presence was very dangerous to German submarine traffic.

For that reason two German two-seater Arado Ar 196 seaplanes were brought to Penang by the auxiliary cruisers *Michel* and *Thor* in the spring of 1944. Naval Lieutenant Colonel Ulrich Horn, himself a pilot, was in command of this *Marinesonderdienst Ost-Asien* [East Asia Naval Special Service]. So that they would be immediately recognisable as friendly to the Japanese forces, both carried Japanese *Hinomaru* markings – the sun symbol from the Japanese flag. The Arado planes were very useful in guaranteeing the safe movement of the U-boats in the Strait of Malacca and the Java Sea. Air surveillance in the area was increased when an additional aircraft, a Japanese Aichi E 13A seaplane, was supplied to the Germans. As well as a three-man crew, this aircraft could carry a 250-kilogram bomb load on its reconnaissance missions.

In addition to securing the safe movement of the U-boats, the Arado seaplanes did sterling service in rescue actions. On the 14th of February 1944 the base in Penang was awaiting the arrival of the former Italian submarine, the UIT 23, which had been sailing under German colours with a mixed German-Italian crew since the Italian capitulation. She was carrying a large number of survivors from the sinking of the German auxiliary cruiser, the *Michel*, and the tanker, the *Brake*. The rescued sailors were on the upper deck when the UIT 23 was sunk in the Strait of Malacca by the British submarine *HMS Tally-Ho*. The survivors attempted to escape from the oil rising from the sunken boat and kept themselves afloat on pieces of wreckage. The British attacker ignored their plight.

When the UIT 23 failed to arrive in Penang as expected, the base commander ordered one of the Arados to search for the submarine. The pilot discovered the carpet of oil from the sunken submarine and the sailors swimming in it. The seaplane landed in the water, but since there was no room in the plane itself five survivors were tied to the floats for each rescue flight and brought to land. The seaplane flew back and forth from the site of the wreck to Penang until the last survivor was saved. The 26-man crew who were inside the submarine when the torpedo hit were all killed.[1]

1   Brennecke, *Jäger...*, p. 341 and www.uboataces.com

The survivors who had been floating in the sea had a lucky escape, because these waters are infested with sharks – it was presumably the layer of oil that saved them. The survivors of the French passenger and merchant ship *SS La Seyne* were less fortunate. On the 14th of November 1909 the ship was on its way from Java to Singapore with 162 people on board when it collided with the British steamer, the *SS Onda* and sank very rapidly. Although the Captain of the *Onda* immediately lowered all his lifeboats, there were only 61 survivors. In a kind of feeding frenzy the sharks had caused a dreadful bloodbath.

The two Arados normally flew from the German base in Singapore, though Lieutenant Colonel Horn occasionally flew his machine to the Japanese naval base at Penang to replace the floats. He spoke a little Japanese and was able to communicate with the Japanese mechanics very well using this and some supplementary sign-language. The Japanese pilots who flew the Aichi E 13A were surprised that changing the floats on the German planes only took a tenth of the time it took to change theirs, because the technology was better developed.[1]

When U-boat traffic was later based more on Batavia, the two Arados were transferred to Batavia. The way to the Indian Ocean through the Sunda Strait was now less dangerous than the Strait of Malacca. The seaplanes once more did very good service in their new station. When Germany capitulated, they were handed over to the Japanese Navy.

There were other German flying boats and seaplanes in the Japanese-occupied Dutch East Indies. The biggest German Naval Squadron was stationed at Surabaya, which had been the biggest Dutch naval flying base. Elly Beinhorn had seen over 60 aircraft there, including 45 Dornier Wal [Whale] flying boats, when she had her engine serviced there.[2]

The archive of the Dornier Museum in Friedrichshafen and Irmgard Loeber's 1939 book revealed that in 1937 the Dutch *Marine Luchtvaart Dienst* ordered 72 new aircraft, including 42 German Dornier DO 24 flying boats. In a document about the strength of the Dutch East Indian army in January 1939 preserved among Hewel's papers, I discovered that the MLD had 72 seaplanes and 18 smaller catapult planes at that time.[3]

The Dornier DO 24 was a very seaworthy trimotor long-distance reconnaissance flying boat that also did good work as an air-sea rescue craft. The 46 Wal flying boats that were sent to the Dutch East Indies in the 1920s needed replacing because of their age: their replacement was the DO 24K flying boat.

---

1   Hiroshi Yasunaga, *Shito no Suiteiai* and www.j-aircraft.com
2   Elly Beinhorn, *Ein Mädchen fliegt um die Welt*, p. 95
3   AA: Pol VIII 1977/41, 740/84671)

The first DO 24K, number X-1, entered service in the Dutch East Indies at the beginning of 1938. X-2 to X-29 were then delivered to the Dutch in quick succession. The last aircraft to be produced in Germany, the X-37, was delivered to the Dutch in December 1939, a few weeks after the beginning of the war.

Up to the German invasion of the Netherlands, Indonesian information suggests that seven machines in total were shipped to the East Indies, but according to the Dornier Museum and the *Dornier Stiftung für Luft- und Raumfahrt* [Dornier Foundation for Air and Space Travel] 37 aircraft had actually been delivered to the MLD for use in the East Indies. Their evidence suggests that the majority of these aircraft were "recaptured" by the German army after the invasion.

Dutch industry was set to work for the German war effort by the German Army. Many items of great military importance were produced, including Dornier DO 24Ks under licence at the Fokker aircraft factory, and the Avio-landa company in Dordrecht. The workforce at the Fokker factory increased rapidly because of a big increase in orders. The licence for the DO 24K only came to an end in 1944.

Another important naval airbase in the Dutch East Indies was Sandar Lampung, previously called Telukbetung or Tanjung Karang. During the Japanese occupation this flying-boat harbour was called the "East Harbour" even though it was right in the west of the archipelago on the Sunda Strait opposite the volcanic island of Krakatau to the south of Sumatra. *Oosthaven* or *Haven Oost* was what it had been called by the Dutch colonial authorities because it was east of the Netherlands. During the Japanese occupation both DO 24Ks and Japanese Aichi E 13A seaplanes were stationed there.

The Dutch had other bases for their seaplanes and flying boats in West Java on Lake Pangalengan, 45 kilometres south of Bandung and on Lake Bagendit near Garut at an altitude of 700 metres. A further squadron of seaplanes was stationed on Sumatra at Lake Toba, the largest inland lake in Indonesia and the biggest caldera lake in the world, from which the aircraft could quickly reach both the west coast of Sumatra and the east coast with the Strait of Malacca.

According to Indonesian eyewitnesses a dismantled DO 24K was transported from Germany to Java on one of the last freight U-boats. After reassembly this aircraft was given to Soekarno's first army, PETA, at the end of 1944. When the Dutch returned, this aircraft – now in the possession of the freedom fighters – was hidden in a lonely bay on the west coast of Sumatra where the Dutch could not find it. During the war of independence from 1945 to December 1945 it was used to transport Soekarno and other leading freedom fighters.

Soekarno also used the East Harbour during the Japanese occupation to fly to various islands in the archipelago on a German Dornier DO 24K. He was recruiting fighters for PETA and trying to win members of various militias and splinter groups of the former Dutch colonial army, KNIL (*Koninklijk Nederlandsch Indisch Leger*) for the independence struggle. The Indonesian archipelago was just made for amphibious planes: isolated bays, broad rivers in the jungle and lonely lakes made landing possible in many different places.

Until the 1970s this Dornier used by Soekarno could be admired at the military air base at Kalijati on Java as a symbol of Indonesia's freedom. Kalijati was where the Dutch had surrendered to the Japanese in 1942, and the room where the capitulation was signed can still be visited.

According to Lieutenant Agusprio Susilo, commander of the base at Kalijati, this last working World-War-Two 24K crashed into a mountain in the mountainous area around the volcano Tangkubanprahu in West Java long ago – probably at the end of the 1970s.

In the spring of 2010 I met a former pilot and officer of the Indonesian Air Force (AURI *Angkatan Udara Republik Indonesia*). He had been retired for some time but still remembered the DO 24K. He told me that several of these flying boats had been used by PETA and the later freedom fighters, and then handed over to the Indonesian Air Force after independence. He had often flown them until the end of the 1970s to take General A. R. Ramli, then the director of the Indonesian state oil company Pertamina to the oil production areas in Borneo (now: Kalimantan) and Sumatra. He had always greatly enjoyed landing these extremely reliable aircraft on the broad rivers in the middle of the Borneo Jungle. He had no idea what had become of them later.

It is no longer possible to establish with any certainty how many of the Dornier flying boats originally ordered reached the Dutch East Indies before the German capitulation in 1945 and how many were captured by the Japanese. The Naval Air Squadron attached to the naval base at Surabaya had at least seven DO 24Ks in action on surveillance duties in the eastern Java Sea. With the two Arados stationed in Batavia, the Japanese Aichi seaplane and a number of Dornier flying boats in the East Harbour and on lake Toba, it adds up to a total of at least 10-15 aircraft.

It could well be that some of the aircraft built in the Fokker factory were transported to the East Indies, first on blockade breakers and then in dismantled form on the transport U-boats. That would not have been a problem technically, because there is evidence that dismantled aircraft were transported to Japan by U-boat:

- 5 Messerschmitt Bf 109E-7, (aka Me 109) fighters, which could also be used as fighter-bombers, night fighters or reconnaissance planes. 34,000 of them were built, more than any other fighter plane in history;
- 1 Messerschmitt Me 210A-1 propeller aircraft capable of carrying a bomb load of 2,000 Kg;
- 1 Messerschmitt Me 163 Komet jet fighter, known to pilots as the *Kraft-Ei* [Power Egg]. This was the first aircraft to fly at more than 1,000 kilometres per hour.
- 1 Messerschmitt Me 262 jet fighter, the first jet fighter to go into full-scale production. Almost 1,500 were produced during the war.

Nevertheless, as eyewitnesses told me, the seven MLD Dornier flying boats were seriously damaged or destroyed by the Dutch when the Japanese invaded at the beginning of 1942, so that other Dorniers must have reached the East Indies during the Japanese occupation. There is no proof of this, but Indonesian eyewitness information makes it almost certain that PETA took possession of one, and possibly several, DO 24Ks after Japan capitulated.

Sasonko Djati, a pilot and Colonel in the Indonesian Air Force, told the journalist Iwan Santosa of the Indonesian daily newspaper KOMPAS on the 21.10.2011 that no flying boats had been in service with the Indonesian Army or Navy since the 1980s.[1]

After 1945 four Messerschmitt Bf 109s were on the airfield at Bandung and fell into the hands of the freedom fighters. They had been given to the Japanese under the terms of the technology exchange agreement. Since Yogyakarta was the provisional capital of Indonesia after independence, and since President Soekarno also resided there the aircraft were flown there. It is not known whether Indonesian pilots were already able to fly them or whether Japanese pilots delivered them. In Dutch air raids on Yogyakarta during their "police action", at least two of these aircraft were destroyed.[2]

---

1   Sources: www.kompas.com on 21.10.2012,
     Dornier Museum Friedrichshafen
     www.wikipedia.org/Dornier_DO_24 and
     Information from eyewitnesses
2   Information from eyewitnesses and Alif Rafik Khan

34. Operations Off the Coasts of Australia and New Zealand

Before turning to U-boat operations in this region, I will describe some operations by surface ships at the other end of the world, since these took place before the deployment of U-boats. Let us take two examples out of many: two auxiliary cruisers and the ships they captured.

The German Fleet was, where the size and number of their ships were concerned, vastly inferior to those of their opponents. Shipbuilding in Germany after World War One was restricted in terms of tonnage by the Versailles Treaty. At the beginning of the Second World War there was a particular shortage of cruisers, and so nine merchant ships were converted into *Hilfskreuzer* (called auxiliary merchant cruisers, AMC, by the Allies) and provided with makeshift armament and armour, as already described. They had extra tank capacity and extra provisions so that they could remain at sea for long periods, even though they had crews of up to 400.

They were not meant to engage in battle with enemy warships, but rather to capture or destroy enemy merchant shipping to cut the Allied supply lines. These nine auxiliary cruisers were very successful: in the Second World War they sank 138 enemy freighters.

The story of the auxiliary cruiser *Kormoran* is interesting, in that her sphere of operations included not just the Indian Ocean, but also activity off the coast of Australia. She was launched for the Hamburg America Line (HAPAG) from the Germania Dock in Kiel in 1938 as the merchant ship *Steiermark*. She was converted into an auxiliary cruiser after the beginning of the war and renamed the *Kormoran*. She appeared on the German navy list as Schiff 41. She had six heavy 150 mm canons, two 37 mm anti-tank canons and five 20 mm anti-aircraft guns. She was also fitted with torpedo tubes, two above the waterline and two below. There was a mine launcher at the stern, and she could carry 390 mines. She also carried a light speedboat and three Arado 196 A1 seaplanes for reconnaissance.

The *Kormoran* was the biggest of the German auxiliary cruisers and entered naval service on the 9th of October 1940 under the command of Captain Theodor Detmers. She set sail on her first voyage from Gotenhafen on the Baltic on the 3rd of December 1940, disguised as a freighter. With her tanks full, she had a range of almost 140,000 kilometres.

The *Kormoran* managed to pass through the Allied blockade in the Atlantic unnoticed. In the South Atlantic she took on fuel and provisions from the supply ship and auxiliary cruiser *Atlantis*. The *Atlantis* had been operating in foreign waters for 622 days without touching land, supplying German submarines operating in the area with provisions and fuel. They had a kind of farm on board with pigs, sheep and chickens to ensure the availability of fresh food.

On her voyage round the tip of Africa the *Kormoran* sank the Greek freighter *Antonius*. In the eastern Indian Ocean the *Kormoran* was again supplied with fuel, provisions and extra ammunition by the supply ship *Kulmerland* without being discovered by the Allies. Her mission was to sail disguised as a Dutch ship under the name *Malakka Straat* and mine Shark Bay near Carnarvon on the west coast of Australia, as it was used as a bolt-hole by Dutch submarines based at Fremantle near Perth.

After completing this mission, Captain Detmers received orders to sail to the Bay of Bengal via Java and Sumatra. Although the *Kormoran* had in only eleven months sunk ten ships and captured the Canadian tanker *Canadolita* as a prize, her last action ended in misfortune.

The last, decisive battle—with the Australian cruiser *HMAS Sydney* – took place on the 19th of November 1941 a good 200 kilometres west of Shark Bay and 1,800 kilometres north of Perth. Since Captain Detmers could not give the *Sydney* the recognition code, the *Kormoran* headed out to sea at high speed. But the *Sydney* was far superior to the *Kormoran* in terms of speed and firepower, and was getting closer and closer, so Captain Detmers ordered his men to hoist the German battle flag and open fire.

The very first hits destroyed the Australian cruiser's bridge and gunnery control centre. The 15 cm shells penetrated the hull and exploded inside the ship, and a torpedo from the *Kormoran* hit the *Sydney*'s bow. The last functioning gun turret on the *Sydney* managed to do serious damage to the *Kormoran*'s engine room. Sailing southwards, the *Sydney* left the *Kormoran* wallowing unmanoeuvrably at the site of the battle.

Fire broke out on the *Kormoran* as well. The electricity supply and the fire extinguishing system failed. When Captain Detmers realised that the engines could not be repaired with the means available on board, he ordered the ship to be scuttled. The crew took to the lifeboats, Detmers leaving his ship last of all. Two lifeboats carrying 106 men reached the western Australian coast near Carnarvon. After four days British ships picked up other survivors. Of the 397 men on board, 316 survived: 20 were killed in the sea battle and 61 drowned.

The Australian Navy only began a search for the *Sydney* after five days. No trace was found of the cruiser: 645 Australian seamen were lost with the ship, the pride of the Royal Australian Navy. Even now legends about the loss of the ship still abound. Only a single life belt was found. What happened? Why didn't the crew use the lifeboats? Why did she sail south and not eastwards to the coast? There are a lot of questions and no answers. The whole of Australia was shocked and appalled. The mystery still exercises historians and authors, but the answer is probably lying at the bottom of the sea, where the wrecks of both the *Kormoran* and, a few days later, the *HMAS Sydney* were discovered in March 2008, about 22 kilometres from each other at a depth of about 2,500 metres.

I should point out once more that this *HMAS Sydney* was not the ship that sunk the German light cruiser *Emden,* but a successor that only entered Australian service in 1935.

Captain Detmers and the other German survivors were interned in Perth as prisoners of war. It was Detmers' second "visit" to Australia – he had been there on a courtesy visit in 1933 on the light cruiser *Köln.* Only a few months after being imprisoned Detmers made an escape attempt in the company of other officers. They dug an escape tunnel, and planned to "capture" a sailing ship in Perth and sail to the Dutch East Indies. Their plan was discovered and so came to nothing.

While he was still in captivity, Detmers was awarded the Knight's Cross by Admiral Dönitz since the sinking of the *HMAS Sydney* was the only time a regular warship had been sunk by an auxiliary cruiser. They were actually supposed to destroy, sink or capture merchant ships. Detmers was given the medal and certificate in the prison camp by the International Red Cross. He and the rest of the *Kormoran*'s crew were released by the Australians in 1947. He died in Hamburg in 1976.[1]

Of course the German Navy also captured enemy merchant ships. These prizes were particularly valuable, not just because of their cargoes, but because they could sail on with an altered name and work in disguise for Germany under a foreign flag. Good examples of this are the auxiliary cruiser *Pinguin* and the minelayer *Passat.* The *Pinguin* was – from a German per-

---

1   Synopsis from following sources:
     Deutsches U-Boot Museum, Cuxhafen-Altenbruch
     Detmers u. Brennecke: *Hilfskreuzer Kormoran,*
     Hamburger Abendblatt, 18th March 2008: *Der tödliche Bluff in der Haifischbucht,*
     Spiegel Online, 16th March 2008: *Wrack des legendären Kreuzers Kormoran entdeckt,*
     Winter: *Duell vor Australien*

spective – a successful, perhaps the most successful auxiliary cruiser in the German Navy. In her short eleven months of operation the *Pinguin* sank or captured 33 ships. Other ships were sunk by the mines the *Pinguin* laid. She was on the German naval list as *Schiff 33*, the Royal Navy feared her under the name of *Raider F*.

In 1936 the *Kandelfels* entered service in Bremen with the DDG-Hansa (*Deutsche Dampfschifffahrts-Gesellschaft Hansa*) as a freighter for trade with South East Asia, and was requisitioned by the navy when the war began. She was converted into an auxiliary cruiser and fitted with six 150 mm guns, a 75 mm canon and several 37 mm anti-aircraft guns. She was also fitted with two torpedo tubes, a mine launcher and camouflaged space for two Heinkel He 114A-2 seaplanes. The ship left Norwegian waters on the 15th of June 1940 under the command of Captain Ernst-Felix Krüder, disguised as a Russian freighter named *Katschura*. She was carrying 16 torpedoes and 300 mines for her own use and another 25 torpedoes and 80 mines to supply other ships off the coast of Africa and in the Indian Ocean. Her mission was to interfere with merchant shipping in the Indian Ocean and lay mines outside Australian ports, and also to destroy Norwegian whalers and their bases in the Antarctic.

When the ship left Norwegian waters and the Russian sphere of influence she changed her name again, becoming the auxiliary cruiser *Pinguin*, a name chosen because she was intended to operate in the Antarctic. German auxiliary cruisers like the *Pinguin* were equipped with all kinds of facilities, like a floating pontoon so that U-boat crews could relax and enjoy more interesting food in the open air on deck when they met to refuel. On board facilities included a sick bay, a fencing strip, an operating theatre, a dental and an X-ray room and a laboratory. Several medical staff cared for the sick and wounded. On the *Pinguin* they had a medical team led by ship's doctor Dr Hasselmann and his assistant Dr Wenzel. They treated not only the 350 man crew of the *Pinguin* but also injured sailors from captured ships or U-boat crewmen who needed intensive care. In spite of the frequently rough seas these two doctors carried out many complicated operations on the storm-tossed ship. If it was possible, the ship's meteorologist, Dr Roll, would try and find calmer waters for them to operate in.

South of the Cape Verde Islands she met the first U-boat, a submarine cruiser commissioned by the Turkish navy but requisitioned by the German Navy at the beginning of the war and put into service as the U-A. The 86-metre U-boat had six torpedo tubes and 105 mm gun in front of the conning tower.

The U-A was the first German U-boat to carry out operations in the South Atlantic under the command of Lieutenant Hans Cohausz. She had sunk several enemy vessels and fired all her torpedoes. The *Pinguin* supplied her with new torpedoes, and with fuel and provisions. The auxiliary cruisers carried these things so that the operational range and time of the U-boats in distant regions could be increased. The high Atlantic swell near the Equator meant that transferring the torpedoes was often a difficult and wearisome process.

Cohausz and the bearded submariners were made heartily welcome aboard the *Pinguin*. After their long voyage in the cramped U-boat, a third of the crew at a time were allowed to relax on the "floating island" that was the *Pinguin* for a few hours. They could finally have a fresh-water shower or a fresh-water bath. Newly shaven and dressed in their Sunday best they could take a walk on the deck or sun themselves in a deck chair. Old sailors' songs were played on the ship's piano and below decks the same film was shown several times so that the whole U-boat crew could watch it. The baker had baked especially crisp rolls and the ship's butcher had slaughtered one of the pigs that were kept in a pen at the stern of the ship for fresh pork schnitzel.[1]

The entertaining time on the *Pinguin* came to an end all too soon and the submariners had to return to their poky home. The U-A left the *Pinguin* on the 18th of July 1940 to operate in a new area round the coast of South Africa. Her six combat missions made the U-A the most successful German submarine of World War Two.

Disguised as the Greek freighter *Kassos* the *Pinguin* sank the British freighter *Domingo de Larrinage* on the 31st of July 1940 near the volcanic island of Ascension in the South Atlantic. The British sailors who survived the attack were taken on board the *Pinguin*.

South of Madagascar in the Indian Ocean one of *Pinguin*'s Heinkel sea-planes spotted a large tanker. It was the Norwegian tanker *Filefjell*, under charter to the Royal Navy, on its way from the Persian Gulf to Cape Town carrying 500 tonnes of oil and aviation fuel. For just such an eventuality, the Heinkel was disguised with British markings. The pilot dropped a message on the deck of the tanker, ordering them to change course and observe radio silence. When the captain disregarded these instructions the seaplane destroyed the radio room with its guns and opened fire on the bridge. The captain of the *Filefjell* surrendered and waited for the *Pinguin* to arrive. Captain Krüder wanted to take the 500 tonnes of oil on board, but other ships hove into view. The *Pinguin* left the *Filefjell* with a German prize crew on board and headed for the newly-sighted ships.

1   Brennecke, *Pinguin*, p. 134ff

The British tanker *British Commander* was taken by the *Pinguin*. Her 45-man crew was taken on board and the ship sunk. The same fate befell the Norwegian *Morviken*: her crew and a fast motorboat were also taken on board. Then the *Filefjell* was made to follow the *Pinguin* to a quiet place off the main shipping routes, where the 500 tonnes of oil and the crew were transferred to the *Pinguin* and the ship sunk. An eventful and exciting day!

Below deck there were prison spaces for a good 200 sailors from captured or sunk ships. The captains of these ships were given cabins to themselves. All prisoners were allowed to take their valuables, clothing and personal effects on board the *Pinguin* and keep them. The prisoners of war were mostly divided according to nationality. They had their own toilets, and they received the same food and cigarette ration as the German crew. Only a few of the British captains complained about the food: they could not understand that on a German warship everyone, from the captain to the cabin boy, received the same food. Class differences were very important on British ships.

Only the Indians serving on British ships caused problems. They were kept in a separate cell with a built-in kitchen where they could cook their own food. The Indians also made a nuisance of themselves with the doctors because they went to see them about every trivial problem.

The Chinese are well-known to be good cooks, clean and very hard-working. On board the *Pinguin* was a Chinese who had been captured on a British freighter. Because of a broken leg he had to be treated in the sick bay for quite a long time. When it healed, he was allowed to help in the galley and did not have to return to the cells.

The prisoners were allowed on deck in groups: when they thronged around the deck, it must have been a peaceful picture, a bit like a passenger liner ... until the alarm bells rang! Then they all had to get below decks as quickly as possible.

The *Pinguin* had attracted so much attention in her disguise as the *Kassos* that she had to change her identity again. She went to an isolated harbour for the transformation, and by the 10th of September 1940 she was no longer recognisable. She now had a black hull, two black funnels with light blue bands and a white superstructure: she was now the British freighter *Trafalgar*. One of the Heinkel seaplanes was lost on take-off in rough seas, so during the repainting the second aircraft, which had been stored below deck, was assembled for action.

Having had so much success in the waters off Madagascar, Captain Krüder wanted to try his luck there just one more time before operating off Australia. On the 12th of September 1940 they sighted the British freighter *Benavon* on its way from London to Singapore. The *Benavon* was armed, and a gun battle developed. The bridge and the radio room on the *Benavon* were destroyed and the ship caught fire. The captain, the deck officers and the radio operator were killed. The 28 survivors were taken on board the *Pinguin*.

Four days later the *Pinguin* sighted the Norwegian freighter *Nordvard* sailing from Fremantle in Western Australia via South Africa to Britain. The *Nordvard* was headed off. The captain and his 30-man crew gave no resistance. The ship was carrying 7,500 tonnes of Australian wheat and other foodstuffs, and so it was captured as a prize. Since there were already about 200 prisoners of war aboard the *Pinguin* from the ships that had already been sunk or captures, 100 of them were transferred to the *Nordvard*, which was manned by a prize crew and sailed successfully to Bordeaux, arriving on the 22nd of November 1940 with its precious cargo.

The plans prepared by Captain Krüder and his navigation officer, Lieutenant Wilhelm Michaelson, required a second ship to lay mines outside Australian ports and in the Bass Strait between South Australia and Tasmania. Between the Sunda Strait and the Christmas Islands south of the western tip of Java the *Pinguin* sighted the Norwegian tanker *Storstad*, which was on its way from British North Borneo (now: Sabah) to Melbourne. She surrendered without resistance and was taken as a prize. In an isolated location south of the Javanese coast the *Storstad* was converted into a minelayer and some of her oil transferred to the *Pinguin*. She was renamed the *Passat* and equipped with 110 mines, and set sail with a mixed German-Norwegian crew under the command of Lieutenant Erich Warning. Captain Krüder was certain that a tanker that was supposed to be heading for Melbourne would not arouse the suspicions of the British and Australians.

The two ships now parted company. The *Passat* mined the seaway from Melbourne to the Bass Strait and the narrow entrance to Port Phillip Bay. She then set course for Adelaide and mined the narrow entry to the port – only ten miles wide – between Kangaroo Island and the mainland.

With incredible boldness the *Pinguin*, unnoticed by the coastal batteries of Forts Phillip and Macquarie, laid mines directly outside the entrance to the port of Sydney. She then mined the port of Newcastle and both entries to Port Hobart on Tasmania. Next she set course for Adelaide and dropped her last mines in the channels heading west from Port Augusta and Port Pirie.

When the mines were laid, the *Pinguin* headed for a pre-arranged rendezvous with the *Passat* 700 nautical miles west of Perth. They met on the 15th of November 1940 after a successful operation unique in the annals of naval operations. While they were laying the mines both ships had kept radio silence to avoid discovery.

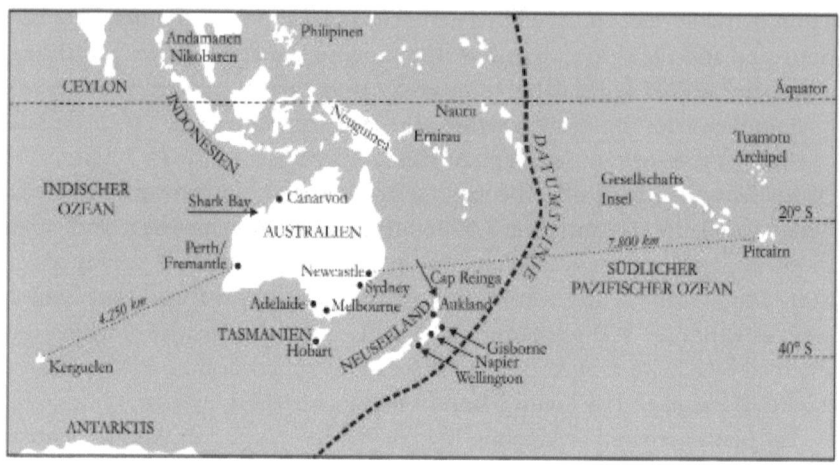

Ill. 84
Widely separated operational areas of the German Navy from 1943-1945 in the
southern Indian Ocean and the South Pacific
Distance Sydney-Pitcairn: 7,800 km,
Distance Perth-Kerguelen: 4,250 km

The Australian coast guard thought that they were far from the shooting war and could not imagine that German ships would pop up next to their fleet headquarters. But Australia soon received a shock. On the 7th of November – the *Pinguin* was still on her way to her meeting with the *Passat* – the British refrigerator ship *Cambridge* hit a mine in the Bass Strait and sank. Only two days later the American freighter, the *City of Rayville* was also sunk by a mine. The Australian and British media all talked about inexplicable explosions underwater or in the ships' holds – no one in Australia could conceive of the Germans being right on their doorstep. But the loss in a very short time of five British, American and Australian ships to the mines laid by the *Pinguin* and *Passat* sent a wake-up call to Australia. The endangered areas were declared off limits by the Australian Navy. In the Australian media they suggested that this bold exploit right under their noses must have been the work of Count Luckner with his "ghost cruiser". Count Luckner had become a legend in Australia because of the boldness of his operations in the region with the auxiliary cruiser, the *Seeadler* [Sea Eagle], a motorised three-master – but since he was born in 1881 he would have been too old for action in the Second World War.

The supply lines for urgently needed materials from Australia to Britain were now seriously endangered, especially since the auxiliary cruiser *Orion* was operating off south west Australia and the auxiliary cruiser *Atlantis* in the eastern Indian Ocean.[1]

On the 11th of November 1940 the *Atlantis* captured the British freighter *Automedon* to the west of Java. She was carrying a great deal of secret British cabinet strategic material intended for the General Staff in the Far East. The papers were sent on to the Embassy in Tokyo on the captured Norwegian tanker *Ole Jacob* and then given to the Japanese. These secret papers were of crucial importance to German and Japanese military planning.

On the 16th of November 1940 the *Passat* resumed her identity as the Norwegian tanker *Storstad*, becoming a back-up for the *Pinguin's* operations. The crew now consisted of 18 Germans and 25 Norwegian volunteers. The very next day the two ships took the large British freighter, the *Nowshera*, which was on the way to Britain from Adelaide. The captain surrendered without any resistance. The *Nowshera* was carrying zinc ore, wheat and wool. The provisions and the 113 crew were taken and the ship with its valuable cargo sunk in Western Australian waters.

On the 20th of November 1940 the large (over 10,000 tonnes) British refrigerator ship *Maimoa* was captured after a short gun battle. She was carrying 5,000 tonnes of frozen meat, 1,500 tonnes of butter, 16 million eggs, flour and other foodstuffs from Fremantle to Britain. After the storerooms on the *Pinguin* and the *Passat* had been filled almost to bursting and the 87 crew transferred, the *Nowshera* was sunk.

On the same day the *Storstad* sighted another British refrigerator ship, the *Port Brisbane*, on her way from Australia to Britain with a similar cargo. Since the *Port Brisbane* was armed, the *Storstad* called on the *Pinguin's* aid. A short gun battle destroyed the *Port Brisbane's* bridge and radio room, killing the radio operator. There was room for only 60 of the 87-man crew and one female passenger on the *Storstad*. The others had to take to a lifeboat in the darkness. Nothing is known of their fate.

On the 28th of November 1940 the *Pinguin* sank another armed British refrigerator ship, the *Port Wellington*, after a gun battle. It was a sister ship of the *Port Brisbane*, carrying food, and also wheat and steel to Britain. In the fight the captain and the radio operator were fatally wounded. 81 British and Australian crewmen and seven female passengers were transferred to the *Pinguin*. The interruption of the supply lines by the *Pinguin*, the *Storstad/Passat* and the *Orion* was beginning to cause the British ever greater problems.

Other auxiliary cruisers and the heavy cruiser *Admiral Scheer* interfered with British supply lines in the western Indian Ocean and around Africa.

---

1   Ibid., pp. 163f

The *Admiral Scheer* had captured Britain's biggest refrigerator ship, the *Dequesa*, as a prize. She had a cargo of canned food as well as 18 million eggs and 7,000 tonnes of Australian frozen meat. Since there was not enough coal on board the *Dequesa* for a voyage to the French Atlantic coast, the ship was kept in the Indian Ocean as the *Verpflegungsschiff* [Provision Ship] *Wilhelmshafen Süd*. Not only the *Pinguin*, but also the auxiliary cruisers *Storstad, Thor* and others ships like the supply ship *Nordmark,* replenished their supplies without emptying the *Dequesa's* giant cold stores.

Since the *Pinguin* had sunk more than ten ships, she had over 300 British, Australian and Norwegian prisoners on board as well as several women. The *Storstad* had also taken prisoners on board from the auxiliary cruiser Atlantis which had rendezvoused with the *Pinguin* and the *Storstad* from the 8th to the 9th of December 1940. Captain Krüder of the *Pinguin,* who was awarded the Knight's Cross at Christmas 1940, regarded it as his duty to save the crews of sunk or captured ships.

He now had all the prisoners transferred to the *Storstad* and ordered her to sail to France. She reached Bordeaux safely on the 4th of February 1941 with almost 550 prisoners. The majority of the captured Norwegian sailors were sent to Norway in March 1941 on the German ship *Donau* and released.

The *Pinguin* now set course for the south-west to attack the Norwegian whaling fleet in the Antarctic, which was under charter to the British government. Her actions there will be summarised as they do not really fit into the context of this chapter.

Partly voluntarily, partly by force, the *Pinguin* captured the entire whaling fleet of factory ships, whaling ships, a supply ship and a whale-oil tanker, fifteen ships in all. Without firing a shot the *Pinguin* took over 20,000 tonnes of whale oil, to a value at the time of more than four million dollars, over 10,000 tonnes of diesel oil and a great deal more.

Some of the Norwegian crews continued to work their ships voluntarily for Germany as if nothing had happened. Two ships, the whale-oil tanker *Solglimt* and the factory ship *Pelagos* were sent to Bordeaux with their cargoes, arriving in March 1941.

The German naval command then ordered the *Pinguin* to bring the rest of the whaling fleet to a rendezvous with the German tanker *Nordmark* south of the island of Tristan da Cunha, a British colony in the South Atlantic. The *Nordmark* had several prize crews on board who would take control of the whaling fleet. One of the whalers was renamed *Adjutant* and ordered to follow the *Pinguin*. The rest of the fleet, under the guidance of the factory ship *Ole Wegger* headed for Europe, arriving – except for two ships – in Bordeaux on the 20th of March 1941. The two ships were stopped by the British corvette *HMS Scarborough* and scuttled by their German-Norwegian crews who were subsequently picked up by the *Scarborough*.

In the meanwhile the *Pinguin* and the *Adjutant* had arrived at Port Gazelle (now: Port Couvreux) on the isolated Kerguelen Islands, a French Antarctic territory of volcanic origin in the southern Indian Ocean roughly 4,000 kilometres from both the South African and southern Australian coasts. The archipelago is an uninhabited, inhospitable bare wasteland which is buffeted day by day by the Antarctic gales of the "Roaring Forties". Stormy winds are followed by snow, rain or hail squalls. The flies have no wings – the storms make it impossible for them to fly, so over time they have lost those unnecessary appendages. The highest temperature in summer is 7-10°C, the water temperature 5-6°. Ten percent of the land surface is covered by glaciers, and the highest point is Mount Ross at 1,850 metres.

At the beginning of the 20th century France had a research station investigating sheep-breeding and the exploitation of the seal population. This was finally abandoned in 1931 because of the unfavourable weather conditions so that by the time of the Second World War the islands were once more uninhabited. The only population left were a large variety of birds, penguins, seals and rabbits. Only a decaying jetty and a few derelict wooden huts remained to show that there had once been a little French settlement. It was an unpleasant place, treeless, without even bushes, avoided by shipping. The only usable vegetable that grew here was the native Kerguelen cabbage which was eaten by whalers and seal hunters because of its high vitamin C content to ward off scurvy. It was here, on this cold, stormy archipelago, cut off from all civilisation, that the German auxiliary cruisers and supply ships rendezvoused. It was the secret "Kerguelen Naval Station".

The German navy already had detailed maps of the Kerguelens because the corvette *Gazelle*, under the command of Captain Freiherr von Schleinitz had already made a scientific expedition there between October 1874 and February 1875 on the orders of Kaiser Wilhelm I. The main reason for the expedition was observing the transit of Venus on the 9th of December 1874, to calculate the exact distance between the earth and the sun: the transit could only be seen south of Australia. The archipelago was also surveyed in detail, although it is hard to believe that the government of the time could have had any economic interest in this tiny, barren group of islands.[1]

---

1   Globus, Band XXIV, No. 22 1876, pp. 344ff and
      Globus, Band XXIX, No. 23 1876, pp. 364ff

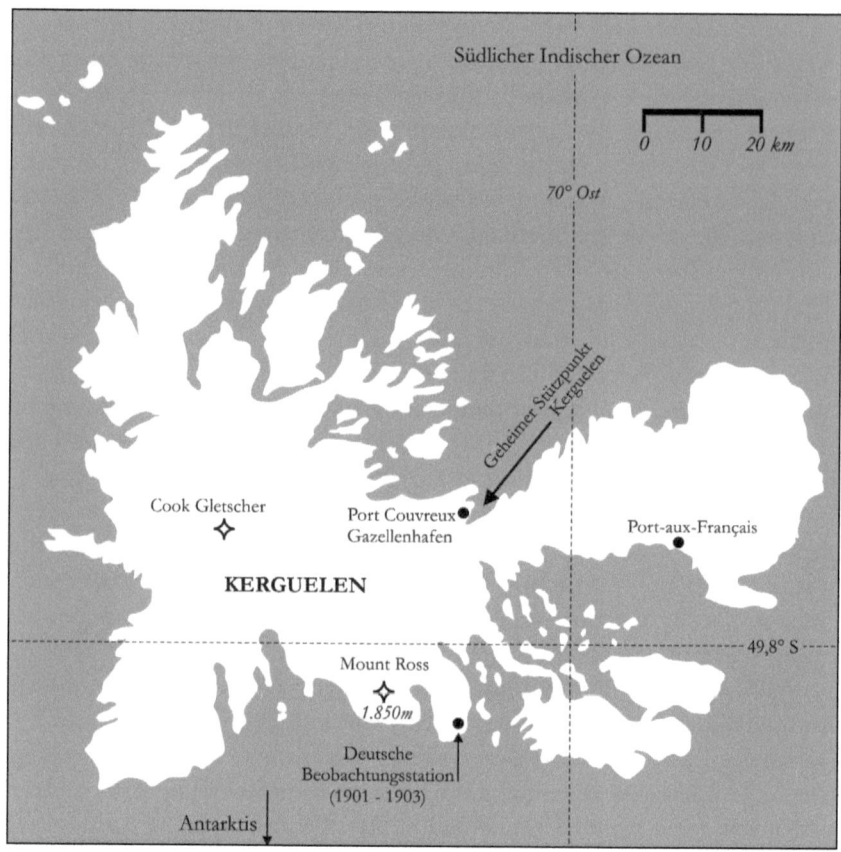

Ill. 85
The Kerguelen Archipelago

On the 24th of December 1898 the research ship *Valdivia* also put into Port Gazelle during the "German Deep Sea Expedition", and another German research expedition to the Kerguelens took place between 1901 and 1903. This was the German Antarctic Expedition under Erich Dagobert von Drygalski, a geographer, geophysicist and polar researcher, on the research ship *Gauss*. The project was to set up a geomagnetic and meteorological observation station manned by five people. The scientists were supposed to produce long-term data for comparison with that produced by the main expedition on the *Gauss*. The *Gauss* was bringing Dr Emil Werth, a biologist, and a sailor named Urbanski as part of the station's staff.

When the *Gauss* arrived at the Kerguelens, they found that the chartered North German Lloyd coastal passenger steamer *Tanglin* had arrived a few days before them, bringing the remaining three staff of the station: the meteorologist Josef Enzensperger, the geographer Karl Luyken and another sailor, Wienke. Enzensperger, the head of the station, had previously been the first scientist at the Royal Bavarian Meteorological Station on the Zugspitze at an altitude of 3,000 metres.

Enzensperger writes of his arrival on the Kerguelens as follows:

11. November [1901]. We've done it! But it has cost us a great deal. What we saw at sea on the 7ᵗʰ of the month was terrifying, and everyone on board said they had never seen anything like it. […] The unbelievably mountainous waves! I measured them at 12 metres high. The captain […] must have felt extremely relieved when he saw the silhouette of a mountainous land emerging through the thick mist […] and we sailed into a lovely fjord landscape in glorious sunshine […] The contrast between the countless islands, the innumerable blue fjords penetrating deep into the land, the steep peaks of the basalt mountains and the ice-covered interior of the island is overwhelmingly beautiful. A pity that the terrible weather so rarely allows us to enjoy this picture unalloyed. […][1]

It is questionable if the passengers were able to enjoy the good food on the *Tanglin* in the stormy seas. The voyage from to the Kerguelens from Singapore and back via Australia took six to seven months.

The *Tanglin* was carrying 200 tonnes of material for the construction of the station and huskies from east Siberia. Because of the bad weather it took ten days until the wood and other building materials, coal and provisions etc. could be unloaded by the Chinese sailors. On the 31ˢᵗ of January 1902 the *Gauss* hoisted anchor and headed on towards the South Pole. The three scientists and the two sailors were left alone on the inhospitable island. When the instruments had been installed, they began the work of collecting data. They also explored the area around the station. The furthest they travelled was 40 kilometres to Gazelle Bay.

Very soon Dr Werth showed symptoms of beriberi – a disease resulting from malnourishment. Enzensperger also became ill and died on the 2ⁿᵈ of February 1903, a week before his 30ᵗʰ birthday. His grave has never been found. Dr Werth's health deteriorated daily.

Finally, four weeks late, the *Staßfurt* of the German Australian Line arrived on the 30ᵗʰ of March 1903 to pick the men up from their lonely is-

---

1   Alberti-Sittenfeld, Conrad, *Die Eroberung der Erde: Der Weiße als Entdecker, Erforscher und Besiedler fremder Erdteile*, p. 499

land. After a two-week voyage the ship reached Sydney, where Dr Werth was brought back to health in a sanatorium.

There is still evidence of the German presence on the Kerguelen. Mount Werth is named after Dr Werth, Karl Luyken Fjord is named after the geographer. The name of the research ship *Gazelle* is found in Gazelle Bay, Gazelle Passage and Port Gazelle (now: Port Couvreux). The Gauss Peninsula takes its name from the research ship.[1]

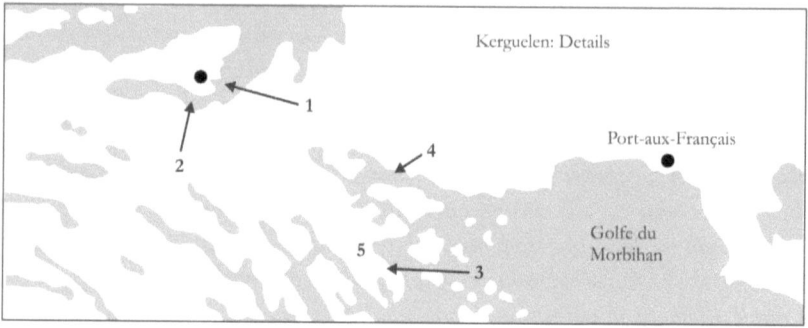

Kerguelen: Details

Port-aux-Français

Golfe du Morbihan

1) Gazellehafen / Port Couvreux
2) Gazelle-Bucht und Gazelle-Fjord
3) Deutsche Beobachtungsstation von 1901 - 1903
4) Karl Luyken-Fjord
5) Halbinsel Gauss / Presqu ile du Gaus

© Horst Geerken *(keine detailgetreue und nicht maßstäbliche Zeichnung)*

Ill. 86
Map of the areas on the Kerguelen Islands visited by the expeditions and the German Navy

Ill. 87
The German scientific observation station set up by the expedition of 1901-1903 in summer

---

1   www.familie-luyken.de

When the auxiliary cruisers *Pinguin* and *Adjutant* arrived at the secret Kerguelen base on the 13th of March 1941 to exchange material and repair the ships, they were therefore able to rely on detailed maps and meteorological information. In the fjord which cuts between towering cliffs into the interior of the island, they met the auxiliary cruiser *Komet*. The entrance to the harbour is concealed and very difficult to find and the harbour itself and the fjord are protected from the strong westerly winds by the high cliffs to the west. After exchanging fuel, provisions, materials and letters to and from home the *Komet* left the next day, the 14th of March 1941.

The *Komet* (previously a freighter, the *Ems*) was the only German ship that, in July 1940, before the Germans attacked Russia, reached the Pacific through the North-East Passage along the northern coast of Siberia with the help of Soviet icebreakers. After her first combat mission – an amazing 516 days – she returned safely to her home port of Hamburg.

In Gazelle Bay the *Adjutant* was converted into a minelayer and the *Pinguin*'s hull was scraped clean of algae and crustacea. An Arado Ar-196 seaplane which had been carried in parts was reassembled. To the great joy of the crews, the supply ship *Alstertor* also arrived at the "Kerguelen Naval Station" with post from home and fresh vegetables.[1]

During the work on the *Pinguin* one of the sailors, Bernhard Herrmann, suffered a fatal accident. He was buried on the island. This, the most southerly German war grave, is still maintained on its isolated island by France at the cost of the Federal German Republic.

After they had filled their tanks with fresh water from a nearby stream, the *Pinguin* and the *Adjutant* left on the 25th of March 1941. The *Pinguin* sailed disguised as the Norwegian freighter *Tamerlane*, accompanied by the *Adjutant,* whose mission was to mine the port of Karachi, then in British India.

The *Tamerlane*, ex *Pinguin,* continued to capture spoils, since the Arado seaplane made it possible to see enemy shipping much earlier, and the *Adjutant* also fanned out and kept a look out. South of the Seychelles the *Tamerlane* sank the British freighter *Empire Light*, capturing 70 British sailors. However, sightings of British shipping decreased considerably since the British had now changed the route for merchant traffic to run along the coast near the British bases.

Another British freighter with a cargo of military equipment, the *Clan Buchanan*, was captured and sunk. 110 British seamen were taken on board the *Tamerlane*. Before the sinking the *Clan Buchanan*'s radio operator managed to send off a distress signal which was received by two British stations. The British Navy in the area was put on alert.

1   Brennecke, *Pinguin*, pp. 225ff

En route from the Persian Gulf to Mozambique the *Tamerlane* sighted the British tanker *British Emperor*. Since she did not obey the order to heave to, the bridge and the wheelhouse were destroyed in a short gun battle – however, the radio operator managed to get off a distress signal. The *British Emperor* caught fire. The crew took to the sea and were rescued by the *Tamerlane*'s lifeboats. The *Tamerlane* sank the burning tanker with a torpedo and set off towards the south east.

The British Navy had increased its activity in the Indian Ocean. The British cruiser *HMS Cornwall*, which was cruising about 500 nautical miles south of the *Tamerlane*, received the *British Emperor*'s distress signal and sailed at full speed towards the *Tamerlane*. This led to a gun battle on the 8th of May 1941, in which the *Tamerlane* at first had the advantage, because several hits damaged the *Cornwall*'s electrical and telephone systems. The *HMS Cornwall* escaped out of range of the *Tamerlane*'s guns to repair the damage.

In the second fight the heavy cruiser *HMS Cornwall* had the advantage. The *Tamerlane* caught fire. Captain Krüder had the lifeboats for the prisoners and his crew launched. Shortly afterwards a shell hit the bridge, and then another one landed in the mine storage area. 150 high-explosive mines tore the *Tamerlane* into thousands of pieces. In a few seconds, she vanished from the surface. The British crew reported that the explosion of the mines caused a jet of flame about 3,000 metres high, like a volcanic eruption.[1]

The *HMS Cornwall* rescued 83 survivors from the *Tamerlane*, 60 German crewmen, 8 British officers and 18 Indians. Now the Germans were the prisoners, and the British and Indians had their freedom.

214 British and Indian prisoners were lost. Most of the officers, including Captain Krüder, were not among the survivors. 555 mostly young seamen went to a watery grave in the Indian Ocean.

Speaking to the German officers, the commander of the *HMS Cornwall*, Captain P. C. W. Mainwaring, expressed his respect for them and Captain Krüder:

You have done the British Empire a great deal of harm. But you have always given us a fair, clean fight. We also know that Captain Krüder did everything he could to avoid unnecessary bloodshed. We also know, from a rescued naval officer, that he treated his prisoners well. I regard it as my duty to thank him and you for that.[2]

During her eleven months at sea the *Pinguin* had travelled almost 110,000 kilometres and sunk or captured a total of 33 ships. She was the German

---

1   Ibid., p. 248
2   Ibid., p. 254

Navy's most successful auxiliary cruiser, but also the first to be sunk by the Allies. Captain Krüder was posthumously awarded oak leaves to his Knight's Cross for his outstanding achievements.

During the battle with the *HMS Cornwall* the *Adjutant* managed to escape. Since the area near India was becoming extremely dangerous for German ships, she was posted to a new field of operations. She was refuelled, provisioned and provided with mines by the auxiliary cruiser *Komet*, though her only weapon was an old pre-World-War-One gun on the forecastle, and then ordered to New Zealand as an auxiliary minelayer. There she laid mines outside the ports of Lyttelton and Wellington and in the Cook Strait and returned safely to the *Komet* in the Indian Ocean.

But what happened to the heavy cruiser *HMS Cornwall*? After a period in dock she operated once more in the Indian Ocean between Colombo and the Sunda Strait. Only a few months after sinking the *Pinguin/Tamerlane* she was sunk, together with her sister-ship *HMS Dorsetshire* on the 5th of April 1942 by a Japanese air attack south of Colombo. 1,122 of the 1,546-man crew were saved. The German prisoners had already been landed safely in Port Victoria on the Seychelles island of Mahé.

British superiority in the Indian Ocean was only lost for a short while. When the Japanese lost the Battle of Midway in the Pacific at the beginning of June 1942, the tables turned in favour of the Allies.

There were other German ships that sailed to Australia and New Zealand and even further east, such as the auxiliary cruisers *Komet* and *Orion*. The *Orion* was the first German warship to operate in Australian waters: off Brisbane, around Tasmania, in the Great Australian Bight in the south of the continent, off Albany in Western Australia and off the North Island of New Zealand. She sank the British merchant ship *Turakina* south of Tasmania on the 15th of August 1940.

Both the *Komet* and the *Orion* operated in the waters of Micronesia in the Pacific off the island of Nauru near the Equator which had been annexed by the German Empire in 1888 "for the protection of German seafarers". Around 1900 the Germans discovered vast deposits of phosphates on the island. After the First World War Nauru became an Australian protectorate and the phosphate deposits were mined by Britain, Australia and New Zealand. All three countries made massive profits – the native population remained poor.

The *Komet* and the *Orion* sank several British and Australian phosphate-carriers on the Pacific near Nauru. Between the 6th and the 8th and again on the 27th of December 1940 they bombarded the port of Nauru. The phosphate loading gear, the oil tanks and other port facilities were destroyed. The consequences for the Australian economy were drastic, since it took months to restore export of phosphate. In 1968 Nauru broke away from Australia to become an independent republic.

The *Komet* and the *Orion* had over 500 Australian and British prisoners on board from the ships they had sunk. Since this meant that supplies on board were used up more quickly than planned, they sailed to the island of Emirau (or Emira) in the Bismarck Archipelago in New Guinea and released the prisoners. They were taken to Brisbane by the Australian Navy soon afterwards.

The auxiliary cruiser *Atlantis* under the command of Captain Bernhard Rogge operated all over the world. In the South Pacific she cruised between New Zealand and the French Polynesian Society Islands. When they reached the remote Tuamotu Archipelago, Captain Rogge allowed his men a short respite on land after so many months at sea.

The *Atlantis* also docked at a small island off Pitcairn Island. Pitcairn is famous because it was settled by Fletcher Christian and his fellow mutineers from the *HMS Bounty*, together with the wives they had acquired on Tahiti, in 1789. The Pitcairns were annexed as a British colony in 1838. When the *Atlantis* arrived, there were about 200 inhabitants on Pitcairn. The crew had to be very careful not to be discovered, as there was a British radio-observation post there.

On the 22nd of November 1941 the long voyage of the *Atlantis* came to an end in an operation in the South Atlantic. After 622 days and 190,000 kilometres at sea, this was the longest voyage by an auxiliary cruiser. In that time she had captured or sunk 22 Allied ships. Now she was attacked by the British cruiser *HMS Devonshire* and severely damaged. One man was killed in the attack. The next day the captain ordered the *Atlantis* to be scuttled. The surviving 305 crew members were taken on board the U 126 and transferred two days later to the supply ship *Python*, a former refrigerator ship used for transporting bananas by the Hamburg shipping line Laeisz.

Only a few days later the *Python* suffered the same fate. She was discovered west of St Helena by the *Dorsetshire* on the 1st of December 1941 and came under fire. Eleven of the crew were killed. The *Python* also had to be scuttled, and now there were several hundred men in the lifeboats, in inflatable boats and in the water – not just the crews of the two ships, but also sailors from captured ships. The *Dorsetshire* sighted German U-boats nearby, and so left the scene of the attack without doing anything for the men in the water.

German Naval High Command organised a major rescue operation. Fortunately there were several German and Italian submarines in the vicinity. The U 68, U-A, U 129, U 124 and the Italian *Luigi Torelli* (which later took Heinrich Foders and the *Würzburg* radar equipment to the "Southern Region"), *Enrico Tazzoli* and *Guiseppe Finzi* managed to take all the survivors on board and take them safely to St Nazaire on the French west coast.

The last German auxiliary cruiser to operate in Australian waters was the *Michel*, which left Yokohama in May 1943 and operated north west of Perth. In June 1943 she sank two tankers which were on the way from Fremantle to the Middle East, killing 47 seamen and passengers. The survivors were taken on board. Thereafter she moved her sphere of operation to the Pacific.[1]

The first submarines to operate in Australian waters were Japanese: the I-10 and I-21 sank six enemy vessels off the east coast of Australia between January and the end of February 1943. In March 1943 the I-6 laid acoustic mines newly developed in Germany outside the port of Brisbane.

German U-boats operating in what was for them unknown territory near Australia and New Zealand received their orders directly from Admiral Dönitz in Germany by radio telegram. Three U-boats were equipped in Java for longer Australian operations: U 862 in Batavia, U 168 and U 537 in Surabaya.

U 537 under Lieutenant Peter Schrewe sailed from Batavia for Surabaya on the 1st of October 1944. There she was prepared for operations off Australia. On 9th of November 1944 she left Surabaya heading for Australia, intending to sail through the narrows of the Selat Bali (only 2.4 kilometres wide) between Bali and Java into southern waters. But only a few nautical miles east of Surabaya the American submarine *USS Flounder* sank her with a torpedo. Her mission to Australia ended with the loss of all 58 of her crew.

We have already mentioned the second boat, the U 168, that was intended to be sent to operate off the Australian coast under the command of Lieutenant Helmut Pich. In the previous weeks Pich had, on two combat missions on Dutch East Indian waters, sunk three Allied vessels and damaged one. In Batavia the U 168 had to give one of its two propellers to the U 532 so that she could return to operations in the Indian Ocean as soon as possible. She then had to travel slowly to Surabaya with only one screw to have a new one, which had arrived shortly before, fitted. She was then to be fitted for operations in Australia together with the U 537.

The U 168 sailed on its relocation voyage from Batavia to Surabaya on the 5th of October 1944. There were 56 men on board, including the ship's me-

---

1   Sources for Auxiliary Cruiser operations:
     Deutsches U-Boot Museum, Cuxhafen-Altenbruch
     www.lexikon-der-wehrmacht.de
     Google: German auxiliary cruiser Pinguin and Pinguin 36
     Chronicle of the war at sea 1939 to 1945
     www.wikipedia: Axis naval activity in Australian waters

teorologist, Dr Balke and the Medical Office, Dr Wenzel. When sailing on the surface through the group of islands off Batavia known as Pulau Seribu (Thousand Islands) all German U-boats were ordered to have all personnel, except those steering the boats, on deck. Allied submarines often lurked among the many islands and coral reefs, and if the crew were on deck there was more chance of surviving a possible attack and swimming to a nearby island.

The dangers of the Pulau Seribu were passed without any problems and the boat then sailed eastwards along the north coast of Java. On the 6th of October 1944 the U 168 was already close to its destination in Surabaya, when it was totally unexpectedly hit in the bow by a torpedo. She sank to the bottom immediately – it was a depth of 45 metres. Some of the men in the bow had been killed or were cut off. In spite of the dangerous depth, Lieutenant Pich organised the ascent of the surviving crew without any oxygen equipment. 28 of them, half the crew, survived surfacing from that dangerous depth. The wreck of the U 168 was found in 2013, of which more later.

The Dutch submarine *Zwaardfis* [Swordfish] under Captain van Goosen had sent off a fan-shot of six torpedoes from a distance of about 900 metres – one of them hit and sank the U 168. In spite of the increasing bitterness of the war, Captain van Goosen acted humanely: against the orders of the Dutch Navy he took the surviving 28 Germans, including Lieutenant Pich, on board. The crew were handed over to Javanese coastal vessels and taken to land and freed. Lieutenant Pich and three other officers were kept and taken to the Dutch naval base in Fremantle. They were handed over to the Australian authorities as prisoners of war. Lieutenant Pich was released from captivity in 1947 and died in Germany on the 18th of March 1997.

As the crew of the *Zwaardfis* later confirmed, the U 168 was lost because of espionage. The Allies used particularly attractive young women with good linguistic skills (for money, of course) to approach the German submariners. Men naturally chat and boast in bed. In this way the Dutch discovered when the submarines were due to sail, what route they were taking and what their destination was. Once they had this information, all they had to do was lie in wait until the enemy came within torpedo range.

Since the other two "Australia submarines" were no longer there, the type IX D2 U 862 was the only one left for the Australia mission. She sailed far into the Pacific and sank a merchant ship off the coast of Australia. The U 862 was equipped with a new FuMo65 Hohentwiel radar system and so was relatively safe from air or sea attack. Unlike the majority of the U-boats operating in South East Asia, the history of the U 862 is documented from the laying of its keel to the time it was surrendered to the Allies by the Japanese. This is largely due to her commander, Captain Heinrich Timm, who survived the war and later occupied a leading position in the Federal German Navy. I would therefore like to summarise the U 862's history, even though it includes more than just its missions in Australia and New Zealand.

8 June 1943: launch of the 1,616 tonne long-range type IXD-2 U-boat by DESCHIMAG AG in Weser, registration number U 862. Interior fitting begins.

7 October 1943: U 862 is ready for service with a crew of 63. The commander was Captain Heinrich Timm. She had four bow and two stern torpedo tubes. After the German Navy decided in the summer of 1943 to deploy submarines to the Indian Ocean, the first group of Monsoon submarines arrived in South East Asia in September 1943.

2 May 1944: A second group of U-boats leaves Kiel heading for Penang and the Dutch East Indies. They include U 862 carrying a heavy cargo for Japan: several hundred bottles of mercury for detonators and batteries, bars of lead, steel, aluminium, unpolished optical glass; drawings, blueprints and models of new German weaponry. Captain Timm sails to various Norwegian ports. A leak is discovered in the fuel tanks and they sail to Narvik for repairs.

3 June1944: U 862 leaves Narvik, sails through the Denmark Strait and travels south down the West African coast

5 July 1944: In the South Atlantic U 862 sinks the American freighter *Robin Goodfellow* travelling from New York to Cape Town.

Early August 1944: U 862 sinks 4 Allied freighters in the Indian Ocean. During the voyage to Penang Timm is promoted to Corvette Captain.

20 August 1944: In the Strait of Mozambique U 862 is attacked by a twin-engined British Catalina flying boat. Radar enables her to shoot down the aircraft.

9 September 1944: After 99 days at sea U 862 arrives in Penang. Captain Timm and the crew are welcomed by Captain Dommes, commander in the "Southern Region" and of the Monsoon submarines in Penang (previously commander of the U 178), and Rear Admiral Jisaku Uozumi, commander of the Japanese naval base, with the German and Japanese national anthems.

11 September 1944: Timm invites Admiral Jisaku Uozumi and Commander Ariizumi Tatsunosuke and the officers of Japanese submarine I-8, which was in Penang at the time, on board U 862. This was followed by an invitation to view I-8.

12 September 1944: U 862 left Penang heading for Singapore through the Strait of Malacca. In the Strait she is escorted for safety by one of the Penang Arado flying boats, which also took Captain Dommes to Singapore. U 862 arrived in the naval port of Seletar in Singapore. The boat is dry-docked for an overhaul. The mercury and other cargo were unloaded. She is loaded with molybdenum and tungsten for Batavia in transit to Germany.

19 September 1944: Timm was awarded the Knight's Cross in a radio telegram from Berlin. 50 crew members were awarded the Iron Cross Class I or II. Timm received the first instructions for his Australian mission from Dönitz. He flew from Singapore to Batavia and Surabaya for discussions with German and Japanese officers, the main purpose of which was to obtain Japanese naval intelligence about trade routes and main centres of merchant shipping in Australian waters. The result was useless. Timm wrote in his diary: *I flew there in a Japanese aircraft. But I discovered nothing at all from the fleet there. The Japanese don't like telling you anything anyway. They smiled. They were very friendly, but they said nothing. There was a Captain there, Fudjy [correctly: Fuja,] with a beard like Wilhelm II's. He invited us to have a beer, and we had to pay the whole bill...*[1] After Timm met with nothing but timorous caginess from the Japanese Navy, it became obvious to him that he would have to rely on his own instinct and experience in this mission in unknown territory.

27 October 1944: British B-24 bombers mined the seaway to Penang in the Strait of Malacca, making it considerably more dangerous for submarines to sail in and out.

November 1944: Penang was attacked several times by the Allies. The German U-boats were transferred to Batavia and the Japanese submarines to Surabaya.

5 November 1944: U 862 left Singapore for Batavia

7 November 1944: U 862 moored in the outer harbour intended for the Monsoon boats in Batavia. The following day she was piloted into the main harbour by Captain Kandeler, commander of the German base in Batavia.

18 November 1944: U 862 left Batavia through the Sunda Strait for a 90-day mission in Australian and New Zealand waters. It was the only combat mission carried out by a German submarine in the Pacific during the Second World War. Timm sailed along the west coast of Australia. Near the most south-westerly point of Australia, Cape Leeuwin, his radar showed strong signals of enemy presence and so he headed far to the south.

---

1   Brennecke, *Haie im Paradies*, p.179

9 December 1944: The U 862 had been near the Port of Adelaide and the Kangaroo Islands for several days without sighting a worthwhile target. He finally sighted the Greek tanker *Illios* south of Adelaide close to the coast of Tasmania. As U 862 made to attack, the strong phosphorescence revealed her bow wave. Inhabitants of Tasmania informed the Australian Navy. When an Australian bomber arrived, U 862 dived and left the area. She was discovered again south of Tasmania and had to dive once more.

24 December 1944: U 862 rounded the southern tip of Tasmania and sailed north along the coast of New South Wales.

25 December 1944: U 862 sank the American Liberty Ship *Robert J. Walker* off the coast of New South Wales with two torpedoes, the only ship sunk by a German submarine in the Pacific during World War Two. Timm remained near Sydney for some time, but when he attempted to attack a large freighter, Australian aircraft appeared again. Because of this aerial surveillance Timm left the area and set course for New Zealand. The reason why U 862 found no suitable targets around Australia and the air surveillance was so intensive was simple: the British had captured an ENIGMA code machine as described before and cracked the German codes. The Australian forces were informed of U 862's plans and so the routes of allied merchant shipping were moved further south.[1] Since the successful attack on the *Robert J. Walker* had taken place at Christmas, they caught up on their Christmas celebrations on the way to New Zealand and also celebrated New Year. They probably played Christmas songs over the boat's loudspeakers: this would have been an exception, as Timm was a great fan of classical music and the only entertainment his crew normally received was piano concertos, sonatas and symphonies.

7 January 1945: She arrived at Cape Reinga at the northern tip of New Zealand.

12 January 1945: Timm cruised near the entrance to Auckland harbour but once again sighted no useful targets.

15 January 1945: In stormy seas Timm sailed to take up a position directly at the entrance to the small port of Gisborne in the north-east of North Island. Again no sensible targets. There were only small ships carrying wood in the port. They observed the evening activities in the small town through binoculars. One night later she tried her luck in Hawke's Bay, sailing right up to the port entrance at Napier on the east coast of North

---

1   Axis naval activity in Australien waters

Island. Once again there were no credible targets – there were only a few coastal freighters in the harbour. Near a bathing resort north of Napier, Timm stopped only a few hundred metres from the coast. The crew could see happy couples dancing in bright lantern-light on the terraces of the hotels. It was peaceful here, while in Germany the Allied bombs were raining down on the cities.

Operating off New Zealand, Captain Timm frequently came so close to land that U 862 could be seen by people on land with the naked eye, giving rise to all kinds of wild speculation and stories in New Zealand. For example, a farmer from Napier, Frank Steiner, claimed that his cows, which were in a meadow near the shore, had been milked during the night by someone unknown in January 1945. During the day he had sighted a U-boat near the meadow. This was attributed to the crew of U 862 wanting to improve their rations by a raid on land. The New Zealand Times reported on the incident in detail on the 18th of January 1994.

This adventure on land by the German U-boat crew was confirmed as a fact in a British veterans' magazine by the New Zealand Air Marshall Sir Rochford Hughes. It is still uncertain whether this whole story is simply a sailor's yarn: Captain Timm refused to confirm or deny the incident as long as he lived.

17 January 1945: On her way to Wellington, New Zealand's largest port U 862 received a command by radio to return to Batavia immediately. Timm later said of this: *If they had just said 'begin return voyage' I might have taken a bit more time, but the 'immediately' meant that I had to leave at once.*[1]

21 January 1945: U 862 rounded the South Island of New Zealand and set course for the Tasman Sea, where she had to battle with more than 10-metre waves.

6 February 1945: 250 nautical miles from Fremantle in Western Australia U 862 sank the American Liberty Ship *Peter Silvester* sailing from Melbourne to Colombo. This was the last attack made by a U-boat in Australian waters and the Indian Ocean before the German surrender.

14 February 1945: After her voyage round Australia and New Zealand U 862 returned through the Sunda Strait. She was escorted for the last few miles by an Arado flying boat and docked at Batavia. Captain Dommes, commander of the "Southern Region", and Captain Kandeler, commander of the Batavia base, held a big reception for Captain Timm and his crew to celebrate their safe return.

---

1   Brennecke, *Haie...*, p. 181

Only then did Timm discover the fate of the other two submarines intended for service off Australia and the reason why he had been ordered to return "immediately". Strong Allied forces were advancing southwards in south East Asia, and Bose's Indian National Army was retreating. If the Malay Peninsula – where the bases at Singapore and Penang were situated – had fallen, they would no longer have been able to contact the U 862 by radio. We will return to her subsequent fate later.[1]

1   Synopsis from the following sources:
     SENSUIKAN! IJN Submarine I-502: Tabular Record of Movement
     © 2001-2010 Bob Hackett & Sander Kingsepp, Revision 5
     Deutsches U-Boot Museum Cuxhafen-Altenbruch
     www.deutsches-u-boot-museum.com

35. Early Freedom Fighters and the Founding of PETA, Pembela Tanah Air

The origin of Indonesian nationalism coincides with the beginning of Dutch colonial rule. Over the course of the centuries the native economy was unbalanced by Dutch enterprises and the forced imposition of monocultures. The dissatisfaction of the indigenous population and their rejection of their colonial rulers grew from year to year. The words Independence and Freedom were spoken ever more loudly.

Tan Malaka, born 1894, was one of the outstanding national freedom fighters of the last century and a passionate Communist. Although he was awarded the title of National Hero by President Soekarno in 1963 he has sadly vanished from most Indonesian school history books as a result of the dogmatic anti-Communism that characterised the rule of the second President, Soeharto, who tried to claim for himself the laurels of independence.

With the help of his native village Tan Malaka studied in Medan on Sumatra and in the Netherlands, where he came into contact with Communist and Socialist ideas. In the 1920s, he was the leading light of the Dutch East Indian Communist Party and trade-union movement. He was elected first chairman of the PKI, the Communist Party of Indonesia, at the end of 1921. Communism had always attracted Asian people, and collective thinking and action is still a part of Asian culture. The dispossessed show a particular interest in Communism, while at the same time there is a great yearning for freedom.

Tan Malaka was the first to call the Dutch colonial government fascist. After they subjected Indonesian nationalists to ever greater reprisals after 1930, even right-wing Netherlanders like Mussert described their mode of government as fascist.[1]

Like everyone who fought for Indonesia's freedom he was cursed and persecuted by the Dutch and pursued from one hiding place to the next. He always managed to find refuge in the isolated and still quite unknown region of Bayah on the south coast of Java to the west of Pelabuhan Ratu. He devoted himself unselfishly with all his strength to getting rid of the Dutch and inarguably deserves great credit for his services to the cause of independence. However, his goal was a Communist Indonesia.

In 1922 he was exiled from Indonesia for his subversive activities, and went to Moscow and Berlin, where he sought out fellow left-wingers. Tan

---

1   See earlier in this book

Malaka was in Berlin from August until November 1922, where he met his fellow-countryman Darsono and made contact with the German Communist party. In 1927, with his help and the support of the Soviet Union, the "South Sea Communist Party" was founded, embracing the Dutch East Indies, Malaya, Siam and Indochina. The Soviet Union was hoping to make use of this to extend their sphere of influence in the region. After living in China, the Philippines, Siam, Burma, Malaya and Singapore, Tan Malaka returned home after twenty years' absence when the Japanese occupied the Dutch East Indies. By this time Soekarno had already allied himself with the Japanese and had a different philosophical view of the future of a free Indonesia from Tan Malaka's.

Tan Malaka's attitude to Soekarno was always critical. In his view, Soekarno and Mohamad Hatta were always too compliant and patient with the Dutch. According to the Dutch historian Harry Poeze, Tan Malaka was shot in the village of Selopanggung in East Java at the foot of Mount Gunung Wiliis on the 21st of February 1949 on the orders of Lieutenant Soekotjo[1] of the Indonesian Army. Now Tan Malaka is once more honoured and there are plans to erect a monument to him.[2]

Their exploitation of the East Indies made the Netherlands one of the richest colonial powers in the world. The profits all went home to Holland: in their view the colony was only there for the profit of the colonists with no regard for the native population. Schools, social security and humane treatment were all neglected. During the centuries of Dutch rule there were all kinds of excesses and crimes. On the plantations in Sumatra, Java and elsewhere the native coolies led a degrading existence as slaves without any human rights. The death rate among them was extraordinarily high as a result of exhaustion, disease and malnutrition. Abuse of power and violence by the plantation owners and overseers were the general rule. Soekarno and his fellow revolutionaries wanted to change this situation for ever, and so it was hardly surprising that their independence movement grew day by day. The more the Dutch tried to suppress the movement with extreme severity, the greater the population's resistance grew. The Indonesians saw that they now had the chance to be independent at last.

Many young educated people who fought for an end to colonial rule in all the countries of East Asia sought their salvation in Communism. Why? Communist ideas, like dispossessing the owners of wealth and property and

---

1   later Brigadier General and Mayor of Surabaya (not related to my friend Otty Soekojo)

2   Workshop Harry Poeze: *Tan Malaka, Left Wing Movement and the Indonesian Revolution*, 20.10.2010 and Jakarta Post, 17.02.2014, p. 6

land reform, as well as the removal of social abuses were tempting ideas for the dispossessed who had been exploited by white colonial rulers for centuries. Collective thinking and action as preached by Moscow was more in tune with Asian tradition and the Asian way of thinking than Western capitalism. In the West it is the amount of time that is valued, in the East it is its quality. In South East Asia the attitude to time and self is basically different from that in the West. There is no such thing as an ego in our sense. You are always a member of a family or a village community, and find your existence justified by fulfilling a specific function within them, an attitude to life not that distant from that of Communism.

After the Russian Revolution in 1917 countless young Asians attended the Moscow University of the Far East. Moscow used this to spread the seeds of Communism in oppressed countries and found many groups whose goal was independence under Communism. Soekarno said on many occasions: *The Communist Part was the only one that consistently opposed the Dutch.*

Soekarno and Hatta fought for many years to achieve Indonesian independence, spending a large proportion of their lives in Dutch prisons or in exile as a result. Now that the Japanese were freeing the imprisoned Indonesian Nationalists, Soekarno and Hatta could once more move freely around the country to spread their message of freedom and independence. In 1942, after 16 years of jail and deportation, Soekarno was at last a free man.

Some of the countries occupied by the Japanese in South East Asia were already on the way to independence with Japan's help. Soekarno, who had been chosen by the Japanese as his country's future leader, received the assurance that Indonesia too could prepare for independence. The Indonesian nationalist movement under Soekarno was not simply tolerated by Japan, but generously supported. Japan held to its idea of Asia for the Asians until the end of the war.

The Japanese began a period of fruitful collaboration with the nationalists around Soekarno and Hatta. They were both working towards freedom from colonialism and, with the help of an admittedly sparse native elite, began to create a rather precarious order. This shaky order was – as it was in the other occupied countries of the "Greater Asian Co-Prosperity Sphere" – continually under attack by the Communist underground movement, which was strongly supported by the USA, France and Britain, who hoped to use the resulting conflict to keep hold of their colonies.

Soekarno was intelligent enough to accept the Japanese occupation in order to be able to build up the country's inward strength and prepare for independence from the Netherlands. He did not regard the Japanese as liberators, but used them as a means to an end and entered into a tactical alliance with them. Shortly after the Japanese Army marched in, he said to his friend Waworunto:[1]

I know that they [Author's note: the Japanese] are fascists. But I also know that this is the end of Dutch imperialism. Things will happen exactly as I foretold: we will have to go through a period of Japanese occupation in order to gain unlimited and permanent independence thereafter.[2]

To prevent chaos the Japanese used Soekarno to keep the multifarious Indonesian people, with all their different ethnicities, languages and religions, together. Although Soekarno had been in prison or in exile for years, the people still remembered him. He was the only person who was known and accepted as leader in the whole giant archipelago. On the other hand, Soekarno also needed Japan in order to receive wide-ranging concessions under their protection.

At this time many politicians, especially from abroad, called Soekarno a collaborator. But Soekarno was just being clever enough to make concessions to the victorious Japanese to get closer to his own goal: preparing to meet the forthcoming return of the Dutch with his own army. The Japanese had already recruited young Indonesians for an Indonesian volunteer force, the *Heiho*. The Japanese propaganda apparatus persuaded these youths to fight for Japan and the "Greater Asian Co-Prosperity Sphere". Over 42,000 of them joined the *Heiho*, 25,000 from Java alone.[3] They were armed, and deployed mainly in Burma, Malaya, Borneo and New Guinea. The force was under Japanese command and fought against the Allies for the Japanese. However, Soekarno wanted an army of his own that would be under Indonesian command and defend the country after independence.

Soekarno got the Japanese government's agreement to prepare for an Indonesian government of which he should be the head. He put all his weight into the balance to receive the maximum concessions for his country from the Japanese and to promote the creation of an independent Indonesian national army.

Under the pretence of supporting the Japanese in their fight against the Allies, Soekarno persuaded the Japanese to allow him to recruit and train Indonesian volunteer militia forces. They were called PETA, *Pembela Tanah Air* (Defenders of the Homeland). The Japanese called them *Kyodo Boei Giyugun*. Soekarno put all his efforts into creating this organisation and led the Japanese to believe that PETA was also ready to fight the Allies. In real-

---

1   I was a friend of his son
2   Adams, *Sukarno*, p.156
3   http://oktorino.tripod.com/id48.html

ity, Soekarno was just waiting for the day when the Japanese troops would withdraw, leaving PETA in a position to deal with the anticipated and feared return of the Dutch. Soekarno's main aim was to use all means to prevent the Dutch from reconquering their rich colonial lands.

In order to create a force that would be capable of action as soon as possible, Soekarno flew to Saigon in 1943, to meet Marshal Terauchi, the Japanese Commander in Chief in the South Pacific. He wanted to get further concessions from the Japanese. He then flew on to Tokyo, where he was given a friendly welcome by the *Tenno*, the Japanese Emperor. A successful journey for Soekarno: he had achieved his medium-term goal. He could now create the national army, PETA, under his command.

In the "Southern Region" 500 million Asians were ruled by the Japanese and so Japan was glad to receive help from indigenous forces. Japan's own means were limited because the demands of army, navy and air force were continually growing. They too had to economise. If one looks at the occupation of the southern areas from a modern perspective, it was not just a matter of atrocities. Japan also did many good things for the benefit of the people they freed from colonial rule.

PETA was officially founded on the 3rd of October 1943 and the oath of allegiance from its Indonesian leaders was taken by the Japanese Lieutenant General Kumakichi Harada in the military base in Bogor on Java. PETA's motto was *Indonesia Akan Merdeka*, Indonesia will be free! The force's banner contained the Rising Sun, symbol of the Japanese Empire, and the Crescent Moon and Star, symbolic of Islam.

*Ill. 88
The PETA
banner*

A large number of Indonesian officers who later served in the regular Indonesian forces received their commissions from the Japanese occupying power. In order to make the force battle-worthy as soon as possible, Soekarno's voice could be heard increasingly frequently on the radio in the East Indies calling for new recruits to PETA. People from all levels of society thronged to this new volunteer army, which was equipped with Japanese weapons.

Ill. 89
A PETA roll call

PETA forces comprised 66 battalions on Java, 20 on Sumatra and 3 on Bali. Soekarno's forecast turned out to be correct. His army had to fight against the returning Dutch and their British allies from October 1945 onwards. Later, during nearly five years of struggle for independence, hundreds of thousands of volunteer freedom fighters formed the backbone of the Indonesian resistance. PETA was the foundation stone of today's Indonesian forces.

I received a great deal of information about PETA from my friends Wibowo and Daan Jahja, who sadly died far too early, my close and trusted colleagues for many years. They were members of PETA from the very beginning and served their country faithfully for five years. In the 1960s they introduced me to many of their fellow fighters.

I was frequently told by these eyewitnesses that Hitler had supported the freedom fighters during the Japanese occupation financially and with military supplies. German officers had even served in PETA as trainers. I followed up this information, and will report my findings in another chapter. Even today many Indonesians feel that Hitler's war in Europe and the German presence in Indonesian waters, but more particularly his invasion of the Netherlands, contributed decisively to the acceleration of Indonesian independence. Soekarno had forecast this development several years before the war. Japan's clearly more important role is mainly undervalued.

36. War Crimes at Sea

The Monsoon boat U 852 commanded by Lieutenant Heinz-Wilhelm Eck sailed from Kiel on the 18th of January heading for Penang and Batavia. On his way to South East Asia she sank the Greek freighter *Peleus*, under charter to the British Ministry of Transport, in the Indian Ocean on the 13th of March 1944. Two weeks later he sank the British ship *Dahomian* off Cape Town and then sailed on up the coast of East Africa. The sinking of the Greek freighter led to a tragic – and fortunately unique – incident. The war was becoming more cruel.

The Peleus had a crew of 35. Some of the survivors of the sinking ship clung on to bits of debris and managed to save themselves on life rafts that had come free as the ship went down. Because of the Laconia Incident (which I will briefly describe below) U-boats had been forbidden to pick up survivors. By now it was night time, and the U 852 sailed slowly among the wreckage and tried to sink the larger pieces of debris and the life rafts with machine guns. Since the life rafts were unsinkable, Eck gave the order to destroy them with hand grenades. When even the hand grenades and shots fired from the 20 mm anti-aircraft guns failed to have the desired effect, Eck gave up with this wild shooting an hour after midnight and sailed away in the direction of the Arabian sea.

What Eck did not know was that an officer of the watch and three sailors from the Peleus had survived the attack concealed behind pieces of debris. They had watched their comrades being slaughtered. 35 days later three survivors were picked up by a Portuguese ship – one survivor had not been strong enough for the strain and had died. Now the massacre was known.

The U 852 then operated off the coast of Somalia. On the 30th of April 1944 Eck sent off a long message to the control centre in Berlin which was intercepted by the British. Using automated radio direction finders the U 852's position was pinpointed. The Allies were well equipped to deal with enemy submarines in East African water. There were air bases in Aden, on the island of Diego Garcia and on the Addu Atoll in the Indian Ocean south of the Maldives. On the 2nd of May 1944 six RAF Wellington bombers from the base in Aden made a surprise attack on the U 852, dropping six depth charges. The attack was so quick that she had no time to defend herself or dive. She was seriously damaged, letting in water and with defective batteries. There was no way she could be saved. Eck decided to beach the

U 852 on the Somali coast. The crew could defend themselves against further air attack using the anti-aircraft guns.

When she grounded on the Somali coast the crew escaped to the land. The submarine was supposed to be destroyed, but the charges did not detonate properly. The British attacked again and killed seven of the crew. 56 of the crew, including the commander and the officers, were captured by the British. The U 852's log also fell into British hands, providing evidence that she had sunk the Peleus and that Eck was responsible for the massacre.

On the 17th of October 1945 the trial of five accused from the U 852 opened. All five were found guilty of war crimes. On the 30th of November 1945 Lieutenant Eck, his 2nd Officer and the Medical Officer were shot. The Chief Engineer and a seaman received long prison sentences. Of all German U-boat commanders, Lieutenant Eck was the one who took the order not to rescue enemy survivors all too literally.[1]

There had previously been a similar incident in the Atlantic, where the Americans were the guilty party: the American destroyer *USS Roper* commanded by Hamilton W. Howe sank the U 85, commanded by Lieutenant Eberhard Greger, west of Florida on the night of the 14th of April 1942. About 40 members of the crew managed to escape the sinking submarine. Captain Howe decided not to save them and dropped 11 depth charges among the swimming survivors. At daybreak the British trawler *HMS Bedfordshire* recovered 29 bodies. Eleven crewmen, some of them severely injured, survived. However, Captain Howe was not called to account for this action. Only three weeks later his ship was sunk by the U 558.[2]

The American submarine *USS Wahoo,* commanded by Dudley Walker Morton, committed a similar war crime off Wewak, in the north of New Guinea. Wewak was the biggest Japanese air base in New Guinea. As a small convoy with attendant supply ships approached the port, two transporters, the *Buyo Maru* and the *Fukuei Maru* were sunk by torpedoes from the *Wahoo*. Over 100 survivors of the *Buyo Maru* were in lifeboats, mostly Indian PoWs from the 2nd Battalions of the 16th Punjab Regiment from Singapore. Captain Morton ordered the lifeboats to be sunk and survivors swimming in the sea to be killed. Although Morton recorded this action in his log, there was never any charge against him for the massacre.[3]

A far more barbarous incident, in which thousands of helpless survivors were literally slaughtered, occurred in 1943 in the Bismarck Sea near New Guinea. A Japanese convoy consisting of 8 destroyers and 8 troop transport-

1   Cameron, *Peleus*
2   Gannon, *Operation Paukenschlag*, pp. 393 f. and 475
3   http://de.wikipedia.org/wiki/USS_Wahoo_SS-238

ers was on its way from Rabaul to Lae, a large town in the south of New Guinea on the 2nd of March 1943. The convoy was discovered, and was attacked several times over the next two days by over 100 bombers and 54 fighters of the US and Australian air forces. All eight troop transports and four destroyers were sunk about 100 kilometres from Finschhafen.[1] Thousands of survivors took to the lifeboats or floated in the sea in their life-jackets. Following orders from US Naval High Command all survivors of sunk vessels were to be liquidated. All day long US and Australian aircraft and patrol boats hunted down the Japanese soldiers and sailors who were swimming in the water. The Japanese claim that 7,000 men were killed in this way, while an Australian memorial gives a figure – almost definitely understated – of 2,890. The true death toll was probably somewhere in the middle. It is however indisputable that this massacre of survivors, the biggest in World War Two, was a breach of the Geneva Convention. No one in the USA or Australia was prosecuted for this war crime.[2]

I would now like to return to Hitler's "Laconia Order" which was passed on to all U-boat commanders by Dönitz at the end of 1942: all U-boats were forbidden to rescue or take on board any survivors from enemy ships that were sunk. This was a consequence of the sinking of the British passenger ship, *RMS Laconia*. The U 156 had already successfully completed three combat missions in the western Atlantic, the Caribbean and near the Panama Canal. She had sunk 16 Allied ships, including 5 tankers, and damaged several more. On her fourth mission she was patrolling off the coast of West Africa under the command of Captain Werner Hartenstein as part of the *Gruppe Eisbär* [Polar Bear Group] consisting of four combat submarines and a supply submarine.

The U 156 had already sunk a British ship off the West African coast when she came upon the British troop transporter *RMS Laconia,* which was on her way from Suez in Egypt to Liverpool. For safety reasons she had chosen to avoid the more direct route across the Mediterranean and sail round the tip of Africa. After four weeks at sea she was already past Cape Town. There were 2,700 on board, 340 of them passengers, many of them women and children fleeing the Afrika Korps' advance into Egypt. There were British and Polish soldiers as well, and 1,800 Italian PoWs from North Africa.

---

1   the natural harbour on the north coast of Papua-New Guinea was discovered in 884 by the German explorer Otto Finsch. During the German colonial era Finschhafen was very important.

2   Samuel Eliot Morison, *Geschichte der Marineoperationen der USA im Zweiten Weltkrieg,* Band 6;
Stahmer, *Japans Niederlage,* p. 151;
wikipedia.org/Schlacht_in_der_Bismarcksee

As the *Laconia,* with her 14 guns, was an armed troop transporter and not marked as a passenger ship carrying prisoners of war, the U 156 sunk her with two torpedoes.

When Hartenstein surfaced he saw 2,700 people struggling for their lives in the water. He then began an unprecedented rescue action, the greatest of World War Two. He informed Admiral Dönitz by radio, and Dönitz showed the courage to behave humanely and ordered other German and Italian ships to the site. Hartenstein also broadcast the following message on the official distress frequency:

If any ship will assist the ship-wrecked Laconia crew, I will not attack, providing I am not being attacked by ship or air force. I picked up 193 men. 4.53 South, 11.26 West. – German submarine.

U 156 remained at the site until other German U-boats and Italian submarines arrived. In the meanwhile, she had picked up 200 survivors and taken them aboard below deck, including a number of women, and was towing four lifeboats with several hundred others. Three other U-boats had each taken a similar number on board or in inflatables. The convoy sailed towards the African coast. On the deck of the U 156 there was a four square metre red cross. There were now more than 1,500 people in assumed safety, including many British women and children. Warships of the French fleet were to meet the convoy at sea and collect the survivors.

The U 156's radio message requesting help was received by the British in Freetown, and since they did not feel it was their responsibility, passed on to the American base on Ascension island. The message was not taken seriously there either, and they intended to send out a single aircraft the next day to look for this dubious German U-boat at the co-ordinates she had supplied. They suspected a trap.

On the morning of the 16ᵗʰ of September 1942 an American Liberator bomber sighted the convoy and, even though it was clearly marked with the red cross, attacked the U-boats and the survivors with depth charges. One of the lifeboats being towed by the U 156 was hit and the submarine herself damaged. Captain Hartenstein and the other U-boat commanders ordered the lines to the lifeboats to be cut and crash-dived. The survivors who had been on the decks of the U-boats and those in the lifeboats were once again alone in the open sea. The American operational controller who ordered the bombing later said in his defence, *"A German submarine is a German submarine. We make no distinction.* He showed no concern whatsoever for the Allied survivors. In international law an attack on defenceless survivors is condemned – as happened with Eck and the U 852. Nothing happened to the American controller.

When Lieutenant Hartenstein informed Admiral Dönitz of the incident by radio, he and the other U-boat commanders were ordered to break off the rescue mission immediately. Many of the *Laconia* survivors drowned. About 500 of them, who had been below decks on the submarines were handed over to a French ship the same day. Other survivors attempted to reach the African coast in the lifeboats. Inexplicably, no British or American rescue attempts were made in this area. Only two of the lifeboats reached the coast, one of them spending 39 days at sea. Only four people reached the coast alive: more than 2,000 were killed in this disaster. The war was going from bad to worse. After this incident Hitler gave Dönitz the "Laconia Order" forbidding the rescue of survivors. For his rescue action, however, Hartenstein was awarded the Knight's Cross by Hitler on the very same day.

Dönitz was charged at the Nuremberg Trials because of this order. The court felt unable to condemn him on this point as the US government had issued similar orders regarding Japanese survivors in the Pacific.[1]

There were also many war crimes on the Japanese side. I will cite just two examples of actions by a Japanese submarine cruiser under the command of Captain Ariizumi Tatsunosuke: the Dutch ship *SS Tjisalak* was actually a passenger ship that was armed with four guns and deployed by the Allies as a freighter between Australia and Ceylon. She was carrying cargo, 80 Dutch, British and Chinese crewmen, ten British soldiers to man the guns and 27 passengers. On the 26th of March 1944 the ship was west of Perth, having sailed from Melbourne. In the early hours of the morning she was attacked by the Japanese submarine I-8 and sunk with a single torpedo. 105 people survived the attack, and were taken onto the deck of the I-8. One after another, the survivors of the *SS Tjisalak* were beheaded with a Samurai sword or thrown into the sea with bound hands and feet. Miraculously, four sailors survived the massacre and were picked up after 30 hours by the American Liberty Ship *SS James O. Wilder*.

The same commander committed a similar crime only two months later. The US Liberty Ship *SS Jean Nicolet* was sailing from Fremantle to Colombo with a cargo of machines, lorries, landing craft and other military equipment. There was a crew of 41, 28 marines to man the guns and 31 passengers. On the 2nd of June 1944 the I-8 sank the *SS Jean Nicolet* with two torpedoes. All 100 people on board were able to take to the lifeboats. Before the ship sank, the radio officer managed to send a distress signal giving the

---

1   Peilard, *The Laconia Affair*
     www.wikipedia.org/Laconia-Befehl

ship's position which was received in Colombo, where an aircraft was immediately dispatched to the site of the sinking.

All the survivors were ordered onto the deck of the I-8 and slaughtered one by one. When the British aircraft from Colombo approached, the I-8 had to abandon the massacre and crash dive. There were now 23 survivors swimming among the corpses. The aircraft dropped an inflatable dinghy and 30 hours later they were all rescued by the British trawler *HMS Hoxa*.

Captain Tatsunosuke returned to Japan in his submarine cruiser after a 64-day operation in August 1945. He was only one day's sailing away from the naval base in Yokosuka when he was informed of Japan's capitulation. He committed suicide on his ship because he was sure that he would be prosecuted by the Allies for his war-crimes at sea. After the war this captain was accused of yet more war crimes: he had sunk 15 Allied ships, none of which had left any survivors. An informant in the crew of the I-8 denounced three other crew members. All three were condemned to death by a US court martial.

After the war almost all Japanese submarine commanders were classified and sentenced by the Americans as Class B war criminals, including 5 admirals, 4 captains, 2 commanders and many other officers and crewmen. They were given prison sentences of between seven and twenty years.

37. Sarangan: A German School on Java

Now, in the middle of the war after the Japanese conquest of the Dutch East Indies, the German state began to take an increased interest in the Germans there. The documents about Walther Hewel in the Berlin archive of the Foreign Ministry show that he took serious action to secure the well-being of those who had been in the Dutch internment camps – mainly women and children – and had now been freed.

In a large number of letters Hewel had previously shown his interest in helping to find missing family members. We can therefore assume that he also intervened in favour of German residents during the Japanese occupation: unfortunately we have no documentary evidence for Hewel's activity during this period.

During his time on Java Hewel had visited the mountain resort of Sarangan, and was therefore aware of the favourable climate and other resources available there. He had met Captain Kandeler, later commander of the Batavia naval base, there in 1935. Presumably the initiative to build a German school in Sarangan was in some way inspired by Hewel and Kandeler.

Ill. 90
German women and children leaving the Dutch internment camp in Batavia carrying the Swastika and the Japanese flag, 1942. Even the tiniest children raise their right arms in the Hitler salute

After the German invasion of the Netherlands in May 1940, schooling for German children had been forbidden in the Dutch East Indies. But now that the Japanese were in charge this was to be rectified. The Germans put pressure on the Japanese to collect all German children of school age together in a boarding school so that they could be educated as "good Germans" in the service of the fatherland.

For some reason the original intention was to separate the children from their mothers. Was this to be like the evacuation of children to the countryside in Germany, with the purpose here of removing them from their mothers' influence? Mothers and children alike protested: the mothers because their husbands had already been taken away and they did not want to lose their children too in these uncertain times; the children because they simply did not want to go to school. Since the internments began two years earlier they had had no schooling on Dutch orders. They had become used to unlimited freedom and did not want to submit to the discipline of a strict school system. The boys had run wild, the girls had helped their mothers in the household. The mothers prevailed: at the end of 1942 all mothers were ordered to move to Sarangan with their children. Sarangan was to be very important for the Germans in Indonesia from 1942 until the end of the independence struggle in 1949.

The picturesque and peaceful village of Sarangan lies at an altitude of 1,400 metres at the foot of the volcano Gunung Lawu on the border between central and eastern Java. It was a small mountain resort for Dutch colonial officials with small family hotels, guest houses and holiday homes. Sarangan, on the shore of Lake Telaga Pasir had a delightful, cool climate. At the end of 1942 this sleepy village was transformed into an anthill of activity and began to fill with life. Today there is a steep road up to Sarangan, but at that time the last few hundred metres had to be covered on foot or on one of the ponies which were always there waiting with their grooms.

It was up here that German mothers and children from all over the vast archipelago that was the Dutch East Indies now met. They were overwhelmed by the sight of Sarangan and its surroundings. There was a glorious view of the 3,200 metre volcano whose tongues of lava ran deep down into the valley; the hills around Sarangan were covered in lush tropical vegetation and the cool waters of Lake Telaga Pasir looked most inviting. After the chaos, humiliation by the Dutch and uncertainty of recent months this was like paradise. Many old friends and acquaintances met again. There were even a doctor and a nurse in the community. The mothers, together with children who had not reached school age, were housed in the little hotels and guest houses scattered around the lake, while the school-age boys and girls were given places in separate boarding schools.

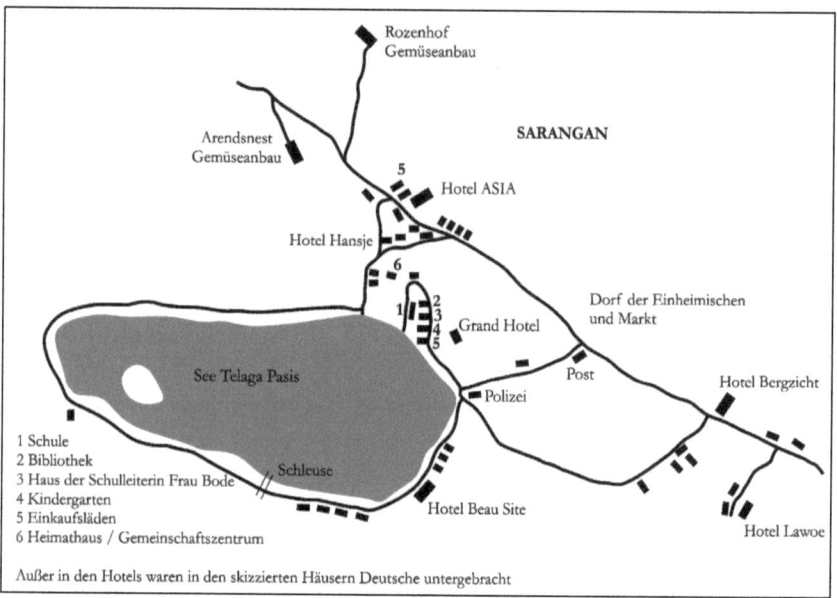

Ill. 91

Sketch plan of the layout of Sarangan

By the beginning of 1943 over 350 Germans, including 175 schoolchildren, had arrived at Sarangan from all over the colony. They were mostly mothers with children, although some children were alone. The children were divided into classes according to what they knew and teaching soon began. The school with its sports field was right next to the lake. Several classrooms were in simple huts made of the local woven bamboo, intended by the Japanese to house Dutch internees: these huts sat oddly with the spruce, well-kept houses in the village.

It was a purely German school with nine classes from elementary to middle school, the biggest German school in East Asia. The German state provided financial support for the school through the German Embassy in Tokyo and the Consulate in Batavia. *Reichs* German mothers were given an allowance, but the *Volks* Germans were left empty-handed. Children of Indos with a German passport were also allowed to attend the school

Above Sarangan there was extensive pasture and cowsheds where German farmers produced milk which was distributed to mothers with small children. Vegetable gardens were also created in terraces along the slopes to provide the Germans with potatoes, carrots, tomatoes, cabbage, onions and salad. There was plenty of cheap fruit available in the village anyway. They produced their own meat and sausages, and a German baker made the bread. There was a pastry shop for tarts, cakes and patisserie. No distinction was made between *Reichs* and *Volks* Germans in the distribution of food. They all helped each other and no one in Sarangan went hungry. Gardeners in the surrounding areas were encouraged to create more vegetable gardens. Their produce was bought from them at fixed prices, and went to the base at Surabaya as well.

The school insisted on discipline, just like schools back in Germany. The pupils marched around the lake to lively tunes: the German youth movements of the *Jungvolk* and the Hitler Youth had arrived in the East Indies.

The Japanese set up a youth organisation like the Hitler Youth for the indigenous young people, the *Badan Pemuda Asia Raya,* the Great Asia Youth Corps, a fanatical, tightly organised troop of young people. Instead of a uniform with shoulder badges and emblems they wore shorts and shirts. The younger members were armed with sticks and the older ones with spades. The Great Asia Youth Corps later played an important role in the fight for independence.

Before they could begin instruction in other subjects, the German schoolchildren had to be taught perfect German. Most of the boys and girls born in the archipelago spoke German mixed with Dutch and Malay words. Since the school was under Japanese patronage, Japanese became the first foreign language from the beginning. The German School was now the *Doitzu Gakko.* A great deal was demanded of the children linguistically. As well as German and Japanese, they were taught English, French and Latin. It was intended that the German School should be equated with the Javanese system, and so Malay was added to the curriculum from the third class onwards. They were also taught history, biology, geometry, physics, chemistry, religion etc.[1] Some of the children were only able to write in the German *Sütterlin*-script that had been in use since the 16th century. Now everyone was made to use the Latin script that had been introduced in Germany in 1941.

The Japanese were closely involved in curriculum and other planning for the school. There was instruction on 6 days a week, sport on 3 days a week. Since there were no cinema or other entertainment facilities, music, games and yoga groups were gradually set up.

On Hitler's 53rd birthday, the 20th of April 1943, the Sarangan German School was officially opened with great pomp and ceremony in the presence of Japanese and German guests of honour. The German representatives had

---

1   Zöllner, *Sarangan*, p. 25
     Information from eyewitness Hardy Zöllner

travelled from Batavia and Tokyo. There were a lot of speeches about final victory, flags were raised and patriotic songs were sung. German boys and girls no longer marched around the lake in step to "one, two, three, four": now it was the Japanese *itchi, ni, sang, shi*. Instead of *Sieg Heil* they now shouted *Kooa sai banzai!* The inauguration of the German School ended with a big sports festival.

The first Principal was Frau Braun, but she soon had to leave Sarangan because she was Jewish. Her successor was Frau Lydia Bode. She had lived for many years with her husband, a missionary from the Rhenish Mission, among the Bataks on Lake Toba in Sumatra. During this time she had translated the New Testament into Batak. Her husband was lost in the sinking of the *Van Imhoff*.

Initially the staff consisted of one male and 15 female teachers. The only male was a German who had lived in Japan for many years and taught German at the university there. Later there was also a Japanese male teacher for the obligatory Japanese language tuition. Sport classes were given by a physiotherapist whose husband, a doctor and Dutch citizen with German roots, had been interned by the Japanese. Few of the female teachers were formally trained. Mothers without any experience were given introductory instruction. In the course of time the number of pupils increased to over 180.[1] Teaching materials like books, exercise books and writing materials did not arrive until some months later by submarine from Germany. They were unloaded in Batavia and then sent on to Sarangan.

A kindergarten was opened for children below school age. Far from the terrible war in Europe the Germans lived as if they were at peace in a self-governing German island in exotic surroundings. There was no orderly schooling back home in Germany because of the daily Allied air raids, and city children were being evacuated to the countryside.

In Sarangan however, school life ran its regular course. The children got up at 6 o'clock in the morning. After their morning exercises they breakfasted in the refectory and then marched in step to school singing hiking songs. For the native population this was a strange sight. Hitler's birthday on the 20th of April and the Midsummer festival the Hitler Youth liked so much were always major events. The children's birthdays were celebrated with flowers, songs and home-made cakes, as was the First of May, Labour Day, with dancing round the maypole. Harvest festival was celebrated on the 1st of October although there were harvests all year round in Sarangan. Shortly after Hitler's birthday they now celebrated Emperor Hirohito's birthday on the 29th of April. The curious natives watched all these festivities over

---

1   Keppner, *Airmolang*, pp. 214 ff

the fence: there were so many festivals in Sarangan and on the German bases now that those of both countries were observed.

The Japanese flag flew over Sarangan next to the Swastika every day, but on Hirohito's birthday Sarangan was transformed into a sea of Japanese flags. Every schoolchild had a little Japanese flag which they waved enthusiastically in honour of the Emperor. On all these special days the children marched singing around the lake to the flag-bedecked sports ground opposite the school, where they would engage in sports competitions. Christmas and New Year were also celebrated communally, with gifts for all of the children.

In Sarangan there were sports competitions, children's parties, amateur dramatics and sailing and rowing on the lake. There were flute, and later on piano lessons, as well as riding and horse-jumping lessons – the children were kept busy from morning to night. There was even a barber and a ladies' hairdresser.

The German School in Sarangan was exemplary, and so it is no surprise that it saw many visitors. In the early months there were visits from a Japanese doctor, representatives of the German Embassy in Tokyo, the Japanese Education Minister, the Civil Governor of Java and the Japanese Commander in Chief in the Pacific. In January 1944 there was a visit from a Japanese professor who had studied in Bonn and spoke perfect German.

After an inspection by representatives of the Embassy in Tokyo to check if the children's education was in line with the requirements of Nazi Germany, some children had to leave. *Volks* Germans were tolerated, but pure Dutch children with no German background in a German school? *No,* said the inspectors, *that cannot happen!*

The *Reichs* Germans in Sarangan had accepted the *Volks* Germans into their community without reservation in that time of mutual necessity, and supported them as well as they could. As a former *Volks* German schoolboy from Sarangan with Dutch citizenship told me, the *Volks* Germans could never mention the fact that they had been at the German School when they returned to the Netherlands after the war. Their parents' pension rights would have been cancelled immediately.

The relationship between the native population and the Germans was excellent and mutually friendly. The German mothers bought food from the peasant women at the local market, the native men found work in the German vegetable gardens or did repair work around the houses. Indonesian women and girls worked as domestic help. Every day the peasant women from the neighbouring villages toiled up to Sarangan to sell their fruit and vegetables. What must they have thought when they saw the young Germans marching around the lake in step, singing lustily?

The young Germans made friends with children of their own age in the villages. When the boys hiked up to the peak of the smoking, 3,265-metre volcano Gunung Lawu, they took their native friends with them, because they knew all the paths through the jungle on that five-hour climb. They also knew what to do about black panthers, snakes and the spirits that lived deep in the woods. On Java and especially around the volcano many things were bewitched. *Hantu,* the natives would say: Spirits!

The natives still say that the area around the sacred volcano abounds with hidden powers and mystic energy. Hidden in the forest on the slopes of the volcano there are ancient Hindu temples like Candi Sukuh, Candi Kethek or Candi Cetho from the middle of the 15th century before Java was converted to Islam. There are still some small Hindu communities in this remote region. In these places the German boys had to rely on the experience of their native friends.

One day two men visited Sarangan: they were two of the few survivors of the wreck of the *Van Imhoff,* who had reached the island of Nias. The shameful story of the *Van Imhoff* and the strange coup d'état on Nias had already reached Sarangan, but now they were hearing the whole unvarnished story from the horse's mouth. One of the men, Herr Fischer, had previously been the representative of the German firm Bosch in the Dutch East Indies. He had become famous as the leader of the coup d'état, which I will now describe in more detail, just as they heard him relate his adventurous tale. The Dutch deliberately allowed hundreds of German civilian internees to die in the sinking of the *Van Imhoff,* including 18 Catholic and 20 Protestant missionaries and ministers. The 65 survivors were rearrested by the Dutch on the beach at Nias and locked up in the police prison in the island's main town, Gunung Sitoli. They were guarded by Dutch soldiers and 38 native policemen, the *Veldpoliti.* The Indonesian policemen, instead of guarding the Germans, allied themselves with them and smuggled weapons to the prisoners. The Indonesians could not understand why they were having to guard Germans who had just defeated their hated colonial rulers in Europe. The Germans were freed on Palm Sunday 1942 and with the help of the Indonesian guards put the Dutch behind bars. Any British or Australians living on Nias were also imprisoned.

In co-operation with leading Indonesian figures on the island, the *Republik Nias Merdeka*, the Free Republic of Nias, was declared. Everything was done with truly German thoroughness: Fischer became the first Prime Minister and Albert Vehring[1], who had managed Emil Helfferich's tea plantation

---

[1] Herr Vehring and other survivors gave sworn evidence of the war-crimes committed by the Dutch when the Van Imhoff, was sunk (e. g. Notar Bernhard Grünewald, Düsseldorf, Urkundenrolle Nr. 61/1949)

on Java since 1928, was Foreign Minister. The inhabitants of Nias rejoiced: they were the first people in the whole Indonesian Archipelago to throw off – with German help – the yoke of 350 years of exploitative colonial rule, more than three years before Soekarno proclaimed the independence of the whole of Indonesia in August 1945.

Although they did not have many weapons, the Germans were able to prevent the native population going on a rampage with looting and lynch justice and keep control of the island's population of around 200,000. Without this temporary German government, neither the Chinese, the Dutch or the Allied PoWs would have survived: the natives would have massacred them without mercy, as even the Dutch admitted after the war. The Foreign Minister, Albert Vehring, sailed the 200 kilometres to Sumatra in a native fishing boat to make contact with the Japanese troops, and then returned with them to Nias.

The Free Republic of Nias lasted a few months until the Japanese occupied the island. The inhabitants welcomed the Japanese with delight and the national anthem *Indonesia Raya*. Three days later on the 20th of April the Germans and Japanese both celebrated Hitler's birthday to shouts of *Sieg Heil* and *Banzai*.

On the 23rd of April 1942 the Germans left Nias. They were now free, and returned to their families or their former work places. Many volunteered to work in the German naval bases. The Dutch, British and Australian prisoners on Nias were taken to Sumatra and Burma to work on the railways there.

Only one German remained on Nias: Doctor Heid, who had been head of the island's hospital in Gunung Sitoli since the arrest of the Dutch – before internment he had worked as a doctor on Java. Only a few months after the coup, in August 1942, he committed suicide.

This curious tale of German-Indonesian relations in the middle of the war, which led to the first independence of a part of Indonesia, is unfortunately practically unknown in modern Indonesia, even though the internationally famous Indonesian writer Rosihan Anwar describes it in his short story collection, *Sejarah Kecil*.[1]

Herr Fischer, who had won the trust and recognition of the Japanese military authorities and the German-embassy in Tokyo by his coup, was now made the head of the German community in Sarangan as a kind of mayor.

One day the Swiss artist Willy Quidort turned up in Sarangan, hoping to sit out the rest of the war there. He had arrived in Bali in 1938, but even as citizen of a neutral country had not been allowed to leave the island after

---

1   Anwar, *Sejarah Kecil*, pp. 79ff

the war began.[1] During the Japanese occupation he was, as a Swiss citizen, a "free guest" and so could, with some restrictions, move about and come to Sarangan. In his luggage he had a gramophone and a large collection of records which he put at the disposal of the community in Sarangan for their rare cultural activities.[2] Quidort was a friend of Walter Spies. He and his wife had lived temporarily as guests in Spies' house in Campuan near Ubud on Bali. Walter Spies wrote to his mother in July 1938 that he had benefited from Quidort's knowledge of painting technique.[3] Quidort had even been allowed to build his own house on Spies' land in Campuan, but he only lived there a short while.[4]

With the approach of the war in the Pacific and American aircraft flying over Java, people even in Sarangan had to prepare for more difficult times. Japanese troops practised fire drill with the women who learned how to work in a bucket chain. Using a straw dummy they were taught how to disable American paratroops with a bamboo spear before they could free themselves from their parachutes.

In February 1945 the older pupils, both male and female, were first pressed into service to plant Djarak on a large stretch of land. Djarak is the plant from whose seeds castor oil is made. The oil was not just used for medicinal purposes, it was urgently needed in Germany for the synthetic fabric and paint industries as well as the production of biodiesel. The oil, not just from Sarangan, was collected in large quantities and sent to Germany by submarine from Batavia and Surabaya. Even though the Russians were already marching towards Berlin, and cities had been destroyed in horrific air-raids, the last reserves were mobilised in Sarangan.

From the age of 16 all *Reichs* German boys from Java were conscripted for military service. The boys from the cities in Java first went to Surabaya for training. The German Consulate in Batavia remembered that there were boys of the right age in the holiday resort of Sarangan and selected about a dozen for military service. The boys were proud and dreamed of heroism and service to the fatherland – all the things that had been drummed into them over the years in the Hitler Youth. The mothers they were leaving behind waved goodbye to them as they left in a Japanese truck for the German base in Surabaya.

On the base there were four concrete tennis courts which became indescribably hot in the tropical sun. This is where the boys from Sarangan

---

1   Rupp, *Ernest A. Christen*, p. 26
2   Keppner, *Airmolang*, p. 290
3   Rhodius, *Walter Spies*, p. 374
4   Ibid., p. 411

were drilled for several weeks until they dripped with sweat. The carelessness of youth was soon forgotten. Their uniform consisted of dark khaki shorts and short-sleeved shirts. They wore long a Japanese bayonet hanging from a broad leather belt. Their dress uniform was grey, with eagle-and-swastika epaulettes sewn by skilled Chinese and Javanese seamstresses. Only the officers were allowed to wear white service and dress uniforms.

To the annoyance of the boys from Sarangan the food on the base was resolutely German: lots of meat, potatoes, dumplings, thick sauces, very few vegetables and a lot of pudding. They had been used to light Indonesian and Chinese food with fish, rice and lots of vegetables from childhood.[1]

If they didn't have a pass, they were not allowed to leave the base after dark. But the boys from Sarangan – like all the sailors – knew about the hole in the fence. So did all the officers, including the base commander, but it still wasn't closed – after all, the officers also occasionally wanted to spend an evening with their Javanese girlfriends. So the Sarangan boys would slip out through the hole to eat the food they were used to in a nearby Javanese restaurant.

Because of their German descent and German blood the children of *Volks* Germans were later also allowed to join the forces. The German naval base at Surabaya was a hive of activity. U-boats arrived and left, freight for Germany was delivered, the U-boats had to be loaded by trustworthy personnel and there was continual hammering and welding. After their voyages of three months or longer around Africa the majority of the submarines needed repairs and had to be overhauled for the return journey. Everybody had to lend a hand.

The children of the Dutch-Germans could hardly refuse the call to the colours, because without German protection the boys and their mothers would have been sent to internment camps by the Japanese. *Reichs* German Indos, children of Germans and native, were disappointed not to be called up. Many of them would also have liked to wear a German uniform and take part in the "Great War".

After basic training some of the boys from Sarangan, now feeling like real men, were posted to the bases at Batavia and Singapore, but the majority stayed in Surabaya to be trained as radio operators or diesel mechanics. They now travelled the two kilometres to the harbour every morning in a heavy Horch open-top truck. These trucks, which had four-wheel drive and four-wheel steering, were developed specially for the German army and produced in great numbers. In the port the young soldiers were allowed to help the senior mechanics who were overhauling the U-boats diesel engines, but they also had to load raw rubber and bars of tin into the submarines' bilges.

---

1   Keppner, *Airmolang*, pp. 363ff

When the young men had passes and went out in their smart dress uniforms and their white sailors' caps, they felt as if they were the base commander himself. They ran after the pretty girls on the Oranje Boulevard hoping that one of them would respond. However, before their first pass was issued the base medical officer had a serious talk with them. As they left, he pressed a packet of contraceptives into their hands.

They didn't really like going to the German recreation centre, the Taifun Hotel, near the base on the Oranje Boulevard, even though their friend and comrade Otto Kühn played dance music there with his Javanese band. They would be under observation by their superiors, the drinks and dancing partners were too expensive for them, but most of all it was too stiff and formal for them there. They had to bow nicely to their partners when asking them to dance and give them the requisite dance ticket – and of course the upper floor of the Taifun Hotel with its more intimate rooms was barred to the boys from Sarangan. Station commander Hoppe thought they were too young for that kind of game.

The Tabarin Bar and Dance Club was near the base, and was visited by Japanese soldiers as well. The establishment was cheaper and less stiff, and the girls there were just as pretty and affectionate. This was the favourite hang out of the Sarangan boys when they had a pass.

The war now became serious in Sarangan too. After an Allied aircraft was spotted flying over Sarangan the Japanese commander ordered all the houses to be blacked out. At night the windows were curtained and the use of electric light reduced. Nevertheless, school carried on as usual by day. More and more sailors from the U-boats docked in Surabaya began to come to the little resort on shore leave. Shortly before the end of the war a film projector and the films *Reitet für Deutschland* [Riding for Germany], *U-Boote Westwärts* [U-boat Westward] and some newsreels were sent to Sarangan from Tokyo. It may have been the projector from the *Scharnhorst*, which had previously been lent to the German colony in Tokyo or one that had been on a U-boat, like that on the U 181 to entertain the crew.

It was during the first days of May 1945, days like any other previously. The sun rose above the forested mountains and the birds sang, rejoicing at every new day. The German mothers, children and men at Sarangan had less to rejoice about: there were rumours going around that Hitler was dead. When the news was confirmed, they were outraged. Hitler dead? Our idol, whom we trusted so blindly? What will happen now?[1]

---

1   Information from the former Sarangan pupil Hardy Zöllner
     Sarangan newsletter of the Friends of Sarangan, Hamburg 1989
     Keppner, *Wie weit bis Airmolang*

38. Operation "Transom"
and the Last German U-Boats
in the "Southern Region" Until the End of the War

Only four weeks after the first of many attacks on the base at Sabang a second base was attacked by the Allies on the 17th of May 1944. Under the code name Operation Transom this attack was aimed at the port of Surabaya, so important for the maintenance and repair of German U-boats. As in Sabang the Japanese were once more caught unprepared.

Once again it was the American aircraft carrier *USS Saratoga*, which after her successful raid on Sabang now bombed the naval base at Surabaya with her aircraft. The following night there was an attack by a second wave of seven US B-24 heavy bombers from the secret air base at Corunna Downs south of Marble Bar in Western Australia.

However, the damage in Surabaya seems not to have been as bad as that in Sabang, because only three weeks later, on the 10th of June 1944, the UIT 25 – which was lying in dock at Surabaya during Operation Transom – sailed from Surabaya for Kobe. She must therefore have only been lightly damaged, if at all. She was commanded by Lieutenant Colonel Alfred Meyer, who had previously been First Officer of the Watch on the U 183. There were only ten German submariners in the crew (transferred from the U 183), the rest being Italian submariners or seamen from the crews of auxiliary cruisers. The UIT 25 travelled several times between the "Southern Region" and Japan, mainly to bring tungsten and molybdenum to the "Southern Region" for further transport to Germany.

Although the majority of U-boats now headed for the base in Batavia, which had not been attacked, several German submarines still docked in Surabaya after Operation Transom: the U 861 on the 3rd of November 1944, the U 537 on the 9th of November 1944 and the U 195 on the 17th of March 1945.

Lieutenant Fritz Schneewind was the first to sail into Penang in the U 511. Now he became one of the last to lose his life in the "Southern Region" just before the end of the war. He took over command of the U 183, which had already sunk a number of Allied ships on combat missions in Dutch East Indies waters, on the 20th of December 1943. First he sailed to the naval dockyard of Kobe in Japan, where new batteries were fitted, not possible in the "Southern Region" itself. German submariners were well aware that submarine batteries produced in Japan were better than those originally fitted in Germany. The capacity was greater and they lasted longer. Was this because raw materials were scarcer or unavailable in Germany during the war, or was Japanese technology superior?

Getting hold of any kind of spare part for the U-boats or telecommunications equipment in the "Southern Region" was a massive problem. If parts were ordered from Germany it took months for them to reach the "Southern Region" by U-boat. It was also difficult to acquire them from their Japanese Axis brothers, since there was constant rivalry between the Imperial Navy and the Imperial Army. A talent for improvisation was needed every day. The following example shows how time-consuming and often unsuccessful the attempt to find spare parts was:

The German base in Singapore had organised two buses for transporting personnel between the port and the various parts of the base, but unfortunately they did not have rubber tyres. There were no suitable tyres at all in Singapore, but they knew that the Japanese had a tyre store on the island of Bali. Captain Hermann Kandeler, commander of the Batavia base, ordered Lieutenant Oskar Herwartz, who was in Batavia at the time with the U 843, to get the tyres from Bali at all costs. Count Maeda was the Japanese liaison officer for the German Navy in Batavia. He gave Herwartz the necessary travel permit and permission to use the ferry to Bali. Herwartz, however, had to promise to bring four tyres for Maeda as well.

Herwartz took the train to Surabaya with five men as "tyre-carriers". There he was refused permission to travel any further, because the travel permit had to be authorised by the Japanese town commander. For six days the commander kept the Germans waiting with promises of "tomorrow", and then he explained with a friendly smile that Bali was heavily fortified and no foreigners – not even their allies, the Germans – were allowed on the island. The ban had been put in place by the Imperial Army command which was in charge of Bali.

After further long-drawn out negotiations, the Japanese interpreter was at least allowed to travel to Bali to sort out the tyre problem. After eight days he returned, exhausted and tyre-less. The mission was a failure.[1]

On the 9th of March 1945 the U 183 returned to Batavia from Kobe. A few days later she set out on her seventh combat mission. She operated in the Java Sea south of Borneo (now Kalimantan) in the Strait of Makassar. On the 23rd of April 1945, only a few days before the German capitulation, she was sunk by a torpedo from the American submarine USS Besugo, com-

1   Thomer: *Unter Nippons Sonne*, pp. 180ff

manded by Captain Miller, which had fired a fan of six torpedoes at the U 183, one of which hit her exactly amidships. Within a few seconds the U 183 had sunk to the bottom of the sea. Only one of the 55-man crew survived: First Mate Karl Wiesniefsky, who had several fractures of his leg. The American submarine picked him up, and he returned home to Germany on the 10th of January 1946 after his release from American captivity.

Fritz Schneewind was one of those lost: he was born on the 10th of April 1917 in Padang (West Sumatra), where his parents had run a German trading station. He spoke fluent Malay and so was predestined for action in the Dutch East Indies: now he found his last resting place in his old home, the Java Sea.

When a place in a dry dock in the naval port of Selatar in Singapore was made available to a German submarine by the Japanese authorities, that submarine, even if it was not 100% seaworthy, had to be sailed there from Penang, Batavia or Surabaya if major repairs were necessary, even if they were only repairs to the outside of the hull.

Therefore the Monsoon boat U 532 under Captain Otto-Heinrich Junker sailed from Penang on the 17th of May 1944, its destination Singapore. Junker had taken over command of the boat in November 1942. In four missions, with 400 days at sea, Junker had sunk 8 Allied ships and seriously damaged two others.

Since the U 532's engines were not capable of producing their full power, she travelled south towards Singapore as close as possible to the coast and had extra air protection from an Arado 169 seaplane. Because of the minimal depth of the water near the coast, the U 532 had to travel on the surface.

In spite of the air escort the U 532 was sighted by the British submarine *HMS Tally-Ho* (which was submerged at the time) and attacked. The *Tally-Ho* had operated successfully near the Andaman Islands and the Similan Islands (a Siamese possession), as well as laying mines off the Sabang base and the east coast of Sumatra. She fired a fan of six torpedoes at the U-boat, but by manoeuvring skilfully Captain Junker managed to avoid all of them – some of them shot past with their deadly cargo only a few metres away. The Strait of Malacca had become very unsafe, but Junker was lucky once again. The next day he docked safely in Singapore about mid-day. After her overhaul the U 532 sailed to Batavia to take on cargo.

Junker left Batavia on the 13th of January 1945 to sail back to Germany with a cargo of rubber and molybdenum. The U 532 was refuelled in the western Indian Ocean by the U 195 on the 8th of February 1945. In the Atlantic Junker sank the British freighter *Baron Jedburgh* on the 13th of March and the American freighter *Oklahoma* on the 28th of March. On the 15th of

May the U 532 surrendered at sea to the British warship *HMS Anthony* and was escorted to Liverpool, arriving on the 17th of May 1945, 117 days after departing Batavia. Captain Junker was one of the few commanders who only lost one of his crew during all his many hundreds of days of operation, and that man was washed overboard in extremely rough seas just before reaching Liverpool. The British escort ship had refused Junker's request to be allowed to sail submerged. He and his crew entered British captivity and were only released in 1948. Junker was given no credit for his positive action in not sinking an unescorted British troop transporter shortly before surrendering either when he was interrogated or when sentence was passed.

The U 859 under Lieutenant Johann Jebsen and the U 861 under Captain Jürgen Oesten reached Sabang on consecutive days in September 1944 after a long voyage including operations in the Indian Ocean. The base had returned to limited functionality after the devastating Allied attack in April of the same year.

On the voyage to Sabang the U 859 had sunk three Allied ships, including the US Liberty freighter *SS John Barry* on the 28th of August 1944. The wreck of the *John Barry* is still lying at a depth of 2,600 metres in the Arabian Sea off the coast of the Sultanate of Oman. She was carrying a cargo of gold and silver ingots as well as coins to the value of several hundred million US dollars.

After a cheerful welcome from their German and Japanese comrades stationed at the base, the two U-boats were to be piloted together from Sabang to Penang to unload the cargo they had brought from Germany. The situation in the Strait of Malacca had become very dangerous because of constant Allied submarine patrols. The protection by Japanese escort vessels near the German bases was generally far from satisfactory, resulting in the loss of at least five U-boats in the stretch of water between Sabang and Penang.

The crews of both U-boats were delighted when their pilots greeted them with big baskets or tropical fruit and cold Japanese beer. They then sailed a zig-zag course towards Penang, where the U 861 arrived safely. The U 859 was less fortunate. After a voyage of more than five months she was sunk only a few miles from her destination by a torpedo from the British submarine *HMS Trenchant*. 19 of the 67-man crew were rescued.

Captain Jürgen Oesten, who had sailed the U 861 safely to Penang was an experienced U-boat commander: the U 861 was his third command; he had previously also commanded the U 61 und U 106. On twelve combat missions he had sunk 20 ships and damaged others, one of which, the British battleship *HMS Malaya,* was so severely damaged that she had to spend many months in dock for repair.

When he set sail from Lorient for the "Southern Region" in the U 861 on the 20th of April 1944, he was already convinced that the war could no longer be won. Before sailing he said:

I felt damned uneasy, because I actually knew that it would achieve nothing – whatever we sank, whoever we killed, none of it was really necessary.[1]

The U 861 sailed to Singapore for overhaul and then operated between Singapore, Batavia and Surabaya. She was then loaded with a new cargo for Germany and sailed from Surabaya for Lorient on the 15th of January 1945. Because of the dangers of the Sunda Strait Captain Oesten decided to take the longer route to the Indian Ocean through the Lombok Strait between Bali and the Island of Lombok. But two American submarines were already lying in wait for the U 861, because her sailing time and course had been betrayed to the Allies by spies. As far as the Lombok Strait the U 861 was escorted by a Japanese Destroyer. When Oesten made a test dive to check the condition of his submarine he noticed that there was an unusually strong undersea current pulling him south from the Lombok Strait. To save fuel he let the boat drift with the current for a whole day and did not surface until night-time.

Some of the crew were suffering from dengue fever, a tropical disease carried by mosquitos. At the time, they thought that cooler temperatures would help to cure the disease, and so Oesten sailed off the normal route directly south towards cooler Australian waters. The use of the strong current in the Lombok Strait and his unusual route towards Australia had saved the U 861, which escaped both its American pursuers.

The U 861 was very fortunate as she crossed the Indian Ocean. Here as in the Atlantic the Allies now had the upper hand. For this reason Oesten kept changing course, and dodged far to the north in the Atlantic. In the North Sea the U 861 collided with an iceberg, but the damage was only superficial. After a voyage of more than three months she arrived safely at the German naval base at Trondheim in Norway on the 18th of April 1945. On the 6th of May 1945 the commander and his crew surrendered to the British, becoming prisoners of war.

In December 1944 and January 1945 the last four U-boats sailed from the "Southern Region" carrying raw materials. Although none of them were lost, they arrived in Europe too late to make any contribution to the war effort.[2]

Let us return to the story of the U 862, the only U-boat, to operate in Australian and New Zealand waters, after her arrival in Batavia on the 14th of February 1945.

---

1   Williams: *U-Boot-Krieg im Atlantik*
2   Krug, Hirama, Sander-Nagashima, Niestlé, *Reluctant Allies*, p. 231

On the 18th of February 1945 the U 862 rendezvoused with the German supply ship *Bogota* and left the port of Batavia the same day. The next day she passed through the Banka Strait.[1] On the 20th of February 1945 she arrived in Singapore for overhaul in the naval dockyard. After the completion of the work and a period of recreation for the crew, she was to sail back to Germany at the end of April. Every available space in the submarine was filled with rubber and molybdenum – they even reduced the number of torpedoes carried to eight to make more room. The Naval High Command in Berlin turned down a Japanese request for her to land Japanese agents in Madras (now Chennai) in southern India.

There were several delays in completing the overhaul and repairs, but the main engines were now ready and had undergone a successful test run. U 862's departure was set for the 12th of May 1945. On the 5th of May 1945 the German Naval Attaché in Tokyo and Admiral of East Asia, Paul Wenneker, sent the code word "Lübeck" to all U-boats in Asia. This was the order to cease all hostilities with the Allies with immediate effect.[2] Nevertheless shortly before the end of the war several U-boats left German ports and some even managed to evade the allied blockade and escape after the German surrender.

U 234, for example, left Kiel for Java on the 25th of March 1945. Because of some technical problems she had to put in to the German naval base in Kristiansand in Norway. On the 15th of April 1945 – only three weeks before the end of the war, she finally set sail for Java. The commander was Lieutenant Johann Heinrich Fehler. His Second Officer was Lieutenant Ernst Pfaff, who was responsible for the cargo. The ship's medical officer was Dr Franz Valentin Walter. They had before them a long voyage via the "Southern Region" to Japan. Hitler himself gave the orders for this mysterious voyage when he finally realised that Germany had lost the war.

The U 234 was actually a mine-layer submarine, but had been converted to carry freight. Her cargo consisted of several large boxes and a large number of smaller ones. Even the torpedo tubes were loaded with cargo. As Lieutenant Pfaff told the American secret service when interrogated, nobody on board knew what was in the boxes. They were not intended for the German bases in South East Asia, but were simply to be transferred to a Japanese sub-

---

1   The Banka Strait, between 11 and 27 kilometres wide, lies between the east coast of Sumatra and the island of Banka

2   SENSUIKAN! IJN Submarine I-502: Tabular Record of Movement, © 2001-2010 Bob Hackett & Sander Kingsepp, Revision 5
Deutsches U-Boot Museum Cuxhafen-Altenbruch, www.deutsches-u-boot-museum.com

marine in Batavia or Surabaya. They were meant for the Japanese Ministry of Defence.

The U 234 was carrying twelve passengers. There was General Ulrich Kessler of the Luftwaffe with his two aides, the radar specialist Ulrich Menzel and Lieutenant Fritz von Sandrart, an air-defence expert. Kessler was to be the new Air Attaché in Tokyo and his aides were to help Heinrich Foders with the *Würzburg* project. There were also four high-ranking German naval officers and specialists to support Admiral Wenneker in Tokyo, and three German civil engineers, specialists in electronics and aircraft construction. Finally there were two Japanese officers, Genzo Shoji and Shinchiro Tomonaga, specialists in rocket technology. They had made a detailed study of the latest weapons and rocket technology in Germany.

Atomic research in Germany was already quite advanced, indeed, Germany could be seen as the birthplace of atomic physics after Otto Hahn discovered nuclear fission and its explosive power in 1938/39. Japan was also working on the development of an atom bomb, but they had no uranium. Three Japanese submarines, the I-52, I-30 and I-29, which were supposed to transport uranium from Germany had been sunk by the Allies. Two of them had been on the way home carrying large quantities of uranium ore. Hitler, in spite of his slogans to the contrary, had obviously given up hope of winning the war, as he was now supporting the Japanese atomic weapon programme with all the means at his disposal.

After the war it was discovered that the U 234 was carrying large amounts of mercury and 560 kilograms of uranium oxide, the raw material for an atom bomb. There was also a dismantled Messerschmitt Me 262, the first jet-fighter in the world, parts for the Me 163 rocket-plane, parts for the newest version of the V2 ballistic rocket and countless boxes of construction plans, technical drawings and research results of the latest German military developments. The cargo weighed about 240 tonnes. The German scientists and engineers were supposed to help arm the Japanese war machine as quickly as possible with the latest German weaponry. If the Third Reich was losing the war, at least Japan should be helped to win it!

At the time the incessant air-raids on Berlin made atomic weapons research more or less impossible, and so the project was continued, though with restricted working conditions in the "atom tunnel" in Hechingen in South Germany.

U 234 never reached Java or Japan. After Germany's surrender on the 7th of May 1945 and the order to all U-boat commanders to give themselves up to the Allies, the U 234 sailed to the USA with her dangerous cargo and surrendered to the US destroyer *USS Sutton* on the 14th of May. The two Japanese officers had previously committed suicide on the U 234. No Japanese officer devoted to his Divine Emperor could fall into enemy hands. Three days later U 234 sailed into Portsmouth on the US east coast.

When American scientists heard of the captured uranium oxide, they were electrified. It was processed into weapons-grade uranium in the atomic research laboratory in Oak Ridge. Was this German uranium used in the US atom bombs that were dropped on Hiroshima and Nagasaki? Some American scientist claim that it was.

39. The German Capitulation

Chaos reigned all over Germany. But in spite of the retreat on all fronts the radio still blared on with special bulletins about victorious battles, miracle weapons and final victory, coupled with *Wir fahren gegen England* [A march: We are sailing against England] and slogans about keeping going. The reality looked somewhat different: Germany was in ruins!

In the middle of 1944 German U-boat losses reached their peak. Only four Allied freighters were sunk for the loss of 23 U-boats.[1] New radar warning devices with resonant names like *Naxos, Hohentwiel* or *Borkum* were constantly being fitted, but none of them solved the problem. In the Indian Ocean and the Java Sea there were fewer U-boats, but they were more successful – almost half of all Allied shipping was sunk. But even here losses were on the increase. In August 1944 8 U-Boats transporting raw materials for Germany were sunk. Since the bulky and heavy loads of the freight U-boats were carried at the expense of fuel reserves, they had to depend on supply ships for refuelling. The supply ships *Charlotte Schliemann* and *Brake* had been sunk: submarines sailing home fully-laden mostly only encountered large oil slicks at the rendezvous points, which meant that the U 532, for example, had to return to Penang.

U 532 made a second attempt to get her vital cargo to Germany. On the 31st of January 1945[2] she left Batavia. Instead of the now non-existent supply ships the U 195 was deployed for that purpose, refuelling the U 532 south of Madagascar. However the U 532 did not succeed in getting her cargo to Germany before the war ended and surrendered off Liverpool on the 10th of May 1945.

There were always individual submarines that reached Europe. U 843 sailed from Batavia under Lieutenant Oskar Herwartz on the 10th of December 1944, fully laden with tin, molybdenum, rubber and other raw materials. On the 9th of April 1945, after a voyage of more than 16,000 nautical miles, she was attacked by a British aircraft just short of her destination in Kiel. The rudder was damaged and she ran into a minefield, hit a mine and sank. 44 of her 56 man crew were lost in the disaster. In 1958 she was raised and her cargo salvaged.

Supplies of raw materials for the war machine were interrupted. The big new type XX freight U-boats with a cargo capacity of 800 tons which could

1   Brennecke, *Jäger - Gejagte*, p. 338
2   Other sources give the 13th of January 1945

have sailed non-stop from the "Southern Region" to Europe were not ready to enter service when the war ended.

After Hitler's suicide, it was clear that the war should be brought to an end as quickly as possible. In his will Hitler named Admiral Dönitz as his successor. The German fleet had been largely sunk, raw materials and steel had been used up and there were no new supplies. A lack of fuel meant that the Luftwaffe could not take off, and people were starving. The soldiers who fled back to Germany had tattered uniforms and holes in their boots. The German armed forces were beaten.

In January 1945, just before the war ended, the German Navy had the largest submarine fleet in its history: around 430 U-boats, most of them unserviceable because of a lack of fuel and trained crews. Their numbers had become meaningless.

The code word *Regenbogen* [rainbow] sent by the naval high Command to all German ships and bases all round the world was the command to cease hostile action immediately in view of the forthcoming capitulation – ten days after Hitler's death.

Dönitz wished to gain time before a total capitulation to enable as many Germans as possible to escape from the east – from East Prussia and Courland. They even used submarines to evacuate civilians and soldiers: they all wanted to avoid capture by the Russians.

Between the 1st and the 4th of May 1945 all U-boat commanders received the order from the High Command to render their craft unusable. Over 200 of the roughly 370 submarines still at sea were scuttled by their crews. The rest were captured by the Allies. The new electro-submarines, which were lying in European harbours and did not yet have trained crews available for combat mission were blown up so that they would not fall into enemy hands.

On the 4th of May 1945, in the course of the capitulation negotiations, the Allies forced Dönitz to rescind the order to destroy the submarines. Many commanders disregarded this second order. The U-boats that were at sea had no choice but to surrender to the Allies, although there were some that crossed the Atlantic and landed in neutral Argentina.

A partial capitulation and armistice agreement was reached with British Field Marshal Montgomery on the 5th of May 1945. British air raids on German cities were stopped. US General Eisenhower, however, would only allow a partial capitulation with a respite of 48 hours – that was all the time the USA would allow for German refugees from the east to reach US-occupied areas. The time won by Dönitz and an amazing rescue action by the German Navy meant that about two million people were saved from the advancing Russians.

From 1935 to 1945 1,155 German U-boats were built and entered service. 15 others were taken over from other powers such as Italy. 652 were lost by enemy action and a further 518 by other causes: scuttling, accident or as gifts to Japan. What a senseless waste of human life and material![1] On the 7th of May 1945 Colonel General Alfred Jodl signed the capitulation in France on behalf of the army High Command. A day later the document was signed again in Berlin, this time in the presence of the Supreme Commander of the Red Army and the commanders of the other German armed services. The long and devastating war, which had cost millions of lives and destroyed towns and cities on both sides, was over.

Japanese officers had totally misjudged the course of the war and their own capabilities even at the point where Germany surrendered. Japanese naval losses in the Pacific were enormous and there was a shortage of modern military equipment. The fighting spirits of their troops had been eroded by tropical temperatures and the length of the war, and yet Japan still believed they could win.

After the German capitulation the German officers on the staff of the bases in Singapore and Penang and the officers from the U-boats docked there were invited to a big farewell reception by the leading Japanese officers before their "open internment". Here the Germans were told in all seriousness that after Japan's victory in the Pacific and East Asia, Japan would reconquer Germany. Only a few months before their own surrender the Japanese were still grotesquely underestimating the opposition.[2]

U 181, commanded by Captain Kurt Freiwald, was in Singapore when Germany capitulated. She had left Bordeaux on the 16th of March 1944 and arrived in Penang on the 8th of August 1944. After a few subsequent operations in the Indian Ocean and voyages between Singapore and Batavia, Freiwald tried to sail back to Germany just before the capitulation. An order by radio from Germany forced him to break off his return voyage and sail back to Singapore.

Here Freiwald revealed to his crew and that of the U 862, which was also in Singapore, that Hitler was dead and that all military action except the defence of Berlin against Soviet troops was at an end. After the capitulation, Vice-Admiral Fukudome Shigeru, Commander of the Japanese 13th Fleet in East Asia came to the German base and informed Captains Freiwald and Timm, as well as Dommes, the "Southern Region" commander, that the submarines would now be taken over by the Japanese Navy. The German

---

1   Deutsches U-Boot-Museum, Cuxhafen-Altenbruch
2   ONI-Review, Kapitän zur See Kurt Freiwald, *German U-Boats in the Indian Ocean*, p. 370

commanders politely but firmly turned down a Japanese suggestion that the two U-boats should continue to operate with German crews under Japanese colours. Vice Admiral Fukudome nevertheless still thanked the German officers for their "selfless and courageous service against the common enemy". The same afternoon Japanese sailors boarded the U 862 and U 181. They lowered the German Naval ensigns and hoisted the Japanese flag.

The staff of the Penang and Singapore bases and the U-boat crews were taken to the Pasir Panjang camp. This was in a rubber plantation area south of Kuala Lumpur in Malaya and should not be confused with that part of the German naval base in Singapore of the same name. There must have been several hundred men, because the transport of the German soldiers and civilians with their luggage required a hundred trucks.

The Germans were accommodated in the village, which had 3,000 inhabitants. They were allowed to move around freely. The officers were put into bungalows and the other ranks into schools and other public buildings. The Japanese were as helpful and friendly as their circumstance allowed. The Germans were even allowed to keep their weapons.

30 men from each U-boat crew were detailed to introduce the new Japanese crews to the running of the two submarines in Singapore. First, however, the German labelling on the controls and instruments had to be changed to Japanese. The submarines were immediately renamed to integrate them into the Japanese fleet.

On the 15th of July 1945 the U 862 as I-502 commanded by Captain Yamanaka Shuaki and U 181 as I-501 were assigned to the Japanese 13th Fleet. They were to be used for training purposes and as transporters between Penang and the Japanese occupied Andamans. On the 1st of August 1945 the first test trips with the new Japanese crews began.

The head of the Batavia base, Captain Hermann Kandeler, who was also Germany's representative in the Dutch East Indies, also declined the Japanese offer to continue fighting on Japan's side with the U-boats lying in Batavia and Surabaya. The Germans were simply glad that for them the war was at last over! In compliance with the terms of a German-Japanese agreement all German military equipment in the "Southern Region" was to be handed over to their Japanese allies. The German naval personnel in Java were also put into so-called "open camps".

In Batavia the U 219 under Captain Walter Burghagen was the last submarine to be made ready for the return voyage to Germany. The crew's attempt to leave the harbour at Tanjung Priok before the foreseeable capitulation was in vain. When the Japanese heard of the capitulation, Japanese sailors led by Rear-Admiral Count Tadeshi Maeda marched up to the submarine and ceremoniously lowered the German ensign and hoisted the Japanese flag. The German U 219 became the Japanese I-505. Tadashi Maeda gave a lofty speech about Japan's soon to be expected victory over the Allies which was translated by the Batavia base interpreter Dr Hupfer.[1]

Ill. 92
Count Tadeshi Maeda, commander of the Japanese base in Batavia

The German crew of the U 219 introduced the Japanese to the running of a German submarine so that she could now operate under Japanese colours with a Japanese crew. After that most of the naval personnel at the Batavia base retired for a well-earned rest at the "U-Boat Meadow" on the Helfferich plantation in the mountains. Some of them, including the base commander Captain Kandeler, had to remain at the disposal of the Japanese in Batavia.

In Surabaya the U 195 entered Japanese service as the I-506. Most of the naval personnel left Surabaya and spread all over Java. Some went to Tretes or Sarangan in the mountains, others to the "U-Boat Meadow" in Bogor in the west. But in Surabaya too the Japanese insisted that a skeleton staff remain in the base.

After the German capitulation the two ex-Italian submarines which were in the naval dockyard in Kobe, the UIT 24 and UIT 25, became the RO-503 and RO-504 in the Japanese navy. These were the only submarines to sail under the flags of all three Axis powers, first Italian, then German and finally Japanese, and these were the only two Italian submarines to survive the war.

The German base commander in Kobe, Lieutenant Kentrat, his officers, the U-boat crews and the German base staff were allowed to remain in their quarters: they all lived in hotels and bungalows. As the US air-raids on Kobe grew heavier all Germans living in Japan were moved to the holiday resorts of Rokko and Hakkone.

1   Keppner, *Wie weit bis Airmolang*, p. 487

Rokko was a Japanese holiday paradise, with excellent hotels and guest houses, as well as superb restaurants. From Kobe's local mountain (over 900 metres high) there was a superb view over the cities of Kobe and Osaka. Here too the Germans had every freedom. At that time Rokko must almost have become a German town, because the navy alone had about 2,000 men stationed in Japan. And then there were several thousand German civilians living in Japan, as well as the refugee women and children from the Dutch East Indies, some of whom were also quartered in Hakkone, 100 kilometres from Tokyo. After the war repatriation of the Germans in Japan did not begin until mid-1947.

In Sarangan there were at first only rumours, but then it became a certainty here too: the Führer had died "in the battle for Berlin" and Germany had surrendered. What would happen now? The Japanese were in control in Sarangan and nobody knew what their plans were. Many German men, sailors and civilians turned up in Sarangan seeking a refuge. On the other hand, many mothers left with their children. Where were they to go? The mood was gloomy.

After the capitulation, lessons at the German School in Sarangan continued as before. They were after all living in a Japanese occupied area, and Japan was still at war. The German Embassy in Tokyo and the German Consulate in Jakarta were closed, which also meant that the financial support for the *Reichs* Germans in the Sarangan community came to an end. Fortunately all the Germans in Sarangan were by now—to a certain extent – self-sufficient, so that the situation was not too bad.

To the delight of the teachers and pupils a large shipment of German schoolbooks and teaching materials, as well as new gymnastic equipment arrived from Shanghai just before the capitulation. The school was now very well equipped.[1]

Nippon's sun was now sinking rapidly in South East Asia. More and more natives were arrested by the Japanese, presumably in desperation. Was it that the native population were not humble enough, or not grateful enough for the "benefits" they had received? The *Kempetai* made people suffer, arresting many of them on the slightest suspicion. All prominent Chinese and Indians living in South East Asia found the *Kempetai* spying on their every step. The situation also worsened in the many prison and internment camps. The *Kempetai* had the power of life and death over thousands of Allied prisoners of war.

For many soldiers of the Third Reich the war did not come to an end with Germany's capitulation. In the SORA (*Sekolah Olahraga*, a training

---

1   Information from the former Sarangan pupil Hardy Zöllner
     Sarangan newsletter of the Friends of Sarangan, Hamburg 1989

establishment for sport and languages) in Sarangan Indonesian cadets were trained, and German officers acted as trainers in the first, provisional military academy in Yogyakarta. German officers and men were also active as trainers in Soekarno's volunteer army, PETA. Sailors and former French Foreign Legionnaires volunteered to fight at the side of Soekarno and his independence movement against the returning British and Dutch. Many made a new home in Indonesia.

Six German sailors, four of them from the crew of the U 195, were unfortunate. They wanted to join the freedom fighters in Bogor, but were discovered by Dutch soldiers in Batavia as they tried to buy provisions. They were imprisoned first in the Glodok prison in Batavia and then on the prison island of Onrust. They were later transferred to Malang as the Dutch were afraid they might be liberated by the freedom fighters.

Ill. 93
Six German sailors captured by the Dutch

German soldiers and sailors were welcome not only among the Indonesian freedom fighters, but also in French Indochina. When they returned to the ruins of Germany after release from prisoner of war camps, the only way out for many German soldiers was the French Foreign Legion; many of them were posted to the Far East. They quite often deserted and joined the Vietminh, the League for the Independence of Vietnam. Former soldiers of the Third Reich were immediately given the rank of officers. They were mostly deployed as trainers for the Vietminh troops, who had no experience of modern warfare.[1]

---

1   Information from eyewitness Foreign Legionnaire Schneider
     Hougron Jean, *Das Mädchen von Saigon,* Soleil au Ventre, Gütersloh 1967, p. 67

40. The Japanese Capitulation

It was impossible for Japanese forces to administer and effectively defend the massive area in East and South East Asia which they had overrun so quickly: it was a front of nearly 10,000 kilometres, stretching from Japan via the Dutch East Indies to New Guinea and including thousands of islands in the Pacific. The Japanese war machine was simply overstretched – on land, at sea and in the air. It was impossible for their forces to be everywhere at once in adequate numbers.

As the German swastika had sunk, so now did the Japanese sun also begin to set. Massive Allied air-raids and the loss of one base after another in the Pacific brought even the Japanese to realise that the war was nearing its end. Japanese politicians began to suggest the possibility of capitulation, but the military were obstinately opposed: soldiers should fight to the death.

The German Reich and imperial Japan must surely have imagined a different ending: Hitler spoke of his "thousand-year Reich" and when the Japanese army took Singapore they renamed it Shonan "for the next 800 years". Neither promise lasted long.

On the 6th of August 1945 the first atom bomb fell on Hiroshima. In fractions of a second it claimed the lives of 80,000 human beings. During the next year a further 100,000 to 165,000 died of the after effects. Only three days later a second atom bomb fell on Nagasaki, causing another 70,000 deaths. War and the mass liquidation of civilians had reached a new dimension. Whether this – unique, thank God – deployment of atomic weapons was justified in moral, political and international legal terms is still the subject of controversy.

It was not just the atom bombs that forced Japan to surrender. Only a day before the bomb was dropped on Nagasaki, the Soviet Union broke the neutrality agreement signed with Japan in April 1941 and declared war on Japan on the 8th of August 1945. The Japanese surrender proclaimed by Emperor Hirohito was announced at midnight on the 14th of August 1945 by US President Roosevelt and the British Prime Minister Clement Attlee. The 15th of August became official known as VJ Day – Victory over Japan, as opposed to VE (Victory in Europe) Day on the 8th of May. On the 16th of August most Japanese troops laid down their arms. However, the US Army did not enter Japan for another two weeks because of a series of typhoons.

To avoid the disgrace of losing the war and subsequent captivity, Japanese generals called on their officers and men to commit Seppuku, the traditional suicide ritual often known in the West as Hara-kiri. Many followed the call. When the Tenno forbade Seppuku (with the Samurai sword) many soldiers decided to blow themselves up with hand grenades – that was still allowed!

On the 2nd of September the Japanese surrender was signed on the US battleship *Missouri* in Singapore. Everything now went very quickly. On the 5th of September the first British troops landed in Singapore. On the 8th of September Japan's surrender in parts of the Dutch East Indies was signed. New Guinea and the Pacific islands followed a day later. On the 9th of September the Japanese army in Nanking (almost a million strong) surrendered to the Nationalist Chinese led by Chiang Kai-shek. This led to brutal violence against the Japanese: the Chinese had not forgotten the Nanking Massacre, and were now taking their revenge.

In was not until the 10th and 11th of September 1945 that Japanese troops in North Borneo and the Dutch East Indian western half of the island of Timor surrendered, so that the surrender in Singapore of the whole of the Dutch East Indian archipelago was not signed until the 13th of September. The capitulation of the Japanese forces in Burma and Malaya followed the same day, Hong Kong on the 16th and finally on the 9th of October the British once more took possession of the Andaman Islands north of Sabang, which were occupied by the Indian National Army.

The Second World War had ended, but the western powers did not want to give up their overseas possessions. France fought on for another twenty years in Indochina and for five years the Dutch waged a shocking and particularly brutal colonial war against Indonesia – which had been independent under President Soekarno since the end of the war.

In the areas occupied by the Allies everything was blooming. The American officers' clubs in Shanghai and Manila were full to bursting with US officers dancing with young "flower girls" to the beat of swing and jazz. In the British clubs in Kuala Lumpur, Rangoon and Singapore there was an equally heady atmosphere, though it was rather more quiet. And in Batavia – now renamed Jakarta – British and Dutch officers made merry in the former Le Chat Noir café on the Jalan Veteran I.

In South East Asia the Rising Sun banner had been replaced by the Stars and Stripes or the Jack. The delicate, tranquil Japanese tea ceremony *O Cha-no-yu* was no longer celebrated in the clubs – it was replaced by vulgar ice cream, hamburgers and chewing gum. Some countries were celebrating the independence the Japanese had brought them, but Indonesia was far from achieving its freedom. The Dutch returned, but the goal of all Indonesians was now to drive out their hated colonial rulers – they had no wish to give up the independence they had achieved with Japan's help.

Rear Admiral Jisaku Uozumi, commander of the Japanese naval base in Penang, where he had welcomed the arrival of the U 862 in September 1944, now signed the document surrendering the Penang base on the 2nd of September 1945 on board the British cruiser *HMS Nelson*. He was wearing his resplendent white uniform with all his decorations, including the DSC (Distinguished Service Cross) awarded to him by the British for his services in the First World War. At his side he carried the Kaiguntō, the Japanese naval officer's sword, which was usually handed down from generation to generation in Samurai families. The Kaiguntō sword was a reminder of the Samurai code of honour.

Ill. 94
Admiral Jisaku
Uozumi signing the
surrender document
in Penang

After signing the surrender, Jisaku suffered a collapse and had to be taken to hospital by a British military policeman. On the way to the hospital the policeman stole the sword and took it home as a souvenir. This was an affront and showed disrespect to a Japanese cultural treasure. I'm sure that the sword did not bring him any luck!

The surrender of the Japanese base in Singapore a few days later was rather more dramatic. On the 28th of August 1945, before the surrender document was signed on the heavy cruiser *HMS Sussex*, the commander of the Japanese 7th Army stationed in Singapore, General Seishiro Itagaki, informed his staff that hostilities were to cease and the conditions of the capitulation must be observed.

About 300 officers then celebrated a rather macabre farewell party for the war in the famous Raffles Hotel with a dinner and copious quantities of sake. Normally the preparations for a ritual *Seppuku* suicide took several months, but now they had to move faster. To end the celebration they all leaned over their *Kaigunto* swords and exploded hand grenades against their bodies. The souls and bodies of the victims were now dedicated to the "Divine Emperor". For generations they had been brought up with Buddhism and its indifference to death as well as heroic enthusiasm for a noble death by self-disembowelment. It must have been considerably less exciting for the Raffles hotel staff who had to clean up the reception room for the Allied victory celebrations that were shortly to follow.[1]

The Japanese had placed the crews of the U 181 and U 862 "Monsoon Boats" and the staff of the naval base in Singapore in the open prison camp at Pasir Panjang in the hot, humid Malayan jungle after Germany surrendered. The survivors of the auxiliary cruisers *Michel* and *Thor*, the supply-ship and prize crews and the staff of the naval base in Penang were also quartered there, including the base commander, Captain Erhardt. Under the Japanese they had been perfectly free in the camp and the surrounding area. This changed when the British regained control.

On the 18th of October 1945 the German seamen were transferred to the dirty stone barracks of the infamous Penjara Changi (Changi Jail) in Singapore. The transfer was commanded by the young British Major Wilson. Major Wilson wanted to teach the Germans a lesson – contrary to all the tenets of British fairness. He ordered them to walk over 30 kilometres through Singapore in the tropical heat. Captain Kurt Freiwald, the last commander of the U 181, mustered the seamen. At his rousing command over 300 men in resplendent white uniforms with white forage caps and polished boots marched off with Captain Freiwald at their head.

Major Wilson did not succeed in humiliating the Germans. Singing catchy German military songs – and even the English *It's a long way to Tipperary* – they marched through Singapore with an escort of Ghurkhas. At the side of the road Malays, Chinese and Indians cheered the Germans on. They were astonished, because they had never seen Europeans performing a military parade through the Crown Colony with an Asian guard. Yelling enthusiastically, they had to be held back by British and Australian paratroopers. The British and Ghurkha guards escorting the prisoners were exhausted and had to be relieved, but the Germans marched on, even though Major Wilson refused their request for water. Dripping with sweat and exhausted, they reached their destination:

---

1   Bayly & Harper, Forgotten Wars: *Freedom and Revolution in Southeast Asia*, p. 49
The Straits Times, Singapore, September 4th, 2005, *The real Japanese surrender'*
www.wikipedia/operation-zipper

Changi Jail, a filthy and vermin-infested prison, which before the Japanese occupation had been used for native criminals, murderers and drug-dealers.

The one who lost face and made a fool of himself was Major Wilson. He showed the contemptuous Asians that European hegemony in Asia was now over. At the end of November 1945 some of the former German submariners were ordered to work outside the camp under British supervision. After the end of November 1945 the conditions in the camp were eased and a maximum of 30 German seamen were allowed to leave the camp by day to remove all the valuable parts from the U-boats that had remained in the „Southern Region". They had to be back in the camp by nightfall because that was when the British officers called the roll.

But very soon they found a way not to have to return to the camp by night and to allow rather more of the German seamen to leave the camp by day. The German officers and men visited the bars in Singapore, danced and enjoyed themselves half the night or worked in the city for hard cash – in dollars. How was this possible?

An Australian infantry battalion was quartered near Changi Jails. The German seamen had quickly made friends with the Australian soldiers and got them to take their places at the roll call. Although often fewer than half the Germans who should have been there were not in the camp, the British officers never noticed the deception. Or were they just turning a blind eye?

A few months later the German naval personnel were shipped to a prison camp on board the RMS *Empress of Australia,* a Canadian Pacific passenger liner converted into a troop transporter. But where? To Canada? Australia? That remains a mystery.[1]

In December 1945 the Tripartite Naval Commission (USA, Britain and the Soviet Union) decided on the destruction of German U-boats U 219 in Batavia, U 195 in Surabaya and ex U 181(now I-501) and ex U 862 (now I-502) in Singapore under British control before the middle of February 1946. The last two were sunk with three explosive charges each in the Strait of Malacca on the 15th of February 1946 by the frigate HMS *Loch Lomond.* The U 181 and U 862 are now lying at a depth of 95 metres at the bottom of the Malacca Strait.[2]

During the war, with very few exceptions, there were only women and children living in Sarangan, while the men were interned in camps in British India, Dutch Guyana and other places. The end of the war brought a change.

1   Brennecke, *Haie...*, pp. 10ff
2   Sensuikan: www.combinedfleet.com/I-502.htm by Bob Hackett & Sander Kingsepp

Many German seamen from the naval bases in Surabaya and Jakarta had had enough of the war by the time Japan surrendered and just wanted to get away. They remembered that Sarangan was a cool holiday resort with a lake where there was a German school and many German women and children. A number of ex-seamen and ex naval officers were attracted there, and were made welcome. For reasons of security the women were glad to have more men around, because Indonesia had become unsafe, with marauding and murdering bands of young men everywhere.

Until the Japanese surrender some of the staff and the boys from Sarangan had been employed in the Surabaya base by the Japanese. Now the former base commander, Lieutenant Hoppe, sent them home. They received their proper pay, together with a bonus, and were allowed to take whatever they wanted from the clothing store. The boys, both *Reichs* and *Volks* Germans, returned to Sarangan heavy laden.

However, many German seamen remained in the bases voluntarily and waited. Waited for what? For whom? The Americans, the British, The Dutch? Even though the Japanese had surrendered, they were still the most powerful military force in the country. No one knew how things would develop.

Unlike Singapore, the Germans in Surabaya and Batavia were treated perfectly correctly by the British, who were the first to arrive from Singapore. As two eyewitnesses[1] told me, the German servicemen in Surabaya and Batavia were actively employed by the British. In Surabaya the bombing had totally destroyed the electric power station. The U 195, renamed I-506 by the Japanese, was docked there.

The British asked the German servicemen to sort out an electricity supply for the barracks in the port, where British and British Indian troops were now to be quartered. They managed this relatively quickly, because they were able to use the U-195/I-506's diesel engines and generators. This produced so much power, in fact, that there was enough to provide a supply for domestic purposes in Surabaya – the first since the war. During the subsequent unrest between Indonesian freedom fighters and the British, the Germans were able to carry on in peace because the port and the military installations were protected by the British. The same happened in Batavia with the U 219: her engines and generators were used to provide the port with electricity.

Very shortly after the end of the war there was an epidemic of newly-weds in the Far East and South East Asia. Many German women had received news that their husbands had died in German camps or on the *Van Imhoff,* and many young girls had become young women by 1946, the first year of peace. New friendships were struck up, people fell in love, and there were a lot of

1   General Otty Soekojo und Admiral Martadinata

weddings and babies. After six long years of war they wanted a new beginning, a new home. The majority of the bonds forged under the tropical sun lasted for life: they all had something very deeply felt in common, the war!

After the capitulation the Japanese soldiers gave their weapons to PETA's native soldiers – and what they didn't give, the freedom fighters took from the depots. Many light and heavy weapons came into the possession of the Indonesians without a fight. Soekarno had declared Indonesia's independence on the 17th of August 1945 and Japan wanted the country to be capable of defending itself against the returning Dutch and maintaining its independence and self-determination. With all the means at his disposal, Soekarno wanted to make sure that no foreign country would in future have the power to make decisions about his country. PETA, a people's army which was now a real fighting force was the key to ultimate freedom and the seed from which the Indonesian armed forces grew. The Third Reich's support of PETA will be described in the next chapter.

Even after the surrender, the Japanese had to help the British to maintain order in several places. It took quite some time before the victorious powers were able to do so alone. The Japanese were allowed to retain their weapons – if they hadn't already given them to PETA.

The British were the first to arrive in Java after the capitulation. The Dutch internees in the Japanese camps now thought that they were going to be released. But that was not to be. They had to stay in their camps and, since the British did not have enough troops, the Japanese continued to guard them. But now they were not so much guards as protectors: the Dutch were only safe in the camps. The Indonesian mob, in the intoxication of freedom, was demanding revenge after centuries of humiliation: they slaughtered any Dutchman they could lay hands on. It was certain death for any Dutch person to be found outside a camp. The mob made no allowances for women and children: several dozen of them were murdered on a train in West Java and their bodies thrown out onto the railway embankment. They even lynched several German seamen because they thought they were Dutch. After that, the others sewed the German eagle from their uniforms on the sleeves of their shirts to make it clear they were German.

It was only in September 1945 that a British regiment, much to their surprise, found the German servicemen at the "U-boat meadow" in Tjikopo. Several of them had collected there after the German capitulation – they felt safe high up in the hills and away from the centres of population. As senior officer, Captain Walter Burghagen, former commander of the U 219 was assumed command of the camp.

One strange incident shows how chaotic the situation was: there were a large number of Dutch internees in a camp in Bogor (then: Buitenzorg). They had to be protected against the Indonesian mob, which wanted to storm the camp. There were too few British to take control, and they did not trust the PETA soldiers, suspecting they were just waiting for a chance to take revenge. So the Scottish commander of the British regiment gave Captain Burghagen and his men the task of guarding the camp. More then 300 German servicemen from Tjikopo now had to put their German uniforms back on and were supplied with small arms, rapid fire rifles and hand grenades by the British. They were taken to the camp in Bogor in 50 Japanese trucks[1] to protect the Dutchmen and Jews in the camp. The losers of the war, whose countrymen had previously been maltreated in the Dutch internment camps, were now rearmed to protect the former tormentors – in German uniform! For several months! Which did not, of course, please the Dutch prisoners – but without German help they would not have escaped the vengeance of the marauding gangs.

The very first night there was an exchange of fire between the Germans and Indonesians, but fortunately no one was injured. The Indonesians had assumed that the Germans had been imprisoned by the British and wanted to free them. This shows how well liked the Germans were by the native population. They nevertheless still had to protect the camp in Bogor several times against rampaging bands of Communist youths and militias.

At the beginning of 1946,when the Dutch returned and assumed command, the German guards were taken to the infamous prison on the island of Onrust. Naval pilot Werner and submariner Lösche of the U 219 succeeded in escaping. Both joined the Indonesian freedom fighters on Java. Werner was later accidentally killed trying to construct a flamethrower for the Indonesians.[2]

The Second World War was very unusual. The victors were not satisfied with gaining territory or new export markets. The Americans had taken it into their heads to re-educate and democratise the Japanese, and to transplant the "American Way of Life" to East Asia. With the enthusiasm of youth Japanese schoolchildren were prepared to learn something new, but the older generation were unimpressed, because the Americans showed a frightening ignorance of Japanese psychology. Older Japanese did not smile at the occupiers out of enthusiasm, but out of tact, because in Asia they hide even catastrophe and pain behind a smile.

---

1   www.bogor.indo.net./indonesien.deutschersoldatenfriedhof, p. 5 (Herwig Zahorka)

2   Ibid., p. 6 (Herwig Zahorka)

After the war the Americans and Japanese were as unlike each other as it is possible for two nations to be. The social hierarchy, tradition and culture of Nippon had developed over millennia, and they had proved successful at all levels. There was no need for trades unions. The business and industrial bosses had for generations shown a fatherly concern for their employees, even in hard times. Japanese from good families treated even their servants with attentive politeness and respect. They didn't need schoolmasters, petty pedagogues in American uniform, who came from a country where circumstances were totally different. For the Americans, the Japanese psyche was a book with seven seals – and the reverse must also have been true. After the war many Japanese wondered why their nation and the Germans were so unpopular in the western world. They came to the conclusion that the world was afraid of their diligence and thoroughness. Conscientious people have always been unpopular.

At the beginning, Japanese-American relations were characterised by deep misunderstandings, which began with the ambiguities of the Japanese language and ended with the ancient traditional state Shinto ceremonies, which were forbidden by the American occupiers. Why were the Americans so arrogantly sure of their own superiority? They had no reason to be! The Japanese had an ancient culture, they were a more genteel race, they behaved better, and in a few decades managed to catch up with the West in matters of technology. This was – unlike the situation in occupied Germany – the collision of two different worlds.

41. German Support for Indonesian Freedom Fighters

When I arrived in Indonesia in 1963, 18 years had passed since the Japanese occupation and 13 since the victory of the independence movement over the Dutch colonial rulers, and yet the events of that time were still very much alive in the thoughts of all Indonesians. Every day my Indonesian friends, who had themselves fought in that struggle, would tell me about their experiences of that time.

I have also interviewed many reliable eyewitnesses who all lived through the Second World War and the Japanese occupation, then training in PETA and the subsequent independence struggle. These men and women came from all levels of society. At the beginning of 1963 there were still over half a million former freedom fighters, militia members and partisans in Indonesia who had formed various veterans' associations. There were therefore plenty of people to speak to who had been there.

I kept hearing from them that Germany had, during the Japanese occupation, provided military material to equip PETA, such as steel helmets, water canteens and cooking utensils. There had also been heavier equipment, like trucks and DKW RT 125, BMW and Triumph motor cycles. They had even been given a Dornier seaplane. My Indonesian friends affirmed that they, like many of their fellow-fighters in the independence struggle after 1945, had fought against the Dutch and British in German steel helmets. They also told me that German officers had trained the Indonesian forces and German seamen had actively taken the part of the freedom fighters. I wanted to follow up this information.

When I came to Jakarta in 1963, I used to be a regular visitor to the street market on the Jalan Surabaya (Surabaya Street). You could find anything there – antiques, radios, stolen goods. The normal shops were almost always empty, but on the Jalan Surabaya almost everything was available. If you were looking for something special, it would be "taken care of". It was an official black market – and thieves' market.

I was surprised to find vast quantities of relics of the German army and the Nazi period there: hundreds of steel helmets, bayonets and Mauser pistols, cooking utensils, water canteens, German army boots etc. As curios I bought a canteen, a cooking pot and a steel helmet. I gave the helmet to an Indonesian friend and former freedom fighter. When he died, his wife used it to decorate his grave.

Given the quantities still available in 1963 the military equipment for PETA must have come from Germany: there was far too much for it to have come only from the supplies in the naval bases.

But how did this military equipment get to Java? Given the Allied superiority in the Indian Ocean and the blockade in the Atlantic, transport by surface freighter could be excluded after 1942. Dönitz could not afford any more losses to his already decimated battle and merchant fleets. So there was only one way: under water by U-boat! The large number of U-boats that reached South East Asia has already been described. But of the few boats whose cargo lists have survived, there is no mention of material destined for PETA in Indonesia. Regrettably, Walther Hewel's diaries for the time after the 31st of December 1941 have not survived the war: they would surely have helped to solve the mystery. After the occupation of the Dutch East Indies by Japan in 1942 and the building of the German bases, there was a lively exchange of goods between Germany and the "Southern Region". But PETA was not even founded until 1943, and so all I have to go on is the evidence of Indonesian veterans of the time.

It seems likely, however, that Hewel used his influence with Hitler to support the independence movement in Indonesia. The country's raw materials were anyway of vital importance to Hitler, and as the entries from Hewel's diaries quoted above show, the East Indies were often the subject of their intimate evening chats. Hewel therefore had every opportunity to make his concerns known. It seems fair to assume that Hitler would allow Hewel, his expert on the region, a free hand to supply German help to PETA.

Hewel not only had the opportunity to gain Hitler's support, he also had other influential helpers. In Berlin there was a triumvirate of high-ranking friends who were very familiar with the people, the culture and the whole Indonesian Archipelago. All three supported the freeing of the country from Dutch colonial rule, though it was the Japanese who played the main part in the creation of PETA.

On the German side, one supporter was Walther Hewel with his personal relationship with Hitler; on the Japanese side, Oshima Hiroshi must surely have been a driving force. He was a general in the Japanese army who was posted to Berlin as Japanese Military Attaché in 1934 and became Japanese Ambassador to Germany in 1940. He was a regular guest of Hitler even before his appointment as Ambassador – in 1936 he had been invited to join the Führer on a trip to Bayreuth.[1] At the end of 1941, after the Japanese attack on Pearl Harbor, Hitler awarded him the Order of the German Eagle in gold.

---

1   Hitler's Meetings: www.forum.axishistory.com

Hewel himself was very close to Hiroshi as can be seen from his 1941 diaries and his personal papers, which show reciprocal invitations in 1939 and later as well as a special invitation from Hiroshi to Walther Hewel on the occasion of the visit of the Japanese Foreign Minister Matsuoka Yōsuke to Berlin in March 1941.[1]

In Dönitz, who became commander of the German U-boat fleet in 1939 and Commander in Chief of the whole German Navy in 1943, Hewel and Hiroshi had another ally. In 1935 Dönitz had cruised East Indian waters for four weeks in the course of a South East Asian voyage as commander of the cruiser *Emden*, visiting Surabaya and Batavia among other places. He therefore had a clear picture of the situation there. Since Hewel was living in Batavia at the time[2], it seems certain that Hewel, because of his leading position as press officer of the NSDAP for the whole of the Dutch East Indies, must have met Dönitz in Batavia. Indonesia's supporters therefore had a third influential, like-minded ally.

Hewel held all the strings: Hitler as financial backer, Oshima Hiroshi as organiser of distribution in the Dutch East Indies and Dönitz as the man who could find free cargo space for them in the U-boats. The Indonesian veterans told me that the U-boats occasionally carried material for PETA as well as freight for Japan on their voyages back from Europe after delivering raw materials from the east.

My Indonesian friend, former freedom fighter Wibowo, took me to the Ancol war cemetery near Jakarta at the beginning of 1964. The bodies of Indonesian freedom fighters were buried beside those of Dutch, British, American and Japanese servicemen. I was surprised to see that most of the Indonesian graves were decorated with German steel helmets. When the cemetery was later moved because of a land reclamation and building project in the area, the majority of the steel helmets I had seen disappeared.

A lot of helmets must have been sent to Indonesia, because in the 1960s there were on the street markets in Indonesia not just original German steel helmets on sale, but also steel helmets with holes punched in them for use as colanders. Even now you can see motor-cyclists on the roads of Java and Bali wearing not modern crash-helmets, but old German steel helmets.

In 2013 I discovered to my surprise the temple guardians at the Hindu temple of Pura Bukit Lan Pucak on Bali, already mentioned before. Instead of the usual winged lions, giant snakes or Dewapala demons they are two almost life-size Japanese soldiers carved in stone – and wearing German army boots. Though this shows the Balinese sense of humour and irony, it also

1   IfZ, ED 100/79
2   he departed for Berlin in 1936

demonstrates the fact that German army boots were supplied to the Japanese in the "Southern Region" during the war.

Ill. 95
Notice at the entrance to the
  Pura Bukit Lan Pucak temple

Ill. 96
Japanese soldier as
Temple Guardian,
Pura Bukit Lan
Pucak Temple

I had been taken there by Agung Gde Rai, owner of the ARMA museum at Ubud in Bali, who told me that he had in the past taken Japanese veterans who had served in the Dutch East Indies during the occupation to the temple, and they had told him that the light Japanese army footwear was unsuited for operations in the jungles of South East Asia. As a result, large numbers of German army boots had been supplied to the Japanese. Some of these had then been handed on to PETA. It was not clear whether the boots came directly from Germany or from the factory in Penang mentioned above.

It was not, however, in purely material ways that Germany was helpful. After the German capitulation a number of German officers worked as trainers for PETA and the first provisional military academy in Yogyakarta. When Indonesia declared its independence on the 17th of August 1945, Soekarno insisted that all Indonesian officer cadets should speak German. All these cadets were taught German in groups by the German teachers in the Sarangan German School, as well as receiving instruction in physical training, as it was called at the time. This is why the Sarangan branch of the military academy was SORA, *Sekolah Olahraga*, sport school. The commander in chief of the Indonesian Navy, Admiral Martadinata, was also trained there. In the 1960s I was able to converse with him fluently in German. The first President of Indonesia, Soekarno, is known to have been an avowed Germanophile.

As I have said before, the veterans frequently told me that a dismantled Dornier DO 24 flying boat had been sent to Indonesia for PETA on one of the last U-boat transport missions, and that this aircraft, which could still be seen at the military airfield of Kalijati on Java, was the one Soekarno himself had used. I strongly doubt if this was actually the case, as the Dutch *Marine Luchtvaart Dienst* MLD (Naval Air Service) had several aircraft of this type in service in the East Indies, and it is likely that the plane at Kalijati had been captured from the Dutch MLD.

There was also a light German World-War-Two patrol boat in service in Sabang in 1969. Since it was in excellent condition, it must have been in PETA hands during the war of independence, otherwise the Dutch would have destroyed it, as they did so much else, when they finally withdrew from Indonesia.

My old friend, the former freedom fighter General Otty Soekotjo told me that at least two Mercedes-Benz *Kolonialwagen* G5s had been in service in the German bases in Batavia and Surabaya. For the time these vehicles were a "technological miracle". They were supplied to the German military between 1935 and 1941. The G5 was a robust all-terrain vehicle whose predecessor had been developed in 1910 for use in the German colony of South West

Africa. It had four-wheel drive and four-wheel steering, as well as a cooling system designed for use in the tropics. It had a turning circle of only seven metres. My friend told me that these vehicles had been handed over to the Japanese military authorities in Batavia after the German surrender. Soekarno had made temporary use of one of them when Japan also capitulated. Later he was driven around in a black Mercedes 190 which can still be seen in his parents' house in Blitar.

Young people in Indonesia increasingly venerate the Nazis. There are even organisations that wear imitation Waffen-SS uniforms to their meetings, and the swastika constantly appears in Indonesian periodicals and on the Internet. Hitler is still honoured for his support of the independence movement, unfortunately ignoring the fact that the Third Reich was a criminal regime that plunged the world into chaos by starting the Second World War.

In the *Museum Sepuluh Nopember* in Surabaya the Indonesian freedom fighters' four week battle against the British in November 1945 is commemorated. The exhibits include powerful photographs and other relics, such as Mauser rifles and bayonets used by the freedom fighters to defend themselves against the British.

The chapter on Subhas Chandra Bose showed that the Third Reich made a significant contribution to the fight for Indian independence. Unfortunately Bose – unlike Soekarno – did not live to see the moment to which he had devoted his entire life. It is a fact that the Third Reich, together with Japan, did, because of the war, directly and indirectly contribute to the Asian peoples' achieving independence after centuries of colonial rule. The German Reich's major contribution was in India and the Dutch East Indies, while Japan had the greater share in supporting all the South East Asian nations.

42. Indonesia's Struggle for Independence

On the 7th of August 1944 the Japanese Prime Minister Koiso Kuniaki announced the intention to grant the Dutch East Indies their independence. The closer the end of the war – foreseeable not a victory – approached, the more the Japanese supported Soekarno's efforts to achieve independence. The PPKI *(Panitia Persiapan Kemerdekaan Indonesia)* committee set up by Soekarno and the Japanese at the beginning of 1945 made preparations for breaking away from the Dutch. Soekarno, later the first President of independent Indonesia, and Mohammad Hatta, later the Vice President, chaired the committee. On the 12th of August 1945 they met Field Marshal Count Hisaichi Terauchi, Commander in Chief of the Japanese army in French Indochina, in Saigon, where they were informed of the impending collapse of the Japanese forces. However, Terauchi also assured them that Indonesia would be given independence in a few days.

After capitulating on the 15th of August 1945 Japan handed over power in the Dutch East Indies to the Allies. Many Japanese soldiers handed their weapons over to the freedom fighters, and where this did not happen voluntarily PETA soldiers disarmed the Japanese. Japanese barracks were stormed and arms depots plundered. All strategic points in the country, such as radio and telecommunications stations, ports and railway control centres were taken over by PETA.[1] There were many Japanese and also German servicemen who joined the Indonesian freedom fighters in what was to be an almost five-year struggle against the British and then the Dutch, until the latter finally left the country.

Japan's sudden capitulation after the Americans dropped the atom bomb came as a complete surprise to the Indonesians, since Japanese troops were still in action all over the "Greater Asian Co-Prosperity Sphere". Soekarno had hoped that Japan would hold out for a few months longer to give him time to create an orderly basis for independence – he and his ministers were not ready for such a swift takeover. There was also the frightening prospect of the imminent return of the Dutch. PEMUDA, the nationalist youth movement, was demanding a quick decision.

On the 16th of August 1945 the commander of the Japanese naval base in Batavia, Rear Admiral Count Tadashi Maeda, summoned Soekarno and Hatta to his residence in what is now Jalan Imam Bonjol No.1. In Dutch colonial times the street had been called Nassau Boulevard, and during the

1   Adams, *Sukarno*, p. 224

Japanese occupation Jalan Meiji Dori. It was clear that Japan was about to capitulate and Maeda urged Soekarno to declare independence before that happened. Whether he had received orders to do so from Japan or whether he was acting on his own initiative against the orders of the Japanese Commander in Chief, General Nashimura, has still not been established.

During the night the text of the declaration of independence was composed in Maeda's house. In the early hours of the morning of the 17th of August 1945, when they wanted to get the official text of the proclamation down on paper, they discovered that the only typewriter in the house was Japanese. Maeda's aide de camp Satzuki Mishima rushed to the house of Captain Kandeler, the former commander of the German base in Batavia, to ask for help. They went to the orderly room of the former German base in the port of Tanjung Priok to get a German typewriter. Only then could the declaration be typed out by Soekarno's secretary, Sayuti Melik, on a German Adler typewriter. It was then signed by Soekarno and Hatta the very same morning.[1] Soekarno and Sayuti Melik had been friends since 1926. As a nationalist, Sayuti had been imprisoned for many years in the concentration camp of *Boven Digoel* in Dutch New Guinea. Sayuti Melik also represented the Indonesian youth movement, PEMUDA, at the signing of the declaration.

Admiral Maeda's residence now houses the *Museum Perumusan Naskah Proklamasi* (Museum of the Declaration of Independence), which is surrounded by Jakarta's diplomatic quarter. The typewriter displayed there is not, however, the one that was actually used: according to the curator the German navy typewriter was handed back to Captain Kandeler immediately after the declaration was completed.

The independent Republic of Indonesia had now been launched by many heroes like Soekarno, Hatta, Sutan Syahrir[2], Bung Tomo and Tan Malaka, who had fought for their country's freedom over many decades and spent several years in prison as a result. Just before surrendering, Japan had kept its promise of independence to Soekarno. The white power of the Dutch was at an end. In fact that was a false conclusion. The brazen obstinacy with which the Dutch tried to regain their former colony knew no limits.[3]

After the 17th of August 1945 the slogan *Sekali Merdeka! – Tetap Merdeka!* (Once independent, always independent!) rang throughout the land, but their elation did not last very long. Firstly, marauding gangs swept through

---

1   Statement by eyewitness General Otty Soeketjo
2   First Indonesian Prime Minister and author of the 1945 *Onze Strijd/ Perdjoeangan/Unser Kampf*
3   Geerken, *Der Ruf des Geckos*, pp. 159ff

the country bringing chaos; then on the 22ⁿᵈ of August 1945 the Japanese announced that they were going to dissolve and disarm Soekarno's PETA and their own Indonesian *Heiho* militia. They did not succeed in doing so. Soekarno had a firm grasp on the power of the state and the new Indonesian forces, even though some of PETA's soldiers were armed only with bamboo spears, machetes or sickles because of a shortage of guns.

Ill. 97
PETA soldiers armed with bamboo spears

By October 1945 Soekarno had merged all the different military and paramilitary groups into the ABRI (*Angkatan Bersenjata Republik Indonesia*), which developed into the modern Indonesian armed forces.

When independence was declared, the Dutch still had not sent any troops to the East Indies. British and British Indian troops who were already in Singapore and Malaya were to prepare the way for the Dutch return under the command of Lord Mountbatten. The main mission of the British was to liberate the Dutch internees and prisoners of war from the camps and take them to British controlled areas. Then Indonesia should be returned to the Dutch step by step as they returned.

When the Japanese camp commanders announced that the war was over the prisoners initially rejoiced. At last the Japanese were no longer the masters! But liberation remained a dream: leaving the camps would have meant certain death for the Dutch, whether men, women or children.

The nationalist youth organisation PEMUDA had its origins in 1928. During the Japanese occupation, this Greater Asian Youth movement based on the Hitler Youth experienced a high point in terms of membership and radicalisation. These young men now saw their chance to revenge themselves on the Dutch for centuries of servitude. After the declaration of independence, there was a vacuum of power until internal order could be restored, a period known as *Bersiap* (Be prepared!). The Japanese had capitulated and given a large number of their weapons to the freedom fighters, the British were initially involved in regaining Malaya and Singapore, and the Kingdom of the Netherlands, so recently freed from the yoke of the Third Reich did not yet have the military power or financial means to re-establish the old power relationship in their colony.

During this *Bersiap* period some individual PEMUDA were totally out of control. They roamed the land robbing and plundering, terrorising the Dutch and Dutch sympathisers among their fellow-countrymen with their red and white banners. The latter included the Chinese and more especially the Indos and the Christian inhabitants of the Molucca Islands. These were groups that had always been all too ready to take the side of the colonists and to volunteer as canon fodder for the KNIL (the Dutch Colonial Army) in the fight against rebellious Indonesians. They were now at the top of the nationalist list for implacable retaliation.

The whole country was seized by nationalist fever: "We are free at last! *Merdeka!* Long live Soekarno!" Even among the older, more settled section of the population there was an explosion of the hatred that had built up against the Dutch for centuries. For the Dutch to leave the camps would have been fatal and the British, who had not expected this development, had to use Japanese and German servicemen to protect the camps against the marauding mobs.

The British occupation force was soon unwelcome, and hostilities against them began, culminating in massacres and war. On the 25th of October 1945 about 6,000 British infantry under the command of General Mallaby landed in Surabaya to – as they said – restore order. The truth of the matter was that the British wished to recapture the town from the freedom fighters for the Dutch. But the British had underestimated the heroic will of the Indonesians. There were skirmishes between British and Indonesian forces, especially since the freedom fighters refused to hand over their weapons when ordered to do so. The freedom fighters in Surabaya were particularly well-equipped with the weapons the Japanese had voluntarily given them.

There was an engagement in which General Mallaby was shot, after which the British military decided to take Surabaya by force. Another 24,000 British troops supported by tanks and aircraft were landed from Singapore. British warships were just off the coast. From the 10th of November 1945 Surabaya was shelled and bombed for three weeks. 200,000 people fled the city, civilians, the aged, mothers with children. British fighters strafed the refugee columns with machine guns. The battle for Surabaya lasted four weeks until the British managed to regain control of the city. K'tut Tantri, better known as Surabaya Sue though born in Glasgow, reported from Surabaya on a secret radio transmitter, becoming famous all over the world.[1]

10, 000 civilians, 16,000 Indonesian and 2.000 British soldiers lost their lives in the fighting – after Indonesia had become independent. Native women were hunted and raped by British Indian soldiers. Because of these events Surabaya was given the title "City of Heroes". Today this massacre by the British Empire would be prosecuted as a war crime committed when there was no actual war.[2] Sutomo, a freedom fighter better known in Indonesia as Bung Tomo (Brother Tomo) played a major role in the battle for Surabaya. The day before the battle he broadcast a stirring appeal to young Indonesians to defend the city:

Hey British soldiers! As long as the Indonesian bulls, the youth of Indonesia, have red blood that can make a piece of white cloth red and white, we will never surrender. Friends, fellow fighters, especially the youth of Indonesia, we will fight on, we will expel the colonialists from our Indonesian land that we love... Long have we suffered, been exploited, trampled on. Now is the time for us to seize our independence. Our slogan: FREEDOM OR DEATH. GOD IS GREAT... GOD IS GREAT... GOD IS GREAT... FREEDOM![3]

Under the government of Indonesia's second President Soeharto Bung Tomo fell into disgrace when he openly criticised rampant corruption. He indirectly accused Soeharto of failing to demonstrate courage during the independence struggle while claiming all the success of Indonesia's achievement of independence for himself. Bung Tomo was jailed. He is honoured today with a monumental obelisk in Surabaya and detailed documentation in the *Museum Sepuluh Nopember* mentioned before.

Violence against the new, now British, occupation forces escalated throughout the country. When a British aircraft made a forced landing in West Java near Jakarta the entire crew was lynched by the local inhabitants. In retaliation British forces destroyed the town of Bekasi.

As was usually the case in the east, the majority of the British front-line troops were Indian. Protests came not just from the Indonesians, but also in

---

1   Ibid., p. 162
2   Dates and Information from the Museum Sepuluh Nopember, Surabaya
3   Museum Sepuluh Nopember, Surabaya (official translation of the original text in Bahasa Indonesia)

India, where demonstrations took place all over the country. They could not accept the idea of Indian troops being used against another Asian country, their Asian brothers. The Indian politician Jawaharlal Nehru called on the Indian troops to lay down their arms. Nehru's protest was successful: as a result, hundreds of Indian soldiers deserted with their weapons to join the Indonesians every day. The British withdrew their troops from Indonesia.

At this time there were 25,000 Dutch volunteer soldiers on their way to Indonesia. In 1946 the Netherlands cabinet headed by Schermerhorn and Drees altered the constitution at short notice to allow them to send 100,000 conscripts to a bloody colonial war in Indonesia. On the 19th of December 2009 Dirk Schümer commented in the *Frankfurter Allgemeine Zeitung*:

Anyone who refused on conscientious grounds, immediately after the German occupation, to invade another country [Author's note: Indonesia] was sentenced to prison and never rehabilitated in civil society afterwards. Anyone who was against the colonial war was regarded in Holland as a deserter and was finished for life in social terms – a worse punishment than that given to the majority of Dutch Nazi collaborators.

Only a few years after the – obviously unjustified – occupation of their country by the German army, which the Dutch justifiably protested against, they were now occupying another free nation, which had been independent since the 17th of August 1945, and were surprised that the Indonesians resisted.

The last British troops left the archipelago in October 1946. The Dutch now set about Soekarno and his forces extremely brutally in order to restore the old power relationships. The Netherlands felt that their colony made them a *middelgrote mogendheid,* a medium power, and that without it they would lose a lot of prestige and become unimportant. They felt that the possession of the East Indies was vital and justified. The Netherlands parliament refused to recognise Indonesia's sovereignty and regarded it as a republic founded by "Japanese collaborators".[1]

While the Netherlands were committing atrocities, there were also Dutch soldiers who deserted and joined the Indonesians. The best-known is probably the later human rights activist Jan Princen. He was not allowed entry to the Netherlands until 1995, when he was seriously ill: they then allowed him to visit his family, but even then there were violent protests. The older generation in particular is unable to swallow the loss of their colony.[2]

---

1   www.wikipedia.org, Indonesian War of Independence, p. 10
     Doel, *Afscheid van Indie*, p. 350
2   Doel, *Het Rijk van Insulinde*, p. 298

In comparison with the Dutch the Indonesians were poorly armed, but PETA's soldiers were fighting for an idea and, in Soekarno, a leader they believed in. The soldiers were young, strong peasants whose discipline was based on that total trust in Soekarno. The lack of modern armament was not the only problem: without proper communication it was not possible to coordinate the operations of the various units. Individual groups often had to operate independently of each other. The only thing that held them together was their belief in their idol Soekarno and their shared objective of independence and self-determination. Although they had superior numbers, the freedom fighters were faced by around 150,000 well-trained and well-armed Dutch soldiers and soldiers of the former Dutch colonial army, the KNIL. This meant that the only hope of success lay in guerrilla warfare.

The Netherlands had unleashed a bloody and cruel war. The sections of the Dutch population that had rightly rebelled against the occupation of their own land by the Germans were heroes to them – but the Indonesian freedom fighters who, only a few years later, were rebelling against the Dutch invaders were terrorists and criminals. The Dutch were applying double standards.

In 1947 and 1949 they tried, in what they called police actions (*Politionele acties*), to neutralise the government of what was now the free Republic of Indonesia and regain control of the country. The Dutch government chose the innocent term "police action" to make the world believe that they were just dealing with a minor internal problem, when it was in fact a colonial war.

The deployment of 80,000 Dutch soldiers against the Indonesian Government in the second "police action" reminded the Dutch historian De Jong of the German invasion of the Netherlands.[1] Yogyakarta, the provisional seat of the new independent government, was bombed in December 1948 and Soekarno and other members of the government arrested and imprisoned. But the Indonesian army's guerrilla war was not halted by this: quite the contrary, it was intensified and the atrocities on both sides escalated.

One of the worst Dutch war criminals was Captain Raymond Westerling, who committed massacre after massacre of the Indonesian civilian population of Celebes, Sumatra and Java. He commanded the Dutch "special unit" DST[2] (*Depot Speziale Troepen*). He was known throughout the whole of Indonesia as "the butcher". When he was interrogating natives, he would hang them up by their feet. He carried out indiscriminate executions, and whole villages were exterminated by him and his henchmen. In South Sulawesi

---

1   Loe de Jong, *Het Koninkrijk der Nederlanden...*, p. 948
2   In some publications this special unit is also called KST (Korps Speziale Troepen)

alone he was responsible for the murder of 40,000 freedom fighters, women and children[1], murdering 400 with his own hands.[2]

There was also a lot of blood on the hands of Fred Ormskerk alias Bikkel, a soldier from Dutch Guyana (now the Republic of Surinam). He joined Westerling's DST as the head of a subordinate unit in 1946. The Dutch liked deploying troops from their South American colony against the Indonesians because they were very experienced in jungle warfare. For the crimes he committed in the service of the Dutch government Ormskerk is said to have been awarded several medals in 1946. The Indonesians insist that this is true, though the Dutch refuse to accept or admit it.[3]

Westerling was recommended for a high Dutch honour by General Simon Spoor, the Commander in Chief of the "Royal Netherlands Army of the East Indies" for his "great achievements". What is certain is that he was a brutal war criminal and should have spent his life in jail. But Dutch justice turned a blind eye.

Best selling Dutch author Geert Mak wrote:

The problem in the Netherlands [… was] the endless denial, the suppression of memories, the refusal to look historical truth in the eye. The Dutch people who were so outraged by similar behaviour on the part of the Americans in Vietnam and the Serbs in Bosnia and Kosovo have always carefully covered up their own My Lais and Oradours. That is also why hardly any […]documents have survived […].[4]

[Author's note: My Lai was a massacre carried out by US soldiers in South Vietnam in 1968. Oradour was a war crime committed by the Waffen-SS, who massacred the inhabitants of the village of Oradour sur Glane in France in 1944.]

The massacre of the civilian population of the village of Rawagede in West Java on the 9th of December 1947 still concerns the Indonesians. The Dutch troops suspected that the Indonesian guerrilla fighter Lukas Kustario was hidden there. They found no weapons and no fighters. Nevertheless they rounded up the villagers and murdered 431 men, youths and invalids. In spite of this war crime and an outraged report by the United Nations, the Commander in Chief, General Spoor, and the Chief State Prosecutor in the Hague did nothing to prosecute the perpetrators.[5]

---

1   Indonesian weekly magazine TEMPO, 25.02 – 03.03. 2013, pp. 32ff
     Geerken, *Der Ruf des Geckos*, pp. 168ff
2   Doel, *Afscheid van Indie*, pp. 284f
3   for details see: Kagie, *Bikkel*
4   Mak, Geert, *Das Jahrhundert meines Vaters*, pp. 433f
5   FAZ Nr. 295, 19.12.2009

The death of General Spoor is surrounded by rumours and speculation. He was lunching in the Yacht Club in Tanjung Priok in Batavia with his aide, the chief military chaplain and other guests on the 20th of May 1949. After lunch he and the two people sitting beside him suffered severe heart trouble. Spoor died five days later, the aide and the chaplain survived after a long illness. Since all the other guests ate the same things and suffered no problems it is assumed that Spoor was poisoned. Indonesians are masters of the art of poisoning.[1]

On the 1st of August 1949 a Dutch Lieutenant opened fire on the guests at an Indonesian wedding in the village of Goenoeng Simpin on the south coast of Java for no apparent reason, killing 26 and wounding 33.[2] Here too the Dutch authorities saw no reason to take action. One could continue with a long list of Dutch war crimes during their "police action". In 1948 the United Nations called the actions of the Netherlands in their former colony "deliberate and ruthless". There were certainly also war crimes on the Indonesian side, but one should not forget that the Dutch were the aggressors, not the Indonesians who were simply defending their independent republic against an attempt to recolonise it. As international pressure on the Netherlands intensified, the Hague tried to split the archipelago into several smaller states, hoping in this way to foster internal conflict. Fortunately, they were not successful.

Most public opinion in the world sympathised with the Indonesian independence movement. In Australia and nineteen Asian countries a boycott of Dutch goods and ships was started in 1948. The case of Indonesia appeared before the United Nations on several occasions, and the Dutch were unable to refute the accusations made against them. The US government threatened to stop Marshall Aid to the Netherlands as they had no desire to finance their colonial war. At a Round Table Conference in the Hague on the 23rd of August 1949 a decision was finally reached under pressure from the US and the UN that the Netherlands would irrevocably and unconditionally renounce their sovereignty over the independent Republic of Indonesia on the 3th of December 1949.

After the UN passed two more resolutions against the Netherlands on the 28th of December 1949, they finally had to cease hostilities. On that same day[3] Soekarno appeared before his people in Jakarta as the first President of Indonesia. Hundreds of thousands had assembled on the Koningsplein (King's Square), which was immediately renamed Medan Merdeka (Free-

---

1   Geerken, Horst, *Der Ruf des Geckos,* pp. 328ff
2   Doel, *Afscheid van Indie,* pp. 294f
3   During summer time in Europe, Jakarta was always one day ahead

dom Square). They were waiting excitedly for a speech by their leader. When Soekarno stepped up to the microphone, he paused for some minutes to enjoy the power of silence. When he finally triumphantly declared: *Alhamdulillah, Merdeka!* (We thank God! We are free!) and *Satu Tanah Air! Satu Bangsa dan Satu Tekad Tetap Merdeka!* (We have a home! We are one nation and are determined to remain independent) wild cheering broke out. The crowd cried out in chorus to their President: *Merdeka!* (Freedom) and *Hidup!*, (Long life!) Indonesia was free, but the international reputation of the Netherlands had suffered severely because of the obstinacy of its politicians.

Ill. 98
President Soekarno outside his palace on the 28th of December 1949

The Communists now went underground. Using the motto *Bhinneka Tunggal Ika* (Unity in Diversity) Soekarno could now unite his gigantic realm regardless of race, religion or language.

Young Indonesians have been well informed by their parents and grandparents about the war crimes committed by the Dutch. It is only now, more than 60 years later, that the Indonesian media are reporting these events more frequently, which is very unpleasant for the Kingdom of the Netherlands because they want to forget. Widows, children and grandchildren of the victims are prosecuting the Netherlands in national and international tribunals – sometimes successfully, as in the case of the Rawagede massacre. One reason why this massacre was finally discussed was my book *A Magic*

Gecko[1], published in Jakarta in 2011. It was reviewed in many Indonesian newspapers and magazines in Jakarta. In August 2013 17 widows were finally awarded 20,000 euros each by the Dutch government. It was a victory for the widows, even if the level of compensation for this war crime was extremely meagre. But at least the Dutch government was finally admitting that this was a crime. However, the Dutch government's agreement to pay the compensation swiftly was mere lip service. At the end of May 2014 only one widow had been paid, and in the mean time two of the others have died. Their ages are between 80 and 100 – and the Dutch Foreign Ministry says that the sums will not be payable to their heirs. So, as the Dutch lawyer Liesbeth Zegveld says, the Dutch legal system is dragging out the process so that this embarrassing problem will solve itself.[2]

Cases against the Dutch kingdom continue. Recently the interests of other victims have been represented in Indonesia and the Netherlands by the KUKB Foundation, (Dutch Debt of Honour Committee Foundation). Efforts are in train to bring the Westerling case before the UN and the International Court of Justice in the Hague: the official complaint was handed to the Dutch Government in May 2012. The aim is to have Westerling declared a war criminal for his acts of terror and to get compensation for the complainants, who are now between 75 and 104 year old, or their heirs. Since it would be extremely embarrassing for the Netherlands if the case were dragged up in public, they will presumably try to settle out of court.[3]

Why do the Dutch, government and people alike, have so much trouble accepting their inglorious colonial past? Is it just a question of the money? The Dutch authorities' major argument against the complaint is that it is out of time. Similar acts by Germans in the Second World War are still prosecuted: once again it is the famous Dutch double standard!

In the Dutch media and among the Dutch public interest in the atrocities committed during the colonial war is – perhaps understandably – surprisingly small. It is only left wing groups that call for atonement. By contrast, the stories of the victims of the German occupation are brought up all the time. Against the run of normal Dutch opinion the Dutch historian Lou de Jong writes in his standard work *Das Königreich der Niederlande im Zweiten*

1   *A Magic Gecko, Peran CIA di Balik Jatuhnja Soekarno*, Perebit Buku Kompas 2011 and *A Magic Gecko, CIA's Role behind the Fall of Soekarno*, Penerbit Buku Kompas, 2011

2   NRC Handelsblad v. 25. Mai 2014, *"Generous Gesture"*, Editor Emilie Outeren, The Hague
    http://7mei.nl/2013/12/31/generous-gesture/

3   TEMPO, 25.02 – 03.03. 2013, p. 40
    Geerken, *Der Ruf des Geckos*, pp. 168ff

Weltkrieg [The Kingdom of the Netherlands in the Second World War]: *Our lady Justitia applies double standards.*[1] But the past will still catch up with the Dutch because in international law crimes against humanity never lapse.

The Indonesians have now been waiting in vain for over 60 years for an official apology from the Dutch royal family for the many crimes committed during the colonial period and the police actions. Even when Queen Beatrix made a state visit to Indonesia in 1995, she could not bring herself to apologise, even though the Indonesian media demanded it. All Indonesians and neutral international observers find it incomprehensible that the Dutch government is now the only one in the world not to recognise the 17th of August 1945 as the official date of Indonesian independence. Is it obstinacy? Stupidity? Hurt pride? Or is it concern about possible claims for compensation? It could be expensive because at the end of the Second World War the Netherlands forces attacked a nation that had been independent since the 17th of August 1945 without any declaration of war.

---

1   Der Spiegel, 4/1988

43. Sarangan After the War

What became of all the Germans in Sarangan after the war? The delightful village that had been their home for many years now became alien and dangerous. No one knew what would happen next. Marauding gangs were making Java unsafe. It began with political conflict between the different groups. The Bersiap period brought chaos and plundering by rampaging gangs and Communist groups. Every night you could hear the fast, outlandish rhythm of the tom-toms, the village drums which warned the villagers of attacks, robberies or fire. They spread news from village to village like lightning. In the areas controlled by the freedom fighters, Soekarno's new government set up administrative structures, schools and barracks.

In collaboration with the new Indonesian authorities in Yogyakarta the German School in Sarangan continued, though at a reduced level. In 1946 at the request of the Indonesian military they accepted young officer cadets and other students. Some German families had to move house: the military had priority.

In Yogyakarta the new Indonesian armed forces had set up a temporary military academy where German seamen and officers from the Surabaya base acted as instructors. The Indonesians responsible for the military academy were impressed by the German School and the sports facilities in Sarangan, which is why the military academy's branch in Sarangan was called SORA, Sekolah Olahraga, (sport school), even though it provided more than just sports.

Initially 14 officer cadets received sport and foreign language instruction there. Since many mothers and children had left Sarangan, class sizes had shrunk. The teachers and the men at Sarangan now had new duties: they were working for the Indonesian military. German, English and French were taught, as well as sport and *klewang*, the Javanese martial art. German men kept SORA's books, German women did secretarial work and ran the kitchen staff.

It was a carefree time for them all. The vegetable gardens produced a rich harvest, but so that the supply of vegetables for the new arrivals would not run out, the German pupils were given the task of creating new vegetable plots. The Germans were paid for their services in kind by the Indonesian military: with rice, sugar, Indonesian cigarettes and Javanese tea and coffee. Paper money was now worthless.

Most meals were eaten together with the young officer cadets. In their free time they took trips into the forest or swam in the lake. The German pupils measured their klewang skills against the cadets. The head of the SORA in Sarangan was Colonel Singgeh, who had a doctoral degree in veterinary science. A school friend of Soekarno's, he was charming, extremely correct and polite.[1] He spoke German well.

One student at the SORA was the future Admiral Martadinata, Commander in Chief of the Indonesian Navy. After 1963 I had several opportunities to meet him and chat about his time in Sarangan and Yogyakarta. He still spoke good German, which he had learned in Sarangan. He confirmed that German naval officers had taught in the first Indonesian military academy in Yogyakarta, including Captain Rosenow, of whom more later. All my conversations with Admiral Martadinata were very friendly and open. He told me that as well as languages and sport he was taught orderliness and discipline at Sarangan, where he had spent a pleasant, carefree time with the Germans. Most of the officer cadets who were trained in the SORA later held senior positions in the Indonesian armed forces under President Soekarno after 1950.

Working with the Indonesian military meant extra security for the Germans living in Sarangan. If there was any danger from the marauding gangs, Indonesian government soldiers moved in to guard them. Both sides saw this collaboration as evidence of the friendship linking the German and Indonesian peoples.

The relationship between Soekarno and the Indonesian military and the Germans was one of great mutual respect and affection. As opponents of the Dutch and as only half friends of the defeated Japanese they saw Germany as their ally of the future.[2] Germans were in demand everywhere, not just as military advisors at the academy. German experts in a wide range of areas – engineers, craftsmen and doctors – who had previously worked for the Dutch colonial government were now needed by the young and inexperienced Indonesian republic. For example, in the workshops in the German naval bases, which had previously produced parts for the U-boats, they now made *goloks* (machetes) and spear points for the freedom fighters' bamboo spears. They often had no other weapons to defend themselves against the advancing Dutch troops.

The Germans in Sarangan gradually began to get the feeling that they had been forgotten in their lonely mountain village. It was like living on an island. Where was the Red Cross to take them home? Some of them lost patience: in February 1947 a few families left Sarangan and tried to get to Europe or Australia via Batavia, now called Jakarta, because the Dutch had

---

1   Keppner, *Wie weit bis Airmolang*, pp. 453 to 460
2   Ibid., p. 394

by now regained control of the major ports in Java, and they hoped leave that way. But in the towns around Sarangan, like Yogyakarta, Madiun and Solo, there was still fierce street fighting between the freedom fighters and the Dutch. Any overland journey was dangerous, as Java was divided into areas controlled by the Dutch, the Japanese and the new Indonesian government. But the Indonesian military provided escorts through the areas controlled by the new republic so that people did not mistake the Germans for Dutch people – without their help no blankes, whites, would have reached the coast.

Many women were not prepared to take the risk and waited for official help from the Red Cross, the Nederlandsch Indische Roode Kruis. Women, men and children wanted to get home to Europe at long last. Rumours kept circulating about a forthcoming evacuation from Sarangan. They packed their cases, but nothing happened. The Germans wrote petitions to the relevant officials in the Centraal Informatie Bureau in Jakarta, but the letters that reached the waiting women from the Red Cross were mostly simply notifications that their husbands had died in Dutch internment camps on Java and Sumatra or in British India or Dutch Guyana. When a positive response did finally arrive, it was simply that some women and their daughters could leave – the others would have to continue to wait in Sarangan.

When the second so-called Dutch "police action" began at the end of 1948, even Sarangan was no longer safe. The Dutch troops were getting closer and closer. Herr Fischer, the Van Imhoff survivor, ex-president of the "Free Island of Nias" and "mayor" of Sarangan, suddenly vanished one night, and no one knew where to. He had simply gone underground, probably to the freedom fighters. The Dutch had been looking for him for some time. They wanted to bring him to book for his coup d'état, which had led to a German transitional government and the first free Indonesian area. The Dutch could not forgive him for this exploit, which had led to the capture of all the Dutch, British and Australians on the island, especially since some of the British and Australians were escapees from Japanese prison camps, who were then executed in Nias by the Japanese.[1] Fischer's successor was Dr Hupfer, the interpreter from the German base in Batavia, who had also withdrawn to Sarangan after the Japanese capitulation.

In December 1958 the Indonesian base commander informed the 50 or so Germans still in Sarangan that they would have to leave because of the superior strength of the Dutch forces. He could no longer guarantee their safety. His soldiers would carry out a scorched earth policy: Sarangan would be demolished and burnt down, so that no habitable buildings, people or animals would fall into Dutch hands. The only booty the victorious Dutch

---

1   Anwar, *Sejarah Kecil,* pp. 85ff

would acquire would be charred beams and soot-covered ruins.[1] The Germans would have to decide whether to escape into the forest with them or to stay on in Sarangan, in which case a few of their houses would be spared. The Germans decided to stay. There were now 52 Germans left – 42 women and children, and ten men, including Dr Hupfer.

Sarangan was still in flames when the Dutch marched in on the 25th of December 1948 and took the Germans prisoner once more. What a sad Christmas Day!

The *Volks* German boys with Dutch citizenship who had had to work for the Germans on the naval bases were now in a very difficult position. They were forced to work for the Germans, since they would otherwise have been interned in a Japanese camp. Now they were collaborators in Dutch eyes. The Dutch secret service PID (Politieke Inlichtinger Dienst) had a long black list of names. The *Volks* German boys were harassed and abused: You claim to be Dutch and worked for the Germans? That was high treason, and could mean the death penalty. They had to carry out hard penal labour and were subjected to harsh brain-washing. Just like the Indos, they fell between two stools.

As had happened with the Japanese, the Germans in Sarangan and in other areas were now faced with forced repatriation. On the 1st of January 1949 the Germans were taken away in open Red Cross trucks. On Dutch orders, they could only take one piece of luggage, which is why so few letters, documents and photographs have survived from their time in Sarangan. A group of women, children and a few men reached Jakarta via Madiun and Semarang. Here the Germans were held in the Chasee camp and the former PoW camp on the infamous prison island of Onrust. Another group had to hold out for weeks in the most primitive circumstances in the Sawahan camp in Surabaya, near the former German naval base. Four years after the end of the war, German women and children were treated like prisoners of war by the Dutch! It took nine long months until, in September 1949, the Germans' Odyssey in the former Dutch East Indies was at an end. The final German women and children were allowed to travel to Amsterdam on the Dutch ship *Willem Ruyss*, and then on to Germany.

As well as the Germans, and some Dutch soldiers, the *Willem Ruyss* also carried returnees, Dutch with German roots, who had been called *Volks* Germans during the Third Reich. German descent was for the Dutch government enough to justify dishonourable dismissal, cancellation of pension rights, imprisonment, abduction and internment, often with fatal consequences.[2] Many of the returning widows arrived in Amsterdam without any

---

1   Keppner, *Wie weit bis Airmolang*, pp. 464ff
2   Ibid., pp. 508f

financial means and were in need of help. The battle for rehabilitation lasted a long time and was often unsuccessful.

The Netherlands left the young republic with a country that had been devastated and a debt of almost 3.5 billion US dollars – the amount the Dutch had spent on their colonial war and the two police actions. For Indonesia and the international community, this seemed a monstrous impertinence. But in 1955, with the agreement of many, even some western, nations, Soekarno unilaterally cancelled this unjust agreement arising from the 1949 Hague Conference. Indonesia could not be made to pay for a war that had been forced upon them![1]

At the end of January 1950, after the international community had forced the Dutch to withdraw, Captain Westerling, created an army, the APRA (Angkatan Perang Ratu Adil) [Army of the Righteous King] made up of Dutch soldiers who had remained in Indonesia and fanatical Communists and Muslims. Capturing parts of Bandung in a coup d'état, he attempted to overthrow the Soekarno government. Westerling set fire to south Bandung, but the Indonesian forces were now capable of concerted action. The Dutch captain's final criminal act failed, and he was forced to flee to Singapore in February 1950.[2]

From 1945 to the end of 1949 Indonesian sources suggest that between 100,000 and 200,000 freedom fighters and even more civilians lost their lives in Dutch "police actions".

This did not end the tension between the Netherlands and Indonesia. After the almost five-year struggle for independence, there was a fourteen-year fight for Dutch New Guinea, the western half of the island. Indonesia, as the successor to the entire Dutch territory in the East Indies, insisted on claiming this part of the colony as well. The Netherlands remained obstinate for reasons of power politics, and clung on to this last scrap of their territory. There was another reason why the Dutch wanted to hang on to New Guinea: they wanted to settle the Indos there and not in "pure-blooded" white Holland.[3] During the colonial period the Dutch had never shown any economic interest in New Guinea, and this part of the island was totally undeveloped.

Because the Netherlands were so unyielding on the question of New Guinea, Soekarno led an anti-Dutch campaign in December 1957, as a result of which tens of thousands of Dutch people who had remained in Indonesia had to flee back to their homeland. Dutch property was confiscated. Relations with the Netherlands got worse and worse until they finally broke

1   Geerken, *Der Ruf des Geckos*, pp. 169f
2   Ibid., pp. 170f
3   www://www.insideindonesia.org/stories/being-indo-22031411, p.7

off all diplomatic and economic relations. At the beginning of 1963 Indonesia occupied their half of New Guinea – an area about the size of California.

Soekarno had previously ordered a number of Russian submarines which entered service at the beginning of 1962, so that Indonesia would be able to protect itself if the Dutch attacked with their navy. It was only after strong international pressure on the Netherlands that the UN agreed to the transfer of power in the former Dutch colony of New Guinea to Indonesia on the 1st of May 1963. Today the territory is called variously West New Guinea or West Papua, and in Indonesia the "Province of Papua". The trauma caused by Dutch New Guinea's survival as a symbol of continuing colonial power in the Pacific was at an end. The red and white flag of Indonesia was at last waving over the whole of the former colony – the Indonesian state now stretched from Sabang to Merauke! By holding on to West Papua the Netherlands did a great deal of economic damage to themselves and Indonesia and gave an enormous boost to Indonesian nationalism.

Ill. 99
Stamp from Sabang to Merauke

Unfortunately Holland was in no way prepared to help her former colony with good will, fairness and good advice – quite the opposite. In revenge for having freed themselves from their colonial masters stumbling blocks were constantly thrown in the path of the young republic.

On the initiative of Hardy Zoellner, a former pupil of the school, a memorial plaque was unveiled in a central position in Sarangan where the Jalan Telaga Sarangan leads directly to Lake *Telega Pasir*, commemorating the friendship between the native population and the Germans who lived there peacefully with them during the war and afterwards. The plaque arouses great interest among both natives of Indonesia and tourists.

Dalam persahabatan Jerman - Indonesia
Sebagai kenang-kenangan
akan sekolah Jerman dan
para ibu Jerman beserta anak-anaknya
yang pernah tinggal di Sarangan
di masa kesukaran tahun
1943 – 1949
In Erinnerung an die *Deutsche Schule*
und die Mütter mit ihren Kindern,
die in der schweren Zeit hier
in Sarangan gewohnt haben.

Ill. 100
Memorial plaque to the German School Sarangan

When I first visited Sarangan in 1963, fifteen years after the German school was shut down and the last Germans left, it was once more a dreamy, picturesque little village, though the ruins left by the scorched earth policy were still there, as were the foundations of the school. Today Sarangan is a popular resort with new hotels round the lake, markets and souvenir shops. Boats towing water-skiers speed over the lake. Loud music blares from loudspeakers. The peaceful time when the German School was there is quite definitely over.

44. The Dutch After the War

From 1933 until the beginning of the war, relations between the Netherlands and Germany were extremely friendly. After his marriage to Princess Juliana, heir to the Dutch throne, in January 1937, Prince Bernhard von Lippe-Biesterfeld's first state visit as a member of the royal house was to Hitler in Berlin. Even at the end of 1939, after the failed assassination attempt on Hitler in the Bürgerbräukeller in Munich, Queen Wilhelmina was the first to send her good wishes and express how glad she was that he had survived. After the war, however, there was no trace of friendly relations.

When it was once again possible to travel to Holland after the war – it must have been between 1948 and 1950 – my mother and I visited our Dutch relations. After crossing the Dutch border, we were insulted and cursed by Dutch people on the train. I was distraught – I was still quite young – what had I done? There were notices on restaurants in Amsterdam and other places: "Dogs and Germans Forbidden". When staying with our aunts and uncles we were asked not to leave the house if possible, but if we had to, then not to speak German aloud. They had to conceal the fact that they had Germans staying with them.

It is bordering on the hypocritical for the Dutch to give the impression that they were just victims in the Second World War. All that Germans heard from the Dutch media was a stream of Nazi Germany, criminals, concentration camps, Holocaust! Such a thing could never happen among us Dutch – yet it did happen! After the war there were no more concentration camps in Germany – thank God! – but the Dutch opened new ones on islands in their former colony in 1950. Thousands of nationalists and their sympathisers were arrested and imprisoned. One of the worst concentration camps was *Boven Digoel* deep in the jungles of Dutch New Guinea. The Dutch quite rightly condemned the Nazi bombing of Rotterdam, but after the war they bombed cities in Java and Sumatra, killing many thousands of civilians. The Dutch were not just victims – as they still try to present themselves – they were also perpetrators.

After the German surrender, young Dutch women who had been friendly with German soldiers during the occupation were made to suffer. They were called *moffenmeiden* and had their heads shaved, then with a swastika painted on their forehead were paraded through the town or taken through the town on open lorries for public show.[1]

1   http://7mei.nl/belanda-tjampur

After 1945 the Dutch behaved as if they – with a very few exceptions – had been on the right side and fought against the Germans in every possible way. They even managed to whitewash any misdemeanours and to wipe their own crimes from memory. And yet it has been shown that the Dutch police, the administration, the railway and many Dutch citizens took an active part in the destruction of the Jews. And the fact that the Netherlands committed war crimes during their "police action" in Indonesia is incontrovertible.[1]

After the war the Dutch government did everything to prevent scandalous details of their inglorious colonial past and their "police Action" from becoming public knowledge. They wanted to forget about the colonisation of the East Indies as soon as possible, since it was something they could by no means be proud of.

Even the reception of the Dutch colonists returning home after three, four or more years in Japanese internment camps or on the Sumatra and Burma railways was extremely restrained. The Dutch in the motherland were looking to the future, and did not want to hear stories about the war in the distant East Indies. They had grown apart from each other, and there was a fear that the new arrivals would provide competition in their economically struggling homeland. They also spoke differently, their Dutch was mixed with Malay words, and they had been spoiled by their comfortable and luxurious colonial life-style. Now they were arriving empty-handed and needed help – there was hardly a word of thanks for their commitment to the homeland. They returned to their cold and estranged native land on the North Sea in three waves. They were not welcome: they were regarded as beggars, and no one was interested in "Indian" problems.

The first wave in 1945/1946 saw about 110,000 Dutch and Indos arrive in the Netherlands. After December 1949 brought the end of their dream of the reconquest of their colony which was now, after pressure from the UN, under Indonesian control, another roughly 100,000 former settlers returned to the Netherlands. The third wave arrived when Soekarno began his anti-Dutch campaign in December 1957 because of the Dutch Government's intransigence over the New Guinea question. The last remaining 50,000 Dutch were now forced to leave Indonesia, returning to a homeland that was alien to them.

All the Indos, mixed-race Dutch citizens, also had to leave their familiar Indonesian home, where they had been born and grown up. At the beginning of the 1930s almost a quarter of all Dutch marriages in the colony were mixed-race. Their Eurasian descendants, called Indos, formed their own so-

---

1   Mak, *Das Jahrhundert...*, p. 476 and
        Bergstein and Bloemgarten, *Remembering Jewish Amsterdam*

cial grouping with their own clubs and schools.[1] It was particularly difficult for them to start a new life in the Netherlands: they all experienced conflict, a lack of recognition, humiliation and trauma. They were Dutch according to their documents, but for the native Dutch they remained Indos, half-castes to be looked down on.

There were also tens of thousands of indigenous soldiers who had fought for the Dutch in the Colonial army, the KNIL, seeking refuge in the Netherlands with their families. Most of them were inhabitants of the Molucca Islands: since their early conversion by the Portuguese, the Moluccas had had a majority Christian population and felt closer to their European colonial masters than to the mainly Muslim native population. During the colonial period they had always been on the Dutch side, and during the war of independence they had fought against Soekarno, whose aversion to them was thus understandable. At the beginning of the 1990s there were 450,000 people living in the Netherlands who had been born, or whose parents had been born, in Indonesia.[2] This is still problematic.[3] Colonial officials and members of the Dutch Colonial army received a miserly payment of 7,500 Gulden (in modern terms about 3,300 Euro), scant reward for so many years under Japanese rule.[4] The time spent in Japanese internment was added to the pension entitlement of white people, but not the Indos who served in the KNIL. They are still fighting for equal treatment.

---

1   Loeber, Irmgard, *Das niederländische Kolonialreich*, p. 40
2   Doel, *Het Rijk van Insulinde*, p. 299
3   Geerken, Horst, *Der Ruf des Geckos*, pp. 172ff
4   FAZ, 15.08.1985, *Beim Wilhelmslied nahmen sie Haltung an*

45. Portuguese Timor's Involvement in the Second World War and its Far-Reaching Consequences

Portugal remained neutral in the Second World War, and yet its colony in Portuguese Timor was dragged into the conflict. Although I can find no evidence that Germany had any contact with Portugal's colonies, I would like to refer briefly to Portuguese Timor, since the effects of the war are still being felt there.

Portuguese Timor, now the Democratic Republic of Timor Leste, better known as East Timor, played an important role in the war, although the neutral half of the island was far away from the world's power-centres in the eastern part of the Indonesian archipelago. The whole island is 476 kilometres long and its maximum width is 102 kilometres. For many centuries the island was a pawn in the games of the colonial powers.

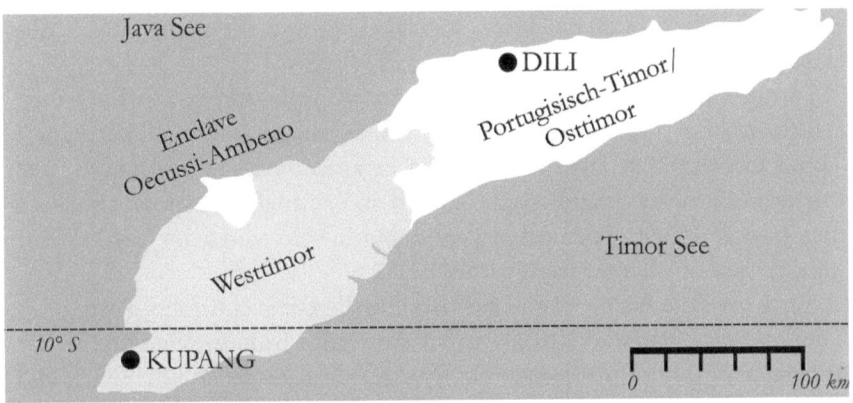

Ill. 101
The Island of Timor

In the 14th century Timor was probably part of the Hindu Majapahit Empire, whose capital was in East Java. At the beginning of the 16th century Portuguese seafarers were the first Europeans to discover the island, and in 1515 Portuguese missionaries began to settle its eastern half. Shortly afterwards the Portuguese built garrisons and trading posts.

In 1640 the Dutch began to settle in the west of the island. For over 200 years they and the Portuguese were at war because they both wanted to claim this economically interesting island for themselves. Sandalwood, which grew on the island, was very much in demand in Europe and therefore very profitable. In 1859 they agreed to divide the island, although quarrels and military skirmished continued. Only in 1919 was the current arbitrary border – dividing villages and tribes – established. Now there were Portuguese Timor in the east with its capital in Dili and Dutch West Timor (Timor Barat) with its capital in Kupang. Peace reigned at first, but the small Portuguese enclave remained a foreign body in the giant Indonesian archipelago.

Portuguese Timor was a permanent trouble spot. The Portuguese ruled with brutal force. The native Timorese were subjected to forced labour and an extremely high poll tax. There were regular indigenous uprisings against Portuguese rule right down to the beginning of the war. Order could only be maintained by large contingents of troops from Portugal's African colonies. After the Portuguese half of the island had been completely deforested and exploited there were floods in the five-month rainy season that led to heavy erosion and drought in the dry season. With nothing more to be squeezed out of it, the Portuguese now totally neglected the colony. There was as good as no infrastructure except in the capital, Dili, and the population in the countryside starved.[1]

Portugal and its colonies remained neutral in the war, but without their agreement the Netherlands and Australia stationed troops in Portuguese Timor in December 1941 to prevent a Japanese invasion. Australia feared that this half of the island might be used as a springboard for an attack on their own continent. Portugal protested, but in vain, and from then on Portugal refused any cooperation with the Allies.

Since the Dutch and Australians had illegally taken control of Portuguese Timor, several thousand Japanese infantry invaded from the west on the 20th of February 1942. At the same time Japanese ships landed 1,500 men at Dili and a further 850 Japanese paratroopers provided support. Japan assured the protesting Government in Lisbon that there would be no problem with restoring Portuguese Timor's neutrality after the war.

There were fierce battles in which there were heavy losses among the Japanese paratroops, but ending in a large number of Allied troops being taken prisoner. A few of them escaped into the mountains in eastern Timor and waged a guerrilla war on the Japanese. On several occasions convoys of US and Australian warships and troop transporters attempted to bring reinforce-

---

1   http://de.wikipedia.org/wiki/Rebellionen_in_Portugiesisch-Timor_
     %281860%E2%80%931912%29

ments from Darwin, but these were attacked by Japanese aircraft and had to return with heavy losses.

The Allied guerrillas were extremely brutal towards the indigenous people in the mountain villages. If they had the slightest suspicion of treachery or were not given sufficient supplies of food, there were serious punishments – including execution. They were supplied with food and weapons by air and sea from Darwin, 650 kilometres away.

The majority of indigenous Timorese initially saw the Japanese as liberators and joined their side. The Japanese created a Black Column (the *Colunas Negras*) from among collaborating and conscripted Timorese and the coloured soldiers from Portuguese Africa. During the Japanese occupation these soldiers terrorised inhabitants of Portuguese descent, and there were also internal struggles between rival groups within the population. Since the Portuguese inhabitants mostly sympathised with the Allies and collaborated with them, about 600 people, mainly Portuguese officials and their families, were interned in camps in October 1942. Many died of diseases because of a lack of medication. The indigenous people's initial enthusiasm for the Japanese also soon waned, and they began to place their hopes of freedom from colonial rule not on Japan but on Australia, which was closer. By the end of 1942 there were over 10,000 Japanese troops stationed on the Portuguese part of the island.

On the Dutch, western half of the island the situation was different. Right down to the end of the war the Japanese were seen as liberators from Dutch rule, and the indigenous population worked closely with the Japanese, actively supporting their military action against the Allies in the east. Here, too, there were far more than 10,000 Japanese troops in action.

In 1943 the Japanese wiped out the last Allied guerrillas in Portuguese Timor: they had suffered severely from the tropical climate and malaria. Some of the troops and some Portuguese civilians had been taken to safety in Australia in Australian ships and a US submarine. Now Japan controlled the whole island in such force that it was unlikely that the Allies would be able to retake it.

The Japanese troops took brutal revenge on those elements of the population that had supported the Allies. The Portuguese colonial administration was eliminated and a new Japanese paper currency issued. Japanese was taught in the schools. Once again there were forced labour and forced prostitution, and what little food there was was seized.

The Allies bombed the capital Dili several times during the Japanese occupation, destroying the Japanese Consulate, the radio station, the hospital, the port and other targets. Shortly before the end of the war the Japanese introduced measures to reinstate the old colonial status quo and Portuguese sovereignty in East Timor – exactly the opposite to what they did in the western half of the island, where they introduced measures – as in the whole of the Dutch East Indies – to ensure independence. These different actions can be explained by the fact that it was possible to foresee that the US would wish to make use of the Portuguese half of the island, which was of great strategic importance as well as possessing major oil reserves. To prevent this, Japan tried to reintroduce the old colonial situation.

At the end of the war Japan surrendered control over the island to the Allies. On the 11th of September 1945 the surrender of the Dutch part of the island was signed on board the Australian ship *HMAS Moresby*. Much to the annoyance of the Netherlands, their representatives were not allowed to be present at the ceremony. This showed that the Allies recognised western Timor as part of independent Indonesia.

On the 26th of September 1945 the official capitulation ceremony for Portuguese Timor took place in Dili. The vast majority of the population wished to be free of Portuguese rule, but at the negotiations in Lisbon the US had favoured retention of colonial status, in return for which the US demanded that they should be able to continue to use the military base on the Azores which had been built during the war. For US political and strategic reasons the people of Portuguese Timor were refused both independence and incorporation into Indonesia.

The first Portuguese transports carrying 2,000 troops reached Dili the next day, the 27th of September 1945, to enforce the return of colonial status. The native revolts against the Portuguese continued: they were put down with great brutality.

Since the Netherlands and Australia had been the first to occupy Portuguese Timor, Portugal demanded that they pay for the war damage caused as a result. In vain.[1]

In 1975, with Portugal's agreement, East Timor declared itself independent. The country descended into chaos, and Indonesian troops marched in to bring about a return to peace. Linguistically the Indonesian troops had no problem, since Bahasa Indonesia was the lingua franca of the country even if Portuguese was preferred. Portuguese was now forbidden by the Indonesian authorities, just as Bahasa Indonesia had previously been. Indonesia's invasion and annexation of East Timor took place with the agreement of the US and Australia. The annexation was even welcomed by the Australian ambassador in Jakarta, because they felt that Indonesia would be a more reliable

---

1   http://home.snafu.de/watchinII_1_05/Port_Timor.htm
     http://de.wikipedia.org/wiki/Schlacht_um_Timor

and solvent partner in the exploitation of the oil resources in the Timor Sea than a small, independent East Timor without any other resources.

The Indonesian military clamped down on the Portuguese-friendly movement Fretlin, which started a guerrilla war against the Indonesian occupiers. Even the visit of Pope John Paul II in October 1989 failed to bring a peaceful solution. It was the first visit by a head of state to the country which, although annexed by Indonesia, had a majority Catholic population.

On the 12th of November 1991 Indonesian troops committed a massacre at a demonstration during the funeral of a Fretlin independence fighter, killing 271 people – Indonesian sources suggest 19. Since the massacre took place under the eyes of foreign journalists it received great international attention, especially since it took place in the heated religious atmosphere of a Muslim state attacking Catholics. Of course, none the previous massacres of the indigenous population by Portuguese Catholics were as interesting to the Western press.

Violence between the two sides escalated. The land, already poor, was laid waste, agricultural areas destroyed. Only when Australian troops landed in the east of the island could some calm be brought to the heated situation. The UN organised a referendum to decide whether the country wished to be part of Indonesia or independent. Bishop Belo played a major role in the forefront of the referendum campaign.

Belo had studied philosophy in Portugal. After the Indonesian annexation of Portuguese Timor he moved to Macao and then to Rome to study Theology. In 1980 he was ordained in there and returned to his homeland during the Indonesian occupation. He was consecrated bishop there in 1988. He engaged actively and publicly in East Timor's campaign for independence and was subjected to repressive measured by the Indonesians. He proposed an independence referendum, though this was strongly influenced and guided by the Catholic church.

I visited East Timor shortly before the referendum in 1999. Among the indigenous population I sensed a general pro-Indonesian feeling, since a great deal of progress had been made during the Indonesian occupation. They praised the work on the infrastructure, which had hardly been there at all during Portuguese colonial rule: the fact that they were now free to travel, free trade with the outside world and the promotion of Bahasa Indonesia as the official language. But the simple country population was being intimidated by the Portuguese section of the population who – since there was no chance of reinstating colonial rule – at least wanted complete independence. I kept hearing that the Catholic Church and Bishop Belo personally were threatening with excommunication anyone who voted to stay with Indonesia. For very

Catholic minded simple people, who relied on the Church, this would mean exclusion from the community. And so in the referendum a majority of 78% voted for independence. New unrest flared up and about 200,000 Catholic East Timorese fled to the Indonesian part of the island. Bishop Belo returned to Portugal, later becoming a missionary in Mozambique.

On the 20th of May 2002 Portuguese Timor finally became independent of Portugal. Today this half-island is really unattractive and hardly able to survive without outside help. Portuguese and Portuguese Eurasians still dominate the indigenous population.

In the Timor Sea between East Timor and Australia, there are considerable off-shore oil and gas resources. Shortly after the annexation of East Timor by Indonesia in 1975, talks began between Indonesia and Australia to define the borders of these off-shore oilfields. This led to the 1989 Timor Gap Treaty, which agreed on mutual exploitation of the oil and gas resources on East Timorese territory. Although the oilfields are considerably closer to East Timor than Australia, the Indonesians agreed that Australia should receive 50% of the income. The people living in East Timor were not consulted, even though the largest deposits are on their territory.

East Timor is now once more a half island, independent within the massive Indonesian archipelago of more than 13,000 islands. Surely this cannot bode well? There will obviously be conflicts in future. And there is some conflict already, not with Indonesia, but with Australia. Since independence there have been border disputes concerning the exploitation of the oilfields. They are the subject of international litigation at the moment.[1]

The agreement between Australia and Indonesia led to the creation of a Zone of Cooperation to deal with exploitation of the resources on East Timorese territory. When independence came, Indonesia abandoned its rights, just when the extraction was moving into profit. Indonesia withdrew at great financial loss. Not so Australia. It insisted on retaining the borders agreed with Indonesia, even though it was established internationally that by far the greatest part of the oil and gas fields are on East Timor's territory. Australia is still delaying talks to define an internationally accepted boundary while making billions of dollars of profit. Presumably the delay will continue until the offshore resources are exhausted. Although there is a campaign in East Timor opposing the occupation of the Timor Sea by Australia, their calls for help are not receiving much attention in the Western media. Tiny East Timor has no hope of defending itself against its powerful southern neighbour.

---

1   The Sydney Morning Herald, 25 January 2014, *East Timor: Oil and troubled borders*,
      www.smh.au/world/east-timor

In 2009 there was an accident on an Australian oil rig and over four million barrels of crude oil leaked into the sea. The oil-carpet polluted not only the south coast of East Timor, but also many Indonesian islands, causing many fishermen to lose their livelihood. It will take a long time for the ecosystem to return to normal.[1]

The USA plans to build a major base on East Timor, including an atomic submarine base, which certainly will not please Indonesia. Since East Timor is as poor as a church mouse and depends on outside financial support it is hardly likely to refuse the American offer. Further problems are bound to crop up.

There is another area that is causing Indonesia unease. On the north coast of Timor, inside Indonesian West Timor, there is the tiny former Portuguese enclave of Oecussi-Ambeno (also Oecusse-Ambeno). In the 1980s a group of New Zealand anarchists founded a fictional state there, the Sultanate of Oecussi-Ambeno. The newly published stamps were very much in demand among collectors. The enclave became independent with East Timor in 2002, but still has border disputes with Indonesia. East Timor and Oecussi-Ambeno, located in the midst of the Indonesian archipelago, are sure to be responsible for further unrest in the future.

---

1   http://www.laohamutuk.org/Oil/curse/OilInTLOilwatch.htm

46. Hitler's Death

On the 7th of May 1945 Germany's unconditional surrender was announced. The war and the dictatorship of the Third Reich were finally over. But Europe lay in ruins. Berlin, the proud and beautiful German capital, was now the "Reich's rubble field". I was only eleven and a few months old, but to judge by what I had experienced in the war I was no longer a child.

During the Third Reich we children were indoctrinated in school, by our surroundings, by the *Jungvolk* and the Hitler Youth. We still believed in the "wonder weapon" and final victory. When we heard that Hitler had avoided his responsibilities by committing suicide, our world collapsed. We couldn't believe it. Hitler had been presented to us as a god, and was adored by us accordingly. There was a lot of speculation, and constant rumours that he was alive and living abroad. We could rely on him and he would be back. But what has Hitler's death to do with Indonesia? Perhaps more than you might think. This is something that has been totally neglected by historians to this very day.

The Red Army led by General Zhukov was surrounding Berlin: Stalin wished to make sure that the Western Allies should have no access to the city. For days there was terrible street fighting in Berlin, even though the Russian forces were hundreds of times more numerous than the defenders.

Hitler gave his last radio address on the 30th of January 1945. Only 12 days before the fall of Berlin, on the 20th of April 1945, Hitler celebrated his 56th birthday, apparently in the Führer bunker in Berlin. Chaos reigned. With him in the bunker were Walther Hewel, his aides, bodyguards, secretaries, his valet Linge, his physician Dr Schenk and other loyal members of his entourage, including his chief pilot, Hans Baur.

The last German *Wochenschau* newsreel no. 755 shows Hitler walking about in the open in the courtyard of the Reich Chancery. He walks along a row of Hitler Youth, inspiring them with the courage to defend Berlin to the last drop of blood – they were hardly more than ten years old. Hitler strokes the cheek of one of them in a fatherly way.

This was what has until now been assumed to be Hitler's last public appearance. His loyal friend and companion Walther Hewel was at his side to present the boys to Hitler.[1] Witnesses who claim to have seen him on his birthday say that they advised him to escape. After this public appearance Hitler is said to have immured himself in his bunker, the safest bunker in

---

1   www.youtube.com/watch?v=vslu5C2M981

*Ill. 102
Hitler's last
appearance,
supposedly on
the 20ᵗʰ of April
1945*

the world, built of concrete several metres thick, nine metres underground. At least, that is the official version, and how this last German newsreel is described in the media. But this is where inconsistencies start to appear.

As the media scientist Anne Luise Kiss, a graduate of the Film and Television University in Potsdam recently demonstrated, the material was not filmed on Hitler's birthday. As she showed, by reason of the background, the filming took place only partly in the Chancery, but also partly in the Hitler Youth's *Auslandshaus*, now the Haus Lenné in Berlin Gatow. This part of the city could not have been reached on Hitler's birthday because of the house-to-house fighting raging there. There were also signs that the film had been cut, and there were continuity errors in, for example, the headgear of a young recruit. Dates on which the newsreel could possibly have been shot were verified by Anna Luise Kiss as the 19ᵗʰ and 20ᵗʰ of March 1945,[1] and so Hitler's last appearance must have been a month earlier than has been assumed. This painstaking research brought Anne Luise Kiss the Brandenburg State prize for young academic of the year 2013.[2]

Hitler's death is officially dated to the 1ˢᵗ of May 1945. Goebbels called it a "hero's death". Roosevelt had died three weeks before. Hitler hoped in vain that the British would now join him against the Soviet Union – Stalin was also afraid of this possibility, which was why he had Berlin so tightly surrounded to exclude the Western Allies.

---

1   Potsdamer Neueste Nachrichten 08.11.2013, *Hitlers letzter Auftritt* by Jan Kixmüller, www.pnn.de/campus/802662/

2   Potsdamer Neueste Nachrichten 1.11.2013, *Hitler, Piraten und Fettleibigkeit* by Jan Kixmüler, www.pnn.de/Campus/800820/

It was not only Graf Stauffenberg who had a chance to kill Hitler. The Russian secret service also had clear opportunities to assassinate Hitler in 1943 and 1944. According to the former Russian General and Minister of the Interior Anatoly Kulikov, both attempts were stopped on Stalin's orders. Stalin was afraid that Hitler's successor would make a separate peace with Britain and the USA to Russia's disadvantage.[1]

On the 2nd of May 1945 when Berlin had fallen and the Führer's bunker was captured, the Russians found no trace of Hitler. Where was he? Was it possible that Hitler could have escaped? Had his place over recent days been taken by a double to enable him to do so? Was the newsreel a fake to fabricate Hitler's presence in Berlin? There were many unanswered questions and much speculation.

Rumours abound about the Ju 390 long-distance bomber which was given the code name *Junkers Lastkraftwagen* [Junkers Truck] by the German Air Ministry. It was a top-secret project. Even the number of them said to have been ready for action before the end of the war, which varies between two and more than seven, is uncertain. There are documents which mention six prototypes and a series production of twenty. One thing that is certain is that the Ju 390 V-1's maiden flight took place in October 1943.

There are said to have been three fully fuelled six-engined Ju 390s on the military airfield at Rechlin[2], north of Berlin, days before the city fell. Rechlin was the most important airfield for testing aircraft and their armaments in the Third Reich. According to the flight logs at Rechlin two Ju 390s were test flown in February and March 1945. Himmler wanted to reserve one of them to escape from Berlin, but they are said to have told him that the aircraft was already booked for someone else. After the German surrender, two of the Ju 390s were found destroyed, but the third has vanished without trace in spite of intensive searches by the USA. Several of these bombers were also said to have been ready and waiting near Oslo. At the end of 1943 Hitler's personal pilot Hans Baur had requested a Ju 390 for government flight. Was it intended as an escape aircraft? Its range was such that you could have flown non-stop to Argentina, or Japanese occupied Manchukuo (Manchuria) and then on to Japan.

The Japanese air force was extremely interested in the Ju 390. According to Albert Speer one of these aircraft was flown to Japan over the polar route. Was Hitler in this one, or another one? According to secret British reports there was also a flight to New York and another non-stop flight to South Af-

---

1   Geerken, *Missbrauchte Kindheit,* p. 204
      Russian News Agency RIA Novosti/Kulikov
2   also Rechlin-Lärz, now: Müritz-Airpark

rica.[1] What is true? What is fiction? There are so many questions about this ghost flight that will probably never be answered.

On the 1st of May 1945, only a day before the fall of Berlin, Waffen-SS Major-General Wilhelm Mohnke and his troops made an attempt to break out. He was an experienced commander and held the Iron Cross. In the middle of April 1945 he was ordered to the Reich Chancery under Hitler's direct command with more than 3,000 men to defend the government area. Although the area was already completely surrounded by the Russians at the time, he made this forlorn attempt with his men and a number of civilians. Mohnke was captured by the Russians, but his men fought on in the west of the city for several days longer. Troops commanded by General Weidling defended a corridor in the west until the last inhabitants of the bunker escaped. If they were going to be captured, then rather the Americans than the Russians. Many of them actually escaped the encirclement and went to ground somewhere. It is hardly likely that Hitler and Eva Braun would have chosen an escape route that bore such little hope of success.[2]

A few days after the fall of Berlin the charred remains of Hitler and Eva Braun were supposedly found near the Führer bunker. The corpses were so burnt that it was impossible to identify them with absolute certainty. Russian doctors concluded that a double was being presented as Hitler's body. The few remaining body parts like the jaw and fragments of skull would have fitted into a cigar box. They were buried and exhumed several times before being taken to Moscow. At first, it was suggested that a gold dental bridge was proof positive of identification as Hitler. But there was still doubt, because the teeth were largely undamaged: Hitler and Eva Braun were supposed to have shot themselves in the mouth as well as taking cyanide. A shot in the mouth, which was what the pieces of skull said to be Hitler's showed to have happened, would have done severe damage to the teeth and the bridge. And the dental evidence was based on a dental technician's "memory". After performing the identification, this witness disappeared into the chaos of Berlin and was never seen again. Shaky evidence of Hitler's death!

Latest research suggests that Hitler had up to four doubles, and Hess and Himmler are also said to have had them. One of Hitler's four doubles was

---

1   Georg, Friedrich, *Hitlers letzter Trumph. Entwicklung und Verrat der Wunderwaffen.* Bd. und II. Deutsche Nachkriegsgeschichte; Bd. 44 + 45 Institut für Deutsche Nachkriegsgeschichte, 2009 and
www.globalecho.org/10324/junkers-ju-390-das-gespensterflugzeug

2   Fischer, *Die Verteidigung der Reichskanzlei 1945*

also said to have been capable of giving speeches in his place. Another double allegedly had the same dental work as Hitler performed.[1]

After the war Scotland Yard, the elite of the British police, made intensive investigations to resolve the question of the double, but the results are classified as secret for 100 years – we still have some time to wait to know the answer.

The Russians did not allow the Allies to inspect the bunker until two months after the end of the war. When the Americans wished to search for more parts of Hitler's body, the Russians blocked them, so that the investigation into Hitler's death was initially entirely in Russian hands. It was only some years later, in the 1970s, that American scientists were given the opportunity to test the remains stored in Moscow for DNA. It is said that they turned out to be from a woman.

Stalin constantly fostered doubts about Hitler's death. Until he himself died, he insisted that Hitler had escaped from Berlin and was still alive. Red Army General Zhukov, who won the Battle of Berlin, was also convinced that Hitler had escaped. He said, *We did not find Hitler* and *Hitler has deceived the world*. Zhukov announced to the world's press on the 9th of June 1945 that there was no sign of Hitler and that his whereabouts were a mystery. He believed that Hitler had flown out of Berlin.[2]

Was it a tactical move by the Russians to send the West on a wild goose chase? Disinformation is a speciality of the secret services. Much later the Russian military claimed that the bodies of Hitler and Eva Braun had been stored in a barracks and not destroyed until 1970. What was the truth and what rumour? There is still no unambiguous proof.

Shortly after the war ended General Zhukov travelled around the devastation in Russia with US General Dwight D. Eisenhower, Supreme Commander of the Allied Forces in Europe, elected President of the USA in 1953. Zhukov later reported that Eisenhower was convinced that Hitler had succeeded in escaping.

Michael Mussmanno, a judge at the Nuremberg trials, writes in his book *Ten Days to Die*, that the Soviets alone are to blame for not capturing or killing Hitler. Hitler's secretaries, his chauffeur, his bodyguard, his telephonist Rochus Misch, and his personal SS aide Otto Günsche may all have confirmed Hitler's suicide, but all their evidence was exactly the same in every detail,

---

1   Peter Fotis Kapuistos, *Pope Sixtus VII*, Athen 2013,
    www.blackraiser.com/nredoubt/iden
    Glenn B. Infield, *Hitler's Secret Life*, New York 1979
    Donald M. McKale, *Hitler's Survival Myth*, New York 1981
2   Der Spiegel 15/1995, Hitlers Höllenfahrt
    www.spiegel.de/spiegel/print/d-9182358.html, p. 2

and looked as if it had been learned by heart. Were these statements an attempt at deceit that had been discussed beforehand? Because later these same people all changed their stories many times causing considerable confusion.[1]

When Hitler finally realised that the war could not be won, he had only three choices: suicide, flight, or capture by the Soviets. Dictators are usually – as many examples right down to this day show – too cowardly to choose suicide. Too high an opinion of their personal worth holds them back from this ultimate step. They have no scruple about sending others to their deaths, but themselves? Hitler certainly did not want to fall into his enemies' hands alive or dead. He knew about the gruesome fate of his Axis partner Mussolini and did not want to end up like that. Until Hitler's death is proven beyond doubt, the only remaining possibility is that he escaped.

Hitler probably decamped days before the battle for Berlin, leaving his double in the bunker. We have shown that his last appearance was on the 20th of March 1945, the *Wochenschau* film of the event being shown four weeks later to make it seem that Hitler was still in the bunker, a deception tactic that had already been used when Subhas Chandra Bose travelled to Japan.[2]

It was possible to fly 2,000 high-ranking Nazis like Göring, Himmler, Eichmann, Bormann, Admiral Karl-Jesco von Puttkamer, Hitler's personal doctor Theodor Morell, Hitler's secretaries Johanna Wolf and Christa Schröder and the fighter pilot Hans-Ulrich Rudel out of Berlin as late as the 23rd of April 1945, after which they went to ground in South Germany, Austria or Spain.

If thousands of Nazi bigwigs managed to escape to South America and other refuges, why not Hitler and Eva Braun as well? Although the western Allies had control of the air, making escape by plane very risky, German aircraft did still manage to get away from Berlin: Hanna Reitsch, the famous German flier and test-pilot flew unharmed from the devastated capital only five days before the city fell, and eleven days before the end of the war. She was said to have been with Hitler before this spectacular flight, but she denied that it was she who had flown him and Eva Braun out.

At least one German jet fighter also managed to break through Allied lines to the west of Berlin three days before the city fell, carrying two passengers. It flew at low altitude and the Allied defences were so surprised that they only managed to get their anti-aircraft batteries into action after it was out of range. It escaped to an unknown destination.

A German pilot who escaped to Chile reported after the war that he had flown Hitler and Eva Braun to Tondern in Denmark on the 30th of April

1   www.theforbiddenknowledge.com
2   see earlier in this book

1945. He claimed that they had then travelled to Kristiansund in Norway, where a convoy of German U-boats was awaiting them. Both Denmark and Norway were still under German occupation at the time.[1]

This version of Hitler's escape by plane was indirectly "confirmed" by another pilot who also lived in Chile after the war. On the 18th of January 1948 the *Diario Ilustrado* of Santiago in Chile reported that this pilot, named "B"[2], had flown troops into Berlin in a JU 52 on the 30th of April 1945. At 16.15 he landed at Tempelhof airport. Only 100 metres away the pilot and his radio operator saw Hitler being seen off by a group of Nazi functionaries beside an Arado 234. The pilot was in the air only 15 minutes later and was unable to witness Hitler taking off in the Arado.

The Arado 234 was a new jet reconnaissance aircraft that had only entered service in 1943. It could reach such high speeds and such a great height that Allied fighters were unable to catch it. Was it one of the wonder weapons Hitler and Goebbels were continually boasting about?

There were rumours, inconsistencies and conspiracy theories about Hitler's whereabouts. Stalin accused the West of protecting Hitler. According to Soviet information he was living comfortably in a castle in the British occupied zone, then he was said to be hiding in Spain, Argentina or Japan. Now he was seen as a shepherd in the Bavarian Alps, now as a croupier in a casino. After the war Heinrich Noll, an unemployed nurse, appeared in Hessen. He looked so like Hitler that passers-by greeted him with the forbidden *Heil Hitler*. He was interrogated by the Americans, but he had nothing to do with Hitler's doubles, he said.[3]

Hitler was never found in spite of intensive searches in South America, Spain and Japan by the Allies and Israel. Japan had claimed that they would reconquer Germany after defeating the Allies. Perhaps that is what he was waiting for? And why were they looking for him, when after the war they obstinately insisted that he was dead?

In Spain his close ally Franco was still in power, there were many Germans living in Argentina who sympathised with Hitler and Argentina's head of state Juan Peron was an admirer of Hitler. Japan was Germany's ally and still had not surrendered. Hitler could have found refuge in any of these countries, and many investigations were made there over the years. But in all these world-wide searches one country was always forgotten: Indonesia, even though Indonesia was the one country where Hitler and Eva Braun could have successfully hidden without any problem. After Germany surrendered,

---

1   News magazine Zig Zag, Santiago de Chile, 16 January 1948
2   the pilot's full name was known to the author of the article and the editors
3   Der Spiegel, 1/1950 v. 5.1.1950 and 7/1950 v. 16.2.1950

Indonesia was still occupied by his Japanese allies. But how could he have got there?

If we assume that Hitler could have escaped from Berlin by air or some other means before the city fell, then his best chance of reaching a country where he would be safe would be by U-boat. There were German U-boats ready for service in the German North Sea and Scandinavia. After his last appearance, probably the 20th of March (see above) an escape from Berlin would have been possible without very great difficulty. He would have had plenty of time to reach any country overseas by U-boat. Even if he did not escape until the 30th of April with the alleged flight to Norway via Denmark, he could still have escaped by U-boat. Ten days after the 30th of April, on the 10th of May 1945, the U 977 set sail from Norway under the command of Lieutenant Schäffer. Officially U 977 ceased to exist, because Schäffer sent several men in an inflatable boat into a fjord in Norway. On landing, they said that their submarine had hit a mine, and that they were the only survivors. The U 977 was then included in the Navy's list of missing vessels. Another manoeuvre intended to deceive?

By that time U 977 had been at sea for a long time. She was equipped with a schnorkel. With an underwater voyage of 66 days, by day even at a depth of 50 metres, Schäffer set a new world record. His route first followed the west coast of Africa, the same route taken by submarines headed for Java and Japan. On the 17th of August 1945, three and a half months after Germany surrendered, and on the day that Soekarno declared Indonesia independent, the U 977 reached the resort and port of Mar del Plata in Argentina. Schäffer and his crew explained the length of their voyage by saying that they had put in to the uninhabited island of Branca in the Cape Verde group and had a relaxed holiday swimming, fishing, sunbathing and partying on deck. They had also celebrated crossing the Equator rather more lavishly than usual.[1] The commander and crew were interned and then handed over to the USA. Soon afterwards rumours, encouraged by the Soviets, began to circulate, suggesting that the U 977 had carried Hitler and other important Nazis to Argentina with a cargo of gold bars, weapons and important plans.

But it would be possible to explain the excessively long voyage (108 days) of the U 977 in a different way. She left Norway as the Soviets stormed Hitler's bunker in Berlin, and then remained at sea for months. This gives rise to many questions. Did the U 977 first divert from her route and sail from South Africa to Java or another Indonesian island? Even if Germany had surrendered, the German naval bases in Batavia and Surabaya were still being used by the Japanese, control of the bases only being handed over after

---

1   Schaeffer, U-977, *Geheimfahrt nach Südamerika*

their own surrender was declared on the 2ⁿᵈ of September 1945. Given the length of the U-boat's voyage, they would have had time to land Hitler und Eva Braun on Java and then sail on to Argentina. Hitler and Eva Braun could then have gone into hiding in Indonesia before Japan surrendered.

In July and August 1945 the media in Argentina and Chile reported sightings of German submarines almost every day. Several U-boats are known to have landed there at the time, such as the U 530 commanded by Lieutenant Otto Wermuth. However, the U 530 could only be considered as Hitler's escape transport if he left almost immediately after his last appearance on the 20ᵗʰ of March. The U 530 also had a schnorkel, and reached Mar del Plata on the 10ᵗʰ of July 1945, long after the capitulation.

Her log book, war diary, code book and maps were no longer on board when the U 530 reached Argentina. None of the crew had any identity papers. It was not even certain if the officer who claimed to be the commander of the U 530 was really Otto Wermuth. In Germany Wermuth was described as tall and fair-haired, in Argentina as short and dark-haired. It was suggested that the commander who sailed the submarine into Mar del Plata had actually only joined her off the coast of Argentina. The normal complement of six rubber life boats was short. No one could give any information about where the missing ones were. There were no torpedoes, weapons or ammunition on board, and there was no gun on deck. Some of the crew said it had been removed before they left Germany, others that it had been removed during the voyage and thrown overboard. All radar and barometric equipment had vanished. The crew gave vague information – or none at all – about what had happened to them and the submarine's route, and most of the officers refused to say anything.[1] It was suspected that the U 530 had come via Japan. It would have been more logical – if Hitler had been on board – to land him on Java. There they could also easily have changed the crew, because there were many trained submariners in the bases. The U 530 raises many questions, not least because the time and port of her departure from Europe are not certain.

There was also a suspicion that the U 530 and U 977 were only bait to divert attention from other U-boats. South American witnesses claim to have seen up to ten other U-boats. The Argentine government refuses to allow research in their state archives for reasons of national security.[2] It is, however, a fact that many U-boats left port in Europe for unknown destinations just before the end of the war and were afterwards listed as missing.

---

1   www.de.wikipedia.org/wiki/U_530

2   www.v-22.de/forum/526, *Ist Hitler im U-Boot nach Südamerika geflohen?*
     www.bild.de/news/2009, *Der Untergang des Dritten Reichs*

It was a book by Argentinian journalist Ladislas Szabo[1] that really set the conspiracy theories alight. He claimed to have interviewed many witnesses who had seen Hitler in Argentina, including two members of the crew of the *Graf Spee*, which was sunk off the Argentinian coast. The book became a best seller and laid the foundation for much further speculation.

There was a persistent rumour that Hitler and his followers had escaped to his ice fortress of New Berchtesgaden 250 kilometres inland from the coast of Antarctica. On the coast there was a base with a U-boat harbour and a garrison of up to 1000 men. New Berchtesgaden was said to have been situated in the partly ice-free territory of New Swabia (*Neu-Schwabenland*), the Third Reich's only secret colony. Hitler's U-boat convoy, they claimed in Argentina, had brought Hitler to this secret Antarctic base through ice metres thick. The Nazis had begun building their hideout in New Berchtesgaden in 1940. As camouflage a whole mountain had been hollowed out. The speculation was also encouraged by statements made by Admiral Dönitz in 1943: he said that the German submarine fleet had now created an earthly paradise for the Führer, an impregnable fortress somewhere in the world.

Papers and magazines all over the world speculated about Hitler's hideout at the South Pole. They reported there had been extensive building activity by German companies in the Antarctic and that large numbers of tractors, sleds, machines and aircraft had been taken there. How much of this is fiction, and how much is truth?

Helmut C. H. Wohlthat – already mentioned several times above – did in fact organise the German South Polar Expedition in 1938/39 under the auspices of Göring. They intended to begin the construction of a base in the ice fields to maintain German whaling rights: before the war Germany had over 50 whaling ships and seven factory ships. Whaling was of great economic importance and was to be expanded, especially since whale oil was also important as a source of glycerine for the production of explosives.

The expedition's ship, the *Schwabenland*, commanded by Captain Alfred Ritscher was provided with the most modern research equipment. She had previously served as a floating base in the South Atlantic for Lufthansa's South American airmail service. On the 17th of December 1938 she sailed for the Antarctic on the first of three planned research expeditions, arriving on the 19th of January 1939. She was carrying two Dornier Wal flying boats – named *Boreas* and *Passat* – which were launched from the ship by steam catapult. At the furthest point that the aircraft could reach over the Antarctic, flags and poles with German insignia were thrown out to establish territorial claims. The new 600,000 square kilometre territory was chris-

1   Szabo, Ladislas, *Hitler está vivo* (Hitler is alive)

tened Neu-Schwabenland. About one hundred German names were given to mountains, glaciers, lakes and geographic features, including the Wohlthat Massif, which is still used. Several survey flights surveyed and photographically recorded an area of 350,000 square kilometres. They discovered an ice-free area with 118 lakes which were free of ice in the Antarctic summer. They named the area the Schirmacher Oasis. The mapping of New Swabia was a major pioneering achievement. After the war Captain Ritscher became president of the German Society for Polar Exploration, and was awarded the Federal Grand Cross of Merit in 1959.

This area in Antarctica was not occupied by the Allies after the German surrender, even though they knew that German U-boats had sailed to the Antarctic several times in the last weeks of the war. It was not until some time after the war that there were expeditions which were to investigate the mystery surrounding Hitler.

Miguel Serrano[1], a Chilean diplomat and close friend of Carl G. Jung and Hermann Hesse, author of many books[2], some of which have been translated into German, organised two expeditions which failed to find any traces of building activity.

The USA sent several mysterious expeditions to the Antarctic, presumably to search for Hitler. In 1946 they sent out what was the biggest expedition ever until that time with the code name Operation Highjump. There were 31 ships, the submarine *USS Sennet* and the aircraft carrier *USS Philippine Sea*. They took provisions for eight months The leader of this 4,700-man expedition was the Antarctic explorer Admiral Richard Evelyn Byrd. Among the journalists accompanying the expedition was Walter Sullivan of the New York Times who later published a book about it[3], complaining about the lack of information about their objectives provided by the military. One striking thing was the large amount of heavy equipment, which made the whole operation suspect, especially since it had to be terminated early and hurriedly with losses of men and material.

The conspiracy theorists saw this as a failed attack on the imagined Nazi base. However, the early cancellation has an easier explanation: in that year the temperatures in the Antarctic were exceptionally low. The expedition had only one ice-breaker, and most of the ships did not have reinforced hulls. This meant that the convoy advanced very slowly, only reaching the Ross Ice Shelf on the 15th of January 1947. Some of the ships were surrounded by ice. To avoid further losses the operation was cancelled. The loss of personnel was officially explained as the

---

1   Ambassador in India, Austria and former Yugoslavia
2   Serrano, Miguel, *Adolf Hitler - El Ultimo Avatar* (Adolf Hitler - The last avatar)
3   Sullivan, *Quest for a Continent*

result of an aircraft crashing in a snowstorm, but some sources suggest that 9 aircraft and their crews had to be left behind, frozen in the eternal ice.[1]

If Hitler had escaped to the Antarctic in March or 1945, he would have arrived at the beginning of the Antarctic winter. How would a U-boat of the time have broken through the metres-thick ice? And Hitler was then supposed to have got through to his fortress at New Berchtesgaden, 250 kilometres inland? A totally absurd idea.[2]

At the end of the 1950s a new conspiracy theory hit the press. The New Berchtesgaden fortress was said to have been destroyed by atomic bombs, concealed behind the pretext of an atom-bomb test code named Operation Argus. Tests were actually carried out in the Antarctic in 1958: three atom bombs were exploded at altitudes of up to 466 miles, a good 2,000 kilometres from Neu Schwabenland. The official purpose of the tests was to investigate the effects of radioactivity on communication and location systems – not to find or destroy Hitler's ice fortress.[3]

Those were just some of the rumours and theories that circulated about Hitler's possible escape at the end of the war. The only known facts are that Hitler last appeared in public on the 20th of March, that a German aircraft with a pilot and passengers on board did manage to escape to the west three days before Berlin fell, that Major General Mohnke made a successful attempt to break out from the besieged government area with people from the Führer bunker just two days later, and that some German U-boats did manage to reach the open sea at the time around the German capitulation. Some arrived in South America after unusually long voyages. Other German U-boats were seen all over South America.

The media are still obsessed with myths and theories about Hitler's death or his possible escape. There is, however, one that we should not reject too hastily. I have already suggested that Indonesia was the only country on earth where Hitler could have gone to ground unrecognised. His trusted friend Walther Hewel, with his expert knowledge of the country, would surely have recommended it. In those final days in the bunker, the "Southern Region" was actually named as a possible escape destination.[4] Java was still in Japanese hands months later and the German bases in Batavia and Surabaya were still intact. A German U-boat could have docked there at the end of the

1   German Antarctic Expedition 1938/39, www.wfg-gk.de/gesvchichte 8.html
2   Summerhayes, *Hitler's Antartic Base: The Myth and the Reality*, 2007, Polar Record, 43 (01)
     DOI: 10.1017/S003224740600578X
3   Wolff, Suttie, Peel, *Atmospheric Environment: Antarctic Snow Record of Cadmium, Copper and Zinc Content during the Twentieth Century*
4   ZDF Info, 11.08.2014, 22.25h, *Hitlers Tod/Das Testament*

European war without any difficulty. Hitler would not even have needed a false passport. And even after Japan capitulated in September 1945 the Japanese kept a certain degree of order on Java and other islands until they were – only partially – disarmed by the British. In the general chaos Hitler could have settled on one of the 13,000 islands in the archipelago unrecognised. On the islands beyond Java there were no printed media or communications facilities for many years after the war. The peasants who inhabited the islands were then, just after the Dutch colonial period, largely illiterate. Who would suspect or recognise Hitler?

The unrest in Indonesia after the declaration of independence[1] would even have aided concealment. Indonesia would have been the safest place for Hitler, especially since the Allies had their eyes on Spain and South America. Hewel's advice would surely have pointed to Indonesia.

Hewel was at Hitler's side in the bunker to the bitter end and Hewel's trust in Hitler seemed unbroken. They were together at that last public appearance in March, and then both vanish without trace. Did they escape together? There is a lot to be said for the idea. If Hitler went to Indonesia then Hewel would surely have accompanied him. He knew the country, he spoke the language, and he understood the people's mentality.

Hewel's body was never found. Another argument against his suicide is the fact that as a diplomat with limited decision-making powers he would presumably have survived the Nuremberg Trials without too much trouble. If Hewel was able to escape, Hitler would also have been able to do so.

On the other side, an interview that Hewel's wife, Blanda-Elisabeth Hewel[2], gave to the British historian David Irving after the war is strong evidence for Hewel having committed suicide. On the 8th of December 1970 Irving wrote as point 7 of his notes on the interview:

She [Frau Hewel] found it entirely in keeping with his [Hewel's] nature, that when the man [Hitler] who had meant so much to him, deceased, he too [Hewel] should want to follow.[3]

There is still a great deal of interest in Hitler in Indonesia, because the Indonesians are absolutely sure: Hitler died in Indonesia! He is supposed to have escaped from Berlin with Eva Braun via Graz and Belgrade to Rome, and then travelled by U-boat to Indonesia. The U 977 and her secret mission to South America is always mentioned. This fascination with Hitler is not confined to the older generation, but is also found among young Indonesian

---

1   Cf. Geerken, *Der Ruf des Geckos*, pp. 159ff
2   née Ludwig, later remarried Blanda-Elisabeth Benteler
3   http://fpp.co.uk/Hitler/Hewel/zs-2241.pdf

students of both sexes. In their eyes Hitler was a genius who helped Indonesia to achieve independence. The Hitler cult can be seen in Nazi emblems on T-shirts, caps and buttons – not only in Indonesia but in other Asian states as well. In Bandung in West Java they even opened a Hitler Cafe a few years ago. Unfortunately Hitler is only seen from the perspective of the independence struggle – his crimes are ignored.

The question of Hitler and Eva Braun in Indonesia was initiated by an article by Dr Sosro Husodo, which appeared in the Indonesian newspaper *Pikiran Rakyat* in 1983. In the article, Dr Husodo describes working with someone he claims to have been Hitler. Since the book *Hitler Mati di Indonesia: Rahasia yang Terkuak*[1] [*Hitler died in Indonesia; the mystery is unveiled*] appeared in 2010, the subject has been of great public interest. The evidence is based on people who claim to have spoken to Hitler personally and a notebook that is said to have been found after his death.

Dr Husodo, who only made his revelations public after the death of the supposed Hitler, first had contact with him in 1960. As a doctor, he received a posting from the Indonesian government to work at the General Hospital, the biggest hospital on Sumbawa, one of the Lesser Sunda Islands, about 300 kilometres east of Bali. Here Dr Husodo claims to have met Hitler, who was working as head of the hospital under the name Dr G. A. Poch. There were hundreds of German doctors working on the outer Indonesian Islands at the time on the invitation of President Soekarno, so that a German doctor on Sumbawa was nothing out of the ordinary.

The longer Dr Husodo worked with the German Dr Poch, the more certain he became that this was Hitler and that his wife was Eva Braun. Dr Poch, by now 71, had no documents to show his medical qualifications and seemed not to have even the most basic medical knowledge. Nevertheless he was highly respected by the native population, who called him "Doktor Jerman", the German doctor. According to Husodo he had looked – though he rarely wore a moustache – exactly like Hitler, he spoke with a typical Austrian accent, his left hand shook and his left foot had a slight limp, two problems that Hitler also had. On visits to Dr Poch's home, Husodo noticed that his wife always addressed him as Dolf – perhaps a pet name for Adolf. Whenever Husodo tried to get him to talk about his time in Germany, Dr Poch always changed the subject. But he made no secret of the fact that he admired Hitler and Goebbels greatly. He was also a Holocaust denier.

At the beginning of the 1960s his wife, the supposed Eva Braun, left him and returned to Germany as Frau Poch.[2] Dr Poch subsequently got to know

---

1   Soeryo Goerinto, *Hitler Mati di Indonesia, Rahasia yang Terkuak*
2   http://www.faz.net/suche/?query=Der+Hitler%2C+der+in+Indonesien+starb

a lady from Bandung called Sulaesih who worked in local government on Sumbawa. They married in 1965.

Dr Poch's death was recorded as having taken place on the 16th of January 1970 at 19:30 in the Rumah Sakit Dr Sutomo Hospital[1] in Surabaya: it was a heart attack.[2] After his death, Dr Poch's second wife Sulaesih returned to her home town of Bandung, where Dr Husodo tracked her down in the suburb of Babakan Ciamis. Sulaesih gave Dr Husodo all Dr Poch's documents, including his driving licence with his fingerprints, his passport and a rather dog-eared notebook. This means that Husodo only received definite proof that Poch was Hitler from his wife Sulaesih after his death.

There were hundreds of names in this notebook – some of them only abbreviated or written in a secret language – and places of residence ranging from Argentina, Chile, Pakistan, South Africa, and Tibet to various Arab states. It seems clear that these are all escaped Nazis, an assumption that is supported by the fact that the name of the Franciscan priest and church historian Dr Draganovic[3] appears several times, with addresses in Genoa (Delegation Argentina da Imigration Europa, Genova, Val Albaro 38) and Rome (Roma, Via Tomacelli 132).

It is well known that the Vatican was close to Hitler. Even after the war they provided a great deal of help to escaping Nazis. The escape routes they used were called rat lines or *Klosterrouten* [monastery routes] by the US intelligence services. This last name was coined because high ranking Vatican figures, including Pope Pius XII and his closest confidant Montini, later Pope Paul VI, gave huge support to the escape of German war criminals. The route was mainly via South Tyrol to Rome and then via Genoa to South America. The head of the organisation was the Croatian fascist Krunoslav Draganovic named in the notebook. Identities were altered and authenticated by the Vatican, visas were arranged and financial and other organisational help provided. Sea passages were mostly provided by the International Red Cross. With Draganovic's help leading Nazis like the pilot Hans-Ulrich Rudel, the Butcher of Lyon, Klaus Barbie, Adolf Eichmann, Dr Josef Mengele and hundreds of others succeeded in escaping from a devastated Germany.[4]

---

1   There are also sources that give Rumah Sakit Karang Menjangan
2   Death and burial register for the cemetery of Makam Islam Ngagel Rejo in Jalan Bung Tomo Street, No. 19 in Ngagel, a suburb of Surabaya
3   also spelt Draganowitch
4   Bruns, *Der Vatikan und die Rattenlinie. Wie die katholische Kirche Nazis und Kriegsverbrecher nach Südamerika schleuste*
     Goni, Odessa: *Die wahre Geschichte, Fluchthilfe für NS-Kriegsverbrecher*
     Steinacher, *Nazis auf der Flucht: Wie Kriegsverbrecher über Italien nach Übersee entkamen*

Sosro Husodo said that as well as Draganovic, the lists contained other names which he could not interpret, with abbreviations and addresses in Argentina. Under Dr Poch's escape route there were only the abbreviations B, S, G, J, B, S, and R, which he assumed to be Berlin, Salzburg, Graz, Jugoslawia, Belgrade, Sarajevo and Rome. Poch's passport had also been issued in Rome –evidence of help from the Vatican?

After Poch's death, his second wife Sulaesih admitted that he had told her in confidence before he died that he was really Adolf Hitler. This is the "evidence" produced in the book *Hitler mati di Indonesia* [Hitler died in Indonesia]. Unfortunately, all my attempts to locate Sosro Husodo's address, or any of his family were unsuccessful. A further look at the documents he was given might have thrown more light on the subject. Even if he was not Hitler, Dr Poch may well have been an important person in the Third Reich.

If Frau Poch, the supposed Eva Braun, did actually return to Germany, then a search could be made for possible family members. In the German telephone book there are several hundred entries for "Poch": it was impossible for me to contact all of them. Perhaps this book will be read by someone in that social circle who could provide information about Dr Poch's actual identity.

I had more success in my search for Dr Poch's grave, which does actually exist. I visited the Makam Islam Ngagel Rejo Cemetery in Jalan Bung Tomo, No. 19, in Ngagel, a suburb of Surabaya. With the help of the cemetery custodian Edi Sumerman I found the grave in a remote part of the cemetery. The grey stone grave, surrounded by an iron fence, bears a memorial tablet inscribed with the name Dr G. A. Poch, without any date or place of birth.

The date of death, the 16th of January 1970, seems to have been added later in paint. The date and time (19.30) of death do agree with the cemetery authority's death and burial register. Edi Sumerman has worked there for about 20 years and affirms that the death date was there in its present form when he entered his post.

If Hitler was buried there, he would have died at the age of 81. His burial in an Islamic cemetery suggests that he may have converted to Islam, in which case he could have married his second wife, Sulaesih, without divorcing his first wife, Eva. According to the same cemetery's register, Sulaesih's death was registered in the Mesjid Darmawangsa mosque in Surabaya by a member of her family named Mohammad. She was buried there, but her grave had already been cleared away, and there was no date of death in the register.

There is, of course, still no conclusive proof that Hitler escaped to Indonesia; nor was there any clue that Walther Hewel could have been there after the war. Hitler's death remains a mystery. Forensic investigation of Dr Poch's grave and a more intensive search for Dr Sosro Husodo's family might bring more clarity.

Hitler wanted his people to see him as a new Messiah, sent by God as a redeemer and liberator, who should be granted divine honours. His model was the mythological Celtic-Germanic Grail knight as represented in Wagner's operas *Lohengrin* and *Parsifal*. Perhaps we should therefore allow his end to remain in complete darkness, like the mystery of the Grail.

Ill. 103
Dr Poch's Grave

Ill. 104
Memorial tablet
on Dr Poch's Grave

47. A German Military Cemetery on Java

If you travel along the old main road from Jakarta to Bandung there is a turnoff to the right just after Bogor which leads high up to the Pangrango volcano. I drove past it hundreds of times on my many business journeys to Bandung. But in my 18 years working in Indonesia, I rarely had the time or opportunity to drive up that road: if you do, you will find, just above the village of Pasis Muncang a monument with the inscription:

DEM TAPFEREN DEUTSCH-OSTASIATISCHEN GESCHWADER 1914
ERRICHTET VON EMIL UND THEODOR HELFFERICH
[ERECTED BY EMIL UND THEODOR HELFFERICH
TO THE VALIANT GERMAN EAST ASIAN SQUADRON 1914]

Beside it there is a German war cemetery with ten graves: the gleaming white gravestones are in the form of Iron Crosses.

Ill. 105
The German Military Cemetery of Artja Domas/Arca Domas

The cemetery and monument stand in a place regarded by the Indonesians as sacred, the Artja Domas (now: Arca Domas), which means: Place of the 800 Statues. For over 1,000 years Hindu kings ruled here, but from the beginning of the 16th century the inhabitants were either driven out or converted by Islamic warriors. According to the legend, the last 800 soldiers of the defeated Pajajaran were turned to stone and dedicated to the Hindu gods in Artja Domas. It is said that 150 years ago the remains of these stone warriors were still lying about, but these ancient statues became fewer over the centuries: collectors helped themselves and the last remaining pieces were used for house and road building.

How do these monuments and a cemetery for fallen German sailors come to be in such a magic place on Java, almost 1,000 metres above sea-level on the side of a volcano? The monument with a seated, meditating Buddha and an elephant-headed Ganesha, the Hindu god of wisdom and prosperity, is more reminiscent of a Balinese temple. At three of the cemetery's corners there are gigantic, ancient waringin trees – Indian fig trees. Many branches bow down to the ground and root themselves in the earth to grow up as new trunks which then link to the ancient trunk. In this way the tree is constantly renewed: they can live for hundreds of years. The waringin is sacred to all Indonesians as a symbol of vital energy. At the beginning of the 1960s there were four trees, one at each corner, but one of them did not survive a great storm.

Emil Helfferich, already mentioned before was a merchant who first traded in pepper and then founded the Straits and Sunda Syndicate. He was a prominent personality among the businessmen in the Dutch East Indies at the beginning of the 20th century. His brother Theodor, whom he called out to join him, was always overshadowed by him.

Before the First World War warships of the German East Asia squadron occasionally visited Java and Sumatra. Out of solidarity with the Imperial Navy the Helfferich brothers always provided a hearty welcome and reception for the officers and crews. The commander of the squadron, Vice-Admiral Count Maximilian von Spee, was also a guest of Emil Helfferich. The brothers had a close relationship with the squadron.

During the First World War the squadron had frequent encounters with the British. In the naval battle of Coronel off the Chilean coast in November 1914 they resoundingly defeated the British fleet. Winston Churchill, then First Lord of the Admiralty, had underestimated the Germans and vowed revenge. Bigger and faster warships whose guns had a range almost twice that of the Germans were sent to hunt down the East Asia Squadron. Only a few weeks later, off the Falklands, came the Royal Navy's vengeance: five German warships were sunk. In the terrible battles of Coronel and the Falklands, thousands of young officers and men on both sides went to their deaths in the cold Antarctic sea.

As related above, the German warship *Emden* had previously been sunk by the Australian cruiser *HMAS Sydney* on the 9th of November 1914 near Direction Island, only 400 kilometres south-west of Java. The German East Asia Squadron had ceased to exist.

After the First World War the training cruiser *Hamburg* was the first German naval vessel to visit the Dutch East Indies in 1926. The Helfferich brothers for some time had been considering where would be the best place for a memorial to the fallen sailors of the East Asia Squadron. They first thought of the Cocos Keeling Islands, because the remains of the wreck of the *Emden* are still visible there today. But because the monument would receive too little attention on that remote and inaccessible atoll, they decided on Artja Domas, which was close to Emil Helfferich's tea plantation at Tjikopo (now: Cikopo), which had often been visited by the officers and men of the squadron before the war. The *Hamburg*'s visit thus provided a good opportunity to unveil the monument in the presence of the captain, the officers and some of the crew.

On the 17th of October 1926 the memorial in Artja Domas was solemnly inaugurated. The site is breath-taking: it is as if the giant volcanic cones all around were keeping watch over it.

Emil Helfferich made the Tjikopo plantation available to German naval personnel during the Japanese occupation as the "U-boat meadow". After the German surrender, a large number of German seamen found refuge there. As senior officer, Captain Walter Burghagen, former commander of the U 219, took command of the camp.

There were also German servicemen who hid with Indonesian friends or girlfriends. The Indonesians always treated the Germans as brothers because they regarded them as like-minded allies against the Dutch. However, the Germans had to be extremely careful not to be taken for Dutchmen. There were some German sailors who wished to remain in Indonesia permanently, many of them joining the Indonesian independence movement. One of the most interesting German personalities who did stay was Herr Schamberger, who later worked in the German Embassy in Jakarta. In the late 1930s he was chief steward on a North German Lloyd passenger liner. He happened to be in Batavia when the war began. He managed to hide with Indonesian friends and so avoid internment by the Dutch. When the Japanese arrived, he was free again, and worked on the German naval bases in Batavia and Surabaya. After the Japanese surrender, he joined the Indonesian freedom fighters, where he must have made a positive impression on Soekarno or someone important in his entourage, because after the Dutch were expelled in December 1949, Soekarno engaged him in 1950 as manager and chef in a newly-built government guest house 800 metres up in the mountains in Tugu, south of Jakarta. When Hjalmar Schacht and his wife were in Indonesia in 1951 at the invitation of President Soekarno, they spent the weekends in that guest house. They were more than a little surprised to be cared for there by a German![1] In June 1952 diplomatic relations between Germany and Indonesia commenced, and Schamberger started work at the Embassy in Jakarta, where I met him in 1963. He worked there until he retired, and then remained in Indonesia for his sunset years.

1   Hjalmar Schacht, *76 Jahre meines Lebens*, p. 672

The memorial grounds at Artja Domas were expanded to include the graves of seamen who died in Indonesia later on. The inscriptions on the gravestones are:

ObLt. Dr Ing. H. Haake, U 196; 1914 – 30. November 1944

Lt. Wilhelm-August Jens; 7. November 1907 – 12. Oktober 1945

Kpt. Lt. Hermann Tangermann; 11. Oktober 1919 – 23. August 1945

ObLt. Friedrich Steinfeld, Kdt. U 195; 15. Dezember 1906 – 30. November 1945

Schiffszimmermann Eduard Onnen; 14. Dezember 1906 – 15. April 1945

Lt. W. Martens; gest. [died] Oktober 1945

ObGefr. Willi Petschow; 31. Dezember 1912 – 28. September 1945

ObLt. Willi Schlummer; gest. [died] 12. Oktober 1945

Two gravestones are just inscribed *unbekannt* [unknown]. Willi Schlummer and Wilhelm Jens were killed in Bogor, because they were mistaken for Dutchmen. The same thing happened to W. Martens who was lynched on a train journey from Jakarta to Bogor. Willi Petschow and Eduard Onnen died at the "U-boat meadow" Tjikopo; Hermann Tangermann died in an accident. The commander of the U 195 and UIT 21, Friedrich Steinfeld, was said by members of his crew, Peter Marl and Martin Müller, to have died of dysentery and malnourishment while imprisoned in Surabaya. At the request of his family, there is also a stone for Dr H. Haake. He sailed from Batavia on the U 196 on the 30th of November 1944 on an operation in the Sunda Strait – the boat was declared missing. There is, however, a rumour in South America that the majority of the 65-man crew were landed in Iqueque in Chile by the ship *Almirante Latorre*, and remained there.

One of the two "unknown" graves could be for Able Seaman Thiel, who was buried with full military honours during the cruiser *Hamburg's* visit in October 1926: he was one of the crew and was killed in an accident on the Javanese railway.[1]

The German sailors had a good life on the Tjikopo plantation. They grew their own vegetables and kept their own animals so there was no lack of food. The mountain climate was cool and healthy in spite of being close to the Equator. Compared with war-torn Germany it was a paradise. A contemporary witness, Abah Sa'ad who was 15 at the time, saw a funeral. He remembers that four sailors carried the coffin followed by dozens of others in white uniforms. For the local inhabitants lining the way it was a very special event. The German sailors at Tjikopo were discovered by a British Ghurkha regiment in September 1945. As I have already written, they were armed by the

---

1   Hans-Georg v. Friedeburg, *32.000 Seemeilen…*, p. 147

British and set to guard the Dutch internees in Bogor from the marauding Indonesian gangs.

Every year on Remembrance Day in November the German Embassy together with numerous German residents in Indonesia holds a ceremony under the giant waringin trees at this site, now called Arca Domas. It would be desirable for the Indonesian government to honour the memory of the Germans who fought for and supported the Indonesian fight for independence by erecting a monument here. Emil Helfferich's plantation at Tjikopo is now Plantation VIII of the Indonesian state plantation company *PTP Nusantara*.

48. Notable Germans Involved in the Development of the Free Indonesian Republic

Captain August Friedrich Herrmann Rosenow

At the end of 1963/beginning of 1964, when I had several discussions about short-wave transmitters for the navy with the Commander in Chief of the Indonesian Navy ALRI (Angkatan Laut Republik Indonesia), Admiral Eddy Martadinata, he had much to say in praise of the German Captain Rosenow, who he said had made an extremely important contribution to the country's independence and the creation of the Indonesian Navy.

Even before the First World War Rosenow had sailed in Dutch East Indian waters as an officer on ships of the Hamburg-America Line HAPAG. He knew the country and its people extremely well. My conversations with Admiral Martadinata inspired me to find out more about Rosenow, and my researches uncovered an eventful life story.

In the First World War Rosenow was interned by the Dutch in a camp in Belawan in North Sumatra. When the war ended, he entered the service of the Dutch colonial government and took Dutch citizenship. From then until the outbreak of the Second World War he worked as a pilot in the waters of the Indonesian archipelago.

He then avoided renewed internment by escaping to Japan in 1940, where he worked as an instructor in a nautical college belonging to the Japanese Navy. In 1942, after the Japanese occupation, he returned to Java. He met Soekarno at this time, and gave him both advice and help. He suggested that Soekarno should found a military academy: the first provisional military academy in Yogyakarta and the SORA in the German School in Sarangan were due to his initiative. Soekarno listened to his expert advice.

When the Dutch returned after the declaration of independence to try and restore their colonial rule by military means, he joined the freedom fighters. During the five year war that followed, Rosenow acted mainly as an instructor of Indonesian cadets in the military academy, having been made an officer in the Indonesian Navy by Soekarno. After Soekarno's public appearance at the end of December 1949, and his declaration: *Alhamdulillah, we are free at last!* the President was able to move into his palace on Medan Merdeka [Freedom Square]. He remembered Captain Rosenow, and made him his main advisor on maritime matters. They both had the long-term view that an archipelago with more than 13,000 islands would need a modern navy and merchant fleet with well-trained seamen for inter-island communication as soon as possible.

The Germans had achieved many pioneering feats in Indonesia, which is why Soekarno was so happy to work with German companies, but it was surely also due to Captain Rosenow that he chose Germany as his partner for the creation of a modern fleet.

In 1963, shortly after my arrival in Jakarta, a remarkable chance led to my meeting Captain Rosenow in person in Tanjung Priok, Jakarta's port, when I was invited on board a HAPAG freighter. Senior officers of the Indonesian Navy and the representatives of a few German companies had been invited to dinner. I was fortunate enough to be one of them. Rosenow was fair-haired, tall and well-built with a wide face and broad shoulders, the image of a real sailor. He was very likeable, and the Indonesian officers held him in the greatest respect. That evening I heard many details about his eventful and adventurous life.

Rosenow was born in 1892 on the Baltic island of Usedom, where he met his future wife on a visit in 1926 – she later accompanied him to the East Indies. They had two daughters. In 1936 he took one of his daughters, who was suffering a serious bout of malaria, to her grandmother on the Baltic to recuperate. Then came the Second World War and the troubles in Indonesia during the War of Independence, so that she was unable to return – Rosenow did not see her again until 1952.

Rosenow persuaded President Soekarno to have a sail-training ship built in Germany for the training of Indonesian cadets. He travelled to Germany at the beginning of 1952 and found the right partner for the project in H. C. Stülcken & Sohn, whose boatyard was opposite the Hamburg *Landungsbrücken*. In the 1930s they had built a 3-masted topsail-schooner as a training ship for the Yugoslavian navy. Based on that ship, a three-master barquentine with a steel hull was now ordered for Indonesia. Since Indonesia was more or less bankrupt, having been bled dry by colonial rule and the War of Independence, payment was in kind: rubber and copra.

He was now to supervise the building of the ship with a young Indonesian naval officer, Captain Oentoro Koesmardjo. This young officer and the daughter Rosenow had left behind fell in love at first sight and headed back to Indonesia to get married. Rosenow was now solely responsible for the ship. In January 1953 she was launched: she was 58.3 metres long, 9.5 metres wide and had a sail area of 1,091 square meters. She started on her voyage to her new home in July 1953: Rosenow was commander and Captain A. F. Hottendorf was responsible for navigation. She arrived safely in the

Indonesian naval base in Surabaya on the 1st of October and was welcomed by Admiral Martadinata after a very successful maiden voyage.

Shortly afterwards the training ship was named *KRI Dewa Ruci* on the suggestion of Rosenow's son-in-law, Oentoro Koesmardjo. The naming ceremony was led by Admiral R. S. Dubijakto, and the ship was given *Dewa Ruci,* the tutelary goddess of the seas, as her figurehead. At the same time she was handed over to her first commander, A. F. H. Rosenow, now promoted to Lieutenant Colonel.

Ill. 106
The Indonesian Sail-Training Ship Dewa Ruci

Since then the Dewa Ruci has sailed all the seas of the world and has been back to Germany several times. She is the pride of the Indonesian Navy and has successfully taken part in many tall-ship competitions. Countless cadets have trained on her. The Dewa Ruci has also contributed a great deal to international understanding, bringing people of other cultures closer to her homeland and its friendly people. In Germany a foundation to support the ship, the "Friends of Dewa Ruci" has been set up with the aid of the Chamber of Industry and Trade.

Rosenow died in Indonesia in 1966. The urn with his ashes was sunk by an Indonesian naval ship in the Sunda Strait near the volcano Krakatau. On

the *Dewa Ruci*'s honour board Rosenow is at the very top as her first commander.[1] He is still greatly honoured in Indonesian maritime circles.

Since Rosenow's time the relationship between Indonesia and Germany in
the field of ship-building has continued to develop. The Meyer shipyard in
Papenburg has so far supplied over two dozen passenger ships with a capacity
of up to 3,000 to the Indonesian state shipping line, P. T. Pelni, to maintain
a regular and reliable service between the main ports of the archipelago.

Dr Hjalmar Schacht

Not many people know that Dr Hjalmar Schacht, President of the *Reichsbank* from 1923 to 1930 and reappointed to the post by Hitler in the Third
Reich, was in Indonesia after the end of the Second World War. He played
a major role in the creation of a stable financial system, and provided useful
suggestions for dealing with the country's financial and economic problems.
Schacht had already done sterling work with the introduction of the German
Rentenmark in 1923: this new currency helped to cut unemployment, end
inflation and stabilise the German mark. This earned Soekarno's admiration,
and he invited Schacht to come to Indonesia with his wife to advise him and
his ministers. After the Second World War other countries, such as Egypt,
Iran, Brazil, as well as American oil companies, also sought his advice.[2]

Schacht studied in Kiel, Berlin, Munich, Leipzig, Paris and London, taking his Dr Phil. degree in Kiel. In 1930 Schacht met Hermann Göring, a
year later Adolf Hitler and Joseph Goebbels. He joined the Keppler Circle,
the "Circle of Friends of the Reich Leader of the SS Himmler", which Emil
Helfferich also belonged to, but he was never a member of the Nazi Party.

In 1933, after being reappointed President of the *Reichsbank* by Adolf
Hitler, he was invited to the White House by President Franklin D. Roosevelt. From 1934 to 1937 Schacht was also Minister for Economic Affairs
and responsible for financing the rearmament of the German forces. In 1937
Schacht was awarded the Gold Medal of the Nazi Party by Hitler.

Schacht was a personal friend of Sir Montagu Norman, Governor of the
Bank of England, sitting with him on the committee of the Bank for International Settlements. As a young man, Norman had studied music in Leipzig, a
period he remembered with affection. He was godfather to Schacht's daughter Inge's third child, who was christened Norman Hjalmar.[3]

---

1   Kowaas: *Dewa Ruci*, p. 432
2   AA, Bestand B 11, Band 696 and Generalanzeiger Bonn v. 08.01.1952
3   Schacht, *76 Jahre meines Lebens*, p. 250

In 1938 Schacht led negotiations in London with the director of the Intergovernmental Committee on Refugees (ICR), George Rublee. They worked together on the Schacht-Rublee Plan mentioned before, which was intended to persuade Britain, the USA and other western states to increase their immigration quotas for German and Austrian Jews.[1]

Schacht's resistance to Hitler's policies grew. Hitler found the concessions Schacht was prepared to make to the Jews too generous, and Schacht had previously distanced himself from the events of Crystal Night. In 1939 Schacht – officially because of his proximity to the opposition and his criticism of Hitler's armament and finance policies – was deprived of all his offices. In 1944 he was arrested and imprisoned in connection with the July Plot to assassinate Hitler. He was interrogated and maltreated in the concentration camps at Ravensbrück and Dachau, in the cellars of the headquarters of the Security Service in Berlin and the death camp at Flossenburg. At the end of the war he was released from the camp at Reichenau near Innsbruck by the Americans, but he did not enjoy his freedom for long. He, together with many others who had risked their lives to fight against Hitler, was tarred with the same brush as the members of the regime and thrown into the Aversa camp near Naples as a war criminal.

After the war, Schacht was acquitted of being a war criminal by the Allies at the Nuremberg trials, but sentenced by a German denazification court to eight years in a labour camp as a *Hauptschuldiger* [one of the main guilty parties]. Schacht was acquitted on appeal in 1948.

The last British pre-war Ambassador in Berlin, Nevile Henderson, wrote in his memoirs – also in relation to Schacht: *It would be extremely unjust not to recognise that a great number of those who attached themselves to Hitler and worked for him and the Nazi regime were honourable idealists. [...] It is possible that Hitler himself was an idealist in the beginning.*[2]

There is very little documentary evidence of Schacht's connection to Indonesia after the war, even though his advice about economic and financial policy was so influential in the initial stages of the republic. However, I was lucky enough to meet Wilhelm Dunsing, a representative of the Hamburg private bank Bankhaus Ludwig, in Indonesia. Hjalmar Schacht was founder and co-owner of the bank under its former name Bankhaus Schacht & Co.

After his arrival in Indonesia in 1967 I had frequent conversations with Wilhelm Dunsing about the economic and political situation in Indonesia. I also found out a great deal about Hjalmar Schacht and his activities in Indo-

---

1   See earlier in this book
2   Schacht, Hjalmar, *76 Jahre meines Lebens*, p. 627

nesia during these talks. I am still in contact with Dunsing's son-in-law, Dierk von Drigalski, who worked in the agrochemical sector in Indonesia for some years.

After the Dutch finally left Indonesia in 1949, the country was destitute. In 1950 an Indonesian delegation led by the Indonesian Finance Minister Jusuf Wibisono visited Schacht in his home in Bleckede on the Elbe. The delegation brought an invitation to Schacht and his wife from President Soekarno, together with a request that he prepare a financial and economic assessment of the country. Schacht agreed to do so.

Professor Soemitro Djojohadikoesoemo (new orthography: Sumitro Djojohadikusumo) the then Industry and later Finance Minister now travelled to Germany as the government's representative to prepare Schacht for his visit to Indonesia. Soemitro was one of the leading ecologists in Indonesia. In July 1951 the Schachts took off for Jakarta with Soemitro. Schacht spent a week in Cairo en route at the invitation of the Egyptian government, while Soemitro continued on to Jakarta to make preparations for Schacht's visit.

In Bangkok the Schachts had to wait six days for one of the rare direct flights to Jakarta. The British authorities in Singapore had issued a regulation that Germans and Japanese could only enter with a visa, and could not leave their hotel during their stay.[1] Schacht understandably decided not to travel via Singapore.

In Jakarta a suite in the Hotel Duta Indonesia, the Hotel des Indes in Dutch colonial times, was put at Schacht's disposal by the Indonesian government. There were two rooms, a spacious loggia and an office with a secretary.[2] The Schachts spent the weekends at the government guest house in Tugu under the tender care of our previously introduced German friend Schamberger. Tugu is about 100 kilometres south of Jakarta in a cool mountainous region.

President Soekarno's choice of Schacht to prepare the report was clearly influenced by a number of factors: that Germany was no longer weighed down by colonial baggage and had no imperialist interest in Indonesia, that Soekarno liked working with German business friends and loved products "Made in Germany" and that in essence he was pro-German. He was familiar with the German language and German culture. After independence, Indonesia became West Germany's main Asian supplier of raw materials.

Schacht's task was by no means simple because the Dutch colonial rulers had blocked the way to Indonesian social advancement for centuries, and had placed no value on educating the indigenous population. Education and intelligence were suspect to the Dutch, as an educated people will defend

1   Schacht, Hjalmar, *76 Jahre meines Lebens*, p. 664ff
2   for the history of the Hotel des Indes see: Geerken, *Der Ruf des Geckos*, p. 41f

itself against oppression and exploitation. Schacht recommended – after the adoption of the necessary financial and economic policies – that a major initiative to educate the people was needed, because there was only a very thin layer of dynamic, foreign-educated politicians beside a broad and sluggish layer of officials and workers, who needed motivation. The illiteracy that was the legacy of the Dutch was also a cause of great concern to Schacht and Soekarno. Schacht supported the measures Soekarno and his Education Minister Wongsonegoro were already taking to train 50,000 new teachers to provide intensive courses in reading and writing for millions of people.

Indonesia's main problem was, however, a lack of hard currency. Schacht suggested that they should use foreign capital to build facilities for the production of Indonesian goods that could be sold on the world market, thus bringing in hard currency. Production should be in the hands of partnerships between Indonesian and foreign – in this case, German – companies. The production facilities should be built at the expense of the companies, who would then recoup the costs from sales revenue. This plan was somewhat optimistic, since it assumed that the costs would be covered within three to five years: the aim was to pay the Germans who built the facilities 20% of the sales revenue.

On the 9th of October 1951 Schacht presented his 65-page report, written in German, to the Indonesian government. Most of Soekarno's ministers and associates spoke German; after independence German was promoted as

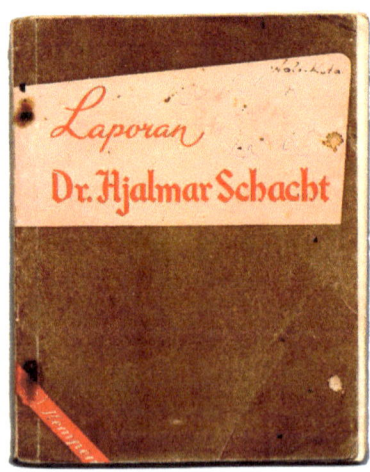

Ill. 107
Hjalmar Schacht's report in book form, 1951

Ill. 108
Hjalmar Schacht in his office in the Hotel Duta Indonesia 1951

the first foreign language taught. In the 1950s more than 150,000 young Indonesians studied in Germany.

Schacht's report was translated by the Indonesian Press and Information ministry and distributed in a German and English handbook to all the leading government officials

Schacht, who described his relations with ministers and important officials in the Indonesian government as always being very friendly and dependable, had written the report in close collaboration with Finance Minister Soemitro.[1]

When Schacht was in Jakarta, the German Federal Republic had still not sent an ambassador to Indonesia. They had not realised in Bonn what an important economic and political role the new state between the Pacific and the Indian Ocean was going to play – for Germany too. It was probably more important to have a German Ambassador in Jakarta than in Rome! In 1952, a year after Schacht's visit, the first German Ambassador to Indonesia, Werner Otto von Hentig, was appointed. This explains why there are hardly any documents worth mentioning about Schacht's visit in the German Embassy in Jakarta and the Foreign Office's Political Archive in Berlin.

A few days before Schacht handed over his report, there was a diplomatic incident. All the important figures in the international community in Jakarta were invited to a reception in Schacht's honour by the UNO representative in Indonesia, Sir Mirza Ismail (Diwan/Prime Minister of Mysore, Jaipur and Bangalore in India) and the Indonesian Finance Minister. At the reception, a Canadian UNO official, Hugh L. Keenleyside, refused to shake Schacht's hand, saying loudly:

I'm sorry, but I cannot shake that man's hand. Everyone who knows Herr Schacht's history will agree with me. [He is] An unprincipled turncoat! A despicable scoundrel. A disgrace to the human race!

Schacht and his wife walked out of the room but the boorish Canadian also had to leave, because Minister Wibisono announced just as loudly:

I think that Mr Keenleyside's presence is no longer required![2]

Keenleyside had only come to Jakarta to cut the UN's 1952 funding for Indonesia. Schacht and the Indonesian government were strongly opposed to this. After Keenleyside had left, Schacht and his wife were brought back to great applause. Keenleyside not only had to leave the reception because of his rudeness – he was expelled from Indonesia the next day.

1   Schacht, *76 Jahre meines Lebens*, p. 672ff
2   Der Spiegel, 16. Januar 1952, *Indonesien: Typisches Fiebertemperament*
      http://wissen.spiegel.de/wissen/image/show.html?did=21058603&aref=
      image028/E0203/SP195203-019-T2P-21058603.pdf&thumb=false

Schacht did more than just work in Indonesia. Soekarno put an aircraft at the Schachts' disposal so that they could discover other areas of the beautiful archipelago than Jakarta and West Java: they visited central Java, Bali and Sumatra. On the 17th of August 1951, Indonesian Independence Day, the Schachts were invited to a ceremony at the palace in Jakarta by President Soekarno.

Harmony reigned at the Schachts' farewell party. Schacht had generously refused to accept any payment for his consultancy work, so as a friendly gesture he was presented with a cheque for the value of one Deutschmark in Indonesian rupiahs. Soekarno's charming wife Fatmawati had taken a particular liking to the Schachts, and she and Frau Schacht had met several times and gone on excursions together. The two couples parted on very affectionate terms.

Schacht was very much in demand in Asia. On his way back he and his wife were invited to spend several days in New Delhi by Jawaharlal Nehru, and they also visited the Maharaja of Mysore at the instigation of Sir Mirza Ismail. There were other discussions in Persia (now: Iran) with Prime Minister Mossadegh and Shah Mohammed, followed by meetings in Cairo with General Naguib, the head of the government and Finance Minister El Emari. Schacht was back home in Germany by Christmas 1951. Shortly afterwards the Schachts were visited in their Munich home by Sir Mirza Ismail. In December 1952 Schacht accepted an invitation to Damascus by the Syrian Government to prepare a report on the creation of a state central bank.

Schacht wrote of his Indonesian experience:

[...] What 75 million people will make of this island state only the future will show. It may disappoint western observers to see that the ideals of modern western democracy are not very highly regarded. This is not true of Indonesia alone, but of almost all Muslim countries. Of course all educated people there unreservedly condemn the excesses and crimes of the Hitler regime. But the social and economic achievements of the early years of the Hitler era are regarded with great interest. There is also the fact that all these people are conscious that they owe their final liberation from colonial rule to the Second World War, which means that they do not condemn the Hitler regime outright.[1]

In 1953 Schacht founded his Bankhaus Schacht & Co in Düsseldorf. In the years following his visit to Indonesia Schacht was frequently consulted on financial matters by the Indonesian government. Nonetheless it was not until 1962 that the Indonesian government built a palm oil pressing plant worth 17 million marks following Schacht's plan. Schacht became person-

1   Schacht, Hjalmar, *76 Jahre meines Lebens*, p. 682f

ally involved in the project by urging the Federal Ministry for Economic Cooperation to provide a deficit guarantee through the state-owned Hermes Guarantee Insurance. The Federal German President also discussed the matter with Soekarno during his state visit in 1962. Schacht ended his banking career a year later, leaving the Bankhaus Schacht & Co, which now continued to operate under the name of Bankhaus Ludwig & Co.

In 1967 the IGGI, the Intergovernmental Group on Indonesia, was founded. 16 donor countries including Germany granted credits to Indonesia. A major bank from each country was to control the distribution of the funds, sending a representative to Jakarta for the purpose. And this is where the minnow among German banks, the Bankhaus Ludwig & Co, enters the game. This private bank was actually far too small to join in with the other international "global players", but the Indonesian Government insisted that the German representative should be Schacht's little bank and not one of the major German banking houses. They had not forgotten Schacht's service in the early days of the Republic and still felt obliged to him as an old friend. And that is why Wilhelm Dunsing, after retiring as a representative of this Hamburg private bank, was posted to Jakarta, where I was able to benefit from the information he provided.

Dunsing was an experienced Asia connoisseur. In 1930 he had gone to Yantai in China to work for Niggemann & Co. In 1947 he took over the organisation of the Chinese Tung Hsi company, founded by Chiang Kaishek and the influential German businessman Werner Jannings. Jannings's unique collection of Bronze Age Chinese weapons can be seen in National Palace Museum in Beijing.

After the Communist takeover in China Dunsing was taken on as an official in the Chinese foreign trade organisation. In February 1951 he and his wife were arrested on suspicion of espionage and imprisoned separately from each other. In 1954 they were deported to Germany. Indonesia was the last station in Wilhelm Dunsing's adventurous career. After that he finally did retire[1]

Hjalmar Schacht died in Munich in 1970 aged 93. His life's motto was always: "States founder for two reasons – wars and bad finances".[2]

---

[1]   http://www.oai.de/de/component/content/article/37-publikationen/ publikationen/778-deutsche-in-china-1920-1950.html
    Ostasieninstitut Hochschule Ludwigshafen am Rhein, *Deutsche in China, 1920-1950*

[2]   Interviews with Wilhelm Dunsing
    Dirk von Drigalski: *Al Andar Se Hace Camino*, Berlin 2011, p. 119
    DER SPIEGEL, 4/1952 pp. 19ff and 4/1964 pp. 26f
    www.wikipedia.org/Hjalmar_Schacht

German doctors in Indonesia

Before the First World War a wave of German doctors went to the Dutch East Indies. This led to the modernisation of the hospitals and the improvement of hygienic conditions and medical care. But at the time many were not allowed to treat the indigenous population. A friend of mine is the daughter of two doctors who practised in Bandung. Since they ignored this Dutch instruction in emergencies, the family was exiled to Dutch New Guinea, where my friend was born.

When the Dutch left at the end of 1949, there were only a handful of native doctors, a gap that Soekarno wished to fill as soon as possible with German doctors. In 1950 he started a major operation to recruit German doctors for Indonesia, and in 1950 and 1951 Indonesian delegations travelled to Germany. Up to 500 doctors accepted the new government's invitation to work as government doctors or consultants in remote regions in the archipelago. Most of them worked in Indonesia between 1950 and 1960. I met many of them when I arrived in 1963 – some of them remained there permanently.

After the war and, in many cases, captivity, large numbers of German doctors were unemployed or working in hospitals without pay. Numbers of them were therefore grateful to receive this offer, even if the pay in Deutschmarks and a sum in local currency was very modest.

One German doctor would care for an average of 100,000 patients. They did not just treat them in a central hospital, but often had to deal with one or two dozen polyclinics widely dispersed in the jungle. There were the normal operations and births, and frequently 200 to 300 patients to deal with in the polyclinics. It was not an easy task, as all the patients insisted on being treated by a Doktor Jerman, a German doctor – from whom they expected miracles. Many of the polyclinics were only accessible by lengthy boat journeys along the rivers through the jungles of Sumatra, Borneo, or Celebes or across the sea to the outer islands.

That may sound romantic at first, but the German doctors had to carry out their duties under very difficult working conditions in a tropical climate. At the time there were no dictionaries, no language courses, no introductions to the country and the people and their mentality. They had to cope with everything on their own. There was a language barrier, an unfamiliar tropical climate, a shortage of medication, and tropical diseases that they often only knew from text books. The nervous disease *latah*, for example, wasn't even in the text books, because it was only found in the Malay region and has only been recognised recently in the west, being defined as a "startle disorder". There was frequently no electricity, and there was also – as in Su-